55 *Victorian Prose Writers Before 1867,* edited by William B. Thesing (1987)

56 *German Fiction Writers, 1914-1945,* edited by James Hardin (1987)

57 *Victorian Prose Writers After 1867,* edited by William B. Thesing (1987)

58 *Jacobean and Caroline Dramatists,* edited by Fredson Bowers (1987)

59 *American Literary Critics and Scholars, 1800-1850,* edited by John W. Rathbun and Monica M. Grecu (1987)

60 *Canadian Writers Since 1960, Second Series,* edited by W. H. New (1987)

61 *American Writers for Children Since 1960: Poets, Illustrators, and Nonfiction Authors,* edited by Glenn E. Estes (1987)

62 *Elizabethan Dramatists,* edited by Fredson Bowers (1987)

63 *Modern American Critics, 1920-1955,* edited by Gregory S. Jay (1988)

64 *American Literary Critics and Scholars, 1850-1880,* edited by John W. Rathbun and Monica M. Grecu (1988)

65 *French Novelists, 1900-1930,* edited by Catharine Savage Brosman (1988)

66 *German Fiction Writers, 1885-1913,* 2 parts, edited by James Hardin (1988)

67 *Modern American Critics Since 1955,* edited by Gregory S. Jay (1988)

68 *Canadian Writers, 1920-1959, First Series,* edited by W. H. New (1988)

69 *Contemporary German Fiction Writers, First Series,* edited by Wolfgang D. Elfe and James Hardin (1988)

70 *British Mystery Writers, 1860-1919,* edited by Bernard Benstock and Thomas F. Staley (1988)

71 *American Literary Critics and Scholars, 1880-1900,* edited by John W. Rathbun and Monica M. Grecu (1988)

72 *French Novelists, 1930-1960,* edited by Catharine Savage Brosman (1988)

73 *American Magazine Journalists, 1741-1850,* edited by Sam G. Riley (1988)

74 *American Short-Story Writers Before 1880,* edited by Bobby Ellen Kimbel, with the assistance of William E. Grant (1988)

75 *Contemporary German Fiction Writers, Second Series,* edited by Wolfgang D. Elfe and James Hardin (1988)

76 *Afro-American Writers, 1940-1955,* edited by Trudier Harris (1988)

77 *British Mystery Writers, 1920-1939,* edited by Bernard Benstock and Thomas F. Staley (1988)

78 *American Short-Story Writers, 1880-1910,* edited by Bobby Ellen Kimbel, with the assistance of William E. Grant (1988)

79 *American Magazine Journalists, 1850-1900,* edited by Sam G. Riley (1988)

80 *Restoration and Eighteenth-Century Dramatists, First Series,* edited by Paula R. Backscheider (1989)

81 *Austrian Fiction Writers, 1875-1913,* edited by James Hardin and Donald G. Daviau (1989)

82 *Chicano Writers, First Series,* edited by Francisco A. Lomelí and Carl R. Shirley (1989)

83 *French Novelists Since 1960,* edited by Catharine Savage Brosman (1989)

84 *Restoration and Eighteenth-Century Dramatists, Second Series,* edited by Paula R. Backscheider (1989)

85 *Austrian Fiction Writers After 1914,* edited by James Hardin and Donald G. Daviau (1989)

86 *American Short-Story Writers, 1910-1945, First Series,* edited by Bobby Ellen Kimbel (1989)

87 *British Mystery and Thriller Writers Since 1940, First Series,* edited by Bernard Benstock and Thomas F. Staley (1989)

88 *Canadian Writers, 1920-1959, Second Series,* edited by W. H. New (1989)

89 *Restoration and Eighteenth-Century Dramatists, Third Series,* edited by Paula R. Backscheider (1989)

90 *German Writers in the Age of Goethe, 1789-1832,* edited by James Hardin and Christoph E. Schweitzer (1989)

91 *American Magazine Journalists, 1900-1960, First Series,* edited by Sam G. Riley (1990)

92 *Canadian Writers, 1890-1920,* edited by W. H. New (1990)

93 *British Romantic Poets, 1789-1832, First Series,* edited by John R. Greenfield (1990)

94 *German Writers in the Age of Goethe: Sturm und Drang to Classicism,* edited by James Hardin and Christoph E. Schweitzer (1990)

95 *Eighteenth-Century British Poets, First Series,* edited by John Sitter (1990)

96 *British Romantic Poets, 1789-1832, Second Series,* edited by John R. Greenfield (1990)

...enment ..., edited ...toph ...

...ssayists, First Series, ... Robert Beum (1990)

99 *Canadian Writers Before 1890,* edited by W. H. New (1990)

100 *Modern British Essayists, Second Series,* edited by Robert Beum (1990)

101 *British Prose Writers, 1660-1800, First Series,* edited by Donald T. Siebert (1991)

102 *American Short-Story Writers, 1910-1945, Second Series,* edited by Bobby Ellen Kimbel (1991)

103 *American Literary Biographers, First Series,* edited by Steven Serafin (1991)

104 *British Prose Writers, 1660-1800, Second Series,* edited by Donald T. Siebert (1991)

105 *American Poets Since World War II, Second Series,* edited by R. S. Gwynn (1991)

106 *British Literary Publishing Houses, 1820-1880,* edited by Patricia J. Anderson and Jonathan Rose (1991)

107 *British Romantic Prose Writers, 1789-1832, First Series,* edited by John R. Greenfield (1991)

108 *Twentieth-Century Spanish Poets, First Series,* edited by Michael L. Perna (1991)

109 *Eighteenth-Century British Poets, Second Series,* edited by John Sitter (1991)

110 *British Romantic Prose Writers, 1789-1832, Second Series,* edited by John R. Greenfield (1991)

111 *American Literary Biographers, Second Series,* edited by Steven Serafin (1991)

112 *British Literary Publishing Houses, 1881-1965,* edited by Jonathan Rose and Patricia J. Anderson (1991)

113 *Modern Latin-American Fiction Writers, First Series,* edited by William Luis (1992)

114 *Twentieth-Century Italian Poets, First Series,* edited by Giovanna Wedel De Stasio, Glauco Cambon, and Antonio Illiano (1992)

115 *Medieval Philosophers,* edited by Jeremiah Hackett (1992)

116 *British Romantic Novelists, 1789-1832,* edited by Bradford K. Mudge (1992)

(Continued on back endsheets)

Sixteenth-Century British Nondramatic Writers
Third Series

Dictionary of Literary Biography® • Volume One Hundred Sixty-Seven

Sixteenth-Century British Nondramatic Writers
Third Series

Edited by
David A. Richardson
Cleveland State University

A Bruccoli Clark Layman Book
Gale Research
Detroit, Washington, D.C., London

The paper used in this publication meets the minimum requirements
of American National Standard for Information Sciences–Permanence
Paper for Printed Library Materials, ANSI Z39.48-1984. ∞ ™

Library of Congress Cataloging-in-Publication Data

Sixteenth-century British nondramatic writers. Third series / edited by David A. Richardson.
    p. cm. – (Dictionary of literary biography: v. 167)
"A Bruccoli Clark Layman book."
Includes bibliographical references and index.
ISBN 0-8103-9362-X (alk. paper)
1. Authors, English – Early modern, 1500–1700 – Biography – Dictionaries. 2. English literature –
Early modern, 1500–1700 – Bio-bibliography – Dictionaries. 3. English literature – Early modern,
1500–1700 – Dictionaries. 4. Sixteenth century – Biography – Dictionaries. I. Richardson, David A.
II. Series.

PR411.S583 1996
820.9'003--dc20   96-20951
[B}   CIP

10 9 8 7 6 5 4 3 2 1

For Donald Cheney, A. C. Hamilton, Brewster Rogerson
and
O. B. Hardison, Jr. (in memoriam)

Teachers, scholars, and "doughtie Doucepere[s]"

Contents

Plan of the Series ix

Introduction xi

Lodowick Bryskett (1546?–1612) 3
   Kenneth R. Bartlett

William Bullein (1520s–1576) 8
   Elizabeth McCutcheon

Edmund Campion (1539–1581)..............................13
   Carolyn F. Scott

Sir Thomas Chaloner (1520–1565) 20
   M. Rick Smith

Miles Coverdale (1487 or 1488–1569) 27
   Richard Y. Duerden

Angel Day (flourished 1586) 37
   Richard Rambuss

Thomas Deloney (died 1600) 41
   Alexandra Halasz

Thomas Drant (early 1540s?–1578?) 48
   Peter E. Medine

John Field (1545?–1588) 53
   Richard Y. Duerden

Robert Greene (1558–1592) 61
   Sandra Clark

Gabriel Harvey (1550?–1631) 77
   Wayne Erickson

Raphael Holinshed (died 1580) 94
   Emily E. Stockard

John Lyly (between 1552 and 1554–1606) 102
   Derek B. Alwes

A Mirror for Magistrates....................................116
   Frederick Kiefer

Alexander Montgomerie (circa 1550?–1598) 128
   David Parkinson

Richard Mulcaster (1531 or 1532–1611) 134
   William Barker

Thomas Nashe (1567–1601?) 142
   Reid Barbour

Richard Pace (1482?–1536)..................................160
   Peter C. Herman

George Peele (1556–1596) 165
   Charles Whitworth

Thomas Phaer (1510?–1560) 171
   M. Rick Smith

Richard Robinson (circa 1545–1607) 177
   James Robertson

Mary Sidney Herbert, Countess of Pembroke
   (1561–1621) 184
   Margaret P. Hannay

Sir Philip Sidney (1554–1586) 194
   Marvin Hunt

Robert Southwell (1561?–1595) 220
   F. W. Brownlow

Edmund Spenser (circa 1552–1599) 228
   Donald V. Stump

Appendix I
Author-Printers, 1476–1599 267
   Sheila Ahern

Appendix II
Documents on Sixteenth-Century Literature......277

Checklist of Further Readings 305

Contributors...315

Cumulative Index...319

Plan of the Series

. . . Almost the most prodigious asset of a country, and perhaps its most precious possession, is its native literary product — when that product is fine and noble and enduring.

Mark Twain*

The advisory board, the editors, and the publisher of the *Dictionary of Literary Biography* are joined in endorsing Mark Twain's declaration. The literature of a nation provides an inexhaustible resource of permanent worth. We intend to make literature and its creators better understood and more accessible to students and the reading public, while satisfying the standards of teachers and scholars.

To meet these requirements, *literary biography* has been construed in terms of the author's achievement. The most important thing about a writer is his writing. Accordingly, the entries in *DLB* are career biographies, tracing the development of the author's canon and the evolution of his reputation.

The purpose of *DLB* is not only to provide reliable information in a convenient format but also to place the figures in the larger perspective of literary history and to offer appraisals of their accomplishments by qualified scholars.

The publication plan for *DLB* resulted from two years of preparation. The project was proposed to Bruccoli Clark by Frederick C. Ruffner, president of the Gale Research Company, in November 1975. After specimen entries were prepared and typeset, an advisory board was formed to refine the entry format and develop the series rationale. In meetings held during 1976, the publisher, series editors, and advisory board approved the scheme for a comprehensive biographical dictionary of persons who contributed to North American literature. Editorial work on the first volume began in January 1977, and it was published in 1978. In order to make *DLB* more than a reference tool and to compile volumes that individually have claim to status as literary history, it was decided to organize volumes by topic, period, or genre. Each of these free-

*From an unpublished section of Mark Twain's autobiography, copyright by the Mark Twain Company

standing volumes provides a biographical-bibliographical guide and overview for a particular area of literature. We are convinced that this organization — as opposed to a single alphabet method — constitutes a valuable innovation in the presentation of reference material. The volume plan necessarily requires many decisions for the placement and treatment of authors who might properly be included in two or three volumes. In some instances a major figure will be included in separate volumes, but with different entries emphasizing the aspect of his career appropriate to each volume. Ernest Hemingway, for example, is represented in *American Writers in Paris, 1920–1939* by an entry focusing on his expatriate apprenticeship; he is also in *American Novelists, 1910–1945* with an entry surveying his entire career. Each volume includes a cumulative index of the subject authors and articles. Comprehensive indexes to the entire series are planned.

With volume ten in 1982 it was decided to enlarge the scope of *DLB*. By the end of 1986 twenty-one volumes treating British literature had been published, and volumes for Commonwealth and Modern European literature were in progress. The series has been further augmented by the *DLB Yearbooks* (since 1981) which update published entries and add new entries to keep the *DLB* current with contemporary activity. There have also been *DLB Documentary Series* volumes which provide biographical and critical source materials for figures whose work is judged to have particular interest for students. One of these companion volumes is entirely devoted to Tennessee Williams.

We define literature as the *intellectual commerce of a nation*: not merely as belles lettres but as that ample and complex process by which ideas are generated, shaped, and transmitted. *DLB* entries are not limited to "creative writers" but extend to other figures who in their time and in their way influenced the mind of a people. Thus the series encompasses historians, journalists, publishers, and screenwriters. By this means readers of *DLB* may be aided to perceive literature not as cult scripture in the keeping of intellectual high priests but firmly positioned at the center of a nation's life.

DLB includes the major writers appropriate to each volume and those standing in the ranks immediately behind them. Scholarly and critical counsel has been sought in deciding which minor figures to include and how full their entries should be. Wherever possible, useful references are made to figures who do not warrant separate entries.

Each *DLB* volume has a volume editor responsible for planning the volume, selecting the figures for inclusion, and assigning the entries. Volume editors are also responsible for preparing, where appropriate, appendices surveying the major periodicals and literary and intellectual movements for their volumes, as well as lists of further readings. Work on the series as a whole is coordinated at the Bruccoli Clark Layman editorial center in Columbia, South Carolina, where the editorial staff is responsible for accuracy of the published volumes.

One feature that distinguishes *DLB* is the illustration policy – its concern with the iconography of literature. Just as an author is influenced by his surroundings, so is the reader's understanding of the author enhanced by a knowledge of his environment. Therefore *DLB* volumes include not only drawings, paintings, and photographs of authors, often depicting them at various stages in their careers, but also illustrations of their families and places where they lived. Title pages are regularly reproduced in facsimile along with dust jackets for modern authors. The dust jackets are a special feature of *DLB* because they often document better than anything else the way in which an author's work was perceived in its own time. Specimens of the writers' manuscripts are included when feasible.

Samuel Johnson rightly decreed that "The chief glory of every people arises from its authors." The purpose of the *Dictionary of Literary Biography* is to compile literary history in the surest way available to us – by accurate and comprehensive treatment of the lives and work of those who contributed to it.

The *DLB* Advisory Board

Introduction

The Early Modern period from 1485 to 1603 in England is commonly referred to as "the Renaissance" and as "the Age of the Tudors," for it can be conveniently divided into the reigns of Henry VII, Henry VIII, Edward VI, Mary I, and Elizabeth I – an unbroken string of idiosyncratic Tudor monarchs. But just as there is no grand unified theory (GUT) in modern physics, there is no single theory, history, concept, or tag for sixteenth-century British nondramatic literature – none at least that inspires widespread and lasting conviction. In matters of literary history, each defining term and every generation of scholarship has been succeeded by new information, interpretations, and labels.

Scholarship about sixteenth-century English writing was dominated in the early twentieth century by historical, philological, and bibliographical work, with the New Criticism especially prominent at midcentury. The latter half of this century – and especially the final third – has seen an explosion of scholarship influenced by Freudian and other psychologies, Marxist theories of history and economics, feminist and gender issues, deconstruction, and a vast array of other French theories. Each has had or is having its day, as the New Historicism, for instance, is succeeded by "New New Historicism," and received studies of the British literary empire are reassessed in light of postcolonial anthropological or ethnographic criticism. The present state of sixteenth-century literary history is nothing less than effervescent, so that canonical features that dominated yesterday are challenged by others today and may be displaced tomorrow.

Two important background studies for sixteenth-century scholarship are Jacob Burckhardt's *The Civilization of the Renaissance in Italy* (1860) and E. M. W. Tillyard's *The Elizabethan World Picture* (1944). Some of the most influential works of the twentieth century include Douglas Bush's *The Renaissance and English Humanism* (1939), Hallett Smith's *Elizabethan Poetry: A Study in Conventions, Meaning, and Expression* (1952), C. S. Lewis's *English Literature in the Sixteenth Century, Excluding Drama* (1954), Mikhail Bakhtin's *Rabelais and His World* (1968), Michael Foucault's "What Is an Author?" (1984), and Stephen Greenblatt's *Renaissance Self-Fashioning from More to Shakespeare* (1980).

Michael J. Marcuse's listings of "Literature of the Renaissance and Earlier Seventeenth Century" (1990) and Leah S. Marcus's essay on "Renaissance/Early Modern Studies" (1992) provide a quick overview of the scholarly status quo. An evolving history of sixteenth-century literature is implicit – often aggressively explicit – in "Recent Studies in the English Renaissance" (annually in the winter issue of *Studies in English Literature*), and readers will quickly spot trends from articles in respected journals such as *English Literary Renaissance* and from reviews in *Renaissance Quarterly* and *The Sixteenth Century Journal*. Although now more than two decades old, *The New Cambridge Bibliography of English Literature* (1974) is an invaluable guide to primary and secondary materials, including literary history. *The State of Renaissance Studies: A Special Twenty-Fifth Anniversary Symposium in Honor of Dan S. Collins* (1995) is a more current critical and bibliographic starting point.

As in *DLB 132* and *DLB 136*, this introduction does not pronounce on what is past or passing, nor does it predict what is to come in our understanding of sixteenth-century literary history. Instead, it highlights some recurrent motifs in the entries making up this volume – motifs and emphases that will inevitably change with the discovery of new documents, reinterpretations of standard texts, and the rise and fall of theoretical schools in the universities. In the last decade of the twentieth century, however, the articles in this volume stress several traits of sixteenth-century British nondramatic literature: an accelerating pace of literary innovation; experimentation across a variety of genres; concern for education and didacticism; substantial work in biography and autobiography; much attention to the artistic and useful potential of vernacular English and of translation from classical and modern languages; a vital humanistic inheritance from Desiderius Erasmus, Sir Thomas More, and their contemporaries; widespread use for political and religious ends; the phenomenon of a popular press among an increasingly literate reading public; and the successful use of writing to obtain patronage.

Innovation. The writers discussed in this volume, like those in *DLB 132* and *DLB 136*, are conveniently labeled "Renaissance authors," but they were far more than literary discoverers and revivers, or adapters and imitators, of "reborn" classical texts. Their works are often strikingly new, even revolutionary. Collectively, their literary biographies document innovation on a scale perhaps unequaled in the entire history of English and in a heterogeneous diversity that almost defies classification. The fact that many of these innovations happen near the end of the century suggests not only that specific political, economic, religious, technical, and literary stimuli continue to be enormously fruitful over decades or even the entire century, but also that change generally provokes further change.

Pride of place for innovation in sixteenth-century England must be given to heroic poetry and especially to Edmund Spenser for *The Faerie Queene* (1590, 1596), which according to Donald Stump "charted a new path for neoclassical epic in English verse." His native models included only the manuscript of Sir Philip Sidney's prose *Arcadia* and possibly Gabriel Harvey's (now lost) vernacular epic from the 1570s, so that Spenser and these contemporaries stand at the forefront of the genre in English. Little more than a decade earlier, England had acclaimed Spenser for his pastoral eclogues in *The Shepheardes Calender* (1579), "the first major published work of 'new poetry' written along the neoclassical lines advocated by nationalist poets such as those of the Areopagus," a literary circle that included Spenser, Sidney, Daniel Rogers, Edward Dyer, Fulke Greville, and Thomas Drant. Synthesized from ancient, medieval, and contemporary sources, *The Shepheardes Calender* borrows an unprecedented variety of meters and forms of pastoral poetry. A structural innovation is its seasonal progression depicting human aging and specifically the outer, physical world that mirrors the inner, emotional world of unrequited love in its protagonist, Colin Clout.

Sidney has come into his own during the last quarter of the twentieth century, and not least as an innovator. In addition to his experiments with the heroic prose romance, he wrote the first epithalamium in English in his *Old Arcadia* (circa 1577–1582); and six of the eleven songs among his sonnets in *Astrophil and Stella* (1582) use a trochaic rhythm hitherto unknown in English. His *Defense of Poetry* (1579–1580), observes Marvin Hunt, "is undoubtedly the most important critical treatise on poetry written by an Englishman during the Elizabethan period," and its digression is the "first example of sustained dramatic criticism in English." Furthermore, in it

Sidney is the first Englishman to mention Dante's Beatrice (from *Paradiso*).

More recently, his sister, Mary Sidney Herbert, Countess of Pembroke, has been recognized as far more than an instrument for memorializing her brother. Her translation of Robert Garnier's *Marc Antoine* (1590), says Margaret Hannay, is "among the first English dramas in blank verse." In addition, her translation of Petrarch's *Triumph of Death* is among the first to interject a female voice into the Petrarchan tradition, providing "an entry into the genre of love poetry for English women."

Translation prompted innovation across many subjects and genres beyond the drama and Petrarchan verse. Thomas Drant, for example, published the first English translation of Horace in 1566–1567. Thomas Chaloner provided the first English version of Erasmus's satiric *Moriae Encomium* (1511) as *The Praise of Folly* (1549). In 1535 Miles Coverdale completed the first Bible published in English. He helped to establish the tradition of congregational singing with his collection of fifteen metrical psalms (1535?) and was thus instrumental in encouraging worship in the vernacular. His translation of Heinrich Bullinger's *Christian State of Matrimony* (1541) helped to introduce the genre of the marriage manual specifically and more generally the tradition of vernacular conduct books.

Other useful texts include Thomas Phaer's translation of *The Book of Children* (1544), the first popular handbook of pediatrics published in English. William Bullein's *Dialogue against the Fever Pestilence* (1564) is the "first literary treatment of the plague in sixteenth-century England" and also "the first utopia (or quasi-utopia) written in English," according to Elizabeth McCutcheon (a dramatic adaptation was actually performed by medical students at the Johns Hopkins University in 1939). In 1586 Angel Day published his *English Secretary,* the first epistolary handbook comprising original English letters rather than translated Latin models. It is also a guide for the career of secretary, setting forth the ideals of humanist rhetorical culture and routes for career advancement. Because it is not restricted to letters of ambassadors, popes, emperors, and others of rank, Richard Rambus shows how it serves as a "proto-professional training handbook," as a "how-to" guide or courtesy manual for the rising middle classes; and with the addition of a dictionary of rhetorical forms, it simultaneously functions as a rhetorical handbook.

The sixteenth century saw a growing market for new ideas about formal education. While Thomas Elyot and Roger Ascham had earlier proclaimed a balanced physical and intellectual regimen for young scholars, Richard Mulcaster in his *Positions* (1581) is among the first to argue for a fully institutionalized program of rigorous physical education on grounds of health (there is, however, no proof that his Merchant Taylors' School routinely practiced sports despite his advocacy). At about the same time at Cambridge University, Gabriel Harvey's three lectures on rhetoric (1574–1575) were among the first printed works in England to promote Ramist pedagogy, stressing Protestant and Copernican sympathies in his attacks against Aristotelian traditions in logic and rhetoric. As Wayne Erikson says, they "preserve an exemplary portrait of his appeal as a teacher, and they are some of the most delightfully endearing and intellectually playful pedagogic works of the English Renaissance." They do, however, represent the "radical fringe" of education theory at English universities.

Several author-printers (that is, writers as well as manufacturers of texts) made a variety of innovations. Among them, Robert Copland introduced the comma in its modern usage into England. In 1551 Humphrey Powell set up the first printing press in Ireland, where he published only works by Protestant Reformers. John Rastell is apparently the only Englishman during the first half of the century to write about voyages of exploration. Best known among his peers, Richard Tottel collected and published the first printed anthology of English poems in 1557, titled *Songs and Sonnets.* Familiarly known as *Tottel's Miscellany,* it was extremely influential on the new directions taken by English poetry during the Elizabethan period.

Nor did originality decline in the final decades of the century. Emily Stockard observes that Raphael Holinshed in 1577 was the "overseer and primary compiler of the first continuous and authoritative narrative account of British history written in the vernacular." Alexander Montgomerie is arguably the first Scottish practitioner of the sonnet. Although Robert Greene was perceived in the 1590s as innovative, his cony-catching pamphlets were actually derivative of earlier rogue literature and hence imitative, like most of his nondramatic work. But he does seem to be the first person in England to try to earn a living purely from writing: "Many things I have wrote to get money, which I could otherwise wish to be suppressed. Poverty is the father of innumerable infirmities."

What is noteworthy about so much of this innovation is that it accompanies or actually embodies genuine literary excellence. For example, Frederick Kiefer notes the claim that Thomas Sackville's 1563 "Induction" to the *Mirror for Magistrates* is "the best [poetry written] between Chaucer and Spenser." Reid Barbour argues convincingly for Thomas Nashe as "the most brilliant, explosive, and inventive prose writer of Elizabethan England." And Donald Stump reminds readers that Spenser's 1590 *Faerie Queene* "won immediate recognition as the finest poetic achievement of its generation."

Furthermore, these innovations and accomplishments were not isolated or passing phenomena. Collectively they were powerful influences upon contemporaries and successors. To take only the prominent example of Spenser, one recognizes with Stump that "in earlier periods he exerted an influence on English culture that rivaled that of any poet in the language" – especially on John Milton and hundreds of eighteenth-century imitations, adaptations, and continuations. "No other English poet except Milton can claim a greater following" among writers of the eighteenth century. In the nineteenth century, "along with Chaucer, Shakespeare, and Milton, Spenser stood as one of the great English sources of inspiration for the Romantic age. . . . Every one of the major Romantic poets was a serious reader of his works." In varying degrees, Spenser's contemporaries left their own influences upon their successors.

Genres. An additional trait of these writers is that they are remarkably diverse, producing both prose and verse on virtually every subject in a variety of nondramatic genres. Prose dialogue, for instance – what Kenneth Bartlett calls the "favorite medium of humanist discourse" – is represented by Lodowick Bryskett's *Discourse of Civil Life* (1606) and by William Bullein's formal medical treatises and his fictional treatment of the plague. As a tool of the Counter-Reformation, dialogue is the form of *Mary Magdalene's Funeral Tears* (1591), the best-known and most influential work of the Jesuit martyr Robert Southwell.

Even in a brief literary career, Southwell managed to write in many genres. His *Epistle of Comfort* (1587) exemplifies the ancient Christian genre of the pastoral letter encouraging the persecuted, even to the point of martyrdom. His dialogue between Mary Magdalene and others on

Easter morning (1591) is less a meditation on remorse than a story about Mary's love for Christ. *Triumphs over Death* (1591) is an epistolary prose elegy, and his *Humble Supplication* (1591–1592) is a graphic reply to Queen Elizabeth's proclamation of October 1591 that stigmatized Catholic priests. His *Short Rule of Good Life* (1596–1597?) is a prose handbook for Catholic laymen wishing to lead a devout life. And among his religious poems, *Saint Peter's Complaint* (1595) is an imitation of the literature of penitence and conversion characteristic of Counter-Reformation Italy.

The genre of prose fiction shows up in this volume at least a generation before Southwell in Bullein's *Dialogue against the Fever Pestilence* (1564), later in John Lyly's wildly popular Euphues volumes (1578, 1580), and again in Day's translated pastoral romance *Daphnis and Chloe* (1587). Sidney's *Arcadia* appeared posthumously in 1590 and 1593. More works by Greene, Nashe, and Thomas Deloney make the last two decades of the century a treasure trove of the most imaginative and heterogeneous prose fiction imaginable.

Greene alone is responsible for a sizable catalogue of diversity, as Sandra Clark documents. His moralizing euphuistic prose imitates Lyly's, although "the proportion of narrative to moralizing throughout is low." In 1584 he published a spate of romances, each with a different patron and printer but preoccupied with two favorite motifs: illicit sexual desire in old men and vindication of a woman's chastity. Moving from extended fiction to collections of novellas, he published several frame-tales in 1587–1588; and although they increased the role of narrative action beyond the minimum in his romances, "Greene rarely loses sight of the concept of literature as a compendium of moral exempla." His "second-phase romances" gradually minimize his Lylian style, extend the narratives to longer accounts, and modulate from the mode of profit to that of delight. *Pandosto* (1588), William Shakespeare's source for *The Winter's Tale* (1611), shows the strongest influence of Greek romance. *Menaphon* (1589), now often considered Greene's best romance, includes interspersed poems in a dozen different meters.

Greene becomes less heavy-handed in the didacticism of his cony-catching pamphlets, although they were written with an explicit aim of social benefit. Despite claims of "documentary realism" (created by "generous detail of names and places"), they are heavily dependent upon models in rogue literature and the jestbooks. His *Disputation between a He Cony-Catcher and a She Cony-Catcher* (1592) is more overtly didactic, with particular stress on the evils of prostitution.

Many of Greene's fictions are semi-autobiographical accounts of the prodigal. Some emphasize exemplary tales and moralizing discourse. In form, *A Quip for an Upstart Courtier* (1592) is a dream debate, but in substance it is social satire in the medieval Estates tradition. The posthumous *Repentance of Robert Greene* (1592) is a collection of fragments, some directly autobiographical, with a first-person confession and recantation "in passionate Puritan style" and a summary of Greene's prodigal life, death, and final prayer. All his life stories use the "single model of prodigality and repentance." Yet his *Never Too Late* (1590), while professing didactic intention, is actually much concerned with "the delight that comes from variety." It is hard to conceive more heterogeneous forebears for English fiction than the works of Greene.

When it comes to satire in prose, Nashe's work seems almost to belong to our own age. His popular *Unfortunate Traveler* (1594) is "the most modern thing in spirit and kind that Nashe ever wrote," according to Reid Barbour — a picaresque mishmash of jests, mirthful caricatures, and realistic prose fiction with an apparent artistic disorder that may actually reflect its theme of a culture in crisis. In contrast to this profoundly disturbing text, *Lenten Stuff* (1599), written at the end of Nashe's life, is a mock-encomium of the red herring (Yarmouth's chief economic resource), with the author's defense of "his right to be trivial."

As a serious apologist for art, Nashe lashed immoral authors and Puritans alike in his early *Anatomy of Absurdity* (1589). He was later hired by the Established Church to help rebut the pseudonymous Martin Marprelate's attacks and essentially came of age as a satirist with his *Almond for a Parrot* (1590), which Barbour describes as having the "trademarks of Nashe's mature invective style." Two years later *Pierce Penniless,* a complaint against public abuse and a satire of worldly follies and vices, made Nashe's career. His petulant quarrels with the Harvey brothers — Gabriel, Thomas, and Richard — are aired and preserved in *Strange News* (1593) and *Have with You to Saffron-Walden* (1596). Typically eclectic, Nashe combines medieval traditions of the homily and "speculum narrative" in the satire of *Christ's Tears over Jerusalem* (1593). In this text, which Barbour describes as showing a "penchant for the horrific and gory," he instructs modern society to see itself in the mirror of Rome's destruction of Jerusalem.

Deloney's prose fiction, by contrast, is more homogeneous: "middle-class" romances about idealized artisans such as shoemakers and their domestic situations. In his posthumously published *Thomas of Reading* (1602), for example, an alliance of king and clothier works for the good of the commonwealth. In structure, Deloney's romances are not loosely organized and episodic but rather are composed of multiple and interwoven plots from a variety of sources and traditions. In theme, Alexandra Halasz shows how they are far from simplistic in dealing with crossing and maintaining class boundaries in "a world in which the middle classes are ascendant."

Deloney also wrote original ballads – a genre at the bottom of any sixteenth-century hierarchy and one that Halasz describes during the 1590s "as the lowest literary form, or as non-literary altogether: 'threadbare trash' or 'trivial trinkets'. " Yet Deloney was the best-known ballad writer of the century for his strongly Protestant, patriotic, and antipapal spirit, and his ballads have a distinctive claim as a lasting literary type: they were published in book form (collected in two full volumes), some having been written originally for book publication and others originally published as broadsides.

From low to high and back again, generic diversity spans geographic as well as temporal and cultural boundaries. In Scotland, it is apparent in the works of Alexander Montgomerie written during the 1580s and 1590s. His dispute with Patrick Hume of Polwart is one of the most notable examples of "flyting," a kind of Scottish court poetry – a precursor of "doing the dozens" or "dissing" – in which contestants vie with each other in verbal abuse and technical virtuosity. More traditionally, Montgomerie is an expert with medieval personification allegory, as in his *Cherrie and the Slae* (1597), in which he extends and elaborates a debate among various mental attributes over choices of bold action versus cautious compromise. He is also notable for complex musical stanzas and a bountiful use of traditional proverbs.

Montgomerie's (and Nashe's *Christ's Tears*, noted above) are not the only works that look back to medieval models. The verse tragedies of the *Mirror for Magistrates* are in the medieval complaint and *de casibus* traditions. From its original publication (1559) through Sackville's "Induction" (1563) to John Higgins's new "Induction" (1574), the *Mirror* reflects the models of Giovanni Boccaccio, Geoffrey Chaucer, and William Langland in its use of the medieval dream-vision and its preoccupation with

history. George Peele's poem for the Order of the Garter investiture of 1593 is cast in a skillful dream device recalling Chaucer and that medieval tradition. In the very book that for many marks the beginning of the Golden Age of the English Renaissance, Spenser's "February" eclogue in *The Shepheardes Calender* uses the medieval beast fable to make a moral point, as does his *Prosopopoeia; or, Mother Hubberds Tale* in *Complaints* (1591). *The Shepheardes Calender* includes more, however, than medieval moralizing fables, for it also integrates pastoral complaint, singing matches, debate, encomium, elegy, and hymn. These genres are represented elsewhere in Angel Day's original encomium of Queen Elizabeth (1587) and in Sidney's pastoral entertainment *The Lady of May* (1578 or 1579). His sister's "Doleful Lay of Clorinda" (in Spenser's *Astrophel* of 1595) is an elegy for his death.

Mary Sidney is currently receiving long-overdue recognition, but she evaded criticism in her own time by confining her work to genres thought appropriate to women: translation, dedications, elegy, and encomium. Her own literary career began after the death of her brother Philip by encouraging works in his praise, editing and publishing his works, and completing his translation of the Psalms.

The noblest genre by sixteenth-century standards – heroic narrative – is represented by Phaer's translation of the *Aeneid* (beginning 1558), which made a Latin classic available in iambic heptameter couplets (fourteeners) familiar to readers from the alliterative ballad stanza. Sir Philip Sidney wrote a prose counterpart in his original and revised heroic romance, *Arcadia* (1583–1584). The masterpiece of the century is Spenser's *Faerie Queene,* which includes the descent of the epic hero to the underworld (Guyon's visit to the House of Mammon in Book II) and the tradition of depicting the hero's genealogy (in *Briton Moniments* at the House of Alma). Heroic grandeur informs even a poem from his *Complaints* volume: *Muiopotmos; or, The Fate of the Butterfly* might be dismissed as trivial mock-epic, but its central stanzas reflect on "one of the great themes of *The Faerie Queene,* the contrast between human folly and shortsightedness and 'The fatall purpose of divine foresight' ."

From his early pastorals through his allegorical masterpiece to his later love poems and complaints, Spenser's oeuvre is a poetic panoply. Remarkably, it parallels Sidney's, for both authors created pastoral, romance epic, sonnets, epithalamia, religious verse (hymns or psalms), and even drama and criticism (although these are lost in Spenser's case). Together with their contemporaries, they laid a large part of the foundation for literary achievement by Milton and others in the next century and beyond.

Education, didacticism. Teaching is an explicit or implicit concern in verse and prose throughout the sixteenth century. Richard Pace's *Benefit of a Liberal Education* (1517) is an early instance. Written during odd moments of an active political and diplomatic career, ostensibly for John Colet's students at St. Paul's, it includes references to many humanists (More, Erasmus, Colet, Thomas Linacre, and others) while dropping in several off-color "merry tales." Pace assumes that education is not its own reward but rather a means to a career in government. (He was nothing if not pragmatic, having served Archbishop Bainbridge until the latter's death, then Cardinal Thomas Wolsey – who was Bainbridge's probable murderer.)

The *Benefit* includes Pace's encomium of learning (specifically theology, law, philosophy, and medicine) followed by orations from personified branches of the liberal arts (music, astrology, astronomy, geometry, arithmetic, rhetoric, and grammar, omitting logic). While it purports to show that nothing can be done without learning, it presents all disciplines "fallen into severe decay" and illustrates the difficulty of "reconciling humanist idealism with political realities." In the end, the text persistently undercuts its theme – that learning leads to advancement, that the liberal arts make one free, that training in Greek and the classics make a better political world – when, Pace concludes, experience proves otherwise.

At once more pragmatic and idealistic than Pace, Richard Mulcaster is notable as the teacher of many Elizabethan and Jacobean men of letters (including Thomas Kyd, Thomas Lodge, and Spenser) and as the author of a commentary on the education of young women. In 1561 he became the first headmaster of the new Merchant Taylors' School, where the first curriculum was in Latin and chiefly for political ends. In contrast to Thomas Elyot and Roger Ascham, he strongly supported public education. His approach to the fifth part of rhetoric is interesting for integrating "indoor sports" – loud speaking and laughing – with more traditional methods of delivering a speech. Mulcaster's *First Part of the Elementary* (1582) addresses problems of vernacular spelling

with proposals to revise English for a more regular and rational orthography. But it is more than a mechanical treatise, for it integrates practical spelling with considerations of lexicography, the theory and politics of language, and a Platonic view (from the *Cratylus*) of relationships between words and things. It was perhaps intended to rival Quintilian's never-completed *De Institutione oratoria*. (See also Gabriel Harvey's radical lectures on Ramist pedagogy in 1574–1575, as noted above.)

Sixteenth-century treatises on educational theory and practice are complemented by pragmatic "how-to" handbooks in prose. As Day's *English Secretary* is to the aspiring professional, for example, so is Southwell's posthumous *Short Rule of Good Life* (1596–1597?) to Catholic laymen; Frank Brownlow calls it "a founding document of Christian social and domestic life in the modern world." It is possible that Lodowick Bryskett's *Civil Discourse* (1606) was conceived as early as the 1560s with equally practical ends as part of an educational regimen designed for the Sidney family, for Bryskett was long involved with the Sidney household, with the Dudleys' marriage aspirations, and with Ireland. (Compare also Phaer's *Book of Children,* Bullein's *Dialogue against the Fever Pestilence,* and Coverdale's translation of Bullinger's *Christian State of Matrimony;* also such practical guides as Chaloner's translation *Of the Office of Servants* [1543] to train servants and clarify their relationships to their masters.)

Less overtly, the *Mirror for Magistrates* is characterized by a didactic quality "so prized by Elizabethans and so disparaged by moderns," according to Frederick Kiefer. Its tales can symbolize self-absorption, vanity, or impulses to introspection. Its stories of miscreants can be viewed as admonitions and models for righteous living by negative example. Its narrative ghosts "express wonderment at the fragility of worldly prosperity, the tendency of things to alter, often for the worse." Its many examples of tragedy in the *de casibus* tradition suggest "that the reformation of conduct may be frustrated by an intractable human nature, easily distracted by pleasure and profit." The best poems in the *Mirror* make the reader feel the pain of loss so that the tales become more than wooden "object lessons in the wages of wrongdoing." Similarly, Holinshed believed that history writing is in itself a moral act and that history serves the chronicler with instructive examples, for instance, "that the rule of a usurper will end badly," as in his account of Macbeth in Scotland.

Even in the realm of prose fiction, a heavy-handed didacticism appears in Lyly's *Euphues: The Anatomy of Wit* (1578), which is actually a plea for academic preferment. Its successor, *Euphues and His England* (1580), is less pedagogic but no less practical as a bid for courtly patronage. As Derek Alwes observes, with its "extravagant patriotism, its lavish praise of Queen Elizabeth, and its dedication to Oxford," it "secures Lyly's position as . . . 'amuseur de la Cour' ." Both volumes were instructive models for an intense but short-lived eruption of imitations. In the next generation, Greene's romances and frame-tales moralize prominently. Moral exempla are conspicuous, for example, in *Penelope's Web* (1587) with its "edifying tales in which virtuous women convert erring men." His "second-phase romances" didactically emphasize human helplessness and the uncertainty of life before a sinister Fortune, and his "semi-autobiographical fictions of the prodigal" include concerns for both delight and teaching, often with prefatory "moralizing discourse." Greene published his cony-catching pamphlets with the explicit aim of social benefit.

As author of poetry, prose fiction, and a landmark treatise on literary theory and criticism, Sir Philip Sidney holds a notably syncretic view of aesthetics and instruction, of writing and the life of the author. As Marvin Hunt says, "the remarkable and very important trait of [his] mind was that he saw the aim of human life to be . . . 'well-doing, and not . . . well-knowing only' ." The equestrian anecdote opening his *Defense of Poetry* is appropriate to that text precisely because he regarded horsemanship as an art both to practice and to contemplate. His definition of "poesy" is an amalgam of Aristotle (mimesis), Plutarch (speaking picture), and Horace (teaching and delighting); thus, imaginative writing in verse or prose is a feigning of images in which delightful teaching is the "right describing note to know a poet by." As a teacher, the poet is superior to both the philosopher and historian; and the epic is the highest genre for teaching and moving "to the most high and excellent truth."

Hence, it is no surprise that *The Faerie Queene* of his contemporary Spenser draws together in heroic romance all that teaches and delights, and that, according to Donald Stump, it can be seen as a late-sixteenth-century climax of constructing both the individual and the society on classical and Christian ideals of civility, with courtesy as the "ground, / And roote of civill Conversation."

Biography, autobiography. Humanistic attention to the individual in society helps to explain the persistence of life writing – both explicit and implicit – throughout this period. The *Mirror for Magistrates,* for instance, is a midcentury collection of ostensibly first-person narratives that are actually poetic biographies by various hands. It is informed by a Renaissance concern with historical continuity and the chronicle tradition, and it includes accounts of women such as Jane Shore (by Thomas Churchyard) and Eleanor Cobham, the wife of Humphrey, Duke of Gloucester (by George Ferrers).

In quite a different vein, Nashe published *Have with You to Saffron-Walden; or, Gabriel Harvey's Hunt Is Up.* This burlesque or mock-biography – part of an exchange of biting invective between the two antagonists – is rather like a Scottish flyting. At the same time, its satire constitutes a kind of self-portrait, for, as Barbour says, "Nashe is more autobiographical here than in his other works." While Erickson suggests that Nashe's hostile portrait is "probably factually accurate," a modern, "enduring sketch of Harvey" is available in Ronald B. McKerrow's account of the quarrel in his 1904 edition of Nashe's works.

For a third perspective on the man usually known (until recently) as "Spenser's friend Harvey," the marginalia in his books provide "one of the most intimate surviving portraits of an English Renaissance figure," according to Erickson. Among the different personae created to represent "his most private aspirations to competence and fulfillment," Axiophilus stands for Harvey as poet, and Eutrapelus (the most frequent persona), as the "eloquent orator, teacher of rhetoric, persuasive man in speech (and in writing) and one who engages in witty jesting and very often in irony." The marginalia were not written for publication, so they record Harvey's "ingenuous psychotherapeutic excursions into his own vulnerabilities" and are testimony to his broad learning and extraordinary self-awareness.

Yet another species of life writing is Richard Robinson's unpublished semi-autobiographical *Eupolemia,* a record of his benefactors he made at the end of his career. It is a unique source for studying professional authorship from 1570 to 1600: "a catalogue of all my labors until [August 1602]," presented to the Lord Mayor and then to James I. As a list of all titles, reprints, purchasers, publishers, and dedicatees, *Eupolemia* provides a tremendous record of how to survive as an author, translator, and compiler at the end of the Tudor era.

In more traditional genres, Greene's "fictions of the prodigal" are semi-autobiographical. Southwell's *Triumphs over Death* (1591) was taken by contemporaries as his "last statement to death and to his own executioners" in a "tone of absolute and exalted resignation" to the will of God. Marvin Hunt observes how autobiography creeps into fiction in Sidney's 1590 *Arcadia,* in which his description of Kalendar's house conveys "the warmth, serviceability, and understated grace of the Sidney home." The conviction of Sidney's family that the goal of life is not just to know but also to do well is conspicuous both in his *Defense of Poetry* and in the *Arcadia,* where a "desire to make all experience educational distinguishes the childhood of Pyrocles and Musidorus." Sidney portrays himself in the eclogues of his prose *Old Arcadia* "as the love-stricken Philisides." In his sonnet sequence, "Astrophil is a refracted version of Sidney himself. . . . Stella is just as certainly a refracted version of Penelope Devereux." In the unlikely context of translating 107 Psalms, Sidney's sister Mary expanded upon metaphors and descriptions in the original Hebrew to incorporate not only her personal experience at court but also the experiences of marriage and childbirth.

Translation, vernacular. For many educated folk in the sixteenth century — and especially for a burgeoning reading public — the language of choice was English instead of Latin. As readership grew, so did the demand for translations of secular and sacred texts as well as for original works in the vernacular.

Virgil, Horace, and Cicero were obvious authors of interest. By 1562 Phaer had translated more of Virgil's *Aeneid* than any Englishman before him, in part for self-conscious literary and linguistic nationalism. But an equally compelling motive, according to M. Rick Smith, was his "stated object of freeing knowledge from the bonds of Latin for the benefit of the literate commoner." He refused "neo-classical diction as well as meter in favor of what he considered a more purely English versification and style" — a choice that was successful for a vast audience in his own time and beyond: in addition to many contemporary encomia, Smith notes that "Phaer's was the best known English *Aeneid* for the entire Elizabethan and Stuart age, displaced only by Dryden's in 1697."

Drant's translation of Horace into English (1566–1567) was the only complete version of the *Satires* and *Epistles* until well into the seventeenth century. Drant also paraphrased Job and Ecclesiastes. As an exercise suggested by his friend and mentor Hubert Languet, Sidney translated Cicero from Latin into French, then into English and back into Latin to improve his mastery of languages — but he demurred at studying German at his age, in part because "it has a certain harshness about it." Spenser included a version of the pseudo-Virgilian *Culex* as "Virgil's Gnat" in his *Complaints* volume (1591). His first publication in 1569 was also a book of poetic translations, not from Latin but from the Italian of Petrarch and from the French of Joachim du Bellay.

On the sacred scene, Coverdale was appointed by Henry VIII to edit the "Great Bible" of 1539. This translation exerted enormous influence on vernacular prose style, especially through Coverdale's version of the Psalms as used in the Book of Common Prayer. Because the Book of Common Prayer and the English Bible are arguably the most influential books in the language, then, as Richard Duerden suggests, a double debt is owed to "the nearly anonymous Coverdale." Soon after Coverdale, Chaloner completed John Cheke's translation of the *Homily of St. John Chrysostom* in 1544. His translation of Erasmus's *Praise of Folly* (1549) takes liberties with accuracy in order to enhance readability in this central humanist text, but his polemical modifications show how translation in the Tudor period was "often a weapon in the religious, philosophical, and political struggles of the day," according to M. Rick Smith. During the last quarter of the century, Richard Robinson was unusual in being able to make a living from publishing, not just translating, texts that are mostly works of Lutheran piety drawn from the first third of the century.

Translation was also a socially acceptable activity for creative women such as Mary Sidney, who completed her brother Philip's translation of the Psalms — in 128 different verse forms. As noted above, her own translation of Garnier's *Marc Antoine* is among the first English dramas in blank verse, and her translation of Philippe de Mornay's *Discours de la vie et de la mort* (1600) is both an oblique commentary on court politics and a denunciation of the vanity of worldly ambition.

For purely practical ends, translation was necessary in the sixteenth century to make legal and medical texts available to English-speaking professionals, as Phaer did during the 1530s and 1540s. His complaint against physicians applies generally to the Latin learned: "how long would they have the people ignorant?" M. Rick Smith observes that "his popularization of medicine and law greatly extended knowledge of these fields among the literate members of all classes, improving the people's overall understanding of their political and social, as well as their physical, bodies."

As the market for English texts grew, both authors and publishers increasingly produced original literature in the vernacular rather than translating from Latin models. Examples include Day and the original English letters of his *English Secretary*. Deloney wrote English ballads and fiction for the newly literate; these and his other works in English provided material that might otherwise have been unavailable to certain kinds of readers. And many printers who were also authors encouraged the development of a literary vernacular, especially by commissioning and printing both translations and original works. Among them, William Caxton, John Rastell, and Robert Copland may be considered among the "earliest promoters of printed English literature," as Sheila Ahern asserts.

Humanism. This concern to develop the vernacular is only one among many that are loosely characterized as "Renaissance humanism." Imitating classical authors is another. Scholarly Gabriel Harvey, for example, was a champion of reformed Ciceronianism in venerating Cicero without idolizing him. He viewed memorizing and imitating a classical writer only as a complement to understanding him and to reading widely in both the ancient and modern authors. Drant's major commitment was to sacred rather than secular texts, but his persistent interest in classical studies filled his sermons with allusions to Aristotle, Cicero, and other ancient authors. His last published volume, *Silva* (1576?), recalls the *Silvae* of Statius and uses both scriptural and classical materials to defend the study of the Ancients as an aid to better understanding and translating the Scriptures.

Throughout the century, humanistic syncretism works to juxtapose if not reconcile seeming incompatibles such as art and morality, Christianity and the classics. The stated purpose of Nashe's *Anatomy of Absurdity* (1589), for example, is to defend poetry against its enemies — both from authors who neglect morality for the sake of obscene pleasure and from Puritans who deprive morality of beauty or power — for the purpose of

true poetry is moral reformation effected by eloquence. Spenser's *Epithalamion* is a "delicate balance between the heavenly and the earthly, the classical and the Christian," says Donald Stump. "A similar, though more puzzling, blend of the classical with the Christian" appears in his *Fowre Hymnes* (1596) which juxtapose pagan Cupid and Venus with Christ and Sapience (Christian wisdom).

Another humanistic concern is the active life as complement or alternative to contemplative and voluptuous modes. Pace's *Benefit of a Liberal Education* (contemporary with More's *Utopia*, 1516) corroborates More's humanistic concern for service to the state, but it also shares More's protagonist Raphael Hythloday's skepticism about the compatibility of service and ideals. Bryskett's *Discourse of Civil Life* helped to extend the humanist culture of Renaissance Italy into England, especially with its emphasis upon "patrician civic responsibility and education," says Kenneth Bartlett. Like Sidney, Bryskett was aware of the respective merits of the active and contemplative lives and was ready to serve his government when needed. Spenser's nationalistic bent is apparent in the political and religious allegory of his *Shepheardes Calender,* probably cultivated by his many relationships with humanist activists such as Mulcaster, Harvey, Bryskett, Sidney, and Sir Walter Ralegh.

Politics, religion. Literary figures are not above meddling in politics and were often drawn into the ongoing battles of the Protestant Reformation in sixteenth-century England. For instance, when ousted from a position of poetic influence at the Scottish court in 1593, Montgomerie became involved with Roman Catholic plots for a revolution in Scotland and was subsequently outlawed. The fifty-seven surviving poems of Robert Southwell are entirely religious as he "always strives to engage his reader in contemplation" of their subject matter. Yet because he served as an underground Jesuit and was thus a threat to the state, he was martyred for his faith.

In 1569 the skillful orator Edmund Campion wrote his *History of Ireland* as "a virtual panegyric extolling England's sovereignty over Ireland," says Carolyn Scott; the book was to affect both government policy and national perceptions, especially through its influence upon Holinshed's *Chronicles* (1578) and Spenser's *View of the Present State of Ireland* (written before 1599; published 1633). Campion was not overtly Catholic until he renounced the Established Church in 1571 and became a Jesuit in 1573. Thereafter he was regarded as a particular threat to the English church and state because of "his oratorical persuasiveness and his attractive character," for Protestant and Catholic authors alike were influenced by his writing and oratory.

Religion and politics permeated education as well as historiography. The main thrust of Mulcaster's ambitious educational program is political, deriving, according to William Barker, from the assumption that "a properly consistent and regulated system of education will enhance the social order of the commonwealth." Emily Stockard comments that Holinshed's *Chronicles* include multiple and conflicting voices in the historical narrative – and thus encouraged religious toleration while expressing "a philosophy of political liberalism that was developed in sixteenth-century England in reaction to the conflicts of the Reformation."

Few religious writers of the period had as much consequence in England as Miles Coverdale and Richard Field. Behind Coverdale's translations of Scripture lay the politically explosive assumption that "reception of the Word would transform behavior." The political strategies of some of the Protestant Reformers are implicit in his dedicatory epistle to King Henry VIII with the first complete Bible in 1535: "it insinuates that the promulgation and reading of an English Bible will increase obedience in the realm," and "it symbolically empowers the king by bestowing upon him a scriptural legitimation," observes Richard Duerden. Coverdale's opposition to the Established Church developed only gradually, in part through commentaries on Scripture that were popular rather than scholarly, calling for personal responses, morally and emotionally. By appealing to common folk, his books ran counter to edicts against Bible reading by women, artificers, laborers, and so forth; copies of at least thirteen of his titles were confiscated and burned by the authorities.

Growing literacy, access to the Scriptures in English, and Coverdale's populist strategy coalesce in John Field, who Duerden reports has been called "the Lenin of Elizabethan puritanism," dedicating all his skills to "further reformation of the English church." His religious writing includes *A Godly Exhortation* (1583), excoriating Sabbath recreations and neglect of churches. While largely covert, his work was enormously influential in disseminating the tenets of Puritanism, especially after 1566. But what may seem to be merely superficial attacks on vestments, ceremonies, and church organization in fact entailed radical revision of the premises of Elizabe-

than government and society as well as the church. A scriptural form of church government, for instance, required the abolition of episcopacy and hierarchy and was thus a threat to royal prerogative and supremacy. Even his materials for a documentary history of Puritanism – on the model of John Foxe's *Acts and Monuments* (1563) and covering the period 1565–1588 – were used before publication as part of the Puritan assault on episcopacy. The work was viewed by Elizabeth's officials as sedition for setting up a democratic counter-authority to the Established Church and state.

These implications and interpretations warrant emphasis, for Field and his successors show, "with a clarity seldom matched, the power of the Word" for political as well as religious persuasion. His literary skill is perhaps best seen in *Godly Prayers and Meditations* (1583), in which his prayers are laced with political propaganda, reproofs of the queen, and legislation for Parliament. Duerden observes that "he teaches all the people who read his little manual that they may pass judgment on rulers, so long as they submit to God's word and give their support to the ministers." A decade earlier, his *Admonition to the Parliament* (1572) "convulsed England as few documents have done," especially for its threat of "popularity" (that is, democratic government by the populace). Although Field has been only newly recognized at the forefront of the Elizabethan Puritan movement, it is no exaggeration to say that a part of his legacy is the Revolution and the Civil War of the seventeenth century.

Even flattery has political and religious implications in the period. In September 1578 Harvey expanded and printed the encomia and admonitions he had presented to Queen Elizabeth in July and included an endorsement of Castiglione's courtier as an exemplary model of courtesy – but also as a subtle and ironic critique of Machiavellian intrusion into English politics by the Roman Catholic French and the Duc d'Alençon. At about the same time, Sidney's "superficially innocuous entertainment," the pastoral *Lady of May* (1578 or 1579), is highly political: ostensibly an encomium of Queen Elizabeth and possessed of some literary merit, it has considerable political and propagandistic value against her proposed marriage to Alençon. The holograph fragment of his "Discourse on Irish Affairs," by contrast, is explicitly political and seems overtly brutal today, but it is typical of Elizabethan English attitudes toward Ireland. Sidney himself was "viewed in his own age as the best hope for the establishment of a Protestant League in Europe."

In Spenser's exactly contemporary *Shepheardes Calender,* Donald Stump observes that the eclogues for May, June, and September "all turn on the controversy between Protestant reform and Elizabeth's more conservative Catholic subjects, which [controversy] was the greatest single threat to her ability to rule." Spenser was for most of his adult life a government official employed in the ongoing English campaign to suppress rebellious Ireland. The topical allegory of his massive *Faerie Queene* often reflects on England, Ireland, and their relationship, especially in Book V.

Women authors were no less implicated than men in religion and politics. Margaret Hannay says that Mary Sidney's translation of Garnier's *Marc Antoine* "helped introduce the continental vogue for using historical drama to comment on contemporary politics." Although there is nothing explicit in it about English politics, it "was particularly appropriate in the turbulent 1590s, when England feared that Elizabeth's death would plunge them into a civil war as bloody as Rome's." Sidney's translation of Philippe de Mornay's *Discours au roi Charles* (1572) — published with *Marc Antoine* (1590) — recalls previous sixteenth-century writers such as Erasmus, More, and Wyatt in its oblique commentary on the danger of civil war and on court politics as a demonstration of the vanity of worldly ambition. Among her sacred works, she used her translation of the Psalms to comment on contemporary politics, especially to urge English intervention in the persecution of Protestants on the Continent. As an aristocratic woman, she was quite bold to publish under her own name.

Readership and popularity. Irrespective of party and sect, sixteenth-century British nondramatic writers found a growing public that was eager to read and willing to pay for their works. Deloney's ballads and prose fiction, for instance, were so popular that they were republished frequently throughout the seventeenth century and into the eighteenth; the earliest surviving copy of *Jack of Newbury* (1619) is apparently the eighth edition, its predecessors having literally been read out of existence by "a culture that was popular and oral."

Among the "university wits" who left a mainstream career at the university to authors such as Harvey, Greene was part of the first generation of professional London writers; he enjoyed an "extraordinary contemporary popularity" and created a unique image of himself as the "archetypal literary prodigal." His *Pandosto* was the most popular English romance after Sidney's *Arcadia,* with twenty-six different editions in 150 years, including several French translations in the seventeenth century. According to Sandra Clark, "His audience appeal was wider than that of any contemporary prose writer." The great diversity of Greene's writing in several genres (see above) demonstrates his appeal across a spectrum from courtly to popular literature. And Lyly's two volumes about Euphues, according to Derek Alwes, were "the most popular works of [English] fiction in the sixteenth century. Ten editions of each text saw print by the end of the century, inspiring dozens of imitators."

Other kinds of writing sold well, too. Southwell's works enjoyed an "extraordinary popularity during his brief English career and the forty years following it." Despite its massive size and high cost, the first edition of Raphael Holinshed's *Chronicles* (1577–1578) was so popular that a second, augmented edition was required in 1587. But the economic pie had some limits, and as early as 1567 Drant responded disdainfully to his printer's concern that while a translation of Horace might be wise it also might not be sellable to a readership taken up with prose romances.

As a literary life became more and more viable as an occupation in the later sixteenth century, the very lack of a distinctive oeuvre by Richard Robinson suggests how wide were the possibilities of surviving by writing. (Curiously, in the midst of a burgeoning London market for print materials, he found law students and legal stationers willing to pay him for copying texts in longhand.) He cobbled together a literary living by transcribing manuscripts, by collecting money from patrons, by translating godly works and compiling miscellaneous texts — and even by selling the "author's copies" that publishers gave him for such work.

Patronage, networking. Behind these popular and economic successes lies another principle: that a successful literary life in sixteenth-century England often depended not only on the marketplace but also on whom the author knew. Robinson's career is instructive, for he made "a remarkably professional pursuit of patronage," including requests to courtiers, citizens, and clerics. His *Eupolemia* includes a record of his benefactors and covers a spectrum ranging from refusal by Queen Elizabeth through a single grudging payment to repeated support for his writing. It also shows how dedications are not merely indexes of dedicatees' interests. Conspicuously, it reveals a lack of consistent support from his many publishers. James Robertson concludes that "Robinson's efforts offer insights into the strategies for survival as an author in Elizabethan society, a business that remained very distant from the clichéd vocabularies of reciprocity and gratitude that formed the language of patronage employed by Robinson and his peers."

Among fiction writers, Lyly's prose shows motives shifting from academic to court preferment, thus giving the modern reader a perspective on the patronage system at large and the different rhetorical strategies it demanded. Informal networking, too, was valuable for stimulus and points of entry to publication. For example, during his years at Christ Church, Oxford, George Peele was a contemporary of Sidney, Edward Dyer, William Camden, and Richard Carew. At other Oxford colleges during the early 1570s, he knew Lyly, Lodge, Edmund and Robert Carey, Matthew Roydon, and John Grange. As Charles Whitworth says, it is "hardly surprising that Peele's talent for poetry and drama flourished at Christ Church in the 1570s," for the college was well known for its dramatic productions. In nondramatic modes Peele, along with several other students at Oxford, was a contributor to *The Phoenix Nest* (1593), one of the best poetical miscellanies of the age. In the case of Greene, his prolific literary life included contact with several well-known figures, including antagonistic relations with Nashe and Harvey.

Harvey's own star has been rising at the end of the twentieth century, giving him a brighter luster in a circle that included Sidney, the Earl of Leicester, Spenser, Dyer, and Daniel Rogers. In a kind of joint publishing venture, he collaborated pseudo-anonymously with Spenser in *The Shepheardes Calender* and two collections of letters (1580). His protracted war of words with Nashe and Greene beginning in 1589 includes, among other things, twenty-two sonnets of slurs on Greene and praise of noble persons. Bryskett was also a friend of Sidney and Spenser and shared some of their experiences in Ireland. His brother Sebastian was in the service of Robert Dudley (the Earl of Leicester and uncle to Sidney), and he was himself in the service of Sidney's father, Sir Henry.

Sidney was a lifelong friend of Fulke Greville from age ten, when they were students at Shrewsbury School, and he developed a friendship in Strasbourg with Hubert Languet, a leading Huguenot. In February 1577 Sidney was accompanied by Greville and Dyer to convey English condolences to the family of Emperor Maximilian II of Austria. He probably knew Edmund Campion while a student at Oxford, and he met him again in Prague in 1577.

Spenser's relationship to Sidney is being actively studied today partly in the context of the literary circle known as the Areopagus. Their affinities are apparent in the *Amoretti* sonnet sequence, which sometimes reads like a reply to Sidney's *Astrophil and Stella*. In addition, Donald Stump notes that Spenser wrote his own elegiac *Astrophel* and collected other elegies and epitaphs for Sidney at the end of his *Complaints* (1591), offering "a belated though impressive tribute to the dead poet-hero who had served as [his] early mentor." Spenser's first job, the result of patronage and networking, was as personal secretary to John Young, Bishop of Rochester. Even in Ireland during the 1580s and 1590s, his literary circle was extensive, including Barnabe Riche, Barnabe Googe, Bryskett, and Ralegh. Ralegh arranged for Spenser's 1589 trip to London to publish the first three books of *The Faerie Queene* and to present the poem to Queen Elizabeth, whose annual pension of fifty pounds "was more than the parsimonious queen granted to any other poet of the period."

Finally, it is notable that Mary Sidney was "the most important nonroyal woman writer and patron of Elizabethan England." Gathering a coterie of writers at Pembroke (her estate in Wilton), she actually played three major literary roles: author, translator, and patron. Her role model as patron endured in her sons William (third Earl of Pembroke) and Philip (Earl of Montgomery, fourth Earl of Pembroke), the "Incomparable Pair of Brethren" to whom Shakespeare's First Folio was dedicated. Clearly, the losses to British literature would be immeasurable were it not for patrons such as these and the broader system of patronage and networking that they represent.

This introduction has described nine large topics that are conspicuous in the articles in this volume: innovation; genres; education and didacticism; biography and autobiography; translation and the vernacular; humanism; politics and religion; readership and popularity; and patronage and networking. It is complemented by similar descriptions of other sixteenth-century British nondramatic writers in *DLB 132* and *DLB 136*.

Note: Titles in the lists of authors' works at the beginnings of the entries have been checked against *A Short-Title Catalogue of Books Printed in England, Scotland, and Ireland and of English Books Printed Abroad 1475–1640,* second edition (1976–1991) and other sources and are given, as far as possible, with the original spellings and punctuation but modernized capitalization. With the exception of Montgomerie's and Spenser's works, titles and quotations in the texts of the entries are modernized in capitalization, spelling, and punctuation to make them more readily accessible to modern readers.

– *David A. Richardson*

Acknowledgments

This book was produced by Bruccoli Clark Layman, Inc. Karen L. Rood is senior editor for the *Dictionary of Literary Biography* series. Samuel W. Bruce was the in-house editor.

Production manager is Samuel W. Bruce. Photography editors are Julie E. Frick and Margaret Meriwether. Photographic copy work was performed by Joseph M. Bruccoli. Layout and graphics supervisor is Emily Ruth Sharpe. Copyediting supervisor is Laurel M. Gladden. Typesetting supervisor is Kathleen M. Flanagan. Systems manager is Chris Elmore. Laura Pleicones and L. Kay Webster are editorial associates. The production staff includes Phyllis A. Avant, Ann M. Cheschi, Melody W. Clegg, Patricia Coate, Joyce Fowler, Stephanie C. Hatchell, Kathy Lawler Merlette, Jeff Miller, Pamela D. Norton, Delores Plastow, Lisa A. Stufft, William L. Thomas Jr., and Allison Trussell.

Walter W. Ross and Steven Gross did library research. They were assisted by the following librarians at the Thomas Cooper Library of the University of South Carolina: Linda Holderfield and the interlibrary-loan staff; reference-department head Virginia Weathers; reference librarians Marilee Birchfield, Stefanie Buck, Stefanie DuBose, Rebecca Feind, Karen Joseph, Donna Lehman, Charlene Loope, Anthony McKissick, Jean Rhyne, Kwamine Simpson, and Virginia Weathers; circulation-department head Caroline Taylor; and acquisitions-searching supervisor David Haggard.

The editor expresses particular thanks to Michael D. Bohnert for his meticulous and reliable assistance.

The publishers acknowledge the generous assistance of William R. Cagle, director of the Lilly Library, Indiana University, and his staff, who provided many of the illustrations in this volume. Their work represents the highest standards of librarianship and research.

Sixteenth-Century British Nondramatic Writers
Third Series

Dictionary of Literary Biography

Lodowick Bryskett

(1546? - 1612)

Kenneth R. Bartlett
Victoria College, University of Toronto

BOOK: *A Discourse of Civill Life, Containing the Ethike Part of Morall Philosophy.* (London: Edward Blount, 1606; London: Printed for William Aspley, 1606).

Editions: *A Discourse of Civill Life,* edited by Thomas E. Wright (Northridge, Cal.: San Fernando State College, 1970);

Literary Works, edited by J. H. P. Pafford (Farnsborough: Gregg International, 1972).

Lodowick Bryskett is usually mentioned as a friend of Edmund Spenser — he may be the model for Thestylis in *Colin Clouts Come Home Againe* (1595), and he is referred to in *Amoretti* 33 — or as the companion of Sir Philip Sidney on the Continent, rather than as a significant literary figure in his own right. However, his *A Discourse of Civil Life* (1606) merits serious study, not so much for its original content as for its importance as a medium for extending the humanist culture of Renaissance Italy into England. His contribution to the transmission of literary culture is illustrated as well by two elegies on the death of his friend Sidney, printed at the end of *Astrophil* in Spenser's *Colin Clout:* "The Mourning Muse of Thestylis" (powerfully echoed in John Milton's *Lycidas,* 1638) and "Pastoral Eclogue upon the Death of Philip Sidney, Knight" (heavily derived from Torquato Tasso's "Selva nella morte del signor Aluigi da Gonzaga" and "Alcippo"). The tradition of paraphrasing Italian lyric poetry was long and respected, beginning with Sir Thomas Wyatt the Elder, who began the practice with his free translation of Pietro Aretino's *I sette salmi de la penitenzia di David* (1534) as *Penitential Psalms* (1549), as well as his versions of works by Petrarch and Serafino dell'Aquila. Thus, Bryskett, whose first language was Italian and who had, like Wyatt, traveled to Italy, went beyond the immediately popular works of Italian literature to present an English translation of treatises on civic humanism and to introduce his English readers to the strong statements of patrician civic responsibility and education found in those sources.

Lodowick Bryskett was probably born around 1546 in his family's house in Hackney, London. He was the third son of Anthony Bryskett (Antonio Bruschetto), a Genoese merchant who had been resident in England from about 1523 but who did not receive letters of denization until 1536. Given the early date of his migration to England, it is probable that Anthony was not an Italian exiled for his religious allegiance, although he is described as belonging to an English parish and hence conforming to the established Protestant Church. Nevertheless, as a member of Michelangelo (the father of John) Florio's Italian Protestant church in London, he was accused of desiring a return to the Mass. Later the elder Bryskett was involved in attempts by Pope Pius IV to renew England's communion with Rome, a clandestine operation in which Anthony's eldest son, Sebastian, was also deeply involved as a messenger, a role occasionally pressed upon Lodowick as well.

Lodowick was educated first at Tunbridge and later, as a result of a lingering illness, by private tutors at home. In 1559 he entered Trinity College, Cambridge, as a pensioner but left before taking a degree. By 1562 he was abroad in Italy acting for the family's commercial interests, most likely with his brother Sebastian, who had been educated at the University of Padua and was a student of philosophy at Rome in 1560. It was at this time that the

A

DISCOVRSE

OF CIVILL LIFE:

Containing the Ethike part
of *Morall Philosophie*.

Fit for the instructing of a Gentleman
in the course of a vertuous life.

By LOD: BR.

Virtute, summa : Catera Fortunâ.

LONDON,
Printed for VVILLIAM ASPLEY.
1 6 0 6.

*Title page for Bryskett's only book, which was influential in transmitting
the ideals of Italian civic humanism into Elizabethan England*

Bryskett family became involved in the work of Gurone Bertano, a papal diplomat with close connections to the Curia and long experience with England (his brother was a leading cardinal at Trent and twice a plausible candidate for the papal throne). Bertano was charged on two occasions to negotiate a reunion of the English and Roman Churches. It is likely that Bryskett was engaged in these secret negotiations, given that his brother was Bertano's secretary and the principal means of transmitting letters from Rome to his father, who in turn passed them to Sir William Cecil, Sir Robert Dudley, or, on at least one occasion, the queen.

To facilitate this clandestine mission and to further Robert Dudley's ambition to marry the queen through papal auspices, Sebastian Bryskett entered Dudley's household in 1564, the year Dudley was raised to the earldom of Leicester. He was accorded the significant pension of two hundred crowns per annum and his maintenance by the earl. That same year or early in the next, Bryskett entered the service of Sir Henry Sidney, Leicester's brother-in-law. This position could have been arranged by Bryskett's father, who had close contacts with the court, especially with Cecil, or more likely through Leicester, who had already involved the Sidneys in his scheme to marry the queen and achieve the crown matrimonial. Early in 1561 Sidney had spoken with the Spanish ambassador, Alvaro De Quadra, on Dudley's behalf, suggesting that Dudley would be disposed to restore Catholic worship and the Roman allegiance in return for assistance in seeking Elizabeth's hand. This project was then pursued by the papacy, leading to the deep involvement of the Bryskett family as conduits of information. It is likely, for these reasons and to further the scheme, that Bryskett was put in Sidney's household, since Leicester made it clear that his entire family was to benefit from his royal marriage. His brother Ambrose was even to be made a cardinal.

The Bertano-Bryskett-Dudley schemes collapsed on the death of Pius IV in 1565. Bryskett remained in the Sidney household, however, traveling with Sir Henry in that year to Ireland, where Sidney had been appointed lord deputy, and accompanying Sir Henry's son, Philip Sidney, to Italy in the late 1560s on a grand tour of the Continent, for which he received twenty pounds. During that time in Italy, he once more made contact with his elder brother Sebastian, receiving letters from him in Venice. Although these might have been simply documents concerning family affairs or unspecific intelligence reports (still probably Sebastian's employment), they might equally have been related to Cecil's continued interest in Bertano and papal policy regarding England, given that a surviving letter of 1573 from Anthony Bryskett to Cecil records Gurone's death.

Bryskett's experience with Philip Sidney on the Continent was eventful: they were in Paris in 1572 during the Saint Bartholomew's Day Massacre. In 1574, however, Bryskett had to return to England because of the death of his father. The fact that Anthony was buried in an English parish churchyard indicates that the family probably was not Catholic but rather attempted to heal the religious division in Europe through private diplomacy. Similarly, this irenic position of the Brysketts might well have been shattered by the events of Saint Bartholomew's Day witnessed by Lodowick. There is no indication that the doubtlessly sincere Protestant Philip Sidney questioned the religion of his companion. Nevertheless, it is likely that Bryskett, like his brother and father, had the confessional flexibility of *un inglese italianato,* an observation reinforced by the marriage of Bryskett's sister, Lucrezia, to a prominent English Italian recusant, Vincent Guicciardine.

Bryskett's connection to the Sidneys resulted in his appointment as clerk of the Privy Council of Ireland under Sir Henry in 1575. Other comfortable sinecure appointments followed: clerk in chancery for the faculties in 1577, general controller for customs on wines in 1579, and secretary to the great soldier Sir William Drury during 1578–1579. The summer of 1581 saw Bryskett with the lord deputy,

Lord Grey of Wilton, on a tour of the northern Irish counties.

Bryskett married during these years; his first child, Philip (probably named after Philip Sidney), was born in 1580. Grey's recall to England in 1582 caused Bryskett to lose his influence temporarily, although by the next year he had secured the position of clerk of the Council of Munster, with Edmund Spenser as his deputy after 1584. Moreover, Bryskett's loss of office resulted in his return to literary occupations, since *A Discourse of Civil Life* had probably been begun by this time; indeed, he might have conceived of the idea as early as the 1560s as part of an educational regimen devised for the Sidney family. If this is the case, Bryskett's recognition of Sir Henry's concern for the bringing up of his family in good and virtuous learning attests to the origin of the work, which also recounts Sidney's accomplishments.

Although *A Discourse of Civil Life* was first printed in 1606, Bryskett had begun it twenty years earlier, after his loss of office in 1582 occasioned by Lord Grey's recall from Ireland, as Bryskett himself acknowledges in the prefatory letter. It is largely a careful translation of *Tre dialoghi della vita civile* (1565) by Giambattista Giraldi, usually known as Cinthio (or Cinzio) from the persona of Cynthius adopted for his Latin poetry. Bryskett added shorter selections from two other humanist treatises: Alessandro Piccolomini's *Della Institutione morale* (1560) and Stefano Guazzo's *La Civil conversazione* (1574). There are, moreover, original passages interpolated into the text that give the entire work a much more personal character than is usually found in a translation. These passages are evident in the opening section of each day's conversation, which together provide an almost domestic charm to the work. Day three, for example, opens with Bryskett not yet fully dressed and looking out his window toward Dublin, when he sees a troop of soldiers approaching. Such passages, together with Bryskett's energetic style in the dialogue – "I cry you mercy, my Lord [Primate], quoth I, if I have stepped into your marches before I were aware" – indicate that *A Discourse of Civil Life* is not just a derivative translation but a powerful statement of the author's voice.

Cinthio's work is a dialogue, a favorite medium of humanist discourse and a genre Bryskett retains, although he adds a frame to place the discussion in his own house near Dublin, to which several friends had repaired to avoid plague. Also, he changes the personae of the speakers from Cinthio's Italians to historical figures Bryskett knew in Ireland. The primary spokesman for the author's point

The first page from a manuscript for Bryskett's elegy for Sir Philip Sidney
(Lambeth Palace Library, Ms. Cod. Tension 841, item 3)

of view thus becomes Bryskett rather than Cinthio's Lelio. Spenser appears, as do the archbishop of Armagh, the chief justice of Common Pleas, the queen's solicitor, four celebrated soldiers, and a Dublin apothecary. These framing passages provide a much more immediate quality to *A Discourse of Civil Life* and render it less of a studied translation. Also, these sections of the work provide useful autobiographical and biographical information concerning the interlocutors, as well as a rationale for Bryskett's having undertaken the work in the first place. Even the location of the dialogue – which may have reflected an actual conversation, although there is no hard evidence – is justified in the dedicatory letter to Lord Grey: "How much more will you esteem my endeavor and be delighted with my translation of those choice grafts and flowers taken from the Greek and Latin philosophy. . . . Neither is it unlikely but that the receiving of so unlooked for a present out of this barbarous country of Ireland will be some occasion to hold it the dearer, as a

thing rare in such a place, where almost no trace of learning is to be seen."

This original material also presents Bryskett's thoughts on the humanist debate between the respective values of the active and contemplative life. Circumstances have led him to be more engaged in private study than he had enjoyed in his previously busy appointments; however, he admits that although he savors these delights, he is still close enough to the government to offer service when required. Also, he is reminded by his guests of the duty implicit in learning, experience, and moral knowledge to serve the commonweal.

It is in the discussion of these fundamental questions of civic humanism that Bryskett fairly acknowledges the guidance of the Italians and specifically of the texts he has chosen to translate in *A Discourse of Civil Life*. Recognizing the difficulty in understanding the subtleties of Plato and Aristotle and other texts of moral philosophy, Bryskett remarks that the Italian humanists have successfully produced useful and accurate syntheses in their own language. He concludes that it is the duty of similarly trained and inspired writers in English to present these important concepts to their people.

Spenser, who is asked to speak on the question of moral philosophy and who has a deep knowledge of Greek classical texts, defers by saying that he is writing *The Faerie Queene,* which will discuss moral virtues in verse. Instead, he suggests that Cinthio's dialogue on "The Ethic Part of Moral Philosophy," translated by Bryskett, be the basis of the discussion. In this way, the translation is integrated into the author's frame, although at the cost of losing the original Italian's socratic energy, which is subsumed by Bryskett's more rhetorical style.

The great significance of *A Discourse of Civil Life* is its value as an instrument for transmitting into the literary and intellectual world of Elizabethan England the fully developed ideals of Italian civic humanism founded upon the appropriate classical models. The Italian sources are heavily concerned with issues of ethics and the responsibilities of the educated, articulate citizen. Bryskett was familiar with such concepts not only from his education but from the example of his own life and family.

The events of the 1598 Tyrone rebellion ruined Bryskett's ambitions and forced him back to England, which he had regularly visited. Thereafter he returned to his initial employment as intelligence operative, possibly through the influence of the earl of Essex (given the connections of the Essex faction with the Sidneys, Walsingham, and Leicester, as well as the links with Ireland).

Bryskett was captured in 1600 in the Netherlands as an intelligencer and exchanged in 1601 for two Catholic prisoners in England, including the Jesuit Fernand Cardin. Returning to England, he discovered his wife had given birth to their daughter, Elizabeth, during his imprisonment in 1600.

Moreover, he was profiting economically. Having benefited from part of his father's property through inheritance and having acquired former monastic land in Ireland, Bryskett in addition purchased English property at Chelsea. He died on his estate in Ireland in 1612.

Biography:

Henry R. Plomer and Tom Peete Cross, *The Life and Correspondence of Lodowick Bryskett* (Chicago: University of Chicago Press, 1927).

References:

Kenneth R. Bartlett, "Papal Policy and the English Crown, 1563–1565: The Bertano Correspondence," *Sixteenth Century Journal,* 23 (Winter 1992): 643–659;

John Erskine, "The Virtue of Friendship in the *Faerie Queene,*" *PMLA,* 30 (September 1915): 831–850;

Raymond Jenkins, "Spenser and the Clerkship in Munster," *PMLA,* 47 (January 1932): 109–121;

Deborah Jones, "Lodowick Bryskett and His Family," in *Thomas Lodge and Other Elizabethans,* edited by C. J. Sissons (Cambridge, Mass.: Harvard University Press, 1933), pp. 243–263;

Alexander Judson, "Spenser and the Munster Officials," *Studies in Philology,* 44 (April 1947): 157–173;

W. P. Mustard, "Lodowick Bryskett and Bernardo Tasso," *American Journal of Philology,* 35, no. 2 (1914): 192–199;

James M. Osborn, *Young Philip Sidney, 1572–1577* (New Haven: Yale University Press, 1972);

Janet Spens, "On Bryskett's Translation of Giraldi's *Discourses,*" in her *Spenser's "Faerie Queene": An Interpretation* (London: Arnold, 1934), pp. 139–144.

William Bullein

(between 1520 and 1530 – 7 January 1576)

Elizabeth McCutcheon
University of Hawaii

BOOKS: *A Newe Booke Entituled the Gouernement of Healthe: Reduced into the Forme of a Dialogue* (London: J. Day, 1558); revised as *A Newe Boke of Phisicke Called ye Gouernment of Health* (London: J. Day, 1558);

Bulleins Bulwarke of Defe[n]ce againste All Sicknes, Sornes, and Woundes (London: J. Kingston, 1562);

A Comfortable Regiment, and a Very Wholsome Order against Pleurisi (London: J. Kingston, 1562); concluding pages printed as "Doctor Bullins Diet for Health" at the end of an anonymous work, *A Briefe and Short Discourse of the Vertue of Balsame* (London: John Perin, 1585);

A Dialogue Both Pleasant and Piety-Full, against the Fever Pestilence (London: J. Kingston, 1564; revised, 1564; revised and enlarged, 1573).

Editions: *A Dialogue against the Fever Pestilence,* edited by Mark W. Bullen and A. H. Bullen, Early English Text Society, extra series 52 (London: Oxford University Press, 1888);

Bulleins Bulwarke of Defe[n]ce againste All Sicknes, Sornes, and Woundes (Amsterdam: Theatrum Orbis Terrarum / New York: Da Capo Press, 1971).

OTHER: Philip Moore, *The Hope of Health Wherin Is Conteined a Goodlie Regimente of Life,* with a prefatory letter, verses, and marginalia by Bullein (London: J. Kingston, 1564);

Flavius Vegetius Renatus, *The Foure Bookes of Flauius Vegetius Renatus, Briefelye Contayninge a Plaine Forme, of Martiall Policye,* translated by John Sadler (London: T. Marshe, 1572) – includes verses by Bullein.

A cleric, physician, and medical humanist, William Bullein wrote several medical works that circulated widely in Tudor England. He was particularly attracted to the dialogue form, using it for instructional purposes in his first two treatises and turning it into an original work of fiction in *A Dialogue against the Fever Pestilence* (1564), the first literary treatment of the plague in sixteenth-century England.

Little is known about the early part of Bullein's life. He was born in the region known as the Isle of Ely, in Cambridgeshire – probably between 1520 and 1530 – but neither his date of birth nor his education has been established. On 9 June 1550 he became rector of Blaxhall in Suffolk, resigning the position by 5 November 1554. Subsequently he practiced medicine, first in the counties of Durham and Northumberland and later in London: on 15 June 1560 he leased a house and garden in the parish of St. Giles, Cripplegate.

Bullein wrote his first book, *The Government of Health* (1558), while living in the north. His claims that he wrote it for "the better understanding of the unlearned" and for "those who lack wherewithall and be furthest from the physicians" are probably exaggerated – his audience would have included other medical practitioners and a social elite – but the book does treat in a simpler and more accessible way material that reappears in his later treatises. It has a Galenic base, and the widely read Bullein drew upon a variety of other authorities, both classical and contemporary, as well as his experience and observations. It is written as a dialogue between John, a young man who has been too interested in "belly-cheer," and Humphrey, an older and wiser man who answers John's questions and counsels moderation in all things. Advice ranges from the importance of simple routines such as combing one's hair or cleaning one's teeth, to the need for a good diet and exercise,

8

The booke of the vse of ficke men, and medicens.

Surfeite, age, and fickenes, are enemies all to health,
Medicenes to mende the bodie, excelleth worldly wealth:
Phificke fhall florifhe, and in daunger will giue cure,
Till death vnknit the liuely knot, no lenger we indure.

Woodcut from the title page for Bullein's Bulwark of Defense *(1562),*
believed to depict the author

to technical information on bloodletting, purging, and medicines.

Shortly afterward Bullein wrote a work on healthful medicines, but the manuscript was among the goods lost in a shipwreck – one of the misadventures Bullein records. Another is recounted in the preface to *Bullein's Bulwark of Defense* (1562). There he also recounts how William Hilton, the brother of Bullein's patron and patient, Sir Thomas Hilton, falsely accused the author of murdering his patient in 1558 and subsequently had Bullein and his wife, Hilton's widow, imprisoned for debt. External sources confirm that Bullein and his wife were in prison in London in 1561, and it was there that he wrote his longest work, *Bullein's Bulwark,* published in folio the next year.

It is a composite text, made up of a series of dialogues, each characterized as a "book." In the first one, "The Book of Simples," Hilarius answers Marcellus's questions about the various uses of herbs, plants, fruits, and meats for medicinal purposes; prevailing ideas about the four humours shape the information given. Hilarius also digresses, giving information about Bullein's life, attacking corruption in the commonwealth, and calling for charity for those in need. A second dialogue, between Soreness and the Surgeon, is far darker in mood; winter is at hand as the two men ponder abscesses and wounds and how best to deal with them.

Both sets of dialogues include illustrations, and it appears that a third "book" would have been devoted to a "large *Anatomy* of the body of mankind," but there is only one such diagram: a skeletal form with the names of a few of the bones. "The Book of Compounds," in effect an exhaustive pharmacopoeia, follows. *Bullein's Bulwark* ends with "The Book of the Use of Sick Men and Medicines," as a personified Sickness asks a tough question: why is it that good medicines sometimes hinder people

A newe booke

Entituled the Gouerne-
ment of Healthe, wherein is vttered manye notable Rules for
mannes preseruacion, with sondry symples and other matters,
no lesse fruiteful then profitable:
colect out of many approued authours. Reduced into the forme
of a Dialogue, for the better vnderstanding of thunlearned.
Wherunto is added a suf-
ferain Regiment a-
gainst the pesti-
lence.
By VVilliam Bulleyn.

Imprinted at Londō by John
Day, dwellyng ouer Aldersgate
beneth saint Martins.

Cum priuilegio ad imprimen-
dum solum.

*Title page for Bullein's first book, which he wrote to assist
"those who lack wherewithall and be furthest
from the physicians."*

more than sickness? Health explains that much depends on the physician's skill in administering the medicine. But the text also considers the fragile state of humankind (this includes a meditation on Job), discusses the perturbations of the mind, and gives advice on living well, advice that includes a summary of Tudor religious principles.

Bullein's shortest work was also published in 1562. *A Comfortable Regiment against Pleurisy* begins with a meditation upon death and gives a brief history of plagues (in general and in England) before explaining the causes of pleurisy and ways to treat it. Like Bullein's other works it includes satiric asides and autobiographical remarks, but it is not in dialogue form and is structurally sloppy. It found an audience,

though; the concluding pages were published with few changes as the anonymous work "Doctor Bullein's Diet for Health" at the end of *A Brief Discourse of the Virtue of Balsam* (1585).

Bullein promised to add thirty more sicknesses to his *Comfortable Regiment*. But only one, bubonic plague, figures in his most important work, *A Dialogue against the Fever Pestilence,* first published soon after a serious outbreak of the plague in London in the spring and summer of 1563. Like Bullein's earlier works the *Dialogue* is in part a medical treatise, and it provides technical information about treatments and medications for the plague. The dialogue form has been otherwise transformed, however, and the work is a seriocomic and original work of art that resists classification. It has been called a colloquy, a drama, a collection of merry tales, a spiritual therapeutic, a medical novel, a Menippean satire, and an anatomy. In addition, like other anatomies it both echoes and parodies various works and forms: besides the medical recipes, it includes a philosophical debate on the nature of the soul, a little anthology of English poetry, topical satire, beast fables, a collection of emblems, a homily and *ars moriendi,* and the first example of a utopia (or quasi-utopia) in English.

There are twelve interlocutors in the *Dialogue:* a beggar, Mendicus; the chief speaker, Civis; his wife, Uxor (later called Susan); their servant, Roger; a rich Italian merchant, Antonius, who is Civis's foil; the doctor, Medicus, in later editions called Dr. Tocrub, after Dr. Burcot, a contemporary charlatan doctor and metallurgist whom Bullein is satirizing; the doctor's apothecary, Crispine; two lawyers, Avarus and Ambodexter, like the doctor, out to get the dying merchant's money; a traveler and teller of strange tales, Mendax; a wholly allegorical figure, Death (Mors); and Theologus, a good divine. Each of the characters has a distinct speech pattern, and, as in an Erasmian colloquy, the conversations are central to the development of the ideas. But the implicit story line is more complex and more fully developed.

The action, which is not staged but conveyed through the dialogues, opens in London, as the beggar knocks at the door of Civis's house and asks for alms. It soon shifts to the house of Antonius, who is dying of the plague and is being treated by the doctor. The latter knows that the merchant is beyond help but wants his gold and gifts. In the second part of the *Dialogue* the action shifts to the road, as Civis, Uxor, and Roger leave London to flee the plague. After stopping for dinner at an inn along the way, they meet Mendax, who tells them about all sorts of marvelous countries, including Taerg Natrib (a utopian antipode of Great Britain). They continue their journey, but soon there is a terrifying thunderstorm, and Death appears, striking Civis. Realizing that he is dying, Civis sends for Theologus, who teaches him the way to the kingdom of Christ.

The *Dialogue* invites comparisons between the deaths of Antonius, who depends on help from the doctor, who abandons him and Civis, who trusts in spiritual counsel; and it can be divided into two parts, one concerned primarily with the body, the other with the soul. The work is also concerned with larger social, political, and moral questions, as well as human nature, and its author seems to be part scientist, satirist, philosopher, psychologist, preacher, and humorist; his vision of London in plague time is a peculiarly comic and ironic kind of physico-theology.

Bullein twice revised his *Dialogue,* which was popular throughout the sixteenth century. Thomas Nashe alluded to it as the model for his *Have with You to Saffron Walden* (1596), and Ben Jonson probably drew upon it for a subplot in *Volpone* (1605–1606). In 1939 a dramatic version, "The Black Dart of Death," was produced by Sanford Vincent Larkey and performed by a group of medical students at Johns Hopkins University. A few verses, a Latin letter, and marginal annotations by Bullein appeared in 1564 in a medical treatise by his friend John Moore, and John Sadler's 1572 translation of Vegetius on the art of war also includes some of Bullein's verses.

Bullein's first wife died sometime before 30 September 1566, when he married Anne Doffield; they had one child, Margaret, who was baptized on 9 January 1567. Bullein died on 7 January 1576 and was buried at St. Giles, Cripplegate.

Bullein's writings say much about how he and others understood the human body and tried to cope with disease and the social, moral, and spiritual problems it represents. Though based upon now-outmoded Galenic medical theory, his works retain their interest as cultural artifacts, giving some sense of how and why medical material was disseminated in sixteenth-century England. They are of further interest insofar as Bullein stressed good diet, exercise, peace of mind, and the recuperative power of laughter, ideas whose importance is being rediscovered in medicine. Bullein has been admired as a plainspoken writer, and in *English Literature in the Sixteenth Century, Excluding Drama* (1954), C. S. Lewis singles out the "civilized prose" of the *Dialogue.* Critics of the work have noted its unevenness, but they have also been struck by its dramatic potential and by the author's humor and satiric sensibility. Bullein remains an interesting, if little-known, writer whose innovations in the dialogue form deserve more recognition.

References:

William C. Boring, "William Bullein's *Dialogue Against the Fever Pestilence,*" *Nassau Review,* 2, no. 5 (1974): 33–42;

A. H. Bullen, *Elizabethans* (London: Chapman & Hall, 1925), pp. 155–181;

Catherine Cole Mambretti, "William Bullein and the 'Lively Fashions' in Tudor Medical Literature," *Clio Medica,* 9, no. 4 (1974): 285–297;

Elizabeth McCutcheon, "William Bullein's *Dialogue against the Fever Pestilence*: A Sixteenth-Century Anatomy," in *Miscellanea Moreana: Essays for Germain Marc'hadour,* edited by Clare Murphy, Henri Gibaud, and Mario A. Di Cesare (Binghamton, N.Y.: Medieval & Renaissance Texts & Studies, 1989), pp. 341–359;

William S. Mitchell, "William Bullein, Elizabethan Physician and Author," *Medical History,* 3, no. 3 (1959): 188–200;

J. Proust, "Le dialogue de W. Bullein à propos de la peste (1564): formulation d'une thérapeutique pour l'âme en péril," in *Le dialogue au temps de la Renaissance,* edited by M. T. Jones-Davies (Paris: Centre de Recherches sur la Renaissance, 1984), pp. 59–73;

Paul Slack, "Mirrors of Health and Treasures of Poor Men: The Uses of the Vernacular Medical Literature of Tudor England," in *Health, Medicine and Mortality in the Sixteenth Century,* edited by Charles Webster (Cambridge: Cambridge University Press, 1979), pp. 237–273;

W. H. Welply, "An Unanswered Question: Bullein and Hilton," *Notes and Queries,* new series 4 (January 1957): 3–6.

Edmund Campion

(25 January 1539 – 1 December 1581)

Carolyn F. Scott
Fu Jen University, Taiwan

BOOKS: *History of Ireland,* incomplete text in *The Firste Volume of the Chronicles of England, Scotlande, and Irelande,* by Raphael Holinshed (London: Printed by H. Bynneman for J. Harrison or Harison, 1577); full text in *Two Histories of Ireland. The One Written by E. Campion, the Other by M. Hanmer* (Dublin: Society of Stationers, 1633);

Rationes decem: quibus fretus, certamen aduersarijs obtulit in causa fidei, E. Campianus (Stonor Park, Henley on Thames: Greenstreet House Press, 1581); English translation by R. Stocke in *An Answere to the Ten reasons of E. Campion. Whereunto Is Added the Summe of the Defence of those Reasons by John Duraeus the Scot, a Jesuit, with a Reply unto It,* by William Whitaker (London: Printed by F. Kyngston for C. Burby and E. Weaver, 1606); republished as *Campian Englished. Or a Translation of the Ten Reasons, in Which E. Campian Insisted in His Challenge, to the Universities of Oxford and Cambridge. By a Priest of the Catholike and Roman Church.* (Rouen?, 1632);

Ambrosia: A Neo-Latin Drama by Edmund Campion, S.J., edited and translated by Joseph Simons (Assen, The Netherlands: Van Gorcum, 1970).

OTHER: "To the Right Honourable Lords of Her Majesty's Privy Council," in *An Answere to a Seditious Pamphlet Lately Cast Abroade by a Jesuite, Conteyning IX. Articles Heere Inserted and Set Downe at Large, with a Discouerie of that Blasphemous Sect,* by William Charke (London: C. Barker, 1581); also in *The Great Bragge and Challenge of M. Champion a Jesuite, Contayning Nyne Articles Here Seuerallye Laide Downe, Confuted & Aunswered,* by Meredith Hanmer (London: T. Marsh, 1581).

Edmund Campion influenced English literature as much by his death as by his literary output. Although he produced only two works of English prose, on two widely divergent subjects, each in its way illuminates major concerns of late-sixteenth-century England. The use of his *History of Ireland* in Raphael Holinshed's *Chronicles of England, Scotland, and Ireland* (1577) provides an example of Elizabethan historiography, reveals England's concern with Ireland, furnishes a source for Edmund Spenser's *View of the Present State of Ireland* (1596), and distinguishes Campion as a master of clear, graceful English prose. "To the Right Honourable Lords of Her Majesty's Privy Council" (1581) – better known as *Campion's Challenge* or *Campion's Brag* – polarized public thinking and solidified government policy pertaining to the relationship between the Church of England and the Roman Catholic Church. The author's execution in 1581 generated both prose and poetry on both sides of the controversy.

Edmund Campion was born on 25 January 1539 in London to the family of a bookseller, Edmund Campion. He was sent to Christ Church Hospital, Newgate Street, for his education. His outstanding scholarly abilities made him the acknowledged head of all London schoolboys, demonstrated by his selection in 1553 as the schoolboy orator for Mary I's solemn entry into London. Campion's prowess as an orator established his career and became the foundation of his reputation. He won a scholarship to St. John's College, Oxford, at the age of fifteen and in 1557 became a junior fellow, earning a B.A. in 1561. He was a highly influential figure at Oxford, where he collected a circle of followers who not only imitated his rhetorical style but also his appearance and manner of walking. When Elizabeth I visited Oxford in 1566, Campion provided the welcoming oration as well as participating in several learned debates. The queen was so impressed by Campion's ability that she recommended him to Robert Dudley, Earl of Leicester, and William Cecil, Lord Burghley. Leicester became the scholar's patron, leading Campion to dedicate the *History of Ireland* to him.

In 1564 Campion received his M.A., which mandated that he take the Oath of Supremacy as a deacon in the Church of England. In spite of having taken the oath, he remained uncertain about the relationship between the established church and Catholic doctrines. He was pressured to make a formal public declaration of his adherence to the Protestant faith, and when it could be avoided no longer he resigned his position at Oxford in 1569 and went to Ireland. There he lived under the protection of James Stanyhurst, the recorder of Dublin, and Sir Henry Sidney, the lord deputy. These men were working on a project to restore Dublin University and hoped Campion would play a leading role in the revitalized institution.

It was during this time that Campion wrote the *History of Ireland.* His primary source is the history compiled by Gerald of Wales (Giraldus Cambrensis), but Campion adds his own material based on research, the reports of friends, and his own observations. According to the dedicatory epistle, he spent only ten weeks writing it in early 1571, although the research had been begun before. During part of this composition period, warrants for his arrest as a papist necessitated frequent moves, which in turn account for the fragmentary nature of the text.

The work begins with a description of the geographical layout of Ireland, names the principal Anglo-Irish families, then describes the landscape and the people, particularly the customs of the "meere Irish" (the native Irish). The text then presents a chronological retelling of the important incidents in Irish history, beginning from the time of Noah and concluding with 1571. In particular Campion tends to focus on the relationships between England and Ireland, and his point of view generally favors the English version of events.

Campion's primary purpose in writing this history seems to have been to promote the need for education in Ireland and to endorse English claims to the country. Contrary to expectation, Campion argues against papal claims to Ireland. His description of the inhabitants makes clear that Ireland would benefit from the presence of an English-sponsored university:

The people are thus inclined: religious, frank, amorous, ireful, sufferable, of pain infinite, very glorious, many

Edmund Campion (sixteenth-century German engraving by an unknown artist)

sorcerers, excellent horsemen, delighted with wars, great alms-givers, passing in hospitality; the lewder sort, both clerk and laymen, are sensual and loose to lechery above measure. The same being virtuously bred up or reformed are such mirrors of holiness and austerity that other nations retain but a show or shadow of devotion in comparison of them.

The work closes with verbatim accounts of speeches made by Stanyhurst and Sidney in the Irish Parliament advocating the need for reform, education, and a strong English presence, transforming the whole book into a virtual panegyric extolling England's sovereignty over Ireland.

The clarity of Campion's prose is also particularly evident in his descriptions of the Irish countryside. The third chapter begins:

> The soil is low and waterish, and includes diverse little islands, environed with bogs and marshes: highest hills have standing pools in their top. Inhabitants (especially new come) are subject to distillations, rheums, and fluxes for remedy whereof they use an ordinary drink of aquavitae, so qualified in the making that it dries more and inflames less than other hot confections. The air is wholesome, not altogether so clear and subtle as ours of England. Of bees good store, no vineyards, contrary to the opinion of some writers who both in this and other errors touching the land, may easily be excused, as those that wrote of hearsay.

These portions of the text, drawn from Campion's personal experience, display his mastery of the language. Even the portions drawn primarily from other sources reveal his ability to make his point with simple elegance. Campion is also aware of himself as a historian and takes pains to delineate those points that have solid support from those that "strain a point of truth." He explains his rationale for including such material, however:

> I hold him unwise that will utterly mistrust the principal because the circumstances vary, or condemn the whole because he could not reach to the undoubted truth of some part. If any man be so delicate that not a jot thereof will sink into his head, who shall control him? Neither he nor we are bound to believe any story besides that which is delivered us from the Scriptures and the consent of God's Church. Let the discreet reader judge of it.

Campion uses the history for his own purposes, but he takes care to present the facts as accurately as possible.

Because of the imminent danger of arrest, Campion had to leave Ireland quickly in 1571 and became separated from his manuscript. It eventually arrived in the hands of his former pupil, Richard Stanyhurst (son of James). Stanyhurst and Holinshed used Campion's text as a basis for the Irish component of Holinshed's *Chronicles*. Holinshed used both Campion's organization and words, expanding on them where necessary for his section of the work, so that a large portion of Campion's text appears verbatim scattered throughout the *Chronicles*. Stanyhurst also borrowed heavily from Campion's material for his part of the volume. Strictly speaking, Holinshed's *Chronicles* cannot be considered the first publication of Campion's *History*, because of the fragmentation caused by the heavy editing. Evidence also suggests that Spenser had access to a manuscript of the *History of Ireland* as he wrote *A View of the Present State of Ireland*. Both authors' works were not published in their entirety until 1633.

In late 1571 Campion returned to England, where he witnessed the trial of Dr. John Storey, a Catholic who had served Mary I in enforcing her ecclesiastical acts. The arguments presented there convinced Campion to embrace Catholicism. He escaped from England and joined the English college at Douai, France, where he was ordained a subdeacon. He traveled to Rome to join the Society of Jesus (Jesuits) in 1573 and was subsequently sent to teach in Prague, where he was ordained as a priest in 1578. In Prague he was professor of rhetoric and philosophy at the Jesuit College and he wrote several plays in Latin, as well as providing Latin orations for a variety of occasions. His quiet life there was disrupted in 1580, when his superiors ordered him to join the Catholic mission to England that was being organized by William Allen.

This mission – designed "to preach the Gospel, to minister the Sacraments, to instruct the simple, to reform sinners, to confute errors" – set Campion at the heart of the Anglo-Catholic controversy, involved him in politics against his will, and inspired his next works of literary significance. Although Campion had no political agenda, the situation in England made it impossible to separate religion and politics. Pope Gregory XIII's machinations in Ireland, the Continental politics of the Catholic monarchs Philip II of Spain and Henry III of France, and the internal pressures of Puritan agitators led Elizabeth and her Privy Council to equate Catholicism with treason. Campion in particular seemed to be a threat because of his oratorical persuasiveness and his attractive character.

Before he began his travels through the English countryside, Campion, aware of the certainty of his eventual arrest, composed his well-known letter "To the Right Honorable Lords of Her Majesty's Privy Council," purportedly in less than half an hour. Not originally intending a challenge, he desired merely to have a written statement of his intentions to be published in refutation of any false reports that might attend his imprisonment. The document began to circulate among Catholics in 1580 and was soon seized by the authorities. Its effect was to galvanize both camps into action. Several Catholics produced their own articles of faith in imitation of Campion. The Protestants responded

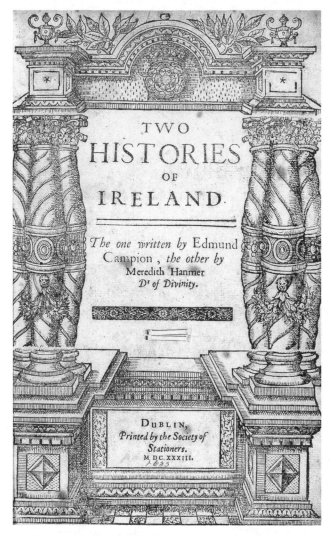

Title page for the first full edition of Campion's history, which had appeared in an abbreviated and altered form in 1577 in Raphael Holinshed's Chronicles of England, Scotland, and Ireland *(courtesy of the Lilly Library, Indiana University)*

with refutations from eminent scholars. The text of Campion's letter was printed in full for the first time in William Charke's 1581 refutation. Refutation and defense escalated as the struggle for the established church continued.

At the center of this storm of controversy was Campion's document enumerating nine points that he wished to assert about his purpose in coming to England, as well as his conviction that Catholicism is the true faith. In *Elizabethan Recusant Prose 1559–1582* (1950), A. C. Southern notes that "the force, and indeed the charm, of the writing lies in the extreme simplicity of the structure and vocabulary." Campion focuses on distancing himself from any charges of personal or political motivations and asks only to be allowed

to the glory of God, with all humility, and under your correction, three sorts of indifferent and quiet audiences: *the first* before your Honors, wherein I will discourse of religion, so far as it touches the commonweal and your nobilities; *the second,* whereof I make more account, before the Doctors and Masters and chosen men of both Universities, wherein I undertake to avow the faith of our Catholic Church by proofs innumerable, Scriptures, Councils, Fathers, history, natural and moral reasons; *the third* before the lawyers, spiritual and temporal, wherein I will justify the said faith by the common wisdom of the laws standing yet in force and practice.

Throughout the letter Campion reveals a fundamental reliance on the truth of what he speaks. Ronald J. Corthell comments that the work "is the story of a man of faith and reason who finds

Last page of a manuscript commentary on Aristotle's Physics, *with Campion's signature at the top and the bottom (Campion Hall, Oxford)* cheerfully to carry the cross you shall lay upon us, and never to despair your recovery while we have a man left to enjoy your Tyburn, or to be racked with your torments, or consumed with your prisons. The expense is reckoned, the enterprise is begun; it is of God, it cannot be withstood. So the faith was planted, so it must be restored.

Campion's death would bear witness to the truth of his assertions concerning martyrdom and lend credence to the rest of his statements.

Before his death, during the year that he was free and traveling England in disguise, Campion wrote a longer Latin work, *Rationes decem* (1581), that expanded many of the points raised in *Campion's Challenge.* Published secretly by his Jesuit companion Robert Persons, the book was distributed by placing copies on every pew of St. Mary's, the university church in Oxford, just before commencement on 27 June 1581. The work takes a scholarly approach to the question of faith and was written to attract the waverers among the intellectuals at Oxford and Cambridge. Again many refutations were prepared against it, leading once more to a full publication of the English translation in an opponent's work in 1606. The *Rationes decem* was popular on the Continent, with six Latin editions and Polish, Flemish, German, and French translations all appearing before 1600.

Although Campion's arrest happened almost by accident, he was finally captured in July 1581 and imprisoned in the Tower of London, where he endured several rackings. Tradition holds that Elizabeth came in person to offer Campion his freedom and ecclesiastical advancement if he would return to the established church. (Although there is little sound evidence to support this tradition, such an offer was made to Campion, probably by the earl of Leicester.) He was also forced to appear in several public debates with Protestant divines, during which his oratorical powers thwarted his opponents to the extent that the council ordered the debates to cease. Neither Leicester nor Sir Philip Sidney, an old friend and the son of his former protector, dared to assist Campion because of the volatile political situation and their own precarious positions. Campion, along with seven others, was tried for treason in November 1581, since the Privy Council feared to try him on the religious grounds that were their actual reason for arresting him. The charges of treason were patently false, even to Protestant observers, and Campion in particular was believed to be innocent of any political wrongdoing and

Rope with which Campion was bound to the hurdle as he was taken from the Tower to Tyburn

himself surrounded by a faithless and unreasonable enemy" and argues that Campion deliberately constructs this vision of himself. Nevertheless, it is effective as a statement of belief and rationality because the power of the language supports the constructed image. The effect of this letter on English recusants intensified with Campion's martyrdom. In his eighth article Campion declares that he and the Jesuits have taken a vow likely to be acquitted. The verdict was guilty, however, and Campion was hanged, drawn, and quartered on 1 December 1581. The eyewitness accounts of his death published by Catholics were countered by Protestant accounts of his seditious activities, arrest, and weakness under torture. Even in death Campion continued to exert an influence on religious controversy and polemics.

The Crown seems to have particularly feared Campion as an opponent in its struggle for control of the church because of his charisma, oratorical prowess, and literary ability. Rather than fitting the image that the government promulgated of the Jesuits in such pamphlets as *The Rat-Trap; or, The Jesuits Taken in Their Own Net* (1641) – "the most cunning engineers, politic underminers, subtle supplanters, and dangerous incendiaries" – Campion represented the acme of British scholarship: he was popular, persuasive, successful, and entirely sincere in his belief. Although only two of his works were published in his lifetime, and those brought into circulation only through the efforts to discredit him, Campion's works continued to generate controversy and provoke discourse for decades after his death. His death itself inspired poetry and ballads along with publications of eyewitness accounts. His time in the public eye was brief, but his writing influenced Protestant and Catholic authors, government policy, and English perceptions of Ireland. The Roman Catholic Church canonized him in 1970. He remains an important figure in the study of recusant literature, Jesuit dramaturgy, Catholic and Protestant martyrologies, and Elizabethan politics.

Biographies:
Richard Simpson, *Edmund Campion: A Biography* (London: Hodges, 1867);
Evelyn Waugh, *Edmund Campion* (London: Longmans, 1935).

References:
Ronald J. Corthell, " 'The secrecy of man': Recusant Discourse and the Elizabethan Subject," *English Literary Renaissance,* 19 (Autumn 1989): 272–290;
Thomas M. McCoog, " 'The Flower of Oxford': The Role of Edmund Campion in Early Recusant Polemics," *Sixteenth Century Journal,* 24, no. 4 (Winter 1993): 899–913;
Peter Milward, *Religious Controversies of the Elizabethan Age: A Survey of Printed Sources* (Lincoln: University of Nebraska Press, 1985), pp. 54–64;
J. H. Pollen, *The English Catholics in the Reign of Queen Elizabeth* (London: Longmans, 1920);
A. C. Southern, *Elizabethan Recusant Prose 1559–1582* (London: Sands, 1950);
Fay Vincent, "A View of Oxfordshire and St. Edmund Campion," *America,* 168 (24 April 1993): 4–15.

Papers:
Edmund Campion's manuscripts for the *History of Ireland* can be found at the British Library and the Library of the College of Arms in London. Manuscripts for two of the Latin plays can be found at the Jesuit College in Prague.

Sir Thomas Chaloner

(1520 – 14 October 1565)

M. Rick Smith
Wichita State University

BOOKS: *In Laudem Henrici Octavi, Regis Angliae, Praestantissimi. Carmen Panegyricum* (London: John Day, 1560);

De Rep[ublica] Anglorum Instauranda Libri Decem, Authore Thoma Chalonero Equite, Anglo. Huc Acessit in Laudem Henrici Octavi Regis quondam Angliae Praestantissimi. Carmen Panegyricum. Item, De illustrium quorundum Encomiis Miscellanea, cum Epigrammatis, ac Epitaphiis nonullis, Eodem Authore (London: Thomas Vautrollier, 1579) – includes *In Laudem Henrici Octavi* and many of Chaloner's Latin epigrams, epitaphs, and elegies.

OTHER: *Of the Office of Servants, a Book Made in Latin by One Gilbertus Cognatus and Newly Englished,* translated by Chaloner (London: Thomas Berthelet, 1543);

An Homily of Saint John Chrysostom upon That Saying of Saint Paul, Bretheren, I would not have you ignorant what is become of those that sleep, to the end that ye lament not, also with a Discourse upon Job, and Abraham, Newly Made out of Greek into Latin by Master Cheke, and Englished by Tho. Chaloner (London: Thomas Berthelet, 1544);

The Praise of Folly. Moriae Encomium. A Book Made in Latin by that Great Clerk, Erasmus of Rotterdam. Englished by Sir Thomas Chaloner, Knight (London: Thomas Berthelet, 1549);

"How King Richard the Second Was for His Evil Governance Deposed from His Seat, and Miserably Murdered in Prison," in *A Mirror for Magistrates* (London: Thomas Marshe, 1559).

Editions: "Ovid's Seventeenth Heroical Epistle, 'Helen to Paris,' Translated into English Verse," in *Nugae Antiquae,* volume 2, edited by Thomas Park (London, 1804), pp. 372–389;

"Translated Out of Boethius' *De Consolatione Philosophiae,*" in *Calendar of State Papers, Domestic Series, of the Reign of Elizabeth, 1601–1603; with Addenda, 1547–1565,* edited by Mary A. E. Green (London, 1870), p. 546; republished in *Queen Elizabeth's Englishings,* edited by Caroline Pemberton, Early English Text Society, Original Series 113 (London, 1899), pp. 150–160;

"How King Richard the Second Was for His Evil Governance Deposed from His Seat, and Miserably Murdered in Prison," in *The Mirror for Magistrates,* edited by Lily B. Campbell (Cambridge: Cambridge University Press, 1938), pp. 110–118;

The Praise of Folie by Sir Thomas Chaloner, edited by Clarence H. Miller (London: Published for the Early English Text Society by the Oxford University Press, 1965);

Thomas Chaloner's "In Laudem Henrici Octavi" (Latin Edition and English Translation), edited and translated by John B. Gabel and Carl C. Schlam (Lawrence, Kans.: Coronado, 1979).

A noteworthy example of Renaissance self-fashioning, Sir Thomas Chaloner remained prominent in the diplomatic and civil establishments of Henry VIII, Edward VI, Mary I, and Elizabeth I during one of the most troubled and dangerous periods of English history. Though briefly recalled from diplomatic service upon Mary's succession in 1553, he enjoyed the trust and favor of all four monarchs. Today Chaloner is of interest primarily as the first English translator of Desiderius Erasmus's *Moriae Encomium* (1509) and the author of the tragedy of Richard II in the 1559 edition of *A Mirror for Magistrates.* Chaloner's *The Praise of Folly* (1549) made widely available a central humanist text at a crucial phase of the English Renaissance when the success of the Reformation hung in the balance, and the future development of Elizabethan literature was being influenced by such scholars, schoolmasters, and statesmen as Thomas Wilson, Roger Ascham, and Sir John Cheke. His translation contributed to the broader foundations of Elizabethan literary culture. His verse tragedy of Richard II must be termed a standard, in many ways backward-looking, example of *de casibus* (the fall [of princes]) or *speculum*

Sir Thomas Chaloner (engraving by Wenceslas Hollar)

principum (mirror for princes) literature. It may have influenced the anonymous *Woodstock* (circa 1592–1595) and William Shakespeare's *Richard II* (circa 1592), though neither play refers directly to it. In the sixteenth century, however, Chaloner's literary reputation stemmed from two long, virtuosic Neo-Latin hexameter poems, *In Laudem Henrici Octavi* (1560) and *De Republica Anglorum Instauranda* (1579).

Thomas Chaloner was the son of Roger Chaloner, a mercer and citizen of London who came from Wales. Roger Chaloner rose under Thomas Cromwell, survived his fall, and, between 1522 and his death in 1550, held many government posts. Thomas was born in London in 1520, as indicated by the inquisition post mortem of his father and the record of his testimony at the trial of Bishop Gardiner in 1550. Chaloner's father married three times; Chaloner's mother was Margaret, the daughter of Richard Middleton.

Chaloner was, according to Henry Peacham's *The Compleat Gentleman* (1622), "brought up" in Cambridge, possibly at St. John's College. As Clarence H. Miller notes, however, this is unlikely since Sir William Cecil, an alumnus of Saint John's, says in an elegy published with the *De Republica Anglorum* volume that he first met Chaloner at court. Chaloner may also have studied at Oxford, but there is no record of his taking a degree at either university.

In his own time Chaloner's fame rested on three distinct kinds of accomplishment: military, diplomatic, and literary. As a young man he appears with George Ferrers in a list presented to Cromwell in 1538 of "gentlemen most meet to be daily waiters upon my said lord and allowed in his house." He accompanied Sir Henry Knyvet on an important and splendid legation to the imperial convention at Ratisbon in 1540. A year later Knyvet, Chaloner, and two other young English gentlemen (identified by Peacham as Henry Knowles and Henry Isam) attended Charles V of the Holy Roman Empire on his disastrous expedition against Algiers. An account reported in 1579 by William Malim and reproduced by Richard Hakluyt states that Chaloner, his arms and legs exhausted from swimming after his ship was wrecked, saved himself by grasping with his teeth (*per dentibus*) a cable thrown from another vessel. Along with Ferrers and Cecil, Chaloner took part in the bloody English victory of Pinkie Cleugh, or Musselburgh, Scotland, on 28 September 1547. He was knighted on the battlefield by Lord Protector Somerset and presented with a jewel by the duchess.

A tireless and prudent servant of the Tudor state, he maintained favor by making himself indispensable in the diplomatic service. Keen linguistic abilities gave him the fluency in written and spoken Latin essential to success in the international diplomatic community. The diplomatic corps formed a mobile subculture that followed the courts of monarchs and emperors about Europe; among them the composition of Latin epigrams, elegies, satires, panegyrics, and didactic epics was an important means of recreation and recognition. Chaloner's command of Latin also naturally led him to take up translation as an outlet for his literary ambitions, and in addition to *The Praise of Folly* he translated *Of the Office of Servants* (1543) by Gilbertus Cognatus and *An Homily of Saint John Chrysostom . . . with a Discourse upon Job, and Abraham* (1544).

Of the Office of Servants is a practical guide to the choice, training, and discipline of good servants, as well as a consideration of what constituted the most godly and just relationship between servant and master. In translating *An Homily of Saint John Chrysostom,* Chaloner completed a work begun by Sir John Cheke, who first translated the sermon from the Greek into Latin, along with related commentary on Abraham and the Book of Job. Protestant reformers favored Chrysostom as a patriarch of the early church, a denouncer of princely and ecclesiastical abuses, and a source of doctrine uncontaminated by the papacy. The sermon and the commentary printed with it reinforced such familiar Protestant themes as salvation by faith and the necessity that the church renounce material in favor of spiritual grandeur.

Chaloner's translation of Erasmus's *Moriae Encomium* is a model of avoidance of pseudo-Latinate diction and sentence construction and is clear on the translator's liberties with the text:

Likewise in all my translation I have not pained myself to render word for word, nor proverb for proverb, whereof many be Greek, such as have no grace in our tongue: but rather, marking the sense, I applied it to the phrase of our English. And where the proverbs would take no English, I adventured to put English proverbs of like weight in their places.

Such frankness about textual liberties was rare, but where Erasmus is circumspect, Chaloner does not hesitate to malign the Catholic hierarchy directly. For example, in her use of polemical epithets, Chaloner's Folly sounds distinctly English and Protestant:

But now (on God's half) longer than of late days, Pope holy fathers of Rome, scarlet cardinals, and blessing bishops have not only followed the steps of princes, as touching their pomp and magnificence, but done also what they can to surpass them.

Examples of such polemical amplification occur throughout the work and show how Tudor translation of Latin texts was more than a cultivated art; it was often a weapon in the religious, philosophical, and political struggles of the day. As satire, Erasmus's *Moriae Encomium* ranges widely and spares few, but its varied attacks tend to coalesce around a thematic anti-Scholasticism. For example, portraying Erasmus's theologians, a *genus hominum mire superciliosum atque irritabile* (a nest of men so crabbed and wasplike) Chaloner depicts their habit of silencing dissent with the charge of heresy.

Or consider Erasmus's *grammatici* (grammarians) as they appear in Chaloner:

A kind of men (doubtless) most miserable, most slavelike, and most contemptuous, unless I did mitigate and relieve the discommodities of their most wretched profession with a certain sweet bait of madness. . . . So lordly a thing they take it, when they fear their fearful flock, with a threatening voice and countenance. So princely an execution, to tear the poor boys' arses with rods and ferules, playing the tormenters and termagants among them, much like the ass wrapped in a lion's skin.

Despite Chaloner's claim to have "eased the sour sense of the Latin," most of the famous passages on princes, nobles, and gentlemen, lawyers, clerks, and schoolmasters remain especially pungent, such as a remark about courtiers: "Now likewise what say you to courtiers? these minion gaybeseen gentlemen, who being for the most part as fawning, as servile, as witless, and as abject as can be devised, would be taken yet among all men for the principal." The spirit of Chaloner's *The*

Praise of Folly so pervades the comic and satiric modes of English literature in the last half of the sixteenth century that it would be hard to identify examples of direct influence or imitation.

The place of Chaloner's contribution to *A Mirror for Magistrates* is harder to determine. In William Baldwin's frame to the tale of Richard, Chaloner ("one of the company" who first compiled the book) instructs his audience to imagine the king's corpse as the narrator of his own story: "And therefore imagine Baldwin that you see him all to be mangled, with blue wounds, lying pale and wan all naked upon the cold stones in Paul's church, the people standing round about him and making moan in this sort."

"This sort" shows little of the fashionable Senecan tragedy-mongering (to use Marie Axton's phrase) prevalent in other sections of *A Mirror for Magistrates,* most notably Thomas Sackville's induction and complaint of the duke of Buckingham. Chaloner's tragedy stands out as homiletic in a collection notorious for homily. Instead of rhyme royal he employs stanzas of ten iambic pentameter lines rhyming *ababbaabab*. The shape of this stanza as well as its alliteration, its narrative pace, and its tendency freely to incorporate emblems and proverbial expressions anticipates, perhaps, the stanza form used by Edmund Spenser in *The Faerie Queene* (1590, 1596):

> The chief conspired by death to drive him down,
> For which exploit, a solemn oath they swore
> To render me my liberty and crown,
> Whereof themselves deprived me before.
> But salves help seld an overlong suffered sore.
> To stop the breach no boot to run or rowne
> When swelling floods have overflowen the town:
> Till sails be spred the ship may keep the shore.
> The anchors weighed, though all the freight do frown,
> With stream and steer perforce it shall be bore.
>
> For though the peers set Henry in his state,
> Yet could they not displace him thence again:
> And where they easily put me down of late,
> They could restore me by no manner pain:
> Things hardly mend, but may be marred amain.
> And when a man is fall'n in froward fate
> Still mischiefs light one in another's pate:
> And well meant means his mishaps to restrain
> Wax wretched moans, whereby his joys abate.
> Due proof whereof in me appeareth plain.

Among humanists and the Latin-fluent diplomatic world, Chaloner's literary fame rested on contributions to two of the chief Neo-Latin genres: the panegyric *In Laudem Henrici Octavi* (published and formally presented to Queen Elizabeth in 1560,

but almost certainly composed during the last years of Henry VIII's reign) and the didactic-epic-pastoral *De Republica Anglorum Instauranda.* Chaloner's two lasting contributions to English literature, his *The Praise of Folly* and the tragedy of Richard II in *A Mirror for Magistrates,* suggest the contradictions inherent in any career that combined classical learning and literary accomplishments in the tradition of Erasmus, Sir Thomas More, and John Colet with full-time service to a state.

Indeed, with *The Praise of Folly* in mind, it is difficult to read *In Laudem Henrici Octavi* without irony. In the Renaissance the composition of Latin praise poems in imitation of the imperial or consular addresses of Claudian and Sidonius was a common school exercise, as well as an occasional humanist employment. The content and plan of such poems was inevitably influenced by the rules for composing speeches of praise in the *Ad Herennium* and in Quintilian's *De Institutione Oratoria.* In his panegyric, Chaloner employs many of the rhetorical devices set forth as appropriate to ceremonial oratory. It would be a mistake, though, to dismiss all such poetry as mere "flattering unction" or sycophancy. Nevertheless, the performance has its embarrassing moments, as when Chaloner's Henry VIII refuses election as Holy Roman Emperor (his candidacy was in fact never taken seriously); or when Henry is solemnly acclaimed for aiding the emperor's troops with money at the battle of Pavia in 1525, while in fact his own military ambitions resulted in poorly led, immensely expensive campaigns for little gain, such as the ruinous French expedition of 1513–1514. Extensive sections of apologia occupy much of the poem, in particular when Chaloner deals with those who complained about tax burdens or criticized Henry's tyranny.

By far the longest section of the poem concerns the Reformation (lines 759–1001). A highly reductive first cause for the immensely complex and agonized process of reform is sought in the personal inspiration of Henry VIII: "Nescio . . . / Quae nova relligio hunc antiquam relligionem / Flectere ad exemplar primaevae relligionis / Impulerit, multo pectus iam numine versans" (I do not know what new faith . . . by an infusion of grace impelled Henry to alter the old faith in accordance with the model of the primeval church). Chaloner treats the Reformation primarily as a struggle against self-aggrandizing prelates and encroachments upon royal authority. Much of the section is spent defending the disestablishment of the monasteries.

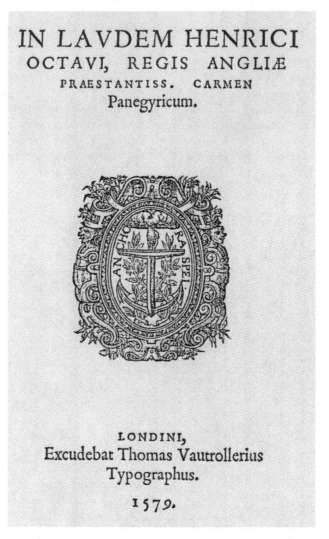

IN LAVDEM HENRICI
OCTAVI, REGIS ANGLIÆ
PRAESTANTISS. CARMEN
Panegyricum.

LONDINI,
Excudebat Thomas Vautrollerius
Typographus.

1579.

*Title page for Chaloner's Latin hexameter poem praising
Henry VIII*

Mythological comparisons abound, equating Henry with Alexander the Great, Telephus, Pollux, Castor, Hercules, and Jove. Invocations of Astraea as well as a personification of Britain are probably aimed at Elizabeth, as is some doubtless unwelcome advice with which the poem closes:

> Aude aliquando tui, nimium cunctata, pudoris
> Vincula felici et plus quam conferre marito,
> Parvulus ut nobis Henricus lusitet aula.
> Qui bene pulcher avum referat, quo pulchrior alter
> Non fuit aut pulchris umquam praestantior actis.

(Dare at some time, having already too much delayed, to bestow the bonds of your modesty on a husband, a man who will be blessed and more than blessed. For then a little Henry will play in the palace for us, a handsome child who happily will bring to mind his grandfather, than whom no man was ever more handsome or more outstanding for handsome deeds.)

De Republica Anglorum Instauranda, a didactic epic of more than six thousand lines, displays even more tendency to avoid direct treatment of political theory and reform. Employing some conventions of the medieval dream-vision poem, Chaloner begins Book 1 in the midst of a desolate pastoral landscape. While he meditates upon the decay of his times and of his people's customs and moral fiber, lamenting the withdrawal of justice from the earth, the goddess Britannia appears. She admonishes him to stop bemoaning the present. Instead he must use her inspiration to compose for the English people an epic vision of an England restored to the joys of the Golden Age. The books that follow contain much prolix advice of a general nature on the settlement of religion, public morals, and the education of youth. The poem culminates in Book 7 with a visit to the sphere of Saturn, revealed as a place of perfect happiness and the source of all public and private virtues. The inhabitants receive the poet enthusiastically and conduct him to the temple for an audience with the god himself, and Saturn takes up most of Book 7 with a dissertation about the reform of England. At the end of the poem the god reiterates that civil order, morality, wealth, and happiness will all be secured if Englishmen only embrace anew the values and customs of rural life, hard work, and obedience to the monarch. Fortunately for England, Elizabeth, and those "many, many bodies" that fed upon her, Chaloner's approach to actual affairs was much more practical. His diplomatic successes probably helped ensure the peace and security necessary to consolidating Elizabeth's position in the early years of her reign.

Almost incessantly busy from 1558 to his death, as Elizabeth's ambassador in Augsburg, in Flanders, and in Spain, Chaloner composed *De Republica Anglorum Instauranda* at Philip II's court between 1562 and 1564. He was largely responsible for the diplomatic maneuver that maintained a balance of power favorable to the English in the critical years following Elizabeth's accession in 1558.

When in 1559 it appeared that Chaloner's earnest request to retire as ambassador to Philip II in the Low Countries might be granted, he advised Sir William Cecil "to send none to King Philip but those perfect in the language and who can as perfectly understand the king, whose soft speech is hard of a young beginner in Spanish to be well at the first comprehended." This advice probably had the unintended effect of ensuring his dispatch once again since, in addition to Latin, he had an excellent command of Spanish and French. He left in November 1561 for a tour of duty in Spain that would almost literally weary him to death with toil and boredom. It soon became evident that his appointment was chiefly ceremonial, and he complained that his lack of instructions and information made him "disgraced as no ambassador in this court is the like." In addition to the *De Republica Anglorum Instauranda,* he composed and sent to Cecil and Elizabeth two books of religious polemic that have not survived.

He returned to Exeter on 1 May 1565, in his own words, "worn to the stumps." His return and his failing health occasioned a series of disputes and recriminations about the settlement of his property. In June 1546 Chaloner married Joanna, the widow of Sir Thomas Legh, but the couple had no children. She died on 11 January 1557. He married his second wife, Ethelreda, daughter of Edward Frodsham, in September 1565, one month before he died. On this basis Miller concludes that his heir, Sir Thomas Chaloner the Younger, was Chaloner's stepson, and not his son by Ethelreda. Chaloner died on 14 October 1565, and at his funeral in St. Paul's, Sir William Cecil was chief mourner.

The extent of Chaloner's Elizabethan reputation is attested by William Malim's 1579 edition of the author's work, which collected much of the Latin poetry and an impressive array of tributes. The latter included, in addition to an elegy by Cecil and Malim's life of the poet, commendatory verses by Laurence Humphrey, William Fleetwood, Christopher Carlisle, and Edward Webb and an epitaph by Walter Haddon translated in *Athenae Cantabrigienses* (1858):

> Nature and art in Chaloner combined,
> And for his country formed the patriot's mind.
> With praise deserved his public posts he filled;
> And equal fame his learned labors yield.
> While yet he lived, he lived his country's pride,
> And first his country injured when he died.

George Puttenham in *The Art of English Poesie* (1589) praises Chaloner's talent for eclogue and pastoral, while Francis Meres in *Palladis Tamia; or Wit's Treasury* (1598) ranks him among the best pastoral poets of his time.

After Henry Peacham's appreciation in *The Compleat Gentleman* (1622), Chaloner received little notice until modern times. In 1965 Clarence H. Miller published a critical edition of Chaloner's translation of the *Moriae Encomium,* with the most complete and scholarly life of Chaloner yet published. Given the charm of Chaloner's *The Praise of Folly,* it is to be hoped that someone will make available an inexpensive modern-spelling edition of Miller's text, allowing all students access to Chaloner's translation, not just textual scholars and specialists. Perhaps as a sign of increased attention to Chaloner and other figures of the mid sixteenth century, John B. Gabel and Carl C. Schlam published an edition and translation of *In Laudem Henrici Octavi* in 1979. Interest, however, in Chaloner's contribution to the influential anthology *A Mirror for Magistrates* as well as in his Neo-Latin poetry will probably remain quite specialized.

Biography:

Clarence H. Miller, "The Life of Sir Thomas Chaloner," in his *The Praise of Folie by Sir Thomas Chaloner* (London: Published for the Early English Text Society by Oxford University Press, 1965), pp. xxix–xlv.

References:

Marie Axton, *Three Tudor Classical Interludes: "Thersites," "Jacke Jugeler," "Horestes"* (Cambridge: Brewer, 1982);

Leicester Bradner, *Musae Anglicanae: A History of Anglo-Latin Poetry 1500–1925* (New York: Modern Language Association of America / London: Oxford University Press, 1940);

Carl C. Schlam, "Sir Thomas Chaloner: *In laudem Henrici octavi carmen panegyricum,*" in *Acta Conventus Neo-Latini Bononiensis: Proceedings of the Fourth International Congress of Neo-Latin Studies, Bologna, 26 August to 1 September 1979,* edited by R. J. Schoeck (Binghamton, N.Y.: Medieval and Renaissance Texts and Studies, 1985), pp. 607–612;

G. Gregory Smith, ed., *Elizabethan Critical Essays,* 2 volumes (Oxford: Oxford University Press, 1904).

Papers:

Manuscript materials related to Thomas Chaloner's diplomatic activity are preserved in the archives of Vienna, Brussels, Bensançon, Simancas, and Venice. The manuscript of Chaloner's "Helen to Paris" translation, along with letters to Sir Nicholas Throckmorton, Lady Northhampton, and others, are among the Sloane Manuscripts in the British Library. There is additional manuscript material in the British Library Cotton-Galba and Cotton-Vespasian series. The British Library Lansdowne manuscript collection preserves an epitome of Chaloner's will and an estimate of how the will may be performed. Other materials are held among the British Library Royal Manuscripts.

Miles Coverdale

(1487 or 1488 – 20 January 1569)

Richard Y. Duerden
Brigham Young University

BOOKS: *The Concordance of the New Testament,* compiled by Coverdale (London: Thomas Gybson, 1535);

A Confutacion of that Treatise Which One J. Standish Made Agaynst the Protestacion of D. Barnes in M.D.XL (Zurich: Christoph Froschauer, 1541).

Editions: *Writings and Translations of Myles Coverdale, Bishop of Exeter,* edited by George Pearson, Parker Society (Cambridge: Cambridge University Press, 1844);

Remains of Myles Coverdale, Bishop of Exeter, edited by Pearson, Parker Society (Cambridge: Cambridge University Press, 1846).

TRANSLATIONS: *A Paraphrasis, Vpon All the Psalmes of David, Made by Johannes Campensis, and Translated oute of Latyne,* attributed to Coverdale (Antwerp: Catherine van Ruremund, 1535);

Johannes Campensis, *Here Followeth the Book of Solomon Called Ecclesiastes,* attributed to Coverdale (Antwerp: Catherine van Ruremund, 1535);

Biblia, the Bible, That Is, the Holy Scripture . . . Translated out of Douche and Latyn in to Englishe (Cologne: Johannes Soter & Eucharius Cervicornus, 1535);

A Faythfull and True Pronosticacion vpon the Yeare M.CCCCC.xxxvi. Gathered out of the Prophecies and Scriptures of God . . . Translated out of Hye Almayne by Miles Couerdale (Southwark: Printed by James Nicholson for John Gough, 1535);

A Spirituall Almanacke (Southwark: Printed by James Nicholson for John Gough, 1535);

Goostly Psalmes and Spirituall Songes Drawen out of the Holy Scripture, with a preface by Coverdale (London: Printed by John Rastell for John Gough, 1535?);

Gulielmus Fullonius, *A Myrrour or Glasse for Them That Be Syke, Translated out of Dutch,* with a preface by Coverdale (Southwark: Printed by James Nicholson for John Gough, 1536);

The Byble, Which Is All the Holy Scripture, translated by "Thomas Matthew" (John Rogers), compiling the translations of Coverdale and William Tyndale (Antwerp: Printed by Matthias Crom for Richard Grafton & Edward Whitchurch, 1537);

The Causes Why the Germanes Wyll Not Go, Nor Consente vnto That Counsel, Called at Mantua (Southwark: James Nicholson, 1537);

Martin Luther, *A Very Excellent and Swete Exposition vpon the Two & Twentye Psalme, Translated out of Hye Almayne into English by Myles Coverdale* (Southwark: Printed by James Nicholson for John Gough, 1537);

Andreas Osiander, *How and Whither a Christen Man Ought to Flye the Horrible Plage of the Pestilence, Translated by M. C. out of hye Almayne* (Southwark: Printed by James Nicholson for John Gough, 1537);

The Original & Sprynge of All Sectes & Orders by Whome, Wha or Were They Beganne, Translated out of Hye Dutch (Southwark: Printed by James Nicholson for John Gough, 1537);

The Faith of the Indians (Southwark: Printed by James Nicholson for John Gough, 1537);

A Goodly Treatise of Faith, Hope and Charite, Translated into Englyshe, with a preface by Coverdale (Southwark: James Nicholson, 1537);

The Bokes of Salomon, Namely: Prouerbia, Ecclesiastes, Sapientia, and Ecclesiasticus, with a preface and epilogue by Coverdale (Southwark: James Nicholson, 1537);

The Newe Testament Both Latine and Englyshe Ech correspondent . . . after the Vulgare Texte, called S. Jeroms, translated by Myles Couerdale (Southwark: James Nicholson, 1538);

The New Testamen Both in Latin and English after the Vulgare Texte: Which Is Red in the Churche, Translated and Corrected by Myles Couerdale (Paris: Printed by Francis Regnault for Richard Grafton and Edward Whitchurch, 1538);

Martin Luther, *An Exposicion Vpon the Songe of the Blessed Virgine Mary, Called Magnificat, Whereunto Are Added the Songs of Salve Regina, Benedictus and Nunc Dimittis*, as John Hollybush (Southwark: James Nicholson, 1538);

The Byble in Englyshe, That Is to Saye the Content of All the Holy Scrypture (Paris: Francis Regnault, 1539; London: Richard Grafton & Edward Whitchurch, 1539);

The Psalter or Boke of Psalmes both in Latyn and Englyshe, Translated out of the Comon Texte in Latyne, Which Customably Is Redde in the Churche (London: Richard Grafton, 1540);

Heinrich Bullinger, *The Olde Fayth,* with a preface by Coverdale (Antwerp: Matthias Crom?, 1541);

Bullinger, *The Christen State of Matrimonye, Translated by Myles Coverdale* (Antwerp: Matthias Crom, 1541);

Martin Bucer and Philip Melanchthon, *The Actes of the Disputacion in the Cowncell of the Empyre Holden at Regenspurg: Concernyng the Christen Relygion, Translated owt of Latyne by Mylys Couerdale* (Antwerp: Catherine van Ruremund, 1542);

The Supplicacion: That the Nobles and Comons of Osteryke Made vnto Kyng Ferdinandus, in the Cause of the Christen Religion, Item, The Kynges Answere, with a preface by Coverdale (Antwerp: Matthias Crom, 1542);

The Maner of Sayinge Grace (Antwerp: Catherine van Ruremund, 1543?);

A Shorte Instruction to the Worlde, printed with *A Christen Exhortacion vnto Customable Swearers,* by John Bale (Antwerp: Catherine van Ruremund, 1543?);

The Order that the Church in Denmarke Doth Vse, Set Forth by Myles Coverdale (N.p., circa 1544); republished in *A Faythful and Most Godly Treatyse Concernyng the Sacrament,* by John Calvin (London: Nicholas Hill, 1548?);

A Shorte Recapitulacion or Abrigement of Erasmus Enchiridion, Drawne out by M. Couerdale (Ausborch [i.e., Antwerp]: Adam Anonimus [i.e., Steven Mierdman], 1545);

The Defence of a Certayne Poore Christen Man: Who Els Shuldhaue Bene Condemned by the Popes Lawe. Written in the Hye Allmaynes Tonge by a Noble Prynce, and Translated by Myles Coverdale (Nurenbergh [i.e., Antwerp: Steven Mierdman], 1545);

John Wyclif, *Uvicklieffes Wicket. Faythfully Ouerseene and Corrected. Hereunto Is Added an Epistle to the Reader. With the Protestacion of J. Lassels Late Burned in Smythfelde: and the Testament of W. Tracie Expounded by W. Tyndall, and J. Frythe. Ouerseene by M. C.* (London: John Day?, 1548?);

Desiderius Erasmus, *The Second Tome or Volume of the Paraphrase of Erasmus upon the Newe Testament,* edited and partly translated by Coverdale (London: Edward Whitchurch, 1549);

Otto Werdmüller, *A Spyrytuall and Moost Precyouse Pearle. Teachyng All Men Howe, Consolacyon in Afflyccyons Is to Be Soughte. Sett Forth by the Duke of Somerset* (London: Printed by Steven Mierdman for Walter Lynne, 1550);

Werdmüller, *A Moste Frutefull, Piththye and Learned Treatise, How a Christen Man Ought to Behaue Himself in the Daunger of Death* (Wesel?: Hugh Singleton?, 1555?);

Werdmüller, *A Godlye and Learned Treatise, Wherin Is Proued the True Iustificacion of a Christian Manne to Come Freely of the Mercy of God in Christ,* with a preface by Coverdale (Wesel?: Hugh Singleton?, 1555?);

Werdmüller, *The Hope of the Faythful, Declaryng the Resurreccion of Our Lorde Jesus Chryst* (Wesel?: Hugh Singleton?, 1555?);

Certain most Godly, Fruitful, and Comfortable Letters of Such True Saintes and Holy Martyrs as in the Late Bloodye Persecution Gaue Their Lyues, edited, with a preface, by Coverdale (London: John Day, 1564);

Ulrich Zwingli, *Fruitfull Lessons, vpon the Passion, Buriall, Resurrection, Ascension, and of the Sending of the Holy Ghost. Gathered out of the Foure Euangelists: with a Plain Exposition of the Same by Myles Coverdell* (London: Thomas Scarlet, 1593).

Editions: *The Holy Scriptures, Faithfully and Truly Translated by Myles Coverdale, Bishop of Exeter, 1535* (London: Samuel Bagster, 1847);

The Hexaplar Psalter, edited by William Aldis Wright (Cambridge: Cambridge University Press, 1911);

The Coverdale Psalter and the Quatrocentenary of the Printed English Bible [facsimile] (Chicago: Lakeside Press for the Caxton Club, 1935).

Miles Coverdale's translation of the Bible (the first complete English version to be published) placed him at the nexus of religious reform, politics, and English literature. As a Bible translator, Protestant reformer, bishop, and preacher, he helped shape the nascent English church. As a translator, he also helped shape the language of English literature, especially through his version of the Psalms, which, in the Book of Common

Miles Coverdale

Prayer, taught rhythms and images of poetic language to generations raised on its cadences. Though a secondary figure, Coverdale achieved several firsts through his translating: in addition to the first complete Bible, he produced the first metrical psalter in English, established the tradition of congregational singing, encouraged worship services in the vernacular, and helped introduce the genre of the marriage manual. His career not only spans the English Reformation but offers a paradigm of it. First an Augustinian friar, he passed through Erasmian humanism into Lutheranism and then on to the doctrines of Swiss reformers and returned from his last exile with the ideas and convictions of nascent Puritanism. Alongside these doctrinal shifts, Coverdale's career traces swings from official patronage to banishment, and his political and ecclesiastical attitudes move from Reformation Erastianism to passive resistance.

Of Coverdale's early life, scholars know only that he was born in York in 1487 or 1488 and loved learning. In 1514 he was ordained priest at Norwich, having evidently studied at Cambridge, where he entered the house of the Augustinian friars. Coverdale may have met Desiderius Erasmus, who taught at Cambridge from 1511 to 1514; he was certainly exposed to the Erasmian ideas that stirred the university. About 1520 Robert Barnes returned to Cambridge from his studies at Louvain (where Erasmus resided from 1517 to 1521) to become prior of the Augustinian friars. Barnes led his friars through Erasmian humanism and into lectures on Paul, then, after his conversion by Thomas Bilney in 1525, into Lutheranism. Coverdale likely joined early reformers such as Bilney, Hugh Latimer, William Tyndale, John Frith, Nicholas Ridley, and Matthew Parker, who gathered in Cambridge at the White Horse tavern, nicknamed "Germany" for the Lutheran views discussed there.

When Barnes was summoned before Cardinal Thomas Wolsey, Coverdale accompanied him to

London to help prepare a defense. After Barnes had done public penance at Paul's Cross on 11 February 1526, he was ordered to live at the house of the Augustinian friars in London. Perhaps Coverdale remained in London as well, for it seems that at about this time he came under the patronage of Wolsey's secretary, Thomas Cromwell. Cromwell owned a house adjacent to the London Augustinian friars, but he initiated his influence over Coverdale in a meeting at a more surprising location: in a letter dated "May Day" and written at "the Augustin's" (whether Cambridge or London is uncertain), Coverdale asks Cromwell "to revocate to your memory the godly communication which your mastership had of me your orator in Master Moor's house upon Easter Eve." In all likelihood this "Master Moor" was the staunch opponent of Protestantism, Sir Thomas More. The letter requests books and expresses a sense of vocation; Coverdale writes, "Now I begin to taste of holy scriptures," to "smell of holy letters," and to "savor of holy and ancient doctors, unto whose knowledge I cannot attain without diversity of books, as is not unknown to your most excellent wisdom."

From this devoted study of the Scriptures, Coverdale soon progressed into a kind of apprenticeship in translating them. Within a year he had cast off his friar's habit and, as a secular priest, was preaching in Essex about Erasmus's ideas and against transubstantiation, confession, and icons. Then, sensing danger, he fled to the Continent. According to John Foxe's *Actes and Monuments* (1559), Coverdale spent 1529 in Hamburg helping Tyndale translate the Pentateuch. He apparently followed Tyndale to Antwerp and may have worked as a proofreader at the press of Martin de Keyser. Foxe reports that when John Rogers came to Antwerp in 1534 as chaplain to the Merchant Adventurers, he fell in with Tyndale and Coverdale, was converted by them, and joined in the work of translating, which in his case resulted in the Thomas Matthew Bible of 1537.

Coverdale's 1535 Bible was the work of a single year. After producing an English version of Johannes Campensis's Latin paraphrase on the Psalms in 1535, he was urged by an Antwerp merchant, Jacob van Meteren, to translate the entire Bible. Because his knowledge of Hebrew and Greek was rudimentary, he drew not from the original tongues but from previous Latin, German, and English versions. The "five sundry interpreters" he followed were, in order of importance to him: the English New Testament, Pentateuch, and Jonah of Tyndale; the 1534 edition of the Zurich Bible (a German-Swiss version by Ulrich Zwingli and others); the German version of Martin Luther; the Latin Vulgate; and the Latin version by the Italian Hebraist Santes Pagninus (1528). On 4 October 1535 the printing was completed, most likely at Cologne by the printers Eucharius Cervicornus and Johannes Soter, though the publication and marketing were taken over from van Meteren by James Nicholson. In late August 1535 Nicholson wrote to Cromwell seeking the king's license for the Bible to go forth.

The Bible did not circulate in 1535–1536 with the king's privilege, but it apparently had his consent. Credit for that permission is due not only to the favor of Cromwell and Anne Boleyn and Henry VIII's ongoing negotiations with Lutheran princes but also to Coverdale's own dedicatory epistle to the king, a copy of which accompanied Nicholson's letter to Cromwell. What may appear flattery in the dedication in fact follows a strategy of some reformers and their official supporters: it insinuates that the promulgation and reading of an English Bible will increase obedience in the realm, and it symbolically empowers the king by bestowing upon him a scriptural legitimation.

Readers of the Bible, too, are admonished and authorized in Coverdale's prologue; Coverdale insists in this and all later writings that reception of the Word would transform behavior, and so he tried every means of spreading the Word in English. Along with encouraging the private reading of vernacular Scripture, he advocates public worship in the vernacular. Soon after completing the Bible, he published a book of *Ghostly Psalmes and Spiritual Songs* (1535?) and thereby instigated a tradition. The hymns, translated from Luther and others, introduced England to the idea of congregational singing, and the fifteen psalms rendered in verse are the earliest collection of metrical psalms in English. Though more like versified theology than poetry, and though often less resonant than Coverdale's own prose psalms, they sometimes have a clear and simple ring: "The angels made a merry noise, / Yet have we more cause to rejoice." They influenced later metrical psalters and hymnals in England and Scotland and appear to have circulated widely: Coverdale's was the only collection of psalms and hymns in 1545 when Henry VIII complained to Parliament that "that most precious jewel, the Word of God, is . . . rhymed, sung, and jangled in every alehouse and tavern."

In 1537 the new Thomas Matthew Bible and a new edition of the Coverdale Bible circulated with

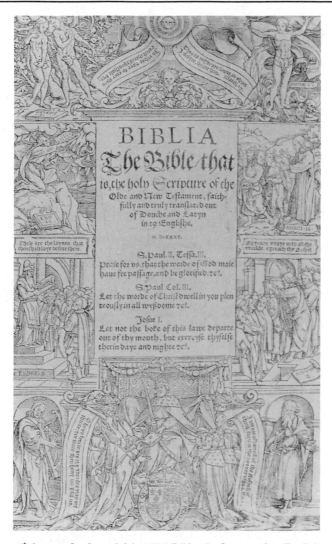

Title page for Coverdale's 1535 Bible, the first complete English version to be published

the king's license. (For the Matthew Bible, John Rogers published with slight revisions Tyndale's Pentateuch and New Testament, added from Tyndale's manuscript Joshua through 2 Chronicles, and then followed Coverdale from Ezra to the end of the Apocrypha. Coverdale thus provided a little less than half of the Matthew Bible.) The Injunctions of 1538 moreover required English Bibles to be set up in every church. Though Coverdale and Matthew Bibles began appearing on stands in many churches, the decision had been made to issue an official Bible "of the largest volume," generally now called the Great Bible.

Coverdale, as the most experienced Bible translator, as a modest and trustworthy subject, and as a longtime acquaintance and supporter of Cromwell, was appointed to edit the Great Bible. Richard Grafton and Edward Whitchurch were to publish it,

and Cromwell both shared the cost with the publishers and directed the operation. Coverdale was instructed to take the Matthew Bible as the basis of his revision, and he selected as aids Sebastian Munster's Hebrew-Latin Bible of 1535 and Erasmus's Latin New Testament. In the spring of 1538 Coverdale and Grafton traveled to Paris, where printing was faster and paper more abundant, and lodged with the printer Francis Regnault. They reported their progress to Cromwell and sent samples of their work in June, August, and September and then again in December just before trouble erupted.

After threatening rumblings along the way from theological conservatives in England and France, all printing stopped in December. The printer Regnault was haled before the inquisitor-general; French authorities seized the printed sheets for twenty-five hundred unfinished Bibles; and Coverdale and Grafton fled to England. Eventually diplomacy recovered the type, paper, and printers so that work could resume in London. Securing the printed sheets was more difficult: some had been publicly burned; four vats full were bought back from a haberdasher to whom they had been sold for cap linings; and the rest may have been recovered in Paris by Grafton in November 1539. The first edition appeared in April 1539. In it Coverdale has thoroughly revised the New Testament and the historical books of the Old – the Tyndale portion – but he saved many revisions of the prophetical and poetic books for the second edition, which appeared in April 1540 with a celebrated preface by Archbishop Thomas Cranmer.

Even amid this haste and trouble, Coverdale produced two additional works, Latin-English diglots of the New Testament and of the Psalms. For all his fervor to spread the Word of God in the vernacular, he loved the Vulgate and wished to appease the conservatives who resented deviations from it inspired by Greek and Hebrew translations, as well as to help both laity and clergy who struggled with Latin. Before leaving for Paris and the printing of the Great Bible, he had left with the printer Nicholson a Latin and English New Testament with a dedicatory epistle to the king; but when he received a copy around midsummer, he was so disappointed over the changes and blunders committed by the corrector that he redid the whole work and in November 1538 issued it from Regnault's press. Sometime in the months after returning to England, Coverdale prepared a Latin-English Psalter that was printed by Grafton in 1540.

In February and March 1539 Coverdale was sending Cromwell reports from Newbury, where he found illegal papist practices and books. Cromwell's opponents were even busier, however, in holding back the surge of Reformation. In June they passed the Act of Six Articles to enforce conformity to the doctrines and practices of transubstantiation, communion in one kind, private masses, monastic vows, clerical celibacy, and auricular confession. A year later Barnes, probably selected as the foremost representative in England of the Lutheran connection, went to the stake, and Cromwell went to the block. With the forces of reaction in the ascendant, and having lost both a mentor and a patron, Coverdale fled again into exile. This time a wife accompanied him, a Scotswoman named Elizabeth Macheson.

Coverdale and his wife were hospitably received in Strasbourg at the home of John Calvin, and they remained in the city about three years. Theologically, Coverdale progressed from Lutheran toward Swiss reformed doctrines. In 1537 and 1538 he had translated short scriptural expositions by Luther and a sermon by Andreas Osiander. During this period of exile he followed his colleagues and predecessors Tyndale and Barnes toward a new emphasis on works that spring from faith, an emphasis for which he found support among the Swiss reformers. He wrote against a treatise by John Standish that had accused Barnes of justly suffering death for "heresy and treason." A primary strategy in the 1541 defense is to repair "the perverting or chopping up of a text of Holy Scripture" by rendering in English and in full scriptural passages that Standish often gave in Latin or in part. A predominant concern of the work is to defend justification by faith in ways that stress the importance of good works, an emphasis characteristic of Swiss reformers.

In 1540 Coverdale translated, revised, and expanded *Brevis commemoratio mortis Christi,* a book by the Swiss reformer Ulrich Zwingli, as *Fruitful Lessons.* The book presents New Testament texts on the passion and resurrection of Christ and on Pentecost, followed by commentaries or sermons stressing the "fruit" – the changes in life and behavior – that faith in such doctrines should produce. In discussing the Lord's Supper, Coverdale retains a Zwinglian sense of communion as commemoration. The commentary is not scholarly but popular in tone, directed to the feelings and character of readers or hearers; it calls on common people to respond emotionally and morally to the texts.

Coverdale also translated two books by Zwingli's successor, Heinrich Bullinger. *The Old Faith* (1541) summarizes the entire Bible chronology to turn back accusations that the reformers are innovators, "new-fangled gospellers," with the claim that the Christian faith they teach was held by the ancient patriarchs as well as the apostles. Coverdale's distance from Luther appears in the prologue, which reclaims the Epistle of James from Lutheran disapproval and even names it the epistle that most speaks to the times. In translating Bullinger's *Der Christliche Ehestand* (1540) as *The Christian State of Matrimony* (1541), Coverdale established yet another genre in English: with this marriage manual in its various editions he helped introduce the tradition of vernacular conduct books.

Title page for Coverdale's revised 1540 Bible, with engravings by Hans Holbein the Younger

During the early 1540s Coverdale also received a doctorate in divinity from Tübingen University. Sometime after 1542, when his brother-in-law, John Macalpine, became by royal invitation professor of divinity in Copenhagen, Coverdale visited Denmark and was deeply impressed with the forms of public worship there. He translated the Danish liturgy in *The Order in the Church of Denmark* (circa 1544), a small book providing both a model for a vernacular prayer book and a manifesto for liturgical reform.

Coverdale soon thereafter received a far humbler post in education than that of his brother-in-law. Through the friendship of Martin Bucer's secretary, Conrad Hubert, Coverdale was appointed schoolmaster and assistant minister at Hubert's hometown of Bergzabern, forty miles north of Strasbourg. Letters from and about him show a gentle and considerate but diligent teacher and minister, concerned with the health of his students and of

Hubert's family, seeking books and paper, catechizing youth, anxious about a lack of piety in the people, troubled by local Anabaptists, and helping fellow exiles find positions. A letter from his friend Richard Hilles to Bullinger in 1545 describes Coverdale as "well loved and honored" throughout the region and notes that "in his leisure hours, for the wider propagation of the kingdom of Christ, he translates into English various religious writings, partly yours, partly of other scholars, and thus greatly benefits and promotes the salvation of those common persons who are eager for the truth."

The conservative reaction in England did not prove to be the catastrophe its beginnings had threatened; Henry issued a general pardon for all heresies and offenses committed before July 1540 and released hundreds of subjects who had been imprisoned. Still, Coverdale's writings after 1540 left him in disrepute, particularly since he wrote for the common folk. In his book on worship in Denmark, he wrote that he longed to return to England and that "all the lawful ways that I could devise, have I sought this great while to obtain license of the higher powers for the same purpose. But it will not be."

A royal proclamation in 1541 reiterated Cromwell's 1538 injunctions calling for English Bibles in every church, but the 1543 Act for the Advancement of True Religion forbade public reading of the Bible by private persons and any reading at all by "the lower sort": "no women, nor artificers, prentices, journeymen, servingmen of the degrees of yeomen or under, husbandmen nor laborers shall read the Bible or New Testament in English to himself or any other, privately or openly." In 1546 a royal proclamation prohibited the possession or reading of Bibles by Tyndale or Coverdale and English books by them and several other reformers (though most authorities must have known that the Great Bibles in their churches by command were virtually all by Tyndale or Coverdale). A few weeks thereafter, copies of thirteen of Coverdale's books were among those gathered by Bishop Edmund Bonner and burned at Paul's Cross.

Through all the books of Coverdale's second exile there runs another intriguing suggestion. Along with the growing emphasis on works as the fruit of faith, he evidences a growing alienation from political and ecclesiastical authority in England. Alongside the scriptural and moral emphasis on obedience, he nurtures a political attitude of resistance. One of the more interesting puzzles in Coverdale's life is how a person who seems by nature so submissive and on principle so obedient could resist first the church in which he was priest and friar, then eventually the church he had helped to shape and the monarch he had recognized and even revered as its head.

His prefaces and postscripts chart the latter stages of this change. In the dedications of his scriptural translations of the 1530s, Coverdale is generally submissive and flattering toward political authority, gentle and conciliatory toward opponents of reform. In the preface to his second New Testament diglot, for instance, he writes, "I am but a private man and owe obedience unto the higher powers." With the death of his patron Cromwell, however, a different tone enters. The prologue to *The Old Faith* appears to wrestle with the execution of Cromwell but still places faith in the king. The defense of Barnes continues to urge the Tudor doctrines of obedience and nonresistance but berates the council and approaches the verge of

criticizing the king. *The Order in the Church in Denmark* appears to be looking back on the translator's submissive attitude from a new position of frustration, as if resistance, though still neither desirable nor possible, is no longer unthinkable. In 1545 he translated *The Defense of a Certain Poor Christian Man*. In the form of a speech delivered before an inquisition tribunal, the text answers eight articles brought against the defendant and in the course of the eight implicitly mounts an attack on the Act of Six Articles, the law of England that helped drive Coverdale out and shattered his ties to power.

After the death of Henry VIII, however, Coverdale felt the favor of the court as never before, for the nobility swung toward Zwinglian positions, and gradually the tone of his work changed again. Edward VI had been on the throne for more than a year before Coverdale was invited to return to England, but soon after his arrival he was appointed royal chaplain and almoner to the dowager queen, Catherine Parr. One of the last books he had completed on the Continent was a 1545 abridgment of Tyndale's translation of Erasmus's *Enchiridion militis Christiani* (1503), and now, apparently at the queen's request and under the further patronage of Anne Seymour, Duchess of Somerset, he edited the second volume of the English translation of Erasmus's New Testament Paraphrases. Under his hand the second volume of paraphrases grew more stridently and polemically Protestant than the first; he inserted the prologue to Romans by Tyndale and antipapal commentary on Revelation by the Swiss reformer Leo Juda. When Parr died in September 1548, Coverdale preached the funeral sermon.

Coverdale was at Windsor Castle when Cranmer and others compiled the Book of Common Prayer. Though there is no certain evidence that he was on the committee, only Cranmer did more to shape the language of the prayer book: the introits, epistles, and gospels were all of Coverdale's translation, taken from the Great Bible.

In 1550, after the duke of Somerset was forced to resign his office as lord protector and was imprisoned, Coverdale provided him a translation of a consolatory tract by the Swiss reformer Otto Werdmüller. If Coverdale shared the sentiments of the tract, then he had retreated far from the frustration and alienation of his exile, back toward a submissive and patient acceptance of adversity.

While working with the government to consolidate the Reformation in England, he even joined efforts to enforce conformity and curb resistance.

Throughout the early part of Edward's reign, Coverdale was in official service: inviting the Strasbourg reformer Paul Fagius to take refuge in England, preaching at Paul's Cross and Westminster Abbey, sitting in judgment on Anabaptists, and serving as preacher to the forces sent to the west countries to quell the first rebellions of 1549. He stayed on in the west, preaching conciliation yet meeting popular resentment of his reformist teachings. He assumed many diocesan responsibilities for the aging and nonresident bishop John Vesey; then in August 1551 the conservative Vesey was removed from the bishopric, and in his stead Coverdale was appointed and consecrated bishop of Exeter.

Coverdale's tenure lasted only until the change in monarchs, for on 28 September 1553, the Privy Council under Mary I ejected him from the bishopric and reinstated Vesey. Coverdale's enemies felt certain he would go to the stake as a heretic. He himself expected as much, writing in August to a member of his diocese to affirm that he was ready to die for his belief and to dispel the rumor that he might recant:

> I have cast my pennyworth's already [and so I know] . . . what this ware will cost me, being fully appointed never to consent to unlawful things for any pleasure of life . . . and steadfastly determined never to return into Egypt, never to kiss the calf, . . . never to forsake, refuse, or recant the word of life. . . . Sure I am, though the flail of adversity beat never so hard, and the wind of affliction blow never so sore, it shall but break my straw and blow away my chaff.

Remaining under a loose house arrest for months, he publicly expressed his solidarity with "mine afflicted brethren, being prisoners," when he signed a declaration of belief by captive Protestants. Meanwhile, his relatives in Denmark persuaded Christian III to intercede. The king wrote to Mary at least twice, and in February 1555 Coverdale was permitted to leave for Denmark.

He soon moved from Denmark to Wesel, where English refugees were gathering around the duchess of Suffolk and her husband, and he became the first minister to the congregation there. It was probably during this time that Coverdale sent to press translations of three more books of popular devotion and instruction by Werdmüller. He was soon invited to return to the school and ministry at Bergzabern, where he stayed for two years. When the refugees in Wesel were asked to leave because their Swiss reformed practices differed from the Lutheran, Coverdale with his wife and two children rejoined them and settled in Aarau, Switzerland, in

August 1557. A year later he moved again, to Geneva, where he served as elder to the Anglican Church under John Knox and joined the work on the Geneva Bible of 1560.

In August 1559, eight months after Elizabeth's coronation, Coverdale returned home, bringing with him from Geneva the convictions that would fire Puritanism. In December he participated in the consecration of Matthew Parker as archbishop, but he wore only a black gown without the vestments of cope or surplice. He joined the household of the duchess of Suffolk as preacher and tutor, and he writes that he and the duchess share "animum a ceremoniis maxime abhorrentem" (the greatest abhorrence to the ceremonies). He refused to resume the bishopric of Exeter, most likely from animus toward vestments and ceremonies, but he continued to preach at Paul's Cross and elsewhere in London. In 1563 Cambridge awarded him a D.D., and the following year on behalf of Cambridge he conferred the degree on Edmund Grindal, bishop of London.

In January 1564 Grindal, who had hoped to procure a bishopric for Coverdale, persuaded him to accept the living of St. Magnus Martyr by London Bridge. Efforts to enforce the wearing of vestments by London clergy led him to resign two years later. Still he preached (sometimes surreptitiously) services eagerly attended by Puritans, until his death on 20 January 1569.

If one accepts the commonplace that the English Bible is the most influential book in the language and that second only to it is the Book of Common Prayer, then a double debt is owed to the nearly anonymous Coverdale. The Bible of 1535 and the Great Bible of 1539 were superseded by translations that followed, but even in them Coverdale's language left memorable traces: "the valley of the shadow of death," "Enter thou into the joy of thy Lord," "Death is swallowed up in victory," "For God so loved the world that he gave his only-begotten son, that whosoever believeth in him should not perish, but have everlasting life." His psalter continued virtually unaltered in the Book of Common Prayer. The 1662 revisers of the prayer book retained Coverdale's psalter in preference to the King James rendering because it was smooth, familiar, and musical. Across five centuries it has exerted its influence on poetry.

During the last century some scholars have adopted a condescending attitude toward Coverdale, claiming that he lacked Tyndale's fire or his scholarship; that he was a toady of government patrons or, later, a stubborn ingrate; and that he imported new ideas to England but originated none. One must concur with the *Dictionary of National Biography* that "in the hour of trouble he was content to remain in obscurity, and left the crown of martyrdom to be earned by men of tougher fibre," but who can endorse such a severe standard? With little drama and with less notoriety, Coverdale followed his conviction that common folk should be free to read, sing, and live by the vernacular word. He lingers at the edges of memory as the ordinary hero of the everyday.

Letters:

Remains of Myles Coverdale, Bishop of Exeter, edited by George Pearson, Parker Society (Cambridge: Cambridge University Press, 1846), pp. 490–532, 591–610;

James Frederic Mozley, *Coverdale and His Bibles* (London: Lutterworth, 1953), pp. 313–318.

Bibliographies:

Mozley, *Coverdale and His Bibles* (London: Lutterworth, 1953), pp. 324–335;

Stanley Lawrence Greenslade, "Introduction," *The Coverdale Bible, 1535* (Folkestone, Kent: Dawson, 1975), pp. 25–27, 29–30.

References:

Frederick F. Bruce, *The English Bible,* revised edition (New York: Oxford University Press, 1970);

Celia Hughes, "Coverdale's Alter Ego," *Bulletin of the John Rylands University Library of Manchester,* 65 (Autumn 1982): 100–124;

Robin A. Leaver, *"Goostly psalmes and spirituall songes": English and Dutch Metrical Psalms from Coverdale to Utenhove, 1535–1566* (Oxford: Clarendon Press, 1991);

James Frederic Mozley, *Coverdale and His Bibles* (London: Lutterworth, 1953);

Alfred William Pollard, *Records of the English Bible* (London: Oxford University Press, 1911);

Ernest Edwin Reynolds, "More, Coverdale and Cromwell," *Moreana,* 10 (May 1966): 77–79;

J. J. Scarisbrick, *Henry VIII* (Berkeley: University of California Press, 1968).

Angel Day

(flourished 1586)

Richard Rambuss
Emory University

BOOKS: *Wonderfull Strange Sightes seene in the Element, over the Citie of London and other places* (London, 1585?);

The English Secretorie. Wherein is contayned, a perfect method, for the inditing of all manners of epistles (London: Robert Waldgrave, 1586); revised as *The English Secretorie. Now corrected, refined & amended* (London: Robert Waldgrave, 1592);

Vpon the life and death of Sir Phillip Sidney: A Commemoration of his worthiness (London: Robert Waldgrave, 1586);

Daphnis and Chloe (London: Robert Waldgrave, 1587).

Editions: *Daphnis and Chloe: The Elizabethan Version by Angel Day,* edited by Joseph Jacobs (London: David Nutt, 1890);

The English Secretorie, facsimile of 1586 edition (Menston, U.K.: Scolar, 1967);

The English Secretary, facsimile of 1599 edition, edited by Robert O. Evans (Gainesville, Fla.: Scholars' Facsimiles and Reprints, 1967).

Angel Day was a rhetorician, poet, and translator whose importance chiefly derives from his epistolary manual *The English Secretary* (1586). This guide to correspondence, or "letter-writer," appears to be the first handbook of its kind to be composed of original English letters rather than translations of Latin models. Responsive to a sixteenth-century vogue for how-to guides, courtesy manuals, and ready handbooks of acculturation aimed at the "middle" and rising classes, *The English Secretary* was one of the most popular Elizabethan letter-writers, republished more than ten times by 1639. It was also one of the most ambitious. In subsequent editions Day augmented his handbook not only with an expanding variety of model letters for the user's instruction and imitation, but also with a relatively detailed treatise on rhetorical forms and figures, a systematic discussion whose usefulness extends well beyond framing simple utilitarian correspondence. Day also appends another treatise to his handbook, a comprehensive account of secretaryship itself, an office here elevated as the embodiment of the ideals of a humanist rhetorical culture. Day's expansive and expanding manual thus delineates in several registers — rhetorical, pedagogical, poetical, and even protoprofessional — the early modern paths that run from letter writing to literacy, from letters to the literary, and from an old notion of the secretary as someone adept at penning letters to an emerging sense of secretaryship as an office of trust and intimacy in the service of a figure of some importance. It is, moreover, along these rhetorical/literary routes that many sixteenth-century literary figures — Sir Thomas More, Roger Ascham, Edmund Spenser, Gabriel Harvey, George Gascoigne, and presumably Day himself — looked for career advancement.

Not much is known about Day's biography, except that he was born around 1550 in London, where his father, Thomas Day, was a parish clerk. On Christmas Day in 1563 Day apprenticed himself for a period of twelve years to Thomas Duxsell, a London stationer. In *The English Secretary* Day implies that at some time he served as a secretary himself (and thus is writing from personal experience); he does not mention, however, whose secretary he was. Since no further biographical records exist, the shape of Day's career is best gleaned from his publications.

Defining the letter in the first edition of *The English Secretary* as "the messenger and familiar speech of the absent," Day enumerates three principles of letter writing: "aptness of words and sentences," "brevity of speech," and "comeliness in deliverance, concerning the person and cause." On

37

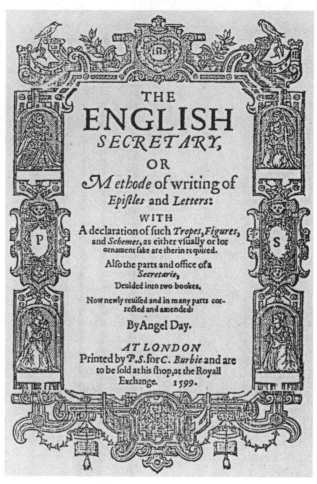

THE
ENGLISH
SECRETARY,
OR
Methode of writing of
Epistles and Letters:
WITH
A declaration of such Tropes, Figures,
and Schemes, as either visually or for
ornament sake are therin required.

Also the parts and office of a
Secretarie,
Deuided into two bookes.

Now newly reuised and in many parts corrected and amended:

By Angel Day.

AT LONDON
Printed by P. S. for C. Burbie and are
to be sold at his shop, at the Royall
Exchange. 1599.

*Title page for Day's letter-writing handbook, the first to use
original English letters rather than translations of Latin models*

this last point the 1599 edition of Day's manual specifies such matters as social rank, age, "manner of living," and occupation – "one platform to courtiers, another to philosophers." Chapter 3 outlines the five parts of an epistle: exordium, narration or proposition, confirmation, confutation, and peroration. Each is theorized and exemplified over the next few chapters, with Day devoting special attention to the composition of proper greetings and farewells. The rest of this first section of *The English Secretary* is given over to Day's classification of letters in four categories: demonstrative, deliberative, judicial, and familiar. Under these general headings he offers instructive examples of more than two dozen kinds of letters, ranging from "Epistles Consolatory" to "Epistles Invective" and "Epistles Amatory."

Much of *The English Secretary* is adapted from what had already been codified in various Latin formularies, chief among which was Desiderius Erasmus's *De conscribendis epistolis* (1522), a treatise Day

paraphrases at length. From this vantage Day's letter-writer appears rather conventional, even derivative. Nor would there be any stigma attached to this method in a literary culture that encouraged and valued imitation of the best models.

Nevertheless, *The English Secretary* is not without its own innovations, particularly by way of what Day provides as model letters. The handbooks of his English predecessors, William Fulwood's *Enemy of Idleness* (1568) and Abraham Fleming's *Panoply of Epistles* (1576), had advertised themselves as translations of only the choicest foreign exemplars of letter writing. Day claims for himself the title of author, however, making the unprecedented boast that he himself composed nearly all of the instructional letters in his manual. In this respect Day puts himself forward as "the English secretary."

Furthermore, his eschewing foreign letters has a nationalistic bias, one that is predicted by the handbook's title: Day's is an *English* letter-writer, offered with the intent of "greatly affecting the benefit of his country." *The English Secretary,* that is, promotes the English language, and does so specifically by promoting the ability of the English to frame proper letters in their native language. Accordingly (and this is another of Day's innovations), the book's model correspondence has been crafted more in accordance with the perceived requirements of its audience. Thus Day proffers sample letters for courtship, "An example Swasory, wherein a Gentlewoman is counselled to marriage" as well as "An example Commendatory . . . recommended to a noble man from his inferior" and "An epistle Expostulatory, touching certain injuries between two friends." Epistles of this sort displace the precedent established by Fulwood and Fleming, with their compendia of essayistic Ciceronian epistles or translations of ambassadorial letters exchanged between emperors and popes. In this way, Day's more familiar letters predict the course of bourgeois English secretaries and letter-writers up to Samuel Richardson's *Letters Written to and for Particular Friends* (1741).

Day's success on this account is backhandedly registered by John Massinger, producer of a rival letter-writer, *The Secretary in Fashion* (1640). In his preface to what is essentially an English translation of Jean Puget de la Serre's *Secretaire a la mode* (1640), Massinger claims that his guide means "to reclaim the idolatrous from adoring that malicious idol *The English Secretary.*" The reader who is not willing to give Massinger's handbook its due, however, is "condemned to the reading of the *English Secretary* as long as thou livest."

Day's ambitions for his letter-writer go beyond providing more-useful and occasionally more-entertaining epistolary models, however. From its first edition Day was annotating his letters, pointing out the specific parts of each letter and their exemplary tropes and figures. In its 1592 edition Day added to *The English Secretary* something no other vernacular manual offered: a compact but thorough dictionary of rhetorical forms and uses, titled "A Declaration of All Such Tropes, Figures, and Schemes, as for Excellency and Ornament in Writing." This addition draws upon the long association of letter writing and rhetoric, so that the expanded version of *The English Secretary* does double duty as a letter-writing manual and a rhetorical handbook, a treatise offering a kind of poetics both for utilitarian epistles and for letters in the sense of the literary.

Beyond his authorship of *The English Secretary,* Day was a man of letters with literary ambitions. He is credited as the author of a pamphlet-length poem titled *Wonderful Strange Sights* (1585?). More

important, Day composed *Upon the Life and Death of Sir Philip Sidney* (1586), a commemorative poem in six-line stanzas. Published in the same year as the first edition of *The English Secretary,* this elegy was dedicated to Sir Francis Walsingham, Sidney's father-in-law and one of the two most important secretaries in the realm. In keeping with the taste for the pastoral established by Spenser's *Shepheardes Calender* (1579), Day also produced a pastoral romance titled *Daphnis and Chloe* (1587), a prose narrative in four books, with lyrics and songs interspersed throughout. Day's version is essentially a translation of Jacques Amyot's French version of the Longus original.

Significantly, Day adds a digression of his own called "The Shepherds' Holiday," which, according to the title page, offers "the praises of a most peerless princess, wonderful in majesty, and rare in perfection." This lengthy encomium of Queen Elizabeth, the "fair Eliza," is placed in the mouth of a reverend, long-winded shepherd named Meliboeus and marks the pastoral community's intention of celebrating "the eternal praises of her divine excellency." These poetic endeavors apparently won Day, if not fame, at least some entrance into Elizabethan literary circles insofar as he joined the company of Spenser, Samuel Daniel, and George Chapman in contributing commendatory verses to William Jones's *Nennio* (1595), a translation of an Italian treatise on the nature of true nobility.

Apart from a few recent exceptions, the critical attention accorded Day has focused on *The English Secretary,* either in its capacity as a popular miscellany of model letters or as one of many sixteenth-century rhetorical guidebooks. But the expanded edition of *The English Secretary* also contains a third section, a thirty-three-page excursus, "Of the Parts, Place, and Office of a Secretary," much of which Day derived from Francesco Sansovino's *Del Secretario* (1565). Day's appended treatise, part of a developing Renaissance discourse on secretaryship, is important for how it describes and even shapes the office, as well as for the way its inclusion further recasts the purview of Day's originally rather humble letter-writer. It was not uncommon for early modern letter-writers and penmanship manuals to present themselves as *Secretaries,* as in Thomas Gainsford's *Secretary's Study* (1616), John Hill's *Young Secretary's Guide* (1687), and even Henry Care's *Female Secretary* (1671). But whereas these manuals are secretaries in that they provide prefabricated letters that could be copied or adapted to serve the epistolary requirements of their users, Day's enlarged manual served as a protoprofessional training handbook for those who looked to become secretaries themselves.

Along these lines, "Office of a Secretary" details the requirements of birth, learning, penmanship, social finesse, trustworthiness, and even physical appearance required of a position that is, Day insists, of far greater importance than is generally admitted. Thus, just as Day's letters exemplify "a perfect method . . . of all manner of Epistles," so too is his secretary a model type, an incorporation of all the processes and skills of humanistic training and gentility. In his endeavor to elevate the office, Day stresses less the secretary's pen and more the uniquely privileged place he occupies in his master's counsels, affairs, and affections. To this end Day foregrounds the etymological linkage between *secretaryship* and *secret,* maintaining that "by the very etymology of the word itself, both name and office in one do conclude upon secrecy." This conjunction is emblematized in Day's striking metaphor, by which the secretary turns into his office, the secret chamber to which the master retires to conduct his private affairs: thus for Day the secretary "is but the closet, whereof another have both the key, use and commandment."

Day was a relatively minor literary figure, and, apart from *The English Secretary,* apparently none of his writings earned subsequent republication. Nonetheless, there is much to be learned from his work concerning the developing rhetorical culture of the sixteenth century as it cast its purview in two directions at once – outward to "the unlearned" and upward "to those that be greatest learned, best advised, discretest governed, and most worthiest ruled." Similarly, *The English Secretary,* as well as what is known of Day's own multiple-track career as a man of letters, can provide more texture to a modern understanding of Elizabethan literary careers. Seldom did they afford the possibility of a single-minded pursuit of literary fame. More often, as Day's manual illustrates, the paths of intellectual, social, and "professional" advancement for the man of letters entailed a dual career. Such careers were composed out of the intersections between the literary domain and the other modes of humanist service or bureaucratic employment (such as, in Day's case, secretaryship) available to those with rhetorical training.

References:

Jonathan Goldberg, *Writing Matter: From the Hands of the English Renaissance* (Stanford, Cal.: Stanford University Press, 1990), pp. 33–78;

Judith Rice Henderson, "Letter as Genre," in *The Spenser Encyclopedia,* edited by A. C. Hamilton and others (Toronto: University of Toronto Press, 1990), pp. 433–434;

Katherine Gee Hornbeak, "The Complete Letter-Writer in English, 1568–1800," *Smith College Studies in Modern Languages,* 15 (April–July 1934): 1–150;

Richard Rambuss, *Spenser's Secret Career* (Cambridge: Cambridge University Press, 1993), pp. 29–61;

Jean Robertson, *The Art of Letter Writing: An Essay on Handbooks Published in England during the Sixteenth and Seventeenth Centuries* (London: University Press of Liverpool, 1942);

Louis B. Wright, *Middle-Class Culture in Elizabethan England* (Ithaca, N.Y.: Cornell University Press, 1935), pp. 139–146.

Thomas Deloney

(died 1600)

Alexandra Halasz
Dartmouth College

BOOKS: *The Gentle Craft. A Discourse Containing Many Matters of Delight* (London: Ralph Blower, 1599);

The Second Part of the Gentle Craft [fragment] (London: Edward Allde?, circa 1600); republished as *The Gentile Craft. The Second Part. By T. D. Newly Corrected and Augmented* (London: Printed by Edward Purslow, 1639);

Strange Histories, of Kings, Princes, Dukes, . . . With the Great Troubles of the Dutches of Suffolke, anonymous (London: Printed for William Barley, 1602);

Thomas of Reading. Or, The Six Worthy Yeomen of the West. Now the Fourth Time Corrected and Enlarged (London: Printed by Ralph Blower for Thomas Pavier, 1612);

Canaans Calamitie Jerusalem's Misery, or the Doleful Destruction of Jerusalem by Tytus (London: Printed by W. Jones for T. Bayley, 1618);

The Pleasant History of John Winchcomb, in His Younger Yeares Called Jack of Newberie. Now the Eight Time Imprinted, Corrected, and Inlarged (London: Printed by H. Lownes, 1619);

The Garland of Good Will. Divided into Three Parts: Containing Many Pleasant Songs, . . . With a Table to Find the Names of All the Songs (London: Printed for E. Brewster and R. Bird, 1628).

Editions: *The Works of Thomas Deloney,* edited by Francis Oscar Mann (Oxford: Clarendon Press, 1912);

The Novels of Thomas Deloney, edited by Merritt Lawlis (Bloomington: Indiana University Press, 1961).

OTHER: *A Declaration Made by the Archbishop of Cologne, upon His Marriage. With the Letter of Gregory the Thirteenth against the Same Marriage, together with the Bishop's Answer,* translated by Deloney (London: Printed by J. Charlewood for J. Wolfe, 1583);

A Most Joyfull Songe, Made in the Behalfe of All Her Maiesties Faithfull Subiects: of the Great Joy, at the Taking of the Late Trayterous Conspirators [folio sheet] (London: Printed by R. Jones, 1586);

A Proper New Ballad, Breefely Declaring the Death and Execution of 14. Most Wicked Traitors the 20 and 21. of September. 1586 [folio sheet] (London: Printed by E. Allde, 1586);

A Proper Newe Sonet Declaring the Lamentation of Beckles in Suffolke, Which Was Most Pittifully Burned with Fire [folio sheet] (Printed by R. Robinson for N. Colman of Norwich, 1586);

A New Ballet of the Straunge Whippes Which the Spanyards Had Prepared to Whippe English Men and Women [folio sheet] (London: T. Orwin and T. Gubbin, 1588);

The Queenes Visiting of the Campe at Tilsburie with Her Entertainment There [folio sheet] (London: Printed by J. Wolfe for E. White, 1588);

A Joyful New Ballad, Declaring the Happie Obtaining of the Great Galleazzo [folio sheet] (London: Printed by J. Wolfe for E. White, 1588);

The Lamentation of Master Pages Wife of Plimmouth, Who Did Most Wickedly Consent to His Murther [folio sheet] (London: Printed for H. Gosson, 1609?);

The Lamentation of George Strangwidge, 1609 [folio sheet] (London: Printed for H. Gosson, 1609?);

The Sorrowfull Complaint of Mistris Page [folio sheet] (London: Printed for H. Gosson, 1609?).

London's best-known ballad writer at the end of the sixteenth century, Thomas Deloney was also a silk weaver and the writer of four fictions featuring artisan and merchant heroes. Two volumes of his collected ballads were published, one of them certainly in Deloney's lifetime. At least two of his prose fictions provided plots for contemporary plays, of which only Thomas Dekker's *Shoemakers' Holiday* (1599) survives. The ballad books and fictions were reprinted frequently throughout the seventeenth century and into the eighteenth. Early editions were read out of existence; the earliest surviving copy of *Jack of Newbury,* for example, is dated 1619 and claims to be the eighth edition.

Aside from the record of his publications and contemporary references to his occupation as a silk weaver and his status as a ballad writer, little is known about Deloney's life. The baptism of a son is recorded in the parish register of St. Giles, Cripplegate, London, in 1586; probably the death of the same son is noted in a garbled entry later the same year. Deloney's death in 1600 is inferred from William Kempe's report in *Kemp's Nine-Days Wonder* (1600) that Deloney "died poorly . . . and was honestly buried" and thus could not have been the writer of ballads about which Kempe complains. Circumstantial evidence allows for a slightly fuller portrait. It is possible that Deloney was from Norwich, or at any rate Norfolk, where Flemish and French Protestant refugees settled and spurred the cloth trades – especially those involving silk – in the fifteenth and sixteenth centuries. His surname is of French origin; he may have been the T. D. who translated Bonaventure Des Periers's sixteenth-century collection of stories, *Les Contes ou les nouvelles recreations et joyeux devis,* published in English in 1583 as *The Mirror of Mirth and Pleasant Conceits,* and the first ballad known to be by Deloney was published in Norwich. Deloney's fictions repeatedly demonstrate familiarity with families and places of Berkshire, another county heavily involved in the silk trade, suggesting that he lived there, most likely in Newbury, for some time. By 1586 at the latest the author was living in London.

Deloney's first known publication was a translation from the Latin of the archbishop of Cologne's declaration and defense of his marriage, together with Pope Gregory's letter in reply and the archbishop's response, printed as a small pamphlet by John Wolfe in 1583. The pamphlet was at once antipapist, strongly Protestant, and patriotic. Later ballads, such as ones about Jesuit conspirators or the war with Spain, demonstrate the same mix of sentiments, which have plausibly been attributed to Deloney. Other evidence complicates the image of a simple-minded patriot, however: in 1595 Deloney and a group of weavers were arrested for having a pamphlet printed that complained to London city officials about competition from foreign workers. A year later Deloney again surfaces in an official record – as the writer of a ballad complaining about the scarcity of corn whom the lord mayor cannot find in order to arrest. The fictions Deloney wrote at the end of his life corroborate a more complicated view of his political and ideological positions, but they also benefit from his decade or more of experience as a ballad writer.

Deloney's ballad-writing practice is attested by surviving ballads from 1586 onward. By the early 1590s contemporaries refer to him as London's exemplary ballad writer. Such references are not exactly compliments; in an era self-consciously concerned with developing an English literature, ballads are most often invoked as the lowest literary form or as nonliterary altogether: "threadbare trash" or "trivial trinkets," as the anonymous writer of *A Defense of Conny-Catching* (1592) puts it. Deloney's ballads are not unusual; they cover a range of topics – journalistic (fires, executions, battles), moralistic (debates between ignorance and truth, or youth and age), and historical (accounts of English kings, legends, and heroes). Like most ballads, they were printed on single sheets with the title of the tune to which they were meant to be sung noted at the top, and they would have been sold for a halfpenny by peddlers who might have sung them to attract attention. Unlike many ballads written for street distribution, Deloney's do not have preliminary verses that situate the ballad singer's performance. Instead they proceed quickly to narrative or dialogue and accomplish their informative, recreative, or educative task efficiently and competently.

What distinguishes Deloney's ballads is the fact that some of them were collected in book form. The first such book, *The Garland of Good Will* (earliest extant edition, 1628), appears in the Stationers' Register with two dates, 1593 and 1596; the second, *Strange Histories, of Kings, Princes, Dukes, . . . With the Great Troubles of the Dutches of Suffolke* (earliest extant edition, 1602), cannot be dated within Deloney's lifetime. *The Garland of Good Will* includes ballads published in the late 1580s and early 1590s as single or half sheets, as well as ballads evidently written for the book. *Strange Histories* appears to have been written as a book: the stories are drawn from Raphael Holinshed's *Chronicles* (1577) and are arranged chronologically. If ballads, at the end of the sixteenth century and now, can be dismissed as nonliterary, it is because they are most often anonymous and, with the exception of folk ballads, ephemeral. By publishing or tacitly consenting to the publication of his ballads in book form,

*Title page for the first collection of Deloney's ballads (courtesy of
the Lilly Library, Indiana University)*

Deloney makes a double claim: for himself as an author and for the ballads as lasting poetic texts. *Strange Histories,* in particular, seems to be a conscious effort to translate Holinshed into a more popular idiom, to create not "threadbare trash" and "trivial trinkets" but poetry that could be disseminated widely, especially among the newly literate.

Deloney also wrote one long poem, *Canaan's Calamity* (earliest extant edition, 1618), drawn from Josephus's second-century account of the destruction of Jerusalem and a prose piece written by Thomas Nashe, *Christ's Tears over Jerusalem* (1593). Both Nashe and Deloney use Josephus's account as the basis of a moral allegory about sixteenth-century London, and sermons of the 1590s simi-

larly refer to the destruction of Jerusalem as a warning to Londoners. The story Josephus tells was especially apt in a decade of scarcity, famine, and plague that drove people to indecent acts. While Nashe's account engages in grotesque, spectacular rhetoric, Deloney's poem is leaner and more circumspect in its moralizing. Unlike Nashe's text, which was printed only once, Deloney's poem was republished at least three times before the English Civil War. Like the ballads in *Strange Histories, Canaan's Calamity* affords access to material that might otherwise be unavailable to less-educated readers or to those who would depend on the reading aloud of others.

In his four prose fictions Deloney repeatedly uses ballads. He represents situations in which ballads are sung (both the weavers and the shoemakers in his stories sing while they work); he uses ballads as commentary on parts of the narrative (after a matter-of-fact summary of the battle of Flodden Field in *Jack of Newbury* the narrator interposes a ballad about it, attributed to "the Commons of England"); and he creates characters, such as Round Robin, Tom Dove, and Anthony Now Now, who are wholly or partly identified with or by their love of music and song. Indeed, it might be argued that for Deloney ballads – their writing, performance, and circulation – were an important figure of his entire writing practice. In any case, his ballads and ballad books were reprinted frequently into the eighteenth century. When, in the later eighteenth and nineteenth centuries, antiquarians began to collect so-called folk ballads, they often could not determine whether a particular song was written by Deloney or merely transcribed, since songs attributed to him seemed also to have circulated independently. All educated guesses aside, the question is finally unanswerable. What can be said, however, is that Deloney's work, from the beginning, was identified and imbricated with a culture that was popular and oral.

Between 1596 and 1600 Deloney wrote the four works that made him a best-selling author: two books about clothiers and two about shoemakers. All of them are historical fictions in that they treat, at least in part, the lives of historical personages. Only two can be dated: *Jack of Newbury,* generally thought to be the first, was entered in the Stationers' Register in March of 1597, and *The Gentle Craft* was entered in October of the same year. The second part of *The Gentle Craft* obviously followed, and the prefatory material to *Jack of Newbury* promises a version of *Thomas of Reading* (1612), but the order of composition and publication for all four books cannot be determined. The two later books, however, can be thought of as sequels, each one continuing a representation of a particular set of artisanal and mercantile practices.

Deloney's fictions have most often been understood as "artisanal romances," that is, as fictions about idealized artisanal figures and situations. *Jack of Newbury,* for example, tells the story of John (Jack) Winchcombe's rise from an apprentice to the manager of a shop to marriage with his former master's widow and thus his own mastery and civic prominence. Yet the story of his rise occupies only two of eleven chapters; two more chapters focus on his influence with the Crown, and the remainder involve characters and events sometimes only loosely connected to Jack's household. Rather than being simply an exemplar of upward mobility, Jack serves as an organizing figure around whom Deloney constructs a complex representation of a large household engaged in a nationally important trade.

To read Deloney's books as artisanal or middle-class romances, or to place Deloney on one side of a class divide, then, is misleading and reductive, for his books are in part about the complications of class, especially the crossing and maintenance of class boundaries. Apprentices rise and become masters; masters rise into civic prominence; masters fall into economic and social disgrace and are redeemed by their brothers-in-trade, by their wives, or by luck; journeymen stay journeymen; gentlemen and princes become apprentices; a soldier becomes a gentleman; a lady becomes a servant. The men who rise to become masters or the men who are masters are no longer artisans: they are merchants – long-distance traders and protocapitalists. Without question Deloney represents a world in which the middle classes are ascendant, but he also represents the costs and complications of that ascendancy.

Because it is organized around an eponymous hero, *Jack of Newbury* is the most visibly coherent of Deloney's fictions. Early critics noted how Deloney was indebted to the jestbook tradition, which used a central figure to organize loosely an episodic narrative. Such a view of Deloney's indebtedness and his technical skill is overly simple. Rather, his fictions, *Jack of Newbury* among them, are composed of multiple narratives that accommodate story elements drawn from a variety of sources and traditions, oral as well as printed, verbal as well as mute. Deloney's characteristic move is to provide a story that situates a name, a place, a song, a proverb, or another story in a network of specific relations of his invention. Anything in the public domain might serve. John Winchcombe's story survives in no chronicle history of the period, yet two John Winchcombes, father and son, were prominent clothiers in Newbury; the son, like Deloney's Jack, served in Parliament in the mid sixteenth century. In seventeenth-century accounts of English history such as Thomas Fuller's *Worthies of England* (1662), Deloney's story becomes the record, much as his ballads became folk/traditional. A story told in the first chapter about Jack's marriage to the widow is drawn from Boccaccio's *Decameron;* a story told about Jack's service at Flodden Field is accurate in the details of the battle, but his presence at the battle and his conversations with the queen there are invented. The final chapter of *Jack of Newbury* involves a discharged soldier, Sir George Rigley, who was knighted but given no income and whom Jack assists, thereby modeling what should have been the Crown's behavior. Both the Rigley family name and the problem of a disbanded soldiery can be found in the chronicles; the story of Sir George, his misfortunes, and his seduction of and benignly coerced marriage to one of Jack's servants are Deloney's invention.

The multiple narratives that compose Deloney's fictions are not simply strung together but rather are thematically interwoven. Weaving is an apt metaphor for Deloney's storytelling; weaving techniques — the handling of multiple threads, the repetition of motifs, the use of emblematic designs — are analogous to his narrative style. In *Jack of Newbury* the weaving is easy to trace. Motifs such as Thomas Cardinal Wolsey's status and conduct as an important self-made man are introduced, laid aside, and reintroduced. Chapter sequences carry the narrative forward while introducing new issues and figures, such as a three-chapter sequence concerning a "gossip" (female friend) and her relation to Jack's wife, which not only illustrates Jack's position but also foregrounds the social relations between women, the marital and domestic economy of the Winchcombe household, and the difference between Newbury and London, as well as introducing another metaphor for Deloney's storytelling practice. Three stories, carefully deployed at the beginning, middle, and end of the book, involve a pig or pigs used as emblems of human animality. By these means, Deloney achieves control and design in his episodic narrative.

In Deloney's subsequent fictions the techniques remain the same, but they are not so insistently related to the artisanal practice of weaving. *Thomas of Reading,* for example, is about clothiers and weavers — there is even a weaving contest between a city journeyman and a country journeyman at one point — but Deloney's metaphoric weaving involves his decision to tell stories about six different merchant-clothiers and their respective wives and households. *Thomas of Reading* opens with a strong image of the clothiers' power: carts bearing cloth literally push the king's entourage off the road. The organizing premise of the fiction is that the clothiers from the northern and western counties periodically meet in or on their way to London and from these meetings develop friendships. The premise allows Deloney to estab-

lish a triple focus: the dispersed country lives in protoindustrial towns, the circuit of roads and inns connecting provincial centers to London, and the economic and political center of London itself. Individual stories are situated within this matrix: the wives desire to go to London or to have London fashions; one of the men misbehaves on the road; Thomas Cole is murdered by innkeepers who want his money. In the opening episode Deloney also establishes a subplot, for he identifies the king (Henry I) as having taken the crown that rightfully belonged to his brother, Robert, duke of Normandy, while the latter was away on a Crusade. Later Duke Robert falls in love with Margaret, the impoverished daughter of an earl who is working as a servant (in the household of a clothier, of course). Deloney represents the king and the clothiers in an alliance that works toward the good of the commonwealth. Duke Robert and Margaret, in contrast, are exemplars of a recalcitrant nobility destined for unproductive, though highly romantic, ends: the duke is judicially blinded, and Margaret enters a convent.

The two parts of *The Gentle Craft* also tell multiple stories, and, like the two books about weavers and clothiers, the first is somewhat simpler in its organization. The first part is divided into three distinct narratives threaded together by the proverb "a shoemaker's son is a prince born." The first two narratives use story elements drawn from a late medieval collection of hagiographies, *The Golden Legend.* The first tells the story of Hugh's ill-fated love for Winifred. Sent away by his ladylove, Hugh has a series of adventures and finally falls in with a group of shoemakers. Meanwhile, Winifred is imprisoned for her faith. Hugh is already a princely type; he becomes a shoemaker out of necessity and a saint by virtue of his decision to join Winifred in prison and martyrdom. The shoemakers take his bones and use them to form the tools of their craft; the tools are henceforth known as "St. Hugh's bones." Although its origins are in hagiography and Deloney remains true to a hagiographic plot, the story of Hugh and Winifred is also a burlesque of both contemporary courtly romances and traditional hagiographies. The second narrative tells the story of Crispine and Crispianus, the patron saints of shoemakers. They too are princes who take refuge among shoemakers and learn their craft; Crispine has a son while he is disguised as a shoemaker, thus literally fulfilling the proverb "a shoemaker's son is a prince born." Deloney transforms the legendary material of his source into romantic comedy and the protorealism that also characterizes his clothier tales. The final narrative is the story of Simon Eyre and how he rose from being an apprentice shoemaker to the lord mayor of London. Eyre's rise depends not on his craft but on a cargo of goods he buys cheap and sells at a profit. More interesting, he is able to buy the goods because he follows his wife's advice and dresses up as a rich man – as the rich man he will become. This is the best known of Deloney's stories because it was the basis for Thomas Dekker's play *The Shoemakers' Holiday* and thus had a doubled circulation. Like Deloney's clothiers, Simon Eyre is what might be called a nominal hero, who serves as a focal point for an examination of the politics of household, city, and nation. The narrative is evenly divided between the stories of Eyre's rise and stories concerning members of his household.

Both parts of *The Gentle Craft* can be distinguished from the clothier books by the shift in the artisanal thematics and because the shoemaker books do not foreground the Crown as insistently. Beginning with the story of Simon Eyre and continuing through part 2, Deloney's concern is with households: the men who head them, the men and women who populate them either as permanent members (wives, journeymen, servants) or as transients (declassed individuals, foreign workers), and the relations between households. The first third of *The Gentle Craft, Part 2,* for example, tells of a historical figure, Richard Casteler, a shoemaker from Westminster whose life Holinshed briefly recounts. Deloney's story involves two women, Long Meg and Gillian, who competitively attempt to woo Casteler, and a coworker, Round Robin, who advises Casteler to lead the women on for the sport of it. Three households are involved, for the women each work at an inn, and three life stories, for Richard Casteler ends up marrying a third woman; Long Meg leaves Westminster and becomes an army follower; and Gillian makes a good marriage after a brief period of depression. Long Meg is a character who exists outside Deloney's work as the heroine of ballads and jestbooks, a virago of popular tradition; Deloney's story gives her an emotional life and history. Round Robin, in contrast, is Deloney's invention and can best be described as a function; he enacts a principle of circulation and repetition, like the musical form after which he is named. By listening and judiciously repeating what he hears, and by singing, he enlivens the domestic lives in which he participates. The themes introduced by a character such as Round Robin can also be seen at the end of the book, in the

story of the Green King, a shoemaker who loses his fortune and leaves his household in the hope of making another. Wandering, he meets a ballad singer who gives him a song. Meanwhile, his wife redeems the economy of the household. When the Green King returns, restored to wealth, he remains committed to wandering and to song; in the final episode he goes "a walking" with his wife, the ballad singer, and some neighbors whose interest in the circulation of song he secures by a bet on the prospect of their perambulation.

As the stories of Round Robin and the Green King suggest, Deloney's fictions are neither simple, protorealistic, nor idealized representations of artisans. Indeed, the story of Simon Eyre suggests demystification rather than idealization. Yet Deloney has almost uniformly been understood as a writer for "simple folk." This reputation arises from two sources: the late-sixteenth-century references that peg him as a debased version of a writer-poet and, paradoxically, the continued circulation of his stories and ballads for two centuries after his death. By the eighteenth century, when the canon of English literature was being institutionalized, Deloney's fictions were printed and circulated as chapbooks, that is, in simplified versions, sometimes rhymed, occupying no more than twenty-four small pages. By the late eighteenth and early nineteenth centuries, such books were considered "children's books."

Beginning with his contemporaries, however, there has also been a more complex appreciation of Deloney. Writing in the margins of his 1598 copy of Geoffrey Chaucer's *Works,* for example, Gabriel Harvey, one of England's most learned men, reminds himself to compare Deloney's stories to Chaucer's tales and fantasizes about writing and publishing Deloney-like stories (though Harvey would have done so anonymously). Simon Eyre's story was not the only Deloney tale adapted for the stage; a play called *The Six Worthy Yeomen,* presumably based on *Thomas of Reading,* does not survive. Moreover, the fictions and the ballads were reprinted, unabridged, for generations. The last trade printing of *Thomas of Reading* was in 1812; it was published by James Ballantyne of Edinburgh, whose partner was Walter Scott, another master of historical fiction.

Yet despite the obvious widespread popularity of his writings, comparatively little critical attention has been directed to Deloney's work. Indeed, its very popularity – the perception that the author "catered for that Elizabethan vulgar," as Francis Oscar Mann puts it in his 1912 edition of Deloney's work — limited critical interest in Deloney until that edition brought the work into view and made reevaluation possible. To date, Deloney's fictions have been recognized in general terms as important forebears of the novel, but little systematic work has been done either on the fictions or on their influence in more than a century of continuous circulation. Deloney is a figure whose accomplishment and influence remain to be fully investigated and assessed.

Bibliographies:

James Harner, *English Renaissance Prose Fiction, 1500–1660: An Annotated Bibliography of Criticism* (Boston: G. K. Hall, 1978), pp. 132–147;

Harner, *English Renaissance Prose Fiction, 1500–1660: An Annotated Bibliography of Criticism (1976–1983)* (Boston: G. K. Hall, 1985), pp. 48–54.

References:

Abel Chevally, *Thomas Deloney: le Roman des Metiers au temps de Shakespeare* (Paris: Gallimard, 1926);

Merritt Lawlis, *Apology for the Middle Class: The Dramatic Novels of Thomas Deloney* (Bloomington: University of Indiana Press, 1960);

David Margolies, *Novel and Society in Elizabethan England* (Totowa, N.J.: Barnes & Noble, 1985), pp. 144–157;

Laura Stevenson, *Praise and Paradox: Merchants and Craftsmen in Elizabethan Popular Literature* (Cambridge: Cambridge University Press, 1984);

Eugene Wright, *Thomas Deloney* (Boston: Twayne, 1981).

Thomas Drant

(early 1540s? – 1578?)

Peter E. Medine
University of Arizona

BOOKS: *Impii Cuiusdam Epigrammatis Quod Edidit R. Shaklockus in Mortem Cuthberti Scoti Apomaxis. Also Certain of the Special Articles of the Epigram, Refuted in English* (London: Thomas Marsh, 1565);

Two Sermons Preached, the One at S. Mary's Spittle 1570 and the Other at the Court at Windsor the Eighth of January (London: John Day, 1570?);

A Fruitful and Necessary Sermon, Specially Concerning Alms Giving, Preached 1572 at Saint Mary's Spittle (London: John Day, 1572);

In Selomonis Regis et Praeconis Illustriss. Ecclesiasten, Paraphrasis Poetica (London: John Day, 1572);

Thomae Drantae Angli Advordingamii Praesul. Eiusdem Silua (London: Thomas Vautrollier, 1576?);

Three Godly and Learned Sermons (London: John Charlewood, 1584).

TRANSLATIONS: *A Medicinable Moral, That Is, The Two Books of Horace His Satires, Englished According to the Prescription of Saint Jerome. Quod Malum Est, Muta. The Wailings of Jeremiah. Also Epigrams* (London: Thomas Marsh, 1566);

Horace His Art of Poetry, Epistles, and Satires Englished, and to the Earl of Ormount by T. Drant Addressed (London: Thomas Marsh, 1567);

Gregory of Nazianzus, *Epigrams and Sentences Spiritual in Verse, Englished by T. Drant* (London: Thomas Marsh, 1568).

OTHER: "In Acta Matyrum Carmen T. Drant," in *Acts and Monuments,* by John Foxe (London: John Day, 1570), sig. iv;

"Thomas Dranta," in *The Four Books of Martial Policy,* by Flavius Vegetius Renatus, translated by John Sadler (London: Thomas Marsh, 1572), sig. 4v;

"In Laudem Lodovici Floodi Thomas Dranta Archdiachonus Leucicensis," in *The Pilgrimage of Princes,* by Lodowick Lloyd (London: John Kingston, 1573), sig. **3v;

"In Annotationes Carteri. Thomas Dranta," in *Dialectica,* by John Seton (London: Thomas Marsh, 1574), sig. 4-4v;

"In Alexandri Nevylli Kettum Thomae Drantae Carmen," in *A Nevylli Angli de Furoribus a Norfolciensium Ketto Duce,* by Alexander Neville (London: Henry Binneman, 1575), sig. a3;

"Thomas Drant, Archdeacon in Praise of This Book," in *Galateo. A Treatise of Manners. Done into English by R. Peterson,* by Giovanni della Casa (London: Richard Newberry, 1576), sig. ii.

Thomas Drant participated in the most forward-looking literary and ecclesiastical movements of the early Elizabethan period. As a protégé of the future archbishop of Canterbury Edmund Grindal, he acquired several important preferments and preached at both Windsor Court (1570) and St. Mary's Spittle (1570 and 1572); judging from the publication of his sermons, he was a successful preacher. In addition to his life as a clergyman, Drant was a man of letters. He reports in *Silva* (1576?) that as an undergraduate he published verse under a pseudonym and that he spent a good deal of time translating Homer. His translations of Horace in the 1560s were the first in English. In addition, his rules for the writing of quantitative verse in English, though never printed and now lost, were important matters of discussion in the circle of Gabriel Harvey, Sir Edward Dyer, Edmund Spenser, and Sir Philip Sidney during the late 1570s. References to Drant as a poet, translator, and theorist occur well into the 1590s.

Drant's origins appear to be middle class; he was born in the village of Hagworthingam, Lincolnshire, probably in the early 1540s, and his father, also named Thomas, was a farmer. Drant matriculated as a pensioner of St. John's College, Cambridge, during Lent 1558 and proceeded B.A. in 1561, M.A. in 1564, and B.D. in 1569. Soon after he left Cambridge in 1569, Drant assumed the readership in divinity at St. Paul's. He claimed that his sermon at St. Mary's Spittle on Easter Tuesday 1570 was a triumph. Thereafter he seems to have suffered from a serious illness, and in *Two Sermons Preached* (1570?) he suggests that he endured slander and straitened financial circumstances. Whatever the exact nature of these reversals, in the course of 1570 he was admitted to the archdeaconry of Lewes, the prebendary of Firles in the church of Chichester, and the rectory of Slinfold in the county of Sussex. Two epigrams reveal that he was married to a woman named Anna and that she preceded him in death, though nothing else is known of her. No evidence suggests that there were children. In view of the cessation of his publishing of new works after 1576, he seems to have died in 1577 or 1578.

The four works Drant published while still at Cambridge reflect his scholarly interests and ecclesiastical politics. The first, *Impii Cuiusdam Epigrammatis Quod Edidit R. Shaklockus in Mortem Cuthberti Scoti Apomaxis* (1565), is a polemical, occasionally satiric miscellany of prose and verse. The target is a Latin epitaph on Cuthbert Scott, a Roman Catholic bishop of Chester, who died in Louvain in 1565 and was commemorated by fellow Catholic Richard Shaklock. Drant reprints Shaklock's Latin verses and parodies them in verses of his own, which include quotations of Hebrew and Greek as well as allusions to Homer. Drant objects particularly to the eulogizing of a heretic, who perverted his pastoral office to advance the cause of falsehood – the Roman Church.

Drant's next publication, *A Medicinable Moral* (1566), similarly reveals humanist and religious interests. It consists of translations of the two books of Horace's *Satires* and the Book of Lamentations – ascribed to the prophet Jeremiah – as well as occasional pieces. The enterprise appears to rest on the premise stated in the opening of his epistle prefatory: "misery from our beginning, and tyranny of appetite to our ending. The one will master us by that we be born, and the other disquiet us to the very moment we die." The works translated are appropriate to such stiff, Protestant morality: "I have brought to pass that [the] plaintive prophet Jeremiah should weep at sin; the pleasant poet Horace should laugh at sin." The third section consists of miscellaneous verses that celebrate virtuous contemporaries and assert particular theological truths and so completes the overall scheme.

The following year Drant republished his translation of the *Satires* in *Horace His Art of Poetry, Epistles, and Satires* (1567). Here his interests seem more literary than in *A Medicinable Moral*. Certainly

the moralistic concerns persist, but Drant also discusses popular literary tastes and even publishing for profit. He responds at length to the printer's concern that though it may "be wise and full of learning," his volume will not be "saleable." The reason is not the poetry of Horace or the English translation but rather "that a scull of amorous pamphlets have so preoccupied the eyes and ears of men that a multitude believe there is none other style or phrase worth gramercy." Drant is probably referring to prose romances. He seems blind to Horace's own concept that literature may please as well as instruct. Such disdainful attitudes toward the growing taste (and market) for popular literature recur among other humanists, including Desiderius Erasmus and Juan Luis Vives, as well as Roger Ascham and Ben Jonson.

The fourth work from Drant's Cambridge days is his rendition of Gregory of Nazianzus into English verse, *Epigrams and Sentences Spiritual in Verse* (1568). Although the translations do not refer specifically to current controversies, the selections embrace themes developed in the usual Protestant attacks on Rome, such as the folly of ignoring the truth and the blasphemy of attaching undue importance to material and sensuous concerns.

Toward the end of his university days, Drant evidently suffered a crisis of conscience over his humanistic pursuits and decided to give up "all things profane, all things pagan." His principal patron, Edmund Grindal, then archbishop of London, seems to have prompted the decision. In Latin verses written in 1568 or 1569, Drant vows that he will no more "turn the pages of Book IV of the *Iliad*. Jesus must be the subject of my singing, as my master, Grindal himself, bids" (*Silva*). He seems in the main to have followed the urgings of his conscience and his patron. During his tenure at St. Paul's he preached, published several sermons, and paraphrased texts from the Old Testament. Even in these specifically religious writings, however, his interest in classical studies persists.

Drant preached to large audiences on several occasions during his first years in London and continued the polemical attacks on Rome with which he began his publishing career. One of the principal charges in *Two Sermons Preached* is against the obscurantism of the Roman rite: "ye chant ye wot not what, ye pray ye wot not what, ye prattle ye wot not what." Citing Jerome's view that ignorance of Scripture is the ignorance of Christ, he dismisses as corrupt Latin editions of the Bible issuing from Louvain. Drant then joins national with ecclesiastical politics in urging the queen to take harsh mea-

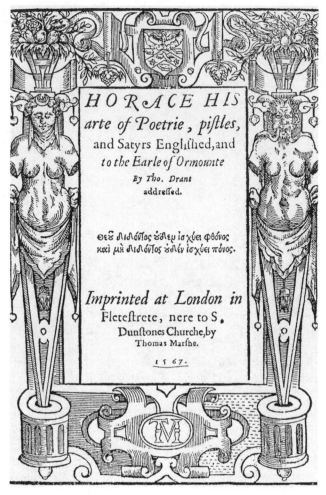

*Title page for Thomas Drant's translation of Horace, the only
complete translation of the* Satires *and the* Epistles
until the late seventeenth century

sures against papists, "the worst traitors to God,
and most rebels to the Prince."

Although the voice of the Protestant divine
predominates in these sermons, Drant's humanism is
also evident. He interlards his preaching with references to Aristotle and Cicero as well as the church fathers and Scripture. He compares himself at one point
in his sermon at Windsor Court to Terence, the
Roman playwright. In fact, Drant's homiletic strategy
frequently recalls the satiric strategy of Horace as he
enforces the ideal of self-knowledge as essential to
conversion and salvation. At other times he sounds
more Juvenalian, becoming apocalyptic in *Three Godly
and Learned Sermons* (1584): "Rough speeches seem
rude, smooth speeches are worse, / Forbearing and
flattering (alas) we see / Doth lead the world into
God's heavy curse." Clearly Drant was self-conscious about his reliance on humanistic disciplines.
Speaking of the connections between classical and

divine eloquence in *A Fruitful and Necessary Sermon*
(1572), he stresses the importance of rhetorical awareness in approaching the Bible: "Nay, let him perfectly
and with judgment read the works of Moses, of Job, of
David, of Solomon, of Isaiah, of Micah. . . . For by the
faithful and close imitation of these men is gotten a
true and godly kind of eloquence."

Drant's "godly kind of eloquence" seems to
have gained him fame. He subsequently fell seriously ill, as he reports in the preface to his first published sermon, and withdrew from London for two
years in an effort to regain his strength. When he
returned, his preaching seemed to have met with
less success, and he claims he endured slander from
vicious adversaries. In view of the circumstances
and his generally grim outlook, his turning to the
Books of Ecclesiastes and Job is understandable.

Drant's biblical paraphrases, *In Selomonis Regis
et Praeconis Illustriss. Ecclesiasten, Paraphrasis Poetica*

(1572), had precedent in the Christian humanist tradition, most notably in Erasmus's paraphrases of Scripture, which enjoyed enormous popularity and eventually official sanction in England. Drant's format consists of a brief "argument" encapsulating each of the twelve chapters, followed by extended paraphrases. The volume concludes with paraphrases of two passages of Job. Drant's paraphrase of Ecclesiastes is presented in carefully written Latin dactylic hexameters, that of Job, in elegiac couplets. They therefore appear more literary than popular. Still Drant takes pains to emphasize the essentially religious inspiration of the undertaking. In one of the prefatory pieces, a Latin "Hymn to the Lord Jesus Christ," he asserts that his faith in Christ is sufficient for his trials as a man and an author, and that "the mount of Helicon, Polyhymnia, the Castilian muses, and the Peierian deities are hateful, pernicious powers and indeed hateful, disagreeable names."

Drant's final published volume, *Silva,* probably appeared in 1576, judging from internal evidence and one bit of manuscript evidence. Its title recalls the *Silvae* of the first-century Roman poet Statius, who toward the end of his career gathered a comprehensive miscellany of his verse. Drant dedicates *Silva* to Grindal, now archbishop of Canterbury, and includes a long piece on his patrons and some three dozen shorter, largely occasional poems. These begin with verses to the queen and include celebrations of various prominent nobles, commendations of several published works, academic exercises on theological questions, autobiographical pieces, and an epitaph on his wife. Many of the pieces can be dated and range from his Cambridge days in the 1560s through 1575.

The volume reflects Drant's abiding interests in humanistic studies and Protestant politics. Besides the classicism of his title, Drant casts the Latin and Greek poems in various classical meters, some of which he identifies in the subtitles, as in the prefatory poem, "Ad Praesulem suum Carmen Iambicum Monocolon Monostrophon" (A Single-Clause Monostrophic Song in Iambics to His Patron). In addition to a commendatory poem on a recent edition of John Seton's *Dialectica* (1574) and a complaint on the poor printing of his Horace, Drant includes the poem "De Principibus Sui Temporis Poetis Qui Tunc Erant Superstites" (On the Principal Poets of His Time Who Then Were Excellent) — nine contemporaries who wrote Neo-Latin verses, men such as Walter Haddon, Theodore Beza, and George Buchanan. There is, as well, Drant's self-consciousness about his humanism, though in this

case he sounds more confident than he had in his earlier publications. In the dedication to Grindal, he anticipates criticism of the volume for its secular form and cites as authoritative precedents Job, David, Solomon, Isaiah, and Moses (as the putative author of the Pentateuch). Adducing contemporary authors Beza and Arias Montanus, he writes that the "more industriously they read the ancient — especially Roman — authors, the more felicitously and wittily do they translate and write."

If Drant is more assertive about his humanism here, his relatively greater confidence may stem from the position he held within political and literary as well as ecclesiastical circles. Besides the good relations he enjoyed with Grindal and Matthew Parker, he dedicates verses to Queen Elizabeth; William Cecil, Baron Burghley; and Robert Dudley (the earl of Leicester and the queen's favorite). The last of these poems includes commendation of such notables as the earl of Oxford and the duke of Suffolk, as well as members of the Leicester circle including Thomas Sackville and Sidney. In addition, between 1570 and 1576 Drant contributed prefatory poems to at least six didactic works, among them the 1570 edition of John Foxe's *Acts and Monuments.*

Another connection to the contemporary literary scene and to the Leicester circle is indicated by Drant's rules for writing quantitative verse in English. Such rules assigned "quantity" to particular syllables and their spelling in order to facilitate the replicating of classical meters in English. Concern for such rules recurred throughout the second half of the sixteenth century in England as classicizing authors sought to establish an aesthetic and a poetic practice that would emulate the achievement of ancient Greece and Rome. Sidney, Spenser, Dyer, and Harvey were among the English poets who experimented with quantitative verse. Drant's rules do not survive, but they are discussed in the Spenser-Harvey correspondence — two letters by Spenser and three by Gabriel Harvey that were published in 1580. When the letters were written, Spenser was a member of Leicester's retinue and living at Leicester House in London. Dyer was there as well, and Sidney — Leicester's nephew and protégé — was a frequent visitor.

References to Drant in the letters reveal his position on the margins of that group of extraordinary young poets. In the letter of 5 October 1579 Spenser commends verses in quantitative meter sent him by Harvey, though he remarks that "once or twice you make a breach in Master Drant's Rules." Responding later in the month, Harvey remarks that he "know[s] not what breach in your gorbellied

Master's rules" Spenser is citing. Though he infers that the rules are sound, Harvey claims that he "neither saw them nor heard of them before" and therefore would most appreciate comparing them with others. He adds that Spenser had held "some prejudice of the man [Drant]" but that he "still remaine[d] a favorer of his deserved and just commendation." Discussion of the rules of both Drant and others evidently persisted over the winter months, and Spenser tried to arrive at consensus in April of the following year. He asks Harvey either to send him his rules or "follow mine, that Master Philip Sidney gave me, being the very same which Master Drant devised, but enlarged with Master Sidney's own judgment." No more was heard of the matter, as Sidney and Spenser at last gave up the doomed project of quantitative verse and followed the accentual verse natural to English.

In view of his uneasiness over secular studies, it is ironic that Drant's principal achievements should have been his efforts in classical studies. His rules gained the attention, however briefly, of several major contemporary poets. Judging from its service to English readers, his translation of Horace was a success; it was the only complete translation of the *Satires* and *Epistles* until well into the seventeenth century. Drant's Horace may not have enjoyed the popularity of Golding's Ovid or Phaer's Virgil, but this apparent neglect probably has more to do with the poetry than with the translation, for there is evidence that Drant's version of Horace satisfied Elizabethan readers and commanded their respect. In his treatise *Of English Poetry* (1586) William Webbe commends (without naming) the "Author . . .

in English . . . of Horace." In 1598 Gabriel Harvey wrote in the margin of his copy of Thomas Speght's edition of Geoffrey Chaucer's works that "Few translate excellently, or sufficiently well; yet methinks neither exquisite Virgil is wronged by Doctor Phaer: nor pithy Horace by archdeacon Drant; nor conceited Ovid by Master Golding." The praise is negative, to be sure, but it comes from one of the most learned men of the age and places Drant in a category with the most distinguished of contemporary translators. Today Drant is primarily remembered as the formulator of the rules for quantitative verse in English, and thus for his influence on the early poetic careers of Sidney and Spenser. Other features of his career merit further attention, however, particularly his wide acquaintance with the literati of his generation and his judgments of their work.

References:

Otto L. Jiriczek, "Zu Drants Horaz," *Jahrbuch der Deutschen Shakespeare Gesellschaft,* 55 (1919): 59;

Jiriczek, "Der Elisabethanische Horaz," *Jahrbuch der Deutschen Shakespeare Gesellschaft,* 47 (1911): 42–68;

William A. Ringler, "Master Drant's Rules," *Philological Quarterly,* 29 (Winter 1950): 70–74;

O. J. Silverman, "A Study of Thomas Drant's *Horace,*" dissertation, Yale University, 1941;

William Webbe, "A Discourse of English Poetrie," in *Elizabethan Critical Essays,* 2 volumes, edited by G. Gregory Smith (Oxford: Oxford University Press, 1904), I: 226–302.

John Field

(1545? – March 1588)

Richard Y. Duerden
Brigham Young University

BOOKS: *An Admonition to the Parliament,* by Field and Thomas Wilcox (Hemel Hempstead?: John Stroud?, 1572);

Certaine Articles, Collected and Taken (As It Is Thought) by the Byshops out of an Admonition to the Parliament, wyth an Answere to the Same, Imprinted We Know Where and Whan, Judge You the Place and You Can. J. T. J. S., by Field and Wilcox (Hemel Hempstead?: John Stroud?, 1572);

A Caueat for Parsons Howlet, Concerning His Vntimely Flighte and Scriching in the Cleare Day Lighte (London: Printed by Robert Waldegrave for Thomas Man and Toby Smith, 1581);

A Godly Exhortation, by Occasion of the Late Judgement of God, at Parris-Garden. Instruction, Concerning the Keeping of the Sabboth Day (London: Printed by Robert Waldegrave for Henry Carre, 1583);

A Most Breefe Manner of Instruction, to the Principles of Christian Religion. By J. F., attributed to Field (London: Printed by John Charlewood for Hugh Singleton, 1587?);

Godly Prayers and Meditations (London: Printed by Richard Read for John Harrison, 1601).

Editions: *The Seconde Parte of a Register, Being a Calendar of Manuscripts under That Title Intended for Publication by the Puritans about 1593,* 2 volumes, edited by Albert Peel (Cambridge: Cambridge University Press, 1915);

Puritan Manifestoes, edited by W. H. Frere and C. E. Douglas (London: Society for Promoting Christian Knowledge, 1954; New York: Burt Franklin, 1972) – includes "An Admonition to Parliament" and "Certain Articles";

The Reformation of Our Church (Amsterdam: Theatrum Orbis Terrarum, 1973);

A Treatise of Dances; A Godly Exhortation, edited by Arthur Freeman (New York: Garland, 1974).

TRANSLATIONS: Jean de l'Espine, *An Excellent Treatise of Christian Righteousnes* (London: Thomas Vautrollier, 1577);

John Calvin, *Thirteen Sermons, Entreating of the Free Election of God in Jacob, and of Reprobation in Esau* (London: Printed by Thomas Dawson for Thomas Man and Toby Cooke, 1579);

Calvin, *Foure Sermons Entreating of Matters Very Profitable for Our Time, with a Briefe Exposition of the lxxxvii. Psalme* (London: Printed by Thomas Dawson for Thomas Man, 1579);

Philippe de Mornay du Plessis, *A Treatise of the Church* (London: Christopher Barker, 1579);

Lambert Daneau, *Two Treatises: The First of Christian Friend Ship: the Seconde of Dice Play* (London: Printed by Henry Middleton for George Bishop, 1579);

Theodore de Beza, *The Other Parte of Christian Questions and Answeares, Which Is Concerning the Sacraments* (London: Printed by Thomas Dawson for Thomas Woodcock, 1580);

Caspar Olevian, *An Exposition of the Symbole of the Apostles, or Rather of the Articles of Faith* (London: Printed by Henry Middleton for Thomas Man and Toby Smith, 1581);

de Mornay du Plessis and Pierre Pellison, *Christian Meditations, Vpon the Sixt, Twentie Fiue, Thirtie, and Two and Thirtie Psalmes . . . And Moreouer, a Meditation Vpon the 137. Psalme* (London: Printed by John Wolfe for John Harrison the Younger, 1581? or 1587?);

Calvin, *Prayers Used at the End of His Readings upon Hosea . . . Translated with Other Necessary Godly Prayers by J. Field* (London: Printed by John Harrison for Henry Carre, 1583);

de Beza, *The Iudgement of a Most Reuerend and Learned Man from Beyond the Seas, Concerning a Threefold Order of Bishops* (London: Robert Waldegrave, 1585?).

OTHER: Edward Dering, *A Sermon Preached before the Quenes Maiestie, the .25. Day of February 1569,* with a preface by Field (London: Henry Denham, 1572?);

Dering, *XXVII. Lectures, or Readings, Vpon Part of the Epistle to the Hebrues,* possibly edited by Field (London: Printed by Henry Middleton for Luke Harrison, 1576);

John Knox, *A Notable and Comfortable Exposition of M. John Knoxes, Vpon the Fourth of Mathew,* edited by Field (London: Printed by Robert Waldegrave for Thomas Man, 1583);

Alexander Nowell and William Day, *A True Report of the Disputation with Ed. Campion, Whereunto is Ioyned a True Report of the Other Three Dayes Conferences,* edited and transcribed by Field (London: Christopher Barker, 1583);

A Parte of a Register, Contayninge Sundrie Memorable Matters, Written by Diuers Godly and Learned in Our Time, Which Stande for, and Desire the Reformation of Our Church, in Discipline and Ceremonies, According to the Pure Worde of God, and the Lawe of Our Lande, compiled by Field (Middleburg: Richard Schilders or Edinburgh: Robert Waldegrave, 1593?).

John Field was one of the most brilliant activists and propagandists of Elizabethan England. He directed all his skills toward a single cause, the reformation of the English church. Field is little known because his work was clandestine and the movement he led was suppressed. But as the leader of the London conference of nonconforming ministers, he became the organizing secretary of the movement; he was, as Patrick Collinson has called him, "the Lenin of Elizabethan Puritanism." The Puritan attack on vestments, ceremonies, and the form of church organization may now seem superficial, but it entailed radical revision of the assumptions behind Elizabethan government and society; its challenges to authority shook the politics of both church and state. One side of the struggle between Puritans and conformists in the English church was public and ideological: the Puritans published and preached their story and arguments in the streets. Another side of the struggle was hidden and practical: avoiding censors, dodging efforts to close down their presses, putting their program into practice through local networks of ministers, enlisting Puritan candidates for Parliament, drafting bills, and planning parliamentary strategy. The best known of the Puritan leaders, Thomas Cartwright, gained his modern fame through his publication of many long volumes in a controversy with his conformist adversary John Whitgift. Field helped write the public pronouncement that launched this controversy, but most of his work was behind the scenes. The nature of that work may be suggested by pointing out that, whereas Cartwright's counterpart was Whitgift and Walter Travers's was Richard Hooker, Field's adversary was Richard Bancroft, a mastermind of espionage in the service of episcopacy. Of the three Puritan leaders, Field was the most active and able, yet his skill in avoiding detection has left him the least known, while his skill in using the press made him the most influential.

John Field was probably born in London in 1545, received B.A. and M.A. degrees from Oxford in 1564 and 1567, and was ordained a priest by Bishop Edmund Grindal of London on 25 March 1566. From the first Field was at the hub of political struggle and religious turmoil. While at Oxford he came under the patronage of the earl of Warwick, a reliable friend of the radical reformers and elder brother of their most powerful supporter, the earl of Leicester, but Field ran afoul of ecclesiastical authority almost immediately. Queen Elizabeth was pressuring Archbishop Matthew Parker to enforce conformity in clerical vestments, and on the day after Field was ordained to the priesthood, more than three dozen nonconforming London ministers were suspended. After a brief return to Oxford, Field was preaching in London again, beyond the bishop of London's jurisdiction, in the parish of Holy Trinity, Minories, a seedbed of London Puritans. By 1570 he was curate of St. Giles, Cripplegate, another Puritan sanctuary, and was meeting regularly in conference with other London clergy intent on pursuing a further reformation. Twenty years later a deposition before the Star Chamber identified Field and Thomas Wilcox as the organizers of the London conference, which soon grew into the center for the dissemination of Puritanism.

In 1571 the Ecclesiastical Commission summoned several Puritan leaders, among them Field, and demanded that they subscribe their complete acceptance of the Thirty-nine Articles, the Prayer Book, and vestments. Field and three others offered to subscribe with reservations, but their compromise was rejected. Suspended from preaching, Field survived by teaching children, while venting his frustration through continued organizing and agitation.

Advocates of reform had been contravened and thrown on the defensive by Elizabeth. Her demand for conformity in clerical vestments focused attention on a single aspect of the Puritan program and threatened to trivialize the movement for reform. Moreover, she thwarted all attempts to reform even such outward and superficial aspects of worship. During the Parliaments of 1566,

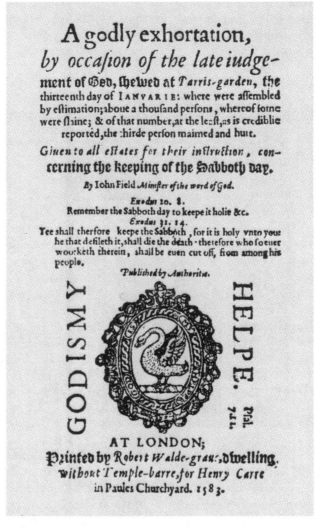

*Title page for John Field's work on the observance of Sabbath,
occasioned by the collapse of a grandstand at
a Sunday bearbaiting*

1571, and 1572 she forestalled or vetoed a series of Puritan initiatives. In June 1572 just before the end of the parliamentary assembly, the doctrinal and ceremonial protests of the Puritans exploded into political hostility with the publication of Field and Wilcox's *An Admonition to the Parliament,* which opened with the claim that "we in England are so far off from having a church rightly reformed according to the prescript of God's word, that as yet we are not come to the outward face of the same."

Two sets of immediate frustrations spurred the *Admonition:* the personal plight of Nonconformists removed from their livings and silenced; and the political deadlock on Puritan initiatives in Parliament. Yet it opened a new stage of Puritan agitation as it probed beyond immediate circumstances to the most dangerous of the issues submerged in the controversy. Previous Puritan pamphlets dealt with particulars of ceremony and dress, but Field and Wilcox launched a full program of reform and sought to articulate its motives and legitimacy. Moreover, though ostensibly addressed to Parliament, the *Admonition* looked beyond monarch or Parliament toward popular authority as it took its arguments to the streets.

The *Admonition* comprises two major parts. The first, mostly written by Wilcox, calls for further reform to bring the church to the true Christian condition of "preaching of the word purely, ministering of the sacraments sincerely, and ecclesiastical discipline." The second part, "A View of Popish Abuses Yet Remaining in the English Church," defends the nonconforming ministers and explains their objections to the Prayer Book, priestly apparel, and the Articles of Religion. But alongside the ostensible arguments run implications that scandalized the prelates: assaults on the existing structure of authority in the church, hints that threatened royal prerogative and implied a dissemination of authority, and insistence on the sole authority of Scripture, which can be wielded even by congregations and laity. A scriptural form of church government, Field and Wilcox claim, requires the abolition of episcopacy and of hierarchy generally, and in its place the institution of Presbyterianism, in which congregations are governed by elders. These two nonconforming ministers, one of them stripped of office by the bishops, call to Parliament and populace to spoil the bishops of office and authority. Their call entailed the demolition of the state church and implied threats to the royal supremacy.

Few modern scholars have paid direct attention to the *Admonition,* though many refer to it in passing, on their way to consider the extended controversy between Cartwright and Whitgift. Yet its publication affected England as few documents have done. The *Admonition* and the commotion it raised received comment in virtually every extant letter from 1573 through 1576 exchanged between the English and the reformers abroad. In many of these letters, as in those between Archbishop Parker and William Cecil, lord Burghley, the great anxiety awakened by the Puritan program was the threat of "popularity," or government by the populace.

While Cartwright and Whitgift plumbed the issues, Field doggedly continued grassroots organizing and agitation. He and Wilcox were arrested in June 1572, perhaps only days after publishing the *Admonition,* and spent the next year and a half in prison, half of that time in Newgate. Even there his primary task was to give the new radical movement a stable and enduring foundation. From prison he continued his correspondence with Puritan ministers, urged unity, encouraged the establishment of Presbyterian organization in local conferences, and wrote a "Confession of Faith" (1572 or 1573) modeled on the Articles of Religion.

The movement gained support, especially among young ministers emerging from the university and among members of their congregations. When Field and Wilcox were moved from Newgate to house arrest at the archdeacon's, the stream of visitors led the bishop of London, Edwin Sandys, to complain that the people flocked to them as if they were going on pilgrimage. Within a year a royal proclamation ordered subjects to surrender all copies of the *Admonition* and the books written in its defense, but as the deadline

for doing so passed, the bishop of London lamented that not a single book had been surrendered and that the whole business was encouraging the populace to challenge established authority and was feeding them with democratic notions.

Not all Puritan sympathizers liked the new radicalism, however. The older and more moderate Puritans had been companions at the universities and in exile with the bishops whom the *Admonition* attacked, and most of them disliked the aggressiveness of the younger radicals coming out of the universities. Field wrote to senior reformers to recruit them for the extremist cause. He also appears to have continued his work as publicist to justify and win support for the new strategies.

Nothing can be found of Field's whereabouts during the year and a half after his release from prison, but Collinson suggests that he was coordinating the publication of a series of books aimed at establishing a respectable pedigree for the new movement: Walter Travers's book on Presbyterian church organization, *Ecclesiasticae Disciplinae* (1574), and Cartwright's translation of it, *A Full and Plain Declaration of Ecclesiastical Discipline* (1574); Cartwright's *Second Reply* (1575, 1577), an installment in his controversy with Whitgift over the *Admonition*; and *A Brief Discourse of the Troubles Begun at Frankfurt* (1574), which traces the movement back to the famed liturgical quarrels between the factions of John Knox and Richard Cox during the Marian exile. These books were all published in Heidelberg, where Cartwright had fled to avoid arrest. Field may have joined him there to oversee the printing, or he may have supervised publication from London.

When Edmund Grindal became archbishop of Canterbury in 1576, the pressure on Puritans eased briefly, and many of them joined in a polemical crusade against Catholicism. By 1577 Field was back in England, where he continued to lead the London conference while also translating into English several sermons, meditations, and discourses of their colleagues in Geneva, France, and Heidelberg: John Calvin, Theodore de Beza, Philippe de Mornay du Plessis, Jean de l'Espine, and Caspar Olevian. He dedicated these translations to the most powerful and reliable friends and patrons of Protestantism in the realm: Robert Dudley, earl of Leicester; Ambrose and Ann Dudley, earl and countess of Warwick; Francis and Elizabeth Russell, earl and countess of Bedford; and Henry Hastings, earl of Huntingdon and president of the Council in the North.

In dedicating de Mornay du Plessis's *A Treatise of the Church* (1579) to Leicester, Field called on the earl to defend the church against "Papists, Arians,

Anabaptists, Libertines, and other heretics of all sorts," who endangered "this florishing commonweal and her Majesty's most royal person, crown, and dignity." The charge of subversion helped to motivate a defense of English recusants by the newly arrived Jesuit missionary Robert Parsons, *A Brief Discourse Why Catholics Refuse to Go to Church* (1580), published under the pseudonym of John Howlet. Parsons included a personal attack on Field as "a strange brainsick fellow, whom Newgate possessed for a long time for his fantastical opinions" and charged the Puritans with disrupting the peace of the realm. Field responded with *A Caveat for Parsons Howlet* (1581), a tirade against the "feigned friendship" and "crafty underminings" of "these parasitical Papists." Field confesses "that I use myself otherwise than my manner is, in roughness of words and sharpness of style, which perhaps some delicate ears will hardly bear," but he justifies his savage attacks with the excuse that "the Scriptures give sufficient warrant . . . of round speech." After Parson's companion Edmund Campion was arrested and executed, Field edited the official record of his disputations with Protestant theologians in the Tower before his trial.

In 1579 Field's patron Leicester persuaded Oxford University to grant him a license to preach; by 1581 he had secured a position as parish lecturer at St. Mary Aldermary. While joining in the official campaign against Catholics and enlisting support for the Puritan preachers, Field also struck out at their competition for the attention of the commoners: plays and other Sunday entertainments. A disaster at a Sabbath-day bearbaiting, in which the grandstands collapsed and seven people were killed and scores injured, provided the occasion for his brief treatise on Sabbath observance, *A Godly Exhortation* (1583). England, he urges, has been richly blessed; indeed, "Our benefits have been greater than ever were bestowed upon any nation excepting neither one or other." How "lamentable," therefore, "that theaters should be full and churches be empty." On Sundays "there is no tavern or alehouse, if the drink be strong, that lacketh any company: there is no dicing house, bowling alley, cock pit, or theater that can be found empty." Here, too, Field directs his words to those empowered to enact change, the lord mayor and aldermen.

Parsons's *Brief Discourse of the Troubles Begun at Frankfurt* concludes with a promise to continue its story in later volumes, and Field was already collecting a documentary history of Puritanism. As organizing secretary of the London conference, he assembled correspondence and writings of Puritans and their sympathizers throughout England and abroad. He gathered and sent to press tracts, papers, and sermons by Knox, de Beza, William Fulke, and Anthony Gilby, even without the knowledge or permission of the authors. He collected the writings of the brilliant, popular, and fearless preacher Edward Dering and may have been the editor of Dering's collected works. And, despite strict censorship of the press, he also preserved and prepared to publish the records and testimonials of Elizabethan Puritanism. These attested to the legitimacy of the Puritan demands and the severity of the oppression they suffered.

The idea and the methods for a documentary history of the teachings and the sufferings of the faithful Field took from John Foxe's *Acts and Monuments* (1559). He had contributed material to the "Book of Martyrs" early in his career; the earliest letter in Field's hand is one he wrote to Foxe from Oxford in 1567. So, as the suspension or imprisonment of preachers persisted, Field amassed the evidence that would link the Puritans with previous martyrs and associate the conformist bishops with the papist ones. He gathered and registered a huge store of documents comprising individual accounts of ministers examined by the High Commission and the bishops, letters and records of the Puritan conferences, treatises on church government, surveys of corruption and ineptitude among the unreformed parish clergy, and petitions to the queen, Privy Council, and Parliament. Most come from the period 1565 to 1588, but a few were added in 1590, and some date as early as the reign of Edward VI. In 1593, five years after Field's death, a selection of these documents was printed in Scotland as *A Parte of a Register,* but most were seized by Bancroft's agents shortly after they were shipped to London.

Even before part of it was published in the Puritans' defense, Field's register was cited in the Puritan assault on episcopacy. The first of the pro-Presbyterian, pseudonymous Martin Marprelate tracts circulated in 1589. Though Field had died a year earlier, he was named among those suspected of being the author. Field was almost certainly not Martin Marprelate, but a contemporary who was examined testified that the first Marprelate tract was written from "some such notes . . . found in Master Field's Study." In the tract, Martin taunts the bishops, "see . . . what a perilous fellow Master Marprelate is. He understands all your knavery and, it may be, keeps a register of them. Unless you amend they shall all come into the light one day."

The *Register,* like Field's earlier efforts, was interpreted by authorities as a seditious means to set

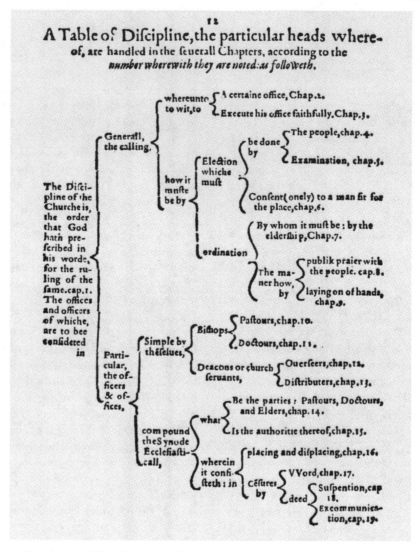

Page from Field's A Parte of a Register, *a documentary history of Puritanism published around 1593 and seized by the queen's agents in London*

up a counterauthority. As early as 1572, when Field and Wilcox first published the *Admonition,* anxious bishops proclaimed that the Presbyterian program, with its government by clergy and lay elders, impugned the royal supremacy over the church and implied popular sovereignty. In 1593, when the copies of the *Register* shipped into London were confiscated and destroyed, Bancroft looked back over twenty years of Puritan agitation, labeling the Puritan efforts "these more political than Christian practices" and claiming that in preparing the *Register* the Puritans' "drift and especial end" was to undermine "the present government of the Church" so that in its place they might "set up and establish their glorious scepter and kingdom." When he was later nominated bishop of London, Bancroft was especially commended for his detection, discovery, espionage, and persecution of Field and his allies.

Field proved able to disseminate his attitudes even more effectively than Bancroft could spy them out, however. No writings of his prove both his sincerity and his skill in propaganda better than his volume of *Godly Prayers and Meditations* (1601), a collection of exhortations to, principles and rules for, and examples of meditation and personal prayer. In the prayers Field devoutly addresses himself and his readers to God yet also insinuates the Puritan public agenda. The prayers are laced with political indoctrination, but in a form that bypasses argument, since they give readers the very words and opinions that are to come sincerely from the heart. By suggesting prayers, Field teaches the godly what their deepest yearnings should be.

In prayers intended to be uttered by all estates from private families to the nobility, and from the universities to Parliament, suppliants express their submission to the Word and its ministers and plead that the ministers' preaching may go unhindered. An "evening prayer for a private family" gives individual households daily occasion to rehearse the flaws in the state's ecclesiastical policy. In two prayers intended for the queen, Field puts self-deprecation in the monarch's own mouth for all the kingdom to overhear. It is of course common to confess one's sins in prayer, but Field's royal persona confesses with a gusto unusual even for this Puritan collection. Where a simple householder prays, "I acknowledge that my sins are great," the queen must thank God that He did "advance me, miserable worm, a most sinful wretch, and the worst of all others, to be above others," and she must admit her subjection to the reproofs of the advocates of Presbyterian discipline: "O open my ears, that I may hear the reprover gladly, and let such as are thy faithful servants in the ministry break my head with that comfortable balm of admonition." Through his prayers Field insinuates legislation into Parliament; he humbles the queen and prescribes her duties; he teaches all the people who read his little manual that they may pass judgment on rulers, so long as they submit to God's word and give their support to the ministers.

In the mid 1580s, as Archbishop Whitgift tightened his enforcement of conformity, Field led the resistance and encouraged fellow Puritans to stand firm. In March of 1585 the High Commission again suspended his license to preach. He coordinated efforts to besiege the Parliaments of 1584 and 1586 with petitions for the relief of suspended Puritan ministers and for reform of the ministry, petitions supported by Puritan surveys that, parish by parish, listed unqualified or degenerate clergy ("Mr. Durden, parson of Mashbury, a careless man, a gamester, an alehouse haunter, a company keeper with drunkards and he himself sometimes drunk. Witnesses, Richard Reynolds, John Argent, etc."). But he also joined in the secret effort to establish Presbyterian church government within the established church, without waiting for Parliament. Ministers were to be called by their congregations; they were to meet monthly in local classes of up to ten ministers to try each other in knowledge, preaching, and practice of the gospel; they were to send representatives from each local classis to semiannual provincial synods; and they were to attend national conferences at Parliament time.

Puritan initiatives in the Parliaments of the 1580s were quashed by the queen's direct intervention. After Field's death in March 1588, the new classis movement, lacking a leader and organizer of Field's talent and drive, withered. Within a year or two several of the powerful patrons whose support Field had nurtured also died: Leicester, Warwick, Bedford, and Walsingham. But the popular propaganda he had initiated gained momentum. When one of his colleagues voiced despair over the opposition of bishops and magistrates, Field snapped an answer that made clear he had already decided the new kingdom of Christ would be reared by the populace: "Tush, Mr. Edmunds, hold your peace. Seeing we cannot compass these things by suit nor dispute, it is the multitude and people that must bring the discipline to pass which we desire."

In the decades after Field's death, history treated him with some duplicity. His youngest child, Nathan, became a noted actor and a playwright; his eldest, Theophilus, became a corrupt Laudian bishop – a legacy strangely incongruous with his own career as preacher against playgoers and prelates. Another part of that legacy, however, was revolution, and its possibility was foreseen by Elizabeth herself in 1590 as she wrote to James VI of Scotland, who would succeed her:

> Let me warn you that there is risen, both in your realm and mine, a sect of perilous consequence, such as would have no kings but a presbytery, and take our place while they enjoy our privilege, with a shade of God's word, which none is judged to follow right without by their censure they be so deemed. Yea, look we well unto them. When they have made in our peoples' hearts a doubt of our religion, and that we err if they say so, what perilous issue this may make I rather think than mind to write.

Field and his successors show, with a clarity seldom matched, the power of the word.

Modern scholars of the English Reformation have often mentioned Field, though he is just as often overlooked entirely, even in major studies. The *Admonition* has been excerpted in anthologies, but even books on "the Admonition Controversy," such as the work of Donald Joseph McGinn or Peter Lake, barely mention its instigator, Field. Collinson's labors restored Field to his position at the forefront of the Elizabethan Puritan movement. It remains, however, to interpret the significance of his texts and legacy.

References:

Patrick Collinson, *Archbishop Grindal* (London: Cape, 1979);

Collinson, "The Authorship of *A Brieff Discours off the Troubles Begonne at Franckford,*" in his *Godly People: Essays on English Protestantism and Puritanism* (London: Hambledon Press, 1983), pp. 191–211;

Collinson, *The Elizabethan Puritan Movement* (London: Cape, 1967);

Collinson, "John Field and Elizabethan Puritanism," in *Godly People: Essays on English Protestantism and Puritanism* (London: Hambledon Press, 1983), pp. 335–370;

G. R. Elton, ed., *The Tudor Constitution: Documents and Commentary,* second edition (Cambridge: Cambridge University Press, 1982);

M. M. Knappen, *Tudor Puritanism* (Chicago: University of Chicago Press, 1939);

Peter Lake, *Anglicans and Puritans? Presbyterian and English Conformist Thought from Whitgift to Hooker* (London: Unwin Hyman, 1988);

Donald Joseph McGinn, *The Admonition Controversy* (New Brunswick, N.J.: Rutgers University Press, 1949);

J. E. Neale, *Elizabeth I and Her Parliaments,* 2 volumes (New York: St. Martin's Press, 1958);

H. C. Porter, ed., *Puritanism in Tudor England* (Columbia: University of South Carolina Press, 1971), pp. 115–152;

Hastings Robinson, ed., *Zurich Letters,* Parker Society 51 (Cambridge: Cambridge University Press, 1842).

Papers:

John Field's unpublished manuscripts for *The Second Part of a Register* are in the Morrice manuscript collection in the Dr. Williams Library, Gordon Square, London. A list of the documents, with summaries and excerpts, is included in Albert Peel's 1915 edition of Field's works.

Robert Greene

(*July 1558 – 3 September 1592*)

Sandra Clark
Birkbeck College, University of London

See also the Greene entry in *DLB 62: Elizabethan Dramatists.*

BOOKS: *Mamillia. A Mirrour or Looking-Glasse for the Ladies of Englande* (London: Printed by T. Dawson for T. Woodcocke, 1583);

Mamillia. The Triumph of Pallas (London: Printed by H. Middleton for W. Ponsonby, 1583?);

Arbasto. The Anatomie of Fortune (London: Printed by J. Windet and T. Judson for H. Jackson, 1584); republished with *Pyramus and Thisbe* (London: Printed by J. Beale for R. Jackson, 1617);

Morando the Tritameron of Loue (London: Printed by J. Charlewood and J. Kingston for E. White, 1584); enlarged as *Morando . . . The First and Second Part* (London: Printed by J. Wolfe for E. White, 1587);

The Myrrour of Modestie, Wherein Appeareth . . . Howe the Lorde Deliuereth the Innocent (London: Printed by R. Warde, 1584);

Planetomachia: or The First Parte of the Generall Opposition of the Seuen Planets (London: Printed by T. Dawson & G. Robinson for T. Cadman, 1585);

Penelopes Web: Wherein a Christall Myrror of Faeminine Perfection Represents . . . Vertues and Graces (London: Printed by T. Orwin? for T. Cadman and E. Aggas, 1587);

Euphues his Censure to Philautus (London: Printed by J. Wolfe for E. White, 1587);

Pandosto. The Triumph of Time (London: Printed by T. Orwin for T. Cadman, 1588); republished as *The Pleasant Historie of Dorastus and Fawnia* (London: Printed by T. Purfoot for F. Faulkner, circa 1635);

Perimedes the Blacke-Smith, A Golden Methode, How to Vse the Minde in Pleasant and Profitable Exercise (London: Printed by J. Wolfe for E. White, 1588);

Ciceronis Amor. Tullies Loue. Wherein is Discoursed the Prime of Ciceroes Youth (London: Printed by R. Robinson for T. Newman and J. Winnington, 1589);

Menaphon, Camillas Alarum to Slumbering Euphues (London: Printed by T. Orwin for S. Clarke, 1589);

The Spanish Masquerado. Wherein . . . Is Discouered the Pride and Insolencie of the Spanish Estate (London: Printed by R. Ward for T. Cadman, 1589);

Greenes Mourning Garment, Giuen Him by Repentance (London: Printed by J. Wolfe for T. Newman, 1590);

Greenes Neuer Too Late. Or, A Powder of Experience (Francescos Fortunes: Or the Second Part) (London: Printed by T. Orwin for N. Ling and J. Busbie, 1590);

Greenes Farewell to Folly. Sent to Courtiers and Schollers (London: Printed by T. Scarlet for T. Gubbin and T. Newman, 1591);

A Maidens Dreame. Vpon the Death of Sir Christopher Hatton (London: Printed by T. Scarlet for T. Nelson, 1591);

A Notable Discouery of Coosenage (London: Printed by J. Wolfe for T. Nelson, 1591);

The Second Part of Conny-Catching (London: Printed by J. Wolfe for W. Wright, 1591); enlarged as *The Second and Last Part of Conny-Catching* (London: Printed by J. Wolfe for W. Wright, 1592);

The Defence of Conny-Catching or a Confutation of Those Two Iniurious Pamphlets Published by R. G., possibly by Greene, as Cuthbert Cony-Catcher (London: Printed by A. Jeffes for T. Gubbins, sold by J. Busbie, 1592);

The Thirde and Last Part of Conny-Catching (London: Printed by T. Scarlet for C. Burbie, 1592);

A Disputation, Betweene a Hee Conny-Catcher, and a Shee Conny-Catcher (London: Printed by A. Jeffes for T. Gubbin, 1592); republished as *Theeves Falling Out, True-Men Come by Their Goods* (London: Printed by W. White for T. Gubbin, sold by R. [i.e., E.] Marchant, 1615);

The Blacke Bookes Messenger, Laying Open the Life and Death of Ned Browne One of the Most Notable Cutpurses (London: Printed by J. Danter for T. Nelson, 1592);

Philomela. The Lady Fitzwaters Nightingale (London: Printed by R. Bourne and E. Allde for E. White, 1592);

A Quip for an Vpstart Courtier: or, A Quaint Dispute . . . Wherein is Plainely Set Downe the Disorders in All Estates and Trades (London: Printed by J. Wolfe, 1592);

Greenes Vision: Written at the Instant of his Death (London: Printed by E. Allde for T. Newman, 1592);

Greenes Groats-Worth of Witte . . . Written before His Death, doubtfully attributed to Greene, edited by H. Chettle (London: Printed by J. Wolfe & J. Danter for W. Wright, 1592);

The Repentance of Robert Greene, doubtfully attributed to Greene (London: Printed by J. Danter for C. Burbie, 1592);

Greenes Orpharion. Wherin is Discouered a Musicall Concorde of Pleasant Histories (London: Printed by J. Roberts for E. White, 1599);

Alcida Greenes Metamorphosis, Wherein is Discouered, a Pleasant Transformation of Bodies into Sundrie Shapes (London: Printed by G. Purslowe, 1617).

Editions: *The Life and Complete Works in Prose and Verse of Robert Greene, M.A. Cambridge and Oxford,* 15 volumes, edited by Alexander B. Grosart (London & Aylesbury: Privately printed, 1881–1886);

The Plays and Poems of Robert Greene, 2 volumes, edited by J. Churton Collins (Oxford: Clarendon Press, 1905);

A Notable Discovery of Coosnage; The Second Part of Conny-Catching, edited by G. B. Harrison (London: Bodley Head, 1923);

The Third and Last Part of Conny-Catching; A Disputation, Betweene a Hee-Conny-Catcher, and a Shee Conny-Catcher, edited by Harrison (London: Bodley Head, 1923);

Greenes Groats-Worth of Witte; The Repentance of Robert Greene, edited by Harrison (London: Bodley Head, 1923);

The Blacke Bookes Messenger; The Defence of Conny-Catching, edited by Harrison (London: Bodley Head, 1924);

Greene's Menaphon; A Marguerite of America, edited by Harrison (Oxford: Blackwell, 1927);

A Critical Edition of "Ciceronis Amor," edited by C. H. Larson (Salzburg: Institut für Englische Sprache und Literatur, Universität Salzburg, 1974);

The Poetry of Robert Greene, edited by Tetsumaro Hayashi (Muncie, Ind.: Ball State University, 1977);

Planetomachia, edited by D. F. Bratchell (Amersham: Avebury, 1979);

Perimedes the Blacksmith; Pandosto, edited by Stanley Wells (New York: Garland, 1988);

Rogues, Vagabonds, and Sturdy Beggars: A New Gallery of Tudor and Early Stuart Rogue Literature Exposing the Lives, Times, and Cozening Tricks of the Elizabethan Underworld, edited by Arthur F. Kinney (Amherst: University of Massachusetts Press, 1990) – includes "A Notable Discovery of Cozenage" and "The Black Book's Messenger."

PLAY PRODUCTIONS: *Alphonsus, King of Aragon,* London, unknown theater, circa 1588;

The History of Orlando Furioso, London, The Theatre, 1588–1591;

Friar Bacon and Friar Bungay, London, unknown theater, 1589–1591;

A Looking-Glass for London and England, by Greene and Thomas Lodge, London, The Theatre(?), circa 1590–1591;

Locrine, attributed to Greene, London, unknown theater, circa 1591;

Selimus, attributed to Greene, London, The Theatre, circa 1591;

The Scottish History of James IV, London, unknown theater, circa 1592;

George a Greene, The Pinner of Wakefield, attributed to Greene, London, Rose Theater, by 1593;

John of Bordeaux, or The Second Part of Friar Bacon, attributed to Greene, London, Rose Theater(?), by 1593.

OTHER: *Gwydonius. The Carde of Fancie,* translated by Greene (London: Printed by T. East for W. Ponsonby, 1584);

The Royal Exchange. Contayning Sundry Aphorismes of Phylosophie and . . . of Morrall and Naturall Quadruplicities. Fyrst Written in Italian, translated, with commentary, by Greene (London: Printed by J. Charlewood for W. Wright, 1590).

Robert Greene's place in the literary scene of the 1580s and 1590s is unique: he was the first person in England to attempt to make a living purely from his writing. Although he thought of himself as a playwright, by far the larger part of his literary output consisted of prose. In a working life of little more than ten years, he experimented with almost every fashionable mode of his day, creating a considerable reputation for himself though never achieving any sort of social or financial security. His popularity and success derived initially from euphuistic novellas and romances that were highly imitative and derivative,

Caricature of Robert Greene in his funeral shroud, from John Dickenson's
Greene in Conceipt *(1598)*

but he was soon able to introduce new kinds of writing to the following he had created for himself. The cony-catching pamphlets of his last years, though dependent on earlier models of rogue literature, were perceived as innovative in the 1590s and influenced his many posthumous admirers and imitators.

Even in Greene's time it was difficult to distinguish the facts of his life from the mass of gossip, conjecture, and controversy with which he was surrounded, and it remains so today. There seems no reason to doubt that the baptismal record of a "Robert Greene, son of Robert Greene," baptized outside Norwich on 11 July 1558 refers to him, but his father may have been either of two men, a Norfolk saddler or a cordwainer-turned-innkeeper who subsequently became comparatively prosperous. Although Greene signed himself "Norfolciensis" (of Norfolk) and "Nordovicensis" (of Norwich), he may have spent a good part of his early years living in South Yorkshire when Norwich underwent a commercial slump in the 1560s and 1570s. Not only were there Greenes recorded in this part of England at this time, but there was also a network of local gentry who, though prosperous, were not known in literary or theatrical circles, and it was these whom Greene selected for his earliest patrons. A Yorkshire connection might also account for the fact that he went to St. John's College, Cambridge, for his B.A.; he entered as a sizar (a student of modest means) in 1575, took his degree in 1580, and then moved to Clare Hall, where he gained his M.A. in 1583.

Greene was married while still a student and may have fathered a son; Fortunatus Greene was buried at Shoreditch on 12 August 1593, though this may have been the child Gabriel Harvey says he had by Em Ball, the sister of the pickpocket Cutting Ball. Harvey cites a letter of Greene's, possibly authentic, in which he records his wife's name as Dorothy or Doll, but she may have been Isabell Beck, who married a Robert Greene in 1579 in

Lincolnshire. Greene gives his protagonist in *Greene's Never Too Late* (1590) a wife named Isabel, and in *The Repentance of Robert Greene* (1592) — doubtfully attributed to Greene — the author says it was in Lincolnshire that he lodged her and their son when he came to London to make his name as a writer. There are indications that he became alienated from his wife and son while living in London, where he pursued a hectic working life as a writer with apparently no other source of income. This life came to a premature end when Greene died in poverty on 3 September 1592 after a period of illness.

Greene's literary life brought him into contact with several well-known figures, some of whose writings flesh out his skeletal biography, though they cannot necessarily be regarded as accurate or truthful. The chief figures are Thomas Nashe and Harvey. The record of Nashe's relationship with Greene dates from 1589, when the former, presumably by invitation, contributed a lengthy preface to Greene's romance *Menaphon* (1589). Greene was by this time a well-known figure on the London literary scene, author of a dozen pamphlets and one or two plays, while Nashe was an unknown; not surprising, Nashe praises Greene's writing and supports him in his enmity with playwright Christopher Marlowe. At the time, Nashe and Greene may have been associated in the anti-Martinist movement — a reaction to a series of tracts in support of Presbyterian church-government published under the pseudonym Martin Marprelate — but then, according to Nashe's *Strange News of the Intercepting Certain Letters* (1592), they drifted apart until shortly before Greene's death.

Afterward Nashe was called upon to defend Greene's reputation during his literary flyting with Harvey, and these exchanges, in Harvey's *Four Letters and Certain Sonnets, especially Touching Robert Greene* (1592) and Nashe's *Strange News of the Intercepting Certain Letters,* have contributed substantially to the creation of the Greene legend. Nashe creates the vivid image of Greene with his "jolly long red peak, like the spire of a steeple" and the details of the "fatal banquet of rhenish wine and pickled herring" that was his last. He also describes Greene's professional skills, particularly the "extemporal vein" that he had praised in the preface to *Menaphon,* recalling how Greene "yarked up a pamphlet in a day and a night as well as in seven year."

Harvey, admitting that he was "altogether unacquainted with the man, and never once saluted him by name," presents Greene's reputation — as a dissolute and bohemian pamphleteer, an associate of whores and cutpurses, and the father of a bastard child — as a matter of common knowledge: "Who in London hath not heard of his dissolute and licentious living; his fond disguising of a Master of Art with ruffianly hair, unseemly apparel, and more unseemly company . . . his villainous cogging and foisting; his monstrous swearing," and so on. Harvey had reason to dislike Greene both for his association with Nashe and for the writer's wounding attack on members of Harvey's family in the first edition of *A Quip for an Upstart Courtier* (1592) — although the passage was subsequently removed. Nashe does not attempt to exonerate Greene from the bulk of Harvey's charges and makes distinct gestures toward dissociating himself from his former friend, although he adds a little human warmth to Harvey's picture, writing that Greene "inherited more virtues than vices . . . his only care was to have a spell in his purse to conjure up a good cup of wine with at all times."

Henry Chettle, another posthumous commentator with an ambiguous attitude toward Greene, revived him as an apparition in *Kind-Heart's Dream* (1592). He sides with Greene and Nashe in the controversy with Harvey but is embarrassed by Greene's attack on William Shakespeare as an "upstart crow" in *Greene's Groatsworth of Wit* (1592). Chettle apologizes for Greene and defends Shakespeare's professionalism: "Myself have seen his demeanor no less civil than he excellent in the quality he professes." Greene's image lived on after his death and made his name a marketable commodity; a spate of pamphlets capitalizing on it soon appeared: *Greene's News Both from Heaven and Hell* (1593) by "B. R.," perhaps Barnaby Rich; *Greene's Funerals* (1594); and John Dickenson's *Greene in Conceipt* (1598) and *Greene's Ghost Haunting Cony-Catchers* (1602), probably by Samuel Rowlands. The chambermaid in *The Overburian Characters* (1616) reads Greene's works "over and over."

Such an image was the creation of Greene himself, which the contributions of Nashe, Harvey — who sneered at Greene's popularity — and Chettle endorse rather than qualify. The most direct biographical information is provided by two posthumous pamphlets of uncertain status: *Greene's Groatsworth of Wit* and *The Repentance of Robert Greene,* put out by different publishers within weeks of his death. Computer-aided stylistic analysis supports long-standing doubts about their authorship, although their style strongly resembles authentic Greene, as does another dubious pamphlet, *The Defense of Cony-Catching*

Morando
The Tritameron of
Loue:

Wherein certaine pleafaunt conceites,
vttered by diuers woorthy perfonages, are perfectly
dyfcourfed, and three doubtfull queftyons of Loue,
moft pithely and pleafauntly difcuffed : Shewing to the
wyfe howe to vfe Loue, and to the fonde, howe
to efchew Luft : and yeeldmg to all both
pleafure and profitt.
(*٭*)

By Robert Greene, Maifter of Artes
in Cambridge.

At London
Printed for Edwarde White, and are
to be folde at his fhoppe, at the little North
doore of S Paules Church, at the
figne of the Gunne.
1584.

Title page for one of the early romances Greene modeled after
John Lyly's Euphues *(1578)*

(1592) by "Cuthbert Cony-Catcher" (ascribed to Greene by R. B. Parker in 1974 and René Provost in 1938, and to Greene and Nashe together by Edwin Havilland Miller in 1954), which adds further detail. But most of the work put out in Greene's last two years, from *Greene's Never Too Late* onward, is engaged to varying extents in the business of self-representation, and in relation to the commercial production of the Greene legend, the actual authorship of the *Groatsworth of Wit* and the *Repentance* is hardly relevant.

Greene's many prose works, written within about twelve years, generally fall into five groups, which roughly correspond to chronological stages in his career: euphuistic romances; frame tales influenced by the novella; second-phase romances informed more by the Hellenistic than the mode of John Lyly's *Euphues* (1578); semi-autobiographical fictions centered on the theme of the repentant prodigal; and cony-catching pamphlets. He seems not to have diversified into playwriting until about 1588, beginning with *Alphonsus, King of Aragon,* an imitation of Marlowe's *Tamburlaine* (1587 or earlier); his precise dramatic output is not certain, but modern scholarship ascribes to him four other plays: *The History of Orlando Furioso* (1588–1591); *Friar Bacon and Friar Bungay* (1589–1591); *The Scottish History of James IV* (circa 1592); and, in collaboration with Thomas Lodge, *A Looking-Glass for London and England* (circa 1590–1591).

Greene's first publication was *Mamillia,* printed in two parts in 1583 but written while he was at the university in 1580. It is closely modeled, both stylistically and thematically, on Lyly's *Euphues,* but the roles of the sexes are to some extent reversed. In part 1 the hero Pharicles, a male equivalent of Lyly's fickle Lucilla, woos the virtuous Mamillia but turns, with no good reason, to the equally virtuous Publia and then, in disgrace, leaves them both; in part 2 Pharicles, like Euphues, reforms, resists the blandishments of a courtesan, faces trial as a spy, and is saved by the intervention of Mamillia in disguise. There is a greater element of narrative interest in part 2, in which Pharicles has various picaresque adventures in disguise, but the proportion of narrative to moralizing throughout is low.

Greene draws on a range of devices to give the moralizing a function within the narrative: it can take the form of soliloquies, long speeches, internal monologues, letters, or a debate on ethical topics by a group of characters, such as the *questione d'amore* of Italianate courtly fiction, as when in part 2 a party of Sicilian courtiers discusses whether men or women are the more constant in love. Sometimes the narrator simply allows himself a digression, on the immorality of Italian men, for example, or on how women suffer from men's fickle behavior.

The narrator addresses his readers as gentlemen and sometimes presents his narrative from a consciously gendered position: "If I may enter into a woman's thought, without offense." Throughout he creates frequent opportunities to express sympathy with women and focuses on them as victims of men's infidelity. As Walter R. Davis observes in *Idea and Act in Elizabethan Fiction* (1969), the conflict between the demands of love and fidelity, central to *Euphues,* is transformed by Greene into one "between the firm faith of woman and the fickleness of man."

Greene's variation on the Lylian model, carried out within the limits prescribed by Lyly's brand of humanist fiction, clearly found a public, as the small barrage of works published the following year indicates. Each has a different printer and a different patron: *Arbasto, the Anatomy of Fortune*; *Gwydonius, the Card of Fancy*; *Morando, the Tritameron of Love* (enlarged in 1587); and *The Mirror of Modesty* all appeared in 1584.

The best of these, *Gwydonius,* is still strongly influenced by euphuistic rhetoric; it continues to employ interior monologues, letters, and other such devices to create a quality of introspection, and it balances masculine vice in Gwydonius against feminine virtue in his sister, Lewcippa. Both stylistic symmetry and interest in action, however, are more pronounced in this work; there are two rulers, each with a son and a daughter, who eventually marry, and the narrative concludes with a double wedding.

In the meantime Greene develops various complications for his hero, in that Gwydonius, at odds with his father, bankrupts himself through prodigality, reforms, assumes a socially humbler identity, and enlists in the service of King Orlanio of Alexandria, who turns out to be his father's enemy. He falls in love with Orlanio's daughter, but their apparent difference in rank obliges her to test him extensively to ensure that he is no fickle fortune hunter. In a dramatic climax featuring the "intrafamilial bloodshed" that Helmut Bonheim in "Robert Greene's *Gwydonius: The Card of Fancie*" (1978) says was to become a favorite situation in Greene's romances, Gwydonius, in another disguise, fights as Orlanio's champion against his own father, an aggressive warrior king, who has invaded Alexandria and committed feats of brutality. Thus Gwydonius has to undergo the "cruel combat between Nature and Necessity" promised in the romance's title, but out of division is created unity: he proves his manhood to his father, reveals his social and moral worthiness to his mistress, and reconciles two warring kingdoms.

Arbasto, the Anatomy of Fortune focuses more narrowly on unhappy love and uncertain fortune. Arbasto loves the disdainful Doralicia, daughter of his enemy, but is in turn loved by her sister, the constant Myrania; love here is not an educative force but "a frantic frenzy which so infecteth the minds of men, as under the taste of nectar they are poisoned with the water of Styx." Arbasto recognizes the irrationality of his behavior but has no power to correct it, and in the end all come to grief in a world subject only to the power of chance.

Philomela, the Lady Fitzwater's Nightingale (1592) also explores the consequences of obsessive passion in a version of the popular Renaissance tale, best known in Miguel de Cervantes's version, "The Curious Impertinent" (1605), in which a jealous husband tests his wife's chastity by persuading a friend to attempt to seduce her. The sufferings to which the impeccably virtuous Philomela is subjected never overcome her love for her husband, and like Mamillia, she intervenes to save him when he is on trial. But the only reward for her virtue is fame in widowhood, because her husband is so overcome when he realizes the true extent of her love that two hours after the trial "in an ecstasy he ended his life."

The Mirror of Modesty, in which Greene takes the role of women's champion, is a retelling of the story of Susanna and the elders in euphuistic style. It draws on two favorite Greene motifs, the vindication of a woman's chastity, located here, uniquely, in a Christian setting, and illicit sexual desire in old men. *Morando* is a transitional pamphlet, its subtitle, *the Tritameron of Love,* suggesting a frame-tale structure, whereas in fact it consists of a debate over three days on "three doubtful questions of love" between a group of knights and ladies in a courtly foreign setting.

Planetomachia (1585), published the following year, has been seen as the last and best of Greene's early work but more convincingly as the beginning of a new phase moving from extended fictions to collections of novellas, comprising *Penelope's Web* (1587), *Euphues his Censure to Philautus* (1587), *Perimedes the Blacksmith* (1588), and *Greene's Orpharion* (1599). The change in form during this phase of composition marks a move away from the exemplary toward the purely romantic and a separation from Lylian humanism; but despite the increasing preference for narratives of action, in the debates with which most of his tales are framed Greene rarely loses sight of the concept of literature as a compendium of moral exempla.

On the title page of *Planetomachia* Greene is described as a "student in physic," and he has put together a patchwork of classical sources, some of them scientific texts not drawn on elsewhere, to give his work an air of authority. The work intersperses learned and rhetorically ornate debate, held between the planets as to which astrological influence bears most responsibility for human suffering, with tragic novellas of passion and revenge in the manner of Matteo Bandello. The third of these novellas begins in a striking way when Jupiter encounters a beautiful woman who holds a human heart in her hand and drinks from two human skulls. She narrates a fast-moving and bloody tale of rivalry, rejected love, and violent revenge from which moral judgment is entirely withheld and no participant vindicated. The tone of this collection is more deterministic than anything in Greene's previous work and darker than in other collections; *Penelope's Web,* for example, contains edifying tales in which virtuous women convert erring men, while *Euphues his Censure* illustrates virtuous qualities of men such as wisdom, fortitude, and liberality.

Unlike Greene's other frame tales, the three in *Perimedes the Blacksmith* are framed by a humble setting and narrated by characters of low social status. In his epistle Greene signals to the gentleman readers to regard this as a novelty: "At last

to Perimedes the blacksmith, who sitting in his holiday suit, to enter parley with his wife, smudged up in her best apparel, I present to your favors." From time to time the wife makes up the fire while the two eat a simple meal and moralize about domestic contentment and the value of wit over wealth, but the tales themselves are not significantly related to the natures of the tellers. Two of them are adapted from Giovanni Boccaccio's *Decameron* (1349–1351), which perhaps accounts for their more rapid style of narration, but the third concerns a virtuous gentleman who wins the hand of a princess and becomes wealthy through his "excellent wit and rare qualities."

Alcida (1617) and *Orpharion,* however, are written with a lighter touch and a defter sense of design. *Alcida* presents three Ovidian-style tales about women, metamorphosed respectively into a stone image, a bird, and a rosebush for their faults of pride, inconstancy, and gossiping. The stories are told by their mother, the melancholy Alcida, to a traveler who has been temporarily shipwrecked on the distant island where she lives. She relates them as examples of fortune "in some unfortunate and cursed aspect"; but the lightness of tone and Greene's elegant handling of the transformation theme neutralize the effects of the moral commentary, especially in the conclusion, where the traveler is rescued by a passing ship, and as he leaves the island he sees Alcida herself transformed by the gods into a fountain.

A similar formula of tales about women, located in a remote pastoral setting, is followed in *Orpharion,* with variations: the tellers of the tales are the ghosts of Orpheus and Arion; one story is tragic, one comic; and they are linked by themes of appetite and of women's power over men. The conclusion is explicitly neutral: in the words of Mercury, "Arion's tale paints out a paragon, a matchless mirror, as well for constancy, as the other for cruelty; these extremes therefore infer no certain conclusions, for they leave a mean between both, wherein I think the nature of women do consist."

While continuing to produce frame tales, the ever-ambitious Greene was also experimenting with a new style of romance, reverting to the extended fiction, but discarding the Lylian mode. He never entirely lost all his euphuistic habits, which persist as rhetorical tics even in the cony-catching pamphlets, but in *Pandosto* (1588) and *Menaphon* he modulated his style from the mode of profit to that of delight.

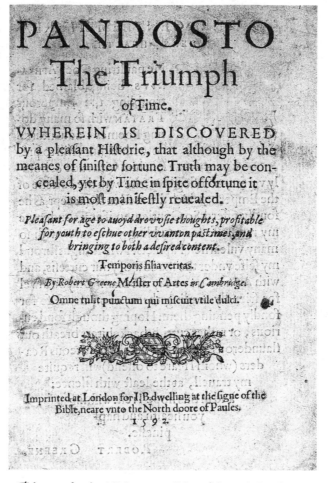

PANDOSTO
The Triumph
of Time.

WHEREIN IS DISCOVERED
by a pleasant Historie, that although by the
meanes of sinister fortune. Truth may be concealed, yet by Time in spite of fortune it
is most manifestly reuealed.

Pleasant for age to auoyd drowsie thoughts, profitable
for youth to eschue other wanton pastimes, and
bringing to both a desired content.

Temporis filia veritas.

By Robert Greene Maister of Artes in Cambridge.

Omne tulit punctum qui miscuit vtile dulci.

Imprinted at London for I. B. dwelling at the signe of the
Bible, neare vnto the North doore of Paules.
1592.

*Title page for the 1592 quarto edition of Greene's best-known
pastoral romance, which served as the inspiration for
Shakespeare's* The Winter's Tale *(1611)*

Pandosto, the Triumph of Time, published in 1588 but written perhaps three years earlier, shows the greatest influence of Greek romance of all Greene's works, though for most readers now its claim to fame is as the source of Shakespeare's *The Winter's Tale* (1611). Those who come to it by this route may be surprised by Greene's greater bitterness; his ending, designed "to close up the comedy with a tragical stratagem," seems deliberately to subvert generic expectations. The romance combines the familiar motifs – infant exposure, storm and shipwreck, apparently doomed romance between lovers of differing rank, a shepherdess revealed to be a princess – with favorite Greene themes such as generational conflict, irresistible passion, and the capriciousness of Fortune. Although King Pandosto recovers his long-lost daughter Fawnia and she is happily married to Prince Dorastus, whose father, King Egistus, is reconciled both to his estranged son and to Pandosto, his childhood friend, the stress throughout lies more heavily on the uncertainty of life and the inability of humanity to alter the course of "sinister fortune" than on the workings of Providence. Pandosto's remorse when he recognizes his jealous error over his wife is as great as Leontes's, but not only is there to be no spiritual regeneration for him, worse is to follow. He succumbs to further violent passions in incestuous lust for his disguised daughter and rage against the shepherd's innocent servant Capnio, and in the end he kills himself for his past misdeeds.

Greene's style reveals a new range and sophistication in *Pandosto.* The syntax is more lucid, less encumbered with euphuism in the narrative sections; the representation of thought processes is distinguished from the narrative by a greater rhetorical complexity, though inner debate can be used to create an almost dramatic mode, as when Dorastus argues with himself the decorum of assuming a shepherd's disguise or Pandosto ponders his feelings for Fawnia. The pastoral scenes between the shepherd, who discovers the baby, and his wife allow for a use of realistic detail and give evidence of the sympathetic interest in low-life speech apparent in *Perimedes*. The shepherd, proud of the pretty baby, "would sing and dance it on his knee and prattle, that in a short time it began to speak and call him 'Dad' and her 'Mam.'" When he goes to meet the king, his wife, "a good cleanly wench, brought him all things fit and sponged him up handsomely." *Pandosto* was the most popular English romance of its time after Sir Philip Sidney's *Arcadia* (1584) and went through twenty-six different editions during the next 150 years, as well as several versions in French translation in the seventeenth century.

Ciceronis Amor: Tully's Love (1589), a romance based on Roman legend, relates a fictional account of how the exquisitely beautiful and virtuous Terentia is sought after by two suitors, one of whom is transformed by the power of love from a simpleton into a hero. But Terentia is bewitched by Cicero's eloquence, despite his humbler birth, and after much soul-searching and inner debate they are united by acclamation of the people of Rome. The narrative is much more straightforward than that of *Pandosto,* and the theme of Fortune's uncertainty is absent. Its stylistic variety includes a letter in Latin and also a Latin poem in elegiacs, with its English translation.

The last of Greene's pastoral romances was *Menaphon: Camilla's Alarum to Slumbering Euphues,* now often thought to be his best. Like *Ciceronis Amor,* it is much concerned with the complications of a love triangle, and Greene goes still further in the exercise of stylistic variety. Nashe in his preface, while locating Greene's work in a context of humanist scholarship, draws attention to the author's range: he is both a "scholar-like shepherd" and enviably gifted with an "extemporal vein in any humor." Nashe does not, however, mention the range of verse styles embodied in the narrative: there are a dozen poems, all in different meters, including roundelays, jigs, madrigals, a verse dialogue in low comic style, two competitive eclogues, and the exquisite lullaby "Weep not, my wanton."

The narrative embodies many of the same romance motifs as *Pandosto,* and their deployment seems influenced by Sidney's *Old Arcadia* (1581), which Greene must have seen in manuscript: it opens with a mysterious oracle and, soon after, a shipwreck. There are also disguises of rank and identity, amorous mismatches, and a complex situation of potential parricide and incest in a family unaware of their true relationships, when a father lusts after his daughter, who is also desired by her son. This son, Pleusidippus, has been kidnapped by pirates and brought up remote from his mother, Sephestia, who is really a princess but living in Arcadia as the shepherdess Samela. Samela is wooed by two suitors, Menaphon, the chief shepherd, and Melicertus, who, unknown to all, is actually her long-lost husband in shepherd's disguise. Noble birth naturally reveals itself; Pleusidippus, unknown and living in exile, dazzles beholders with his childish beauty, and later with his deeds of chivalry, and when Melicertus sings in praise of Samela's beauty, she is disconcerted by his eloquence.

Stylistic and social distinction are closely related, and Greene sometimes uses his characters' stylistic consciousness to comic effect. Melicertus is exercised as to how to woo Samela: "esteeming her to be a farmer's daughter at the most . . . yet at length recalling to remembrance her rare wit," he confronts her in obtrusively euphuistic style "as if Ephebus [a character in *Euphues*] had learned him to refine his mother tongue." Samela responds mockingly in kind, as if she "had learned with Lucilla [also from *Euphues*] in Athens how to anatomize wit." Davis, not quite accurately, calls references such as these "Greene's final gesture of freedom from John Lyly." There is considerable comedy in *Menaphon,* and overall the mood is lighter than that of *Pandosto;* as at the climax of *Cymbeline,* the elucidation of the oracle reunites separated kinsfolk and discloses true relationships.

After *Menaphon* Greene changed his mode and, presently, his motto. In *Greene's Never Too Late* he began a series of fictions using an autobiographical model, and in the second part (1591) he switches from the Horatian motto *Omne tulit punctum qui miscuit utile dulce* (he wins all the prizes who mingles the useful and the pleasing), which he had first used in 1584, to *Sero, sed serio* (late but sincere).

The two parts of this work consist largely of the extended story of Francesco, a well-born but impoverished prodigal, who elopes with Isabel (the daughter of a country gentleman), leaves her to make his fortune in the city, and there falls into the snares of the courtesan Infida. "Seeing a means to mitigate the extremity of his want," he takes up playwriting with some success, but Infida is (predictably) inconstant, and he manages to cast her off, eventually returning, a reformed man, to Isabel, whose chastity has prevailed against the advances of Bernardo.

The story is presented amid many excrescences, including the framework provided by a mor-

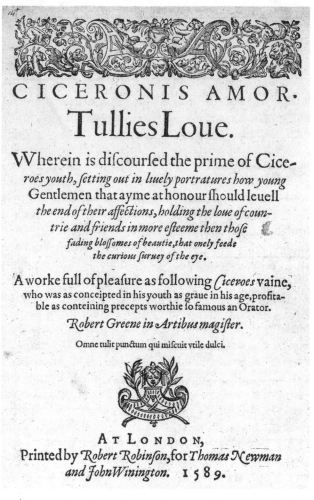

CICERONIS AMOR.

Tullies Loue.

Wherein is difcourfed the prime of Cice-
roes youth, fetting out in liuely portratures how young
Gentlemen that ayme at honour fhould leuell
the end of their affections, holding the loue of countrie and friends in more efteeme then thofe
fading bloffomes of beautie, that onely feede
the curious furuey of the eye.

A worke full of pleafure as following Ciceroes vaine,
who was as conceipted in his youth as graue in his age, profitable as conteining precepts worthie fo famous an Orator.

Robert Greene in Artibus magifter.

Omne tulit punctum qui mifcuit vtile dulci.

At London,
Printed by *Robert Robinfon*, for *Thomas Newman*
and *John Winington*. 1 5 8 9.

Title page for Greene's fictional account of the orator Cicero's
youth, based on Roman legend

alizing palmer who narrates it, a critical digression by the palmer on the ethics of theater, and a lengthy pastoral tale, told to Francesco and Isabel by the host of an inn. Though Greene in his prefatory matter insists on his didactic intentions, he is still concerned with the delight that comes from variety; there is also some reversion to the manner of the euphuistic romances. The conflict between the impulses to profit and delight, which critic Richard Helgerson sees as central to Greene's work, is evident.

Next came *Greene's Mourning Garment* (1590), similar in structure to the second part of *Never Too Late* in that they both combine a prodigal-son story with an inset pastoral tale; in his conclusion Greene promises that the book would be "the last of my trifling fictions." In *Greene's Farewell to Folly* (1591), which followed, he hints that his next move would be in the direction of satire: "As I renounce love for a fool and vanity as too unfit for

a gentleman, so I discover the general abuses that are ingrafted in the minds of courtiers and scholars." These abuses are unfolded in three exemplary tales, each prefaced by a moralizing discourse, a technique familiar from the days of pamphlets such as *Euphues his Censure*.

Greene's Vision, Written at the Instant of His Death (1592), published posthumously, seems also to belong to this series, for at the end Greene, speaking in propria persona, promises John Gower, here enlisted as one of the narrators, to "end my *Nunquam sera est* [never too late]" and tells him to "look as speedily as the press will serve for my mourning garment." But the address to the gentlemen readers is signed "yours dying," and it adopts a tone of last-minute recantation: "Now I am sick . . . I crave pardon of you all, if I have offended any of you with my lascivious pamphletting. Many things I have wrote to get money, which I could otherwise wish to be suppressed. Poverty is the father of innumerable infirmities." The work consists of a dream vision in which the ghosts of Geoffrey Chaucer and Gower each relate to the narrator (Greene) a tale illustrating the dangers of jealousy. Chaucer's is a fabliau, based on the *Decameron,* representing the "pleasant vein" of "amorous works" that Greene has followed too long; Gower's exemplary tale of a jealous man converted by a chaste wife is the mode the author has come to prefer.

In his summary Greene promises to concentrate on matters of more import, such as "political axioms, or acanonical precepts that may both generally and particularly profit the commonwealth." He had already made token gestures in this direction with *The Spanish Masquerado* (1589), a chauvinistic piece capitalizing on the defeat of the Armada, and *The Royal Exchange* (1590), a collection of aphorisms partly translated from Lorazio Rinaldi's *Dottrina della virtù, et fuga de' viltii* (1585) but also culled from other sources, including Mantuan (Baptista Spagnnoli) and Pierre La Primaudaye.

Perhaps the otherwise rather miscellaneous but in its time popular *A Quip for an Upstart Courtier,* in which Greene offended the Harveys, could be included in this autobiographical group. Like *Greene's Vision,* it is a dream debate between two antagonists, but the substance is social satire in the Estates tradition. The participants, Clothbreeches and Velvetbreeches, argue as to which of them, the traditional Englishman speaking for "ancient gentility and yeomanry" or the Italianate upstart with his fashionable clothes and gentlemanly airs, has the greater right to residence in the commonwealth; a jury of twenty-four assorted social types, including as its last member a downat-the-heels poet, hears the cases and finds in favor of Clothbreeches.

Social benefit is most explicitly the aim of Greene's final series, written in the last year of his life. With the publication of the trendsetting cony-catching pamphlets, Greene completed the spectrum of his appeal from courtly to popular: *A Notable Discovery of Cozenage* and *The Second Part of Cony-Catching* (entered together in the Stationers' Register for 13 December 1591 and presumably published together), *The Third and Last Part of Cony-Catching* (entered 7 February 1592), *A Disputation between a He Cony-Catcher and a She Cony-Catcher* (not entered), and *The Black Book's Messenger* (entered 21 August 1592, two weeks before Greene's death); *The Defense of Conny-Catching* by "Cuthbert Cony-Catcher" (entered 21 May 1592) may also belong to this group.

In prefacing these short pamphlets with yet another motto, *Nascimur pro patria* (we are born for our country), Greene was developing a further public role for himself, as civic patriot and heroic journalist, entering the camp of the enemy in order to save his countrymen. In describing the tricks and devices of cardsharpers, pickpockets, and other kinds of London petty criminals who operated in organized gangs, Greene claims that he is exposing "such pestilent and prejudicial practices, as of late have been the ruin of infinite persons, and the subversion and overthrow of many merchants, farmers, and honest-minded yeomen" (*A Notable Discovery*).

But his claims to documentary realism are compromised by his lifelong habit of basing his work on familiar literary models and also by his irrepressible fictionality. His accounts of the London underworld of the 1590s owe much to the tradition of rogue literature from earlier in the century, particularly Gilbert Walker's *Manifest Detection of the Most Vile and Detestable Use of Diceplay* (1532) and Thomas Harman's *Caveat or Warning for Common Cursetors* (1566), which provided both narrative models and also factual detail. A further formal model existed in the jest-book tradition, in which collections of comic anecdotes or "merry tales," usually involving some kind of trickery, were often grouped round a central figure, as in *Tarlton's News out of Purgatory* (1590) or *The Cobbler of Canterbury* (1590).

This is not to say that the cony-catching pamphlets were not concerned with the mechanics of cozenage; the operations of Barnard's Law, the Prigging Law, Vincent's Law, the exposure of the arts of the foist, the nip, the horse stealer, and the dishonest collier appealed to the reading public, as is evident from the speed with which this series of pamphlets appeared and was followed by imitations. An air of authenticity is created by the generous detail of names and places as well as the author's references to the dangers incurred in his underworld investigations, threats of revenge from angry cony-catchers, and the provision of extra information from grateful friends and well-wishers. In a sense Greene had discovered a new way of presenting frame tales.

But Greene the reporter does not supersede Greene the storyteller. The claims to personal acquaintance with some of the rogues and their victims must be weighed against the evident jest-book origins of many of the anecdotes, betrayed by the neatness of the plotting or the way in which the outcome is made to depend on some twist of for-

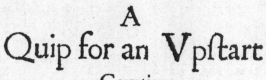

*Title page for the 1606 quarto edition of Greene's popular
1592 pamphlet, a debate between Clothbreeches and
Velvetbreeches, which offended the courtier Gabriel
Harvey and his brother Richard*

tune or play on words. The interest in the narrative arts of realism, hinted at in the frame tales and the comic sections of the later romances, is well displayed in *The Last Part of Cony-Catching*, which consists entirely of tales supposedly composed from notes supplied to Greene by a helpful justice of the peace.

The first of these, "a pleasant tale how an honest substantial citizen was made a cony, and simply entertained a knave that carried away his goods very politicly," describes how a cony-catcher adroitly feigns acquaintance with a naive country serving girl working in a prosperous city household in order to rob her employers. In its use of Greene's fine command of social detail, the narrative does not conceal his admiration for the cleverness of the trickster. Having researched his subject thoroughly, the knave persuades the girl that he is her relative by giving authentic news of her family; she is de-

lighted to show off "so neat a youth" to her employers, whose approval the youth wins with gifts of "a good gammon of bacon, which he closed up in a soiled linen cloth, and sewed an old card upon it" and "a good cheese . . . with inscription accordingly on it, that it could not be discerned, but that some unskilful writer in the country had done it." The mistress of the household invites him to dinner, having "beautified the house with cushions, carpets, stools, and other devices of needlework," and getting out her best linen and plate "to have the better report made of her credit amongst their servant's friends in the country." So well goes the evening that the thief lets himself be persuaded to stay the night, during which time he has no difficulty in making off with all the valuables. In conclusion Greene replaces the heated denunciations of the criminality of the cony-catchers that had appeared in earlier pamphlets with a low-key comment of greater moral neutrality: "how this may

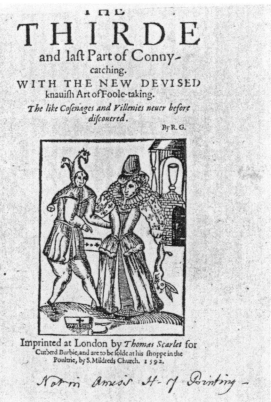

Title pages for four of Greene's cony-catching pamphlets

forewarn others, I leavc to your own opinions that see what extraordinary devices are nowadays, to beguile the simple and honest liberal-minded."

The second group of cony-catching pamphlets, including *The Defense of Cony-Catching,* is more experimental in form. *The Defense* is supposed to be a riposte by one of the cony-catchers whom Greene has exposed, issued in revenge on Greene for spoiling his livelihood and also to show the triviality of cony-catching in comparison with the much greater malpractices of those in conventional positions of power. It is really a pretext for publishing some familiar tales about the dishonesty of stock figures such as lawyers, millers, and usurers; its main effect is to publicize Greene's other work, and it concludes with a puff for a work entered in the Stationers' Register shortly before Greene's death, *The Repentance of a Cony-Catcher,* which Cuthbert Cony-Catcher claims will expose the abuses perpetrated by keepers in the Newgate and Marshalsea prisons. Greene never wrote the work, however.

A Disputation between a He Cony-Catcher and a She Cony-Catcher discards claims to the disclosure of criminal secrets and new information, reverting to a more overtly didactic manner with a particular stress on the evils of prostitution. The first part is a dialogue between Laurence, a thief, and Nan, a whore, about which of them does the greater damage to society. Nan, with the aid of many stories of cony-catching exploits, proves that not only are women as skilled in thieving as men but they can exercise far more power to harm through the exploitation of their sexuality. Greene is not entirely successful in negotiating the stylistic problems of relating Nan's boastful account of her sexual techniques to her hortatory manner, but he does try to create realistic speech styles for his disputants and to locate their encounter in a contemporary London setting.

The second half of the pamphlet is an exemplary story, told in the first person, of "the conversion of an English courtesan," which draws on a traditional tale found as far back as Hrotswitha but more likely was adapted by Greene from Desiderius Erasmus's *Colloquies* (1518). It tells of a prostitute who takes her client at his request to the darkest room possible for their trade and is converted when he points out that even there they are watched by God. This story of a female prodigal, who is also a faithless wife reclaimed by a constant husband, constitutes an interesting variation on Greene's familiar model of admonition, rebellion, and repentance in a young man.

The Black Book's Messenger, a cruder production, also refers to this model; it combines cony-

catching material with the first-person repentance mode that dominates the last works put out in Greene's life. "The Black Book" itself was to be a directory of the London criminal fraternity, as promised in *A Disputation,* but it never appeared; Chettle makes Greene's ghost allude to it in *Kind-Heart's Dream.* In *The Black Book's Messenger* Ned Brown, "a notable cutpurse and cony-catcher," begins his tale as a hardened reprobate, boasting, with anecdotes, of his incredible wickedness. But there is a jarring moral transition between the last "merry jest" he has to relate and the repentant speech he utters on the scaffold; the narrator finally informs the reader that Ned was hanged in France after robbing a church.

Greene's Groatsworth of Wit and *The Repentance of Robert Greene* were published posthumously and addressed to their readers by their respective publishers, William Wright and Cuthbert Burbie. The former somewhat resembles *Never Too Late* as a prodigal-son fiction, but the prodigal's image is split, uniquely, between two brothers, Roberto and Lucanio. The former is despised by their father, a usurer, because he is a scholar, whereas Lucanio wins approval through his devotion to money-making. Lucanio takes up with Lamillia, a prostitute, who milks him of all his wealth and brings him to degradation and early death. Roberto leaves his wife and "becomes famoused for an arch-playmaking poet" in London; he too goes to the bad and becomes so poor that he has "nothing to pay but chalk, which now his host accepted not for current." Then he finds one remaining groat of his father's money, which recalls him to his moral senses. At this point Greene drops his fiction and identifies himself with Roberto; the "groatsworth of wit" is spent on a series of admonitions, some of them directed "to those gentlemen his quondam acquaintance, that spend their wits in making plays," whom he urges to find "a better exercise." *The Repentance of Robert Greene,* possibly a rival publication to the *Groatsworth,* is a collection of fragments, some of them directly autobiographical. It consists largely of a first-person confession and recantation, induced by a reading of Robert Parsons's *Book of Resolution,* written in passionate Puritan style, a summary of Greene's prodigal life, a narration of his death, and a concluding prayer.

Greene's many retellings of his own life never diverge much from a single model of prodigality and repentance, but his literary career was extraordinarily varied and experimental. Not only was he successful in a range of established prose modes, but in introducing new or remodeled ones he was able to create his own public. Even taking into account his habits of wholesale borrowing and of recycling his own material, he was astonishingly prolific. His audience appeal was wider than that of any other contemporary prose writer; initially he directed his work to the tastes of a genteel readership, but he soon extended his range to accommodate more-bourgeois values. The cony-catching pamphlets involve themselves directly in contemporary lowlife and also develop a newly personal relationship between writer and reader, which is amplified in his posthumous works. But sadly for Greene the conditions for authorship in his day were such that however hard he tried, he could not fulfill them; however great his popularity, however ingenious his self-publicizing, he could never make enough money to sustain the life of the writer as he invented it in his fictions.

In the twentieth century Greene's reputation as a prose writer has tended to rest on his cony-catching pamphlets, once regarded as examples of naive realism. But recent interest in self-fashioning and other forms of fictionalizing in the Renaissance has increased awareness of the part that self-promotion played in almost all of Greene's literary activities. It has also reawakened interest in the prose romance, and Greene's considerable output in this genre is worth more attention than it has so far found. Even in the 1590s Gabriel Harvey bitterly opined in his *Four Letters and Certain Sonnets, Especially Touching Robert Greene* that only Greene could satisfy the large popular appetite for romance: "The Countess of Pembroke's *Arcadia* is not green enough for queasy stomachs, but they must have Greene's *Arcadia:* and I believe, most eagerly longed for Greene's *Faerie Queene.*" Greene's extraordinary contemporary popularity and his unique creation of a self-image as the archetypal literary prodigal render him ripe for reassessment, particularly given current concern with the cultural context for the production of literary texts.

Bibliographies:

Tetsumaro Hayashi, *Robert Greene Criticism: A Comprehensive Bibliography* (Metuchen, N.J.: Scarecrow Press, 1971);

William Nestrick, "Robert Greene," in *The Predecessors of Shakespeare,* edited by T. P. Logan and D. S. Smith (Lincoln: University of Nebraska Press, 1973), pp. 56–92;

A. F. Allison, *Robert Greene 1558–1592: A Bibliographical Catalogue of the Early Editions in English (to 1640)* (Folkestone: Dawson, 1975);

James Seay Dean, *Robert Greene: A Reference Guide* (Boston: G. K. Hall, 1984);

James L. Harner, *English Renaissance Prose Fiction 1500–1600: An Annotated Bibliography of Criticism 1976–1983* (Boston: G. K. Hall, 1985), pp. 198–242;

Kevin J. Donovan, "Recent Studies in Robert Greene (1968–1988)," *English Literary Renaissance,* 20 (Winter 1990): 163–175.

References:

Eckhard Auberlen, *The Commonwealth of Wit: The Writer's Image and His Strategies of Self-Representation in Elizabethan Literature* (Tübingen: G. Narr, 1984), pp. 157–177;

Warren B. Austin, *A Computer-Aided Technique for Stylistic Discrimination: The Authorship of "Greene's Groatsworth of Wit"* (Washington, D.C.: U.S. Office of Education, 1969);

Norbert Bolz, "Are Robert Green's Autobiographies Fakes? The Forgery of *The Repentance of Robert Greene,*" *Shakespeare Newsletter,* 29 (December 1979): 43;

H. Bonheim, "Robert Greene's *Gwydonius: The Card of Fancie,*" *Anglia,* 96 (1978): 45–64;

D. Allen Carroll, "The Badger in *Greene's Groatsworth of Witte* and in Shakespeare," *Studies in Philology,* 84 (Fall 1987): 471–482;

Carroll, "Greene's Upstart Crow Passage: A Survey of Commentary," *Research Opportunities in Renaissance Drama,* 28 (1985): 111–127;

Sandra Clark, *The Elizabethan Pamphleteers: Popular Moralistic Pamphlets 1580–1640* (Rutherford, N.J.: Fairleigh Dickinson University Press, 1983);

G. Coggins, "Greene's Repetitions as Solutions to Textual Problems," *Analytical and Enumerative Bibliography,* 5, no. 1 (1981): 3–15;

Charles W. Crupi, *Robert Greene* (Boston: Twayne, 1986);

Walter R. Davis, *Idea and Act in Elizabethan Fiction* (Princeton: Princeton University Press, 1969);

Richard Helgerson, *The Elizabethan Prodigals* (Berkeley: University of California Press, 1976), pp. 79–104;

Jaroslav Hornat, "*Mamillia*: Robert Greene's Controversy with *Euphues,*" *Philologia Pragensia,* 5, no. 4 (1962): 210–218;

John C. Jordan, *Robert Greene* (New York: Columbia University Press, 1915);

Arthur Kinney, *Humanist Poetics: Thought, Rhetoric, and Fiction in Sixteenth-Century England* (Amherst: University of Massachusetts Press, 1986), pp. 181–229;

Nancy R. Lindhcim, "Lyly's Golden Legacy: *Rosalynde* and *Pandosto*," *Studies in English Literature,* 15 (Winter 1975): 3–20;

V. L. MacDonald, "The Complex Moral View of Robert Greene's *A Disputation between a Hee and Shee Conny-Catcher*," *Shakespeare Jahrbuch* (Weimar), 119 (1983): 122–136;

MacDonald, "Robert Greene's Courtesan," *Zeitschrift für Anglistik und Amerikanistik,* 32, no. 3 (1984): 211–219;

MacDonald, "Robert Greene's Innovative Contributions to Prose Fiction," *Shakespeare Jahrbuch* (Weimar), 117 (1981): 127–137;

David Margolies, *Novel and Society in Elizabethan England* (London: Croom Helm, 1985), pp. 105–143;

Edwin Havilland Miller, *The Professional Writer in Elizabethan England* (Cambridge, Mass.: Harvard University Press, 1959);

Miller, "The Relationship of Robert Greene and Thomas Nashe," *Philological Quarterly,* 33 (October 1954): 353–367;

Charles Nicoll, *A Cup of News* (London: Routledge & Kegan Paul, 1984), pp. 122–134;

R. B. Parker, "Robert Greene and *The Defense of Cony-Catching*," *Notes and Queries,* 219 (March 1974): 87–89;

René Pruvost, *Robert Greene et ses romans (1558–1592)* (Paris: Société d'edition les belles lettres, 1938);

Irving Ribner, "Greene's Attack on Marlowe: Some Light on *Alphonsus* and *Selimus*," *Studies in Philology,* 52 (April 1955): 162–171;

Brenda Richardson, "Robert Greene's Yorkshire Connexions: A New Hypothesis," *Yearbook of English Studies,* 10 (1980): 160–180;

Paul Salzman, *English Prose Fiction 1558–1700: A Critical History* (Oxford: Clarendon Press, 1985), pp. 59–69;

Paul A. Scanlon, "The Later Prose Romances of Robert Greene," *Cahiers elisabéthains,* 24 (October 1983): 3–15;

Phoebe Sheavyn, *The Literary Profession in the Elizabethan Age,* revised by J. W. Saunders (Manchester: Manchester University Press, 1967);

Samuel Lee Wolff, *The Greek Romances in Elizabethan Prose Fiction* (New York: Columbia University Press, 1912), pp. 367–458.

Gabriel Harvey

(July 1550?–7 February 1631)

Wayne Erickson
Georgia State University

BOOKS: *Ode natalitia, vel opus eius feriae, quae S. Stephani protomartyris nomine celebrata est. In memoriam P. Rami* (London: Thomas Vautrollerius, 1575);

Gabrielis Harueii Ciceronianus, vel oratio habita Catabrigiae (London: Henry Bynneman, 1577);

Gabrielis Harueii rhetor, vel duorum dierum oratio (London: Henry Bynneman, 1577);

Gabrielis Harueii Valdinatis; Smithus, vel musarum lachrymae; pro obitu T. Smithi, equitis. (R. Harveij lachrymae) (London: Henry Bynneman, 1578);

Gabrielis Harueij gratulationum Valdinensium libri quatuor (London: Henry Bynneman, 1578);

Three Proper, and Wittie, Familiar Letters, bound together with *Two Other, Very Commendable Letters of the Same Men's Writing, Both Touching the Foresaid Artificial Versifying and Certain other Particulars, More Lately Delivered unto the Printer* (London: Imprinted by Henry Bynneman, 1580);

Three letters, and Certaine Sonnets: Especially Touching Robert Greene (London: Imprinted by John Wolfe, 1592); republished as *Foure letters, and Certaine Sonnets* (London: John Wolfe, 1592);

Pierces Supererogation or a New Prayse of the Old Asse (London: Imprinted by John Wolfe, 1593);

A New Letter of Notable Contents. With a Straunge Sonet, Intituled Gorgon (London: Printed by John Wolfe, 1593).

Editions: *Letter-Book of Gabriel Harvey, A.D. 1573–1580,* edited by Edward John Long Scott (London: Camden Society, 1884; New York & London: Johnson Reprint, 1965);

The Works of Gabriel Harvey, D.C.L., 3 volumes, edited by Alexander B. Grosart (London: Huth Library, 1884–1885; New York: AMS Press, 1966);

Gabriel Harvey's Marginalia, edited by G. C. Moore Smith (Stratford-upon-Avon: Shakespeare Head, 1913);

Four Letters and Certain Sonnets, edited by G. B. Harrison (London: Bodley Head, 1922; New York: Barnes & Noble, 1966);

Ciceronianus, Latin/English edition, translated by Clarence A. Forbes, Studies in the Humanities 4 (Lincoln: University of Nebraska Press, 1945);

"Rhetor: The First Lecture by Gabriel Harvey," Latin/English edition, translated and edited by Robert M. Chandler, *Allegorica,* 4 (Summer–Winter 1979): 146–290.

OTHER: "G.H. po eodem," in *Posies,* by George Gascoigne (London: Imprinted for Richard Smith, 1575);

"De Discenda Graeca Lingua Greeke," in *Lexicon Graeco-Latinum, repurgatum studio E. Grant,* by Jean Crespin (London: Printed by Henry Bynneman, 1581);

Academiae Cantabrigiensis lachrymae tumulo nobilissimi equitis, D. Philippi Sidneii sacratae per Alexandrum Nevillum (London: Printed for Alexander Neville, 1587) – includes Harvey's "Academiae Cantabrigiensis lachrimae, in obitum clarissimi Equitus, Domini Philippi Sidneii"; "De subito et praematuro interitu Nobilis viri, Philippi Sydneii, utriusque militiae, tam Armatae, quam Togatae, clarissimi Equitus: officiosi amici Elegia"; and "Ad illustrissimum Dominum Leicestrensem protheoreticon."

Broad-minded, ambitious, well read, and socially inept, Gabriel Harvey was probably one of the most visible literary personalities of his day. Out of a prosperous middle-class background, he carved a multiform personal and public career. He became an eminent and controversial university teacher and scholar who challenged the orthodoxy of Aristotelian logic, conservative humanist pedagogy, Galenic medicine, and Ptolemaic cosmology by endorsing Ramist, Paracelsian, and Copernican models; he taught Latin rhetoric, Greek, civil law, and medicine. In addition, Harvey was a skilled Latin poet; a fringe member of the political and literary circle surrounding Sir

to Saffron-walden.

Lord of *Oxford*, but in the single-soald pumpes of his aduersitie, with his gowne cast off, vntrussing, and readie to beray himselfe, vpon the newes of the going in hand of my booke.

The picture of Gabriell Haruey, as hee is readie to let fly vpon Aiax.

If you aske why I haue put him in round hose, that vsually weares Venetians? It is because I would make him looke more dapper & plump and round vpon it, wheras otherwise he looks like a case of tooth pikes, or a Lute pin put in a sute of apparell. Gaze vppon him who list, for I tell you I am not a little proud of my workmanship, and though I say it, I haue handled it so neatly and so sprightly and withall ouzled, gidumbled, muddled, and drizled it so finely, that I forbid euer a *Hauns Boll, Hauns Holbine,* or *Hauns Mullier* of them all (let them but play true with the face) to amend it or come within fortie foote of it. Away away, *Blockland, Trusser, Francis de Murre,* and the whole generation of them will sooner catch the murre and the pose tenscore times ere they doo a thing one quarter so masterly. Yea (without *Kerry merry buffe* be it spoken) put a whole million of *Iohannes Mabusiusses* of them together, and they shall not handle

Woodcut caricature of Gabriel Harvey in Thomas Nashe's
Have With You to Saffron-Walden *(1596)*

Philip Sidney and Robert Dudley, Earl of Leicester; an intimate friend of Edmund Spenser; a persistent and antagonistic participant in a notorious war of words with Thomas Nashe; a prodigious annotator of the books in his vast library; and a proponent of beautiful handwriting, of consistent phonetic orthography, and of marking the beginning of the year at 1 January instead of 25 March (Lady Day). A quintessential Renaissance intellectual, Harvey aspired to embody his version of the *uomo universale* through encyclopedic learning and searching critical consciousness. His writings — letters; university lectures; elegiac, celebratory, and commendatory verse in English and Latin; marginalia; and an outpouring of defensive invective leveled at Nashe

and Robert Greene — bear directly on events in his life, making the life and works mutually revelatory.

The eldest of at least six children of John and Alice Harvey, Gabriel Harvey was born, probably in July 1550, in the northwest Essex town of Saffron Walden, forty-five miles north of London and fifteen miles south of Cambridge. During his boyhood he lived in the large family home on the west end of the town common, close by the mansion of Sir Thomas Smith (later principal secretary to Queen Elizabeth), who, until his death in 1577, was Harvey's mentor and elder friend. Harvey's father, a yeoman farmer, master ropemaker, and active local citizen, became treasurer of the town's governing corporation for the year 1572–1573, owned substantial property in and around Saffron Walden, and prospered sufficiently to pay for the education of at least his three eldest sons – Gabriel, Richard, and John Jr. – as pensioners at Cambridge.

Gabriel seems to have excelled in the rigorous training afforded him at the local grammar school, initiating habits that characterize his lifelong independence of mind: writing occasional verse from age nine, celebrating and disputing the claims of authoritative texts, and often igniting controversy among those of settled opinions. He matriculated at Christ's College, Cambridge, on 28 June 1566, quickly exhibiting his promising intellectual abilities and securing lifelong friendships with William Lewin, his tutor, and Sir Walter Mildmay, brother-in-law of Sir Francis Walsingham. Duly receiving his B.A. in 1570, Harvey was not elected fellow of Christ's, probably because he chose to eschew the requisite study of divinity; rather, with the probable assistance of Sir Thomas Smith, he was elected fellow of Pembroke Hall on 3 November 1570. Soon after, Harvey may have met a Pembroke undergraduate named Edmund Spenser, who had matriculated in 1569 and would become his intimate friend. Harvey may have found a soul mate in Spenser, but his new friend could do little to mitigate the controversy that soon descended on Harvey when, in March 1573, he stood ready to seek grace for the granting of his M.A. degree.

A group of Pembroke fellows led by Thomas Neville, later master of Trinity College (1593–1616), sought to block Harvey from taking his degree, charging him with unsociability and nonconformity, official accusations that barely concealed personal animosities and class prejudice. Harvey rehearses the details of this dispute in letters to John Young, nonresident master of Pembroke; to Humphrey Tyndale, friend and Pembroke fellow; and to his father (collected in Harvey's *Letter-Book*, 1884). The controversy over Harvey's degree exposes strengths and apparent weaknesses in his character that would follow him throughout his life, winning him devoted friends and resolute enemies and creating intellectual triumphs and social embarrassments. Two characteristics stand out: Harvey's apparent awkwardness in social settings and his pronounced freedom of thought. He apparently never succeeded in perfecting the combination of effortless grace, decorum, and diplomacy – *sprezzatura* – that he eloquently praised in his writings. Owing to insecurities bred of self-consciousness about his middle-class origins, coupled with his always outspoken questioning of received opinions, Harvey's

behavior, especially among his social betters, might have sometimes appeared pompous, vain, or even politically dangerous.

Harvey's long first letter to Young spells out Neville's accusations and Harvey's extemporaneous responses to the Pembroke fellows in assembly. These proceedings, while exposing Harvey in public action, offer an absorbing and sobering account of sixteenth-century academic life. Neville's first accusation goes to the heart of the social matter: "He laid against me my *common* behavior," Harvey writes, "that I was not familiar like a fellow, and that I did disdain every man's company." Harvey answers that his familiarity toward certain fellows was subtly shunned, so he was "constrained to withdraw [himself] somewhat for fear of offending." Neville next charges that Harvey "could hardly find in [his] heart to commend any man" and that he often criticized those praised by common consent. Thus provoked, Harvey admits that he "cast out" a controversial truism: "it were better for a man to be thought arrogant than foolish." Neville's third accusation, pitifully telling, alleges that Harvey "made but small and light account of [his] fellowship" because, unlike Neville, he was unable and unwilling to consider the degree worth a hundred pounds. Amid some bickering, Harvey asserts that money ought not be the issue.

Finally, writes Harvey, Neville focuses on the central intellectual issue: "that I was a great and continual patron of paradoxes and a main defender of strange opinions, and that commonly against Aristotle, too." Harvey forthrightly justifies his opinions by calling on the authority of four sixteenth-century writers: Philipp Melanchthon, Peter Ramus, Cornelius Valerius, and Sebastianus Foxius Morzillus. Regarding Aristotle, Harvey reminds his accusers that he has highly commended the esteemed philosopher in public and in private but that he cannot "take it for scripture whatsoever [Aristotle] has given his word for." Specifically, Harvey states his five chief propositions against Aristotle's philosophy: "the earth is not eternal, the sky is not of the fifth nature . . . the sky is not animated, nothing is physically infinite in force, and virtue is not within our power" (translations from Latin and Greek by Virginia F. Stern in *Gabriel Harvey: His Life, Marginalia, and Library,* 1979). Harvey suggests, after pointing out his authorities' sanction of his views, that topics such as these should replace the "stale questions" consistently debated by the Pembroke fellows. He mentions other details of his behavior that seem to offend some of his colleagues and admits that after three hours the disputation be-

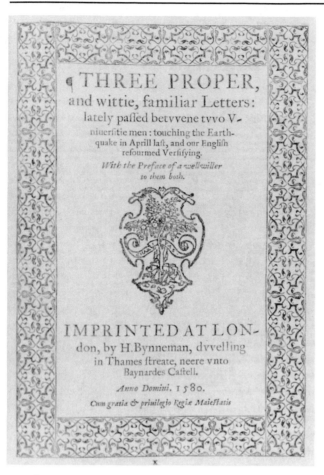
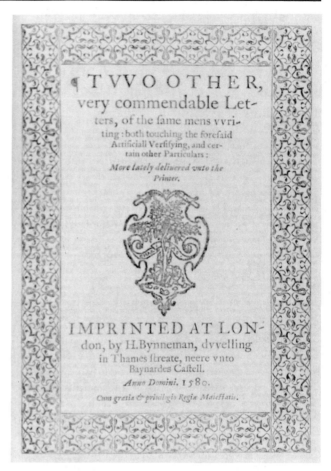

Title pages for the two-part publication of letters between Harvey and Edmund Spenser, published shortly after the appearance of Spenser's Shepheardes Calender *(1579)*

came tiresome; Harvey was left, understandably, *ad miserandum* (approaching misery).

In the next few days matters only became worse as Harvey attempted, without success, to make peace. Finally, on the advice of Tyndale, he retired to Saffron Walden; also at Tyndale's urging, Young appeared at Cambridge, arranged for Harvey's degree, appointed Harvey Greek lecturer beginning 10 October 1573, and, after Harvey's attackers persisted, reprimanded the leaders. Meanwhile, the university awarded Harvey first place in the *Ordo Senioritatas,* and he proceeded with his Greek lectures, two of which were eventually printed as "De Discenda Graeca Lingua Greeke," near the end of the 1581 edition of Jean Crespin's *Lexicon Graeco-Latinum.* Harvey quickly achieved academic success at Pembroke, becoming bursar in 1573, university professor of rhetoric for three years (1574–1576), and senior treasurer in 1575. Amid a demanding and rewarding academic life, Harvey produced his first printed works in 1575: a commendatory Latin poem signed G. H., one

among several introducing the *Posies* of his friend George Gascoigne; and *Ode natalitia,* a tribute to Ramus composed, Harvey says, on Saint Stephen's Day, 26 December, the day commemorating that saint's martyrdom and thereby calling attention to the martyrdom of Ramus during the Saint Bartholomew's Day Massacre of 24 August 1572. Harvey's poem consists of two eclogues: one presents a student succeeding at school by using Ramus as a guide; the other praises Ramus's work and appeals to others to carry it on.

With a view toward making public his academic success, his embrace of Ramist pedagogy, and, perhaps by implication, his qualifications for state service, Harvey published in 1577 three of his university rhetoric orations: two in *Rhetor,* delivered as the first two lectures of spring term 1574 and 1575, and another, *Ciceronianus,* delivered as the inaugural lecture of Easter term 1576. In all three Harvey promulgates views on Latin instruction that stand at the cutting edge of contemporary Continental thought and represent the radical fringe of pedagogic theory at the English universities. As such, they probably inspired his brightest students and disconcerted many of his colleagues. In essence, Harvey champions reformed humanist Ciceronianism, instructing his students to venerate rather than idolize Cicero. Toward this end, students must supplement conventional memorization of phrase books and exercises in imitation with attempts at understanding the exemplary person behind the brilliant style, and they must follow Cicero's advice by reading widely in ancient and modern authors. Because, according to Harvey, rhetorical skill presupposes proficiency in dialectic, students should study Quintillian's *Instituto Oratoria* (96 A.D.) as a Roman model consistent with Rudolph Agricola's *De Inventione Dialectica* (1480) and the clear Ramist distinctions between logic/dialectic and rhetoric incorporated into the *Rhetoric* (1548) of Audomarus Talaeus(Omer Talon), Ramus's friend and fellow reformer. As historical documents, Harvey's orations are among the first printed works in England to promote Ramist pedagogy, stressing Protestant and Copernican sympathies against Aristotelian methods in logic and rhetoric.

According to Harvey, his lectures were heavily attended by Cambridge undergraduates and others; he estimates a crowd of four hundred at his first *Rhetor* lecture and goes on, exposing a characteristic faux pas, to name some senior colleagues who draw few to their own lectures. Harvey's rhetorical peformances preserve an intimate and exemplary portrait of his appeal as a teacher, and they are some of the most delightfully endearing and intellectually playful pedagogic works of the English Renaissance. The *Rhetor* lectures, the first on nature and art and the second on practice of rhetoric, explicitly advertise and enact Ramist theory; the *Ciceronianus,* more general in application and more focused on a broad critique of Italianate Ciceronianism, invites comparison with Erasmus's more disdainfully satiric attack in his own *Ciceronianus* (1540). Erasmus's dialogue invites the reader to laugh at others; Harvey's oration provokes a smile through critical self-judgment. Yet the end is the same, for Harvey finds Ramus's Cicero in Erasmus.

Harvey opens his *Ciceronianus* with memories of his recent studious *otium* in rustication in Saffron Walden where, leaving the literature of the Greeks to sustain himself on that of the Latins, "now your friend Tully invited me to breakfast, now Julius Caesar himself to lunch, now Virgil to dinner, now the others to their desserts, which were very delightful for a change." This personal invitation to the joys of study introduces Harvey's candid self-

exposure, a pedagogic strategy bound to attract his students: he proceeds to disclose his own folly of embracing radical Ciceronianism, implicating himself with specific examples. He then rehearses his transformation after reading Ramus: the Italian humanists came to appear "partly hyperfinical, and partly not quite perspicacious," for Ramus had "revealed the marvelous and exquisite sympathy and symphony of heart and tongue [and] . . . presented a Marcus Tully recognizable not by some wart or by trinkets of identification but by his whole body and mind."

Harvey outlines in detail for his students "an imitation not superstitious and worse than servile but free and enlightened," uniting "dialectic and knowledge with rhetoric, thought with language." As he nears the end of his discourse, he becomes thoroughly inspiring, intimating that a reformed Ciceronianism might "realize in actuality for the public weal what we conceive in mind and imagination for our own delight." He concludes, not surprisingly, with a version of the modesty topos, admitting that his remarks may have seemed more disorderly and unrefined than his audience may have expected.

On 12 August 1577 Harvey lost an influential friend and patron with the death of Sir Thomas Smith, a man whose honored statesmanship and broad learning embodied Harvey's most exalted aspirations. Harvey began his elegiac tribute to Smith the day after the funeral and published it in January 1578 as *Gabrielis Harveii Valdinatis; Smithus, vel musarum lachrymae,* a series of solemn and accomplished Latin verse laments by the Muses; Spenser apparently borrowed both the name and the design for his *Tears of the Muses* (1591). Harvey's poems offer commentaries on Smith's accomplishments in the disciplines governed by the various Muses and mention, in the appropriate contexts, Smith's favorite classical authors and contemporary associates. In addition, the volume includes a dedicatory poem to Sir Walter Mildmay, three poems to John Wood (Smith's nephew and secretary), a "Hymn of the Graces," an elegy by Harvey's brother Richard, and an etched portrait of Smith. The volume worthily displays Harvey's esteem for his elder friend.

About this time, Harvey apparently began to set his sights on employment beyond the university: he may have met Sir Philip Sidney; Sir Edward Dyer; Daniel Rogers; and Robert Dudley, Earl of Leicester, as early as 1576; he was probably among those scheduled to attend a conference of Protestant princes in Germany early in 1578, a diplomatic mission canceled by Elizabeth; and he was soon to find himself among the mighty and powerful when Elizabeth came to Audley End near Saffron Walden on 26 July 1578. During the queen's stay he took part with other Cambridge masters in a Latin disputation won by his own team and was afforded the opportunity to mix socially with the assembled notable persons. *In Have with You to Saffron Walden* (1596), Nashe provides an unusually lighthearted and perhaps not altogether fallacious portrait of Harvey's behavior on the occasion:

> There did this our Talatamtana or Doctor Hum thrust himself into the thickest ranks of the noblemen and gallants, and whatsoever they were arguing of, he would not miss to catch hold of, or strike in at the one end, and take the theme out of their mouths, or it should go hard. In self same order was he at his pretty toys and amorous glances and purposes with the damsels, and putting bawdy riddles unto them.

Whatever the truth of the satirist's description, the occasion – during which the queen allowed Harvey to kiss her hand and remarked to Leicester on Harvey's Italianate good looks – inspired Harvey to produce a complex verse tribute to the most powerful members of the realm. Before the queen left Audley End, he presented to her four folio sheets of Latin verse written in his beautiful Italian hand, including his own encomiums; an epigram by Abraham Hartwell, fellow of King's College, Cambridge; and an ode by Janus Dousa, the governor of Leyden and a member of the Sidney circle. On 15 September 1578 Harvey presented to Elizabeth the expanded, printed version of the work while she was visiting Hadham Hall, Hertfordshire, the estate of Harvey's friend Arthur Capel. This volume, *Gratulationum Valdinensium,* comprises four books: one addressed to Elizabeth; one to Leicester; one to William Cecil, Earl of Burghley; and one to Oxford, Hatton, and Sidney. Each section bears its own title page, dedication, and heraldic insignia. An earnest display of cultural self-fashioning, the work comprises both praise and opinion: sometimes rapturous, sometimes mildly sycophantic, sometimes politically incautious, and sometimes brilliantly adept.

Harvey's multiform work reflects the historical moment in his own life and in that of his nation. George L. Barnett's 1945 article identifies Harvey's poems to Sidney as concise and informed endorsements of Baldassare Castiglione's vision of the courtier as the exemplary model of courtesy, even when the Italian model conflicts with English humanist doctrine; Harvey's Sidney exemplifies this ideal of achieved courtesy. In his 1941 article

Thomas Hugh Jameson provides a contemporary historical context that makes more-radical claims about Harvey's political purpose. Jameson analyzes the apparent additions to Harvey's manuscript made between 30 July and 15 September 1578, during which time Protestants in the Low Countries suffered significant setbacks and emissaries of the duke of Alençon joined the English court at Audley End to offer the queen the duke's marriage proposal. The additions include an *Epilogus* to Elizabeth and the poems labeled *nova carmina* at the end of the sections addressed to Leicester and Burghley. In a critique of Machiavellian intrusion into English politics, Harvey intimates the danger, using popular anti-Machiavellian language to disguise his purpose while emphasizing the irony of the situation. "Machiavelli, that is, about whom there was this foolish hue and cry, was dead; but the people who were the real exemplars of his supposed methods were not only very much alive, but were seeking to gain entrance into England. Their ambassadors were even then at the English court!"

In his second *Epilogus* to the queen, Harvey depicts Italians forcing their way into the English court; and in the final poems to Leicester, Harvey presents three satires on Machiavelli. In the third Alençon becomes "the Florentine Mercury or Machiavelli's apotheosis." Finally, in the *Epilogus* to Burghley, Harvey remembers that the St. Bartholomew's Day Massacre had interrupted the previous de Medici suit for the queen's hand. Jameson wonders, finally, how Harvey got away with his temerity, proposing that Harvey perhaps escaped censure because he was subtle and because he was the first to protest the new match. The public and private implications of Harvey's anthology invite further study.

During late summer 1578 Harvey began preparing for the November expiration of his Pembroke fellowship. Having recently embarked on an intensive study of civil law, he sought a dispensation to forgo the expected study of divinity. Although supported by Leicester and William Fulke, master of Pembroke, Harvey was denied his request but soon found a new academic home at Trinity Hall, an appropriate place to study civil law; probably assisted by Henry Harvey, master of Trinity and perhaps a relative, Harvey was elected fellow on 18 December 1578.

Two days later he met Spenser in London, having perhaps not seen his friend since spring, when Harvey's early defender John Young had left Cambridge to become bishop of Rochester, taking Spenser with him as secretary. Spenser greeted the new Trinity fellow with gifts of jestbooks and satiric tales, in one of which (T. Murner's *Merry Jest of a Man Called Howleglas,* circa 1528) Harvey records the details of the event, which bespeak Spenser's jocose advice that the serious scholar and future doctor of law take an occasional vacation into lighter intellectual territory. Spenser also gave Harvey the jestbook of John Skoggin (circa 1480); the *Merry Tales* of John Skelton (1567); and *The Pleasant History of Lazarillo de Tormes* (1573), a translation of the famous Spanish picaresque prose romance. Spenser insisted that Harvey read these books by 1 January or surrender his four-volume edition of the works of Lucian. The sophisticated yet intimate intellectual play that characterizes this episode illustrates the quality of the public/private literary relationship between Harvey and Spenser during the following year and a half, which would see the pseudonymous publication of Spenser's *Shepheardes Calender* (1579) and the related publication of letters between the two friends.

When the *Shepheardes Calender* appeared with a dedication to Sidney in late 1579, it included, along with Spenser's twelve eclogues, a prefatory epistle to Harvey and extensive scholarly and mock-scholarly annotations by "E. K." Although often identified as Edward Kirke, a Pembroke contemporary of Harvey and Spenser, the actual identity of E. K. remains a puzzling and contested issue. In his 1945 biography of Spenser, Alexander C. Judson suggests that perhaps Spenser, Harvey, and Kirke worked together to prepare the book's editorial material, aiming "to mystify the public and to accomplish certain ends, such as stimulating interest in the works of Harvey and Spenser." Others have argued that E. K. may be Harvey's and Spenser's invented persona for their collaborative work on the volume's subtly allusive ancillary matter.

Two recent approaches to the issue, though differing in emphasis, support Harvey's active participation in Spenser's publishing event. S. K. Heninger Jr. identifies E. K.'s contributions almost exclusively as Harvey's, proposing that Harvey co-opted the publication in order to model the typographical layout of the *Calender* after the 1571 Venice edition of Jacob Sannazaro's *Arcadia,* with the explicit purpose of flattering and announcing allegiance to Sidney. In contrast, Louise Schleiner imagines Spenser and Harvey collaborating to write the epistle and to create a Harveyan persona in E. K., most of whose glosses Schleiner attributes to Spenser, who uses Harvey as "the conceived audience or model reader" for the whole work.

A recent entry in the debate, Louis Waldman's 1991 article, argues convincingly that Spenser observes a time-honored humanist convention by hellenizing his name as Edmundus Kedemon, employing the Greek for procurator, an extension of *spenser* as butler or steward. Whatever the case, Harvey's role in Spenser's *Calender* includes not only his part of the E. K. persona but also his identity with the fictional character Hobbinol, steadfast protector of pastoral safety and sanity and intimate friend of Colin, who has been purloined and perplexed by the enervating Rosalind, much to Hobbinol's distress. Hobbinol appears in the eclogues for January, April, June, and September, where E. K. reveals Spenser's identity as Colin and Harvey's as Hobbinol and lists several of Harvey's works, some of which are not extant. Hobbinol plays a similar role in Spenser's 1595 *Colin Clouts Come Home Againe.*

Following the publication of Spenser's *Calender,* Henry Bynneman, Harvey's publisher, entered in the Stationers' Register on 30 June 1580 and soon after printed a two-part volume of letters between Harvey and Spenser. The first part — *Three Proper, and Witty, Familiar Letters* — includes one letter by Spenser and two by Harvey composed in April 1580; the second — *Two Other, Very Commendable Letters* — includes one letter by each, composed in October 1579. If the prefatory "To the courteous buyer, by a wellwiller of the two authors" can be believed, the authors were not "privy to the publication," at least the first three letters being had "at the fourth or fifth hand . . . by means of a faithful friend, who with much entreaty had procured the copying of them out, at *Immerito's* hands"; the wellwiller hopes the authors are not displeased. Perhaps they were not, for the whole enterprise, hard on the heels of *The Shepheardes Calender* and consistent in tone and apparent purpose with that work's ancillary material, seems likely, behind the prefatory smokescreen and the transparent anonymity of Immerito and G. H., to have been a joint publishing venture, cautiously and ironically obfuscated before the ubiquitous public eye.

Whatever the case, here were letters between the "new poet" (from Westminster and Leicester House) and the most accomplished Latin poet in Cambridge, both moving on the edges of an elite Protestant literary group and both embarked on the composition of epic poems (Harvey's lost *Anti-cosmopolita* — entered in the Stationers' Register on 30 June 1579 — was, unlike *The Faerie Queene,* apparently never published, owing perhaps to the lack of

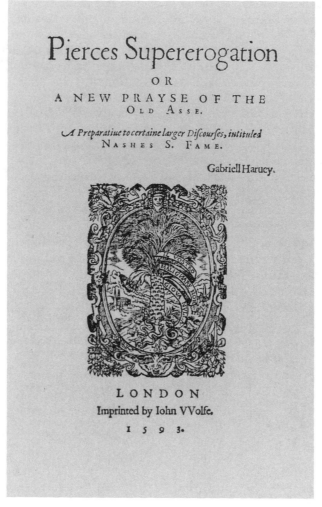

Title page for Harvey's response to Nashe's Strange News of
Intercepting Certain Letters *(1593), part of the
well-known Harvey-Nashe pamphlet war*

sought-after patronage from Leicester). Written in a
context of politico-religious controversy concerning
the proposed marriage of Elizabeth to the young
Catholic Duke of Alençon (mentioned only once,
implicitly, by Spenser as "that old great matter still
depending"), the letters record fascinating interper-
sonal engagement in an atmosphere of court politics, intellectual inquiry, and literary creation. For
practical purposes, the letters announce their authors' proposed publications, advertise their approaches to the Leicester-Sidney circle, and exploit
their verbal skills. The letters to Spenser may present Harvey at the height of his powers, still full of
relatively confident aspirations before being pulled
into the defensive posture that controversy, personality, and family loyalty stamped upon his later
works. In these letters, however, would-be court intellectuals create and rehearse part of the pulse of
their time.

Spenser's first letter, apparently the first composed, introduces the literary/cultural milieu at
Leicester House, where Sidney and Sir Edward
Dyer have "prescribed certain laws and rules of
quantities of English syllables for English verse";
thus, Spenser announces the avant-garde experiment in writing English verse in classical quantitative meter, a central topic of the letters. Additionally, he worries about the social risks of publication
and dedication; offers Harvey "a few *Iambics*" in English and a long Latin poem on the public fate of the
poet; asks Harvey to keep the verses relatively private; announces his imminent departure on a Continental mission for Leicester; and avers that
Harvey's quantitative verse experiments will be for-
warded to Sidney and Dyer.

In his answer, written from Trinity Hall
within ten days, Harvey encourages Spenser to
"tarry the tide" and publish, praises the literary ex-

periments of Sidney and Dyer, teases at inconsistencies in Spenser's trimeters, and discusses in detail technical matters of classical versification in English. Harvey doubts Spenser's immediate departure in Leicester's service but advises him, should he go abroad, to embody both Ulysses and Aeneas, both Minerva and Venus: "the politic head and wise government of the one, and the amiable behavior and gracious courtesy of the other." These letters, published at the back of the volume, being "more lately delivered unto the printer," create a comprehensive general introduction or an uncontroversial conclusion.

Spenser's opening letter of the volume encourages Harvey to publish; mentions the earthquake of 6 April 1580; praises Harvey's English hexameters; refers to discussion of literary particulars with Sidney, Dyer, and Thomas Drant (author of certain syllabic rules); and names several of Spenser's unpublished works, including his *Dreames,* with E. K.'s extensive glosses. This brief letter introduces Harvey's two long and biographically significant ones. The first, his so-called earthquake letter, includes one of his most delightful pieces of writing, a humorous and ironic display of rhetorical skill in the best contemporary Erasmian/Ramist neohumanist idiom. When the earthquake hit, Harvey writes, he was playing cards with some men and women in Essex. At first, he jestingly blames the disturbance on the incessant "wrangling" of the women, then on someone moving something upstairs, then, after receiving word that the turbulence was widespread, on an earthquake indeed. The women begin praying, and one of the men asks Harvey what the scholars at Cambridge have to say about earthquakes. In answer, Harvey produces a mock-scholarly discourse parodying the opinions of some Cambridge natural scientists, according to whom the earth, encumbered by prodigious spring rains, belches and vomits its way toward sobriety. Harvey enlivens his satiric discourse with bits of silly superstition and pseudoscholarly technical terminology. In the face of the ladies' pronounced skepticism about this "great doctorly learning," one of the gentlemen elicits Harvey's serious opinion on the natural or supernatural source of the earth's spasm. "Master H.'s short, but sharp and learned judgment of earthquakes" follows, a careful and comprehensive Ramist analysis employing strict Aristotelian logical divisions between the material and formal internal causes and the efficient and final external causes. Impatient with superstition and sectarian religious propaganda, as evidenced in earthquake pamphlets and sermons advertising God's wrath and exhorting

the populace to repent, Harvey presents a scientifically progressive natural explanation, noting that God's absolute place as final cause need not, indeed must not, cancel more-immediate terrestrial causes.

Harvey's letter continues with some words about his literary work and then a detailed and satiric discussion of what is and is not being read at Cambridge. Near the end of the letter he hurls a series of caustic epithets at his unnamed but easily identified enemy, Dr. Andrew Perne, who had recently undermined Harvey's candidacy for public orator at Cambridge. A postscript instructs Spenser to show the letter only to Sidney and Dyer. In his final letter Harvey discusses quantitative verse, offers several examples, and evaluates Spenser's literary works, issuing his famous judgment on the piece of *The Faerie Queene* he had seen — that in it Spenser had allowed "Hobgoblin [to] run away with the garland from *Apollo.*"

The letters brought Harvey trouble from various quarters. His satiric portraits incensed Cambridge authorities, initiating the author's formal apology to the university. More immediately damaging, his contemptuous and slightly veiled attacks on Perne could only intensify the latter's enmity, which emerged in various ways once Perne became vice chancellor of Cambridge early in 1581. Perne was not the only one angry about the attack, however: because Harvey had referred to Perne as Spenser's "old Controller," Sir James Crofte, powerful controller of the queen's household, mistakenly saw himself as the object of abuse until someone, perhaps Mildmay, cleared up the misunderstanding.

An additional aspect of the controversy involved one of Harvey's English verse experiments, a satire on the Italianate gentleman titled "Speculum Tuscanismi," which, apparently at the instigation of John Lyly, was perceived by the irascible Edward de Vere, Earl of Oxford, as a personal attack. Harvey seems to have been successful in convincing Oxford otherwise, or, more likely, Oxford had more pressing concerns and more dangerous libelers to pursue than Harvey. In all probability, Oxford was the object of Harvey's "bold satirical libel," for the author, ever a ready and even indiscreet defender of Sidney, must have had in mind the recent tennis-court quarrel between Sidney and Oxford over the French marriage, during which Oxford called Sidney a "puppy." Whatever the truth in this matter, Harvey's later life makes clear that the significant actor in this little drama was Lyly, not Oxford. The incident may be seen as the first act in Harvey's protracted and debilitating quarrel with a group of London professional writers including Lyly, Robert Greene, Thomas Nashe, and, marginally, Christopher Marlowe.

Harvey's troubles over his letters to Spenser failed to stymie his being chosen to succeed the latter as Leicester's secretary after Spenser left for Ireland with Lord Grey in late summer 1580. As might be expected, however, Harvey did not stay long at court, his ostentatious dress and behavior, according to Nashe, moving Leicester to tell him "he was fitter for the university than for the court or his turn." Returning to Cambridge in late 1580 to resume his legal studies, Harvey soon found himself publicly parodied in the witty Latin play *Pedantius,* performed at Cambridge on 6 February 1581, which mercilessly satirized him in the title character. The play depicts the aspiring humanist Ciceronian pedant making his way through Castiglione and Ramus, failing as lover and courtier and reduced to selling his beautifully annotated library to meet financial obligations. Harvey seems to have endured this social embarrassment in silence, reconciled to his reputation as a brilliant but awkward nonconformist intellectual and inured to the reactionary prejudices of certain university associates, who clearly both scorned and envied his moderate but sustained academic success.

In May 1583 Harvey was appointed to a vacancy in the office of the university proctor but, because of Perne's machinations, was denied his expected place as master of Trinity Hall following the death of Henry Harvey in February 1585. For some reason, he was not inaugurated at Cambridge after being granted his LL.B. on 10 July 1584; rather, he was incepted doctor of civil law at Oxford on 12 July 1585, given a medical fellowship at Pembroke from 1584 to 1585, and incorporated doctor of civil and canon law at Oxford on 10 July 1586.

Meanwhile, Harvey faced renewed controversy after the publication in 1583 of his brother Richard's *Astrological Discourse upon the Conjunction of Saturn and Jupiter* and his brother John's *Astrological Addition,* both prognosticating dire events for 28 April 1583 and both addressed to Gabriel. Upon the nonappearance of cataclysmic events, the Harvey brothers were duly satirized in print. Gabriel, appropriately learned in astrology but consistently skeptical, nonetheless came to the defense of his brothers, taking his first reluctant step away from independence and into the maelstrom of family loyalty that would come to consume his literary career, if not his intellectual energies.

The scope of abuse soon widened to include satiric insinuations about the elder John Harvey's

honorable trade: in Giordano Bruno's *Cena de la ceneri* (1584) and later in John Florio's *Second Fruits* (1591), Gabriel appears as the pedant fool Torquato amid allusions to the twisting requisite to ropemaking and, supremely insulting, to the ropemaker's supplying the hangman, a connection exploited by Harvey's later antagonists. Richard Harvey stilled his pen for a while, and Gabriel got on with his life, serving a relatively unsuccessful tenure as advocate at the ecclesiastical Court of Arches, befriending the knowledgeable Paracelsian apothecary John Hester, and contributing three Latin poems to a Cambridge commemorative volume to Sidney, *Academiae Cantabrigiensis lachrymae,* published in February 1587.

Having been dormant for several years, the storm of abuse again began to break over the heads of the Harveys in 1589, when Nashe's dedication to his *Anatomy of Absurdity* deplored Ramist logic and Lyly's *Pap with a Hatchet* (1589), an anti-Martinist tract addressed "To the Father and the two Sons, Huffe, Ruffe, and Snuffe," resurrected Gabriel's libels in his earthquake letter and irresponsibly named him "notable coach companion for Martin." Lyly's piece, which lured the Harveys into the Marprelate controversy, was probably commissioned by the bishops, who enlisted sympathetic or merely ambitious professional writers to compose against the Puritan pamphlets of the pseudonymous Martin Marprelate.

In response to Lyly, Harvey wrote *An Advertisement for Pap-Hatchet and Martin Marprelate,* a defense against personal attacks and an objective discourse on religious controversy, dated 5 November 1589 but not published until 1593. Brother Richard soon chimed in, calling for peaceful reconciliation between the Martinist parties while attacking the anti-Martinists in his *Plain Percival* (1590) and *A Theological Discourse of the Lamb of God and His Enemies* (1590). Richard's prefatory epistle to the *Lamb of God* attacks the twenty-two-year-old Nashe for his presumptuous censure of such writers as Sir Thomas More, Roger Ascham, Thomas Watson, and Gabriel Harvey in his preface to Greene's *Menaphon.*

Richard Harvey's gratuitous deprecation of Nashe might represent the immediate cause of what would become the Harvey-Nashe quarrel, an archetypal late-Elizabethan battle of words between members of two middle-class literary groups. On one side stood the Harvey brothers — Gabriel the doctor of law, Richard the clergyman, and John the medical doctor — whose university training had led them to positions in the mainstream culture. On the other side stood the "university wits," who left the main-

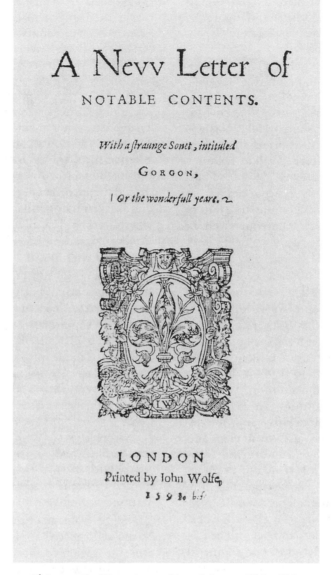

A Nevv Letter of

NOTABLE CONTENTS.

With a straunge Sonet, intituled

GORGON,

Or the wonderfull yeare.

LONDON

Printed by Iohn Wolfe,

1 5 9 3.

*Title page for Harvey's pamphlet epistle to publisher John
Wolfe, the writer's last entry in the quarrel with Nashe*

stream to join the first generation of London professional writers.

Robert Greene, the most prolific and notorious member of the latter group, entered the fray in July 1592 when he published *A Quip for an Upstart Courtier; or, A Quaint Dispute between Velvet Breeches and Cloth Breeches,* which included, before the passage was excised after the first issue of the first edition, a satiric portrait of John Harvey and his three sons. The episode depicts an encounter between the narrator and the ropemaker, who is on his way to visit his three sons in Cambridge: one, a clergyman, kisses his parishioners' wives; another, a physician, ruined his reputation by advertising astrological predictions; and the eldest, a "wondrous-witted" doctor, helped initiate the ill-fated poetic experiments in classical meter and was "clapped in the Fleet" for libels in his letters. The ropemaker concludes that "honest parents may have bad children," to which an attendant collier responds that the ropemaker cannot be honest because his mother must have been a witch, for just as witches say their prayers backward, so the ropemaker works backward – backing up along the ropewalk as he twists the strands of hemp – creating "fatal instruments."

Harvey was incensed; not only was Greene's assertion that Harvey had been imprisoned (by Crofte) probably a lie and his scurrilous abuse of the father's trade deeply hurtful, but brother John had died suddenly in July, before *A Quip* appeared.

Gabriel, as executor, was embroiled in a bitter quarrel with his brother's widow, Martha, daughter of the wealthy Justice Thomas Meade, over the dispensation of her husband's estate.

As a consequence of legal difficulties with Martha Harvey or hoping to take his own legal actions against Greene, Harvey was probably in London soon after Nashe published his *Pierce Penniless His Supplication to the Devil* in August 1592. Nashe's lengthy satire on Elizabethan life and on the lack of financial support afforded literary talent includes several attacks on Richard Harvey. Provoked and disturbed, Gabriel took up his fighting pen in defense of himself and his family, composing letters during August and September that appeared in print in December 1592 (after Greene's death on 5 December) as *Four Letters and Certain Sonnets, Especially Touching Robert Greene.*

The volume opens with a short letter by Harvey's Saffron Walden friend Christopher Bird, who recommends Harvey to his London merchant friend Demetrius and closes with satiric words on *A Quip* and a damning sonnet about Greene. In the second letter Harvey rehearses to Bird his doings in London, including a detailed account of Greene's wretched death and its ignominious aftermath; additionally, he discourses on the relative appropriateness of satiric invective among authors ancient and modern. In the long third and shorter fourth letters, written 8–11 September and addressed to every favorable or indifferent reader, Harvey defends himself and his family, advises the talented Nashe to go straight, celebrates contemporary literary figures, and humbly admits his own human frailty. The last part of the volume includes twenty-two "Funeral Sonnets," Harvey's memorial to Greene, and a varied collection of slurs on Greene and praise of notable persons. Spenser's encomiastic sonnet to Harvey concludes the volume.

From September 1592 to April 1593, amid a serious outbreak of the plague, Harvey most probably lived on the premises of the London stationer and printer John Wolfe, employed as reader and copy editor. Nashe had left the city, but in January 1593 John Danter printed *Strange News of the Intercepting Certain Letters,* Nashe's response to Harvey's *Four Letters.* The pamphlet is a defense of Greene and an attack on Harvey in Nashe's inimitably witty colloquial style. Harvey answered with *Pierce's Supererogation,* dated 27 April 1593 though probably not published until October.

Harvey divides his rambling, stylistically elaborate, and sometimes obscure discourse into three parts, each about seventy pages in the original edi-

tion. In the first part he complains that he would rather be engaged in his own studies than writing against Nashe, refutes specific charges, and labels Nashe "St. Fame," who will do anything for money and notoriety. The second part is Harvey's 1589 attack on Lyly, *An Advertisement for Pap-Hatchet.* In the third part Harvey exploits his broad learning to construct enigmatical retorts and digressions that challenge Nashe – here named Braggadoccio – to respond if he dare; additionally, he presents an Erasmian encomium to the ass, Nashe's favorite epithet for Harvey, and introduces with high praise a learned gentlewoman who is prepared to write against Nashe. Prefatory and appended to the text are commendatory letters and sonnets by Barnabe Barnes, John Thorius, and Anthony Chute, three young writers associated with Wolfe.

During the summer of 1593, in a fit of repentant religiosity reminiscent of Greene, Nashe wrote *Christ's Tears over Jerusalem,* a call for Londoners to repent, lest their sinful behavior bring down their city as that of the Jews had brought down Jerusalem. In the spirit of the work, Nashe's prefatory epistle includes contrite and complimentary remarks to Harvey and a general farewell to satire and misspent hours. Soon after *Christ's Tears* appeared in early September, Harvey wrote *A New Letter of Notable Contents,* dated 16 September 1593 and published, perhaps concurrently with *Pierce's Supererogation,* soon after 1 October, when it was entered by Wolfe in the Stationers' Register.

The twenty-six-page epistle to Wolfe treats Nashe's purported apology as ironic hyperbole and presents a learned discourse on literary and philosophical value, concluding that Nashe remains a victim of timely advantage and immediate gratification, the ravages of myopic ambition. Appended to the text is some dynamic and complex topical poetry by Harvey, beginning with the sonnet "*Gorgon*; or, The Wonderful Year," in which Saint Fame, poised to "connycatch the world" in 1593, finds his ambition dwarfed by more-notable events on the Continent and in London, where Marlowe's "sky-surmounting breath" had been extinguished. Warning Nashe to "Beware the next bull-beggar of the town," Harvey bids a welcome adieu to the protracted war of words, which had probably been both exhilarating and enervating.

Although intermediaries perhaps sought peace between the parties in late 1593, Nashe published a scathing renewed attack on Harvey in his revised preface to the second edition of *Christ's Tears* in 1594 and refused any reconciliation when the two antagonists occupied adjacent rooms at the Dolphin in Cambridge in late 1595. Late in 1596, Nashe published his magnum opus on Harvey: *Have with You to Saffron-Walden; or, Gabriel Harvey's Hunt Is Up.* Nashe is at his witty best in this thorough satiric biography of Harvey, most of which, given allowance for exaggeration, is probably factually accurate. Harvey and Nashe apparently published nothing more against each other, but Nashe received one final whipping in print. In a railing epistle, Nashe had dedicated *Have with You* to Richard Lichfield, a barber at Trinity College, Cambridge. Lichfield's response, a violently abusive attack on Nashe (sometimes dubiously attributed to Harvey), was published in 1597 as *The Trimming of Thomas Nashe, Gentleman, by the High-Titled Patron Don Ricardo de Medico Campo, Barber Surgeon to Trinity College in Cambridge.*

Although Nashe mentions in his 1599 *Lenten Stuff* that he planned to publish an answer to *The Trimming,* he never got the chance because Harvey and Nashe were silenced by fiat on 4 June 1599. On that date Archbishop Whitgift and Bishop Bancroft, the official licensers of the press, ordered a wide-ranging, and therefore ultimately vain, confiscation and censorship of books. The decree, entered at Stationers' Hall, forbade the printing of satires, epigrams, plays, and unsanctioned English histories. The texts ordered to be confiscated, burned, and not published included, in addition to all works by Harvey and Nashe, John Marston's *Pygmalion,* Marlowe's translation of Ovid's *Amours,* Joseph Hall's satires, John Davies's epigrams, and the *Caltha Poetarum.* Despite the ban, Nashe published *Summer's Last Will and Testament,* a comic play, in 1600; he died in 1601 at about age thirty-four.

Harvey, meanwhile, had retired to Saffron Walden following his father's death in July 1593, living either with his mother, who was buried on 14 April 1613, or at another of his family's properties. He made one more bid for an academic position when he unsuccessfully sought to become master of Trinity Hall upon the death of Thomas Preston in 1598, but he was, by this time, probably comfortable in his quiet life in Saffron Walden, where he apparently remained until his death. During those years Harvey continued his studies, provided legal and medical advice to local citizens, and occasionally visited Cambridge and London.

His quiet life was interrupted in 1608 when his sister Mary, who had married in 1600, brought suit against him for nonpayment to her of sixty pounds stipulated in her father's will to be paid within four years. Harvey failed to respond, a negligence that,

according to Irving Ribner's research into Chancery Court records, branded Harvey a wanted man by late 1608. Whether he paid up, hid out in Saffron Walden, went to prison, or finally traveled to the Continent is not known, for nothing more about the controversy is extant and, as Stern points out, there is no solid evidence about Harvey's life for the following twenty years. Richard Harvey died in June 1630, and Gabriel was made executor, only to die himself on 7 February 1631, leaving no will; his sister Alice Lyon was appointed to administer his estate.

Harvey's most cherished possession, his enormous and comprehensive library, was probably sold piecemeal after his death. According to Stern's estimate, Harvey owned close to thirty-five hundred volumes in 1596, with thirty-four years of collecting ahead of him. In comparison, Cambridge University Library contained 457 books and manuscripts in 1582, and John Dee's celebrated library contained, he estimated in 1583, close to four thousand volumes. Moreover, Harvey annotated most of his books with marginalia that span his adult lifetime: from 1565, when he entered Cambridge, to 1626, when he was seventy-six. Harvey's marginalia, predominantly in Latin but often in English and occasionally in Greek, Italian, French, or Spanish, are written in his several beautiful hands. They record studied observations on varying topics, including Harvey's remarks on personal aspirations toward the ideals enshrined in his beloved books; as such, they present one of the most intimate surviving portraits of an English Renaissance figure.

Several twentieth-century scholars have investigated Harvey's annotated books, and study has accelerated in recent years. G. C. Moore Smith published a limited but trenchant selection of marginalia in 1913; Harold S. Wilson published further informed commentary in 1948; and Virginia F. Stern in 1979 catalogued and analyzed marginalia from 180 of Harvey's books, fixing a location on 129 of them. More recently, Lisa Jardine and Anthony Grafton have situated some of Harvey's marginalia in a context of English Renaissance reading habits, concluding that his annotations sometimes record work as a scholar-reader for several notable persons; for instance, they identify Harvey's readings of his folio Livy with Thomas Smith Jr. in 1571, Philip Sidney in 1577, and Thomas Preston, master of Trinity Hall, in 1584, in addition to private reading and commentary. Stern classifies Harvey's marginalia in categories that indicate the broad range of his learning: oratory and eloquent written expression, history and politics,

Notes by Harvey on the blank final page in his copy of D. Ioachi Mi Hopperi Frisii, I. C. Eqvitis
Avrati *(1530; British Library)*

modern languages, gentlemanly learning (manners, horsemanship, and martial strategy), jurisprudence, cosmology and other sciences and pseudosciences, medicine, literature, and philosophical outlook and personal observation. Harvey signified references to these and other topics by using at least seventeen conventional and personal abbreviations, symbols, and astrological signs.

Furthermore, and most remarkably, Harvey created six personae that constitute his portrait of himself in roles embodying his private aspirations to competence and fulfillment. Axiophilus represents the poet, the "lover of the worthwhile"; Angelus Furius, the Italianate Harvey, is "angelic in speech and a fury in action"; Eutrapelus, the most frequent persona, portrays the "eloquent orator, teacher of rhetoric, persuasive man in speech (and in writing) and one who engages in witty jesting and very often in irony"; Eudromus is "the pragmatic, hurrying competitive man of the world . . . constantly striving to excel"; Chrystechus refers to "the man with the golden skill" in a field, most often law; and Euscopius, a persona of Harvey's later years, represents "the sharp-sighted man" whose rational comprehension enables him to prosper amid disappointment.

Harvey's personae appear most abundantly in a thick octavo Italian volume of sententious sayings including the last quarter of Lodovico Domenichi's *Facetie, motti, et burle, di diversi signori et persone private* (1571), an added book by Thomoso Porcacchi (1574), and Ludovico Guicciardini's *Detti et Fatti* (1571). Between the late 1570s and at least 1608, Harvey filled the wide margins of this volume with annotations. The commentary attributed to the various personae celebrates personal achievements and records earnest exhortations to embrace contentment in the face of failure. Had it been written for publication, this commentary would appear vainly self-deceptive; but, in its strictly private context, Harvey's self-analysis records his ingenuous psychotherapeutic excursions into his own vulnerabilities. Taken in their entirety, Harvey's copious marginalia stand as testimony to the broad learning and extraordinary self-awareness of this singular and eminent Renaissance intellectual.

Harvey seldom received praise from his pre-twentieth-century biographers. Rather, influenced by Nashe's satiric portrait of an arrogant, ambitious, obnoxious, and pitiable pseudolearned son of a ropemaker, most early biographers — themselves scholars and academics — flattered themselves by embracing the notorious, gifted, and apparently avant-garde Nashe. Theirs is an incomplete and pa-

rodic representation of the Harvey his friends knew — the smart, loyal, witty, and self-revealing teacher and scholar. Although a few pernicious enemies made Harvey's life more difficult than it might have been, some of his friends preserved the memory of his best self. Among words of praise from his contemporaries, those of Sir William Bird, a prominent Saffron Walden resident, stand out as exemplary and compare favorably with Spenser's portraits of Harvey and Hobbinol. Harvey reiterates the words of his friend in marginalia to Guicciardini as if they were addressed to his Axiophilus persona. If these are not Bird's exact words, they are surely close, and they depict the person to whom Harvey aspired: "I never saw that man angry, never sad, never fearful, never irresolute, never unmindful of himself or others, never thrown into confusion on any occasion. I have not known a man more mindful of kindnesses or more forgetful of injuries; I do not know anyone whose principles and actions emanate so much from himself."

Virtually alone in the nineteenth century as one who acknowledged this view of Harvey, Henry Morley, in his short 1871 essay, wrote vehemently against the received opinion of "the encyclopedists." Morley emphasizes Harvey's friendly connections with Sidney and Spenser, his lack of shame about his class and heritage, his less-than-enthusiastic reception of his brother Richard's unfortunate astrological projections for 1583, his skeptical response to earthquakes, and his understandable but — given Greene's death — untimely entrance into his quarrel with the professional writers. Morley knew he was up against strongly received opinion: "Hardly a definite fact has been stated, real or imaginary, which has not had a turn given to it unfavorable to the good name of this much misrepresented scholar."

Such misrepresentation, which persists in some quarters to this day, climaxes clamorously in Alexander B. Grosart's scathing portrait of Harvey in his 1884 edition of the author's works. Grosart opens by disparaging Harvey's latest defender, Edward Long John Scott, who acknowledges Harvey's better qualities in his 1884 edition of the *Letter-Book*. Grosart proceeds to traduce Harvey with palpable contempt for most of his eighty pages of biographical and critical introduction. But here and there, amid the attack, Grosart forces himself to recognize the most obvious and persistent bits of information on Harvey's behalf, such as his close friendships with Sidney and Spenser.

Grosart also admits that Harvey's "English books in warfare with Greene and Nashe have a certain go to them, a certain vigor, a dexterous, apt-worded, wary fence, and . . . an astounding vocabulary." Of Harvey's Latin oratory, Grosart concedes "technical scholarship, and a certain elegance of composition," a combination that "drew about him crowds of undergraduates, and won him praise as a lecturer." Indeed, Grosart cannot deny the "brilliance in thought and (rhetorical) expression" of Harvey's *Ciceronianus*, and he recognizes Harvey's expertise in Latin poetry, even to the point of suggesting that Harvey's verse celebration of Sidney would reward study.

But such concessions to Harvey's gifts exist within a torrent of abuse aimed partly at Morley's "pugnacious 'Apology'" but primarily at what Grosart views as Harvey's unforgivable moral failure: with "self-conceit so malignant and malignancy so self-conceited," Harvey libeled the dead Greene, Marlowe, and Perne. Of Harvey's defense of himself and his family against Greene's attack, Grosart asserts that "nothing viler, baser, more heartless, exists in our language." He concludes that "His learning was heavy, but not solid . . . his 'rhetoric' magniloquent rather than eloquent; his verse fluent and smooth, but without inspiration; his temperament, vain, cantankerous, malignant; his long life a melancholy failure; his books a tomb, not a monument. I would not, however, leave the friend of Edmund Spenser blamable and despised merely."

During the early twentieth century, Harvey's reputation began a slow ascent, exemplified in the evenhanded and occasionally laudatory descriptions of him in Ronald B. McKerrow's 1904 edition of Nashe's works and in G. C. Moore Smith's 1913 selective edition of Harvey's marginalia. McKerrow, in addition to providing a superb concise review of the Harvey-Nashe quarrel, offers an enduring sketch of Harvey. Moore Smith's portrait depicts Harvey as "the man of the Italian Renaissance: the man who aims at universal knowledge; who can sympathize with the intellectual detachment of Machiavelli and the audacious license of Aretine; who yet would make scholarship a means rather than an end." While Alexander C. Judson, in his 1945 biography of Spenser for the *Variorum*, counterpoises his praise of Harvey with a throwback to nineteenth-century appraisals, Harold S. Wilson, in his introduction to a translation of the *Ciceronianus* in the same year, admits Harvey's personal limitations without damning him and calls him "one of the most learned men of his age."

Most subsequent biographical notices of Harvey follow suit; two stand out. In his 1956 investigation of the contemporary background of Shakespeare's *Love's Labor's Lost*, W. Schrickx exposes fas-

cinating corners of Harvey's expertise and influence, concluding that Harvey "may perhaps lay claim to Coleridge's famous epithet 'myriad-minded,' so diverse were his interests and so engrossed was his attention by all contemporary currents of thought. Alchemy, medicine, emblems, astronomy and astrology, botany, rhetoric, education, mathematics, philosophy, all these were Harvey's province." Virginia F. Stern, in her 1979 biography, which includes an introduction to Harvey's library and marginalia, adds languages, jurisprudence, chemistry, pharmacology, and navigation to Harvey's areas of expertise. While she admits that *sprezzatura* "seems to have been alien to Harvey's nature," she strenuously defends and celebrates him at every turn, rendering a portrait that his friends would probably have applauded as a worthy tribute to the man they knew. This is the man who, in his 1578 Latin poem about the queen's remarking on his Italianate good looks, echoes mock-heroically Virgil's protest against Aeneas's seemingly unjust treatment at the hands of the gods and concludes by giving himself some sound advice that remained an ideal and a warning for the rest of his life:

(Nor will it pain me to record the verse
Sung by Apollo as he plucked my ear:
Oh, may I always recollect his warning)
"Don't credit more what others say of thee
Than what thyself dost say unto thyself."
    – translation by Grosart

Letters:
The Works of Edmund Spenser: A Variorum Edition, volume 9, edited by Edwin Greenlaw and others (Baltimore: Johns Hopkins University Press, 1932–1957), pp. 1–18, 441–477;
Spenser: Poetical Works, edited by J. C. Smith and E. de Selincourt (London: Oxford University Press, 1966), pp. 609–643.

Bibliography:
The Works of Thomas Nashe, volume 5, edited by Ronald B. McKerrow (London: Sidgwick & Jackson, 1910), pp. 163–175.

Biography:
Virginia F. Stern, *Gabriel Harvey: His Life, Marginalia, and Library* (Oxford: Clarendon Press, 1979), pp. 3–134.

References:
Warren B. Austin, "Gabriel Harvey's 'Lost' *Ode* on Ramus," *Modern Language Notes*, 61 (April 1946): 242–247;

George L. Barnett, "Gabriel Harvey's *Castilio, sive Aulicus* and *De Aulica*: A Study of Their Place in the Literature of Courtesy," *Studies in Philology,* 42 (January 1945): 146–163;

Josephine Waters Bennett, "Spenser and Gabriel Harvey's *Letter-Book,*" *Modern Philology,* 29 (August 1931): 163–186;

Jonathan Goldberg, "Colin to Hobbinol: Spenser's Familiar Letters," *South Atlantic Quarterly,* 88 (Winter 1989): 107–126;

Edward George Harman, *Gabriel Harvey and Thomas Nashe* (London: Ouseley, 1923);

S. K. Heninger Jr., "The Typographical Layout of Spenser's *Shepheardes Calender,*" in *Word and Visual Imagination: Studies in the Interaction of English Literature and the Visual Arts,* edited by Karl Josef Höltgen, Peter M. Daly, and Wolfgang Lottes (Erlangen: Universitie-Bibliothek Erlanger-Nurnberg, 1988), pp. 33–71;

Thomas Hugh Jameson, "The 'Machiavellianism' of Gabriel Harvey," *PMLA,* 56 (September 1941): 645–656;

Lisa Jardine, "Humanism and Dialectic in Sixteenth-Century Cambridge: A Preliminary Investigation," in *Classical Influences on European Culture A.D. 1500–1700,* edited by R. R. Bolgar (London: Cambridge University Press, 1976), pp. 141–154;

Jardine and Anthony Grafton, "'Studied for Action': How Gabriel Harvey Read His Livy," *Past and Present,* 29 (November 1990): 30–78;

David C. McPherson, "Aretino and the Harvey-Nashe Quarrel," *PMLA,* 84 (October 1969): 1551–1558;

Edwin Haviland Miller, "Deletions in Robert Greene's *A Quip for an Upstart Courtier (1592),*" *Huntington Library Quarterly,* 15 (Winter 1951–1952): 277–282;

Henry Morley, "Gabriel Harvey," in his *Clément Marot and Other Studies,* 2 volumes (Geneva: Slatkine Reprints, 1970), 2: 229–247;

Irving Ribner, "Gabriel Harvey in Chancery — 1608," *Review of English Studies,* 2 (April 1951): 142–147;

Louise Schleiner, "Spenser's 'E.K.' as Edmund Kent (Kenned/of Kent): Kyth (Couth), Kissed, and Kunning-Conning," *English Literary Renaissance,* 20 (Autumn 1990): 374–407;

W. Schrickx, *Shakespeare's Early Contemporaries: The Background of the Harvey-Nashe Polemic and "Love's Labour's Lost"* (Antwerp: De Nederlandsche Boekhandel, 1956);

Gerald Snare, "Satire, Logic, and Rhetoric in Harvey's Earthquake Letter to Spenser," *Tulane Studies in English,* 18 (1970): 17–33;

Louis Waldman, "Spenser's Pseudonym 'E. K.' and Humanist Self-Naming," *Spenser Studies,* 9 (1991): 21–31;

Harold S. Wilson, "Gabriel Harvey's Method of Annotating His Books," *Harvard Library Bulletin,* 2 (Autumn 1948): 344–361;

Wilson, "Gabriel Harvey's Orations on Rhetoric," *English Literary History,* 12 (September 1945): 167–182;

Wilson, Introduction to Harvey's *Ciceronianus,* translated by Wilson, Studies in the Humanities 4 (Lincoln: University of Nebraska Press, 1945), pp. 1–34.

Papers:

Harvey's letters to John Young, Humphrey Tyndale, and his father, along with drafts of letters to Spenser, personal notes, transcriptions of poetic juvenilia, and other biographical documents from the years 1573 to 1580, are preserved in British Library Sloane Manuscript 93; the British Library also holds a commonplace book by Harvey (Additional Manuscript 32,494), and a manuscript of a poem by Harvey to Lord Burghley (Lansdowne Manuscript 120, folio 12). Cambridge University Library holds several letters (Baker Manuscript 36, pp. 107–14). Virginia F. Stern has identified the location of 129 volumes containing Harvey's marginalia: 29 are in the British Library; 13 in the Houghton; 10 in the Folger; 8 each in the Huntington and the Bodleian; 7 at the Rosenbach Foundation; 4 in the Newberry; 14 in collections at Cambridge; 10 in collections at Oxford; 15 in private collections; and 11 in other libraries.

Raphael Holinshed

(died 1580)

Emily E. Stockard
Florida Atlantic University

BOOK: *The Chronicles of England, Scotlande, and Irelande,* 2 volumes (London: Printed by Henry
Bynneman for J. Harrison, 1577); enlarged as
*The First and Second Volumes of Chronicles. (The
Third Volume.) Newlie Augmented and Continued by
J. Hooker Alias Vowell Gent. and Others,* 3 volumes (London: Printed by Henry Denham, at
the expenses of J. Harison, G. Bishop, R. Newberie, H. Denham, and T. Woodcocke, 1587).

Editions: *Holinshed's Chronicles of England, Scotland,
and Ireland,* 6 volumes (London: Printed for J.
Johnson; F. C. & J. Rivington; T. Payne;
Wilkie and Robinson; Longman, Hurst, Rees,
& Orme; Cadel & Davies; and J. Mawson,
1807);

*Shakespeare's Holinshed: The Chronicle and the History
Plays Compared,* edited by W. G. Boswell-Stone
(London: Laurence & Bullen, 1896);

Holinshed's Chronicles as Used in Shakespeare's Plays, edited by Allardyce and Josephine Nicoll (Lon-
don: Dent, 1927; New York: Dutton, 1959);

*Shakespeare's Holinshed: An Edition of "Holinshed's
Chronicles," 1587; Source of Shakespeare's History
Plays, "King Lear," "Cymbeline," and "Macbeth,"*
edited by Richard Hosley (New York: Capri-
corn Books, 1968);

Holinshed's Irish Chronicle, edited by Liam Miller and
Eileen Power (Atlantic Highlands, N.J.: Humanities Press, 1979).

Although Raphael Holinshed led a life remarkable for its obscurity, he was the overseer and
primary compiler of the first continuous and authoritative narrative account of British history written in the vernacular. *The Chronicles of England, Scotland, and Ireland,* or *Holinshed's Chronicles,* as the work
has come to be known, was first published in 1577.
An expression of national pride, the chronicle genre
flourished during the Tudor period and satisfied a
growing interest in English history. Chronicles
characteristically attempted to provide all available
information and borrowed outright from other historians, often other chroniclers. As C. S. Lewis describes the tradition in his *English Literature in the Sixteenth Century* (1954), "The 'English story' is a sort of
national stock-pot permanently simmering to which
each new cook adds flavouring at his discretion."
Holinshed's version represents the culmination of
this tradition. His work is also distinguished by its
association with William Shakespeare, who used
the augmented 1587 edition (published after Holinshed's death and sometimes referred to as
"Shakespeare's Holinshed") as source material for
thirteen of his plays.

Raphael Holinshed is thought to have been the
son of Ralph Holinshed of Sutton Downes, Cheshire.
School records indicate that he may have been educated at Christ's College, Cambridge, where a certain
Holinshed matriculated in May 1544 and resided as a
scholar until 1545. According to Anthony à Wood's
Athenae Oxonienses (1691–1692), Holinshed then became "a minister of God's word" (as perhaps was
his father). During the 1560s — the early years of
Elizabeth I's reign — he began to work as a translator in the London printing office of Reginald
Wolfe, printer to the queen, to whom Holinshed
in his dedication says he was "singularly be-
holden." It was in Wolfe's shop that Holinshed
undertook the project that would bear his name.

Around 1548, with the patronage of Archbishop Thomas Cranmer, Wolfe had designed a
work that displayed the fondness for monumental
all-inclusiveness typical of sixteenth-century English literary endeavors. Planning to assemble a universal history and cosmography complete with
maps and illustrations, he began with the notes of
antiquarian and historian John Leland. When
Wolfe died in 1573, after twenty-five years of work

on the project, Holinshed continued it under the direction of publishers George Bishop, John Harrison, and Lucas Harrison, who reduced its scope to histories and descriptions of England, Scotland, and Ireland. Even so, the project's size demanded a collective rather than individual effort, and the contributors saw themselves primarily as translators, compilers, and editors rather than authors. Although William Harrison and Richard Stanyhurst aided in the writing and compilation, *The Chronicles of England, Scotland, and Ireland* was published in 1577 under the name of Raphael Holinshed.

A brief description gives a sense of the size, scope, and spirit of this work. The first edition comprises two folio-sized volumes, each about sixteen hundred pages in length, printed in double columns of black-letter Gothic type and well illustrated with woodcuts of much-described activities (battles, hangings, and murders) and historical figures. This feature gives the first edition a sophisticated graphic presentation that subsequent editions lack. Even though it was much reduced from Wolfe's original plan, the *Chronicles* had in its time a reputation as an exceptionally bulky work. When satirist Thomas Nashe (not a friend of chroniclers) sought to impress his readers with the amount of space necessary to recount the history of the red herring, he claimed it would "require as massy a tomb [i.e., tome] as Holinshed."

The first volume of the *Chronicles* is divided into three parts, devoted in order to England, Scotland, and Ireland, each containing first a description and then a history of that nation. The histories of Scotland and Ireland extend roughly to the time of publication; the first volume of the history of England stops at 1066, and the second volume continues with events after the Norman Conquest. Each section includes a list of authors whose histories have been incorporated into it. The second volume, compiled entirely by Holinshed, is devoted to English history following the conquest and consists of 1,586 pages of text (not numbered consecutively), a 98-page index, 4 pages of "faults escaped," and a list of historians living in the time of Elizabeth I (not including Holinshed).

This general description of the *Chronicles* should not be construed as suggesting any unity or systematic presentation, for the editors often made do with inadequate sources that were close at hand, so that the final form of the book is shaped very much by available material as well as by the inclinations of individual contributors. In the dedication to William Cecil, Lord Burghley, Holinshed apologizes for the book's size and disorder but explains that "I was loath to omit anything that might increase the reader's knowledge, which causeth the book to grow so great." Likewise, he admits that "I have not so orderly disposed [my sources] as otherwise I ought, choosing rather to want order, than to defraud the reader of that which for his further understanding might seem to satisfy his expectation."

Although the entire work is dedicated to Burghley (lord treasurer and the queen's chief minister), individual sections carry separate dedications to others, including Burghley's political enemies. The "History of Scotland" is dedicated to the queen's favorite, Robert Dudley, Earl of Leicester, and the "History of Ireland" is dedicated to Leicester's brother-in-law, Henry Sidney, lord deputy of Ireland. Both men were rivals of Burghley, and the relations between Leicester and Sidney were sometimes strained as well. Harrison dedicates the "Historical Description of Britain" to his patron, William Brooke, Baron of Cobham (a friend of the queen), whose daughter married Burghley's son, Robert. Elizabeth Story Donno speculates that Leicester's jealousy of Cobham's ancient lineage may have led to some of the expurgations from the second edition of the *Chronicles*. Harrison's dedication of the "Description of Scotland" to Thomas Seckford differs in kind from the others. A minor legal official, Seckford assisted Harrison in gathering information about rivers and streams for the "Description of Britain" and collected maps of the realm that were omitted from Wolfe's initial plan. These multiple dedications, additional title pages for the "History of Ireland" and the "History of Scotland," and new paginations for each division indicate the substantial independence and the distinctive qualities of the individual sections of the *Chronicles*.

A survey of the descriptive sections displays the book's variety of approaches. The first section, a "Historical Description of Britain," by William Harrison, provides information on topics ranging from natural to religious history. A sample of chapter titles reveals the range of the spectrum Harrison offers, from the speculative ("Whether it be likely that ever there were any giants inhabiting in this island") to the more solidly historical ("Of the wall sometime builded for a partition between England and the Picts") to the mildly sensational ("Of the marvels of England," "Of venomous beasts"). His chapters appeal to the naturalist ("Of the air and soil of the country," "Of English dogs," "Of woods and marshes"), the manufacturer ("Of quarries of stone for building," "Of salt made in England," "Of the manner of building and furniture of our houses"), and the generalist ("Of food and diet of the English," "Of degrees of people in the commonwealth of England"). He offers information to the practical as well as to the curious. A table, titled "How a man may journey from any notable town in England, or from London to any notable town in the realm," records the number of miles between stops along these routes.

Compiled by the Oxford-educated Dubliner Richard Stanyhurst, the "Description of Ireland" is hardly as luxurious in detail as the "Description of Britain." Among Stanyhurst's primary sources were the *Topographia Hibernica* (1185) of Giraldus Cambrensis, the first Anglo-Irish historian, and *Two Books of the Histories of Ireland,* by Stanyhurst's tutor and friend, the Jesuit martyr Edmund Campion, whose work was not published until 1633. Both Stanyhurst and Holinshed write of their debt to Campion's history of Ireland and regret the fact that it is short and was, as Stanyhurst explains in the dedication to Sidney, "huddled up in haste." Informed by Campion's sympathetic tone, the "Description" displays particular interest in the Irish language and begins by explaining the etymology of the name *Ireland.* A chapter titled "Of the nature of the soil, and other incidents" is primarily concerned with the legend of Saint Patrick.

To fill many pages of the description, however, Stanyhurst depends largely upon lists of places and people – "The names of the cities, boroughs, and haven towns in Ireland," "Of the lords spiritual of Ireland," "The lords temporal, as well English as Irish, which inhabit Ireland," and "The names or surnames of the learned men and authors of Ireland." Perhaps with these lists Stanyhurst hoped to improve the reputation of his birthplace for his English readers. In the chapter titled "The disposition and manners of the meer Irish, commonly called the wild Irish," the author warns his readers "not to impute any barbarous custom that shall be here laid down, to the citizens, townsmen, and the inhabitants of the English Pale, in that they differ little or nothing from the ancient customs and dispositions of their progenitors, the English and Welshmen, being therefore as mortally behated of the Irish as those that are born in England."

The "Description of Scotland" is less a reflection of the compilers' interests than are the other descriptions. It consists of passages translated by Harrison from John Bellenden's 1536 Scottish translation of Hector Boece's *Historia Scotorum* (1526). The description is weighted toward geographical detail, particularly rivers and lakes. A short discussion of natural history features the salmon, while the cultural description emphasizes old ways of life in order to point out their subsequent decline.

The historical sections of the *Chronicles* share the inconsistencies of the descriptions – inconsistencies common to chronicles in general and acknowledged by Holinshed in the book's dedication. The histories of Scotland and Ireland consist of earlier works pieced together. Holinshed translates the rest of Boece's *Historia Scotorum* to make up most of the "History of Scotland." For the "History of Ireland" he includes his own summarized translation of Giraldus's *Expugnatio Hibernica* (circa 1188) but relies primarily on Campion's "huddled up" history. The "History of Ireland" comprises 115 pages (much shorter than the 518-page "History of Scotland"), and the dedication to Sidney, lord governor of Ireland, acknowledges its shortcomings. But while Holinshed complains about his lack of source material, he is concerned that Campion get his "due deserved praise" and rejoices at the arrival of his assistant Stanyhurst, who completed the Irish history by writing an account of the years 1509 to 1547.

Following Harrison's "Historical Description of Britain," Holinshed's work begins with the "History of England" and follows previously written histories in both format and content. Organizing his material by the reigns of kings, Holinshed adopts the principle popularized in 1534 by the Italian historian Polydore Vergil in the *Anglicae Historiae Libri 26,* written at the request of Henry VII. He begins recording history after the Flood, describing how rule of the island passed from Noah's descendants to the giant Albion, a son of Neptune, and then to Hercules. In this attempt to reconcile biblical and classical history, Holinshed tries to establish answers to two vexed questions: who were the earliest inhabitants of the island and why was it called "Albion"? At the coming of Brute, the legendary founder of England, Holinshed makes a major division in the history and begins numbering kings. By his count, which follows Geoffrey of Monmouth's *Historia Regum Britanniae* (circa 1136), King Lear is the tenth ruler; he is also the last one that Holinshed numbers.

In constructing his narrative, the chronicler weaves together several sources. For the history of Richard III, he uses both the English and Latin versions of Sir Thomas More's biography of Richard, inserts material from fellow chroniclers Edward Hall and Richard Grafton describing Richard's coronation (an incident More omits), and then concludes with material found in Hall. In consulting a greater variety of sources than other chroniclers, Holinshed employs the scholarly approach of the humanists. He searches out the sources used by more-recent authorities, prints conflicting accounts, and supplies lists of sources and side-note citations that are the forerunners of modern footnotes and bibliographies.

The stories of Richard III and Macbeth illustrate Holinshed's characteristic unwillingness to omit important sources and his habit of including contradictory accounts, as in his handling of the reigns of the Scottish King Duncan and his assassin, Macbeth. Holinshed uses Boece's narrative as the source of this history, but he remarks in a side-note that "This agreeth not with our English writers" and finishes the side-note by giving the English version of events. In his preface Holinshed justifies his refusal to select from among the different accounts that he collected:

> concerning the History of England, as I have collected the same out of many and sundry authors, in whom what contrariety, negligence, and rashness sometime is found in their reports, I leave to the discretion of those that have perused their works: for my part, I have in things doubtful rather chosen to show the diversity of their writings, than by overruling them and using a peremptory censure to frame them to agree to my liking, leaving it nevertheless to each man's judgment to control them as he sees cause.

Like other chroniclers, Holinshed sought to report the information as it came to him rather than to impose his beliefs on the narrative by selecting the version he believed to be correct, but he could be driven to editorialize. Typically he inserts his voice into the narrative in parentheses and side-notes. Reporting Richard III's public refusal of the crown, Holinshed remarks in the margin, "O singular dissimulation of King Richard." When Richard asks the nobles to transfer their love to his nephew, the young prince and heir, Holinshed underscores the obvious: "King Richard spake otherwise than he meant."

Despite Holinshed's occasional insertion of his personal beliefs, his *Chronicles* are primarily a collection of narratives and so serve as a compendium of beliefs and concerns typical of the time. For example, the story of Macbeth from Boece's history displays the concern found in other chronicles for the kind of leadership that would protect order within the realm. Within the context of foreign invasions of Scotland and internal rebellions against the crown, Duncan and Macbeth are set up as opposite

types of rulers – both unsatisfactory. Duncan is "too soft," and although he inherits a peaceful kingdom, his negligence in punishing lawbreakers invites rebels to disrupt the commonwealth. Macbeth is "cruel" but is able to subdue the rebels whom Duncan fears. Both extreme types of leaders create circumstances in which innocent people, specifically women and children, are slaughtered. Duncan's too-lenient reign encourages the rebellion of Macdowald, who, trapped by Macbeth, "first slew his wife and children, and lastly himself, lest if he had yielded simply, he should have been executed in most cruel wise for the example to others." Macbeth gets credit for having put the realm in order and later usurps the crown from the ineffectual Duncan. In the course of protecting it, however, he turns tyrant and has Macduff's family slaughtered. As king, Macbeth threatens the kingdom much like the rebels who had sprung up during the reign of Duncan. After his defeat Macbeth's severed head is presented to the new king as the rebel Macdowald's had been presented to Duncan.

For the chronicler history served an exemplary function, and the story of Macbeth teaches a lesson found elsewhere in English Renaissance writing – the rule of a usurper will end badly. Initially, Macbeth's taking of the crown is justified by the order that he maintains during the early part of his reign. It is only a matter of time, however, before the usurper's true nature shows itself, with Macbeth "instead of equity practicing cruelty." Holinshed deviates slightly from his source to emphasize how the human conscience brings about rough justice: "For the prick of conscience (as it chanceth ever in tyrants and such as attain to any estate by unrighteous means) caused him ever to fear, least he should be served of the same cup as he had ministered to his predecessor." In Shakespeare's play this image of the cup, which Holinshed introduces into the historical narrative, appears as a "poisoned chalice" that Macbeth knows may be turned to his own lips. In both versions this fear provokes his cruel suppression of the Scottish nobility and ultimately brings about his death.

Holinshed takes other opportunities to point out lessons to be gained from the story of Macbeth. In the side-notes he interprets the circumstances that prompt Macbeth to kill Duncan as if to warn the reader not to repeat these mistakes. When Macbeth mulls over the prophecy made by the "weird sisters" that he will be king, Holinshed remarks that "Prophecies move men to unlawful attempts." Following Boece, his concluding statement summarizes

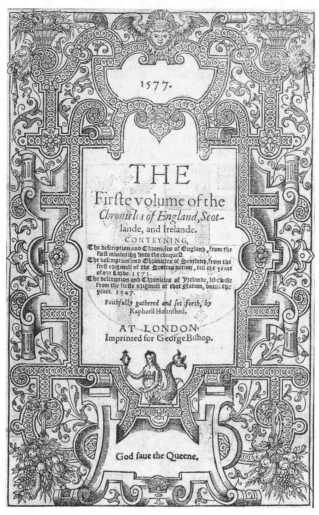

1577.

THE
Firſte volume of the
Chronicles of England, Scot-
lande, and Irelande.
CONTEYNING,
The deſcription and Chronicles of England, from the
firſt inhabiting vnto the conqueſt.
The deſcription and Chronicles of Scotland, from the
firſt originall of the Scottes nation, till the yeare
of our Lorde. 1571.
The deſcription and Chronicles of Yrelande, likewiſe
from the firſte originall of that Nation, vntill the
yeare. 1547.

Faithfully gathered and ſet forth, by
Raphaell Holinſhed.

AT LONDON.
Imprinted for George Biſhop.

God ſaue the Queene.

*Title page for the first edition of Holinshed's influential history
(courtesy of the Lilly Library, Indiana University)*

the moral exemplum to be found in Macbeth's reign: "in the beginning of his reign he accomplished many worthy acts, right profitable to the commonwealth (as ye have heard), but afterwards by illusion of the devil, he defamed the same with most terrible cruelty."

Furthermore, in the preface, Holinshed expresses his related belief that historical writing is a moral act. Complaining that he has been pressed into a duty for which he is not fit, he admonishes those more capable "not to forget their native country's praise (which is their duty) the encouragement of their worthy countrymen, by elders' advancements and the daunting of the vicious . . . to which end I take chronicles and histories ought chiefly to be written." At the end of the "History of England" he again emphasizes the importance of historical writing, this time in the form of an encouragement to historians, especially anonymous

ones: "I wish such to go forward in well doing and to remember that virtue cannot always be hidden but in time their names will be remembered among the best, that those that are virtuously given by their worthy praise be encouraged to follow their steps and endeavor themselves according to duty to advance learning and necessary knowledge in their country."

In his effective anonymity Holinshed resembles those historians he encourages, and critics remark that his consciously chosen method of compiling contradictory historical accounts furthers this anonymity. The modern editors of the *Irish Chronicle* call his writing "completely self-effacing" and contrast him to Richard Stanyhurst in this regard. Similarly, Stephen Booth remarks that "whereas the lesser contributors show their personalities and quirks, Holinshed has no mannerisms that suggest anything at all about the sort of person he might have been." Clarence Brownfield admits to reading between the lines and speculates that Holinshed's

> personal habit of mind led him to sympathize with the traditions of the Merrie England of his childhood. He had deep respect for the scholastic training of her Universities, and on the rare occasions when the personal predilections of the author peep through his work he appears as an old-time conservative in no way given to 'innovations and new fangles.' He was a true historian in the sense that he did his best to attain objectivity.

As an example, Brownfield cites Holinshed's appreciation of the scholarship of both Catholic and Protestant martyrs during the reign of Mary Tudor and his lack of comment on the passing from the reign of Mary to that of Elizabeth.

Holinshed's relative objectivity succeeded in satisfying the English censors. After printer Henry Binneman began selling copies of the *Chronicles* in 1577, the Privy Council ordered alterations of only two passages, both in Stanyhurst's Irish section, which concerned the archbishop of Dublin and the rebellion of the ninth earl of Kildare. Despite a high price owing to its size, the corrected version sold well enough for a second edition to be planned.

Holinshed was not involved in the production of the revised edition. He died in 1580, three years after the first publication of the *Chronicles*. In accordance with his will, where he describes himself as steward to Thomas Burdet of Bramcote, Warwickshire, all his property, including notes, books, and manuscripts, passed to Burdet.

For the second edition booksellers Lucas Harrison and George Bishop, partners in the first venture, were joined by Thomas Woodcock, Ralph Newberie, and Henry Denham. With Holinshed dead and Richard Stanyhurst unavailable, the revision, apparently under the direction of John Hooker (alias Vowell), was undertaken by William Harrison, Francis Thynne, John Stow, and Abraham Fleming, who edited as well as contributed to the new version. The only deletion from the first edition was the removal of Holinshed's summary of Giraldus's *Expugnatio Hibernica,* which Hooker replaced with a complete translation. Among other additions were those Harrison made to his "Description of England," those Thynne made to the Scottish section, and the continuation by Thynne and Stow of the English history to 1586.

As an editor and contributor, Fleming had the greatest impact on Holinshed's book. Besides including aids to the reader such as indexes and headings, he altered Holinshed's tone by inserting pas-

sages that give the book a more obvious Protestant slant. Nevertheless, the second edition did not fare as well as the first at the hands of the censors. For reasons not entirely clear, the Privy Council ordered five sections removed from the continuations of the English and Scottish histories, including 156 pages of the new English history. Apparently it was feared that some of the material might offend King James in Scotland. On the basis of evidence she admits to be tenuous, Donno has suggested that the removal of sections of the English history may have been the result of political jealousies among members of the Privy Council, particularly Burghley and Leicester.

Holinshed's 1577 edition of the *Chronicles* was published at a time when the genre was enjoying its greatest popularity. But by the end of the century this form of historical writing had come under attack, denigrated by scholars because of its increasing association with popular audiences. Among those who deplored it on the grounds of intellectual inferiority, the Cambridge-educated Gabriel Harvey wrote of "many asses who dare to compile histories, chronicles, annals, commentaries," and included Holinshed among those "not cognizant of law or politics, nor of the art of depicting character, nor are they in any way learned."

The inconsistency of historical accounts made the chroniclers easy targets for such derision. Although Holinshed's preface makes clear that he was attempting to provide his readers with all available information, advances in data collection made it impossible for this inclusive method to produce a readable text. New methods of historiography pioneered by Stow and John Speed emphasized historical accuracy as a principle of selection. By the end of the sixteenth century the heyday of the chronicle as a source of historical information had passed.

When the 1587 edition of the *Chronicles* was next republished, it had become valuable because of its scarcity, prized not because of the history it reported but for the history it embodied. The editors of the 1807–1808 edition, who restored the pages expunged by the Privy Council, thought highly enough of Holinshed's book to select it over other Renaissance histories. With this "rarest and most important of our ancient chronicles," they planned to test the appetite of both specialists and general readers. The advertisement for the edition appeals to the antiquarian's curiosity; it portrays the "Description of Britain" as containing "the most curious and authentic account of the manners and customs of our island in the reign of Henry VIII and Elizabeth, in which it was written." The book is valuable, it asserts, not only because it "possesses all the force and value of contemporary evidence, collected by a most skillful observer," but also because "the peculiar style and orthography in which the work is written furnish a very interesting document to illustrate the history of the English language."

Critical interest in Holinshed has continued along these historical lines. Scholars examine the *Chronicles* when they analyze the development of the English historiographic tradition as its orientation changed from theological and moral to political. Described by F. J. Levy as "grafting new scholarly methods onto an old root," Holinshed has a pivotal place in this transition. One strand of this historiographical inquiry continues the sort of criticisms that Holinshed's contemporaries leveled against the chroniclers: that they were not scholars and that they recounted the English national myth when they should have provided analysis that would lead readers to understand the past.

While noting the neglect of social and cultural materials in the chronicle tradition, Arthur B. Ferguson singles out Harrison's "Description of England" as an exception, citing it as "a monumental contribution" to social history but pointing out that "it was deliberately segregated" from the specifically historical sections of the book. On the other hand, Annabel Patterson overturns the traditional criticisms of the work while examining the *Chronicles* from the perspective of a cultural historian. She finds Holinshed's inclusive methodology to express a philosophy of political liberalism that developed in sixteenth-century England in reaction to the conflicts of the Reformation. By including multiple voices in his historical narrative, Holinshed aimed to encourage religious toleration and to create a well-informed and critical middle-class readership.

A look at the publication history of Holinshed's *Chronicles* reveals another primary source of interest in the work — Shakespeare's dramaturgy. With one exception (1979), editions after 1807 have been based on the 1587 edition, or "Shakespeare's Holinshed"; publications made to serve Shakespearean scholarship have included only the sections that he used as source material. When critics refer to Holinshed's *Chronicles,* they are usually referring to the 1587 edition edited by Abraham Fleming rather than by Holinshed. Charles Lethbridge Kingsford suggests, for example, that "Holinshed copied Hall's prejudices rather than Stow's impartiality, and the colour which he thus gave to his

narrative reappears naturally in Shakespeare's plays, and has in consequence been stamped on popular opinion."

But because Shakespeare used the 1587 edition of the *Chronicles,* arguments that Holinshed influenced Shakespeare are problematic. Some scholars have pointed out that Fleming rather than Holinshed is responsible for the prejudices in the work. Both Brownfield and Booth contrast Holinshed's relative objectivity to the partiality of the 1587 edition. Brownfield calls the 1587 editors "literary propagandists," and Booth describes the "Continuation of the English History" as "urgently and often violently, and sometimes grotesquely Protestant and patriotic."

Critics debate the sort of influence that the *Chronicles* might have exerted over Shakespeare. R. Mark Benbow argues that Fleming's view that God is actively at work in the world of men "suggests a source for the strong affirmative note in Shakespearean tragedy. However tragic the individual story may be, good ultimately emerges if not for the individual at least for the state and cosmos." According to Benbow, although this providential view of history was implied in Holinshed's edition, Fleming developed it "into an articulate philosophy of history." Booth, on the other hand, argues that an affinity exists between Shakespeare and Holinshed in their manner of presenting material to the reader, asserting that the *Chronicles* "are the work in English literature that most fully shares the most peculiarly Shakespearean of Shakespeare's traits — the ability constantly to shift the perceptions of a reader or audience from one set of principles for judgment to another." Booth reckons Fleming's additions as "one more voice to the multitude already speaking in Holinshed's narrative."

Both C. S. Lewis and Booth comment on Holinshed's prose style, examining his method of editing his sources. In *English Literature in the Sixteenth Century* Lewis traces the transmission of a particular passage from Jean Froissart (in Berner's English translation) to Grafton to Holinshed and concludes that "there is nothing that can be called original composition except in Froissart: yet at the same time Grafton and Holinshed are not exactly transcribing. We are in a world where our modern notions of authorship do not apply." Booth, however, praises Holinshed's style: "Holinshed writes over a million words, but he is the only member of the project who is never dull." In the case of Holinshed modern readers have only these words, appropriately concluded with an exhortation to anonymous historians, to indicate what the man might have been.

References:

R. Mark Benbow, "The Providential Theory of Historical Causation in *Holinshed's Chronicles:* 1577 and 1587," *Texas Studies in Literature and Language,* 1 (1959–1960): 264–276;

Stephen Booth, *The Book Called Holinshed's Chronicles* (San Francisco: Book Club of California, 1968);

Clarence Brownfield, "Holinshed and His Editors," *Times Literary Supplement,* 7 August 1937, p. 576;

Sarah C. Dodson, "Abraham Fleming, Writer and Editor," *University of Texas Studies in English,* 34 (1955): 51–66;

Elizabeth Story Donno, "Some Aspects of Shakespeare's Holinshed," *Huntington Library Quarterly,* 50 (Summer 1987): 229–248;

Arthur B. Ferguson, *Clio Unbound: Perceptions of the Social and Cultural Past in Renaissance England,* Duke Monographs in Medieval and Renaissance Studies 2 (Durham, N.C.: Duke University Press, 1979);

Charles Lethbridge Kingsford, *English Historical Literature in the Fifteenth Century* (Oxford: Clarendon Press, 1913), pp. 271–274;

F. J. Levy, *Tudor Historical Thought* (San Marino, Cal.: Huntington Library, 1967), pp. 182–186;

Annabel Patterson, *Reading Holinshed's "Chronicles"* (Chicago: University of Chicago Press, 1994);

Patterson, "Rethinking Tudor Historiography," *South Atlantic Quarterly,* 92 (Spring 1993): 185–208;

D. R. Woolfe, "Genre into Artifact: The Decline of the English Chronicle in the Sixteenth Century," *Sixteenth Century Journal,* 19, no. 3 (1988): 321–354.

Papers:

Raphael Holinshed's only known extant manuscript, a translation of Florence of Worcester for the *Chronicles,* is held in the British Museum (MS Harleian 563).

John Lyly

(between 1552 and 1554 – November 1606)

Derek B. Alwes
Clark University

See also the Lyly entry in *DLB 62: Elizabethan Dramatists*.

BOOKS: *Euphues. The Anatomy of Wyt* (London: Printed by T. East for G. Cawood, 1578);

Euphues and His England. Containing His Voyage and Aduentures (London: Printed by T. East for G. Cawood, 1580);

A Moste Excellent Comedie of Alexander, Campaspe, and Diogenes (London: Printed by T. Dawson for T. Cadman, 1584); republished as *Campaspe* (London: Printed by T. Dawson for T. Cadman, 1584);

Sapho and Phao (London: Printed by T. Dawson for T. Cadman, 1584);

Pappe with an Hatchet, Alias, A Figge for My God Sonne (London: Printed by J. Anoke & J. Astile for the Bayliue of Withernam [T. Orwin], 1589);

Endimion, The Man in the Moone (London: Printed by J. Charlewood for the Widdow Broome, 1591);

Gallathea (London: Printed by J. Charlwoode for the Widdow Broome, 1592);

Midas (London: Printed by T. Scarlet for J. Broome, 1592);

Mother Bombie (London: Printed by T. Scarlet for C. Burby, 1594);

The Woman in the Moone (London: Printed by J. Roberts for W. Jones, 1597);

Loves Metamorphosis. A Wittie and Courtly Pastorall (London: Printed by S. Stafford for W. Wood, 1601);

Six Court Comedies, edited by Edward Blount (London: Printed by W. Stansby for E. Blount, 1632) – comprises *Endimion, Campaspe, Sapho and Phao, Gallatea, Midas,* and *Mother Bombie.*

Editions: *The Complete Works of John Lyly,* 3 volumes, edited by R. Warwick Bond (Oxford: Clarendon Press, 1902);

Euphues, The Anatomy of Wit; Euphues His England, edited by Morris W. Croll and Harry Clemons (London: Routledge, 1916);

Alexander and Campaspe, edited by W. W. Greg (London: Printed for the Malone Society at Oxford University Press, 1934);

Mother Bombie, edited by Kathleen M. Lea, with the assistance of D. Nichol Smith (London: Printed for the Malone Society at Oxford University Press, 1948);

Gallathea and Midas, edited by Anne B. Lancashire (Lincoln: University of Nebraska Press, 1969; London: Arnold, 1970).

PLAY PRODUCTIONS: *Campaspe,* London, Blackfriars theater, 1583–1584;

Sapho and Phao, London, Blackfriars theater, 1583–1584;

Gallathea, London, Paul's theater(?), 1585–1588(?);

Endimion, Greenwich, at Court, 2 February 1588;

Love's Metamorphosis, London, Paul's theater, circa 1588–1590;

Mother Bombie, London, Paul's theater, 1588–1590(?);

Midas, London, Paul's theater, 1589–1590;

The Woman in the Moon, London, unknown theater, 1591–1594(?).

C. S. Lewis's remark in *English Literature in the Sixteenth Century, Excluding Drama* (1954) about Philip Sidney's *Arcadia* (1590, 1593), that "What a man thinks of it . . . tests the depth of his sympathy with the sixteenth century," is perhaps even truer of John Lyly's *Euphues: The Anatomy of Wit* (1578) and *Euphues and His England* (1580). They were the most popular works of fiction in the sixteenth century: ten editions of each text saw print by the end of the century, inspiring dozens of imitators, although the phenomenon had largely run its course by the time Elizabeth died in 1603. As Merritt Lawlis says in *Elizabethan Prose Fiction* (1967), "It is as 'Elizabethan' as Elizabeth herself."

John Lyly was in many respects a genuine child of his age. His grandfather, William Lily, was one of the early humanist figures to bring the Re-

¶ *EUPHVES.*

THE ANATOMY
OF WYT.

Very pleaſant for all Gentle-
men to reade, and moſt neceſ-
ſary to remember:

wherin are contained the delights
that Wyt followeth in his youth by the
pleaſauntneſſe of Loue, and the
happyneſſe he reapeth in
age, by
the perfectneſſe of
Wiſedome.

¶ By Iohn Lylly Maſter of
Arte. Oxon,

¶ Imprinted at London for
Gabriell Cawood, dwel-
ling in Paules Church-
yarde.

811472.1   N

Title page for Lyly's best-known book, one of the most popular
works of fiction in the sixteenth century

naissance to England. A friend of Desiderius Erasmus and John Colet, William Lily was the first headmaster of St. Paul's School; and the Latin grammar that he, Colet, and Erasmus produced became identified as "Lily's Grammar" and remained a universal school text through the eighteenth century. John Lyly's uncle George continued the family's humanist tradition, becoming the secretary of the erudite Reginald Cardinal Pole, Henry VIII's exiled kinsman. Lyly's father, Peter, was registrar and/or notary of the cathedral church of Canterbury, an ecclesiastical position of currently uncertain status, but he was no doubt well educated, and he married Jane Burgh, who brought both lands and important connections to the Lyly family. It is fairly safe to assume that the son of the headmaster of St. Paul's would provide a good education for his own son, so it is likely that John Lyly attended the Cathedral Grammar School in Canterbury.

The exact date and place of John Lyly's birth are unknown, but records of his years at Oxford University indicate that he was born between 1552 and 1554. By 1562 he resided with his parents and a growing number of siblings in Canterbury. Given the paucity of hard evidence regarding Lyly's youth, biographers necessarily turn to his fiction for autobiographical testimony. In *Euphues and His England* Euphues and Philautus pass through Canterbury on their way to the court in London, and the city is described as "an old city somewhat decayed yet beautiful to behold; most famous for a Cathedral Church, the very majesty whereof struck them into a maze." In Canterbury they meet Fidus, who is generally regarded as Lyly's self-portrait (though

G. K. Hunter thinks the passage may apply more accurately to Lyly's father). Fidus tells them, "I was born in the Weald of Kent, of honest parents and worshipful, whose tender cares (if the fondness of parents may be so termed) provided all things even from my very cradle until their graves that might either bring me up in good letters or make me heir to great livings." In addition to the portrait of Fidus, Lyly apparently provides an account of his experience at Oxford when he has Euphues complain about conditions at Athens (generally understood to represent Oxford): "I cannot but lament Athens, which having been always the nurse of philosophers, doth now nourish only the name of philosophy."

Lyly's relation to Oxford University is central to an understanding not only of his early biography but of his two well-known prose works and of his career as courtier. When Euphues condemns the "disorder in Athens" – "Such playing at dice, such quaffing of drink, such dalliance with women, such dancing" – the reader is reminded of Gabriel Harvey's remarks about Lyly's career as the "fiddlestick of Oxford," which Harvey describes as consisting of "horning, gaming, fooling and knaving" – though one must keep in mind that Harvey is writing as Lyly's enemy.

In the second edition of *Euphues* (1579), Lyly adds an epistle "To My Very Good Friends the Gentlemen Scholars of Oxford," apparently in recognition of the fact that Euphues' criticism of life at Oxford had given offense to that community. The epistle is not an apology, however: "I speak this, Gentlemen, not to excuse the offense which is taken, but to offer a defense where I was mistaken." Because the best defense is a good offence, Lyly proceeds to condemn Oxford in his own voice.

Biographers have speculated at length about Lyly's three years in the "country," but it seems most likely that he is speaking metaphorically about the scholastic discipline of philosophical disputation offered at Oxford, an assumption supported not only by what is known of the curriculum at Oxford at that time but also by the remarks of Anthony à Wood, who reports in *Athenae Oxonienses* (1691–1692) that Lyly was "always averse to the crabbed studies of logic and philosophy. For so it was that his genie being naturally bent to the pleasant paths of poetry . . . did in a manner neglect academical studies." Wood's testimony is suspect because he wrote at least one hundred years after Lyly's university career and was perhaps influenced by Lyly's more spectacular later career at court, but his remark about the "crabbed studies" certainly conforms to Lyly's criticism of his alma mater.

Wood's suggestion that Lyly was naturally inclined to poetry instead of academics during his university career, however, is disputed by the fact that Lyly's first career choice was not that of a writer but rather a fellow at Oxford. In 1574 Lyly wrote a letter to William Cecil, Lord Burghley, asking him to procure letters from the queen to the authorities of Magdalen, commanding that Lyly be admitted there as fellow. He concludes the letter with a promise to be diligent in his pursuit of learning. The passage sounds like the true voice of William Lily's grandson, the voice of a young man expecting and desiring to carry on the family tradition of humanist scholarship. The question that arises in the study of Lyly's life is what happened to transform the young university scholar into the witty courtier who entertained Queen Elizabeth with his graceful comedies, and the answer is *Euphues*.

After taking his M.A. at Oxford in June 1575 and being disappointed in his pursuit of a fellowship, Lyly apparently decided to pursue advancement at the other venue open to educated gentlemen – the court. This turning point is presumably chronicled in Fidus's account of himself when he says,

being of the age of twenty years, there was no trade or kind of life that either fitted my humour or served my turn but the Court; thinking that place the only means to climb high and sit sure.

I was there entertained as well by the great friends my father made as by my own forwardness. Where, it being now but honeymoon, I endeavored to court it with a grace (almost past grace), laying more on my back than my friends could well bear, having many times a brave cloak and a threadbare purse. Who so conversant with the ladies as I? Who so pleasant? Who more prodigal?

By the time Lyly had fully accommodated himself to the role of court entertainer, he could give to one of his characters in *Sapho and Phao* (1584) a speech praising the court at the expense of the university: "In universities virtues and vices are but shadowed in colors, white and black; in courts showed to life, good and bad. There, times past are read of in old books. . . . Here are times in perfection, not by device as fables, but in execution as truths. . . . What hath a scholar found out by study that a courtier hath not found out by practice?" It is unlikely, however, that this speech reflects Lyly's priorities during the composition of *Euphues,* whose anticourtly sentiments are so prevalent, in fact, that Theodore L. Steinberg has characterized this work as an "anti-courtesy book." During the period that

Lyly was composing *Euphues* he was also pursuing an M.A. by incorporation at Cambridge University (which he received in 1579), so it is reasonable to assume that he was still entertaining hopes for some sort of academic career as late as 1579, and it is as an elaborate plea for academic preferment that *Euphues* can perhaps best be read.

The general intentions or expectations of authors in the Renaissance can sometimes be inferred from the identity of the dedicatee, but in the case of *Euphues* virtually nothing is known about William West, Lord Delaware. It has been suggested that Lyly may have worked as tutor to Delaware's children, but such suggestions can only be speculation. If Lyly were trying to use *Euphues* as a means to solicit patronage for an academic career, it might seem more logical to dedicate it to someone such as Lord Burghley, but of course the serious-minded Burghley did not patronize works of fiction. Echoes and hints of Burghley's presence nevertheless abound in Lyly's fiction.

In his 1574 letter to Burghley (even discounting the inevitable extravagance of language) Lyly seems to indicate that Burghley has already begun to serve as his patron: "In the gracious bounty shown, most noble Peer, to me your foster-son, and in your gratuitous and unlooked-for interest, effort, and extraordinary pains on my behalf, I recognize with all becoming humility your good and kindly disposition toward men devoted to learning." It has also been suggested that Lyly modeled his character Eubulus ("good counsel") on Elizabeth's most trusted counselor. Such an identification is by no means inappropriate, given Burghley's active interest in the education of some of the most important young men of the period, including his ward, the earl of Oxford, to whom Lyly dedicated *Euphues and His England*. Burghley even published a letter he had written for his son Robert, filled with Eubulean precepts (some of which appear verbatim in *Euphues and His England*).

In his letter to Burghley, Lyly describes himself as "a rash and inexperienced youth, one who lacks the ripe judgement bestowed by advancing years, the sound character formed by chaste rule of life, the learned equipment furnished by the teaching of the arts." This is, of course, a portrait of Euphues at the beginning of his story (when he meets Eubulus), and insofar as Euphues is Lyly (an identification Lyly explicitly acknowledges in the dedicatory epistle to *Euphues and His England*), his story is the story of Lyly's transcending his youthful limitations through the acquisition of experience in the world and through the humanist study of classical literature.

As Richard Helgerson has shown, *Euphues* participated in an end-of-the-century fashion for fictions based on the Prodigal Son story. What distinguishes the Elizabethan redactions of the story, however, is that the biblical conclusion of paternal forgiveness and generosity is missing. Elizabethan prodigal-son stories focus only on the components of admonishment, rebellion, and repentance. Lyly's *Euphues* is no exception.

At the beginning of his narrative, Euphues is a young man of great promise but no accomplishment. His name, which Lyly probably got from Roger Ascham's *Schoolmaster* (1570), means "he that is apt by goodness of wit, and appliable by readiness of will, to learning." When he meets Eubulus, however, Euphues proves himself incapable of learning from the old man's precepts. Eubulus asks, "Is it not far better to abhor sins by the remembrance of others' faults than by repentence of thine own follies?," but Euphues refuses to see the applicability of Eubulus's advice to himself. Euphues concludes by mocking the old man's fatherly solicitation and goes off in pursuit of worldly experience, leaving Eubulus to prophesy in soliloquy: "Seeing thou wilt not buy counsel at the first hand good cheap, thou shalt buy repentance at the second hand at such an unreasonable rate that thou wilt curse thy hard pennyworth and ban thy hard heart." Not surprisingly, this is precisely what happens.

The plot of Euphues' adventures is simple; it is the repentance and the advice that Euphues feels qualified to dispense in his turn that take up the majority of the book. After leaving Eubulus, Euphues first meets Philautus ("self-love") and pledges eternal amity to him. (That Philautus is intended to represent Euphues' own narcissism is made explicit by Euphues' remark that "I view in him the lively image of Euphues.") Euphues then accompanies Philautus on a visit to Philautus's lover, Lucilla. Euphues falls in love with Lucilla on first sight; she returns his love; and they betray Philautus, who breaks off his relationship with both of them; Lucilla then quickly rejects Euphues for another lover, Curio. When Philautus learns that Euphues has suffered his fate, he forgives him and their friendship is restored. Euphues has learned his lesson, issues his farewell to "women all," and returns to his university to immerse himself in his studies and compose moral treatises and letters of advice with which the book ends.

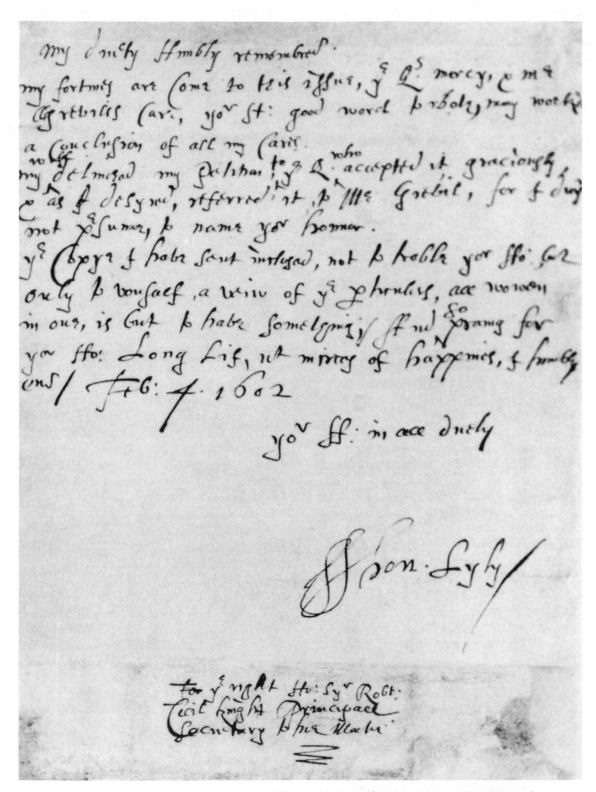

Letter from Lyly to Sir Robert Cecil, dated 4 February 1602–3 (Hatfield Library, Hatfield House)

The treatises are translations or paraphrases of properly classical texts by Ovid and Plutarch, but the most revealing piece of advice is the almost verbatim reiteration of the advice Eubulus had given him at the beginning of the story, which Euphues prefaces with the remark: "And here I cannot choose but give you that counsel that an old man in Naples gave me most wisely, although I had then neither grace to follow it, neither will to give ear to it; desiring you not to reject it because I did once despise it." In this prodigal-son story the rebellious son proves his repentance by assuming the voice of the father – by becoming the father. The point of the biblical parable was to depict God's fatherly love and mercy for wayward sinners; the focus of the Elizabethan prodigal-son stories is on the submission of sons to fathers.

The consequences of a stubborn refusal to submit to the will of the father are portrayed in *Euphues* in the prodigal-daughter story of Lucilla. Obstinately rejecting her father's advice, Lucilla perseveres in her willfulness only to end up dying "in great beggary in the streets." So that there can be no question of the justice of Lucilla's self-inflicted suffering, Lyly gives her a speech acknowledging the error of her ways: "since I am an example to all women of lightness, I am like also to be a mirror to them all of unhappiness. Which ill luck I must take by [*sic*] so much the more patiently, by how much the more I acknowledge myself to have deserved it worthily."

If the penalty for obstinance is poverty and death, the reward for submissiveness is wisdom and, presumably, a kind of success. Success for Euphues comes in scholarship. Having returned to his university in Athens, Euphues "gave his mind to the continual study of philosophy, insomuch as he became public reader in the university, with such commendation as never any before him." Euphues' career, as Hunter has said, "reads like the pipe-dream of a disappointed don." That this dream of academic success was Lyly's own and that *Euphues* was written at least in part to solicit support for Lyly's request for an Oxford fellowship are supported by Euphues' critique of the abuses at Athens, which concludes with the self-serving observation: "How such abuses should or might be redressed in all universities, especially in Athens, if I were of authority to command, it should be seen, or of credit to persuade those that have the dealings with them, it should soon be shown." Furthermore, in the epistle to the gentlemen scholars appended to the 1579 edition, Lyly says, "concerning myself, I have always thought so reverently of Oxford, of the scholars, of

the manners, that I seemed to be rather an idolater than a blasphemer."

It seems likely, therefore, that Lyly wrote *Euphues* at least in part to demonstrate his compliance with the values of men such as Burghley in the hope that the "fatted calf" of preferment would be forthcoming. Although such hopes remained frustrated, the extraordinary success of *Euphues* persuaded Lyly that there were other avenues to advancement, and he turned again to his fictional hero, but this time to tell an entirely different story.

Much has been made of the delay in the publication of *Euphues and His England*. Lyly ended the first book with the apparent promise of a sequel "within one summer," but his second work did not in fact appear until 1580. The interval probably does not need any explanation, since the promise may have simply been the conventional one of "if this work is accepted, I will write another" used by so many contemporaries. If, in fact, the composition of the sequel took longer than Lyly expected, however, it should come as no surprise, since he completely transformed his story, his tone, and his sense of audience for the later work.

Although some modern readers have argued for a thematic consistency between the two Euphues books, the differences far outweigh the similarities, as Lyly himself recognized: "Twins they are not, but yet brothers; the one nothing resembling the other. . . . So may it be that had I not named Euphues, few would have thought it had been Euphues." Where the first volume was thoroughly anticourtly in sentiment, the second is decidedly sympathetic to courtliness; where the first was radically misogynist, the second tends toward uxoriousness; where the majority of the first book was devoted to moral treatises, the second is almost entirely dedicated to narratives of courtly love; and where the first ends in a kind of neoplatonic ladder of love in which Euphues rejects women to pursue philosophy and rejects philosophy to pursue divinity, the second ends in the thoroughly secular marriages of Camilla and Surius and Philautus and Frances. Like Philautus and Euphues at the end of the first narrative, the two books go very much their own ways: "the one was so addicted to the court, the other so wedded to the university."

The differences in tone and subject matter between the two books are delineated most clearly in the epistles that preface them. Of *Euphues* Lyly says, "I think there be more speeches which for gravity will mislike the foolish than unseemly terms which for vanity may offend the wise"; he concludes "To the Gentlemen Readers" with "I submit myself to

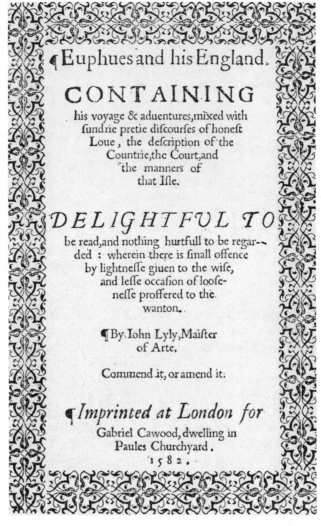

¶Euphues and his England.

CONTAINING

his voyage & aduentures, mixed with
sundrie pretie discourses of honest
Loue, the description of the
Countrie, the Court, and
the manners of
that Isle.

DELIGHTFVL TO

be read, and nothing hurtfull to be regarded : wherein there is small offence
by lightnesse giuen to the wise,
and lesse occasion of loose-
nesse proffered to the
wanton.

¶By Iohn Lyly, Maister
of Arte.

Commend it, or amend it.

¶Imprinted at London for

Gabriel Cawood, dwelling in
Paules Churchyard.
1582.

Title page for the 1582 edition of Lyly's sequel to Euphues,
*which presents a more sympathetic portrayal of court
life than had its predecessor*

the judgement of the wise and I little esteem the censure of fools." *Euphues and His England,* on the other hand, is introduced by an epistle "To the Ladies and Gentlewomen of England John Lyly Wisheth What They Would," in which the author declares that "Euphues had rather be shut in a lady's casket than open in a scholar's study." This change obviously reflects Lyly's consciousness of the (perhaps unanticipated) female audience of the first book, but the shift is also illustrated by the change in dedicatee. Whoever Lord Delaware may have been, it is known that the earl of Oxford was a poet, a playwright, and the most Italianate courtier in Elizabeth's court.

In his biography of Lyly, Albert Feuillerat characterizes this shift as a "régression morale" from the serious humanism embodied in the didactic treatises of the first volume to the courtly enter-

tainment of the second. It is clear, however, that Lyly is simply recognizing the realities of patronage. It is the second book, with its extravagant patriotism, its lavish praise of Queen Elizabeth, and its dedication to Oxford, that secures Lyly's position as what Feuillerat calls with some disdain "amuseur de la Cour."

Despite all the clues in the prefatory material, however, the shift in tone in *Euphues and His England* is not immediately apparent. The narrative begins with Euphues relating a tale for Philautus's instruction that is very much like Euphues' own story in the earlier work. It is a story of a father who bequeaths wise advice to his son instead of wealth and of a son who rejects the advice and goes out into the world to seek adventure. On his way, Callimachus meets a hermit who tells him his own tale of experience and warns him against making the same mistakes. Like Euphues in the first book, Callimachus denies the applicability of the advice to himself. In the end, of course, Callimachus's experience proves to be just as unfortunate as the hermit's or any other prodigal son's, and when he returns to the hermit's cell at the end of his travels it is to admit that "I find too late, yet at length, that in age there is a certain foresight which youth cannot search, and a kind of experience unto which unripened years cannot come, so that I must of necessity confess that youth never reineth well but when age holdeth the bridle."

At this point, however, this prodigal-son story becomes less like the original *Euphues* and more like the biblical parable, for the hermit turns out to be Callimachus's uncle, who is holding the father's wealth for Callimachus when he becomes wise enough to handle it. In this case, filial submission is immediately (if indirectly) rewarded by a father who is both wise and generous. It is not simply that the moral rigor of the first book has been moderated; the whole process of storytelling has become more self-conscious in the second book. Instead of the narrative serving as exemplum for a moral conclusion or mere pretext for a sermon, Euphues (and, one assumes, Lyly) is more conscious of storytelling as a performance. Although Euphues is ostensibly telling this story for Philautus's edification, he is actually addressing a larger audience within the narrative. When Euphues begins his tale, "The other[s] that were then in the ship flocked about Euphues." It may also be a function of this increased self-reflexivity that Lyly is apparently poking fun at Euphues by having him tell a story about the dangers of travel while on ship from Italy to England.

Lyly is still not through ringing changes on Euphues' story, however. When Euphues and Philautus reach England, they first meet Fidus, who regales them with his own prodigal-son story, which is in some respects even closer to the original Euphues story. Like Euphues, Fidus meets an old man who gives him good counsel, which Fidus rejects. Like Euphues, Fidus falls in love with a woman who is already in love with another man. Unlike the misogynistic first volume, however, the sequel represents women as models of faithfulness and restraint. Unlike Lucilla, Iffida rejects Fidus's importunate advances and remains constant in her love for Thirsus.

Again the differences between the two women are emphasized by the similarities. Lucilla debates with herself the dilemma of choosing between Euphues' new love and Philautus's old love — "And canst thou, Lucilla, be so light of love in forsaking

Philautus to fly to Euphues? . . . Why Euphues doth perhaps desire my love, but Philautus hath deserved it. . . . Aye, but the latter love is most fervent; aye, but the first ought to be most faithful" — and ends up choosing Euphues. Iffida, on the other hand, poses the question to Fidus — "Wouldst thou have me inconstant to my old friend, and faithful to a new? . . . tender love maketh greatest show of blossoms but tried love bringeth forth sweetest juice." It is not a dilemma for Iffida; she already knows the answer and challenges Fidus to recognize the validity of her position. As a result, she is not forced to choose one man and reject the other but can offer Fidus a kind of compromise — "for the great good-will thou bearest me I can not reject thy service, but I will not admit thy love. . . . If to talk with me or to continually be in [my] company may in any respect satisfy thy desire, assure thyself I will attend on thee as diligently as thy nurse and be more careful for thee than thy physician."

The remainder of the book (more than two-thirds of the total) is devoted primarily to the recounting of Philautus's amorous pursuit of Camilla, which generally recapitulates the story of Fidus and Iffida. Camilla virtuously rejects Philautus's advances because she is in love with Surius, and finally Philautus accedes to reality and reaches a kind of compromise in the reciprocated love of Frances. As in *Euphues,* Euphues and Philautus have a falling out and are ultimately reconciled, and there are lengthy disquisitions and the exchange of letters; but, unlike *Euphues,* in the end things are resolved within the conditions of this world. It is this sense of compromise, of balance, leading to accommodation and resolution, that most clearly distinguishes *Euphues and His England* from its predecessor.

In *Euphues* all arguments, debates, or issues consist of choosing between contradictory and mutually exclusive positions. This characteristic was probably the result of contemporary scholastic training in which students were required to argue *in utramque partem* — taking both sides of a single issue — so that the emphasis was on the skill in arguing rather than the correctness of the conclusion. The problem that arises, as Lyly points out, is that too much information can be paralyzing: "Too much study doth intoxicate their brains. 'For,' say they, 'although iron the more it is used the brighter it is, yet silver with much wearing doth waste to nothing. . . . For neither is there anything but that hath his contraries.'"

A good example of the frequent dramatization of this dilemma in *Euphues* occurs in Euphues' debate about the value of friendship:

I have read . . . and well I believe it, that a friend is in prosperity a pleasure, a solace in adversity, in grief a comfort, in joy a merry companion. . . . Can any treasure in this transitory pilgrimage be of more value than a friend . . . ? But whither am I carried? Have I not also learned that one should eat a bushel of salt with him whom he meaneth to make his friend? That trial maketh trust? That there is falsehood in fellowship?

Both alternatives are at one time or another true, but the characters in *Euphues* are not capable of choosing confidently between the competing possibilities.

Lyly is not, however, arguing that secure conclusions are unavailable to the human intellect; such epistemological despair is obviously contrary to the didactic enterprise at the heart of *Euphues*. The narrator frequently intrudes precisely to make certain that the lesson is not missed: "Here ye may behold, gentlemen, how lewdly wit standeth in his own light." While acknowledging the difficulty of making informed decisions, however, Lyly also stresses the urgency of making the correct choice by pointing to the dramatically different ethical consequences implicit in each choice: "if wit be employed in the honest study of learning, what thing so precious as wit? If in the idle trade of love, what thing more pestilent than wit?"

The question is how does one learn to apply profitably the often contradictory lessons contained in history, mythology, or natural history? The answer is apparently experience. Of Euphues' debate about friendship, the narrator says, "Although there be none so ignorant that doth not know, neither any so impudent that will not confess friendship to be the jewel of human joy; yet whosoever shall see this amity grounded upon a little affection will soon conjecture that it shall be dissolved upon a light occasion." It is the specific instance, the consequences of specific actions, not the general precept, that determines the truth.

It has often been remarked that *Euphues* is a treatise in praise of experience as the basis for knowledge – as Euphues says, "It is commonly said, yet do I think it a common lie, that experience is the mistress of fools; for in my opinion they be most fools that want it"; but at the same time there is an insistence on the wisdom of being able to learn from someone else's experience – "Is it not far better to abhor sins by the remembrance of others' faults than by repentance of thine own follies?" The problem with the knowledge that comes from experience is that it often comes too late. As Philautus says after Euphues has betrayed him with Lucilla, "I perceive at the last (although, being deceived, it

be too late) . . . that friendship, though it be plighted by shaking the hand, yet it is shaken off by fraud of the heart."

If one sees *Euphues* as a plea for academic advancement through the patronage of such paternal figures as Burghley, this central paradox between experience and precept may be seen as the inevitable result of Lyly's attempting simultaneously to distinguish himself as a man of experience and to ingratiate himself as a follower of paternal precepts. Interestingly, Burghley's letter to his son embodies the same paradox, characterizing his "precepts" as "such advertisements and rules for the squaring of thy life as are gained rather by much experience than long reading." But he expects his son to avoid similar experiences by reading the precepts. It is perhaps a universal paradox, but it works itself out in particularly clear and poignant terms in Lyly's *Euphues*. In the same section ("Euphues and His Ephebus") in which Euphues claims the distinction of personal experience – "Of all these things I may the bolder speak having tried it true, to mine own trouble" – he can conclude only by recapitulating the same advice Eubulus had given him at the beginning of the story, from which he had signally failed to profit.

Theodore L. Steinberg has suggested that Euphues' failure to follow advice inevitably dooms his own advice to ineffectiveness, and *Euphues* therefore represents finally a parody of advice books. Such an interpretation, however, does not adequately account for the long, solemn, almost turgid, didactic passages in the book. In *Euphues* the paradoxical relation between experience and precept is felt as troubling, not as comic.

In *Euphues and His England* this paradox is still not comic, but, like so much else in the sequel, it is less troubling because those giving advice are themselves aware of the limits of its efficacy. As the hermit is telling his story to Callimachus in an attempt to spare him a repetition of his mistakes, he stops himself to acknowledge – not with anger or frustration but with a kind of gentle acceptance – that his words are probably falling on deaf ears: "Such a quarrel hath there always been between the grave and the cradle, that he that is young thinketh the old man fond and the old knoweth the young man to be a fool." Such a recognition does not, however, prevent the hermit from dispensing advice, because it is his duty: "But, Callimachus, for the towardness I see in thee I must needs love thee, and for thy frowardness of force counsel thee."

Unlike *Euphues,* in which worldly experience leads finally to a rejection of the world, *Euphues and*

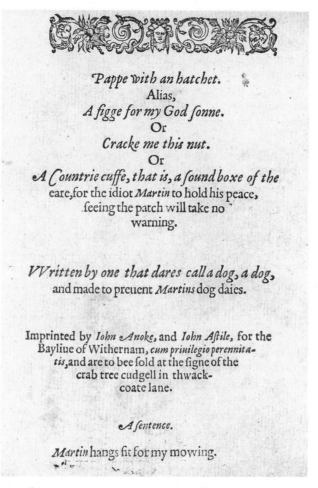

Pappe with an hatchet.
Alias,
A figge for my God sonne.
Or
Cracke me this nut.
Or
A Countrie cuffe, that is, a sound boxe of the
eare, for the idiot *Martin* to hold his peace,
seeing the patch will take no
warning.

VVritten by one that dares call a dog, a dog,
and made to preuent *Martins* dog daies.

Imprinted by *Iohn Anoke,* and *Iohn Astile,* for the
Bayliue of Withernam, *cum priuilegio perennita-*
tis, and are to bee sold at the signe of the
crab tree cudgell in thwack-
coate lane.

A sentence.

Martin hangs fit for my mowing.

Title page for Lyly's pamphlet in the Martin Marprelate
controversy, written at the behest of the Anglican bishops

His England is filled with instances of an acceptance of the way things are, a sense of accommodation with reality, even occasional playfulness. When the Eubulus-figure in *Euphues and His England* gives Fidus advice about the court, he is careful to allow some courtly exercises: "Which things as I know them all to be courtly, so for my part I account them necessary." His only warning is that Fidus dallies too much with women. Even Euphues repudiates the extreme misogyny of the "Cooling Card" (a paraphrase of Ovid's *Remedia Amoris* he had offered as his final word on women in *Euphues*), confessing himself "rash . . . to give so peremptory sentence." When Euphues is called upon later in the book to act as judge in a "questione d'amore," he carefully balances the two sides of the debate and argues in favor of the mean.

The moral earnestness of the first book becomes so relaxed in the sequel, in fact, that Lyly even feels comfortable poking fun at himself. When Euphues tells Philautus that "talk the more it is sea-soned with fine phrases the less it savoreth of true meaning," it is impossible to imagine that Lyly did not see its application to his own work. And when Psellus, the magician Philautus goes to for a potion to make Camilla love him, offers a "merry" account of the efficacy of magic, his examples sound remarkably like a parody of all the examples from natural history the other characters keep reciting: "The herb Carisium, moistened with the blood of a lizard and hanged about your neck, will cause Camilla (for her you love best) to dream of your services, suits, desires, deserts, and whatsoever you would wish her to think of you; but being wakened she shall not remember what she dreamed of."

This is not to suggest, however, that *Euphues and His England* is not a serious work. If Lyly has chosen more to entertain than to preach in his second work, it is only because he believes it will ultimately be more persuasive. Like Lyly's first book, *Euphues and His England* is at least in part a plea for patronage. When Euphues and Philautus debate the

111

relative merits of spiritual and physical love, Lyly (as narrator) takes Philautus's side, arguing that wooing should ultimately come to "full fruition" – "For they that live by the view of beauty still look very lean, and they that feed only upon virtue at board will go with an hungry belly to bed." Although the passage has a genuinely comic tone, Lyly is surely glancing at his own, so far unsuccessful, courting of favor.

Even on the issue of patronage, however, *Euphues and His England* takes a more balanced, more accommodating position. Although Euphues again returns to his university at the end of the story, he acknowledges that he was "willing to live in that court," claiming that he would stay there if he could: "I would Fortune had dealt so favorably with a poor Grecian, that he might have either been born here or able to live here." He concludes with a demonstration of his courtly skills in his "Glass for Europe," which praises both Burghley and Elizabeth by name.

Under the patronage of the earl of Oxford, Lyly did manage to stay at court, where he wrote and produced his elegant comedies, which are now appreciated primarily for their effect on Shakespeare's later plays, but his services were never rewarded with any formal position at court, and he remained at the margins of power as an "amuseur de la Cour."

It would be unreasonable to leave a discussion of Lyly's Euphues works without mentioning the famous (or infamous) prose style to which they gave a name. It is appropriate that *euphuism* was coined by Lyly's adversary Gabriel Harvey, for the word has been a term of disapprobation and even disgust for most of the four hundred years of its existence. George Saintsbury characterized it in his *A History of Elizabethan Literature* (1887) as "eccentric and tasteless," and J. J. Jusserand in *The English Novel in the Time of Shakespeare* (1890) called Lyly's style "immoderate, prodigious, monstrous." More recently C. S. Lewis has called *Euphues* a "monstrosity" and a "fatal success." As Walter N. King asserts in his essay "John Lyly and Elizabethan Rhetoric" (1955), "Lyly has . . . become a major whipping boy in English literature."

What is most remarkable, however, is that the transition from literary phenomenon to literary whipping boy occurred in Lyly's own lifetime. In the early 1580s the two Euphues books were being reprinted at an astonishing rate, and imitators were eagerly jumping on the bandwagon. In *Don Simonides* (1584) Barnaby Riche writes of Lyly as one "who can court it with the best and scholar it with the most, in whom I know not whether I should more commend his manners or his learning, the one so exquisite, the other so general"; and in *A Discourse of English Poetry* (1586) William Webbe writes of "the witty discourse of his *Euphues* . . . his singular eloquence and brave composition of apt words and sentences."

The reaction was also beginning in 1586, however. In his epistle to the reader of *Albion's England,* William Warner warns of the danger "that to run on the letter we often run from the matter; and being over-prodigal in similes, we become less profitable in sentences and more prolixious to sense." By 1589 the parodies of euphuism began to appear with Robert Greene's *Menaphon* – subtitled *Camilla's Alarum to Slumbering Euphues in His Melancholy Cell at Silexedra* – and Shakespeare joins the fun with a speech he gives to Falstaff in the first part of *Henry IV*. Probably the earliest critique of euphuism (though not published until 1595) occurs in Philip Sidney's *Defence of Poetry*:

> Now for similitudes in certain printed discourses, I think all herbarists, all stories of beasts, fowls and fishes are rifled up that they may come in multitudes to wait upon any of our conceits; which certainly is as absurd a surfeit to the ears as is possible; for the force of a similitude not being to prove anything to a contrary disputer, but only to explain to a willing hearer, when that is done the rest is a most tedious prattling, rather over-swaying the memory from the purpose whereto they were applied than any whit informing the judgment, already either satisfied or by similitudes not to be satisfied.

In fact, it was the different style of Sidney's *Arcadia* that replaced euphuism in popularity after its publication in 1590.

When Edward Blount republished Lyly's comedies in 1632, he introduced them with a favorable acknowledgment of Lyly's former popularity – "All our ladies were then his scholars, and that beauty in Court which could not parley euphuism was as little regarded as she which now there speaks not French" – but it was merely the praise of nostalgia. Blount says he has "digged up the grave" of Lyly in order to publish his plays. Blount's most significant remark, however, is his statement that "Our nation [is] in his debt for a new English which he taught them," for that is surely true. Through its brief but enormous popularity as well as through the almost virulent reaction against it, euphuism introduced the possibility of an artistic style for prose.

The stylistic qualities of euphuism have been enumerated and analyzed repeatedly, so only the briefest discussion is necessary here. As the comments cited above indicate, the most distinguishing characteristic of euphuism for Lyly's contemporaries was its liberal use of similes drawn from natural history — the ultimate source of which was Pliny; but, as Morris W. Croll has shown in his and Harry Clemons's 1916 edition of Lyly's works, the more immediate source was probably Erasmus's *Similia*. Many of them are more or less reasonable and straightforward, even if not always true, but some of them strike the modern reader as preposterous. Looking for something in nature to which to compare Euphues' perfidy, for instance, Philautus says: "I see now that as the fish Scolopidus in the flood Araris at the waxing of the moon is as white as the driven snow and at the waning as black as the burnt coal, so Euphues which at the first increasing of our familiarity was very zealous is now at the last cast become most faithless." *Euphues* is also filled with similes drawn from history and mythology, as well as such "unnatural natural history." And the effect of such rhetorical abundance is even further enhanced by Lyly's frequent use of proverbs.

Other characteristics of euphuism consist of what Croll calls "figures of sound" — "isocolon" (successive phrases of equal length), "parison" (correspondence of parts of speech), and "paramoion" (similarity in sound — alliteration, assonance, rhyme). Frequently all three occur in the same passage, as when Euphues tries to excuse himself from providing the after-dinner discourse at Lucilla's: "I may well make you weary but never the wiser, and give you occasion rather to laugh at my rashness than to like my reasons."

For Croll even the characteristic use of similes and antithesis in euphuism is merely part of the "sound design." Jonas A. Barish, however, argues in his essay "The Prose Style of John Lyly" (1956) that the constant use of antithesis is the defining characteristic of euphuism, and that it is not a figure of sound but a figure of thought — "by sheer frequency of repetition it comes to be felt as a major insight." He concludes that Lyly's style is in fact identical with his substance: "One would scarcely need to go further for the moral of *Euphues* than the style, which offers for our inspection the world as antithesis."

In addition to trying to decide what exactly euphuism is, scholars have also devoted considerable time and energy determining where it comes from. C. S. Lewis has shown the general trajectory of euphuistic elements in the works of such writers as Roger Ascham, Thomas Wilson, Thomas North, and George Pettie, but the immediate source of full-blown euphuism remained a perplexing question until William Ringler apparently put the matter to rest in his essay "The Immediate Source of Euphuism" (1938) by demonstrating that all the early euphuists had been students at Oxford and therefore had had the opportunity to hear the Latin lectures of John Rainolds, which embodied all the qualities of euphuism as employed by Lyly and his contemporaries.

It is not surprising that euphuism would have such academic origins, but the history of Lyly's use of the style ironically exhibits a movement from the university to the court to the gutter. In 1589 Lyly was apparently employed as reader of new books for the bishop of London. In *John Lyly* (1905) J. Dover Wilson remarks, "This connexion with the censorship of the day is interesting, as showing how Lyly was drawn into the whirlpool of the *Marprelate* controversy." The scurrilous Marprelate pamphlets were pseudonymous attacks on the clerical hierarchy of the established church published by radical Puritans. The bishops enlisted writers such as Lyly and Thomas Nashe to try to defeat "Martin Marprelate" at his own game. The result in Lyly's case was *Pap with a Hatchet. Alias, a Fig for My Godson* (1589).

Lyly's pamphlet has its virtues, including a few clever tales and a metaphor of a chess game that gets at the heart of the controversy from the loyalist position: "If a Martin can play at chess as well as his nephew the ape, he shall know what it is for a scaddle pawn to cross a bishop in his own walk. Such dydoppers must be taken up, else they'll not stick to check the king." Nevertheless it is hard not to sympathize with Hunter's comment in *John Lyly: The Humanist as Courtier* (1962) that the work is "a lamentable performance, turgid and tasteless." To his credit, Lyly seems sensitive to the tastelessness he was obliged to assume in the pamphlet war: "I was loath so to write as I have done, but that I learned that he that drinks with cutters must not be without his ale dagger, nor he that buckles with Martin, without his lavish terms."

With *Pap,* Lyly's career as a prose writer comes to an end. The only other writings outside of his dramatic works are his famous petitionary letters to Queen Elizabeth of 1598 and 1601. Elizabeth had apparently led Lyly to believe that he was going to be granted the reversion of the post of Master of the Revels, and when it was instead given to Sir George Buc, Lyly wrote:

If your sacred Majesty think me unworthy, and that after ten years tempest I must at the court suffer shipwreck of my time, my hopes, my wits, vouchsafe in your never-erring judgment some plank or rafter to waft me into the country where in my sad and settled devotion, I may in every corner of a thatched cottage write prayers instead of plays – prayers for your long and prosperous life and a repentence that I have played the fool so long, and yet live.

Three years later he wrote again:

Thirteen years your Highness' servant, and yet nothing; twenty friends that though they say they will be sure, I find them sure to be slow; a thousand hopes, but all nothing; a hundred promises, but yet nothing. Thus casting up the inventory of my friends, hopes, promises and time the *summa totalis* amounteth in all to just nothing.

Hunter sees these letters as "a despairing comment on the Humanist dream of Eloquence to move princes," but Lyly had recognized the element of frustration inherent in courtship as early as 1578. When Euphues confesses his love to Lucilla, "minding . . . that he should neither take hold of her promise, neither unkindness of her preciseness, she fed him indifferently with hope and despair, reason and affection, life and death."

Despite his lifelong failure to secure a position at court, however, it was not entirely true that the influence of Lyly's friends amounted to nothing. It was no doubt through the agency of his friends at court that he was seated in Parliament in 1589, 1593, 1597, and 1601; and Hunter rightly points out that "membership in Parliament was an honour that few Elizabethan writers achieved." It was also probably through his connections at court that Lyly met and married, in 1593, Beatrice Browne, an heiress and a relative of Burghley's aunt, whom Hunter characterizes as "quite a prize in the marriage market for the Canterbury registrar's son." Nevertheless, by the time Lyly died in 1606, unrewarded by the court he had tried so hard to serve in his own way and "all but ignored by the literary world which earlier had acclaimed him as its brightest star," as Joseph W. Houppert writes in *John Lyly* (1975), it is hard not to believe that he had looked back on his life as a disappointment.

The decline in popularity of Lyly's Euphues books that began so precipitously in his own lifetime has continued to a large extent to the present day. Even those who succeed in reading the first volume are rarely motivated to proceed to the sequel. Yet the current fascination with Elizabethan power politics and its manifestations in courtship and patronage would suggest that Lyly is ripe for reassessment. It is not simply that his Euphues

works represent appeals for courtly patronage, however; it is that they record, in quite dramatic terms, a shift in the sort of patronage Lyly solicited and therefore provide insights into the whole patronage system and the different rhetorical strategies it demanded.

The shift in tone and subject matter between *Euphues* and *Euphues and His England* has, of course, escaped no one who has studied both texts, but recent emphasis has typically been less on the political implications of that shift than on the moral implications. In "'A Large Occasion of Discourse': John Lyly and the Art of Civil Conversation" (1991) Catherine Bates traces a move "away from a 'bourgeois' delineation of love-making, with its implicit critique of court mores, to a growing appreciation of courtly models of love." In her 1992 revision, however, she transforms this social-class distinction into explicitly moral categories when she discerns "a growing preoccupation on Lyly's part with the highly ambivalent relation between licit and illicit sexuality."

Arthur F. Kinney also emphasizes the moral component of Lyly's shift in tone and material. Although he identifies an "overall movement from sophistry to spirituality in *Euphues*," it is in *Euphues and His England* that "the initial *display of wit* . . . is transformed into a sobering *commitment to values*." The possibility, however, that the values to which Lyly was committed are less ethical than professional remains worth exploring.

Bibliography:

S. A. Tannenbaum, *John Lyly: A Concise Bibliography* (New York: Tannenbaum, 1940).

Biography:

Albert Feuillerat, *John Lyly: Contribution à l'Histoire de la Renaissance en Angleterre* (Cambridge: Cambridge University Press, 1910; New York: Russell & Russell, 1968).

References:

Jonas A. Barish, "The Prose Style of John Lyly," *ELH,* 23 (March 1956): 14–35;

Catherine Bates, "'A Large Occasion of Discourse': John Lyly and the Art of Civil Conversation," *Review of English Studies,* 42 (November 1991): 469–486;

Bates, *The Rhetoric of Courtship in Elizabethan Language and Literature* (Cambridge: Cambridge University Press, 1992), pp. 89–110;

Walter R. Davis, *Idea and Act in Elizabethan Fiction* (Princeton: Princeton University Press, 1969), pp. 109–121;

Richard Helgerson, *The Elizabethan Prodigals* (Berkeley: University of California Press, 1976), pp. 58–78;

Joseph W. Houppert, *John Lyly* (Boston: Twayne, 1975);

G. K. Hunter, *John Lyly: The Humanist as Courtier* (London: Routledge & Kegan Paul, 1962);

Walter N. King, "John Lyly and Elizabethan Rhetoric," *Studies in Philology,* 52 (April 1955): 149–161;

Arthur F. Kinney, *Humanist Poetics* (Amherst: University of Massachusetts Press, 1986), pp. 133–180;

G. Wilson Knight, "Lyly," *Review of English Studies,* 15 (April 1939): 146–163;

David Margolies, *Novel and Society in Elizabethan England* (Totowa, N.J.: Barnes & Noble, 1985), pp. 20–63;

Richard A. McCabe, "Wit, Eloquence, and Wisdom in *Euphues: The Anatomy of Wit,*" *Studies in Philology,* 81 (Summer 1984): 299–324;

William Ringler, "The Immediate Source of Euphuism," *PMLA,* 53 (September 1938): 678–686;

Theodore L. Steinberg, "The Anatomy of *Euphues,*" *Studies in English Literature,* 17 (Winter 1977): 27–38;

J. Dover Wilson, *John Lyly* (Cambridge: Macmillan & Bowes, 1905).

Papers:

A few of Lyly's autograph letters are extant, including four addressed to Sir Robert Cecil (Hatfield House) and one addressed to Sir Robert Cotton (British Library).

A Mirror for Magistrates

Frederick Kiefer
University of Arizona

Renaissance editions: *A Myrroure for Magistrates,* by William Baldwin and others (London: Thomas Marshe, 1559; revised and enlarged, 1563; revised, 1571); revised and enlarged again as *The Last Parte of the Mirour for Magistrates. Newly corrected and amended* (London: Thomas Marshe, 1574; revised, 1575; revised again, 1578; revised and enlarged again, London: Henry Marshe, 1587);

The First Parte of the Mirour for Magistrates, Containing the Falles of Princes from the Comming of Brute to the Incarnation, by John Higgins (London: Thomas Marshe, 1574; enlarged, 1575); enlarged again as *The Mirour for Magistrates. Newly Imprinted, and Enlarged* (London: Printed by H. Marsh for Thomas Marsh, 1587); enlarged again as *A Mirour for Magistrates. Newly Enlarged with a Last Part,* edited by R. Nichols (London: F. Kyngston, 1610 [i.e., 1609]); republished as *The Falles of Unfortunate Princes* (London: Printed by F. Kingston for W. Aspley, 1619);

The Seconde Part of the Mirrour for Magistrates, by Thomas Blenerhasset (London: Printed by Thomas Dawson for Richard Webster, 1578).

Modern editions: *Mirror for Magistrates,* 3 volumes, edited by Joseph Haslewood (London: Lackington, Allen, 1815);

The Mirror for Magistrates: Edited from Original Texts in the Huntington Library, edited by Lily B. Campbell (Cambridge: Cambridge University Press, 1938; New York: Barnes & Noble, 1960);

Parts Added to the Mirror for Magistrates by John Higgins and Thomas Blenerhasset: Edited from Original Texts in the Huntington Library, edited by Campbell (Cambridge: Cambridge University Press, 1946).

Although among the most popular and influential books published during Queen Elizabeth's reign, *A Mirror for Magistrates* (1559) is virtually unread today. Because the work is so little known, students of literature have blithely accepted the notion that the *Mirror for Magistrates* is as monolithically doctrinaire and simplistic as its headnotes imply.

Nothing could be further from the truth. The *Mirror for Magistrates,* a series of biographies written in poetry and joined by prose interludes, manifests the heterogeneity of its multiple authorship and the writers' efforts to make sense of lives that do not conform to one pattern. In subject and treatment the *Mirror for Magistrates* is diverse, encompassing a profusion of case studies, disparate evaluations of the forces that drive history, and considerable variations in attitude and tone. Although belonging to a period that C. S. Lewis dubbed the drab age in his *English Literature in the Sixteenth Century, Excluding Drama* (1954), the *Mirror for Magistrates* contains poems of considerable subtlety and sophistication. In addition, unlike their medieval predecessors, the poets cast their narratives in the first person, imbuing them with immediacy and liveliness. The ghostly narrators engage the reader by their urgency, inviting him or her to share their quandaries in life and astonishment at their fate. From its first publication in 1559, the *Mirror for Magistrates* exerted a strong appeal: its success inspired additional, enlarged editions, culminating in ninety-one poems in the 1610 edition, and a small library of tragic complaints by other authors. Even more important, the *Mirror for Magistrates* helped to shape the very concept of tragedy in plays by Christopher Marlowe, Thomas Kyd, William Shakespeare, and their contemporaries.

The *Mirror for Magistrates* was envisioned as a continuation of the instructive biographies initiated by Boccaccio's *De Casibus Virorum Illustrium* (circa 1356–1360), which numbered among its descendants Geoffrey Chaucer's *Monk's Tale* (circa 1380–1394), Laurent de Premierfait's *De la ruine des nobles hommes et femmes* (circa 1400), and John Lydgate's *Fall of Princes* (1431–1438). In fact, it was a printer of Lydgate's work, John Wayland, who proposed that William Baldwin, an author and translator, extend the biographical portraits down to their own time and place. Daunted by the scope of the project, Baldwin was reluctant to undertake it without assistance, and so Wayland recruited others to help. They included three men who successfully negotiated the political currents of the mid-sixteenth-century court: George Ferrers, Thomas Phaer, and Thomas Chaloner.

George Ferrers was born around 1500, the son of Thomas Ferrers of St. Albans. He earned a bachelor's degree in canon law at Cambridge in 1531 and published *The Book of Magna Carta, with Divers Other Statutes,* a collection of translations from Latin and French into English, in 1534. Thomas Cromwell secured for him an appointment at court, and, following the death of Henry VIII, whose will left Ferrers some money, he served the lord protector, the duke of Somerset. In 1541 Ferrers married Elizabeth Bourchier, and in 1548 he received from Edward VI certain properties that had been leased by his wife's first husband. After the death of his first wife, Ferrers married Jane Sowthtrote in March 1546, and she bore him a son. In that decade Ferrers was involved in an important conflict over parliamentary privilege. Raphael Holinshed reports that in 1542 Ferrers, who represented Plymouth, was arrested in London; at issue was a surety for the debt of a man named Weldon. The speaker of the House of Commons ordered Ferrers's release, and there ensued at the jail a brawl between the parliamentary sergeant-at-arms and the officials who held Ferrers. The sheriffs were called and they too rebuffed the sergeant. Subsequently Ferrers was released and those responsible for detaining him were briefly imprisoned. Henry VIII himself approved the exemption from arrest of a burgess. Ferrers went on to represent Plymouth in the Parliaments of 1545 and 1553; he represented Brackley in 1554–1555 and St. Albans in 1571. His literary skill led to his being named the master of the king's pastimes for the Christmas season of 1551–1552 at Greenwich. Ferrers also served as lord of misrule for the Christmas festivities of 1552–1553 and was himself entertained that January by the lord mayor of London. Queen Mary appointed Ferrers lord of misrule in 1553–1554.

Ferrers also took an interest in history, for John Stow records that he "collected the whole history of Queen Mary, as the same is set down under the name of Richard Grafton." He contributed to history even more directly by accompanying the duke of Somerset on a military expedition into Scotland during the first year of Edward's reign and by helping to put down the rebellion of Sir Thomas Wyatt in 1554. In 1555 he reported to the Privy Council that Princess Elizabeth was in league with John Dee, the astrologer. The implied hostility of this action perhaps explains why Ferrers faded from prominence when Elizabeth was crowned in 1558; he did, however, serve as an official who handled confiscated or forfeited property in Essex and Hertfordshire in 1567. He also wrote a speech for address to the queen when she was entertained at Kenilworth in 1575. Late in life he married again (November 1569); his third wife was Margaret Prestone. He died in January 1579 and was buried at Flamstead, Hertfordshire. Ferrers was praised by Francis Meres in 1598 as among "our best for tragedy," a reference to his contribution to the *Mirror for Magistrates,* and by George Puttenham in *The Art of English Poesie* (1589), though both mistakenly give his first name as Edward.

Baldwin, Ferrers, Chaloner, and Phaer apparently formed a collegial group. Chaloner had worked with Ferrers on courtly entertainments for the Christmas season of 1551–1552, while Baldwin assisted Ferrers in 1552–1553, when the two men roomed together. Collaboration on the *Mirror for Magistrates* must have fostered the bonds of friendship. Chaloner wrote an epitaph for Thomas Phaer, and Phaer's will specified that the inscription on his tomb be written by Ferrers.

In the prose interludes of the *Mirror for Magistrates* these poets are represented as sitting together, listening to one another's narratives, and responding to what they hear. At the first meeting, to which Baldwin brought his copy of John Lydgate's *Fall of Princes,* they discussed whose lives were to be recounted and by whom. Ferrers suggested beginning with the reign of Richard II and volunteered to compose the stories of Robert Tresilian and Thomas of Woodstock. Evidence from this and later editions indicates that Chaloner wrote the story of Richard II, and Phaer (who lived for part of his life in Wales), that of Owen Glendower. (It is also possible that one or more of these poets wrote other poems in the *Mirror for Magistrates* to which their names are not attached.)

The poets also agreed that all the ghostly narrators should address themselves to Baldwin. His authorship of the remaining unassigned narratives is plausible, if uncertain. By his own testimony he had more offers of help than collaborators. In the dedication of the *Mirror for Magistrates* he reports of the project: "When I first took it in hand, I had the help of many granted, and offered of some, but of few performed, scarce of any: so that when I intended to have continued it to Queen Mary's time, I have been fain to end it much sooner." In his 1563 address to the reader, Baldwin says that seven men attended the meeting at which the *Mirror for Magistrates* was planned, but if poets other than those named above actually contributed, their names are not recorded.

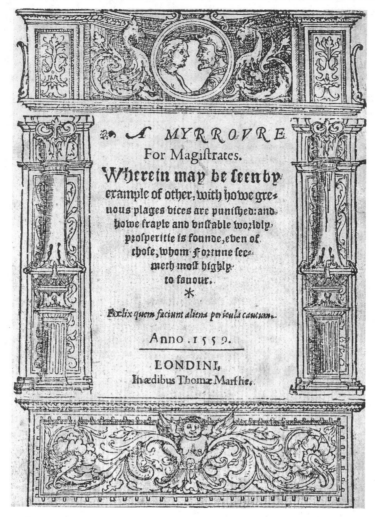

Title page for the first edition of the series of instructive biographies that would become one of the most influential books of Elizabethan England (courtesy of the Lilly Library, Indiana University)

Baldwin encountered an even more serious problem than reluctant partners. His 1559 dedication reveals that an earlier attempt to publish had been halted: "the work was begun and part of it printed four years ago, but hindered by the Lord Chancellor that then was, nevertheless, through the means of my Lord Stafford, lately perused and licensed." Mary's chancellor, Bishop Stephen Gardiner, suppressed the *Mirror for Magistrates,* evidently because its accounts were largely based on Edward Hall's 1548 chronicle, which was specifically banned in a proclamation of 13 June 1555; sympathetic to the goals of the Reformation, Hall was anathema to the Catholic queen. All that remains of the 1555 *Mirror for Magistrates* is a single leaf of text bearing the running title *A Brief Memorial of Unfortunate English Princes,* together with several copies of a title page. That page, bound with an undated edition of Lydgate's *Fall of Princes* (printed by Wayland), reads: *A Memorial of Such Princes, as Since the Time of King Richard the Second, Have Been Unfortunate in the Realm of England.* When the *Mirror for Magistrates* finally appeared in 1559, Thomas Marshe, a Protestant, was the printer.

Narrated by the ghost of Robert Tresilian, chief justice to Richard II, the first story in the *Mirror of Magistrates* is representative of the poems that follow. More important than specific incidents is the overall significance of Tresilian's life and its application to the present: "Learn by us ye lawyers and judges of the land / Uncorrupt and upright in doom always to stand." Sacrificing personal integrity to self-aggrandizement, Tresilian tailored his judgments to the king's whim: "for world's vain promotion, / More to man than God did bear our whole devotion." Although his crimes may have been particular to his office, Tresilian delivers gnomic advice that may apply to anyone: "Happy and twice happy is he that wisely can / Content himself with that which reason doth require." This kind of moralizing lends the *Mirror for Magistrates* its characteristically didactic quality, so prized by Elizabethans and so disparaged by moderns.

If the ghostly narrators sound solemn and sententious, it is because they enjoy an advantage conferred by a finished life. They have lived and died and pondered the meaning of their experience. Representing the intrusion of the next world into this one, they exhort Baldwin not only to listen but also to write down their advice so that others may avoid their mistakes. Tresilian's mood, for example, is imperative: he urges his interlocutor to print, enroll, record, and engrave his story. Like other complainants in the *Mirror for Magistrates,* he assumes that his advice in written form will prove both permanent and efficacious. His interlocutor fails to observe, however, that Tresilian's career illustrates the vulnerability of the written word: by his interpretation of the law, the chief justice perverts its meaning. Also problematic is the effort of this and the other ghosts to hector their listeners into goodness. The persistence of the *de casibus* tradition, from Boccaccio to Baldwin, indicates that the reformation of conduct may be frustrated by an intractable human nature, easily distracted by pleasure and profit. Perhaps this recognition leads the narrators to wring every last lesson from history, as though their intensity could somehow render their counsel effectual. This same recognition is, in part, responsible for the multiplication of stories in subsequent editions. The poets seem to feel that their exhortations will prove the more efficacious through sheer accumulation.

What keeps the narratives from becoming disembodied sermons is their wistful quality. The ghosts express wonderment at the fragility of worldly prosperity, the tendency of things to alter, often for the worse. Tresilian says of his experience, "A change more new or strange seldom hath been seen." He and the other narrators, moreover, remember what it was like to be caught up in the hurly-burly of life, prey to passion and self-interest. Although the remembrance is intended to be admonitory, the speakers ruefully recall the intoxication of power, the pride of office. By evoking that past, they also implicitly acknowledge its attraction. A misty nostalgia colors nearly all of the poems.

The mixed nature of the *Mirror for Magistrates* — detached yet urgent, didactic yet wistful, concerned with the soul yet alert to the claims of this life — is

suggested by the title of the work and its symbolism. As a physical object, a looking glass reflects whatever face or form confronts it. By its function a mirror implicitly signals the fleeting nature of life: the face of a sitter may be quickly transformed by makeup or mood, the changing appearance emblematic of a larger flux. For this reason Dame Fortune was sometimes depicted holding a mirror representing the fragility of worldly existence. A mirror may suggest too an inordinate attention to transient things; it can symbolize self-absorption, even narcissism. Appropriately, mirrors became an accoutrement of personified Vanity, who studies her own reflection in Renaissance engravings and woodcuts. A mirror, however, can suggest something else altogether: an impulse toward introspection and the reform of behavior prompted by self-knowledge. Significantly, Renaissance artists and sculptors commonly represent the cardinal virtue of Prudence as holding a mirror. To the extent that a mirror suggests virtuous conduct, it also implies a guide for future action. Although containing stories of miscreants, the *Mirror for Magistrates* provides a model for righteous living.

The individual mirrors of the *Mirror for Magistrates* teach by negative example. Baldwin says in his dedication, "here as in a looking glass, you shall see (if any vice be in you) how the like hath been punished in others heretofore, whereupon admonished, I trust it will be a good occasion to move you to the sooner amendment. This is the chiefest end, why it is set forth, which God grant it may attain."

To discover suitable instances, the poets consulted the chronicles of Edward Hall and Robert Fabyan, along with Sir Thomas More's acccount of Richard III. What they found, however, did not always advance their purpose, as this prose interlude following Roger de Mortimer's account reveals: "whereas Master Hall whom in this story we chiefly followed, maketh Mowbray accuser, and Bolingbroke appellant, Master Fabyan reporteth the matter quite contrary. . . . Which matter . . . is more hard to decide than needful to our purpose, which mind only to dissuade from vices and exalt virtue." The poets, then, are led by their overriding concern to compensate for what the chroniclers omit or fail to agree on. The ghost of John Tiptoft, Earl of Worcester, undoubtedly speaks for the poets themselves when he says,

Unfruitful Fabyan followed the face
Of time and deeds, but let the causes slip:
Which Hall hath added, but with double grace,

Title page for Thomas Blenerhasset's sequel to A Mirror for Magistrates, *covering figures who lived before the reign of Richard II, the starting point of the 1559 volume (courtesy of the Lilly Library, Indiana University)*

For fear I think lest trouble might him trip:
For this or that (sayeth he) he felt the whip.
Thus story writers leave the causes out
Or so rehearse them, as they were in doubt.

In order to exalt virtue, the poets can scarcely countenance such doubt; they need to explain causation. The format of the narratives is consistent with this objective: the stories are told by the ghosts of people who, for the most part, understand why things happened as they did. Thus, the ghostly narrators know more than did the chroniclers.

In keeping with the celebration of virtue, downfalls are related to misdeeds, crime to punishment. According to a headnote, for example, the fall of Tresilian came about "for misconstruing the laws, and expounding them to serve the prince's affections." The poems, however, are rarely as clearcut as this generalization suggests, for the narrators describe not only divine retribution but also the operation of chance and even the phenomenon of unmerited adversity. Although they describe the ways of God's providence, the narrators also chronicle the play of Fortune, the traditional personification of mutability and contingency. Modern readers, in an effort to reconcile the activities of God and a personified Fortune, have sought to identify the one with the other, positing Fortune as a Dantean executor of providence. Although one poet in a prose link calls Fortune "righteous" in punishing tyrants, that word is never applied to Fortune in the poems. Typically, Fortune conceals her true nature, flattering and deceiving her prey; the poems term her "double" and "false." In short, Fortune is a cunning and treacherous temptress, hardly what is expected in the servant of a rational, benign providence. The poems themselves, then, suggest that for Baldwin and his collaborators, as for other sixteenth-century writers, Fortune is malign, encouraging conduct that brings downfall in this world and perdition in the next.

Scholars have long sought to divide the contents of the *Mirror for Magistrates* according to the assignment of causation: in some stories divine providence dictates the outcome; in others, Fortune. The poems themselves, however, resist such rigid classification. Even those that celebrate divine justice allow some scope for the capricious and random; those that trace God's retributive hand may also invoke Fortune, a long-lived creation of pagan culture. The soundest generalizations about the narratives acknowledge that the relationship of providence and Fortune varies from poem to poem, reflecting the author's attitude. When the poet is most confident that he understands the justice of God's ways, he denies the phenomenon of chance and implicitly rejects Fortune by restricting her role or excluding her from the narrative. However, when injustice seems to prevail and when a character's death lends itself to no easy explanation, the poet forgoes a too strident assertion of providential design and allows Fortune to become the presiding deity of the narrative. Dame Fortune may not represent an ultimate explanation for the demise of a good man (for example, Thomas Montague, Earl of Salisbury), but this personification allows the inexplicable and the irrational to be localized and objectified.

The *Mirror for Magistrates* concludes with the story of Edward IV, written decades earlier by John Skelton. A brief paragraph follows the poem: "When this was said, every man took his leave of others and departed: and I the better to acquit my charge, recorded and noted all such matters as they had willed me." So abrupt is this ending that it suggests a project left unfinished. This impression is reinforced by the prose interlude following the penultimate poem, which looks forward to additional stories prepared at Baldwin's direction: "This day seven nights hence, if your business will so suffer, let us all meet here together again. And you shall see that in the mean season I will not only devise upon this myself but cause divers others of my acquaintance, which can do very well to help us forward with the rest. To this every man gladly agreed."

The fruits of that meeting are apparent in the second edition of the *Mirror for Magistrates* (1563), which bears the same title as the first but has this heading preceding the added material: *The Second Part of the Mirror for Magistrates*. In a new address to the reader, Baldwin explains what happened at the meeting called for in the first edition:

The time being come when (according to our former appointment) we should meet together again to devise upon the tragical affairs of our English rulers, I with such stories as I had procured and prepared, went to the place wherein we had debated the former part. There found I the printer and all the rest of our friends and furtherers assembled and tarrying for us, save Master Ferrers, who shortly after according to his promise came thither.

Upon his arrival Ferrers explains that he was delayed while obtaining additional narratives from friends: he presents his own story of the duke of Somerset, Thomas Churchyard's tragedy of Jane Shore, and unspecified others. Baldwin says that the printer, Thomas Marshe, gave him the biographies of Lord Hastings by John Dolman, and of Richard III by Francis Seager. Baldwin himself presents the tragedies of Henry, Duke of Buckingham, by Thomas Sackville, of the Blacksmith by Master Cavyll, and unspecified others. No authorship is indicated for the story of Anthony Woodville, Lord Rivers and Scales, or of the poet Collingbourne. All together eight new narratives are added to the original nineteen, along with Sackville's induction.

Little is known of Dolman, Seager, and Cavyll. Of the three, Dolman, the son of Thomas, a Newbury clothier, was the most conventionally successful. He translated *Those Five Questions Which Mark Tully Cicero Disputed in His Manor of Tusculanum* (1561), printed by Thomas Marshe. The title page calls Dolman "student and fellow of the Inner Temple," to which he was admitted in 1560; he was admitted to the bar ten years later; in 1586 he was called to the bench. In the dedication of *Five Questions* the author calls himself the "daily orator" of John, bishop of Sarum; he also says that upon leaving university, he "began to apply himself to the study of the common laws of this realm" but found himself drawn to the study of philosophy, which earlier he had pursued.

Francis Seager was, like Dolman, a translator. He produced *Certain Psalms Select out of the Psalter of David* (1553); only a fragment of his translation of a work by Alain Chartier remains: *A Brief Declaration of the Great Miseries in Courts Royal* (1549). He also wrote *The School of Virtue, and Book of Good Nurture for Children, and Youth to Learn Their Duty By* (circa 1550), a conduct book for children, composed in couplets.

Cavyll is the most obscure of these poets; even his first name is unknown. Lily B. Campbell suggests that he may have been Humphrey Cavell, "who was a member of the Middle Temple, and who was returned to Parliament in 1552/3, 1554, and 1555," but this is uncertain. In 1571 the abbreviated name "Ca." was attached to the tragedy of the Mortimers and may possibly refer to Cavyll. Biographical information is readily available about Sackville and Churchyard, however.

Baldwin's contribution to the 1563 *Mirror for Magistrates* appears to have been less substantial than it had been in 1559. A new paragraph added to the dedication describes the encouragement of Lord Stafford: "Through his lordship's means, I have now also set forth another part, containing as little of mine own as the first part doth of other men's." In explanation Baldwin says, "I have been called to another trade of life"; the prose section before Jane Shore's story in the *Mirror for Magistrates* of 1587 reveals that he had become "a minister and a preacher." There are, however, several indications within the prose interludes of 1563 (for example, following the narratives of Lord Hastings and of the Blacksmith) that at least some of the new poems were actually completed much earlier, when Baldwin was assembling the original edition.

The 1563 edition differs from that of 1559 chiefly in two respects: the greater length of the poems and their literary distinction. The most celebrated of the new poems is not a tragedy at all but Sackville's induction. Drawing inspiration from Virgil's account of Aeneas's descent into the underworld, from Dante's account of the wayfarer's descent into hell, and from the medieval genre of dream visions, Sackville presents a journey through a winter landscape during which the narrator, guided by Sorrow, encounters a series of personifications, including Remorse, Dread, Revenge, and Misery. Baldwin explains how this poem, which some commentators claim is the best between Chaucer and Edmund Spenser, came to be written: Sackville

> purposed with himself to have gotten at my hand, all the tragedies that were before the Duke of Buckingham's, which he would have preserved in one volume. And from that time backward even to the time of William the Conqueror, he determined to continue and perfect all the story himself, in such order as Lydgate (following Bocchas) had already used. And therefore to make a meet induction into the matter, he devised this poesy.

Sackville's tragedy of Buckingham, which subtly orchestrates Fortune and Providence, is scarcely less accomplished than his induction. The duke's path to perdition consists of crimes committed at the behest of Richard, Duke of Gloucester. Buckingham acknowledges the justice of his end, but Dame Fortune gradually assumes prominence as he describes his own guilty feelings and growing horror at Richard's villainy. As the assertion of providential design gives way to a recognition of Fortune's perversity, so too the reader's indignation at his transgressions yields to compassion at his plight. Churchyard's description of Jane Shore actually identifies this mistress of Edward IV with Dame Fortune; Shore's admission that "for a time a goddess' place I had" suggests the correlation between her nature and Fortune's. In this portrait of an overreacher who becomes herself a casualty of Fortune, culprit and victim prove to be one and the same.

Just as the 1559 edition looks forward to the composition of additional narratives, so too does the *Mirror for Magistrates* of 1563. Following the story of Jane Shore, Baldwin proposes

> in another volume hereafter, to discourse the residue from the beginning of King Henry the Seventh, to the end of this king and queen's reign (if God so long will grant us life) and I beseech you all that you will diligently perform such stories as you have undertaken, and procure your friends such as be learned, to help us with the rest: for there is in this part matter enough to set all the poets in England in work, and I would wish that every fine, apt wit would at least undertake one.

Baldwin, who died in 1563, did not live to complete the work. In 1571 Thomas Marshe printed a third edition, seeming to promise the additions that Baldwin had anticipated: to the familiar title this *Mirror for Magistrates* adds the words *Newly corrected and augmented*. This cannot, however, be the volume that Baldwin envisioned in 1563, for the 1571 *Mirror for Magistrates* contains no new material; it merely rearranges slightly the contents and deletes Baldwin's second preface (to the new matter of 1563). In 1574 another edition appeared: it too includes the poems that had appeared earlier, but it carries a new title — *The Last Part of the Mirror for Magistrates*. This title was intended to distinguish the work from an entirely new book produced by the same printer in the same year: *The First Part of the Mirror for Magistrates*.

The author of *The First Part* was John Higgins, who, following his tragic complaint of Mempricius, offers an autobiographical digression, informing the reader that he is not yet thirty years old; has studied languages, chiefly Latin and French, during the previous ten years; taught grammar for two years (circa 1568–1570); worked for another two years enlarging Richard Huloet's *Dictionary* (1572), which he dedicated to Sir George Peckham; translated "Aldus' phrases" (by which he probably means

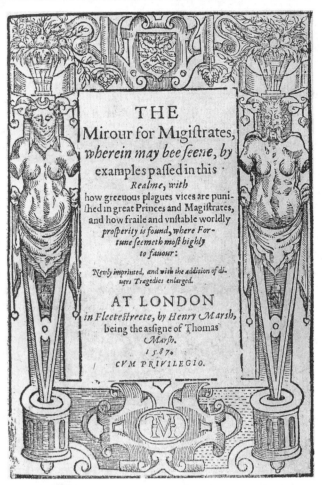

Title page for the 1587 expanded edition of A Mirror for
Magistrates, *which excludes Blenerhasset's work but
includes poems by John Higgins on history prior to
the reign of Richard II (courtesy of the Lilly
Library, Indiana University)*

some work printed by the Venetian Aldus Manutius); and added "flowers" to a work based on Terence. By this last remark Higgins refers to *Flowers or Eloquent Phrases of the Latin Speech Gathered out of All the Six Comedies of Terence* (1575), half of which consists of his additions to an earlier selection by Nicholas Udall (1533). Both the *Dictionary* and *Flowers* were printed by Thomas Marshe, who also printed, in 1572, *The Four Books of Flavius Vegetius Renatus,* containing a poem in rhyming fourteeners by Higgins.

In 1711 Thomas Hearne wrote a letter to Sir Philip Sydenham indicating that Higgins "was a poet, antiquary and historian, a man of great industry, well read in classic authors, and was withal very well skilled in French." Hearne also reports that Higgins was "a student of Christ Church in Oxford." Finally, the title page of Higgins's 1585 work, *The Nomenclator or Remembrancer of Adrianus*

Junius . . . Containing Proper Names and Apt Terms for All Things under Their Convenient Titles, reveals that the author retained his interest in languages and dictionaries. The *Dictionary of National Biography* credits Higgins with *An Answer to Master W. Perkins, concerning Christ's Descension into Hell* (1602), though this book bears no obvious connection to the poet's work. The *Short Title Catalogue* distinguishes between the poet and the controversialist. Higgins died in 1602.

Higgins's induction to the 1574 *First Part,* inspired by Sackville's, represents the author as obtaining a copy of the *Mirror for Magistrates* from the printer, reading it, and lying down to rest. Presently Somnus appears, calls his servant Morpheus, and bids him show to Higgins "from the first to the end, / Such persons as in Britain Fortune thralled." He finds himself in a large hall at the end of which "there seemed a dusking isle / Out of which he gan the Britains call." There one by one the ghosts of the departed appear before Higgins to recount their stories. A precedent for this dream vision appears not only in Sackville's induction but also in the 1559 *Mirror for Magistrates,* in which Baldwin describes himself as becoming drowsy and, in his sleep, being confronted by Richard Plantagenet, Duke of York. What Higgins does, however, is to create a continuing dream vision: at the end of each narrative one ghost departs and another arrives, while the poet remains asleep. This transition, usually a stanza or two, has the function of the prose links in the *Mirrors* of 1559 and 1563.

Higgins says that he was inspired by something Baldwin had written: "It were (sayeth he) a goodly and a notable matter to search and discourse our whole story from the beginning of the inhabiting of this isle." The invocation of Baldwin's name and the appropriation of his title suggest an essential similarity to the *Mirror for Magistrates,* though Higgins deals with history antecedent to Richard II's reign (hence his title, *The First Part*). His sixteen tragedies, beginning with Albanact, the son of Brute, and proceeding to Nennius, a Briton killed by Julius Caesar, trace both the certainty of retributive justice and the field of unpredictable circumstance, as do Baldwin's narratives. But Higgins's moralism is more severe than that of his predecessors and his poetry less accomplished. He fails to share, moreover, Baldwin's interest in the machinations by which power is acquired and retained. Higgins is more concerned with instruction of a general ethical nature than with connecting biography and politics.

Like his predecessors, Higgins was dependent upon the chroniclers; he consulted, among others, Richard Grafton, Thomas Lanquet, John Stow, and Matthew of Westminster. Finding inadequate detail, he improvised: "I was often fain to use mine own simple invention (yet not swerving from the matter) because the chronicles . . . in some such places as I most needed their aid wrote one thing: and that so briefly that a whole prince's reign, life and death, was comprised in three lines." What seems to have guided Higgins is his conviction that righteous living depends on observing those virtues particularly associated with classical antiquity. Significantly, he begins his dedicatory epistle by quoting Plotinus on temperance, which he defines as "to covet nothing which may be repented: not to exceed the bands of measure, and to keep desire under the yoke of reason." He goes on to say that "there are three other cardinal virtues which are requisite in

him that should be in authority: that is to say, prudence, justice, and fortitude."

The narratives are intended to exemplify the catastrophes that ensue when people fail to practice those virtues. For example, following the story of Morindus, who "was exalted to the kingdom, waxed cruel, and at last was devoured by a monster," the narrator says, "Here mayst thou see of fortitude the hap, / Where prudence, justice, temperance hath no place: / How suddenly we taken are in trap, / When we despise good virtues to embrace." As a corollary of this insistence, Higgins concludes his *Mirror for Magistrates* with the story of Nennius, described in the headnote as "the very pattern of a valiant, noble, and faithful subject." So unexpected is this account in a collection of miscreants that Higgins feels obliged to justify its inclusion. To omit the praiseworthy, he says, "Is like, as if a man had not the skill, / To praise the good but discommend the ill."

In his 1574 address to the reader, Higgins indicates his intention of composing other tragedies: "God willing thou shalt as fast as I can prepare them, have other books from my hands which may please thee again." In 1575 *The First Part* was republished, and to it was added a seventeenth narrative, that of Irenglas. *The Last Part* was also republished in 1575 by Thomas Marshe, who undoubtedly intended that the two parts would be bound as one book.

The next substantial installment of the *Mirror for Magistrates,* however, came from Thomas Blenerhasset, whose title, *The Second Part of the Mirror for Magistrates* (1578), identifies the scope of his collection: Britons who lived in the Christian era (and thus subsequent to those chronicled by Higgins) but before the realm of Richard II (and thus prior to those figures chronicled by Baldwin and his comrades). Blenerhasset wrote twelve poems — about Guidericus, Carassus, Queen Hellina, Vortiger, Uter Pendragon, Cadwallader, Sigebert, Lady Ebbe, Alurede, Egelrede, Edricus, and Harold. Despite his appropriation of Higgins's intended title, Blenerhasset appears to have had no direct connection with his predecessor. The printer of this collection was not Thomas Marshe but Richard Webster. When Higgins produced his promised additions in 1587, he took no notice of Blenerhasset's contributions.

Blenerhasset is thought to have been the son of William, who lived in Horsford, Norfolk. He is known to have married and had several children: a daughter was named Margaret, and his sons were named Lennard and Samuel. His family was close to his brother Edward, who was knighted in 1603, and to the family of Samson Lennard, the translator and genealogist. In addition to the *Mirror for Magistrates,* Blenerhasset wrote *A Revelation of the True Minerva* (1582), a narrative poem. His epistle to the 1578 *Mirror for Magistrates* records that he had been a student at Cambridge, where he translated Ovid's *De remedio amoris.* He also says that he wrote his contribution to the *Mirror for Magistrates* while a soldier on the isle of Guernsey, where he served Thomas Leighton, "Her Majesty's lieutenant there." *The Calendar of State Papers for Ireland* records Blenerhasset as a freeholder in 1589, and in *A Direction for the Plantation in Ulster* (1610) Blenerhasset, who calls himself "one of the undertakers" (holders of crown lands) at Clancally in Fermanagh, indicates that although he settled in Ireland, he found it impossible to build a manor without the protection of a strong castle; accordingly he makes a plea for securing the country by force. Blenerhasset died on 11 March 1624.

In contrast to Higgins, Blenerhasset returns to the format of the *Mirror for Magistrates* in its early editions: he links the poems with prose sections, which he calls inductions. But Blenerhasset also distinguishes his transitions from those of his predecessors: "Higgins used . . . Morpheus, the god of dreams, but I dream not: the other had Baldwin for their hearer, but I have diligent Inquisition, who can find out all things, and Memory, who knoweth all things, for the arbiters of my matter." Personifications of Memory and Inquisition thus replace the conferences that Baldwin held with his friends. Blenerhasset explains that these abstractions are appropriate because, when he wrote the tragedies on Guernsey, the few books he had with him supplied little information about historical personages, and so he had to depend on his memory and invention. Blenerhasset's personifications, alas, cannot rival the charm of Baldwin's prose interludes. Like Higgins, Blenerhasset also lacks the poetic skill of the earlier poets. He writes somewhat defensively in his epistle, "if you chance to see the meter, or matter not so well polished, as beseemeth, then remember that they whose falls I have here penned, were not of late time, but such as lived presently after the Incarnation of Christ: and I have not thought it decent, that the men of the old world should speak with so garnished a style as they of the latter time."

Also published in 1578 was a new version of *The Last Part,* printed by Thomas Marshe. This presents the contents of the 1563 *Mirror for Magistrates,* but with two important additions: the tragedies of Humphrey, Duke of Gloucester, and of his wife, Eleanor Cobham. These narratives, composed by George Ferrers, were intended for the *Mirror for Magistrates* of 1559, which lists them in its contents and refers to them in a prose link. The two stories were also to have appeared in the 1571 *Mirror for Magistrates,* which similarly lists them in the contents; the words *Newly corrected and augmented* on the title page almost certainly refer to the stories of this husband and wife. Perhaps living relatives of the historic figures discouraged publication of accounts dealing with witchcraft. Whatever the reason for the delay, Eleanor's story prompts a discussion among the poets. One comments, "I marvel much where she learned all this poetry touched in her tale, for in her days learning was not common, but a rare thing, namely in women." Ferrers replies that her husband was a learned man, "a patron to poets and orators," and so "no marvel therefore though the duchess brought some piece away."

In 1587 Henry Marshe, "the assign of Thomas Marshe," printed a new *Mirror for Magistrates,* one that ignores Blenerhasset's previous work. Following the epistle and preface by Higgins and the commendatory verses by Thomas Newton are seventy-four numbered poems. The forty by John Higgins deal with history prior to the reign of Richard II: fourteen poems that he had written earlier; rewritten versions of Bladud, Forrex, and Porrex; and twenty-three new poems dealing with personages of the later Roman era. Also included are the accounts of Eleanor Cobham and her husband, and the contents of the 1563 *Mirror for Magistrates.* There are four new poems, chronicling James IV of Scotland; the battle of Brampton, or Flodden Field; Thomas Wolsey by Churchyard; and Sir Nicholas Burdet. The last is said in a prose link to have been brought by Holinshed, but the historian may simply have obtained it from someone else. Of the new poems the best is Churchyard's, which would later guide Shakespeare's treatment of Cardinal Wolsey in *Henry VIII* (1613). The effect of the additions is to embellish slightly the treatment of recent history, especially that of Scotland, and to expand greatly the treatment of antiquity. Aesthetically, the poems dealing with the fifteenth and sixteenth centuries are the more accomplished, but since the poems are numbered consecutively and are not divided into parts (first, second, last), the overall effect is one of coherence. Each life is unique, of course, but all are subject to the forces that operate throughout history.

In 1609 Richard Niccols brought the *Mirror for Magistrates* to its final form in a book printed by Felix Kyngston. Niccols, who was born in London

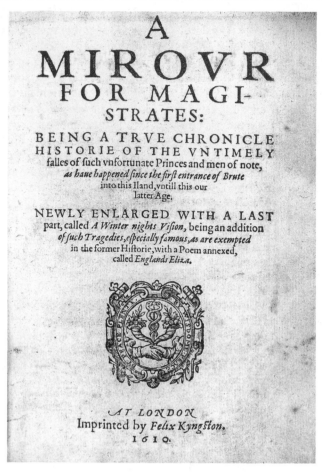

Title page for the 1610 edition of A Mirror for Magistrates,
*the final form of the collection (courtesy of the Lilly
Library, Indiana University)*

in 1584 and who died in 1616, as a youth journeyed on a military expedition to Cádiz with the earl of Nottingham, to whom he would later dedicate the tragic narratives in his *Mirror for Magistrates*. Having received his B.A. from Magdalen Hall, Oxford, in May 1606, Nichols settled in London where he became a prolific author, writing poetry in the manner of Spenser and Drayton. His contribution to the *Mirror for Magistrates* is his best-known work. Representing a conflation of the previous editions, his *Mirror for Magistrates* consists of four sections, each with a title page; these bear the date 1610, except for the second, dated 1609. There is no evidence, however, that the second part was ever issued separately; pagination is continuous throughout.

The first section, called *A Mirror for Magistrates,* contains forty-nine tragedies, from Albanact to Harold; ten of these are Blenerhasset's. The second title page reads, *The Variable Fortune and Unhappy Falls of Such Princes as Hath Happened Since the Conquest.* This section has thirty poems, beginning with

Sackville's Induction: it presents the contents of the 1563 *Mirror for Magistrates,* along with the stories of Humphrey, Eleanor, Burdet, and Wolsey from 1587, and the story of Cromwell (which had been printed in 1607) by Michael Drayton. The poems dealing with Scotland are dropped. The third part is called *A Winter's Night Vision: Being an Addition of Such Princes Especially Famous, Who Were Exempted in the Former Histories.* The additions are by Niccols: Edmund Ironside; Prince Alfred; Godwin; Robert, Duke of Normandy; Richard I; King John; Edward II; the two sons of Edward IV; and Richard III. Niccols prefaces each of his poems with a brief argument and with a woodcut illustrating the personage. The fourth section is titled *England's Eliza; or, The Virtuous and Triumphant Reign of That Virgin Empress of Sacred Memory Elizabeth, Queen of England, France, and Ireland.* Including this last, there are ninety-one numbered poems. The paean to a virtuous queen is, of course, utterly out of keeping with the original intent of William Baldwin. The coherence of the overall work also suffers, for Niccols eliminates the prose interludes that were so important to the 1559 and 1563 editions of the *Mirror for Magistrates;* and he omits the transitional stanzas by which Higgins linked the parts of his dream vision. This book was republished in 1619, 1620, and 1621.

The persistent popularity of the *Mirror for Magistrates* – from Baldwin to Niccols – expresses pride in English nationalism, fascination with God's ways, and confidence that the past represents a storehouse of practical instruction. The impulse that produced the *Mirror for Magistrates* was not very different from that responsible for the chronicles of Hall and Holinshed, though the poems engage the reader in a more immediate way. For example, Baldwin's Worcester, who has killed for his king, asks: "What would mine enemies do in such a case, / Obey the king, or proper death procure?" Such real-politik personalizes history. Modern scholars have tended to find a falling off in the later editions as poets departed from the examination of choices that were political as well as moral. In a sense, however, it was the subject matter that dictated the shift: the accounts of obscure pre-Christian figures were of necessity less specifically political than the accounts of more-recent figures whose careers were better known and whose circumstances were more nearly contemporary. Admittedly the quality of the poetry written by Higgins, Blenerhasset, and Niccols does not match that of their predecessors. There remains, however, an essential continuity, for all of the versions constitute a meditation on the meaning of human suffering, whatever its proximate cause. The greatest poems, especially those by Sackville and Churchyard, make the reader feel the pain of loss, however just. In sharing that emotion, the poems become much more than object lessons in the wages of wrongdoing.

Although the legacy of the *Mirror for Magistrates* is most apparent in those poems that treat English history, from Drayton's *Barons' Wars* (1603), to Samuel Daniel's *Civil Wars* (1595), to Thomas Lodge's *Tragical Complaint of Elstred* (1593), it also finds expression on the Elizabethan stage. The opening speech of Andrea's ghost in Kyd's *The Spanish Tragedy* (1592) is redolent of the *Mirror for Magistrates* as is the viceroy's disquisition on misfortune in the same play. The ghost of Hamlet's father, by the careful description of his death and by his plea for action on the part of the listener, has a precedent in the *Mirror for Magistrates* ("Remember me," says Glendower to Baldwin), and so does Hamlet's final impulse to have his story told aright. Tamburlaine's victims sound like the speakers of the *Mirror for Magistrates* brought to life, as do the defeated characters in Shakespeare's *Henry VI* plays (1589–1592) and in *Richard III* (1591–1592). Tamburlaine astounded Elizabethans by defying the strictures of the *de casibus* world, while Shakespeare's conquering hero, Henry V, transcends that world entirely, becoming "the mirror of all Christian kings." The penchant of tragic figures, from Edward II to Macbeth, to turn sententious when confronting doom has a precedent in the *Mirror for Magistrates,* where the speakers display a high degree of self-awareness and self-definition. And the deposition scene of *Richard II,* where the king requests and then smashes a mirror, evokes the tragic figures chronicled by Baldwin.

The sense of tragedy animating these plays is not so different from that of Baldwin, Sackville, and Churchyard; the practice of Elizabethan playwrights, who acknowledge both the principle of personal responsibility and the force of awesome circumstance, was powerfully shaped by the meditations on adversity that fill the *Mirror for Magistrates.* Francis Meres was surely right in 1598 to group "the author of the *Mirror for Magistrates*" with Marlowe, Kyd, and Shakespeare as among "our best for tragedy."

Bibliography:

Jerry Leath Mills, "Recent Studies in *A Mirror for Magistrates*," *English Literary Renaissance,* 9 (Spring 1979): 343–352.

References:

Alan T. Bradford, "Mirrors of Mutability: Winter Landscapes in Tudor Poetry," *English Literary Renaissance,* 4 (Winter 1974): 3–39;

Lily B. Campbell, *Tudor Conceptions of History and Tragedy in "A Mirror for Magistrates"* (Berkeley: University of California Press, 1936);

Willard Farnham, *The Medieval Heritage of Elizabethan Tragedy,* corrected edition (Oxford: Blackwell, 1956), pp. 271–303;

Frederick Kiefer, *Fortune and Elizabethan Tragedy* (San Marino, Cal.: Huntington Library, 1983), pp. 30–59;

William Peery, "Tragic Retribution in the 1559 *Mirror for Magistrates,*" *Studies in Philology,* 46 (April 1949): 113–130;

Wilbraham F. Trench, *A Mirror for Magistrates: Its Origin and Influence* (Edinburgh: Privately printed, 1898);

Louis R. Zocca, *Elizabethan Narrative Poetry* (New Brunswick: Rutgers University Press, 1950), pp. 16–35.

Alexander Montgomerie
(circa 1550? – 1598)

David Parkinson
University of Saskatchewan

BOOKS: *The Cherrie and the Slaye* (Edinburgh: Robert Waldegrave, 1597); published as *The Cherrie and the Slae . . . Prented According to a Copie Corrected be the Author Himselfe* (Edinburgh: Robert Waldegrave, 1597); revised edition (Edinburgh: J. Wreittoun, 1636);

The Mindes Melodie, Contayning Certayne Psalmes of David Applyed to a New Pleasant Tune (Edinburgh: Robert Charteris, 1605, 1606) — includes translations into Scots verse of fifteen psalms, the canticle *Nunc Dimittis* (from Luke 2:29–31), and the *Gloria Patri;* Psalms 1, 2, and 23 are attributed to Mongomerie, who may have written the whole collection;

The Flyting betwixt Montgomerie and Polwart (Edinburgh: Andrew Hart, 1621).

Editions: *A Choice Collection of Comic and Serious Scots Poems, Both Ancient and Modern,* edited by J. Watson (Edinburgh: J. Watson, 1706–1711) — includes *The Flyting betwixt Montgomerie and Polwart, The Cherrie and the Slae,* and four shorter poems;

The Ever Green, Being a Collection of Scots Poems Wrote by the Ingenious before 1600, edited by Allan Ramsay (Edinburgh: Printed by Thomas Ruddiman for Allan Ramsay, 1724) — includes *The Cherrie and the Slae* and three shorter poems;

Poems of Alexander Montgomerie, edited by David Laing (Edinburgh: Printed by James Ballantyne for W. & C. Tait, 1821);

Poems of Alexander Montgomerie, edited by James Cranstoun, Scottish Text Society, original series 9–11 (Edinburgh: William Blackwood, 1887); supplementary volume, edited by George Stevenson, Scottish Text Society, original series 59 (Edinburgh: William Blackwood, 1910);

Alexander Montgomerie: A Selection from His Songs and Poems, edited by Helena Mennie Shire (Edinburgh: Saltire Society, 1960).

OTHER: Thomas Davidson, *Cantus, Songs and Fancies* (Aberdeen: John Forbes, 1662) — includes four of Montgomerie's lyrics set to music.

The most brilliant Scottish writer of the later sixteenth century, Alexander Montgomerie was an extremely productive poet whose poems range widely in tone and style. Besides the longer poems for which he is perhaps best known — *The Cherrie and the Slae* (1597) and *The Flyting betwixt Montgomerie and Polwart* (1621) — Montgomerie was the author of many sonnets and lyrics, as well as courtly entertainments and psalm translations. Of all the poets associated with the court of King James VI of Scotland, Montgomerie was the one with the most dazzling, catastrophic career.

In his poems Montgomerie refers to particular circumstances of his life; for instance, he alludes to his birthday "on Easter Day at morn" in "The Poet's Complaint of His Nativity" (1589–1593); his imprisonment in "The Poet's Complaint against the Unkindness of His Companions When He Was in Prison" (1589?); and his frustration at the king's failure to guarantee payment of his pension in sonnet 16. Despite this tendency to disclosure, many biographical facts remain unknown, among them the year of the poet's birth. It is known, however, that he was a younger son of John Montgomerie, the Fourth Laird of Hazelhead, in Ayrshire, in southwest Scotland. Through his mother, Margaret Fraser, whose great-grandfather was Sir John Stewart of Darnley, Montgomerie was related to James VI.

Because a short, coarse invective against a Highlander appears ascribed to Montgomerie in that celebrated collection of Scottish verse, the Bannatyne Manuscript (National Library of Scotland, Advocates' Ms. 1.1.6), substantially completed in 1568, it has been assumed that he must have achieved maturity before that date. This assumption is by no means certain, for the poem in question seems to be a later addition to the manuscript, as are the copies in Bannatyne of six other poems ascribed to Montgomerie — one of these, indeed, not to Alexander but to a Robert Montgomerie.

Perhaps greater credence should be given to the evidence in a series of Latin poems commemorating Montgomerie's death, in which the expatriate Scottish monk Thomas Duff alludes to the poet's untimely end in his prime. Duff also refers to Montgomerie's being reared a Calvinist, fighting in military campaigns abroad, and attaining the rank of captain before converting to Catholicism, apparently in Spain or at least under Spanish influences; at any rate, Duff has it that Montgomerie was honored by Philip I of Spain.

Montgomerie's career as poet at the court of James VI essentially began in 1579, in which year James turned thirteen and entered his majority. Having been cloistered in Stirling Castle with the great scholar George Buchanan as his principal tutor, James emerged onto a complex political scene. His mother, the staunchly Catholic Mary, Queen of Scots, was imprisoned by the monarch whose heir James might become, Elizabeth I of England. Becoming master of his own court, James thus became the target of intense pressure from both France and England. From the outset of James's personal reign, Montgomerie seems to have been associated with Catholic interests. In a later poem (sonnet 17) Montgomerie refers to Esmé Stewart, Sieur d'Aubigny, as his former master; the poet may well have come to court at the time of that Catholic nobleman's arrival from France in September 1579.

While several of Montgomerie's early poems for courtly entertainments (including "The Navigation" and "The Cartel of the Three Venturous Knights" (1579), speeches introducing a masque and a tournament, respectively) are largely devoted to praising a king embarked upon the first year or so of his reign, the most notable of these poems is entirely abusive: *The Flyting betwixt Montgomerie and Polwart* (composed circa 1580). As a variety of poetry at the Scottish court, flyting is a contest in verbal abuse between two poets in which each seeks to outdo the other in technical display as well as sheer insult. For Montgomerie and his opponent, Patrick Hume of Polwart, the model was *The Flyting of Dunbar and Kennedie,* written eighty years earlier for the court of James IV of Scotland. Like their predecessors in this game, Montgomerie and Polwart proceed from an exchange of shorter invectives into longer, lurid fantasies in which each offers a grotesque genealogy and description of his opponent. It would seem as if the whole *Flyting* was performed before James, perhaps in fun, but also as a contest for primacy as court poet, with the monarch as adjudicator: in a later poem (sonnet 27) Montgomerie recalls that the young king "laughed some time for to look / How I chased Polwart from the chimney nook."

Montgomerie rose in James's favor during the early 1580s. One of his particular recommendations may have been that he brought to the Scottish court a refreshing familiarity with the contemporary French lyric. He offered translations from Clément Marot ("A Bonny No" and "The Elegy," out of Marot's "De Ouy et Nenny" and third elegy) and Pierre de Ronsard (three sonnets, out of "Pardonne moy Platon," "Qui vouldra voir," and "Heureuse fut l'estoille"); indeed, it may be argued that Montgomerie was the earliest Scottish practitioner of the sonnet form. No less important, his lyrics were early on set to music as part-songs, some of them having been written expressly for this purpose.

While enjoying favor as a poet at court, Montgomerie was involved in other kinds of transactions. During the winter of 1580 he was one of the buyers of an English ship, the *James Benaventor,* from a Southampton merchant, Henry Giles. Helena Mennie Shire has argued that in this purchase Montgomerie was acting as an agent of King James, or even of the imprisoned Queen Mary. To be sure, the court of the young James was subject at this time to powerful Catholic, pro-French influence, embodied by Montgomerie's patron Stewart, now the close confidant of the king and honored by him with the title of duke of Lennox. Montgomerie's unusual purchase did not pass unnoticed by the English admiralty.

By this time, however, Montgomerie had plenty to engage his attention in court affairs. A trio of sonnets entitled "A Lady's Lamentation" in the Ker Manuscript reflects the scandal over the discovery of adultery at court. Two such cases occurred in early 1581, one involving the countess of Angus, the other the countess of March. Another, more happy court event celebrated by Montgomerie was the wedding of his kinswoman Margaret Montgomerie, daughter of the earl of Eglinton, to Robert, Lord Seton. One of the translations from Ronsard, "O Happy Star, at Evening and at Morn" (sonnet 50), can also be associated with this event. Among his other courtly functions at this time, the poet thus aspired to chronicle the fortunes in love of notable female contemporaries.

The displeasure with which the Protestant nobility and their supporters regarded the religious, political, and moral tendencies of James's court led to action. A force led by Lord Ruthven took over the royal household and captured the king (the "Ruthven Raid," August 1582). The king's favorite, the duke of Lennox, was driven back to France, to die there a year later, and James's household was reformed: only those committed to the Protestant cause were allowed access to the king. A Catholic and suspected of political intrigue, Montgomerie was not included in the reformed royal household.

These straitened circumstances did not last. In June 1583 James escaped his rigorously Protestant captors, and before long his court seemed to be returning to its old course. Once again, Catholic lords and courtiers gained access to the king, Montgomerie among them. Back at court, the "master poet" was granted a pension of five hundred merks deriving from the revenues of the archbishop of Glasgow. This pension may have been a mark of high royal favor, but it was also part of the windfall of Glasgow revenues to various Montgomeries that followed upon the hotly disputed appointment of Robert Montgomerie to the see.

In 1583 it seemed as if Montgomerie's star had risen for good. With such studies of the art of poetry as George Gascoigne's "Certayne Notes of Instruction" (1575) as a model, King James was compiling his "Short Treatise Containing Some Rules and Cautels ['Pitfalls'] to be Observed and Eschewed in Scots Poesy" (1584). This groundbreaking treatise on the principles of Scots prosody and diction drew most amply from the poems of Montgomerie for its illustrative examples. An alliterative thirteen-line stanza is drawn from the beginning of the "Second Invective" of *The Flyting betwixt Montgomerie and Polwart,* as is a rhyme royal stanza from the beginning of the complaint "To Thee, Echo" (miscellaneous poem number 8) and, interestingly, the eighth stanza of Montgomerie's longest and most ambitious poem, *The Cherrie and the Slae.* James's treatise was included in the volume *Essays of a Prentice in the Divine Art of Poesy,* printed in Edinburgh in 1584 by Thomas Vautrollier; even though the king included Montgomerie's verses without ascription, he had paid their author the compliment of holding them up for emulation by Scottish poets.

Through the palmy years of close association between James VI and Montgomerie, the king was aspiring to become a poet in his own right; Montgomerie served him toward this end, both as adviser and, less formally, as colleague in a series of literary projects, not all of which were strenuous or exalted. Indeed, in James's own mock-heroic "Admonition to the Master Poet to Beware of Great Bragging" (1584), the seventeen-year-old king jocularly calls the boastful soldier Montgomerie "Beloved Sanders, master of our art" and goes on to tease the poet about having lost miserably in a horse race. Boasts had now led to a fall, and rival poets at court were laughing. The position of greatest favor was also one of vulnerability.

Such rivalries between poets may have been fed by political conflict. In the ongoing struggle between Protestant and Catholic for dominance at James's court, Montgomerie was unable or unwilling to function simply as a poet. In June 1586 he left Scotland to fight in the rebellion against the Spanish occupation in the Low Countries. The mission was intercepted at the outset by an English ship; Montgomerie's bark (containing sixty Scottish soldiers as well as contraband coal and salt) was boarded, and Montgomerie was questioned. He and his company proceeded to the Low Countries as reinforcements to the Scottish contingent James had committed to the English expeditionary force led against Spain by the earl of Leicester. Part of the Scottish regiment of Bartholomew Balfour, Montgomerie's company would have been involved in the capture of Doesborch on 2 September 1586 and the siege of Zutphen later that month. At Zutphen, Montgomerie may have had a brief opportunity to meet Sir Philip Sidney before that poet was mortally wounded during the siege. Montgomerie was engaged on the Protestant side in the Low Countries; according to James, however, he visited Spain before returning home in 1588.

By the time Montgomerie arrived, Catholic hopes for Scotland and England had plummeted with the execution of Mary, Queen of Scots, in 1587 and the catastrophe of the Spanish Armada in 1588. Montgomerie proceeded to make his way by writing: he composed sonnets flattering such personages as James's chancellor, Lord Maitland; and it may have been at this time that he presented translations of several psalms to the General Assembly of the (Protestant) Church of Scotland in an offer to translate the whole book — an offer officially rejected in 1601, three years after the poet's death. For all Montgomerie's efforts to write himself back into his former position of honor at court, however, it would seem that poets such as the Protestant, pro-English William Fowler — whose translation of Petrarch's *Trionfi* (1343–1350) was completed in December 1587 — were now setting the style for the king.

Still, financial prospects looked fair. Montgomerie's pension, which had lapsed during his absence, was confirmed by James in March 1589.

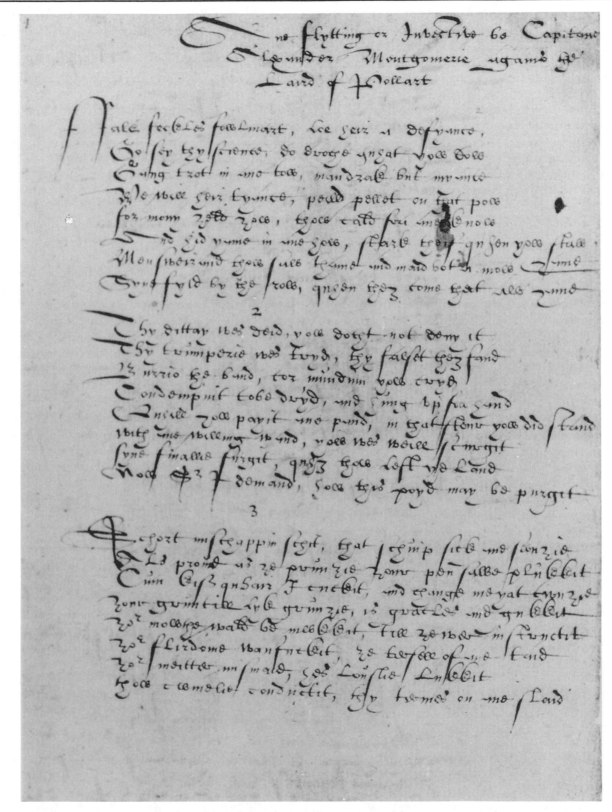

First page of Montgomerie's manuscript for The Flyting betwixt Montgomerie and Polwart *(Tullibardine Ms.; Maggs Brothers catalogue, no. 462, 1925)*

Within three years, however, William Erskine, claimant to the Bishopric of Glasgow since 1585, began an action challenging Montgomerie's right. Clusters of sonnets mark the poet's waning fortunes at law: one group first praising and then excoriating his own lawyer; another, "To the Lords of Session"; and yet another, to James himself, moving from ingratiation to bitter complaint.

With defeat in 1593 came incarceration. Once released, Montgomerie withdrew into his native district in southwest Scotland and became involved in a plot to capture and garrison Ailsa Craig, a rocky island in the mouth of the River Clyde, to be used as a base for Catholic revolution in Ireland and Scotland. Montgomerie does not seem to have been on hand during the capture of Ailsa Craig late in 1596 or during its recapture in March 1597, during which his relative Hugh Barclay of Ladyland – with whom Montgomerie had recently exchanged jocular sonnets – cast himself into the sea to drown rather than be taken by James's officers. Nevertheless, Montgomerie was among those summoned by the Privy Council to answer the charge of treason; he was outlawed for failing to appear.

At this time, when Montgomerie's fortunes would seem to have been at their lowest, his long poem *The Cherrie and the Slae* was first published. This earliest printed edition did not include the complete poem but broke off in the midst of the sixty-seventh stanza. A second edition followed the same year, and from the same publisher, Robert Waldegrave, with the optimistic subtitle "Printed According to a Copy Corrected by the Author Himself." This edition included many changes but no more of the poem; it still broke off incomplete. It is as if the printer Waldegrave had obtained first one, then another manuscript copy, neither of which is likely to have come into his hands with the author's permission. In any case, the fugitive Montgomerie was hardly in a position to forestall or respond to unauthorized printings of his work in an unfinished state.

That is not to suggest that the poet had not proceeded toward completion of his long poem, drafts of which had been circulating at court and perhaps beyond at least as early as 1584, the year King James's "Short Treatise" appeared, with a stanza from *The Cherrie and the Slae* included. At some point in a career that had moved steadily further from the focus of royal favor, Montgomerie revised and augmented *The Cherrie and the Slae*. Appearing in print in 1615 (no copies of this edition survive) and again in 1636, the complete version of the poem was darker and more bitter than the in-

complete first printed version. The pleasant springtime scene with which the poem originally opened becomes rather more sinister in the revision, and Cupid, the first personage the narrator meets in this scene, is more obviously the tempter than had been the case in the earlier version; most important, the personification allegory at the heart of the poem, in which various mental attributes argue in favor of either bold action or cautious compromise, has been extended and elaborated in the revision.

In the second version of *The Cherrie and the Slae,* the narrator rashly accepts Cupid's proffered loan of bow, arrows, and wings: flying out of control, he crashes and wounds himself with one of the arrows. Tormented by his wound, the narrator sees, high on a dangerous crag, an enticing cherry tree; far more accessible is a sloe bush, with its bitter berries. While Courage and Hope urge the narrator to seek refreshment by climbing to the Cherry, the opposing mental tendencies of Dread, Danger, and Despair warn him against such a hazardous, futile effort and recommend that he satisfy his thirst with berries from the Sloe. The debate becomes more productive with the arrival of Experience, Reason, Wit, and Skill, all of whom gradually work toward resolution of the problem. The narrator approaches the tree, at which point the ripe cherries fall; he eats and is refreshed. The poem ends praising God, who has reclaimed the narrator from death to life.

The Cherrie and the Slae is noted for its full working-out of internal struggle in the form of personification allegory and also for its complex, musical stanza and the bounty of proverbs its personages employ to support their arguments. In the allegory of the Cherry and the Sloe religious significance has been found, with the sweet Cherry as the fruit of Catholicism and the bitter Sloe as the emblem of Calvinist Protestantism. That would not have been the sort of reading to endear the poem to a largely Protestant Scottish audience, however, but in the seventeenth and eighteenth centuries, *The Cherrie and the Slae* was a favorite, especially among lawyers, who relished its ingenious interweaving of proverb and argument.

In death, Montgomerie was as much a figure of controversy as he had ever been. According to the last of the memorial poems by Duff, efforts to have Montgomerie buried on consecrated ground were frustrated by church authority. Supported by the common people, Catholic nobility petitioned the king to oppose the Kirk Assembly on this matter. A riot erupted, during which commoners sympathetic to the Catholic cause occupied the churches and rang the bells. It would seem that the bailiffs of the Canongate Church in Edinburgh gave in to this pressure: on 29 August 1598 they answered a summons from the presbytery of Edinburgh to answer for burying "Alexander Montgomerie, poet, a papist, in their church contrary [to] the acts of the General Assembly."

Not unmoved by the death of his former favorite poet, King James wrote an "Epitaph on Montgomerie," in which he asked whether "the prince of poets in our land" should "go thus to grave unmourned" and recalled Montgomerie's "flow and grace, / His sugared style, his weighty words divine": "Though to his burial was refused the bell, / The bell of fame shall aye his praises knell."

Although several of Montgomerie's poems were republished through the seventeenth and eighteenth centuries, his most celebrated poem, *The Cherrie and the Slae,* was the target of critical disfavor from the late eighteenth century well into the twentieth for its mingling of stanzaic complexity with the supposedly exhausted machinery of personification allegory. Nor, until recently, has the range of style and tone in his sonnets and lyrics (from biting invective to fawning praise to sober confession) been appreciated. Montgomerie remains a tantalizing figure, one whose poetry has much to reveal about the crises of literature, politics, and religion in late-sixteenth-century Scotland.

Bibliography:

William Geddie, *A Bibliography of Middle Scots Poets,* Scottish Text Society, original series 61 (Edinburgh: William Blackwood, 1912), pp. 329–356.

Biographies:

Mark Dilworth, "New Light on Alexander Montgomerie," *Bibliotheck,* 4 (1965): 230–235;

Helena Mennie Shire, "Alexander Montgomerie: The Opposition of the Court to Conscience," *Studies in Scottish Literature,* 3 (1965–1966): 144–150;

John Durkan, "The Date of Alexander Montgomerie's Death," *Innes Review,* 34 (1983): 91–92.

References:

Lois Borland, "Montgomerie and the French Poets of the Early Sixteenth Century," *Modern Philology,* 11 (1913–1914): 127–134;

R. D. S. Jack, *Alexander Montgomerie* (Edinburgh: Scottish Academic Press, 1985);

Roderick J. Lyall, "Alexander Montgomerie and the Netherlands, 1586–89," *Glasgow Review,* 1 (1993): 52–66;

Lyall, "Montgomerie and Marot: A Sixteenth-Century Translator at Work," *Etudes Ecossaises,* 2 (1993): 1–15;

David Parkinson, "Alexander Mongomerie, James VI, and 'Tumbling Verse'," in *Loyal Letters: Studies on Medieval Alliterative Poetry and Prose for Gerrit Bunt,* edited by L. A. J. R. Houwen and A. A. MacDonald (Groningen: Egbert Forsten, 1994), pp. 281–295;

Parkinson, "Montgomerie's Language," in *Bryght Lanternis: Essays on the Language and Literature of Medieval and Renaissance Scotland,* edited by J. Derrick McClure and Michael R. G. Spiller (Aberdeen: Aberdeen University Press, 1989), pp. 352–363;

Helena Mennie Shire, *Song, Dance and Poetry of the Court of Scotland under King James VI* (Cambridge: Cambridge University Press, 1969).

Papers:

Collections of Alexander Montgomerie's papers are at the British Library (Harleian Manuscript 7578); the Edinburgh University Library (Manuscripts De.3.70 and Laing III.447 and III.467); the Henry E. Huntington Library (Manuscript HM 105, the Tullibardine Manuscript); Magdalene College, Cambridge (Pepys Manuscript 1408, the Maitland Quarto Manuscript); the National Library of Scotland (Advocates' Manuscript 1.1.6, the Bannatyne Manuscript); the Scottish Record Office (Ms. RH 13/38); William Andrews Clark Memorial Library of the University of California, Los Angeles (the Taitt Manuscript); and the Würzburg University Library (Manuscript M.ch.q.62, containing Thomas Duff's poems).

Richard Mulcaster

(1531 or 1532 – 1611)

William Barker
Memorial University of Newfoundland

BOOKS: *The Quenes Majesties Passage,* attributed to Mulcaster (London: R. Tottell, 1559);

Positions Wherin those Primitive Circumstances Be Examined, Necessarie for the Training Up of Children (London: Thomas Vautrollier, 1581);

The First Part of the Elementarie Which Entreateth of Right Writing of Our English Tung (London: Thomas Vautrollier, 1582);

Cato Christianus. In quem coniiciuntur ea omnia, quae in sacris literis ad parentum, puerorumque pietatem videntur maxime pertinere (London: Valentine Sims, circa 1600);

Catechismus Paulinus, in usum Scholae Paulinae conscriptus (London: Printed by John Windet for Matthew Law, 1601);

In mortem serenissimae Reginae Elizabethae. Naenia consolans (London: Printed for Edward Aggas, 1603);

The Translation of Certain Latin Verses Written upon her Majesties Death, Called a Comforting Complaint (London: Printed for Edward Aggas, 1603).

Editions: *Positions,* edited by Robert Hebert Quick (London & New York: Longmans, Green, 1887, 1888);

The First Part of the Elementarie, edited by E. T. Campagnac (Oxford: Clarendon Press, 1925);

Positions, edited by Richard L. DeMolen (New York: Teachers College Press, 1971);

"Richard Mulcaster's Preface to *Cato Christianus* (1600): A Translation and Commentary," edited and translated by William Barker and Jean Chadwick, *Humanistica Lovaniensia,* 42 (1993): 323–367;

Positions Concerning the Training Up of Children, edited by Barker (Toronto: University of Toronto Press, 1994).

Richard Mulcaster, a schoolmaster, taught in London – first at Merchant Taylors' School, later at St. Paul's School. He is remembered today as a teacher of many Elizabethan and Jacobean men of letters and as the author of *Positions* (1581) and *The First Part of the Elementary* (1582). In these books he criticizes the prevailing practices in schools and offers his own corrective system, based on a political theory of education generated from his own practice and from certain classical models. Along the way, he has much to say about physical education, the education of young women, reading, writing, spelling, and the English language, all of which radiate outward from the author's concern to establish a truly public and consistent form of education. Even the style of his writing, Mulcaster assures his reader, self-consciously mirrors his political and theoretical project.

Richard Mulcaster was born in Carlisle, in northern England, in 1531 or 1532. The earliest record of his life is his matriculation at King's College, Cambridge, in 1548, which establishes that he was then sixteen years of age and that he had been an Eton scholar. Eton was not then a large school for rich men's sons so much as a foundation for the training of worthy boys who had been picked out as potential servants of the church. The movement from Eton to King's was normal for the brighter students. Mulcaster broke the pattern two years later by switching colleges and moving to Peterhouse. After graduating in 1552 with the B.A. from Cambridge he again moved, this time to Oxford, where as a member of Christ Church he received the M.A. in 1555. The reason for his change of universities is uncertain. There is a record of an "R. Muncaster" (a normal variant of his name), a servant accused of stealing from his master, Dr. John Caius, the well-known medical scholar and a powerful presence at Cambridge; if this was Richard Mulcaster, then the removal to Oxford is easily explained, but the record is obscure.

POSITIONS
VVHERIN THOSE PRI-
MITIVE CIRCVMSTANCES
BE EXAMINED, WHICH ARE NE-
CESSARIE FOR THE TRAINING
vp of children, either for skill in their
booke, or health in their bodie.

VVRITTEN by RICHARD MVLCASTER, *mafter
of the fchoole erected in London anno. 1561. in the pa-
rifh of Sainct Laurence Povvntneie, by the vvorfhipfull
companie of the merchaunt tailers of the faid citie.*

Imprinted at London by Thomas Vautrollier
dvvelling in the blacke Friers by Ludgate
1581

Title page for Mulcaster's first treatise on education

With his academic training Mulcaster was destined for teaching or the church – ultimately he ended up doing both. Yet his first known employment was surprisingly different. In January 1559 Queen Elizabeth was welcomed into London by an elaborate pageant put on by the city fathers and merchants. A document in the court of aldermen for the city of London states that "R. Muncaster" was to be paid forty shillings for the "making of the book containing and declaring the histories set forth in and by the City's pageants at the time of the Queen's Highness coming through the City to her coronation . . . which book was given unto the Queen's grace." It may be that this book is the basis for the well-known pamphlet *The Queen's Majesty's Passage* (1559), which some scholars attribute to Mulcaster. There is no suggestion that he helped to plan and execute this pageant for the queen, though later he did actually write pageant material for two lord mayors.

At the same time, and no doubt connected to his activity with these city merchants, Mulcaster

was elected member for Carlisle in Elizabeth's first Parliament. This was unusual and may have had something to do with his domicile in London; that is, he was there and was seen as an acceptable candidate, even though he may have had no special training or interest in politics. It is unusual that he preceded his father, who had been an alderman in Carlisle and who became a member of Parliament some years after his son.

Mulcaster's excellent education and involvement in political activities brought him to the attention of a London merchant named Richard Hilles, who put up most of the money for a new school in St. Lawrence Pountney, a parish of London. As was common, this new foundation was established under the aegis of a guild, hence its name, Merchant Taylors' School. In 1561 Mulcaster was appointed the first headmaster of this new school. If his claim in *Positions* is correct that he had by 1581 taught for "two and twenty years," then he may have begun his work as a schoolmaster in 1559 at another school, though this would have overlapped with his term as MP. But his name is always associated with Merchant Taylors' School, where he taught for twenty-five years.

From the start, Merchant Taylors' School was intended to be an important institution. The founding statutes were modeled in part on those written in 1508 by John Colet for St. Paul's, a school managed by the rival Mercers' Company. The Merchant Taylors' statutes limited the number of boys to 250, making it the second largest school in England (only Shrewsbury, with about 400 boys, was larger). Mulcaster ran the school with only three ushers or assistant masters. It must have been a busy operation. The boys usually began their schooling at about seven years of age, with some knowledge of reading but not much else, and were immediately set to mastering the one skill that all schools of the time were principally made for — the reading and writing of Latin. Boys in some better schools such as Merchant Taylors' also learned Greek, usually in the upper levels, and they might even have started some Hebrew (boys at Merchant Taylors' were examined in 1572 in the Hebrew psalms). But the main work was to take them through a primarily Latin curriculum that started with simple prayers, catechism, and Cato and ended, some seven years later, with Horace and Cicero. This "Renaissance puberty rite," as it has been called by Walter J. Ong, was an introduction by strict physical, social, and religious indoctrination of the young scholar to a dominant — and international — scribal culture, in a time when still only a minority of men and women could read and write the vernacular.

Mulcaster seems to have been a very successful schoolmaster if one may judge by his pupils. They include Thomas Lodge, Thomas Kyd, Edmund Spenser, and several bishops: for instance, Thomas Dove and the well-known preacher and scholar Lancelot Andrewes. In part his success stemmed from the location and function of the school. Many of his pupils came from families that were of a middling degree and relatively uneducated; they were seeking advancement and found it with Mulcaster and Merchant Taylors'. Their success does not entirely account for the high regard in which they held their old master after they left him. Lancelot Andrewes, for instance, kept a portrait of Mulcaster over his study door and on his death left a bequest to Mulcaster's son. There is an interesting description of Mulcaster's work as a teacher in *Liber Famelicus* (1858), a memoir by another grateful former pupil, Sir James Whitelocke, a judge of the Court of King's Bench under James I:

I was brought up at school under Mr. Mulcaster in the famous school of the Merchant Taylors in London, where I continued until I was well instructed in the Hebrew, Greek, and Latin tongues. His care was also to increase my skill in music, in which I was brought up by daily exercise in it, as in singing and playing upon instruments, and yearly he presented some plays to the court, in which his scholars were only actors, and I one among them, and by that means taught them good behavior and audacity.

Mulcaster, then, had some breadth in his curriculum. There is a record of his having taken his scholars to perform at least six times before Elizabeth's court.

Mulcaster was a schoolmaster of unusual ambition. Not only was he successful in the classroom and with his court performances, but he gained the notice of Continental humanists who visited or lived in England. He had close connection with Emanuel van Meteren, a Dutch émigré, who worked as a businessman in London and who also wrote an important history of the Low Countries. Through van Meteren he met several remarkable scholars, including Janus Gruter, Carolus Utenhovius, and Janus Dousa. He wrote a letter to Abraham Ortelius, the well-known cartographer, asking him for advice on further reading about art (in it he mentions he has already had a look at the writings of Pliny; Vitruvius; the Italian humanist Caelius Rhodiginus, or Ricchieri; and even Albrecht Dürer). It is likely that his acquaintance with these humanists encouraged him to set down his thoughts on education.

Though Mulcaster wrote introductory verses to several books, his first full-length publication — at least the first he acknowledges to be his — was *Positions* (or theses, positions taken in argument), published in 1581. This work was followed by *The First Part of the Elementary* a year later. Both books are part of a much longer projected work that was to have begun with *Positions* as an introduction, then was to have proceeded through all five subjects of a projected "elementary" or preliminary program: reading, writing, drawing, music for voice, and music for instrument. There are hints that he intended to go even further, through "the whole course of learning," with some thoughts on the grammar-school curriculum as well — in other words, an English work that would rival in scope the great *Institutio oratoria* (96) of the Roman rhetorical teacher Quintilian. Mulcaster finished only the beginning of the work; in the *Elementary* he gets only as far as English spelling, or "right writing" (as he literally translates the term *orthographia*), which he

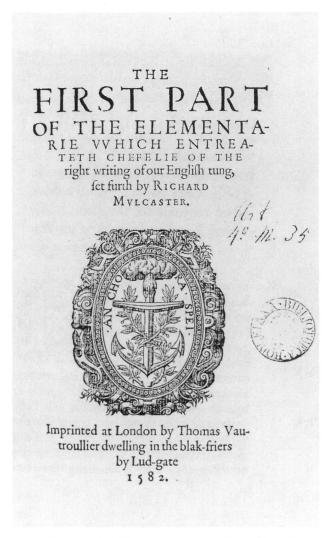

THE
FIRST PART
OF THE ELEMENTA-
RIE VVHICH ENTREA-
TETH CHEFELIE OF THE
right writing of our Englifh tung,
fet furth by RICHARD
MVLCASTER.

Imprinted at London by Thomas Vau-
troullier dwelling in the blak-friers
by Lud-gate
1 5 8 2.

*Title page for Mulcaster's approach to the problem of
teaching "right writing"*

felt had to be cleared up before he could even begin to discuss the problem of reading, his first topic.

The main thrust of Mulcaster's project is political. With many glances back to the *Republic* and *Laws* of Plato, the *Politics* of Aristotle, and the *Cyropaedia* of Xenophon, Mulcaster argues in both books that a properly consistent and regulated system of education will enhance the social order of the commonwealth. He is not interested, except as a side issue, in the education of the nobly born. In this he is different from his predecessors. Thomas Elyot's *Book Named the Governor* (1531) is specifically interested in the training of a public servant who is well born and who is destined for high office; Roger Ascham's *Schoolmaster* (written sometime before Ascham's death in 1568; published 1570) describes the work of a private tutor in a noble household, a far cry from the teacher in a hall or room full of restless boys from all social conditions.

Unlike these earlier writers, Mulcaster is strongly in favor of a truly public education. In his scheme, all children – rich or poor, male or female – will have access, at least in the early stages, to this schooling, and the curriculum will be consistent from school to school, teacher to teacher. His proposed reform is broad; for instance, to produce consistency among teachers he argues for a reorganization of the traditional faculties of the universities, proposing a faculty for teaching (which harks back to the medieval grammar faculty). The nobly born will not study at home but will attend the public school ("making the private public," as he says). Even girls (at the time a remarkable concession) will have a thorough instruction in reading and writing and a good start in classical literature, though because the state does not allow them to profess these subjects, they will not go as far in the curriculum as the boys. The chapter in *Positions* on the education of women is as ambivalent as anything written on the subject by his contemporaries; in part the chapter may have been generated by Mulcaster's concern to flatter Queen Elizabeth, to whom he dedicated the book.

One of the most extended discussions of any subject in *Positions* is that of physical education. Despite the tradition of antiquity, which argued for what Mulcaster translates as "a wise mind, and a healthful body" (echoing Juvenal's *mens sana in corpore sano*), more than a thousand years of schooling from the early Middle Ages through the Renaissance maintained a clear separation between the cultures of the book and the body. Clerks went to school; noble youths went hunting – or so conventional wisdom held. This changed in the later Renaissance in two ways: the higher classes became increasingly involved in the literary culture but maintained their love for sport; and as the schools increasingly welcomed and educated the wealthy nobility, they gradually made room in their curricula for sport, though the notion of a truly balanced program within an institution is really a creation of the nineteenth century.

Mulcaster is one of the first writers in English who would bring into the traditional school setting a rigorous program of physical education, designed specifically for the young scholar. Of course, Elyot and Ascham were both strongly in favor of sport; Ascham's *Toxophilus* presents in the first half a brilliant persuasion for archery as an almost intellectual sport. Although both Elyot and Ascham argue from ethical and cultural grounds for a balance, they did not call for sports to be institutionalized in public schools. Mulcaster takes a slightly different approach. He argues for sport in schools and bases his arguments on reasons of health. In the early chapters of *Positions,* he first outlines the necessity for health in the young and how to maintain it. Following the humor-based system of ancient physicians (above all the second-century medical philosopher Galen), Mulcaster explains how the natural moistness and warmth of children should be maintained by proper diet and exercise. He then divides and discusses in detail the appropriate sports for indoors and outdoors. Aspects of the first part of his program – indoor sports – must have seemed odd or even absurd to his contemporaries. Such exercises as loud speaking, holding one's breath, and even laughing are presented as seriously as dancing or fencing. Yet these unusual exercises were well known in antiquity and are entirely defensible within the categories of Galenic medicine, not to mention rhetorical education, in which loud speak-

ing and holding the breath, for instance, are important in delivery, the fifth part of rhetoric.

Mulcaster's program for outdoor sports would, however, have seemed more familiar to his English contemporaries. Swimming, running, riding, shooting the longbow, and hunting were the traditional sports of a feudal warrior class that had by the early part of the sixteenth century been transformed into the gentry. Mulcaster wishes to see all the traditional sports as part of a regular school program, under the supervision of his training master. As Mulcaster progresses sport by sport, he carefully analyzes each one for its benefits and drawbacks and subjects each to the scrutiny of the Galenic categories. Everyone knows, he asserts, that a child is hot and moist in his physical complexion, but if a child sits for long hours in study, his body will suffer. Will the sport sufficiently excite the natural heat of the body in order to overcome the coldness brought on by too many hours in the classroom and the library? Or will it too suddenly dry out the body that by its nature must retain a great deal of this youthful moisture? Every aspect of the sport is considered in the light of the humoral balance of the child or scholar practicing it.

The long section on sports is based almost directly on the *De arte gymnastica libri sex* (Six Books on the Art of Gymnastics, 1569) by the Italian physician Hieronymus Mercurialis (Girolamo Mercuriale), but Mulcaster shows considerable skill in the way he selects his material and redirects it to an English audience interested in the education of children. Mercurialis, for instance, outlines the benefits and drawbacks of a great many classical sports that Mulcaster leaves out; and the earlier work never really discusses archery or the English form of football (which was still a free-for-all ancestor of rugby, soccer, and American football). Mercurialis is primarily the source for the medical doctrine Mulcaster uses to support his introduction of sports into the school curriculum. Ironically, despite Mulcaster's sustained defense of physical education, there is no evidence that any sports were routinely practiced at Merchant Taylors' under his headship.

Another important subject in his two educational treatises is the problem of "right writing." *The First Part of the Elementary* begins with an analysis and defense of a proposed elementary program, modeled on classical Greek precedent but modified for the English classroom. This program begins with reading. Mulcaster quickly identifies a problem, however: how can one teach a child to read if the English spelling is inconsistent from one text to the next? Other contemporaries, such as William

Page from The First Part of the Elementary *with the beginning
of Mulcaster's list of approximately eight thousand
proposed spellings of English words*

Bullokar and John Hart, had also addressed themselves to the inconsistent state of English orthography, but they had proposed reforms of the alphabet, substituting new letterforms to reproduce English sounds. Indeed, theirs was similar to humanist scholars' response to the same problem elsewhere in the other vernaculars of Europe, which, because of the rise of printing, were seen to be chaotic and in need of reform.

Mulcaster also saw a need for reform in spelling, but in his allegorical interpretation sound (the original phonetic force of the letters) is modified by reason (the *ratio,* or intellectual organization, of the alphabetic representation of sound) and by custom (the practices as they have evolved in the history and culture of the language). Although he is a re-

former, then, he is a cautious one; his revised spelling system is shaped especially by custom (a concept he seems to have picked up from Quintilian). He presses in his *Elementary* for a regularization of English spelling but insists on the retention of many distinctive features. Thus, to choose one of hundreds of examples, he would retain the final *e* (he calls it the "qualifying *e*") to mark a long syllable, as in *these* or *those,* but also *kepe* (for our *keep*) or *sene* (for *seen*); the lack of the final *e* marks a short syllable, as in *ar* for *are.*

Because of the importance of custom in his system, in many ways his revised spelling system was close to the practice of his contemporaries (*ar* is a normal sixteenth-century variant of *are*) and moreover seems close to that of present-day English (for instance, in the title of his book, he allows the spellings *right writing,* despite the obvious problems of *igh* and *wr,* though he prefers *tung* to *tongue*). How well it works can be seen in the actual text of *Elementary,* which is by and large spelled according to its own system (though, like his contemporaries, Mulcaster was himself rather inconsistent if one looks at the spellings in his very few extant English manuscripts). At the end of his theoretical considerations, in a "General Table" he appends a list of some eight thousand correct spellings (some of them, as one would expect in a sixteenth-century English printed book, are misspelled).

Like many would-be reformers of English spelling, Mulcaster shows himself to be a cross between a genius and a crank. His reform in itself may not be terribly important; it has been dismissed by historians of spelling and English pronunciation (though Ben Jonson thought some of what Mulcaster had to say good enough to crib without acknowledgment in his *English Grammar*). Yet within this system of "right writing" there is embedded a theory of language that shows Mulcaster on one side of a debate as old as Plato's *Cratylus* on the nature of language and meaning. "Words be voluntary, and appointed upon cause," he says, arguing that each thing is given a name appropriate to it, that the thing and the word used to nominate it are deeply related. This is a modification of an Adamic view of language (following the story in Genesis where Adam names the creatures); it is also manifested to some extent in the allegory of *The Faerie Queene* by Mulcaster's pupil Spenser.

To Mulcaster, when you know the word, "the thing is half known," and a knowledge of words leads to a power or control over contingency, the way that Adam's knowledge of the "forces" of words gave him privilege in creation. The oral form of language is the starting point of this form of knowledge. Knowledge of the written word, which has a system with its own reason and custom, may also lead back to a greater mastery of speech. A dictionary is one device that would aid in this mastery:

> It were a thing . . . no less profitable than praiseworthy, if some one well learned and as laborious a man would gather all the words which we use in our English tongue, whether natural or incorporate, out of all the professions, as well learned as not, into one dictionary, and besides the right writing, which is incident to the alphabet, would open unto us therein both their natural force and their proper use.

Such a project was a long time coming in English, but Mulcaster was able to connect the need for lexicography with a theory and politics of language and with the practical concerns of spelling reform.

At the end of the *Elementary* is a "Peroration," a concluding statement in defense of the general procedure of argument adopted in both treatises; it is Mulcaster's best sustained piece of writing. Because of its patriotic claims for the English language, it is the most-often quoted section in Mulcaster: "I love *Rome,* but *London* better, I favor *Italy,* but *England* more, I honor *Latin,* but I worship the *English.*" Such a claim is actually not so much a defense of English as it is of Mulcaster's decision to write his books in English and in the particular hard style he adopted. Latin would have been quite easy for him and would have gained him an international readership, so his choice to write in the vernacular reflects his political commitment to the English situation. If indeed there is a connection between words and things (as Mulcaster maintains), then by writing carefully in an impoverished language like English he can, in a sense, create the reality of the kind of education he wishes to see. Furthermore, by using a hard English style, he can introduce a complexity to the subject matter as well as enrich the language. Easiness (that is a plain or clear style) is for Mulcaster no virtue: "If easy understanding be the readiest learning, then wake not my Lady; she learns as she lies." His hard style he calls Ciceronian; he models his elaborate isocolons, parisons, internal rhymes, and prosopopoeias after the patterns described by Cicero in his *Orator* and other works. Though many modern readers find Mulcaster's style little to their taste, he was praised as a writer by Gabriel Harvey in *Pierces Supererogation* (1593), and Harvey also refers to *Positions* several times in his copious manuscript annotations.

Positions and *The First Part of the Elementary* represent the high point of Mulcaster's career as a schoolmaster and writer. In 1586 he quit Merchant Taylors' School, apparently because his pay was not enough. For the next ten years there are scraps of evidence suggesting Mulcaster continued as a freelance master and as a preacher (though when he was ordained is not known). In 1596, however, his fortunes turned. The Mercers' Company, who governed St. Paul's School, turned to Mulcaster for help in a crisis: the high master had refused to leave the school (apparently after being dismissed), so Mulcaster taught the boys in a temporary school a short way off. When the old master was gone, Mulcaster was named as his replacement. He remained until his retirement twelve years later a venerable figure, terrifying to boys and perhaps a figure of fun to some outsiders — the biographer Thomas Fuller describes him as *plagosus Orbilius,* a reference to Horace's hard-hitting schoolmaster. Though this was the heyday of St. Paul's adventure into theater, the revival of the "children of Paul's" is credited to Edward Pearce, the choirmaster.

Mulcaster's two late textbooks, both dedicated to the Mercers, reflect his continuing concern with curriculum at the beginning levels. The *Catechismus Paulinus* (1601; first published, 1599 or 1600) is a modification, in Latin elegiacs, of the Church of England catechism promulgated several decades earlier by Alexander Nowell; it is written for boys at the beginning of their schooling. The *Cato Christianus* (circa 1600), a follow-up text, is not at all like the traditional Cato, but a series all in Latin of verse tales with moral interpretation taken largely from the Old Testament. In the preface Mulcaster explains that the work is to replace the old Cato, which is pagan. He also describes his teaching practice at St. Paul's and, in line with his two earlier English treatises, inveighs against the inconsistent, disorganized, and too-hurried schooling of his day.

Mulcaster's last published work was a long poem in Latin on the death of Elizabeth, *Naenia consolans* (1603), which he translated into English as *A Comforting Complaint.* It is a conventional yet deeply patriotic work that expresses the author's gratitude to the queen. The English verses are not distinguished by their quality. Considering her legendary parsimony, Elizabeth had made surprising gifts to Mulcaster (though extant letters show he had to press for favors from the court). He received rents of land and church livings, one of which was the prosperous Stanford Rivers in Essex, just outside of London. It was to Stanford Rivers that Mulcaster retired in 1608, and it is there he died in 1611.

Despite his avowed conservatism and adherence to custom — or perhaps because of them — Mulcaster's English writings have a radical quality. Though not really a philosopher, he constantly works back to first principles. Though an original by the standards of his age, his ideas never really caught on. If history seems to have moved toward many of his positions, it may be because he was so careful to analyze and criticize those contemporary practices that laid the basis for subsequent change in education. His great interest lies as an acute critic of his own time. Later writers rarely refer to him (exceptions are Charles Hoole and John Newton in the mid seventeenth century), but today his two major books are regularly referred to by scholars writing on the history of education and on English Renaissance culture.

References:

William Baldwin, *William Shakspere's Small Latine & Lesse Greeke,* 2 volumes (Urbana: University of Illinois Press, 1944);

Richard L. DeMolen, *Richard Mulcaster (c. 1531– 1611) and Educational Reform in the Renaissance* (Nieuwkoop: de Graaf, 1992);

F. W. M. Draper, *Four Centuries of Merchant Taylors' School 1561–1961* (London: Oxford University Press, 1962);

Jonathan Goldberg, *Writing Matter: From the Hands of the English Renaissance* (Stanford, Cal.: Stanford University Press, 1990), pp. 27–41;

Walter J. Ong, S.J., "Latin Language Study as a Renaissance Puberty Rite," *Studies in Philology,* 56 (1959): 103–124;

Joan Simon, *Education and Society in Tudor England* (Cambridge: Cambridge University Press, 1966).

Papers:

Richard Mulcaster's letter to Sir John Puckering dated 4 September 1593 is preserved at the British Library (Harleian Ms. 6996, fol. 35), as is his letter to Sir Julius Caesar dated 25 November 1605 (Lansdowne Ms. 161, fol. 25 [24]).

Thomas Nashe

(November 1567 – 1601?)

Reid Barbour
University of North Carolina

BOOKS: *The Anatomie of Absurditie: Contayning a Breefe Confutation of the Slender Imputed Prayses to Feminine Perfection* (London: Printed by J. Charlewood for Thomas Hacket, 1589);

An Almond for a Parrat (London, 1590);

Pierce Penilesse His Supplication to the Diuell (London: Printed by Richard Jones, 1592; republished, London: Printed by Abell Jeffes for John Busbie, 1592);

Strange Newes, of the Intercepting Certaine Letters (London: Printed by John Danter, 1593);

Christs Teares ouer Ierusalem (London: Printed by James Roberts for Andrew Wise, 1593; republished, London: Printed for Andrew Wise, 1594);

The Vnfortunate Traueller. Or, The Life of Iacke Wilton (London: Printed by T. Scarlet for C. Burby, 1594; revised and enlarged, 1594);

The Terrors of the Night or, A Discourse of Apparitions (London: Printed by John Danter for William Jones, 1594);

Haue with You to Saffron-Walden: or, Gabriell Harueys Hunt Is Vp (London: Printed by John Danter, 1596);

Nashes Lenten Stuffe, Containing, the Description of Great Yarmouth. With a New Play of the Praise of the Red Herring (London: Printed for N. L. and C. B., 1599);

A Pleasant Comedie, Called Summers Last Will and Testament (London: Printed by Simon Stafford for Water Burre, 1600).

Editions: *Pierce Penniless's Supplication to the Devil,* edited by J. Payne Collier (London: Shakespeare Society, 1842);

The Complete Works of Thomas Nashe, 6 volumes, edited by Alexander B. Grosart (London: Privately printed, 1883–1885);

The Choise of Valentines, edited by John S. Farmer (London: Privately printed, 1898);

The Works of Thomas Nashe, 5 volumes, edited by R. B. McKerrow (London: A. H. Bullen, 1904–1910); republished, with corrections and sup-

plementary notes, edited by F. P. Wilson (Oxford: Blackwell, 1966);

The Unfortunate Traveller, edited by H. F. Brett-Smith (Boston: Houghton Mifflin, 1920);

Pierce Penniless, His Supplication to the Devil, edited by G. B. Harrison (New York: Dutton, 1924);

The Unfortunate Traveller, edited by Samuel C. Chew (New York: Greenberg, 1926);

Thomas Nashe: Selected Writings, edited by Stanley Wells (Cambridge, Mass.: Harvard University Press, 1964);

Thomas Nashe: "The Unfortunate Traveller" and Other Works, edited by J. B. Steane (New York: Penguin, 1972);

Preface to Robert Greene's "Menaphon" (New York: Garland, 1973);

Thomas Nashe's "Summer's Last Will and Testament": A Critical Modern-Spelling Edition, edited by Patricia Posluszny (New York: Peter Lang, 1989).

OTHER: "To the Gentlemen Students of Both Vniversities," in *Menaphon,* by Robert Greene (London: Printed by T. O. for Sampson Clarke, 1589);

"Somewhat to Reade for Them That List," in *Syr P.S. His Astrophel and Stella,* by Sir Philip Sidney (London: Printed by J. Charlewood for Thomas Newman, 1591).

Thomas Nashe claimed in *Strange News* (1593) that he had "written in all sorts of humors privately . . . more than any young man of my age in England." He left in manuscript an erotic poem dedicated to "Lord S," published late in his short life a show written for Archbishop John Whitgift, and helped in the composition of plays — though there is no passage in any extant play that can definitely be attributed to him. Whatever the scope and range of his private or lost works, his publications and persona are more limited and intense: Nashe was the most brilliant, explosive, and inventive prose writer of Elizabethan England. He loved prose and

The trimming of Thomas Nashe.

But fee, what art thou heere? *lupus* in *fabula*, a lop in a chaine? Nowe firra haue at you, th'art in my fwinge. But foft, fetterd? thou art out againe: I cannot come neere thee, thou haft a charme about thy legges, *no man meddle with the Queenes prifoner*, now therefore let vs talke freendlye, and as *Alexander* fayd to hys Father *Phillip*, who beeing forely wounded in the thigh in fight, and hardly efcaping death, but could

E 2   not

Caricature of Nashe in chains, in Richard Lichfield's The Trimming of Thomas Nashe *(1597)*

wrote it with an energy and a verve that impressed, irked, and intimidated his contemporaries, from barbers to scholars to bureaucrats. Nashe's pamphlets have their putative subjects: the abuses of learning, the seven deadly sins, the fall of Jerusalem, a rogue at large in Europe, the economy of red herring, nightmares, and the foolish doctor from Saffron Walden. For Nashe, however, prose is the enduring topic; he was obsessed with its powers, its spontaneity, and its reception. The prose writer took pride in his favorite "extemporal" vein, with its huge words, its scattershot metaphors, and its parody of styles. Indeed, while his prose has a penchant for invective and an aversion to set patterns, Nashe loved to try on formal styles for a paragraph or two, though he often balked at any charge that his work was derivative. It would be misleading, however, to suggest that he was interested in prose apart from the world in which he lived. His life was as strange and explosive as his prose, and he was forever trying to decide just how the two – prose and life – relate.

The legends and myths surrounding Nashe's life have filled more volumes than the scant number of facts known about him. He was born in November 1567 in the coastal town of Lowestoft, the son of a minister and his second wife. His family moved to nearby West Harling in 1573, where the boy received his earliest education, probably at home. In 1581 or 1582 Nashe arrived in Cambridge, but scholars have debated the month of his arrival, based on a remark the writer made in *Lenten Stuff* (1599) that he had lived in Cambridge "for seven year together lacking a quarter." It is certain that in October 1582 he matriculated as a sizar at St. John's College. Nashe stayed in Cambridge beyond his B.A. in 1586 to work on a master of arts, but he left for London in 1588. Nashe remarked later that he might have been a fellow had he not chosen to leave the university, perhaps for lack of funds in the wake of his father's death in 1587.

With his first manuscript in hand, Nashe came to London, perhaps with the hope of making a living from his wits. His earliest works were pieces of literary criticism, always mixed with social commentary, as was the fashion. The first of these published (though not the first written) was his prefatory epistle to Robert Greene's *Menaphon* (1589). Not long after came Nashe's exercise in euphuism, *The Anatomy of Absurdity* (1589). Two years later appeared a preface to the pirated edition of Sir Philip Sidney's *Astrophil and Stella*. The Sidneys may not have been pleased with the epistle, which was removed from the authorized edition.

The Anatomy of Absurdity is a relatively safe and tame work for Nashe. Its style is more euphuistic than any other of his works, and the targets of its satire and criticism are either traditional or supportive of the establishment. Euphuism was the prose style made popular by John Lyly in the decade just before Nashe brought *The Anatomy of Absurdity* to London. Its chief features include an obsessive pursuit of syntactic balance, antithesis, and parallelism and a copious accumulation of similes and analogies garnered from a variety of compendiums. Alliteration, internal rhyme, learned allusion: all indicate Nashe's intention to create a highly patterned style. Indeed, his stated purpose is to defend art against its enemies, most notably the authors who neglect morality for the sake of obscene pleasure and the Puritans who love morality but deprive it of any beauty or power. As Nashe puts it, "nothing is more odious to the auditor, than the artless tongue of a tedious dolt, which dulls the delight of hearing, and slacketh the desire of remembering."

Nashe's defense of poetry leads him to the conclusion that the best art is the most obscure and idealized. He aspires to sound like Edmund Spenser, George Chapman, or Roger Ascham: the purpose of true poetry is moral reformation, but only eloquence, strengthened by learning and experience, can effect such reform. The orator or poet must navigate between the extremes of brevity and windiness but in all cases "persuade one point thoroughly, rather than teach many things scatteringly." In much of this apology for poetry, one thinks of Nashe's favorite extemporal vein only by contrast. Although he can moralize and obscure, Nashe typically aims for prose with the solidity of a pudding, the power of a tempest, and the focus of a schoolchild. In *The Anatomy of Absurdity*, however, he attempts a grand style in his praises for Elizabeth, in

his dedication of the work to Charles Blount, and in the description of Deucalion's flood: "the springs broke forth and overflowed their bounded banks, the watery clouds with pashing showers unceasingly sending down their unreasonable moisture, augmented the rage of the ocean, so that whole fields and mountains could not satisfy his usurping fury." In theme and style, his satires against women are heavily euphuistic.

In defense of art, Nashe gives the first of his many anatomies of Puritanism. The Puritans, he says, are hypocritical, ignorant, and subversive. They oppose learning and threaten commonwealths with their insubordination. The genesis of these schismatics is, however, somewhat understandable to Nashe: young scholars lack money, lose parents or patrons, have their studies interrupted, and so are forced into preaching too early. In order to forge a career, these young men must make a name for themselves, and strict obedience will not do that. In good humanist fashion, Nashe advises these young scholars on the best ways to succeed, but he already understands how hard it is to steer between the offices of the servant and the self-promotion of the extemporal wit.

In the preface to Greene's *Menaphon,* Nashe returns to many of the absurdities attacked in his first work: the abuses of learning, ignorant Puritans, trite literary fashions. But the style of his invective is not grounded in any one tradition of artifice. For the first time, rather, Nashe proposes an ideal of prose that he embraces for the remainder of his career: the extemporal vein. He prizes "the man whose extemporal vein in any humor will excel our greatest art-master's deliberate thoughts; whose inventions, quicker than his eye, will challenge the proudest rhetorician to the contention of like perfection with like expedition." As Nashe makes clear elsewhere, it is somewhat misleading to call this style an "ideal," insofar as the new breed of professional writers, poor and unpatronized in London, are forced into the rash publications so despised in *The Anatomy of Absurdity* as antithetical to art. Yet here art is demoted, spontaneity promoted. At times, Nashe seeks some authority in the past for his extemporal rhetoric, but he is also attracted to its revolutionary and even dangerous potential.

In contrast to the extemporal vein, Nashe berates playwrights and actors who flaunt the heavens with their pretentious blank verse; plagiarists who rely entirely on the leftovers of Ariosto and Cicero, and who cannot finally tell the difference between a vulgar ballad and true poetry; and in particular dullards who leave their proper trades and translate

Senecan tragedy line by line. This attack on the Senecan vein is the best-known part of the epistle, mainly for what may be topical allusions to Thomas Kyd and Christopher Marlowe: "the sea exhaled by drops will in continuance be dry, and Seneca, let blood line by line and page by page, at length must needs die to our stage; which makes his famished followers to imitate the kid in Aesop, who, enamored with the fox's newfangles, forsook all hopes of life to leap into a new occupation." But Nashe resorts to the attack on the Senecans as an escape from the more political satire against those arrogant young scholars who turn the world upside down. Playwrights, after all, were easier and safer targets than Puritans.

Nashe often promises his reader that he will produce great works and advertises the future miracles he aims to perform. Self-promotion requires that the extemporal wit adopt several styles in order to prove his range. Thus, the Nashe who rails against "the swelling bombast of bragging blank verse" can turn mellifluous on occasion, as he does in the preface to the pirated edition of Sidney's *Astrophil and Stella:* "for here you shall find a paper stage strewed with pearl, an artificial heaven to overshadow the fair frame, and crystal walls to encounter your curious eyes, while the tragicomedy of love is performed by starlight." The epistle has less to do with Sidney than it does with Nashe's own idea of prose. At first glance he appears to devalue his "heavy-gaited" style because it "cannot dance, trip, and go so lively, with 'oh my love, ah my love, all my love's gone,' as other shepherds that have been fools in the Morris time out of mind." He may be sorry that his style plods like a "Gravesend barge," the meaning of which may have something to do with his pursuit of artificial styles. One suspects, however, that Nashe wants nothing to do with the verse of these shepherds. The preface goes on to say that good and bad in literature are matters of opinion; but for all his admiration of Sidney, Nashe suggests a rivalry between his brand of prose and the fashionable verse of the day.

These early works reveal a Nashe who is breaking onto the literary scene in London but not quite prepared to make his mark. It was once believed by readers of Nashe that *The Unfortunate Traveller* was his watershed; counting editions, one would have to say that *Pierce Penniless* was the turning point in his career; but over the last few decades, critics have decided that if any one text – or any one literary event – transformed Nashe from an interesting but second-rate prose stylist into a

phenomenon, it was his participation in the Marprelate controversy and the pamphlet *An Almond for a Parrot* (1590).

By 1590 Nashe was involved in one of the most serious controversies of his day. In 1588 a series of tracts attacking the established church began to appear under the pseudonym Martin Marprelate. These pamphlets divided their space between presenting the necessary points of reformation and making a mockery of the bishops in power. The bishops in turn attempted to answer the arguments of Marprelate, but their ponderous, solemn style was no match for his satire. At last the church hired such wits as Nashe, Greene, and John Lyly to burlesque Martin on stage and in print. Their collaboration in this effort has made it difficult for modern scholars to decide Nashe's share, but most agree now with Donald J. McGinn's claim that Nashe wrote the last and best of these anti-Martin pamphlets, *An Almond for a Parrot.*

Critics agree that *An Almond for a Parrot* features the trademarks of Nashe's mature invective style. Many of these rhetorical strategies were learned from or at least encouraged by the "sauciness" of Martin himself. At the most local level, the style features letter-leaping, or alliteration; mock-honorific addresses to and a running dialogue with the opponent; mundane analogies for the most serious points; the conflation of high with low, learned with colloquial, and abstract with material; gargantuan and inventive epithets; a taunting pugnacity toward the rival; and a penchant for telling the scandalous anecdote or for parodying the habits of the foe, in Nashe's case the antiepiscopal Puritans. One Puritan divine

> came off with this unmannerly comparison: there is an ugly and monstrous beast in our tongue called a hog, and this ugly and monstrous beast in boistrous and tempestuous weather lifts up his snout into the air, and cries "wrough, wrough." Even so (dear people) the children of God in the troublesome time of temptations, cry "Our help is in the name of the Lord."

Marprelate argued that bishops are unscriptural, that they are vicious in their nonresidency and unqualified in their preaching, that the Bible dictates a presbyterian discipline in the church, and that bishops will only ruin the queen with their Romish inquisitions of true believers. Martin has his fun with the bishops, addressing them with mocking titles, exposing the flaws in their tedious books, and revealing their vices. But he also has a serious purpose, the reformation of the English church.

The record of Nashe's christening in November 1567 (Lowestoft Parish Registers, St. Margaret's, Lowestoft)

In *An Almond for a Parrot*, as in *The Anatomy of Absurdity*, Nashe combines mirth and sobriety. The mirth is apparent from the opening address to the clown Will Kempe, in which the target is not so much Martin as the typical epistle to a noble or courtly patron. Here Nashe is a parodist but also a fighter, calling Martin into the back alley with the hope that the authorities will not intervene in their quarrel. With the express purpose of beating Martin at his own game, "Mar-Martin" unleashes the extemporal style:

> It was told me by the undaunted pursevants of your sons, and credibly believed in regard of your sins, that your grout-headed holiness had turned up your heels like a tired jade in a meadow, and snorted out your scornful soul like a measled hog on a muck-hill, which had it not been false, as the devil would have it, that long-tongued doctress, Dame Law, must have been fain (in spite of inspiration) to have given over speaking in the congregation, and employ her Parrot's tongue instead of a wind-clapper to scare the crows from thy carrion.

This passage has the boisterous wordplay, compounds, and similes often pursued by Nashe in his juxtaposition of high and low, of inspiration and excrement. Virtually every phrase is a mock thrown at what Nashe feels are pathetic outlaws. In calling Martin and his fellows "hoddy-polls" (fools), in addressing the Puritan pamphleteer John Penry as "his Welchness" and playing on his name, in satirizing the pulpit-pounding style of the Puritans and their silly rhetoric, Nashe defends the queen's supremacy, social order, and episcopal decency. But he also recognizes that his own authorial stance and voice are close to Martin's: "I speak plain English, and call thee a knave in thine own language." Nashe's persona, Cutbert Curry-knave, vows to overwhelm his enemy provided that "authority do not moderate the fiery fervence of my enflamed zeal." Just short of ten years later, the authorities put out Nashe's fire altogether.

With Martin undone, Nashe earned the good graces of Whitgift. The young wit was at Croydon with the archbishop in the autumn of 1592, where he wrote and (one supposes) helped produce *Summer's Last Will and Testament* (published 1600). This "show" — it is distinguished as such from plays — proves Nashe a poet of considerable merit, not just in the well-known lyric "Adieu, Farewell, Earth's

Bliss" but also in the blank verse spoken by several of the allegorical personae.

The summer of the title is twofold, representing both Henry VIII's clown Will Summers and the season. The jester is a surrogate for Nashe, speaking in what he calls an extemporal prose, criticizing the allegory and commenting on whatever subject arises. He resembles Shakespeare's character Falstaff, counting the hours in food and drink. Like Falstaff, too, he complicates the master/servant relationship, suggesting rebellion in the very manner of his obedience. Like Nashe, he is concerned about those auditors or readers who will dissect the work for its topical or political subtexts and have the author persecuted for what he never intended. The season summer is grave and sober next to the clown, introducing the chief theme of the show, the inevitability of death and decay. As autumn approaches, nature itself withers. But there is also plague in England, a more staggering form of mortality.

In staging the cycles of festival and Lent and their strange disruptions, the show comments on the social problems of the nation as well. The "will and testament" of the title involves a simple narrative premise: Summer is a master who will receive accounts from his servants and then decide which one is his worthy successor. Much of the show is given over to their various positions: Spring is a prodigal son who believes that resources should always and immediately be spent; Solstitium (Solstice) prizes balance and moderation above all things, while Sol is the lavish servant who loves to display the riches of the master as if they were his own. Orion, accused of bringing with him the heat of the dog days, borrows from Sextus Empiricus a paradoxical defense of hounds. Autumn and Winter bicker between themselves as the natural heirs of Summer. Autumn is associated with scholars, which provokes Winter into an assault on poetry, philosophy, and learning in general. Winter is accused of destroying all things. There are also hoarders in the bunch: Harvest is said to be miserly while Christmas hates expenditure and hospitality.

However much Nashe aimed to please Whitgift, the question of the servant's proper use of resources is a vexing one for the prelate and his monarch. Nashe may be a critic of the humanist and mercantilist penchant for hoarding resources, be they natural, monetary, or imaginative, but the show has no easy prescription for the servants competing for the power left by the passing summer. Its language evokes, moreover, the perils of the servant who, like Nashe, is asked to perform the dirty task of cleaning up the corruption in the kingdom.

No master or servant is free from the plague or from general decay. The queen is praised throughout the show, but she can arrest the seasons or the epidemic only for a moment. She may be the "most sacred dame," but "Brightness falls from the air, / Queens have died young and fair, / Dust hath closed Helen's eye." Not even Croydon is safe from disease and cold weather: "Gone is our sport, fled is poor Croyden's pleasure." Nor is the clever author of the entertainment free from harm: "Wit with his wantonness," the lyric warns, "Tasteth death's bitterness." The community of disease leads Nashe to liturgy – "Lord, have mercy on us" – but the plague can also isolate the singer – "I am sick, I must die" – whose position in the kingdom is unstable at best.

Back in London, Nashe already had something of a reputation; his work for Greene and with Lyly confirms this. But his career was made with the publication of *Pierce Penniless His Supplication to the Devil* (1592). Pierce was not just Nashe's most popular creation; it came to be his persona, much more so than the hero of his protonovel, *The Unfortunate Traveller* (1594), finished in June 1593.

Pierce Penniless is traditional in a risky fashion. Its "supplication to the devil" may be a standard complaint against social abuses, framed by the popular medieval device of the seven deadly sins, but the work proved troublesome to Nashe's readers for at least two reasons: Pierce's recourse to hell and the political fable of the bear and fox. Its prose, moreover, aspires to overwhelm the reader with its physicality and nervous, sometimes pulsing energy. A letter from the publisher encourages the reader of *Pierce Penniless* to be patient with its odd arrangement, most notably its deferral of any address to the reader until the end. In the preface to the second edition Nashe complains about the perverse, self-serving reader who "seeks to show himself a politician by mis-interpreting." But in the end Nashe tries to answer the reader's objections.

The text proper introduces a melancholy figure of discontent: Pierce has repented his youthful follies and devoted himself to study but reaps only abuse or neglect for his efforts. Cobblers, he claims, thrive while poets and scholars go hungry. Pierce is so distraught that he paints his agony in verse, but his last recourse is virtually Faustian: he will sell his soul to the devil if Lucifer will liberate gold from its miserly prison. In supplicating the devil, Pierce satirizes the follies and vices of the world around him, beginning with his search for the devil at Westminster and the Exchange. The rest of the plot is simple: Pierce finds a spirit in the body of a professional perjurer (the Knight of the Post) to deliver his supplication to the devil; the knight reads the supplication, only to find that it is a satire on the seven deadly sins in their new and fashionable guises; each portrait of sin is filled with anecdotes and jests but also with personifications in which Nashe unleashes the full force of his invective prose. Finally, Pierce asks the knight to tell him all about the nature of devils and hell, for which Nashe translates a learned treatise on demonology.

Nashe's invective has an acute eye for details and a love for incongruous comparisons. It represents the most mundane or basic materials of the world – dung, pudding, and cloth – and heaps its own verbal inventions. Although his pace is uneven, Nashe often delivers the qualities of a vice at a breathtaking rate. He is also deft with narrative – with the jests and anecdotes of which he is so fond. But he seems to celebrate and to underscore the fully stuffed personification. Usury, for instance,

> clad in a damask cassock, edged with fox fur, a pair of trunk slops [loose trousers], sagging down like a shoemaker's wallet, and a short thread-bare gown on his back, faced with motheaten budge [fur]; upon his head he wore a filthy, coarse biggin [night-cap], and next it a garnish of night-caps, which a sage button[ed] cap, of the form of a cowshard [cow dung], overspread very orderly: a fat chuff it was, I remember, with a gray beard cut short to the stumps, as though it were grimed, and a huge, worm-eaten nose, like a cluster of grapes hanging downwards.

Nashe is clearly trying to amaze his readers with a prose he claims could never be borrowed: "New herrings, new, we must cry, every time we make our selves public, or else we shall be christened with a hundred new titles of idiotism." Such prose may have learning and artifice, but it can hardly derive its heritage from the muse of Spenser or Sidney. It should, however, daunt Nashe's personal enemies, for instance Gabriel Harvey and his brothers, whose foolish books are targeted as a means for illustrating an "indifferent pretty vein in spur-galling an ass."

While the Harveys may number among the enemies of true art, their social aspirations are a little more understandable to Pierce. In a remark that caused the authorities some discomfort, Nashe condemns the Danes for their static hierarchies; indeed, the problem with scholars such as Pierce is their dearth of career options. The enemies of poetry and theater cannot see that these arts should be praised precisely because they inspire the youth of a nation to clean up their language, to pursue honor and vir-

tue, and to fight for their monarch. Under the rubric of sloth, Nashe – or rather Pierce – claims that the theater encourages a healthy rivalry and activism; at the very least it keeps citizens out of pubs and brothels and away from the emperor whose policies they might dislike.

Some of the jests and anecdotes are clear in their relevance to Pierce, for instance, the one in which the raillery of a madcap satirist is severely punished by an offended lord. The fox and bear fable, however, eludes its several topical interpretations. Nashe insists that it is simply a portrait of tyranny and hypocrisy, but he allows for some resemblance to the Marprelate controversy. In general, *Pierce Penniless* epitomizes Nashe's own complex position as an Elizabethan author. Nashe admits that he wants his version of the seven deadly sins to be novel, but he is somewhat wary of its bold dalliance with the social, political, and religious ills of the day. Perhaps anxiety motivates his translation of a learned treatise on demons. Yet even here the issues are controversial, for the nature of hell and the reality of demons are points on which atheists, Puritans, and papists disagree. Pierce reminds his readers that the best remedy against the devil is faith and that the poor author can find hope in patrons such as his own Amyntas. But even if Amyntas is the earl of Derby, as scholars believe, he seems as fabulous to Pierce as the fox and the bear.

Years later Nashe would admit that most of his writing was wasted in private for patrons, not allowed to stand the test of publication as *Pierce Penniless* had successfully done. The only extant example of this manuscript industry is Nashe's erotic poem in the vein of Ovid's *Amores,* "The Choice of Valentines," dedicated to the "Lord S" – either the earl of Southampton or Ferdinando Stanley. The couplets of this poem chronicle the speaker's visit to a brothel, where his failure to maintain an erection leads his mistress to find an artificial substitute. It was, however, Gabriel Harvey – the Cambridge scholar and doctor of law from Saffron Walden – rather than any mistress who gave Nashe his best opportunity to demonstrate machismo in print.

The year 1593 was a landmark for Nashe, for he wrote two other major works: *The Terrors of the Night* and *Christ's Tears over Jerusalem*. Both have complex histories. The former was begun in February, when Nashe was visiting Robert Cotton, and was registered for publication on 30 June. But it was not published at that time, perhaps because it treated a controversial witch trial. Nashe added some material to the pamphlet in 1594, and in October it was registered again and soon published.

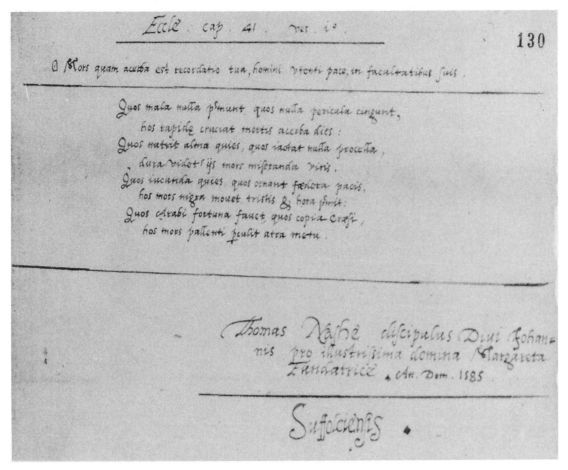

A presentation copy, in the hand of a scribe, of Nashe's Latin verses on Ecclesiasticus *(Public Records Office, State Papers, Dom. Add. Eliz., vol. 29, fol. 167)*

Also in 1594 *Christ's Tears* was republished for two remarkable reasons. The first edition had apologized to Nashe's worst public enemy, Gabriel Harvey, and offended the aldermen of London. In the second edition Nashe retracted both the apology and the offense. Even so, London officials sought to examine Nashe, who escaped to the Isle of Wight with his new and best patron, Sir George Carey. Nashe met Carey probably while the latter was at Windsor Castle in late 1593; he stayed with Carey, the governor of the isle, through Christmas and into the next year. By February Nashe was back in London, where he may have witnessed the trial of the queen's physician.

Despite his pursuit of a patron in the first half of the 1590s, Nashe's most fervent attention was paid to the ongoing quarrel with his nemesis, Gabriel Harvey. The origins of the battle extend back to 1580, the date of Harvey's letters and sonnets to Spenser. But it was Lyly's ridicule of Harvey in 1589 that probably led Richard Harvey, Gabriel's brother, to attack the anti-Martinists in his *Plain Per-*

cival. Nashe was brought into the squabble when Richard's other work of 1589, *The Lamb of God,* upbraided the author of the preface to *Menaphon* for his Martin-like presumption in appraising the great authors of the day. Not until 1592 did the camp of Greene, Lyly, and Nashe respond, with Greene's *Quip for an Upstart Courtier;* but the passage ridiculing the three Harvey brothers (including John) and their rope-making father was deleted soon after the work saw print. Some scholars believe Nashe wrote that section of Greene's work, but he entered the dispute for certain in *Pierce Penniless,* abusing Richard for his sham astrology, obscure origins, opposition to Aristotle, and "lumpish" theology.

From this point onward, Nashe and Gabriel Harvey were in the ring together. The battle was waged at a variety of speeds, sometimes at a plod and other times in a whirl. It was fought for ideological and personal reasons, but also for no real reason at all. Nashe liked to portray Harvey as a seditious innovator and a vain, boorish fool; but Harvey greeted Nashe with the same charges of endangerment to good order and high art. Harvey saw some promise in him and liked to advise the young proser, but this angered Nashe more than anything else.

The main events of the flyting began when Harvey took on Nashe in *Four Letters* (1592); Nashe reponded with a point-by-point satire in *Strange News* (entered in the Stationers' Register 12 January 1593). Efforts were made to reconcile the two, the culmination of which was Nashe's apology to Harvey in the first issue of *Christ's Tears*. Either just before or just after this public apology, Harvey attacked Nashe again in *A New Letter of Notable Contents* (1593), published along with *Pierce's Supererogation* (1593). Thinking that Harvey had refused his apology and humiliated him, Nashe denied him a meeting when they stayed at the same Cambridge lodging in 1595, then published *Have with You to Saffron Walden* (1596). To this burlesque of Harvey's life and works, the only response was *The Trimming of Thomas Nashe* (1597), written by the same Cambridge barber, Richard Lichfield, to whom the mock epistle of *Have with You* is dedicated.

Strange News is Nashe's most derivative work since it clings to its enemy text, Harvey's *Four Letters*. Nashe begins with a mock dedication to William Beeston, whose devotion to poetry and drink inspires the author's madcap wit. Among his enemies Nashe includes the misinterpeters of his works and the calumniators who say that he can write only satire. The main target is, of course, Harvey. Nashe assails his opponent for failing to defend his rope-making father, for promoting his own foolish poetry with its "strange words," for bearing such an unjustified grudge against Nashe, and for being so vain. Nashe puts himself on the side of orthodoxy and the establishment, and Harvey with the forces of discontent and novelty in the kingdom. Ironically, Nashe is compelled in the course of this satire to defend Pierce Penniless against the charges that the persona is a traitor, desperado, or satanist. Nashe points out that he has spent time with a lord – he means Whitgift – in a "house of credit." Among the many contrasts between his own powerful, nimble prose and Harvey's lumbering style, Nashe virtually elevates language over truth. One can imagine why Harvey could turn the charge of self-promotion and dangerous innovation back on Nashe. For the sake of good order and received wisdom, then, Nashe aligns his "declamatory" prose with national interests and locates its place in a tradition stretching from Archilochus to Pietro Aretino.

The Terrors of the Night recapitulates Nashe's interest in demonology but in such a mixed and sometimes skeptical fashion that it also illuminates his concepts of prose and the author. Critics tend to read this work as lightweight, careless, and cynical in its exposure of popular superstitions, that is, in its contribution to what one historian has called the "decline of magic." Nashe in fact adopts a feckless pose from time to time. In one such case he compares his prose to a dream insofar as he is only half awake in writing the book. Dreams themselves, like devils and demons, receive a poignant, if ambivalent, treatment in the pamphlet.

The work is a haphazard account of the causes of fear in human souls. It includes the more religious view that sin produces guilt and, consequently, nightmares. This position holds that the devil encourages despair, assailing the bad conscience at night when hope ebbs low. At the same time, Nashe demythologizes the nightmare and attributes bad dreams to diet or memory. Even when he depicts the guises of the devil or the close packing of spirits into a small space, one glimpses at times the ironic skepticism about superstition forthrightly stated elsewhere.

Nashe may tire of his "drumbling subject," but even the mundane explanation of terror is clearly a serious subject for him. He offers vivid images of the melancholy dream, the "bubbling scum or froth of the fancy, which the day hath left undigested." Dreams resemble arrows that have overshot their mark, or the afterglow of the sun; they are ripples in or blisters on the brain. Some dreams fulfill wishes, for instance, the poor dream of gold. But the several images of torture warn the reader that there is a deeper connection between this work and *Pierce Penniless* than just an interest in the nature of demons and fairies.

Like *Pierce Penniless,* this treatise on dreams concerns the status and obligations of the author. *The Terrors of the Night* is an important work for Nashe because it was patronized by the Carey family, dedicated to Elizabeth Carey (Sir George's daughter), and written in part under their protection. Nashe wants to please them, as well as the original commissioners of the piece who have asked the author to investigate nightmares. The purpose of the pamphlet is to satisfy the friends of a gentleman who died after having strange visions. These friends, associated with Robert Cotton, whom Nashe visited in February 1593, want to know whether the old man died saved or damned and whether the dreams were real or illusory. Herein lies the anxiety of the author, whose obligations require either that he report the truth or invent it. Nashe is concerned about overstepping his limits,

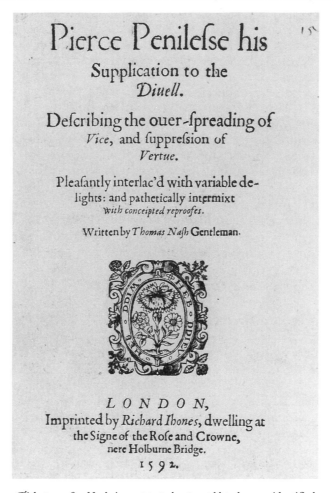

Title page for Nashe's most popular pamphlet; he was identified with the title character for the rest of his career.

displeasing his patron, or abusing the truth. He ends with the most traditional and somber warning for all readers to avoid sin; but it is difficult for the author to rest easy when his own extemporal prose may be blessed, cursed, or, worst of all, ignored.

Nashe had good reason to fear the perils of authorship. *Pierce Penniless* was popular but received some criticism from political readers. *The Terrors of the Night* had trouble getting into print, probably because it dealt with a recent instance of witchcraft. The flytings with Marprelate and Harvey were earning Nashe the reputation of a "young Juvenal" whose only vein was raillery. With *Christ's Tears* the writer attempts to clean up his act. In the first edition he apologizes to Harvey, bids farewell to trivial and satiric works, elevates his style, adopts the pose of minister and prophet, and commits himself to the business of saving London from its manifold sins. The structure of the work is modeled on the "looking glass" narratives that instruct modern society to see itself in the mirror of the past – in this instance, the Roman destruction of Jerusalem. Thus, the main purpose of Nashe's homily, if it can be called that, is confined to the second half of the piece, which traces the family tree of the deadly sins as they are instantiated in the social practices of London.

In an effort to bestow some gravity on *Christ's Tears,* Nashe clutters its style with huge and compound words, with coinages ending in *-ate* or *-ize,* and with alliteration. Readers must make their way among *preludiately, mummianized, gross-brained formallity, purely pacificatory suppliants, assertionate, oblivionize,* and *luciferious passionate-ambitious.* Scripture serves, however, to authorize this inventive yet ponderous style. On two occasions Nashe sets forth the idea that every word of Scripture is a powerful cement or cornerstone. It should not be handled carelessly or often, no matter what the conviction of those Puritans whose sermons are a mass of quotations from the Bible. In contrast to these sectaries, Nashe selects key words from the Gospels – for instance, *gather* and *stone* – and repeats them in a variety of forms.

Nashe also seeks to elevate *Christ's Tears* by way of prosopopoeia, that is, in giving voice to an impressive persona, in this case to Christ. But Nashe's Jesus, overcome with personal failure, laments his replacement by the Romans, who punish the obdurate people of Jerusalem. Even more disturbing is the voice of Miriam, the Jewish woman who kills and eats her son in response to the famine racking Jerusalem, then defends her cannibalism at some length. Nashe is not inventing Miriam any more than he is the rest of the story, but throughout the text he displays a penchant for the horrific and gory. Every motion is a violent one; every street or river is clotted with blood and corpses. The reader is not far from the terrors of the night but even closer to the gruesome Europe of Jack Wilton.

Christ's Tears scarcely redeemed Nashe from his past transgressions. Rather, it caused him more distress than any previous work. For one thing, the sermon is just as satiric as anything else he wrote, and its attack on the abuses and bribery of London officials landed him in trouble. The second edition (1594) keeps the censure of atheists, Puritans, and upstarts but softens the depiction of the aldermen. In the same edition, however, a cantankerous Nashe retracts his apology to Harvey, promising to heed the advice of Machiavellians who trust no one. Moreover, Nashe proudly defends his style against detractors who find it too self-advertising at best, too profane at worst. Appealing to the church fathers for support of his fervent rhetoric, Nashe goes further to justify his new words – the *-ize* terms in particular. With metaphors taken from alchemy, economics, and botany, the author claims that he has re-created an English more powerful than the weak and harsh monosyllabics of old. Once again, the extemporal wit tries to found his prose on the rock of the true church, the established government, and the good patronage of the Careys, but the result is tense and problematic.

In the second edition of *Christ's Tears,* Nashe also attacks misreaders of *The Unfortunate Traveller,* a text in which he tries once more to write in a new vein, to find a patron, and to tell a cautionary tale. There is, however, one major difference between the two narratives: Jack Wilton is no savior. Between service and rebellion, he struggles for survival in a Europe of violence, cultural malaise, and disorder.

For twentieth-century readers predisposed to the novel, *The Unfortunate Traveller* is considered Nashe's major work. Scholars may not agree on how closely it approximates the novel form – some think it is picaresque; others find in it a mishmash of styles and genres – but they concur that it is the most modern thing in spirit and kind that Nashe ever wrote. Dedicating the work to the earl of Southampton, the author promises "some reasonable conveyance of history, and variety of mirth." Indeed, more than before, Nashe is intent on telling an often complex story, one interrupted or elaborated by set speeches or descriptions. He is tentative about what he considers "a clean different vein from other my former courses of writing." From start to finish, his narrator, Jack Wilton, is self-conscious about the tale – about whether readers will like it, about how characters and the narrator himself know things, about the relation between plot and digression. He confesses to having a selective memory for detail, but the scenes of this work are remarkably acute and graphic, even if (or especially because) they don't quite add up.

Some readers have argued that the apparent disorder of the work is its theme – that Nashe sets out to show a culture in crisis, a Europe torn by religious dissent, sham academics, rampant violence, and bogus romanticism. Another view holds that Nashe is testing the boundaries of fiction itself, measuring the extent to which it can be taken seriously. From the beginning, Jack moves in several directions. First there is what might be called the main narrative. Jack starts with Henry VIII in battle against the French in Tournay and Térouanne; from the France of 1513 he travels in time and space back to the English court at Windsor, onward to the Continental battles between France and Switzerland, then to Münster (1534) and the slaughter of the Anabaptists by the imperial forces. Back and forth he goes, meeting the earl of Surrey on his way to England, turning round to visit Rotterdam, Wittenburg, and various Italian cities, returning at last to the English court camped at the famous Field of the Cloth of Gold in 1520. But such a sketch of settings hardly conveys the convolutions and nightmares of misfortune that Jack and his companions encounter.

The mischievous Jack is introduced through a series of his most memorable jests. He is also fond of describing his own social status, giving the reader a character of the court page but also a catalogue of his fashionable clothes. He may value his most prized possession, an extemporal wit, over the highest authorities. But like Nashe, Jack knows when to apologize, as he does to the church when he presumes to sermonize against the Puritans or in favor

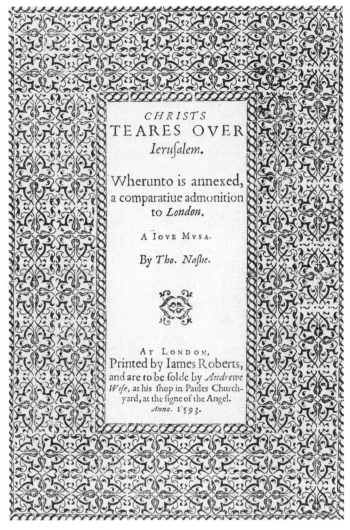

CHRIST'S
TEARES OVER
Ierusalem.

Wherunto is annexed,
a comparatiue admonition
to London.

A Iove Mvsa.

By Tho. Nashe.

At London,
Printed by Iames Roberts,
and are to be solde by Andrewe
Wise, at his shop in Paules Church-
yard, at the signe of the Angel.
Anno. 1593.

Title page for Nashe's pamphlet comparing the condition of London to
the Roman sack of Jerusalem

of good works, and as he does to Surrey when he masquerades as the earl.

At several points in his disconcerting survey of sixteenth-century Europe, Jack introduces set speeches or blazons featuring his powers of caricature, invective, parody, and even grandiloquence. No matter how self-centered he appears, most of his set pieces attempt to capture the "wonderful spectacle of bloodshed" that Europe has become. He pauses over the deserved but pitiful slaughter of the Anabaptists. Faced with the physical deformity and pervasive mortality caused by the sweating sickness and the plague, he is almost forced to turn them into jests. But this he cannot do, for during the plague he is witness to the brutal rape of Heraclide. Jack himself is subject to violence: he is imprisoned on several occasions and threatened with a horrible death by anatomy. The whole world is unstable,

slippery: doors open and Jack falls through. No one is trustworthy, and no position is unassailable.

With one gory execution after another, Nashe returns to his fascination with the basic materials of existence and with torture and terror. Some readers have called this tendency "realism"; by any name it epitomizes a culture in crisis, from which humor and trickery offer no permanent way out. The great heroes of the period are portrayed, the humanists Sir Thomas More and Desiderius Erasmus, the reformer Martin Luther, the magus Cornelius Agrippa. But Jack tends to prefer mirthful caricature over a record of serious disputes; or if this reborn culture is fascinating, its wonder verges on illusory magic. In one scene, Agrippa conjures up the image of Cicero in order to show his audience how the great orator managed to win a case for the most guilty of clients. The point of this scene appears to be an indictment of a humanist culture besotted with its heroes, shaky in its grasp of truth, and committed to shiny surfaces.

Jack's own hero is Aretino, who represents the freedom of the satirist to tell the established powers how wrong they are. But Jack is also fascinated with the glamours concealing the violence of this world. He marvels over the earl of Surrey's tournament in which the most elaborate, ridiculous, and obscure suits of armor are paraded. He describes a walking tour of Rome and a merchant's banqueting house; the latter is virtually a paradise on earth yet with its machinery visible behind the elaborate artifice. Jack loves to parody the rhetorical modes of the day, the ceremonial, homiletic, disputative, romantic, Petrarchan. But they all give way, or so he thinks, to the *sprezzatura* of his own prose. In the end, however, Jack finds his wits at the mercy of the strange forces governing the universe – or leaving it ungoverned. What with the treachery of prostitutes, atheists, outlaws, Jews, the Pope, the Puritans – with a world of violence and instability, Jack converts to honesty in the end. He marries his mistress, returns to his king, and utters his amazement at destiny. But this conversion of the rogue may be just another parody in a world where style and performance are the only means of survival. Like Odysseus, Jack comes home – but only after proving that his name is trouble.

Nashe's activities between 1594 and 1596 are something of a mystery. He did some traveling, in one case to Lincolnshire but perhaps elsewhere in England. He was long in the employment of the printer John Danter and lived at Danter's house for some time. By his own testimony, Nashe wrote little or nothing for the press during these years, though much for private patrons. Only two items survive in manuscript: "The Choice of Valentines," an erotic poem of uncertain date, and a letter sent to William Cotton in 1596. The letter reveals a Nashe still overcome by the official censure of *Christ's Tears*, frustrated in his attempts to write for the theater and the press, caught between country friends and London audiences, and mirthfully obscene. Many of his attempts to find a patron seem to have failed. Charles Blount, Ferdinando Stanley, and Henry Wriothesley each received praises from Nashe, but none offered any lasting protection. For much of the 1590s Nashe appears to have been poor. In *Have with You* he even embraces Harvey's charge that poverty has landed him in the Fleet.

Nashe's final satire on Gabriel Harvey, *Have with You to Saffron Walden*, is a mock-biography, complete with a fictive letter from Harvey's tutor, an account of Harvey's birth, and a portrait. In ad-

dition to this sustained piece of burlesque, Nashe has comic images for every facet of Harvey's life and works, from the sheer bulk of his books to the wrinkles on his face. Everything about Harvey bothers his opponent: he is at once silly in his vanity and dangerous in his heterodoxies. He is portrayed in a variety of funny settings, posing in front of the mirror, failing to pay his debts, whining in prison. At some moments, though, Nashe seems almost to pity Harvey, if not to identify with him. For instance, Harvey is described enduring total isolation in London during the plague, risking life and limb just for the unlikely chance of undoing Nashe.

Nashe seems weary of the whole contest, resents being put in the ring with Harvey, and protests that such writers as he can rely only on their wits. However funny or inventive his satire, Nashe is more autobiographical here than in his other works. He describes his poverty, his travels in England, and his dwelling in London. He paints a self-portrait of a man who is always in good company, who feels no urgent need to answer Harvey, and who is the furthest thing from that lonely image of the poor writer in plague-stricken London. But Nashe admits that he has wasted much of his efforts in the service of noblemen and courtiers who never treated him fairly, and that he is closer to the fiction of Pierce Penniless than he has allowed heretofore.

Nashe still promotes his own extemporal wit and superior prose, but he is also worried that his public image will be damaged by his flyting with Harvey. Giving the work a dialogue format prevents him from appearing so isolated: his interlocuters are men of credit who are clearly on his side, even when they criticize him for his wasted efforts or idleness. Calling himself "Pierce Penniless," Nashe continues to praise the heroes of the establishment, now Lancelot Andrewes, and to bring his academic learning to bear on the shameless ad hominem assaults. He also feels compelled to apologize for his prose, however – to defend its power but also to search for the reasons why he has come short of greatness or believability. For all the outright mockery of the piece, Nashe is intent on measuring the triviality of his life in prose.

Nashe had some involvement with the burgeoning theater of the 1590s. In 1594, for reasons not altogether clear, his name appeared with Marlowe's on the title page of *Dido, Queen of Carthage*. A satiric play, the lost *Isle of Dogs*, sent Nashe running from the authorities in 1597. As the official investigator was confiscating his papers, Nashe was mak-

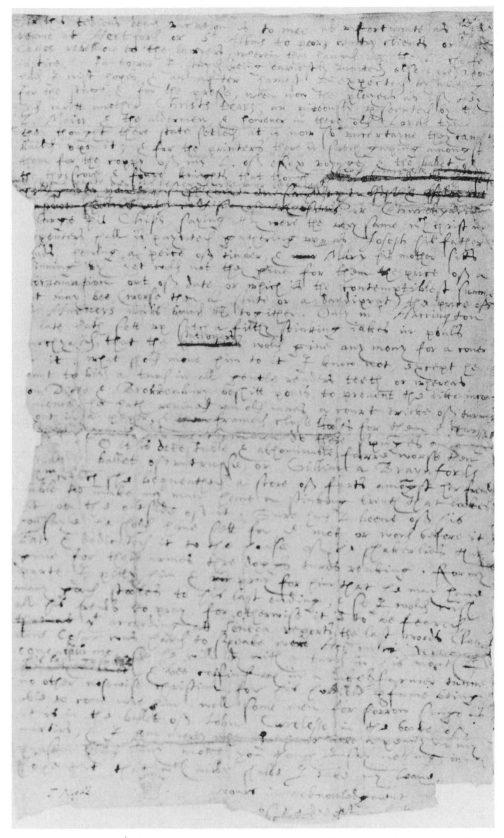

*Letter from Nashe to William Cotton, August–September 1596 (British Library, Cotton Ms. Jul.
C 3, fol. 280)*

ing his way back to the east coast. In Great Yarmouth he found a hospitality not equaled since his brief stay on Wight. In 1598, during Lent, he was working on his last major pamphlet, *Lenten Stuff,* a description of Yarmouth with a mock encomium for its major resource, the red herring.

Written in exile from the *Isle of Dogs* scandal, *Lenten Stuff* insists that triviality is the best course for a proser to take. The mock-dedication to a barber, the praise of red herring, and the comic retelling of Hero and Leander are each a playful fiction that upholds the author's noninvolvement in the serious work of philosophy, politics, or history. The word *lenten* in the title refers to the season when Nashe began to write the text, but it also suggests that his prose is empty. Defending his right to be trivial, he launches a frontal assault on readers who find political matter in his words, and he taunts them with the possibility that they are making much out of nonsense — out of phrases that he simply tossed off, without any semantic or thematic intention.

Between the mock-dedication and the encomium for fish, Nashe gives his reader a walking tour of Great Yarmouth. Exact records are presented of its history, economy, and topography, though these facts — Nashe insists that they are documented — are rendered with the author's love of mock-grandiloquence, physicality, and madcap invention. Both the praise of the town and of its major resource, the herring, are vintage Nashe, filled with jests and anecdotes, with a nervous attitude toward the reader, with an explosion of conceits, and with a juxtaposition of the honorable and the vulgar. But when he turns from the town to its herring, Nashe protests that his encomium is fictive, related more to incredible romance, beast fable, and myth than to historical documents. The praise of the fish is still economic, even as the praise of Yarmouth is mythic. But in this time of anxiety and trouble, Nashe renders unto Yarmouth what he owes it, then proclaims a separate space for his creations.

Nashe may have found in the local economy of Yarmouth the perfect emblem of his own status. The prosperity of the coastal town is said to epitomize the greatness of England; but at the same time the herring industry stands in opposition to an England in which the best resources are abused, manipulated, taxed, and vexed. The same holds true for Nashe. Nothing could be more ironic than the publication of *Summer's Last Will and Testament* just after Whitgift and Richard Bancroft proscribed the works of their onetime servant. In *Lenten Stuff* Nashe is dismayed that his inventions could be read

against his devotion to political and religious orthodoxy. But he defies any reader, official or lay, to suppress the elusive but undeniable power of his prose and the imagination behind it.

In *Lenten Stuff* Nashe promises to answer *The Trimming of Thomas Nashe* and all those enemies who have abused him during this period of forced absence from London. He apparently never answered his foes, and in 1601 Charles Fitzgeffrey published a Latin epitaph for the dead satirist. One of the greatest mysteries about Nashe's life is when, where, and how he died. In his last years the pressures of authorship only increased for Pierce Penniless; on 1 June 1599 his onetime patron Archbishop Whitgift joined with Bishop Bancroft in consigning Nashe's works to the fire. With Harvey and other satirists, Nashe was considered too contentious for a government that had relied on his invective just ten years earlier.

Perhaps the authorities who hired Nashe against the Marprelates always worried that his volatile prose was dangerous to law and order. Nashe was orthodox in so many ways; as R. B. McKerrow asserts, it was Harvey who had all the newfangled ideas. But no matter how shallow or deep his commitments to a contested establishment, Nashe wrote a prose that resisted outside intervention or control. As scholars have shown, these tensions are seen everywhere in Nashe — in his uses of learning, in the explosion of analogies on every page, in his addresses to the authorities or his estimation of the value of "singularity," in his parody of the latest styles or genres, and in the modern authors that he prefers.

Nashe was something of a phenomenon in the 1590s. Even the author of *The Trimming of Thomas Nashe* admitted that he was famous. Some readers were offended by his extemporal wit and so dubbed him a filthy malcontent, more suited to perverse raillery and base dildo poems than to true art. Others prized the invective of this "young Juvenal." Greene and Thomas Lodge, among others, admired him for his liberty in satire, yet warned him that he must protect himself from enemies. Indeed, a common theme in literature about Nashe — and there was a spate of it — is the mirthful and resilient yet pitiful author, one who manages to keep the other unfortunates laughing, though his own plight is perhaps worst of all. In the Parnassus plays, Ingenioso, who is clearly Nashe, pursues one patron after another; the other scholars in the same position look to him for a wit that sustains them, for a spirit that compels them onward. In the end, Ingenioso and the "jerking" fire of his satire topple over into eccentricity, not to say madness, from which only the Isle of Dogs can supply an ironic exile with Furor and Phantasma. The poor scholars know that this, the most impressive and gifted of the university wits, has been wasted on – but also punished by – the world. As they eulogize Nashe in propria persona, "whose muse was armed with a gagtooth, and his pen possessed with *Hercules'* furies," the scholars hold that he had the greatest share of "mother wit," and that no cultural hero can match this gentle yet fiery spirit.

For Thomas Dekker, too, "Pierce" has an unconfined wit, passionate spirit, and revolutionary prose. In one text he imagines Nashe in hell, railing against "dry-fisted patrons" for the amusement of Marlowe, Greene, and George Peele. John Selden records an anecdote that portrays Nashe as a social malcontent who attacks mayors and aldermen, the English Aretino whom princes would do well to fear. In the 1640s, however, the ghost of Nashe is summoned to defend the established church as once he did against the schismatics of the late 1580s. Others remember Nashe not for his politics but for his trivia, the defense of red herring above all.

To some extent, then, the Nashe phenomenon was simple. Here was the man who had written the most powerful prose of the age; Michael Drayton believed that he deserved the poet's laurels in spite of his medium. This "proser" may, moreover, have contributed to a growing rift between poetry and prose, though any such rivalry is sketchy in Nashe's own day. But the simple somehow produced complex effects and responses. How can it be that Nashe was banned and exiled – Lichfield depicts him in chains and anticipates his execution – yet memorialized as the great defender of the establishment? Were Cutbert, Pierce, and Jack friends or enemies of the state? At one and the same time, Thomas Nashe appears to be the most sociable and solitary figure of his day. At one and the same time, his work seems busy and idle, significant and nugatory.

One finds Nashe summed up in the strangest places. In Harvey's *Pierce's Supererogation* the doctor cites, for the sake of fairness, the praises given Nashe by a gentleman. It is hard to tell the extent to which this passage is ironic. The gentleman declares that good humanists will devote their fine and neat artistry to the flights of Hermes, Plato, Orpheus, and other "marvelous eggs in moonshine." But Nashe, with his "smart pamphlet of knavery," understands that "life is a gaming, a juggling, a scolding, a lawing, a skirmishing, a war; a comedy, a tragedy: the stirring wit, a quintessence of quicksilver; and there is no dead flesh in affection, or cour-

age." The extemporal wit always tries to maintain a basis in art, humanism, and classical learning. But the gentleman captures the late-sixteenth-century conviction that in the prose of Nashe, readers hold life itself – its materials, its drama, its hopes and frustrations – in their very hands. The implications of this prose were vexed and troubled, and Nashe must have longed for some stable place in the world of power, the kind of place that John Donne and Ben Jonson sought. It is not so strange that eighteenth-century biographers fancied Nashe a clergyman, for Pierce and Jack had this fantasy, and so perhaps did Nashe as he made his way to Wight or Yarmouth.

Bibliographies:

Samuel A. Tannenbaum, *Thomas Nashe: A Concise Bibliography* (New York: Samuel A. Tannenbaum, 1941); supplemented by Robert C. Johnson in *Elizabethan Bibliographies* (London: Nether Press, 1968);

Robert J. Fehrenbach, "Thomas Nashe," in *The Predecessors of Shakespeare: A Survey and Bibliography of Recent Studies in English Renaissance Drama*, edited by Terence P. Logan and Denzell S. Smith (Lincoln: University of Nebraska Press, 1973), pp. 107–124;

James L. Harner, *English Renaissance Prose Fiction, 1500–1660: An Annotated Bibliography of Criticism* (Boston: G. K. Hall, 1978), pp. 335–338;

Fehrenbach, "Recent Studies in Nashe (1968–1979)," *English Literary Renaissance*, 11 (1981): 344–350.

Biography:

Charles Nicholl, *A Cup of News: The Life of Thomas Nashe* (Boston: Routledge & Kegan Paul, 1984).

References:

Don Cameron Allen, "*The Anatomy of Absurdity*: A Study in Literary Apprenticeship," *Studies in Philology*, 32 (1935): 170–176;

George T. Amis, "The Meter and Meaning of Nashe's 'Adieu, Farewell Earths Blisse,' " *English Literary Renaissance*, 9 (1979): 78–85;

Eckhard Auberlen, *The Commonwealth of Wit: The Writer's Image and His Strategies of Self-Representation in Elizabethan Literature* (Tübingen: G. Narr, 1984), pp. 179–209;

C. L. Barber, *Shakespeare's Festive Comedy: A Study of Dramatic Form in Its Relation to Social Custom* (New York: Meridian Books, 1963);

Reid Barbour, *Deciphering Elizabethan Fiction* (Newark: University of Delaware Press, 1993);

Peter Berek, "Lyly, Nashe, and *Love's Labor's Lost*," *Studies in English Literature*, 23 (1983): 207–221;

Michael R. Best, "Nashe, Lyly, and *Summer's Last Will and Testament*," *Philological Quarterly*, 48 (1969): 1–11;

Fredson T. Bowers, "Thomas Nashe and the Picaresque Novel," in *Humanistic Studies in Honor of John Calvin Metcalf* (Charlottesville: University of Virginia Studies, 1941), pp. 12–27;

Sandra Clark, *The Elizabethan Pamphleteers: Popular Moralistic Pamphlets, 1580–1640* (Rutherford, N.J.: Fairleigh Dickinson University Press, 1983);

Elizabeth Cook, "'Death proves them all but toyes': Nashe's Unidealising Show," in *The Court Masque,* edited by David Lindley (Manchester: Manchester University Press, 1984), pp. 17–32;

Jonathan V. Crewe, *Unredeemed Rhetoric: Thomas Nashe and the Scandal of Authorship* (Baltimore: Johns Hopkins University Press, 1982);

A. K. Croston, "The Use of Imagery in Nashe's *The Unfortunate Traveller*," *Review of English Studies*, 24 (1948): 90–101;

Walter R. Davis, *Idea and Act in Elizabethan Fiction* (Princeton: Princeton University Press, 1969), pp. 189–237;

Margaret Ferguson, "Nashe's *The Unfortunate Traveller*: The 'News of the Maker' Game," *English Literary Renaissance*, 11 (1981): 165–182;

Kenneth Friedenreich, "Nashe's *Strange News* and the Case for Professional Writers," *Studies in Philology*, 71 (1974): 451–472;

Madelon S. Gohlke, "Wit's Wantonness: *The Unfortunate Traveller* as Picaresque," *Studies in Philology*, 73 (1976): 397–413;

C. G. Harlow, "Nashe's Visit to the Isle of Wight and His Publications of 1592–4," *Review of English Studies*, new series 14 (1963): 225–242;

Harlow, "Thomas Nashe, Robert Cotton the Antiquary, and *The Terrors of the Night*," *Review of English Studies*, new series 12 (1961): 7–23;

Richard Helgerson, *The Elizabethan Prodigals* (Berkeley: University of California Press, 1976);

G. R. Hibbard, *Thomas Nashe: A Critical Introduction* (London: Routledge & Kegan Paul, 1962);

Stephen S. Hilliard, *The Singularity of Thomas Nashe* (Lincoln: University of Nebraska Press, 1986);

Devon L. Hodges, *Renaissance Fictions of Anatomy* (Amherst: University of Massachusetts Press, 1985), pp. 36–49;

R. G. Howarth, *Two Elizabethan Writers of Fiction: Thomas Nashe and Thomas Deloney* (Cape Town: University of Cape Town Press, 1956);

Lorna Hutson, *Thomas Nashe in Context* (Oxford: Clarendon Press, 1989);

Hutson, "Thomas Nashe's 'Persecution' by the Aldermen in 1593," *Notes and Queries,* new series 232 (1987): 199–200;

Ann Rosiland Jones, "Inside the Outsider: Nashe's *Unfortunate Traveller* and Bakhtin's Polyphonic Novel," *English Literary History,* 50 (1983): 61–81;

David Kaula, "The Low Style in Nashe's *The Unfortunate Traveller*," *Studies in English Literature,* 6 (1966): 43–57;

Arthur F. Kinney, *Humanist Poetics: Thought, Rhetoric, and Fiction in Sixteenth-Century England* (Amherst: University of Massachusetts Press, 1986), pp. 304–362;

Richard A. Lanham, "Tom Nashe and Jack Wilton: Personality as Structure in *The Unfortunate Traveller*," *Studies in Short Fiction,* 4 (1967): 201–216;

Charles Larson, "The Comedy of Violence in Nashe's *The Unfortunate Traveller*," *Cahiers elisabéthains,* 8 (1975): 15–29;

Agnes M. C. Latham, "Satire on Literary Themes and Modes in Nashe's *Unfortunate Traveller*," *English Studies,* new series 1 (1948): 85–100;

Alexander Leggatt, "Artistic Coherence in *The Unfortunate Traveller*," *Studies in English Literature,* 14 (1974): 31–46;

E. D. MacKerness, "*Christ's Tears* and the Literature of Warning," *English Studies,* 33 (1952): 251–254;

David Margolies, *Novel and Society in Elizabethan England* (Totowa, N.J.: Barnes & Noble, 1985);

Donald J. McGinn, "Nashe's Share in the Marprelate Controversy," *PMLA,* 59 (1944): 952–984;

McGinn, *Thomas Nashe* (Boston: Twayne, 1981);

Barbara C. Millard, "Thomas Nashe and the Functional Grotesque in Elizabethan Prose Fiction," *Studies in Short Fiction,* 15 (1978): 39–48;

Neil Rhodes, *Elizabethan Grotesque* (Boston: Routledge & Kegan Paul, 1980);

Rhodes, "Nashe, Rhetoric and Satire," in *Jacobean Poetry and Prose: Rhetoric, Representation and the Popular Imagination,* edited by Clive Bloom (New York: St. Martin's Press, 1988), pp. 25–43;

Kiernan Ryan, "The Extemporal Vein: Thomas Nashe and the Invention of Modern Narrative," in *Narrative: From Malory to Motion Pic-*

tures, edited by Jeremy Hawthorn (London: Arnold, 1985), pp. 40–54;

James L. Sanderson, "An Unnoted Text of Nashe's 'The Choise of Valentines,'" *English Language Notes,* 1 (1964): 252–253;

Margaret Schlauch, *Antecedents of the English Novel, 1400–1600* (London: Oxford University Press, 1963);

Alice Lyle Scoufos, "Nashe, Jonson and the Oldcastle Problem," *Modern Philology,* 65 (1968): 307–324;

Louise Simons, "Rerouting *The Unfortunate Traveller*: Strategies for Coherence and Direction," *Studies in English Literature,* 28 (1988): 17–38;

Raymond Stephanson, "The Epistemological Challenge of Nashe's *The Unfortunate Traveller,*" *Studies in English Literature,* 23 (1983): 21–36;

Travis L. Summersgill, "The Influence of the Marprelate Controversy upon the Style of Thomas Nashe," *Studies in Philology,* 48 (1951): 145–160;

Wesley Trimpi, "The Practice of Historical Interpretation and Nashe's 'Brightnesse falls from the ayre,'" *Journal of English and Germanic Philology,* 66 (1967): 501–518;

Robert Weimann, "Fabula and Historica: The Crisis of the 'Universall Consideration' in *The Unfortunate Traveller,*" *Representations,* 8 (1984): 14–29.

Papers:

R. B. McKerrow knew of three manuscript copies of "The Choice of Valentines": in an unnamed collection (MS. 538, volume 43, folios 295v–298v); in the Bodleian Library (Rawl. MS. Poet. 216, folios 94, 96–106); and in the Dyce Collection at South Kensington (No. 44). In 1964 James L. Sanderson added a fourth: in the Philip and A. S. W. Rosenbach Foundation Museum in Philadelphia (MS. 1083/15. folios 9v–11v). The letter to William Cotton is in the British Library (Cotton MS Jul C III, folio 280). There is also a presentation copy of Nashe's Latin verses on *Ecclesiasticus* in the Public Records Office (State Papers, Dom. Add. Eliz., volume xxix, folio 167).

Richard Pace

(1482? – 28 June 1536)

Peter C. Herman
San Diego State University

BOOKS: *De fructu qui ex doctrina percipitur* (Basel: Printed by John Froben, 1517);

Oratio Richardi Pacei in pace nuperinne composita (London: Printed by Richard Pynson, 1518);

Praefatio. D. Richardi Pacei in Ecclesiasticen recognitem ad Hebraicam veritatem (London: Printed by Richard Pynson, 1526).

Edition: *De fructu qui ex doctrina percipitur (The Benefit of a Liberal Education),* edited and translated by Frank Manley and Richard S. Sylvester (New York: Ungar, 1967).

TRANSLATIONS: John Fisher, *Contio quam Anglice habuit reverendus pater Joannes Roffensis versa in Latinum per R. Paceum* (London: Printed by J. Siberch, 1521);

Plutarch, *Opuscula de garrulitate de Anarchia . . . Richardo Paceo Anglico interprete* (London: Printed by Richard Pynson, 1530?).

Richard Pace (pronounced "Pacey") was an ambassador and courtier in the service of King Henry VIII; he also acted as the king's secretary. On the surface Pace enjoyed a successful, even brilliant political career that combined humanist leanings with political success. He belonged to the generation of younger, reforming humanists who entered government service and befriended such luminaries as John Colet, Desiderius Erasmus, and Sir Thomas More. Pace acted on the king's behalf in several delicate diplomatic missions, including arguing for Henry's attempt to become the Holy Roman Emperor; he was appointed (though did not serve) as reader in Greek at Cambridge; he was granted a series of highly lucrative benefices, including the deanery of St. Paul's; and he attended the Field of the Cloth of Gold, where he preached a sermon, later published, on the benefits of universal peace. He devoted his few moments of leisure to learned pursuits.

Somewhat like More, who produced *Utopia* (1516) during a break in negotiations, Pace wrote

De fructu qui ex doctrina percipitur (1517; translated as *The Benefit of a Liberal Education,* 1967), a defense of good learning, during a lag in diplomatic maneuvering. During other pauses he translated a sermon by John Fisher and some of Plutarch's works. Toward the end of his life he published a preface to Ecclesiastes. Pace's contemporaries denounced *The Benefit of a Liberal Education* when it appeared, yet, as its modern editors point out, the very reasons for their disapproval are the reasons why the book remains of interest today. The text's confusions illustrate the extreme difficulty, if not impossibility, of reconciling humanist idealism with political realities.

Richard Pace was born around 1482. What little is known about his early years comes from a biographical passage in the *Benefit:*

> Now Music demands her place. She has a claim on me particularly since she singled me out when I was still a boy among boys. For when I was a page in his household, Thomas Langton, the Bishop of Winchester, the predecessor of the one now living, noted that I was talented in music far beyond my years (or so he thought, perhaps because he loved me too much) and said, "The boy's bright; he was born for greater things." A few days later, he sent me to Italy to study liberal arts at the University of Padua, which was then in its prime, and kindly paid the expenses himself since he encouraged all learning.

Langton died in 1501, bequeathing to Pace ten pounds a year for seven years in order to subsidize his education, of which Pace took full advantage. From Padua, Pace went to Ferrara, where he met Erasmus in 1508. He also studied Greek at Bologna under Paulus Bombasius, who later became a friend and who would contribute an epigram and an introductory epistle to the *Benefit.* Pace's humanist accomplishments were sufficiently recognized that when he was about twenty-one, he delivered in Venice an oration on the study of Greek, which was printed afterward in Basel by the humanist publisher John Froben. Erasmus also praised him in a letter to Charles Blount, Baron Mountjoy as "a young man so well equipped with knowledge of [Greek and Latin literature] as to be able by his genius alone to bring honor to England, and of such purity and modesty of character as to be worthy of your favor."

For humanists, however, learning was not supposed to be its own reward but a preparation for a career in government, and in 1509 Pace duly joined the service of Langton's nephew, Archbishop Christopher Bainbridge, Henry VIII's newly appointed agent at Rome, whom he served until Bainbridge's death in 1514. From about September 1513 Pace's diplomatic letters to Henry and to Thomas Wolsey appear regularly. If Erasmus can be trusted, Pace seems to have immersed himself in his diplomatic work to the exclusion of his studies; Erasmus wrote in a letter dated 21 December 1513: "Pace seems to me to forget his scholarship and to assume a style more agreeable to Midas than the Muses." Erasmus's choice of Midas may have been dictated by Pace's sartorial splendor. A Venetian ambassador once came before the Pope wearing a black gown trimmed with black satin, "made in the style adopted by Pace, the English ambassador."

Pace's humanist training meant that he initially approached government service with an eye toward reform and putting ideals into practice. The diplomatic morass into which he was plunged sorely tested the humanist conception of the learned courtier-diplomat leading his prince to virtuous action. His investigation into Bainbridge's death and its aftermath, along with his complex negotations with the Swiss and Holy Roman Emperor Maximilian I, are essential for understanding the peculiarities of the *Benefit*.

When Bainbridge died after a sudden illness, Pace suspected poison. Proved right by an autopsy, he immediately launched into an investigation that ultimately pointed toward (although the charge was never proven) Silvester de Giglis, bishop of Worcester, who acted as Wolsey's agent in Rome and was instrumental in Wolsey's being made a cardinal. In addition, Bainbridge had his own quarrel with Wolsey; one of his last letters to Henry complained about Wolsey's mistreatment of Bainbridge's servants at York and of Giglis's treachery to him and Henry in Rome. Like many courtiers, most notably John Skelton, Bainbridge considered Wolsey an upstart.

Although Cardinal Wolsey was not implicated in Bainbridge's murder, he clearly profited from it by receiving, with the barest form of legality, Bainbridge's bishopric, his estates in York, and his personal fortune. Bainbridge's will appointed Pace executor; and even though Bainbridge left a considerable sum of ready money and plate, Wolsey demanded more from the estate than Pace claimed was due to him. Even further, the money that should have been put toward fixing up the estate Wolsey spent on his own castles in Hampton Court and Moor Park. In sum, Pace had every reason to despise Wolsey, the man who abused Bainbridge's servants, employed his probable murderer, and used his old patron's death to enrich himself. Yet Pace also realized that he needed the newly appointed cardinal of York. To prosper, he had to swim with the tide and enter Wolsey's service. By 25 September 1514 Pace was writing cordially to Wolsey, and in April he became Wolsey's secretary. The unctuousness of his praise of Wolsey in the *Benefit* is staggering.

From 1515 to 1525 Henry and Wolsey sent Pace on a long series of diplomatic missions. At the time he wrote the *Benefit,* Pace was engaged in negotiations with the Swiss and Maximilian, an exercise that also put into relief the gap between humanist ideals and political reality. The French had surprised everyone by defeating the Swiss at the Battle of Marignano, and Henry wanted to contain their power. Thus, in October 1515 Pace embarked on a secret mission to convince the Swiss and Maximilian to join forces and throw the French out of Milan. This was the second time that he was entrusted with such a mission. Henry had proposed a joint invasion of France in 1514, but England's coming to terms with France led to its abortion. Nonetheless, the mission began promisingly, and before long both the Swiss and the emperor's troops were at Milan's gates. At that point, however, things began to fall apart. Maximilian, for reasons still unclear, suddenly decided to retreat, taking the gunpowder with him. The Swiss demanded their money, even throwing poor Pace into prison to ensure payment. The funds finally arrived, only to be largely pilfered by the departing imperial troops. Pace remarked in a letter to Wolsey dated 10 April 1516 that an opportunity bright enough to move an ass, let alone an emperor, had been thrown away.

The petty jealousies of his fellow ambassador, Sir Robert Wingfield, who resented having been passed over for the king's secretaryship, added to Pace's burden, as did the sudden shift in English policy in 1516. The bellicose Henry wanted to invade France, but Wolsey did not, and the cardinal enlisted Pace's aid in fabricating an appeal from the allies to stop Henry. Even so, if Wolsey did not want an English incursion, he had no objections to hiring Swiss mercenaries, and so Pace once again found himself stirring the allies to "resume their

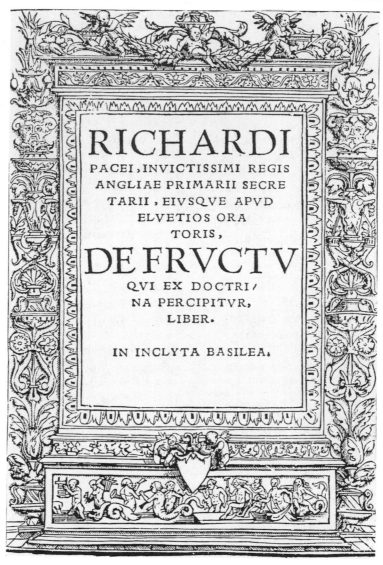

RICHARDI
PACEI, INVICTISSIMI REGIS
ANGLIAE PRIMARII SECRE
TARII, EIVSQVE APVD
ELVETIOS ORA
TORIS,
DE FRVCTV
QVI EX DOCTRI/
NA PERCIPITVR,
LIBER.

IN INCLYTA BASILEA.

Title page for Pace's first book, which argues that "a learned man is best at the things that really matter"

hearts and eftsoons valiantly set forth for the exterminating the French out of Italy," as he put it in a letter to Wolsey dated 23 June 1516. By this time Pace's health, never robust, started to give out, and he was heartily sick of Swiss greed, Maximilian's caprices, Wingfield's maliciousness, and, no doubt, Wolsey's "politic" diplomacy. It was during a lull in these labyrinthine proceedings that Pace managed to write the *Benefit*.

The Benefit of a Liberal Education begins with three prefatory letters from Pace to "All professors of knowledge," to students, and to John Colet, and the text consists of a praise of learning followed by orations from the various personified branches of learning in praise of themselves. Pace speaks in his own voice about theology, law, philosophy, and medicine. Then follow speeches from Music, Astrol-

ogy, Astronomy, Geometry, Arithmetic, Rhetoric, and Grammar, who at the end of her oration merges rather clumsily into Art and then back into Pace. They praise themselves, dispraise their competitors, and include a variety of "merry tales" to spice up their orations, some of a decidedly off-color variety. Although the putative audience for the book was made up of Colet's students at St. Paul's, the number of references to Pace's humanist friends and teachers, in particular More, Erasmus, Colet, and Thomas Linacre, along with the stories about the author, demonstrates that he also meant the work as a kind of in-joke.

The purpose of the *Benefit*, as its title suggests, is to prove that nothing can be done without learning, that "a learned man . . . is best at the things that really matter." Learning is essential if one is to receive preferment: "a lawyer is nothing and can do nothing without learning, which is the only thing that makes him a lawyer." The problem, however, is that Pace was simply not convinced of his subject. Although he doubtless intended the squabbles as a joke, the constant bickering of the various sciences is hardly an edifying display. Many of the examples of learning are less than thrilling, such as the recovery of Roman marbles "that taught Angelus Politianus to write *Vergil* and not *Virgil,* which was the way it was usually spelled for five hundred years before." Useful, perhaps, but it hardly merits Pace's exclamation, "God only knows what we owe to inscriptions!" Nor would this example inspire a recalcitrant schoolchild to devote himself to learning. Furthermore, most of the sciences admit that their practice has fallen into severe decay. Geometry, for example, after speaking at length about its superiority to everything else, admits that "No one, or almost no one teaches me these days." Rhetoric similarly admits that there are no contemporary orators like Demosthenes and Cicero. Today, all the arts "are like some worthless, but rare thing." Music admits that

> the times in which music flourished so remarkably . . . have changed, and most of this art has died out through man's neglect. For everything our musicians do today is insignificant if we compare it with what the ancients did. There are hardly one or two people today who know what harmony is, though they're always talking about it.

More is at stake, however, than the standard humanist complaint that the Ancients did everything better, for learning was being ignored by those in power, a fact that undermines the whole purpose of Pace's book. As Grammar says:

> And it's generally agreed that that's why those ancient princes and famous kings desired learning very much and wanted nothing more. They all wanted to maintain learned men, brought together at great cost, for they thought they'd finally get the glory if they had a wise man, that is to say, a learned man, in the house as their close companion to teach them. If that were done nowadays, no doubt our age would be more distinguished. For the greater the wisdom of the prince, the better the condition of the people, and the more secure from the many evils which come from having public affairs badly handled through stupidity. In our century it's rarely done.

Consequently, Pace, through his various mouthpieces, is always bemoaning the state of Europe. Rhetoric enjoins his audience to consider that "In your father's time . . . everything was done better and more intelligently than it is now."

Ironically, Pace uses his friend Erasmus as an example of how learning fails to lead to glory. There is no one in Europe more learned or more famous than Erasmus, Pace asserts, and so all of the centers of power, "the popes, the cardinals, kings, and princes with one accord seem to fight over him." And yet, he reports that Erasmus has said, "while they struggled so hard for him, he was poor and miserable because men nowadays marvel at the learned more willingly than they take care of them."

Perhaps the book's most telling anecdote comes in the introductory letter to Colet, in which Pace recounts the story of a nobleman who declares that he would rather see his son hanged than see him pursue humanist studies. Pace attempts to rebut him by demonstrating that the future humanist would "be preferred to your son," who has mastered only the arts of hunting or hawking, "and using the freedom that learning gives, they would say to your face, 'We would rather be learned, and thanks to learning no fools, than to be proud of our stupid nobility.' " The passage illustrates a shift in government power away from the nobility and toward those competent to handle an increasingly complex government bureaucracy. Nonetheless, the force of the nobleman's charges remains because he does not speak from ignorance. First, he quotes Greek, and he, too, knows that Erasmus is a "pauper." Second, Pace himself, as shown above, more or less agrees that learning does not automatically lead to preferment. Third, alcohol, not Pace's retort, finally silences the nobleman: "And so I was saved not by Apollo, who saved Horace from a blowhard, but by Bacchus, who saved me from an argument with a madman" – demonstrating once more learning's impotence. Finally, it is hard to reconcile "the freedom that learning gives" with Pace's admission, in his letter to "all professors of knowledge," that

> I am free by nature, but not by choice. For I have bound myself to serve my invincible king as the servant of the wise Cardinal of York. To serve one's country exceeds all freedom. And so, since I am dependent on the will of another and cannot remain here, but must go away – I know not where nor how – I preferred, if it should turn out that way, to die like a man, not a beast, that is, to leave behind something [the *Benefit*] to be remembered by.

In sum, although Pace intends his work to demonstrate, as the title says, the benefits of learning, its primary purpose is undone by the author's doubts. Humanist theory would claim that learning leads to advancement, that the liberal arts make one free, and that training in Greek and the classics leads to a better political world. Reality has taught Pace otherwise, and that knowledge keeps breaking through his text.

The *Benefit* confounded Pace's intended audience, and Erasmus was especially annoyed. Writing to Pace in March 1518, he charges that "you have made me absolutely notorious with the ill report of my poverty, although I seem to myself almost a Midas" (even so, Erasmus also suggested that Pace atone for his sin by appealing to patrons on his behalf). The book, he says, is incoherent, and he advises Pace to confine himself to translations from the Greek. Pace followed this advice.

For the remainder of his life Pace devoted himself to his political career, not humanist scholarship. In 1519 he began receiving a series of lucrative benefices, which culminated in his succeeding Colet as dean of St. Paul's in 1520. He attended the Field of the Cloth of Gold and was present at the burning of Luther's works in May 1521, and he later translated Bishop John Fisher's sermon there into Latin. After Pope Leo X died on 2 December, Pace was dispatched again to Rome to represent Wolsey in his bid for the papacy. When he reached Florence in 1522, he received word that Adrian VI had been elected, and while awaiting instructions he passed the time translating Plutarch.

Pace's physical and mental health had started to deteriorate precipitously, however. Erasmus, who did not hold a grudge, blamed the decline on Pace's diplomacy. Forgetting for a moment the last time Pace had devoted himself to literary composition, Erasmus wrote to Lupton: "a plague on these embassies and counter-embassies! Pace was born for the Muses." In March 1524 Pace begged Wolsey to recall him, and he finally reached London on 17 November. At that point Pace fades from from the political scene, although he retained sufficient importance for Gasparo Spinelli, the secretary to the Venetian ambassador, to describe in a letter to his brother the comforting details of Pace's retirement to Sion monastery:

> I went to Sion to visit the Reverend Richard Pace, who leads a blessed life in that beautiful place. He wears his clerical habit, and is surrounded by such a quantity of books, that for my part I never before saw so many in one mass. He has rendered himself an excellent Hebrew and Chaldean scholar, and now, through his knowledge of those languages, has commenced correcting the Old Testament, in which, as likewise in the Psalms, he found a stupendous amount of errors. He has also corrected the whole of Ecclesiastes, and in a few days will publish them.

This contentment did not last. There were rumors that Wolsey had turned against Pace because he represented the old, discredited policy toward France, although in an undated letter to his brother Pace asserted that "Whatever is spoken here of my lord cardinal's evil mind against, it is untrue." Despite periods of lucidity, Pace's madness progressed to the point that he had to be placed in the custody of the abbot of Beaulieu. He died on 28 June 1536 and was buried at St. Dunstan's, Stepney.

Richard Pace's career continues to be of interest because it illustrates so many of the currents of the early- and mid-Henrician era. The *Benefit* confirms that More's weighing the problem of service in the first book of the *Utopia* was a concern shared by other contemporaries; it also provides a window onto the everyday lives of such people as More, Colet, and Erasmus. Pace deserves more attention than he has received, and with luck the current movement in scholarship toward rethinking the Henrician era will lead to further work on the *Benefit*.

Biography:
Jervis Wegg, *Richard Pace: A Tudor Diplomatist* (London: Methuen, 1932).

References:
Peter Gwyn, *The King's Cardinal: The Rise and Fall of Thomas Wolsey* (London: Barrie & Jenkins, 1990), pp. 62–65, 74–81;

Peter C. Herman, "Rethinking the Henrician Era," in *Rethinking the Henrician Era: New Essays on Early Tudor Texts and Contexts,* edited by Herman (Urbana-Champaign: University of Illinois Press, 1994), pp. 1–15;

James McConica, *English Humanists and Reformation Politics: Under Henry VIII and Edward VI* (Oxford: Clarendon Press, 1965);

A. F. Pollard, *Wolsey* (London: Fontana/Collins, 1965);

J. J. Scarisbrick, *Henry VIII* (Berkeley: University of California Press, 1968);

Edward J. Surtz, "Richard Pace's Sketch of Thomas More," *Journal of English and German Philology,* 57 (Fall 1958): 36–50.

Papers:
Richard Pace's dispatches from 1514 to 1524 are in the Public Record Office, London, and it is likely that others remain undiscovered in various diplomatic archives.

George Peele

(circa 25 July 1556 – 9 November 1596)

Charles Whitworth
University of Montpellier

See also the Peele entry in *DLB 62: Elizabethan Dramatists.*

BOOKS: *The Araynement of Paris: A Pastorall* (London: Printed by H. Marsh, 1584);

The Device of the Pageant Borne before Wolstan Dixi Lord Maior of London (London: Printed by E. Allde, 1585);

A Farewell. Entituled To the Famous and Fortunate Generalls of Our English Forces: Sir J. Norris & Syr F. Drake. Whereunto Is Annexed A Tale of Troy (London: Printed by J. Charlewood, sold by W. Wright, 1589);

An Eglogue. Gratulatorie. Entituled: To the Honorable Shepheard of Albions Arcadia: Robert Earle of Essex (London: Printed by J. Windet for R. Jones, 1589);

Polyhymnia: Describing the Honourable Triumph at Tylt (London: Printed by R. Jones, 1590);

Descensus Astrææ. The Device of a Pageant Borne before M. William Web, Lord Maior of London, 1591 (London: Printed by T. Scarlet for W. Wright, 1591);

The Honour of the Garter. Displaied in a Poeme Gratulatorie: Entitled, To the Earle of Northumberland. Created Knight of That Order, and Installd Anno Regni Elizabethæ. 35. die Iunij 26 (London: Printed by the Widdowe Charlewood for F. Busbie, 1593);

The Famous Chronicle of King Edward the First (London: Printed by A. Jeffes, sold by W. Barley, 1593);

The Battell of Alcazar (London: Printed by E. Allde for R. Bankworth, 1594);

The Old Wiues Tale. A Pleasant Conceited Comedie (London: Printed by J. Danter, sold by R. Hancocke & J. Hardie, 1595);

The Love of King Dauid and Fair Bethsabe (London: Printed by A. Islip, 1599).

Editions: *The Life and Works of George Peele,* 3 volumes, general editor Charles Tyler Prouty (New Haven: Yale University Press, 1952–1970) – nondramatic works are in volume 1, *The Life and Minor Works of George Peele,* edited by David H. Horne (1952);

George Peele: Selected, edited by Sally Purcell (Oxford: Carcanet, 1968).

PLAY PRODUCTIONS: *Iphigenia,* Peele's translation of Euripides' play, Christ Church, Oxford, circa 1579;

Entertainment for Count Palatine, Christ Church, Oxford, May 1583;

The Arraignment of Paris, London, at Court, 1584;

The Pageant before Woolstone Dixie, streets of London, 29 October 1585;

The Pageant for Martin Calthrop, streets of London, 29 October 1588;

The Battle of Alcazar, London, The Theatre, circa 1590;

Edward I, London, The Theatre or Curtain Theater, circa 1590–1592;

Descensus Astrææ, streets of London, 29 October 1591;

The Old Wifes Tale, London, unknown theater, circa 1591–1594;

David and Bethsabe, London, unknown theater, by 1594.

OTHER: *The Phoenix Nest,* edited by R. S. (London: Printed by J. Jackson, 1593) – includes poems by Peele;

Englands Parnassus, edited by Robert Allott (London: Printed for N. Ling, C. Burby & T. Hayes, 1600) – includes poems by Peele;

Englands Helicon (London: Printed by J. Roberts for J. Flasket, 1600) – includes poems by Peele.

George Peele is more difficult to place in the Elizabethan literary landscape than many of his immediate contemporaries. Each of his plays is different from the others, so he is not readily identifiable as a writer primarily of comedies or tragedies or histories; he also practiced hybrid dramatic forms, known variously and vaguely as "entertainments" or "pageants" or "shows." His few surviving non-dramatic works are in a variety of minor, sometimes esoteric genres, while his name does not figure among the practitioners of more highly visible ones such as the sonnet sequence, prose fiction, Ovidian "minor epic," verse satire, or classical translation. Peele's modern literary reputation rests largely on one short play: the strange, delightful fantasy/folk-tale/comedy *The Old Wife's Tale* (circa 1591–1594), published in quarto in 1595. His few other plays — the pastoral *Arraignment of Paris* (1584), the biblical *David and Bethsabe* (by 1594), the historical *Edward I* (circa 1590–1592), and the semihistorical *Battle of Alcazar* (circa 1590) — are never performed, and neither they nor his nondramatic works are often read today. In his own time, however, Peele had a formidable reputation as a poet and scholar; he was, with John Lyly, Christopher Marlowe, Thomas Lodge, Robert Greene, and Thomas Nashe, one of the so-called University Wits active on the London literary and theatrical scene in the 1580s and early 1590s. He acquired a reputation shortly after his death as a dissolute, pox-ridden bohemian, and that posthumous image — for which there seems to be little hard evidence — remained attached to his name until modern scholars, notably Thorleif Larsen and David H. Horne, subjected the traditional account to scrutiny.

George Peele was born on or around 25 July 1556. He came by his writing gifts legitimately. His father, James Peele, a Londoner, was a clerk and teacher of bookkeeping, writing, and arithmetic who wrote textbooks on accountancy. His *Manner and Form How to Keep a Perfect Reckoning* (1553) is the earliest surviving English work on double-entry bookkeeping; *The Pathway to Perfectness* (1569), on the same subject, is in dialogue form, with verses interspersed. The elder Peele also wrote several pageants for the City. In 1562, when George was six, his father became clerk of Christ's Hospital, a charitable institution administered by the Corporation of London. Founded by Edward VI and occupying the site of the former Grey Friars' monastery in Newgate, the hospital was an orphanage and school for the poor, where Peele the elder also taught writing and arithmetic. George, as son of the clerk, would have had free schooling within the grounds until, in 1571 at the age of fourteen, he went to Oxford.

A student of Christ Church, Peele resided at first in Broadgate's Hall across the street (on the site of the present-day Pembroke College), then moved into the college itself. Among his contemporaries at Christ Church were Sir Philip Sidney, Sir Edward

Dyer, William Camden, Richard Carew, and three writers of Latin plays: Richard Edes, Leonard Hutton, and William Gager. Also at Oxford in the early 1570s were Lyly, Lodge, Edmond and Robert Carey (sons of Lord Hunsdon), Matthew Roydon, and John Grange. Christ Church was famous for dramatic productions in its splendid great hall. Twice during her reign, in 1566 and 1592, Queen Elizabeth visited Christ Church, and on both occasions Latin plays were performed in her honor; on the latter, it was Hutton and Gager who provided them. Gager provides a record of what was probably Peele's first effort at dramatic writing, when he was still a student at Oxford, a translation of one of Euripides' *Iphigenia* plays. Gager wrote two Latin poems to Peele praising his translation. The poems survive; Peele's translation, sadly, does not.

It seems to have taken Peele a rather longer time than usual to complete his B.A., which was awarded in 1577. Perhaps poetry and drama distracted him from logic, rhetoric, philosophy, and the other university subjects during that interval. He wasted no time in proceeding to the M.A., however, which he took just two years later, having been granted a dispensation allowing him to proceed to the higher degree in less than the statutory three years.

Peele remained in Oxford for two more years. In 1580 he married a girl of sixteen, Ann Cooke, the daughter of a successful Oxford merchant who died a few months before her marriage, leaving her a substantial inheritance. Several complicated lawsuits against the Cooke estate kept the young couple and Ann's mother, who had remarried shortly after her husband's death, preoccupied for years. They also inevitably ate into the legacy, for despite various profitable investments he made with part of it, Peele seems later to have suffered a chronic cash shortage.

Although Peele moved back to London in 1581, his tangled financial and legal affairs took him frequently to Oxford in the next few years; possibly his wife and children remained there for some time after 1581. There is a record of payment to Peele for his contribution to Christ Church entertainments during the visit of a Polish nobleman in 1583; though no longer officially a member of the college, he was called on when outside help with dramatic productions was needed. It is likely that he had begun working in the London theatrical milieu from 1581 and that this experience and his earlier efforts as an amateur college dramatist recommended him to the organizers of the entertainment, who included his friend Gager, the author of two Latin

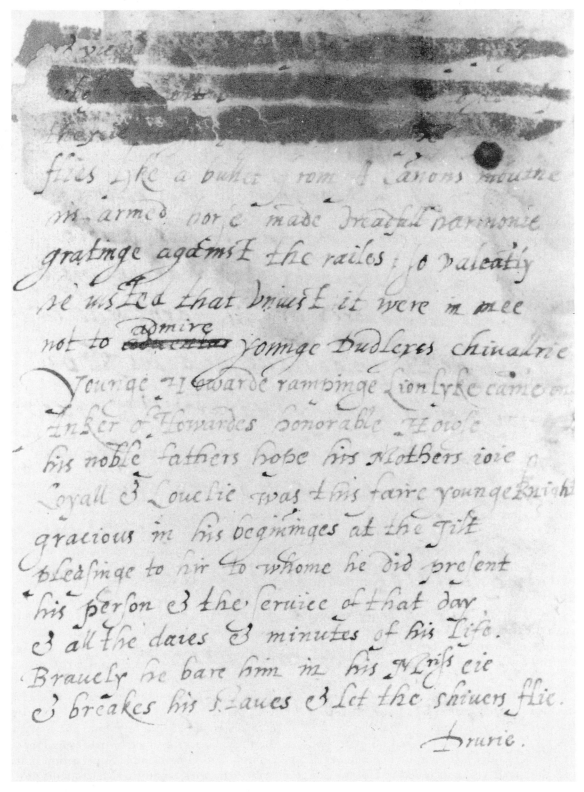

flies lyke a bullet from the Canons mouthe

in armed horse made dreadfull harmonie

gratinge against the railes; so valeatly

he ustd that briuest it were in mee

not to ~~admire~~ yonnge Dudleyes chinalrie

Younge Howarde rampinge Lion lyke came on

Inker of Howardes sonorable Howse

his noble fathers hope his Mothers ioie

loyall & Louelie was this faire younge knight

gracious in his beginnges at the Tilt

pleasinge to hir to whome he did present

his person & the seruice of that day

& all the daies & minutes of his life.

Brauely he bare him in his Mriss eie

& breakes his staues & let the shiuers flie.

Drurie.

Page from the damaged manuscript for Peele's poem commemorating Accession Day (17 November) 1595, the last known work by Peele (British Library, Add. Ms. 21432) plays for the occasion. Several of Peele's plays were written in the 1580s: *The Arraignment of Paris*; the *Hunting of Cupid,* of which only fragments remain — one of them in the outstanding miscellany *England's Helicon* (1600) — and the topical *Battle of Alcazar* near the end of the decade.

Peele's earliest surviving nondramatic work probably dates from a few years following his Oxford graduation. *The Tale of Troy,* not published until 1589 (and the only one of his minor works to have a second edition, in 1604), probably was written around 1580–1581. The scholarly Peele knew the various classical versions of the Troy story, of course, but his principal debt seems to have been to William Caxton's *Recuyell of the Historyes of Troye.* The main stylistic influence, curiously, in view of the classical epic subject, was also English, Spenser's *Shepheardes Calender* (1579). Spenserian archaisms abound in Peele's book, and it is difficult to imagine that it was not written at the height of the vogue of Spenserian imitation in the years immediately following the appearance of that pastoral sequence. It must have appeared even more anachronistic in 1596 than it did in 1589, though Peele may by the later date have made the revisions in the belated edition of 1604, of which no copies survive. Ill and in financial difficulty, Peele in desperation sent his eldest daughter to William Cecil, Lord Burghley with an inscribed copy of the poem and a plea for money. Presumably he considered it the most appropriate of his works to offer in such circumstances; if so, he had misjudged: Burghley filed the appeal among others he had received from cranks, and the impoverished Peele was soon dead.

In less than five hundred lines Peele could not hope to do more than summarize the great legend, and that is what he did — from Paris's early career as a shepherd on Mount Ida (much of the imitation of Spenser's pastoral idiom occurs in this passage) to Aeneas's flight from the doomed city and his welcome by Dido at Carthage. The work is the longest of the ten or so surviving verse compositions that comprise Peele's nondramatic oeuvre. Clearly, large-scale productions in nondramatic modes were not to his taste. In this respect he stands apart from his fellow "wits" Lyly, Greene, Lodge, Nashe, and Marlowe, all of whom wrote prose fiction or long narrative poems; Lodge wrote both. The number of lines in all the verse works included in Horne's edition totals less than twenty-four hundred, roughly equivalent to one medium-length play. Peele made much use of his first and longest poetical work: besides its several late reincarnations — in the 1589 quarto, in the appeal to Burghley in 1596, and in

the posthumous revised edition of 1604 — it also served its author as the principal source for his first play, the pastoral *Arraignment of Paris*.

The Tale of Troy was apparently included in the 1589 volume to lengthen a seventy-six-line pamphlet titled *A Farewell,* addressed to Sir John Norris and Sir Francis Drake on the occasion of their much-heralded but ill-fated expedition to the Azores to place their candidate, Don Antonio, on the Portuguese throne and destroy the Spanish fleet in an intended follow-up to the rout of the Armada the year before. The patriotic lines of blank verse have, like most of Peele's occasional pieces, little more than historical interest today. In the brief prose dedication (one of only two examples of Peele's nondramatic prose) and the first lines of the poem, the author alludes to the legend of London's founding by fugitives from Troy.

More interesting from a literary viewpoint is the companion piece Peele produced a few months later to welcome home another illustrious member of the doomed Norris-Drake expedition, Robert Devereaux, Second Earl of Essex, who had set out against the express orders of the queen. *An Eglogue Gratulatory* (1589) is entirely in the *Shepheardes Calender* idiom and is Peele's only purely pastoral composition. It borrows not only the dialogue form of Spenser's work but also two of his characters: Piers and Palinode from the May eclogue. Unlike the partly Spenserian *Tale of Troy,* the *Eglogue* was clearly composed expressly for the event, as it contains references to Essex's personal heroism in the failed invasion attempt.

On at least three occasions — in 1585, 1588, and 1591 — Peele provided the City with pageants as his father had done; the texts of two of the three shows survive. One of them, *The Pageant before Woolstone Dixie* (1585), is the earliest extant complete lord mayor's show. The text of 130 lines presents speeches for various allegorical characters, including London itself, and for several nymphs. The 1591 pageant, *Descensus Astrææ,* written for the inauguration of William Web as lord mayor, is slightly longer and more ambitious. Astræa appears as a shepherdess on top of the pageant, but there is no Spenserian pastoral this time. She is attended by the three Graces and such virtues as Hope, Faith, Charity, and Honor, while Superstition (a friar), Ignorance (a priest), and two Malcontents plot in vain to overthrow the chaste maiden Queen. The elaborate political allegory in classical guise is typical of civic pageants and royal entertainments of the Tudor Age, forerunners of the Jacobean and Caroline court masques. The City and its guilds and companies had often called upon leading poets to provide such pageants; there are early-fifteenth-century examples in some of the mummings written by the unofficial poet-laureate John Lydgate. Peele is the first Elizabethan author of note to contribute such shows to the City; he was followed by other poet-dramatists such as Thomas Dekker, Anthony Munday, Thomas Middleton, and Ben Jonson.

In 1593 Peele contributed a 111-line poem in quatrains, *The Praise of Chastity,* to *The Phoenix Nest,* one of the best of the poetical miscellanies of the period. There is a distinct Oxford presence among the contributors. The main one was Lodge; others included Sir Walter Ralegh; Nicholas Breton; Edward de Vere, Earl of Oxford; Sir Edward Dyer; Sir William Herbert; and Peele's friends Richard Edes, Matthew Roydon, Thomas Watson, and Greene. Apart from *The Praise of Chastity* and *Descensus Astrææ,* Peele's nondramatic output in the 1590s consisted of just three occasional poems, judging by the extant oeuvre. He continued to write plays during those years, however, including his best achievements in the dramatic mode, *David and Bethsabe* and *The Old Wife's Tale.*

Two of Peele's three poems were written for royal occasions: the Accession Day Tilts held in November each year in commemoration of Elizabeth's accession to the throne. *Polyhymnia* and "Anglorum Feriæ" were Peele's contributions to the festivities in 1590 and 1595, respectively. Such celebrations saw late-Tudor pageantry at its grandest, and it is impossible to gain an impression of the whole multimedia event merely from the written texts. There were special circumstances in both the years in which Peele provided poems. In 1590 Sir Henry Lee, who had been the queen's champion since the first such event in 1559, made his last appearance in that capacity, at the age of fifty-seven, and at the same time a new champion, the earl of Cumberland, was installed in the office. Peele's three-hundred-line text partly describes the appearance of each of the thirteen pairs of contestants and gives a vague impression of the combats, though he does not name the victors – these were more token than real fights, a ceremonial breaking of lances, nothing like the medieval tournaments in which, though ostensibly a game, life and limb were at serious risk. The cast was star-studded in 1590: Lee and Cumberland made up the first pair; they were followed by Lord Strange, the earl of Essex, Fulke Greville, Sir Charles Blount (Baron Mountjoy), Robert Carey (son of Lord Chamberlain Hunsdon), Thomas Sidney (younger brother of Philip), and Everard

Digby, later executed as a conspirator in the Gunpowder Plot.

The 1595 *Anglorum Feriæ* survives only in a badly defaced manuscript. A privately printed edition from the nineteenth century fortunately survives to piece out the manuscript. The additional cause for celebration in 1595 was the queen's escape from an assassination attempt allegedly plotted by her personal physician, the Portuguese Jew Dr. Lopez. Peele's poem, with the hyperbole due on such occasions, extols "Elizabeth by miracles preserved / From perils imminent and infinite." This time no fewer than five earls were among the combatants: Cumberland (the queen's champion), Essex, Sussex, Bedford, and Southampton, Shakespeare's patron. Several of the participants from the 1590 tilts were again present. Peele's 335-line blank-verse text gives rather more detail of the heraldic devices of the "runners" than had been the case in 1590. Again, description of the glittering pageantry, admiration of the skills of the knights, and praise of the queen comprise the agenda. *Anglorum Feriæ* is the last work by Peele that survives. He was obviously ill in January 1596, when he spoke of "long sickness" in the letter to Burghley, and he died on 9 November.

The third of the occasional pieces Peele wrote in the 1590s was for another kind of courtly ceremony, an Order of the Garter investiture in 1593. Among the five inductees was the earl of Northumberland, to whom Peele dedicated the poem and who paid him three pounds for it in June. *The Honor of the Garter* is the longest of Peele's nondramatic works after *The Tale of Troy.* Counting the verse prologue and epilogue, it runs to just over 500 lines, though the poem itself is 425 lines. The work is of interest on several grounds, despite its apparently merely occasional significance. For one thing, it is better poetry than Peele usually managed on such occasions. Furthermore, there is considerable literary interest in Peele's skillful use of the dream device and first-person narrative, reminiscent of the works of Geoffrey Chaucer.

In the work the dreamer sees a procession of Garter knights surrounding Windsor Castle and recounts the history of the order from its founding by Edward III in the fourteenth century. He incorporates the famous motto *Honi soit qui mal y pense,* as would Shakespeare a few years later in *The Merry Wives of Windsor,* performed on a similar occasion. In the prologue Peele gives what seems to amount to his personal pantheon of English poets, living and dead. He mentions Sidney first, as in a class of his own, then Spenser ("Hobbinall"), John Harington, Samuel Daniel, Thomas Campion, and Abraham Fraunce, all still alive, and Chaucer, John Gower, Thomas Phaer, Thomas Watson, and Marlowe, all dead, the latter less than a month in his grave; Peele's must be among the first posthumous mentions of Marlowe to appear in print. Significantly perhaps, only one member of this group, Marlowe, wrote for the popular stage as Peele had done. Peele's true inclination lay in the direction of learned and classical poetry – a translation from Euripides, after all, had been his earliest literary effort – and like many of his contemporaries, he may have felt that the theater was a last but necessary resort for a man who hoped to live by his pen alone.

The end of the year 1596 marks the end of a literary epoch. When Peele died at age forty the heyday of the University Wits was past, and many of his friends and acquaintances had passed from the literary scene. Greene was dead and the literary careers of Lyly and Nashe were virtually over, as were those of Edes, Gager, Dyer, Roydon, Henry Constable, Barnabe Barnes, Fraunce, Harington, Gabriel Harvey, and other lesser luminaries of the Elizabethan Golden Age. Lodge abandoned poetry and set out at the end of the year to study medicine at Avignon. Spenser published no more after the 1596 *Faerie Queene,* Books I–VI. A new generation – dramatists, verse satirists, pamphleteers, essayists, and translators – took over the scene. The posthumous publication of Peele's *David and Bethsabe* and a second edition of *Edward I* in 1599, passages from *The Hunting of Cupid* in *England's Helicon* and *England's Parnassus* (both 1600), and the revised *Tale of Troy* (1604) were mere echoes of a dead poet. The 1607 joke book *The Merry Conceited Jests of George Peele* had nothing to do with his poetry and little, except by way of innuendo and inconsequential pleasantry, with George Peele.

Peele as nondramatic author is virtually unknown today. It is the plays, particularly *The Old Wife's Tale,* that interest critics and occasionally producers. The entertainments receive some attention from historians of theater and pageantry. In the nineteenth century Peele, like many other "minor" Elizabethans, attracted the energies of indefatigable amateur scholars such as Alexander Dyce and A. H. Bullen, who produced editions of his works in 1828–1839 and 1888, respectively. A modern reader without access to a scholarly library and Horne's edition is just as likely to come across Peele's poems in a second-hand copy of Dyce's edition. While a modern-spelling edition of the plays is justified, the poems remain too ephemeral or esoteric to inspire the interest of most publishers. Sally

Purcell's modest 1968 collection remains the sole attempt in this century to salvage George Peele the poet for the common reader.

Bibliographies:

Thorlief Larsen, "A Bibliography of the Writings of George Peele," *Modern Philology,* 32 (1934): 143–156;

David H. Horne, "Bibliography," in *The Life and Minor Works of George Peele* (New Haven: Yale University Press, 1952), pp. 283–294;

Charles W. Daves, "George Peele," in *The Predecessors of Shakespeare: A Survey and Bibliography of Recent Studies in English Renaissance Drama,* edited by Terence P. Logan and Denzell S. Smith (Lincoln: University of Nebraska Press, 1973), pp. 143–152;

George Watson, ed., *The New Cambridge Bibliography of English Literature* (Cambridge: Cambridge University Press, 1974), I: 1431–1434;

Kevin J. Donovan, "Recent Studies in George Peele (1969–1990)," *English Literary Renaissance,* 23 (Winter 1993): 212–220.

References:

L. R. N. Ashley, *George Peele* (New York: Twayne, 1970);

David M. Bergeron, *English Civic Pageantry 1558–1642* (London: Edward Arnold, 1971);

A. R. Braunmuller, *George Peele* (Boston: Twayne, 1983);

Thomas Clayton, "'Sir Henry Lee's Farewell to the Court': The Texts and Authorship of 'His Golden Locks Time Hath to Silver Turned,'" *English Literary Renaissance,* 4 (Spring 1974): 268–275;

G. K. Hunter, *Lyly and Peele* (London: Longmans, 1968);

Thorlief Larsen, "The Early Years of George Peele, Dramatist, 1558–1588," *Transactions of the Royal Society of Canada,* 22 (1928): sections 2271–2318.

Papers:

The British Library holds a manuscript of *Anglorum Feriæ* in Peele's hand (Ms. Add. 21437) and his 1596 letter to Burghley (Ms. Lansdowne 99, no. 54). A receipt signed by Peele for his payment for the entertainment at Christ Church in 1582 is in the college's Disbursement Book for that year. There is a manuscript of *Polyhymnia* (Ms. 216) in the library of St. John Baptist College, Oxford. An extensive list of manuscript material relating to the life and works of Peele is given in Horne's 1952 edition (pp. 283–286).

Thomas Phaer

(1510? – August 1560)

M. Rick Smith
Wichita State University

BOOKS: *A Newe Boke of Presidentes in Maner of a Register, wherin Is Comprehended the Very Trade of Makying All Maner Euydence and Instrumentes of Practyse,* attributed to Phaer (London: Edward Whitchurch, 1543).

Editions: *The Will of Thomas Phaer,* edited by Peter Cunningham (London: Shakespeare Society, 1849);

The Boke of Chyldren, edited by A. V. Neale and Hugh R. E. Wallis (Edinburgh & London: E. & S. Livingstone, 1955).

TRANSLATIONS: *Natura Breuium Newly Corrected in Englysshe, with Dyuers Addicions* (London: Robert Redman, 1530?);

Jehan Goeurot, *A New Booke Entyteled the Regiment of Lyfe: With a Syngular Treatise of the Pestilence* (London: Edward Whitchurch, 1543?);

Virgil, *The Seuen First Bookes of the Eneidos Conuerted into Englishe Meter by T. Phaer* (London: Printed by John Kingston for R. Jugge, 1558);

Virgil, *The Nyne Fyrst Bookes of the Eneidos Conuerted into Englishe Vearse by T. Phaer* (London: Printed by Rowland Hall for Nicholas England, 1562);

Virgil, *The Whole .XII. Bookes of the AEneidos. The Residue Supplied, and the Whole Newly Set Forth, by T. Twyne* (London: Printed by William How for Abraham Veale, 1573);

Virgil, *The .XIII. Books of AEneidos. The Thirtenth the Supplement of Maphaeus Vegius. Now the Second Time Setforth* (London: Printed by William How for Abraham Veale, 1584).

Edition: *The Aeneid of Thomas Phaer and Thomas Twyne. A Critical Edition Introducing Renaissance Metrical Typography,* edited by Steven Lally (New York & London: Garland, 1987).

OTHER: Philip Betham, *The Precepts of War* (London: Edward Whitchurch, 1544) – includes a commendatory rhyme royal stanza by Phaer;

"Howe Owen Glendouer Seduced by False Prophesies Tooke vpon Him to Be Prince of Wales, and Was by Henry then Prince therof, Chased to the Mountaynes, Where He Miserably Dyed for Lacke of Foode," in *A Mirror for Magistrates* (London: Thomas Marshe, 1559).

Thomas Phaer's achievements are of three distinct kinds: legal, medical, and literary. As a poet Phaer collaborated on the first edition of *A Mirror for Magistrates;* he also translated more of Virgil's *Aeneid* than any Englishman before him, publishing seven books in 1558 and completing two more books and part of the tenth before his death in 1560. Although the complete Scots *Aeneid* of Gavin Douglas appeared in 1553 and Henry Howard, Earl of Surrey's translation of books 2 and 4 in 1557, Phaer's *Seven First Books of the Aeneid* (1558) and his *Nine First Books of the Aeneid* (1562) marked the most complete English versions of Virgil's poem by a single hand until John Vicars's *Twelve Aeneids of Virgil* (1632). Phaer also translated notable medical and legal works, including a guide to the compilation of briefs or writs known as the *Natura Brevium* (*On the Nature of Writs*) (1530?) and *The Regiment of Life* (1543?), a popular handbook of practical medicine previously translated into French by Jehan Goeurot. He also produced a popular legal handbook for laymen, *A New Book of Precedents in Manner of a Register* (1543), that saw more than twenty-five editions before 1583. He wrote the first popular English handbook of pediatrics ever published, *The Book of Children* (written, 1544; published, 1955).

Thomas Phaer, or Phayer, said to be the son of Thomas Phaer of Norwich, was probably born in 1510 in Pembrokeshire and was possibly of Flemish origin. Whatever his ancestry, he considered himself Welsh; his daughter Eleanor married a Welshman; and he remained in Wales for most of his life, primarily at his seat in the Forest of Cilgerran, where he died sometime after mid August 1560.

Two other daughters, Mary and Elizabeth, were alive at the time of his death, and his will, dated 12 August 1560, appointed his wife, Anne, his "sole and full executrix."

Phaer was educated at Oxford, which he left to take up residence at the Inns of Court. Early in his career he established his role as a popularizer of knowledge, and his prefaces reflect a rare sense of social consciousness. He remarks in the *New Book of Precedents* that in the study of formal legal terms and procedures of law

> can no man complain for losing of his time, for he shall be well and virtuously occupied, yea every good person that can write and read and intendeth to have anything to do among the commonwealth, must of very need, for his own advantage, apply his mind somewhat unto this kind of learning.

After gaining recognition for his translations of the *Natura Brevium* and *The Regiment of Life* and for his *New Book of Precedents,* Phaer became solicitor to Queen Mary and King Philip in the court of the Welsh marches. He records in the dedication to Queen Mary from the *Aeneid* of 1558 that he was commended to the queen's service "by your right noble and faithful counselor William, Lord Marquess of Winchester, my first bringer-up and patron." It is unlikely that any monarch, however, let alone Mary and Philip, would have rewarded him with the post of solicitor in Wales for merely popularizing legal terminology and procedure. Rather, Phaer's command of Latin and his reputation as a lawyer (and possibly his Catholicism) sufficiently warranted the appointment.

That Queen Mary was his principal patron is suggested not so much by the dedication of the *Aeneid* as by the care with which he recorded the date of completion of each book, along with the number of days each took to translate, clearly indicating that he transmitted the work to her as he completed it. Whatever merited such favor, before Phaer's time the common reader was barred from the *Aeneid,* as well as from most medical and legal knowledge, because of a general ignorance of Latin.

In the preface to *The Book of Children* Phaer vows to remove the barriers to such knowledge: "I shall never cease, during my breath, to bestow my labor to the furtherance of it . . . even to the uttermost of my simple power." In the same spirit, he identifies his mission as "to do them good that hath most need, that is to say, children," and he complains of physicians,

> why dissimule they their conniving? how long would they have the people ignorant? why grudge they physic to come forth in English? would they have no man to know but only they? Or what make they themselves? Merchants of our lives and deaths, that we should buy our health only of them, and at their prices, no good physician is of that mind.

Phaer's medical writings and translations are marked by considerations of practice rather than theory; they are decidedly not the work of a typical midcentury doctor of physic, who was quite unlike the present-day medical doctor. Genuine practitioners were members of craft guilds, officially recognized as barbers, "barber-surgeons," or surgeons. Some who practiced medicine, such as Phaer, came to the craft as amateurs and were looked down on as "empirics" by doctors of physic. The faculties of medicine at Oxford and Cambridge produced medical doctors whose expertise was philological or theoretical and whose activities rarely went beyond commentary and advice based on Aristotle, Galen, or Avicenna. Phaer practiced for twenty years before formally studying medicine at Oxford and taking the M.B. and M.D. degrees in 1559.

Both *The Book of Children* and *The Regiment of Life* prescribe specific, material, medical-based remedies for specific ailments and complaints. Though one short section of *The Regiment of Life* concerns the theory of the effects of misbalanced humors (and probably did much to broadcast popular ideas about humors, humor psychology, and the effects of humors on physiology), the rest of the work provides instructions for the diagnosis and treatment of diseases, all classified according to the part of the body affected. The discussion of each ailment includes two or three pharmaceutical recipes, and most of the entries end with a regimen of diet, rest, and exercise to hasten recovery and prevent relapse.

The Book of Children likewise offers recipes for plasters, simples, and "glisters." The diagnostic and descriptive matter suggests considerable firsthand experience with the treatment of patients. Hence it provides additional evidence that Phaer practiced medicine throughout the years when he was officially recognized only as a solicitor. His popularization of medicine and law greatly extended knowledge of these fields among the literate members of all classes, improving the people's overall understanding of their political and social as well as their physical bodies.

Phaer saw little difference between his dedication to making legal and medical knowledge available to anyone who needed it and his achievements as poet and translator. He appears, however, to have turned to poetry and verse translation as an avocation after achieving renown in law and medicine. His verse tragedy of Owen Glendower first appeared in a supplement to John Wayland's edition of John Lydgate's *Fall of Princes* (1555?), concerning "the fall of all such as since that time were notable in England"; hence its composition predates his *Aeneid*. The tragedy of Glendower then appeared in *A Mirror for Magistrates* beginning with the first edition (1559).

If the Wayland supplement to Lydgate's *Fall of Princes* was a suppressed form of *A Mirror for Magistrates,* then Phaer, along with George Ferrers and Thomas Chaloner, belonged to the original circle of writers who conceived and planned a work that helped determine the course of Elizabethan literature. Direct attribution of the tragedy to Phaer, however, is missing from William Baldwin's prose link in the 1559 *Mirror for Magistrates*. Ferrers edited the prose link in the 1578 edition to read, "I will pray Master Phaer who of late hath placed himself in that country, and haply hath met with his ghost in the forest of Cylgerran that he will say somewhat in his person." On this basis and on the appropriateness of the poem's Welsh subject and setting, Campbell accepted the attribution; also, the tragedy was traditionally associated with Phaer.

Phaer's contribution follows Chaloner's tragedy of Richard II. Composed in familiar rhyme royal stanzas (Chaloner's tragedy is in ten-line stanzas), it exhibits such standard *Mirror for Magistrates* themes as the lament against fortune and the sure fate of all pretenders. In Ferrers's prose link Phaer introduces Glendower "like the image of death in all points (his dart only excepted) so sore hath famine and hunger consumed him." But although Phaer adopts the convention of having Glendower speak as a revenant, the usual Senecan stage properties are missing, and the ghost delivers a sober meditation on how poor upbringing, greed, and delusions furthered by false prophecy contributed to its fate. In *Narrative and Dramatic Sources of Shakespeare* (1962), Geoffrey Bullough identifies Phaer's tragedy as a possible source for Glendower in William Shakespeare's first part of *Henry IV,* but unlike Shakespeare, Phaer has Glendower starve to death in the wilderness, deserted by his followers and pursued by the Prince of Wales.

Phaer's great contribution to English Renaissance literature, however, was his translation of the *Aeneid*. Steven Lally justly claims that "no translation of the *Aeneid* was as widely read during the English Renaissance," and he attributes Phaer's moti-

vation to self-conscious literary and linguistic nationalism. But surely Phaer's own stated object of freeing knowledge from the bonds of Latin for the benefit of the literate commoner was motive enough. Nevertheless, a modern audience might expect some explanation as to why Phaer chose to translate Virgil's epic into iambic heptameter couplets.

Phaer's choice of the heptameter line was one way of claiming the *Aeneid* as an English national epic. Such a gesture accorded well with Tudor mythology about the origins of the English monarchy in an ancient house founded by the Trojan Brutus. Further, while Chaucer's narrative mode remained mostly unfamiliar, highly allusive, and courtly, written in a distinctively medieval, even foreign-sounding language, popular English narrative poetry in alliterative ballad stanzas was widely known. With his views on the translator's mission, Phaer naturally chose the most familiar narrative mode available, and his choice was a successful one.

William Caxton's *Boke yf Eneydos* (1490) consisted more of material from medieval Troy books than from Virgil's poem, while Douglas's 1553 translation "into Scottish metir" was published only once. Surrey's 1557 translation of books 2 and 4 is generally held to be crucial for the subsequent development of blank (unrhymed) verse in Elizabethan England, with far-reaching consequences for both drama (from *Gorboduc,* 1562, to the works of Shakespeare) and epic (from Christopher Marlowe's translation of Lucan's *Pharsalia,* published in 1600, to John Milton's *Paradise Lost,* 1671). But Phaer's version of the *Aeneid* was the best known for the entire Elizabethan and Stuart age, displaced only by John Dryden's in 1697. Phaer's choice of the heptameter couplet influenced the practice of Arthur Golding in his 1567 translation of Ovid's *Metamorphoses* and of George Chapman in his 1598 translation of Homer's *Iliad,* while his refusal of neoclassical diction and meter in favor of what he considered a more purely English versification and style may have contributed to the vocabulary and methods of Edmund Spenser's archaizing in *The Shepheardes Calender* (1579) and *The Faerie Queene* (1590, 1596).

Nevertheless, Phaer's *Aeneid* must not be considered an example of archaizing. Phaer made no self-conscious effort to medievalize Virgil's epic; he was instinctively drawn to the English poetic form most associated with telling stories, and this undoubtedly was the ballad stanza, the formal narrative version which consisted of rhymed fourteen-syllable lines. Phaer's fourteen-

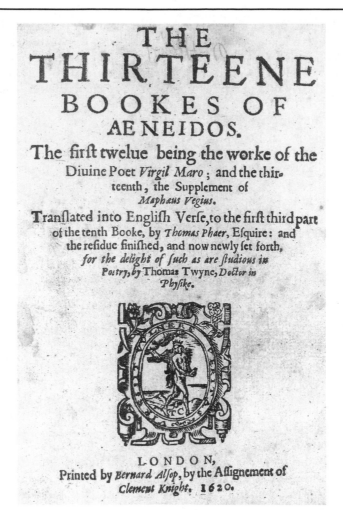

THE
THIRTEENE
BOOKES OF
AENEIDOS.

The firſt twelue being the worke of the
Diuine Poet *Virgil Maro*; and the thir-
teenth, the Supplement of
Maphæus Vegius.

Tranſlated into Engliſh Verſe, to the firſt third part
of the tenth Booke, by *Thomas Phaer*, Eſquire: and
the reſidue finiſhed, and now newly ſet forth,
for the delight of ſuch as are ſtudious in
Poetry, by Thomas Twyne, *Doctor in*
Phyſike.

LONDON,
Printed by *Bernard Alſop*, by the Aſſignement of
Clement Knight. 1620.

Title page for a 1620 edition of Thomas Phaer's translation of
Virgil, the most complete English version of the Aeneid *until*
John Vicars's 1632 translation (courtesy of the Lilly Library,
Indiana University)

ers and his homely diction sound odd to twentieth-century ears conditioned by centuries of blank verse. But Phaer firmly believed that he was translating the *Aeneid* into everyday speech, in a familiar form, believing that his *Aeneid* would chiefly benefit writers.

The qualities of Phaer's translation are apparent in a comparison of the death of Polites in versions by Phaer, Douglas, and Surrey. Phaer's translation is notable for general accuracy, and, rendering *concidit* as "felled . . . to death," he has even availed himself of the Latin verb's apparent etymology:

> Behold where 'scaping from the stroke of Pirrhus fierce
>   in fight
> Polites, one of Priam's sons, through foes and weapons
>   pight,
> Through galleries along doth run, and wide about him
>   spies

> Sore wounded then, but Pirrhus after him 'sues with
>   burning eyes
> In chase, and now welnere in hand him caught and
>   held with spear,
> Till right before his parents' sight he came, then felled
>   him there
> To death, and with his gushing blood his life outright he
>   shed.

Although Phaer's lines are longer, Douglas resorts to considerable periphrasis:

> Bot lo, Polytes, ane of Priamus sonnys
> Quhilk from the slauchter of Pyrrys away run is,
> Throw wapynnys fleyng and his ennemyss all,
> Be land thowgangis and mony voyd hall;
> Woundit he was, and come to seik rescew.
> Ardently Pyrrus gan him fast persew,
> With grondyn lance at hand so neir furthstrekit,
> Almaist the hed hym twichit and arekit,
> Quhil at the last, quhen he is cummyn, I weyn,

174

Befor his faderis and his moderis eyn,
Smate hym down ded in thar sycht quhar he stude,
The gaist he yald with habundans of blude.

Surrey perhaps succeeds better than Phaer in communicating Virgil's sense of violent pursuit but occasionally does so at the expense of clarity:

But lo Polites, one of Priam's sons,
Escaped from the slaughter of Pyrrhus,
Comes fleeing through the weapons of his foes,
Searching all wounded the long galleries.
And the void courts: whom Pyrrhus all in rage
Followed fast, to reach a mortal wound:
And now in hand welnere strikes with his spear.
Who fleeing forth, till he came now in sight
Of his parents, before their face fell down,
Yielding the ghost, with flowing streams of blood.

From this passage Phaer seems to have borrowed the word *welnere;* but while in Surrey the word hobbles the line in which it occurs, it makes a wonderful third foot in Phaer's heptameter. Thus, any assessment of Phaer's *Aeneid* cannot ignore its accuracy nor the skill with which he employs the heptameter. With the translation of the *Aeneid,* Phaer won a literary reputation comparable to those he already enjoyed in law and medicine.

Ferrers, in accordance with a request in the poet's will, wrote the epitaph on Phaer in the church of Cilgerran, Pembrokeshire. Chaloner, Phaer's friend and fellow collaborator on the first edition of *A Mirror for Magistrates,* wrote a fine epitaph that appeared in a collection of Chaloner's Latin poetry in 1579. In addition, Barnabe Googe provided a highly appreciative epitaph in his *Eclogues, Epitaphs, and Sonnets* (1563):

But wonder more may Britain great,
    where Phaer did flourish late,
And barren tongue with sweet accord
    reduced to such estate
That Virgil's verse hath greater grace
    in foreign foot obtained
Than in his own, who whilst he lived
    each other poets stained.

This might seem like excessive praise to modern readers; it would certainly seem unwarranted to Lally, who censures Phaer for the "accentual restraints of the fourteener couplet" that "cannot ... match the metrical sophistication of Surrey." Lally also praises Surrey for the "protean strength" of his metrical style and complains that "the constrained couplet form and evenly measured accent of Phaer's line imposes a regularity that loses the spirit" of Virgil. Lally has trouble explaining why sixteenth-century commentators lavished praise on Phaer's *Aeneid,* and he seems to have found the answer in their failure to understand that Surrey had realized the impossibility of imitating Virgil in English quantitative verse.

This explanation is insufficient, however, to account for the high regard in which Phaer's translation was held. William Webbe in *A Discourse of English Poesie* (1586) singles out Phaer as the best among English translators of Latin poetry, and Thomas Nashe, in his preface to Robert Greene's *Menaphon* (1589), exalts Phaer's "famous Virgil" with its "heavenly verse" over the "hissed barbarism," the "extremity of clownery," and the "thrasonical huff-snuff" of Bishop Stanyhurst. George Puttenham in *The Art of English Poesie* (1589) reveres Phaer along with Golding and mentions Thomas Twyne's continuation. Francis Meres in *Palladis Tamia* (1598) commends "these versifiers for their learned translations ... among us, Phaer for Virgil's *Aeneid,* Golding for Ovid's *Metamorphosis.*" Such extracts show that enthusiasm for Phaer's *Aeneid* cannot be laid to the commentators' lack of scientific understanding of English meter. The extent and variety of acclaim indicates an intelligently appreciative audience that was broad, loyal, and persistent.

Until Steven Lally published his edition of the Phaer-Twyne *Aeneid* in 1987, Thomas Phaer was known chiefly for his medical treatises. This situation was in part because of the fact that the only biographies of note both occur in histories of medicine (John Ruhräh's *Pediatrics of the Past,* 1925, and Sir George Frederic Still's *The History of Pediatrics,* 1931). A 1974 article by Boyd M. Berry approaches Phaer solely from the standpoint of his pediatrics and his views on children; it suffers from extreme views (for example, that Phaer articulates "a paranoid vision of the world which resonates with the utopian and apocalyptic thought of the period") and extraordinary errors (to cite a single, but characteristic, example, that Phaer's prefaces are the "stuff of militant Protestantism"). Apart from its value as an example of computer-generated collation applied to a sixteenth-century text and its importance as a contribution to the study of sixteenth-century stress and Renaissance metrical typography, Lally's edition of Phaer's *Aeneid* has made readily accessible an important and justly celebrated Renaissance English translation. It should also restore balance to assessments of Phaer's achievements and stimulate renewed interest in his life and the period during which he flourished, not to mention his importance in the history of law, medicine, and literature.

References:

Boyd M. Berry, "The First English Pediatricians and Tudor Attitudes Toward Childhood," *Journal of the History of Ideas,* 35 (October–December 1974): 561–577;

Luis García-Ballester, "Academicism versus Empiricism," in *The Medical Renaissance in the Sixteenth Century,* edited by A. Wear, R. K. French, and I. M. Lonie (Cambridge: Cambridge University Press, 1985), pp. 246–270;

V. Nutton, "Humanist Surgery," in *The Medical Renaissance in the Sixteenth Century,* edited by Wear, French, and Lonie (Cambridge: Cambridge University Press, 1985), pp. 75–99;

John Ruhräh, *Pediatrics of the Past* (New York: Hoeber, 1925), pp. 71–98;

G. Gregory Smith, ed., *Elizabethan Critical Essays,* 2 volumes (Oxford: Oxford University Press, 1904);

Sir George Frederic Still, *The History of Pediatrics* (Oxford: Blackwell, 1931), pp. 69–72, 94–100.

Papers:

The manuscript of books 1–3 of Thomas Phaer's translation of the *Aeneid* is in the British Museum (Lansdowne Ms., No. 36529, fols. 10, 21, 36).

Richard Robinson

(circa 1545 – 1607)

James Robertson
University of the West Indies, Mona

BOOKS: *The Vyneyarde of Vertue, Collected into a Tripartite Order,* compiled by Robinson (London: Thomas Dawson, 1579; expanded, 1591);

The Auncient Order, Societie and Unity Laudable of Prince Arthure and His Knights of Ye Round Table in London with a Threefold Commendation of Archery (London: John Wolfe, 1583).

Editions: "*Richard Robinson's Eupolemia* (1603)," edited by George McGill Vogt, *Studies in Philology,* 21 (1924): 629–648;

A Brief Collection of the Queens Majesties Most High and Most Honourable Courts of Requests, edited by R. L. Rickard, Camden Miscellany 20, third series 83 (London: Camden Society, 1953), pp. 1–36.

TRANSLATIONS: *Certeyn Select Historyes for Christians Recreation Translated out of Latin Prose into English Verse* (London: Henry Kingston, 1576);

Francisco Patrizi, *A Moral Methode of Civile Policie* (London: Thomas Marsh, 1576);

A Record of Ancyent Historyes Intytled in Latin Gesta Romanorum (London: Thomas Easte, 1577; revised, 1602);

Robinsons Ruby an Historical Fiction Translated out of Latin Prose into English Verse (London: John Charlewood, 1577);

The Dyall of Dayly Contemplation for Synners, Morall and Devyne Matter in English Prose First Published in Print 1499, Corrected and Reformed (London: Hugh Singleton, 1578);

Philip Melanchthon, *Godly Prayers, Meete to Be Used in These Later Times* (London: Henry Denham, 1579);

Melanchthon, *A Godly and Learned Assertion and Defence of the True Churche* (London: Thomas Dawson, 1580);

Nicholas Hemming (Niels Hemmingsen), *A Godlie and Learned Exposition upon the XXV Psalm* (London: Thomas Vantrollier, 1580);

John Leland, *A Learned and True Assertion of the Life of Prince Arthure* (London: John Wolfe, 1582);

Victorinus Strigelius, *Part of the Harmonie of King Dauids Harpe* (London: John Wolfe, 1582);

Strigelius, *A Proceeding in the Harmonie of King Dauids Harpe* (London: John Wolfe, 1583);

Urbanus Regius, *An Homilye of Good and Evill Angels First Preached at Zella in Saxony, Anno 1539* (London: John Charlewood, 1583);

Regius, *The Solace of Sion and Joy of Jerusalem* (London: Richard Jones, 1587);

Strigelius, *A Second Proceeding in the Harmonie of King Dauids Harpe* (London: John Charlewood for Abraham Kitson, 1592);

Strigelius, *A Third Proceeding in the Harmonie of King Dauids Harpe* (London: Valentine Symes for Richard Banckworth, 1595);

Strigelius, *A Fourth Proceeding in the Harmonie of King Dauids Harpe* (London: Valentine Symes for Richard Bankworth, 1596);

Strigelius, *A Fift Proceeding in the Harmonie of King Dauids Harpe* (London: Peter Short for Matthew Lownes, 1596);

Emanuel van Meteren, *A True Discourse Historicall, of the Succeeding Gouernours in the Netherlands,* by Robinson and Thomas Churchyard (London: Martin Lownes, 1602).

Edition: John Leland, *A Learned and True Assertion of the Life of Prince Arthure,* part 2, in *The Famous Historie of Chinon of England,* edited by W. E. Mead, Early English Text Society, original series 165 (Oxford: Oxford University Press, 1925 [i.e., 1923]).

Richard Robinson, although a minor author, enjoyed striking success in winning major patrons, including Sir Philip Sidney, for his translations and compilations. Robinson's manuscript *Eupolemia, Archippus, and Panoplia* (1603; published 1924), a semi-autobiographical record of his benefactors compiled at the end of his career, is a unique source for the study of professional authorship in the 1570s through the 1590s, when he was working as both a legal copyist and a published author. The very lack of distinction in Robinson's oeuvre means that his experiences illuminate the wider possibilities for making a living as a writer in Elizabethan London.

Richard Robinson was a Londoner; the exact date of his birth is unknown. It is hard to reconcile a comment that he was age fifty-eight on 25 May 1603 with an earlier claim that he had been laboring in London for thirty-one years in 1595 — since it is known that he left school to go to London at fourteen — though the second comment does coincide with the dedication of *A Moral Method* (1576) to Sir William Allen, which acknowledges benefits "received from time to time these twelve years." This evidence would, however, suggest that he was born around 1545 and that he would have finished his education in the optimistic years of Elizabeth I's accession. The texts he chose to translate over the rest of his career continued to reflect the values of years when Protestant worship was restored. In the first few years of Elizabeth's reign he left Newark, where he had studied for seven years at the free grammar school, to undertake an apprenticeship with William Allen, a member of the Leathersellers' Company and a future alderman of London and knight. Neither his company's records for apprenticeships nor the city's records of freedoms survive from this period.

Robinson always remained a citizen of London, but he apparently left the leather trade. In 1565 he received two crowns for dedicating a manuscript, *The Spanish Inquisitor,* to the earl of Hertford. He had earned his freedom by apprenticeship, and the "custom of London" allowed him to work in any city craft, so there was nothing to preclude a citizen and leather seller of London from becoming a professional copyist. Given both the prestige and charitable resources of the Leathersellers' Company, he would have had little reason to transfer to a minor guild such as the Scriveners' Company even if he were making his living transcribing texts for sale.

A manuscript of Robinson's *Brief Collection on the Court of Requests,* "A treatise of the several judicial courts in England," is annotated "Anno Domini 1588 . . . 29 Junii." It is adapted from a mid-sixteenth-century manuscript, "Description of the Courts of Justice in England," although Robinson's text expands the section on Parliament. Robinson later developed an elaborate grudge against an apprentice to a legal stationer, whose master had refused to buy a book "of fees and charges in divers courts at the Common Law" that Robinson had transcribed to earn money during the 1593 plague. The project

suggests one way that he was accustomed to earning extra cash. He continued to produce copies of this compilation, including one dated 1603, with "Jacobus" replacing Elizabeth's regnal years. Parts of a further copy, with the completion date 26 October 1603, also suggest that Robinson maintained this sideline until the end of his career. What appears atypical in Robinson's activities as a legal copyist is that from 1570 he began to have some of his translations and compilations published and that he made a living from this new work.

Most of the present-day knowledge of Robinson's publications comes from a major failure of judgment on his part. In 1595, at what he hoped would prove the climax of his career as a translator of Protestant pamphlets, he presented a dedication copy of his translation of a Lutheran academic's commentary on Psalms 17–45 to Queen Elizabeth; despite her gracious commendations for Robinson's goodwill, his subsequent plea "for some relief in money" was unsuccessful. The queen was accustomed to fending off importunate suitors. Robinson's plea for reward was passed along to Sir Julius Caesar, one of the royal masters of requests, who told Robinson that as Elizabeth had not commissioned the work, she would not pay any wages. Robinson later claimed he left Richmond Palace "as a poor man."

This rejection — and Robinson's earlier successes — are recorded in a rambling appeal for assistance, his *Eupolemia,* compiled ten years later. This appeal was part of a wider lobbying campaign. He initially presented "a catalogue of all my labors until that day" to the lord mayor of London in August 1602. The same year Robinson tagged a variant list of publications onto a dedication to the queen's almoner that he added to a lightly revised edition of the *Gesta Romanorum* (1577), a work attributed by Robinson to John Leland, which had proved one of his most successful compilations; indeed, it remained a schoolteacher's standby for another generation. The fullest version of the *Eupolemia* that has survived, however, was compiled for Elizabeth. Robinson was already writing this volume to deliver to the queen in February 1602 — when he added a reference to Sheriff Thomas Smith's imprisonment in the Tower after the earl of Essex's unsuccessful rising — but it remained incomplete when she died a year later and was then redirected to James. The manuscript is preserved in the British Library, alongside several other cranky petitions to the king. What proves most remarkable about Robinson's career is that he had suffered few brush-offs until his attempt to impress the queen.

G. C. To the Tranſlator.

```
F  irme frendſhip feares no feeble foes, faith triumphes ouer all:
I  t may be toſt and wrapt in woes, but downe it cannot fall,
D  id Chriſt diſdaine for frendes to die, their fatall doomes to pay?
E  uen God for man, iuſt for vniuſt, his ſoule to pledge did laye
L  ooke then on frendſhips force, to foes, and ſee it more abound:
I  n his triumphes we victors were, and riches great haue found,
S  ome captaines of his hoaſt, and ſome his guides and prophetes are
A  nd ſome Apoſtles for to plant, of watring ſome haue care.
M  uſe not therefore, that Prophets ſpeake darke ſpeeches which be wiſe:
I  n huſkes moſt tart, and ſhelles moſt hard, the pleaſant kernell lies.
C  ould greater ſecretes be conceiude, then lurke in Dauids ſonges
V  nknowen to purblinde Iewes, to whom of right the law belongs.
S  trigelus tels them plaine, to thoſe that latine language knowes;
D  eep myſteries in termes moſt plaine, to ſtudious heads he ſhowes.
E  uen he the huſke and ſhel hath broke, to kernell you may come,
F  know his ſpeech all cannot reach, he ſpeaketh but to ſome.
E  xchangde for engliſh pleaſant phraſe, he hath his romiſh ſtile.
S  incerely Robinſon hath dealt, the vulgar ſpeech to file,
T  herefore praiſe God as author chiefe, for to reueale the ſame.
E  ſteeme the Princelie Scribe, whoſe pen theſe ſacred ſonges did frame.
T  hanke Strigell for the light he gaue to darkeſome ſpeech of Harpe
C  ount Robinſons indeuours ſuch, as Momus may not carpe
H  ow great a ſigne is this to thee, the frend of God to be:
R  euealing of his ſecrete will, and giftes beſtowed on thee,
I  f ſeruantes may not know the will, and maſters treaſure great:
S  ure frendes and ſonnes enioy them both, they ſeede on daintieſt meate.
T  his haſt thou treaſure, lock and key, at will to take and chuſe:
I  n wretched ſtate thou art enthralde, if thou ſuch giftes refuſe.

F  Frend Robinſon, thou haſt a frend, if thou like faithfull be:
E  Euen God and Chriſt thee to defend, gainſt all loquacitie,        (pleaſe
A  All tinckling Cymbals ceaſe your ſoundes, vaine heads & mindes to
R  Reſt curious workemen of vaine artes, your ſalue helps no diſeaſe.
E  Egs of the Cockatrice you lay, and weaue the Spiders cloth:
G  Goodly to view, no gayne to vſe, but ſhame and poyſon both
O  Only Gods will to know and teach, is wiſedome, ioy and bliſſe
D  Down with vaine toyes, exalt all hands, and hearts that brings vs this.
E  Gruch not good will its vertues meede, let labouring bees be fed:
C  lo ſte bee the drones that ſpende ſ ſwete, that toyling bees haue bred.
```

FINIS,

Page from Robinson's 1583 translation A Proceeding in the Harmony of King David's Harp, *with an acrostic poem by George Close. The acrostic reads, "Fidelis amicus dei est et Christi. [A faithful friend is God, and Christ.] Feare God, GC."*

Robinson's apparent intention in the recension presented in *Eupolemia* was to show that he had always been at the service of Elizabeth's godly cause: being "virtuously brought up, and in my elder years betaking me to the war from my study and pen, as a preferred friend to true religion and virtue, and a practicing enemy against hypocrisy and vice." It would demonstrate his eligibility for a royal nomination to the reversion of a place at an almshouse, which, he claimed, had been granted to an old soldier who already had a place elsewhere. Presumably in an attempt to show that his Protestant fervor remained clear from suspect religious enthusiasms, Robinson also provided a list of all his titles and reprints, noting who had "perused and allowed" each item, who his publisher was, and who had received the dedication. Recording each shilling and block of author's copies that he had received for his publications over thirty years demonstrates Robinson's retentive memory. His omission of his repeated recopyings of the *Brief Relation*, however, suggests a division between Robinson's transcriptions and his translating – which may say more about his views of godly service to the state than how he actually made ends meet as a professional writer. In any event, this second request for royal patronage proved as unsuccessful as his first.

Despite this autobiographical source, plus long-winded dedications and some references among the records of the Leathersellers' Company, Robinson's activities remain difficult to assess. The occasional scholarly attention he receives acknowledges a diligent translator, with modern critics following his contemporaries' example in barely discussing Robinson's work as a copyist, though this activity seems to have opened important doors for him in legal and antiquarian circles. Dedicatory verses by Thomas Buckminster – a prolific compiler of almanacs – to the third volume of Robinson's translation of a commentary on the Psalms commend the project. Even here, however, the subject rather than the substance of Robinson's project earns the praise: Buckminster proclaims that Robinson brought "labors much, and pains" to his endeavors, receiving little credit for his skill. Subsequently, in describing the elderly Robinson as a co-author in a translation of part of Emanuel van Meteren's *Historia Belgica* – a text that Robinson claimed to have translated "much graced" and transcribed "in my simple Roman hand" for its author, a leading Dutch merchant and litterateur in London – Thomas Churchyard's preface briefly commends Robinson for his "great pains" but then goes on to defend him as "a man more debased by many than he merits of any, so good parts are there in the man."

Subsequent generations have found little to add. In his 1925 edition of Robinson's translation of John Leland's *Asserto Arturii inclytissimi Regis Britanniae* (translated as *A Learned and True Assertion of the Life of Prince Arthur,* 1582), W. E. Mead judges Robinson's prose "reasonably clear and intelligible" but complains that reading "his verse aloud gives about as much pleasure as chewing sand." A paleographically and typographically accurate edition of the *Eupolemia* was published by George McGill Vogt in 1924, and it provided the basis for a reassessment by R. B. McKerrow of the procedures underlying the record provided by the Stationers' Company Registers, who licensed individual books for the press. Vogt's edition has also inspired a description of the mechanics of literary patronage in Michael Brennan's *Literary Patronage in the English Renaissance: The Pembroke Family* (1988). Otherwise twentieth-century readers continue to turn to Robinson's translation of Leland's tendentious life of King Arthur, since it is still the only English translation of this pamphlet; but, along with the relative convenience of a modern Early English Text Society edition, the work remains more a testimony to ebbing latinity than to the virtues of Robinson's text. Leslie Alcock, a modern historian of sub-Roman Britain, points out that even in a key nine-word Latin inscription – allegedly found in Arthur's tomb at Glastonbury – Robinson's translation manages to differ "at four points from Leland's despite the fact that he had Leland's printed text before him." For someone who received benefactions from many of the leading patrons of his day, Robinson and his oeuvre have typically been dismissed briskly.

Robinson's success in finding patrons has wider implications for putting the language of dedicatory epistles into their social context. Robinson's letters of dedication are as grateful as those of any of his contemporaries, but his testimony in the *Eupolemia* undercuts expectations for treating dedications as an index of dedicatees' priorities. His is a freelance translator's guess at his would-be patrons' interests. Elizabeth was not the only recipient who declined to encourage his work. The sponsors Robinson found covered a wide social range, while their support covered the whole spectrum – from refusal to a single grudging payment to repeated gifts at subsequent reprints and support for later projects.

It was a risky policy, as was demonstrated in an instance in which Robinson had sent the dedication copy via a member of the earl of Warwick's household and the earl "rendered me no reward for the same" – though the widowed countess subsequently rewarded Robinson for two reprints. So, too, his codedication of Victorinus Strigelius's *Fifth Proceeding* (1596) to the city aldermen and to Bishop Aylmer of London provided the bishop's secretary with an occasion to refuse "to present it for me unto his Lord the Bishop." In another near misstep, in which Lord Keeper Egerton complained that Robinson "should have made him privy to it, before I had dedicated it unto him," Robinson chose a particularly public venue to press his unsolicited honor onto Egerton "at his new entering unto [the] office" of lord keeper. Disaster was averted only when "a virtuous lady in the City" accepted the dedication instead and gave Robinson "the double value thereof." Such instances warn against modern readers interpreting dedications as a mirror of dedicatees' interests.

Yet Robinson's *Eupolemia* also notes a longer list of successes in maintaining contacts that reached well beyond London: in the church, with such leading clergymen as Dean Alexander Nowell of St. Paul's and Dean Gabriel Goodman of Westminster Abbey; at court, with such officials as Sir William Winter, the surveyor of the Royal Navy, and Arthur Grey, Lord Wilton, a staunchly Protestant lord lieutenant of Ireland, along with Sir Henry Sidney and his son, Sir Philip, who received Robinson's translations of Philip Melanchthon. Alongside these national figures were several lord keepers as well as less prominent lawyers such as David Lewis, an admiralty judge, and some more unexpected figures such as the earl of Rutland, who nevertheless proved "many times before and since

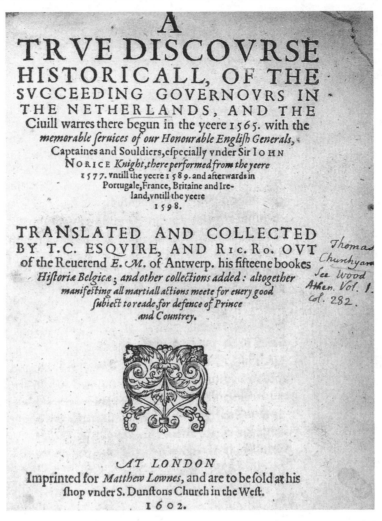

A
TRVE DISCOVRSE
HISTORICALL, OF THE
SVCCEEDING GOVERNOVRS IN
THE NETHERLANDS, AND THE
Ciuill warres there begun in the yeere 1565. with the
memorable seruices of our Honourable English Generals,
Captaines and Souldiers, especially vnder Sir IOHN
NORICE *Knight, there performed from the yeere*
1577. vntill the yeere 1589. and afterwards in
Portugale, France, Britaine and Ire-
land, vntill the yeere
1598.

TRANSLATED AND COLLECTED
BY T.C. ESQVIRE, AND RIC. Ro. OVT
of the Reuerend E. ᴄM. of Antwerp. his fifteene bookes
Historiæ Belgicæ; and other collections added: altogether
manifesting all martiall actions meete for euery good
subiect to reade, for defence of Prince
and Countrey.

AT LONDON
Imprinted for *Matthew Lownes,* and are to be sold at his
shop vnder S. Dunstons Church in the West.
1602.

Title page for Thomas Churchyard and Robinson's translation of Emanuel
van Meteren's Historia Belgica, *the last of Robinson's works*
published in his lifetime (courtesy of the Lilly Library,
Indiana University)

my best benefactor and patron," and two generations of the Uverdale family of Protestant gentry from Dorset.

Nor did Robinson completely lose his touch in his last years, when he tended to do best offering his texts and reprints to the aldermen of London or to his own leather sellers' guild. Here his choice of texts to translate – mostly Lutheran piety from the first third of the sixteenth century, where he proved adroit in avoiding theological minefields – allowed him to appeal to a broad spectrum of patrons through the 1570s and 1580s. Windfalls from these dedicatees were unpredictable but could be extensive. Sir Christopher Hatton's generosity on receiving a translation of Strigelius's *Proceeding of King David's Harp* in 1583 was so liberal that Robinson did not need to peddle further copies and could refrain "from troubling my friends abroad for one whole year's space afterwards." In other instances further sums could be expected for republications: Dean Goodman gave Robinson eight shillings for the first edition of a translated sermon and two shillings more for two subsequent editions that were equipped with additional dedications, besides being "every year since my thankful benefactor for other labors presented unto him." On other occasions Robinson's sale of author's copies of his pamphlets proved almost as remunerative. Judge Lewis rewarded him with twelve shillings for dedicating a translated sermon, but Robinson then "made benefit of 25 books," which he sold at a shilling each.

Alongside these high-profile dedicatees, further sets of contacts smoothed Robinson's work. In the preface to his *First Proceeding* (1583) Robinson acknowledges the "help of a rare well-disposed divine," George Close, preacher of St. Magnus' Church in

London and Robinson's former schoolfellow, who also wrote him a preface and an acrostic poem. Otherwise in a petition for assistance Robinson makes little mention of his origins or any kin beyond his wife and family – demonstrating that his membership in wider kinship networks would hardly help an appeal for royal charity. But in cobbling a literary living together, Robinson's ties to his guild and to London's aldermanic elite proved invaluable. After disasters and near-disasters in 1595 and 1596, when Robinson presented his translations of Strigelius's *Third Proceedings* and *Fourth Proceedings* to the queen and Lord Keeper Egerton, Robinson codedicated his *Fifth Proceeding* to the bishop of London, which also proved unsuccessful, and to the lord mayor and aldermen of London, who were more generous. Yet, with increasing demands on the aldermen's attention and charity in the 1590s, this source of funds also dried up. Even at this stage Robinson continued to have successes in dealing with his own guild – remaining the only person to dedicate books to the Elizabethan Leathersellers' Company – and he turned to their charity again in his last years when courtly and aldermanic patronage failed him.

Other contacts with legal and antiquarian circles are less clear, though they may well relate to Robinson's manuscript work as a copyist, but they led him to some of his most profitable texts. His *Brief Collection* may be the "old copy w[hi]ch" he had been given by a "learned temporal lawyer, one Mr. W. L. of worthy memory" – William Lambarde, an antiquary who had died in 1601, remains a candidate as this early mentor. Robinson also acknowledged assistance from both John Stow, the citizen antiquary, and William Camden, the master of Westminster School, "for the interpretation of hard British and Welsh terms" in translating Leland's Arthurian tract, which also incorporated annotations by Stephen Bateman, a parson of Newington Buttes. Robinson's compilation *The Laudable Society, Order, and Unity of Prince Arthur with a Threefold Commendation of Archery* (1583), which Bateman "perused and allowed" before it was published, should also be seen in this context. A paragraph commending Robinson's *Third Proceeding* to the reader was written by Richard Mulcaster, the headmaster of the Merchant Taylors' School in London, who had earlier been a member of van Meteren's circle of Protestant émigrés and antiquarians. Conspicuous, however, is the absence of any consistent support from Robinson's many publishers.

Robinson's *Eupolemia* stresses the godly component in his translations, although several of his more successful efforts had addressed the antiquarian issues of a manuscript copyist. Two further pa-

tronage coups appealed to the military and antiquarian interests of his municipal patrons rather than their piety. In 1583, when the London archery society – supported by Thomas Smith, the wealthy farmer of the London customs farm – performed with Smith "representing himself [as] Prince Arthur," not only did Smith give Robinson five shillings for the dedication of his *Laudable Society of Prince Arthur,* but "his 56 knights gave" the leading men of the club a shilling and six pence each, while "every Esquire for his book" paid eight pence each "when they shot under the same Prince Arthur at Mile End Green."

Subsequently Robinson was able to turn to advantage his service during the Armada crisis, in which he had trailed a pike in his ward's contingent of the London trained band. Eleven years later he copied out lists of the officers of the city's militia companies in 1588 and 1599. He initially presented these to the captain of his own unit and then, with a recommendation from Baptist Hickes, the leading retail mercer in London, Robinson could offer further copies to all the trained band officers, who generally felt obliged to reward his efforts.

After such coups the end of Robinson's career was disappointing. In 1595 he was obliged to pawn his household movables, books, and the "very gown from my back." In 1598 he was also obliged to sell the lease that he held of a house in Harp Alley, off Shoe Lane in St. Bride's parish. Robinson claimed that this crisis followed his failed attempt to get money from the queen. For all the effort that had gone into the *Eupolemia,* Robinson's petition to King James appears to have proved unsuccessful. After making a career navigating an Elizabethan world in which courtly and civic patrons would pay for translations of Lutheran piety, antiquarianism, or godly belligerence, Robinson blamed the difficulties of his last years on individuals and mischance. He could not recognize that "the Phoenix of the feminine sex, our most redoubted Hester and gracious sovereign lady Queen Elizabeth" of his many prefaces did not acknowledge the value of his endeavors, or that by the end of her reign his most supportive patrons were all dead. In 1603 the Leathersellers' Company made a grant of five shillings to Robinson at Christmas, but his Christian name was omitted in the manuscript, which suggests that he had followed his appeals to the lord mayor and to the Crown with another to his guild. As an elderly member of the company fallen on hard times, he was a candidate for corporate charity. In 1607 two further payments – of thirteen shillings, four pence, and of five shillings – were given to a "Widow Robinson." No will or record of Robinson's having made a will survives.

The historian is left with a sketch of a career that bridged not only copying legal manuscripts and publishing translations of moral texts but also involved a remarkably professional pursuit of patronage that for twenty years managed to appeal to the tastes of courtiers, citizens, and clerics. Robinson's work illustrates the uneven acceptance of print among different groups of readers – with law students (and legal stationers) continuing to pay him for longhand copies of outlines when other types of text had been in print for generations. His success in targeting the dedications for his translations also testifies to the continuing appeal of material from the early sixteenth century or from more-moderate Lutherans across a wide spectrum of Elizabethan society in the 1570s and 1580s.

In the last years of Elizabeth's reign, however, Robinson's endeavors were less successful. Overconfidence may have made him too ambitious in the dedicatees he targeted, but the taste of the times seems to have shifted as well. As a citizen and leather seller of London, Robinson continued to have access to municipal patronage, which seems to have allowed him to survive. However, in his last years he seems to have been retreating from print and reverting to producing the manuscript texts of his youth. But at this stage in his career he no longer had the antiquarian contacts who had helped him in his earlier years. Robinson's vicissitudes seem to suggest a more complicated relationship between copying, print, and patronage than one might initially expect.

The Elizabethan literary worlds that Robinson navigated, on the edge of the city, the court, and the Inns of Court, all remain in need of investigation. As further copies of Robinson's legal transcripts surface, they should provide information about when he wrote them and, perhaps, who bought them. Were these texts standbys that a professional copyist turned to when plague struck and the stationers' shops had few customers? More usefully, investigating Richard Robinson's career illuminates the shadowy inhabitants of the antiquarian circles in the Elizabethan London of William Lambard's generation. The more prominent figures in these groups are familiar enough, but their interrelations with the Protestant émigrés or with figures from the Inns of Court have been overshadowed by the search for precursors of the elite gatherings of the Jacobean Society of Antiquaries. Above all, Richard Robinson's efforts offer insights into the strategies for survival as an author in Elizabethan society, a business that remained distant from the clichéd vocabularies of reciprocity and gratitude that formed the language of patronage employed by Robinson and his peers.

References:

Leslie Alcock, *Arthur's Britain: History and Archaeology, A.D. 367–634* (London: Allan Lane, 1971);

J. H. Baker, *English Legal Manuscripts in the United States of America, a Descriptive List: Part 2, Early Modern and Modern Periods (1558–1902)* (London: Seldon Society, 1990);

Michael Brennan, *Literary Patronage in the English Renaissance: The Pembroke Family* (London: Routledge, 1988);

Thomas Corsar, Introduction to Robinson's *A Golden Mirror* (Manchester: Chetham Society, 1851);

R. B. McKerrow, "Richard Robinson's *Eupolemia* and the Licensers," *Library,* 11 (1930): 173–178;

R. L. Rickard, Introduction to *A Brief Collection of the Queens Majesties Most High and Most Honourable Courts of Requests,* edited by R. L. Rickard, Camden Miscellany 20, third series 83 (London: Camden Society, 1953).

Papers:

The manuscript of Richard Robinson's autobiographical *Eupolemia, Archippus, and Panoplia* is in the British Library (Ms. Royal 18 A, lxvi, ff. 1–37v). Copies of his *Brief Collection* are more scattered. In 1953 R. L. Rickard edited a copy titled "A Brief Collection of the Queen's Majesty's Most High and Most Honorable Courts of Records" (Library of New College, Oxford, Ms. 325) and compared it to another version with the title "A treatise of the several judicial courts in England, their Jurisdiction, Officers and Manner of Proceeding Therein" (All Souls College, Oxford, Ms. 125). A copy dated 1588 with the title "A breviatt concerninge the memorable states and conditions of the queenes majesties honorable courts of record" is in the Houghton Library at Harvard University (Ms. fMS. Eng. 976). Parts of another copy are in the British Library (Ms. Cotton Vespasian E VIII, fols. 2–12, and Cotton Titus A XXVI, fols. 208–230). A later copy is at the University of Kansas (Kenneth Spencer Research Library, Ms. D. 152[6]), and another is in the Philadelphia Free Library (Ms. LC 14.41 [26]). The Bodleian Library, Oxford, also holds Robinson's translation of part of van Meteren's *Historia Belgica* (Ms. Tanner 255).

Mary Sidney Herbert, Countess of Pembroke

(27 October 1561 – 25 September 1621)

Margaret P. Hannay
Siena College

TRANSLATIONS: *A Discourse of Life and Death. . . . Antonius, a Tragoedie by R. Garnier. Both done in English by the Countesse of Pembroke* (London: Printed by J. Windet for William Ponsonby, 1592);

The Tragedie of Antonie. Doone into English by the Countesse of Pembroke (London: Printed by P. Short for William Ponsonby, 1595).

OTHER: "The Doleful Lay of Clorinda," in *Astrophel. A Pastorall Elegie Upon the Death of the Most Noble and Valorous Knight, Sir Philip Sidney,* by Edmund Spenser (London: Printed by T. Creede for William Ponsonby, 1595);

"A Dialogue between Two Shepherds, *Thenot* and *Piers,* in Praise of *Astrea,*" in *A Poetical Rapsody Containing, Diverse Sonnets, Odes, Elegies, Madrigalls, and Other Poesies, Both in Rime, and Measured Verse,* edited by Francis Davison (London: Printed by V. Simmes for J. Baily, 1602);

"To the Angell Spirit," erroneously attributed to Samuel Daniel, in *The Whole Workes of Samuel Daniel Esquire in Poetrie* (London: Printed by N. Okes for Simon Waterson, 1623).

Editions: *The Works of Mary Sidney, Countess of Pembroke,* edited by Robert G. Barnwell (London: John Wilson, 1865);

The Countess of Pembroke's Antonie (1592), edited by Alice Luce (Weimar: Emil Felber, 1897);

Two Poems by the Countess of Pembroke, edited by Bent Juel-Jensen (Oxford: Privately printed, 1962);

The Psalms of Sir Philip Sidney and the Countess of Pembroke, edited by J. C. A. Rathmell (New York: New York University Press, 1963);

The Tragedy of Antony, in *Narrative and Dramatic Sources of Shakespeare,* volume 5, edited by Geoffrey Bullough (New York: Columbia University Press, 1966), pp. 358–405;

"The Triumph of Death" and Other Unpublished and Uncollected Poems by Mary Sidney, Countess of Pembroke (1561–1621), edited by Gary F. Waller (Salzburg: University of Salzburg, 1977);

The Countess of Pembroke's Translation of Philippe de Mornay's "Discourse of Life and Death," edited by Diane Bornstein (Detroit: Michigan Consortium for Medieval and Early Modern Studies, 1983);

Antonius in *A New Variorum Edition of Shakespeare: "Antony and Cleopatra,"* edited by Marvin Spevack (New York: Modern Language Association, 1990), pp. 479–524;

The Sidney Psalms, edited by R. E. Pritchard (Manchester: Carcanet, 1992);

"The Tragedy of Antonie (1595)," in *Renaissance Drama by Women: Texts and Documents,* edited by S. P. Cerasano and Marion Wynne-Davies (London: Routledge, 1996), pp. 13–42;

Collected Works of Mary Sidney Herbert, Countess of Pembroke, edited by Margaret P. Hannay, Noel J. Kinnamon, and Michael G. Brennan (Oxford: Clarendon Press, forthcoming 1997).

Mary Sidney was the most important non-royal woman writer and patron in Elizabethan England. Without appearing to transgress the strictures against women's writing, she composed a sizable body of work, evading criticism by focusing on religious themes and by confining her work to the genres thought appropriate to women — translation, dedication, elegy, and encomium. Even more important to her success was her identity as the sister of Sir Philip Sidney. She began her public literary career after his death by encouraging works written in his praise, publishing his works, and completing his translation of the Psalms. Except for some business correspondence, all of her extant works were completed or published in the 1590s. Tantalizing later references indicate that she continued writing and translating until her death, but all subsequent works have been lost, probably to fire: her primary residences of Wilton and Baynards Castle burned in the seventeenth century. The extensive family

Mary Sidney Herbert, Countess of Pembroke; miniature by Nicholas Hilliard
(Victoria and Albert Museum, London)

correspondence mentioned by her brothers and other contemporaries has also been lost; her only surviving personal letters were written to her uncle, Robert Dudley, Earl of Leicester, in 1578 and to Robert Sidney's wife, Barbara Gamage, in 1591, offering the services of a nurse.

The daughter of Sir Henry Sidney and Mary Dudley, Mary Sidney was born on 27 October 1561 at Tickenhall near Bewdley, Worcestershire, on the Welsh border while her father was serving as lord governor of the marches of Wales. He had been a companion of King Edward, who died in his arms. Her mother, a well-educated woman who was a close friend of Queen Elizabeth, was the daughter of the earl of Northumberland, the virtual ruler of England in King Edward's final years, and the sister of Elizabeth's favorite, Robert Dudley. Lady Sidney was badly scarred by smallpox after nursing the queen and thereafter rarely appeared at court.

While Mary's brothers, Philip, Robert, and Thomas, were preparing to enter the university, she and her younger sister, Ambrosia, received an outstanding education for women of their time, includ-

ing training in Latin, French, and Italian language and literature, as well as more typically feminine subjects such as needlework, lute playing, and singing. After Ambrosia died in 1575, Queen Elizabeth invited the Sidneys to send Mary to court, away from the "unpleasant" air of Wales.

When Mary was fifteen she became the third wife of Henry Herbert, Earl of Pembroke, one of the richest men in England and an important ally of her father and her uncle, the earl of Leicester. Although a 1578 letter to Leicester shows her struggling to please these two powerful earls, she quickly grew into her role as countess of Pembroke. As mistress of the primary Pembroke estate at Wilton, their London home, Baynards Castle, and several smaller estates, the countess encouraged literary and scientific endeavors among her friends and household. Between 1580 and 1584 she bore four children: Katherine, who died in childhood; Anne, who died in her early twenties; William, who became the third earl of Pembroke; and Philip, whom King James created earl of Montgomery and who eventually succeeded his brother as fourth earl of Pembroke. Her sons were the "Incomparable Pair of Brethren" to whom Shakespeare's First Folio was dedicated.

Mary Sidney began her writing career in the late 1580s, after her three surviving children were out of infancy and after she had experienced a devastating series of deaths in her family. Her three-year-old daughter, Katherine, died in 1584 on the same day her son Philip was born. The death of her father in May 1586 was quickly followed by her mother's death in August. Because all three of her brothers were serving with the English forces sent to help free Protestant Holland from the occupying forces of Catholic Spain, Mary was the only one who could represent the family at the funeral. In the autumn, while seriously ill herself, the countess learned that her brother Philip had died on 17 October from infection of a wound received at Zutphen. All England and Holland mourned his death; several collections of elegies and his splendid funeral (delayed until February for financial reasons) helped to establish the Sidney legend. Overcome by illness and grief and fearing invasion by the Spanish Armada, Mary Sidney remained in the country for two years.

In November 1588 Sidney returned to London in a splendid procession and began to honor her brother by her activities as patron, translator, and writer. The stream of elegies for Sir Philip had dried up quickly after the death of the earl of Leicester, who had rewarded those who honored his nephew; Mary Sidney stepped into that role, encouraging a second wave of elegies, including works by Thomas Moffet, Abraham Fraunce, and Edmund Spenser. Her first known literary work, "The Doleful Lay of Clorinda," was published in 1595 with Spenser's "Astrophel" in a collection of elegies. Although some critics have attributed the poem to Spenser, evidence of Sidney's authorship includes her 1594 letter to Philip Sidney's friend Sir Edward Wotton, asking for his copy of a poem of mourning that she had written long ago and now needed; Spenser's parallel treatment of Lodowick Bryskett as "Thestylis" and the countess as "Clorinda"; the parallel separation of "Clorinda" from "Astrophel" and from "The Mourning Muse of Thestylis" by the use of borders and introductory stanzas in the first publication of the "Lay"; Spenser's own references to the countess in "Astrophel" and in *The Ruines of Time* (1591); and stylistic similarities to the countess's other works.

The most probable scenario is that the countess worked with Spenser assembling poems printed earlier in *The Phoenix Nest* (1593) and revising her poem written shortly after Philip's death. Spenser

then wrote "Astrophel" for the volume, as well as stanzas introducing the other elegies. In "The Doleful Lay of Clorinda" Sidney uses pastoral language to mourn the death of one who was the "Joy of the world, and shepherd's pride." A more personal note is sounded in her lament for the "merry maker" of riddles and poems. She follows convention in the final apotheosis, showing her brother living in heaven "in everlasting bliss" while those below mourn his absence.

Sidney next turned to translation — a form of writing, like elegies for male relatives, deemed suitably feminine. Her boldness lay in publishing under her own name, a most unusual action for an aristocratic woman. Like her brother Philip, the countess was deeply influenced by Continental writers and sought to bring European literary forms and themes to England. Two translations from French, *A Discourse of Life and Death* (dated "The 13 of May 1590. At Wilton") and *Antonius* (dated "At Ramsburie. 26. of November 1590"), were published together in 1592.

Sidney's translation of Robert Garnier's *Marc Antoine* (1578), among the first English dramas in blank verse, helped introduce the Continental vogue for using historical drama to comment on contemporary politics, a method of indirect political statement that was continued through her patronage and that of her sons. Samuel Daniel's *Cleopatra* (1594) was written as a companion to her translation, and William Shakespeare's *Antony and Cleopatra* (circa 1606) was directly influenced by her *Antonius*.

Garnier's work is based on Plutarch's *Life of Antonius* but dramatizes only his final days. As the play opens, Antonius, once the most powerful man in the Roman Empire, has become so besotted with love for the Egyptian queen Cleopatra that he has thrown away his power and his marriage to Caesar's sister, Octavia. At war with Octavius Caesar, he has lost the battle of Actium by foolishly fleeing with Cleopatra and is now besieged in Alexandria. The play is written in the form of Senecan closet drama, emphasizing character rather than action. Major events take place offstage; the drama consists of a series of soliloquies, interspersed with discussions with servants and friends, and comments by a chorus, representing "first Egyptians and after Roman soldiers." Acts 1 and 3 are devoted primarily to Antony, acts 2 and 5 to Cleopatra, and act 4 to Octavius Caesar. Antony and Cleopatra learn to stop blaming fate or each other and to accept responsibility for the devastating consequences of their abandoning public duty for private pleasure. As in Greek drama, the chorus comments on the action, the characters, and particularly on the consequences of the ruler's acts for the people.

While there are no explicit references to English politics, the play was particularly appropriate in the turbulent 1590s, when England feared that Elizabeth's death would plunge them into a civil war as bloody as Rome's. The form of the closet drama, more suitable for reading aloud on a country estate than for acting on the public stage, was popular enough that *Antonius* was published in 1595 and was followed by similar works on historical themes by Samuel Daniel; Thomas Kyd; Samuel Brandon; Fulke Greville, first Lord Brooke; William Alexander (later earl of Stirling); and Elizabeth Cary, Viscountess Falkland.

Published with *Antonius* was Sidney's translation of Philippe de Mornay's *Discours de la vie et de la mort* (1576), one of a series of translations undertaken by Philip Sidney and his Continental friends to support Mornay and the Huguenot cause. A close friend of Philip Sidney, Mornay had visited England in 1578 and had probably met the countess on that trip. His meditation on death as the beginning of true life was particularly suited to the countess's grief over the recent deaths in her family. Like *Antonius,* the *Discourse* also served as an oblique commentary on court politics, demonstrating the vanity of earthly ambition as had previous sixteenth-century writers such as Desiderius Erasmus, Sir Thomas More, and Sir Thomas Wyatt. Like *Antonius,* Mornay's work emphasizes the dangers of civil war, although the author concludes that "we find greater civil war within ourselves." The theme is Christian stoicism: "Happy is he only who in mind lives contented: and he most of all unhappy, whom nothing he can have can content."

The Countess of Pembroke also translated Petrarch's "The Triumph of Death" (written 1348, published 1470) from Italian, preserving the original terza rima form. She may have translated the other five poems of the *Trionfi,* since the only extant manuscript is a transcript of a copy Sir John Harington sent to his cousin Lucy, Countess of Bedford, on 19 December 1600, along with three of the countess's 107 Psalms and some other pieces; certainly Thomas Moffett's suggestion in his *Silkworms* (1599) that Sidney "let Petrarch sleep, give rest to sacred writ" indicates a substantial project.

Like the *Discourse,* "The Triumph of Death" offers consolation to the bereaved; the poem also permitted the countess to interject a female voice into the Petrarchan tradition. English Petrarchanists had focused on the first part of the *Canzoniere,* sonnets in which Laura is given little chance to speak. In "The Triumph of Death" the spirit of Laura eloquently describes the experience of death, the joy of heaven, and her love for Petrarch. Even though the original was written by a man, Mary Sidney's vibrant and eloquent Laura provided an entry into the genre of love poetry for Englishwomen.

Sometime in the early 1590s, probably while she was completing her Petrarch translation, the countess had begun the work for which she is known, her metric translation of Psalms 44–150 that completes and revises a project her brother Philip had begun in his final years. Although the Psalms have always been an important part of Judeo-Christian worship, translating them into the vernacular for private meditation and public singing had become a particularly Protestant activity in the sixteenth century. When the countess first began her metric versions, she remained fairly close to the phrasing and interpretation familiar to her from Miles Coverdale's prose version in the Great Bible, incorporated into the *Book of Common Prayer.* Her more polished versions, transcribed by Sir John Davies of Hereford in the Penshurst manuscript, evidence a scholarly process of revision, however. Choosing Protestant scholarship based on the original Hebrew, the countess revised her *Psalms* to be closer to the Geneva Bible than to the Great Bible, with considerable reliance on Théodore de Bèze (in the original Latin and in Anthony Gilby's English translation), on John Calvin, and on *Les Psaumes de David mis en rime Françoise, par Clément Marot, et Théodore de Bèze* (1562). References are also made to other Continental versions and to earlier English metrical Psalms, such as those by Anne Lok and Matthew Parker.

The countess used 128 different verse forms for the 107 Psalms she paraphrased (Psalm 119 has twenty-two sections), making her achievement significant for metrical variety as well as for content. Like her Genevan sources, the countess uses the Psalms to comment on contemporary politics, particularly the persecution of "the godly," as Protestants called themselves. By expanding metaphors and descriptions present in the original Hebrew, Sidney also incorporates her experience at Elizabeth's court, as well as female experiences of marriage and childbirth.

The *Psalms* were essentially completed by 1599, the date recorded on the Tixall Manuscript owned by Dr. Bent Juel-Jensen. This manuscript also includes the unique copies of two poems, "To the Angel Spirit of Sir Philip Sidney" and "Even Now That Care," a dedicatory poem to Queen Eliz-

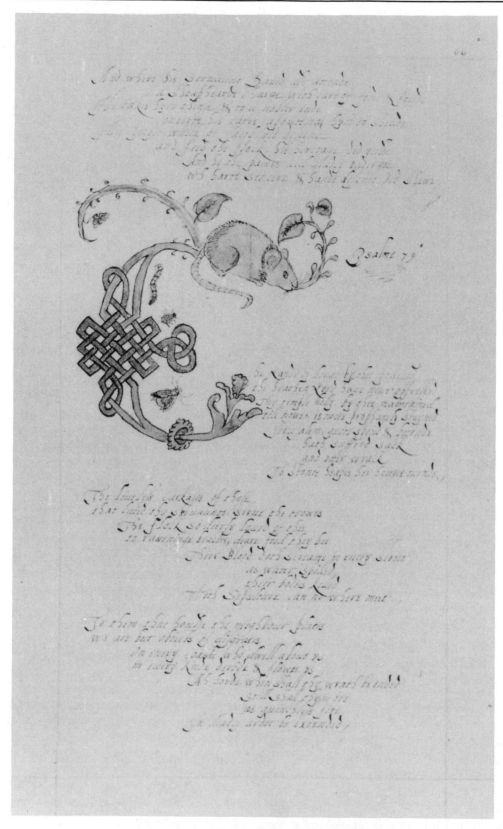

*Page from an ornamented scribal copy of Mary and Philip Sidney's translation of the Psalms
(Sotheby's, London, auction catalogue, 22 July 1980)*

abeth. In "Angel Spirit" the countess makes the traditional gesture of humility, saying as other writers had done that her ability is not equal to the task of praising her brother. She calls the paraphrase of the Psalms a "half-maimed piece," begun by "thy matchless Muse," the rest pieced together by herself. As in several of her Psalms, she develops a metaphor from accounting, adding up the sum of her woes. Unlike "The Doleful Lay of Clorinda," Sidney's final elegy for her brother avoids pastoral conventions in order to make a direct statement of her loss and of her determination to honor him by her writing; her tears have "dissolved to ink." The poem is signed, "By the Sister of that Incomparable Sidney," paralleling her self-designation as "Sister of Sir Philip Sidney" in a business letter of 8 July 1603 to Sir Julius Caesar.

As Beth Wynne Fisken has shown, the humility of Sidney's phrasing in "Angel Spirit" partly masks the boldness of her literary initiative. Her literary career was both inspired by her brother and enabled by his death; as his literary heir, she could accomplish things usually restricted to the male prerogative by using (consciously or unconsciously) the traditionally feminine role of grieving relative to create a public persona. Her grief was undoubtedly genuine, but so was her poetic ambition.

"Even Now That Care," Sidney's dedicatory poem intended for presentation to Queen Elizabeth, continues in praise of her brother, presenting his death as a martyrdom for the Protestant cause and reminding Elizabeth that he would not have died if she had favored him as she should have. By using the Protestant code in phrases such as "these most active times" and by comparing the monarch to King David, Sidney was urging the queen to act on behalf of Continental Protestants. The poem may also provide evidence that the countess had worked on the *Psalms* from the beginning, for she says that they originally had two authors but now only one is left. In an apt metaphor, Sidney claims that Sir Philip set up the warp, the structural threads, while she wove the web, or completed the work. Together they have woven a cloth that becomes a "livery robe" for the queen to present as she sees fit.

Her praise of Queen Elizabeth continues in "A Dialogue between Two Shepherds, *Thenot* and *Piers*, in Praise of *Astrea*." Like the *Psalms* manuscript, it was apparently intended for presentation during the queen's visit to one of the Pembroke estates, most likely the visit to Wilton planned for August 1599. Using the familiar form of pastoral dialogue, Mary Sidney adapts the conventions of the encomium, or poem of praise, to question the adequacy of language. Platonic Thenot debates the nature of poetic language with Protestant Piers, who says that one need only tell the truth plainly. Since it is a dialogue, the countess need not be identified with either position, but Piers concludes that only silence is adequate for the queen's praise, an ambiguity that calls into question the genre of the encomium itself.

Sidney would have been particularly anxious to please the queen at this time, since she was seeking a suitable position at court for her eldest son, William, a teenager ready to begin his public career. An obsequious letter written in January 1601 gives the queen even more extravagant praise than "Astrea." Written in Sidney's own hand with unaccustomed neatness, it employs the thickest flattery to recall the queen's kindness in bringing her to court when she was a girl, asks similar favors for her son, and is signed in the extreme lower right corner, the position of most humility.

Sidney had need of the queen's favor. The earl of Pembroke, a man in his late sixties who had long been struggling against serious illness, was drawing near death. William would not come of age until April 1601, leaving the countess, her children, and all the Pembroke property vulnerable to the Court of Wards. Pembroke died on 19 January 1601. Instead of comforting his mother, young William added to her problems when he seduced and abandoned Mary Fitton, one of the queen's maids of honor. By refusing to marry his pregnant mistress, he incurred Elizabeth's fury and blotted a promising career. Although he was finally released from Fleet Prison on grounds that his health was failing, William was not able to obtain a suitable position at court until the queen died and James came to the throne. These events may account for the period of estrangement from his mother indicated by Robert Sidney's correspondence.

Under Queen Elizabeth the countess of Pembroke had held a position of honor and some power; in the opening years of James's reign the widowed dowager countess lost her influence at court. She turned from literary endeavors to administration. Trying to protect the family property in Cardiff from popular uprisings against the seigneurial hold of the Pembrokes, she lodged charges of jewel theft, piracy, and murder against several residents of Cardiff, particularly Edmund Mathew. Mathew was allied to the Herberts by marriage but had turned against them after Pembroke jailed his older brother, William, for piracy. The convoluted cases can be traced through the countess's correspondence and the records of the Star Chamber.

Sidney holding a copy of her translations of the Psalms;
engraving by Simon van de Passe

In 1604 Sidney's son William married Mary Talbot, the daughter of the earl of Shrewsbury; her son Philip married Susan de Vere, the granddaughter of Lord Burghley; and her niece Mary Sidney married Sir Robert Wroth. Arrangements for Anne's marriage were apparently thwarted by a recurring illness, although she had been well enough to participate in Ben Jonson's *Masque of Blackness* in January. The countess took her to Cambridge for the best medical care, but Anne died there, probably in December 1606.

From 1608 to 1614 there is a hiatus in the records of Mary Sidney's life. From 1614 through 1616, however, there are detailed accounts of her journey to the fashionable Continental resort of Spa and her amusements there. By that time her son William had matured into a leader of the anti-Spanish party at court and her son Philip had become one of James's favorites, so Sidney apparently left politics

to them. Her role as literary patron had also been assumed by her sons; only a few writers, such as her old friends Samuel Daniel and Sir John Davies, continued to dedicate works to her. Her religious and political activities of the 1590s were reputedly replaced by amusements that included shooting pistols with the countess of Barlemont, taking tobacco, playing cards, dancing, and flirting with her handsome and learned doctor, Sir Matthew Lister. That romance may be reflected in the courtship of Simena and Lissius in Lady Wroth's pastoral drama *Love's Victory*. Letters attributed to Mary Sidney by John Donne the Younger indicate that she continued to write and to exchange manuscripts with friends, but any such works have been lost.

As a mature woman Sidney also undertook acts of self-definition: after her new daughter-in-law Mary Talbot adopted her signature, "M. Pembroke," Sidney used the usual male signature "Pembroke," distinguished from that of her son by the surrounding "S fermé," or closed *S,* to represent Sidney. She also adapted the Sidney crest of a pheon, or arrowhead, into her own device — two pheons intersecting to form an *M* for Mary and crossed by an *H* for Herbert. She began to use that device to seal her letters and had it carved in a recurring motif (along with the Sidney porcupine and the Dudley bear with ragged staff) on a stone frieze that decorated Houghton House, a home she had designed and built on land granted to her in Bedfordshire by the king. She asserted her role as writer in the portrait engraved by Simon van de Passe, which shows her holding her translation of "David's Psalms."

Sidney's final years seem to have been relatively cheerful. Reconciled with her sons, she presided over local society in Bedfordshire, fiercely protected her property through legal suits, and continued to enjoy the company of Sir Matthew Lister. She also maintained a London home and occasionally took part in court activities, such as the funeral of Queen Anne in 1619, when she visited with friends and relatives, including Lady Wroth and Anne Clifford. As the mother of the earls of Pembroke and Montgomery, she was honored by the king, who visited her at Houghton House in July 1621. In the 1590s she had been praised for her writing and patronage, for her music and her needlework, and for her Protestant piety. In the seventeenth century she became part of the legend of Sir Philip Sidney and was praised both as a writer and for personal qualities: her "virtue, wisdom, learning, dignity," as Aemilia Lanyer wrote. Sidney was usually linked with her brother, as she had desired. John Donne, for example, praised the pair as the Moses and Miriam who "Both told us what, and taught us how to do. . . . They tell us why, and teach us how to sing" in their translation of the Psalms.

Mary Sidney died from smallpox at her home on Aldersgate Street in London on 25 September 1621; she is buried under the choir steps of Salisbury Cathedral with her husband and sons. No contemporary monument survives, but a brass plaque commemorating them was installed by the sixteenth earl of Pembroke in 1963. The most familiar eulogy is that of William Browne, written in hopes of patronage from her son William, praising her as "Sidney's sister, Pembroke's mother." Certainly she played those roles well, but she was also a writer, translator, editor, patron, administrator, and Protestant activist. A woman who used all the resources available to her — her husband's wealth, her own

position as a Sidney, her brother's legendary death — she stretched the boundaries of what was possible for a woman and became a role model for seventeenth-century women writers, including Aemilia Lanyer and Mary Sidney, Lady Wroth.

Although Sidney was renowned in her time, so much so that one seventeenth-century manuscript identifies Sir Philip as "brother to the Countess of Pembroke," her reputation suffered a subsequent decline, reducing her to a mere shadow of her brother. Earlier in this century her part in editing the *Arcadia* was denounced as bowdlerizing; her translation of Garnier and her literary patronage were (despite chronological improbabilities) termed attacks on Shakespeare; and her other works were either dismissed as worthless or attributed to male writers. The process of reevaluating Sidney's patronage and literary works was begun by Frances B. Young in her 1912 biography and continued by scholars such as John Rathmell, Coburn Freer, Gary Waller, Mary Ellen Lamb, Michael G. Brennan, Noel J. Kinnamon, Barbara Kiefer Lewalski, Beth Wynne Fisken, and Susanne Woods. Included in virtually all recent Elizabethan anthologies, Mary Sidney is now recognized as the most important literary woman of her generation, one who helped to open possibilities for other women writers.

Bibliography:

Josephine Roberts, "Recent Studies in Women Writers of Tudor England II: Mary Sidney, Countess of Pembroke," in *Women in the Renaissance,* edited by Kirby Farrell, Elizabeth H. Hageman, and Arthur F. Kinney (Amherst: University of Massachusetts Press, 1988), pp. 265–269.

Biographies:

Frances B. Young, *Mary Sidney, Countess of Pembroke* (London: David Nutt, 1912);

Margaret P. Hannay, *Philip's Phoenix: Mary Sidney, Countess of Pembroke* (New York: Oxford University Press, 1990).

References:

Virginia Walcott Beauchamp, "Sidney's Sister as Translator of Garnier," *Renaissance News,* 10 (Spring 1957): 8–13;

Elaine Beilin, *Redeeming Eve: Women Writers of the English Renaissance* (Princeton: Princeton University Press, 1987), pp. 121–150;

Diane Bornstein, "The Style of the Countess of Pembroke's Translation of Philippe de Mornay's *Discours de la vie et de la mort,*" in *Si-*

lent but for the Word: Tudor Women as Patrons, Translators, and Writers of Religious Works, edited by Margaret P. Hannay (Kent, Ohio: Kent State University Press, 1985), pp. 126–148;

Michael G. Brennan, "The Date of the Countess of Pembroke's Translation of the Psalms," *Review of English Studies,* new series 33 (November 1982): 434–436;

Brennan, "Licensing the Sidney Psalms for the Press in the 1640s," *Notes & Queries,* 229 (September 1984): 304–305;

Brennan, *Literary Patronage in the English Renaissance: The Pembroke Family* (London: Routledge, 1988);

Brennan, "Nicholas Breton's *The Passions of the Spirit* and the Countess of Pembroke," *Review of English Studies,* 38 (May 1987): 221–227;

John Briley, "Mary Sidney – A 20th-Century Reappraisal," in *Elizabethan and Modern Studies Presented to Professor Willem Schrickx,* edited by J. P. Vander Motten (Ghent: Seminarie voor Engelse en Amerikaanse Literatuur, 1985), pp. 47–56;

John Buxton, *Sir Philip Sidney and the English Renaissance* (London: Macmillan, 1954), pp. 173–204;

T. S. Eliot, "Apology for the Countess of Pembroke," in his *The Use of Poetry and the Use of Criticism* (London: Faber & Faber, 1933), pp. 37–52;

Mary C. Erler, "Davies's *Astraea* and Other Contexts of the Countess of Pembroke's 'A Dialogue,'" *Studies in English Literature,* 30 (Winter 1990): 41–61;

Beth Wynne Fisken, "The Art of Sacred Parody in Mary Sidney's *Psalmes,*" *Tulsa Studies in Women's Literature,* 8 (Fall 1989): 223–239;

Fisken, "Mary Sidney's *Psalmes*: Education and Wisdom," in *Silent but for the Word: Tudor Women as Patrons, Translators, and Writers of Religious Works,* edited by Hannay (Kent, Ohio: Kent State University Press, 1985), pp. 166–183;

Fisken, "'To the Angell Spirit . . .': Mary Sidney's Entry into the 'World of Words,'" in *The Renaissance Englishwoman in Print: Counterbalancing the Canon,* edited by Anne M. Haselkorn and Betty S. Travitsky (Amherst: University of Massachusetts Press, 1990), pp. 263–275;

Coburn Freer, "The Countess of Pembroke in a World of Words," *Style,* 5 (1971): 37–56;

Freer, "Mary Sidney, Countess of Pembroke," in *Women Writers of the Renaissance and Reformation,* edited by Katharina A. Wilson (Athens: University of Georgia Press, 1987), pp. 481–521;

Freer, *Music for a King: George Herbert's Style and the Metrical Psalms* (Baltimore: Johns Hopkins University Press, 1972), pp. 89–108;

Margaret P. Hannay, "'Do What Men May Sing': Mary Sidney and the Tradition of Admonitory Dedication," in *Silent but for the Word: Tudor Women as Patrons, Translators, and Writers of Religious Works,* edited by Hannay (Kent, Ohio: Kent State University Press, 1985), pp. 149–165;

Hannay, "Literary Reconstruction: Written Texts and Social Contexts of Aristocratic Englishwomen," in *Attending to Women in the Renaissance,* edited by Travitsky and Adele Seeff (Newark: University of Delaware Press, 1994), pp. 35–63;

Hannay, "'This Moses and This Miriam': The Countess of Pembroke's Role in the Legend of Sir Philip Sidney," in *Sir Philip Sidney's Achievements,* edited by M. J. B. Allen, Dominic Baker-Smith, and Arthur F. Kinney (New York: AMS Press, 1990), pp. 217–226;

Hannay, "'Unlock my lipps': The *Miserere mei Deus* of Anne Vaughan Lok and Mary Sidney Herbert, Countess of Pembroke," in *Privileging Gender in Early Modern England,* edited by John R. Brink (Kirksville, Mo.: Sixteenth-Century Journal Publishers, 1993), pp. 19–36;

Pearl Hogrefe, *Women of Action in Tudor England* (Ames: Iowa State University Press, 1977), pp. 105–135;

Bent Juel-Jensen, "The Tixall Manuscript of Sir Philip Sidney's and the Countess of Pembroke's Paraphrase of the Psalms," *Book Collector,* 18 (Summer 1969): 222–223;

Dennis Kay, *Melodious Tears: The English Funeral Elegy from Spenser to Milton* (Oxford: Oxford University Press, 1990), pp. 58–62;

Noel J. Kinnamon, "A Note on Herbert's 'Easter' and the Sidneian Psalms," *George Herbert Journal,* 1 (1978): 44–48;

Kinnamon, "The Sidney Psalms: The Penshurst and Tixall Manuscripts," *English Manuscript Studies,* 2 (1990): 139–161;

Tina Krontiris, *Oppositional Voices: Women as Writers and Translators of Literature in the English Renaissance* (London: Routledge, 1992), pp. 69–73;

Mary Ellen Lamb, "The Countess of Pembroke and the Art of Dying," in *Women in the Middle Ages and the Renaissance: Literary and Historical Perspectives,* edited by Mary Beth Rose (Syracuse, N.Y.: Syracuse University Press, 1986), pp. 207–226;

Lamb, "The Countess of Pembroke's Patronage," *English Literary Renaissance,* 12 (Spring 1982): 162–179;

Lamb, *Gender and Authorship in the Sidney Circle* (Madison: University of Wisconsin Press, 1990);

Lamb, "The Myth of the Countess of Pembroke: The Dramatic Circle," *Yearbook of English Studies,* 11 (1981): 194–202;

Barbara Kiefer Lewalski, *Protestant Poetics and the Seventeenth-Century Religious Lyric* (Princeton: Princeton University Press, 1979), pp. 241–245, 275–276;

Steven W. May, *The Elizabethan Courtier Poets: The Poems and Their Contexts* (Columbia: University of Missouri Press, 1991);

Josephine A. Roberts, "Huntington Manuscript of Lady Mary Wroth's Play, *Loves Victorie,*" *Huntington Library Quarterly,* 46 (Winter 1983): 156–174;

Jean Robertson, "Drayton and the Countess of Pembroke," *Review of English Studies,* new series 16 (1965): 49;

Kenneth Thorpe Rowe, "The Countess of Pembroke's Editorship of the *Arcadia,*" *PMLA,* 54 (March 1939): 122–138;

Ernest Schanzer, "*Antony and Cleopatra* and the Countess of Pembroke's *Antonius,*" *Notes & Queries,* 201 (April 1956): 152–154;

Louise Schleiner, *Tudor and Stuart Women Writers* (Bloomington: Indiana University Press, 1994);

Richard Todd, "'So Well Atyr'd Abroad': A Background to the Sidney-Pembroke Psalter and Its Implications for the Seventeenth-Century Religious Lyric," *Texas Studies in Literature and Language,* 29 (Spring 1987): 74–93;

Gary Waller, "The Countess of Pembroke and Gendered Reading," in *The Renaissance Englishwoman in Print: Counterbalancing the Canon,* edited by Haselkorn and Travitsky (Amherst: University of Massachusetts Press, 1990), pp. 327–345;

Waller, *Mary Sidney, Countess of Pembroke: A Critical Study of Her Writings and Literary Milieu* (Salzburg: University of Salzburg Press, 1979);

Waller, " 'This Matching of Contraries': Calvinism and Courtly Philosophy in the Sidney Psalms," *English Studies,* 55 (February 1974): 22–31;

Franklin F. Williams Jr., "The Literary Patronesses of Renaissance England," *Notes & Queries,* 207 (October 1962): 364–366;

Alexander Maclaren Witherspoon, *The Influence of Robert Garnier on Elizabethan Drama* (New Haven: Yale University Press, 1924), pp. 84–95, 181–189;

Susanne Woods, *Natural Emphasis: English Versification from Chaucer to Dryden* (San Marino, Cal.: Huntington Library, 1984), pp. 169–175, 290–302;

Rivkah Zim, *English Metrical Psalms: Poetry as Praise and Prayer, 1535–1601* (Cambridge: Cambridge University Press, 1987), pp. 185–210.

Papers:

Mary Sidney's jointure is in the Houghton Library, Harvard University; her correspondence, either holograph or with holograph signature, is held in collections at the British Library; the Lambeth Palace Library; the Robert H. Taylor Collection, Princeton University Library; the Public Records Office, London; the Dudley Papers at Longleat; and the Cecil Papers at Hatfield House. No holograph manuscripts of Mary Sidney's works survive.

Sir Philip Sidney

(30 November 1554 – 17 October 1586)

Marvin Hunt
North Carolina State University

BOOKS: *The Countesse of Pembrokes Arcadia [The New Arcadia]* (London: Printed for William Ponsonby, 1590);

Syr P. S. His Astrophel and Stella. To the End of Which Are Added, Sundry Other Rare Sonnets of Diuers Gentlemen (London: Printed by J. Charlewood for T. Newman, 1591); revised as *Syr P. S. His Astrophel and Stella. Wherein the Excellence of Sweete Poesie Is Concluded* (London: Printed by J. Danter for T. Newman, 1591);

The Countesse of Pembrokes Arcadia. Now Since the First Edition Augmented and Ended [composite version of the *New* and *Old Arcadias*] (London: Printed by J. Windet for William Ponsonby, 1593);

An Apologie for Poetry (London: Printed by J. Roberts for Henry Olney, 1595);

The Defence of Poesie (London: Printed by T. Creede for William Ponsonby, 1595);

The Countesse of Pembrokes Arcadia. Now for the Third Time Published, with Sundry New Additions of the Author (London: Printed by R. Field for William Ponsonby, 1598) – includes *The Lady of May* and *Certain Sonnets*.

Editions and Collections: *The Complete Works of Sir Philip Sidney*, 4 volumes, edited by Albert Feuillerat (Cambridge: Cambridge University Press, 1912–1926);

The Countess of Pembroke's Arcadia [The Old Arcadia], edited by Feuillerat (Cambridge: Cambridge University Press, 1926);

The Poems of Sir Philip Sidney, edited by William A. Ringler Jr. (Oxford: Clarendon Press, 1962);

An Apology for Poetry; or, The Defence of Poetry, edited by Geoffrey Shepherd (London: Thomas Nelson, 1965);

A Defence of Poetry, edited by Jan van Dorsten (Oxford: Oxford University Press, 1966);

The Countess of Pembroke's Arcadia, edited by Maurice Evans (Harmondsworth: Penguin, 1973);

The Countess of Pembroke's Arcadia: The Old Arcadia, edited by Jean Robertson (Oxford: Clarendon Press, 1973);

Miscellaneous Prose of Sir Philip Sidney, edited by Katherine Duncan-Jones and Van Dorsten (Oxford: Clarendon Press, 1973);

The Countess of Pembroke's Arcadia [The New Arcadia], edited by Victor Skretkowicz (Oxford: Clarendon Press, 1987);

Sir Philip Sidney (Selections), edited by Duncan-Jones (Oxford: Oxford University Press, 1989).

TRANSLATION: *The Psalmes of David* (Chiswick: Printed by C. Whittingham for R. Triphook, 1823).

The grandson of the duke of Northumberland and the heir presumptive to the earls of Leicester and Warwick, Sir Philip Sidney was not himself a nobleman. Today he is closely associated in the popular imagination with the court of Elizabeth I, though he spent relatively little time at the English court, and until his appointment as governor of Flushing in 1585 he received little preferment from Elizabeth. Viewed in his own age as the best hope for the establishment of a Protestant League in Europe, he was nevertheless a godson of Philip II of Spain, spent nearly a year in Italy, and sought out the company of such eminent Catholics as the Jesuit martyr Edmund Campion. Widely regarded, in the words of his late editor William A. Ringler Jr., as "the model of perfect courtesy," Sidney was in fact hot-tempered and could be surprisingly impetuous. Considered the epitome of the English gentleman-soldier, he saw little military action before a wound in the left thigh, received on 23 September 1586 during an ill-conceived and insignificant skirmish in the Netherlands outside Zutphen, led to his death on 17 October at Arnhem. Even his literary career bears the stamp of paradox: Sidney did not think of himself as primarily a writer, and surprisingly little of his life was devoted to writing.

Sir Philip Sidney; portrait by an unknown artist (National Portrait Gallery, London)

Philip Sidney, the first child of Sir Henry Sidney and his wife, Mary, née Dudley, was born in 1554 at Penshurst in Kent, "on Friday the last of November, being St. Andrews day, a quarter before five in the morning." Present at the birth were his royal Spanish godfather and his maternal grandmother, whose husband, John Dudley, Duke of Northumberland, and son Guildford had been beheaded in 1553 following the failure of the Northumberland plan to place Guildford's wife, Lady Jane Grey, on the throne.

It was an auspicious beginning to an often fatherless childhood. In 1559 Queen Elizabeth appointed Sir Henry lord president of the Marches of Wales, a post that required him to spend months at a time away from home. As painful as his absence from his family must have been to Sir Henry, his absence from Penshurst could only have compounded his distress. In the 1590 *Arcadia* Sidney recalled in the character Kalander's house the warmth, serviceability, and understated grace of the Sidney home:

The house itself was built of fair and strong stone, not affecting so much any extraordinary kind of fineness, as an honorable representing of firm stateliness; the lights, doors and stairs, rather directed to the use of the guest than to the eye of the artificer, and yet, as the one chiefly heeded, so the other not neglected; each place handsome without curiosity, and homely without loathsomeness, not so dainty as not to be trod on, nor yet slubbered up with good fellowship – all more lasting than beautiful (but that the consideration of the exceeding lastingness made the eye believe it was exceeding beautiful).

The dominance of women in the poet's early life was doubtless formative. Sidney's skill in portraying female characters, from the bewitching, multifarious Stella of *Astrophil and Stella* (1591) to Philoclea and Pamela, the bold, beautiful, and articulate princesses of the *Old Arcadia* (written circa 1581) and the *New Arcadia* (1590; written circa 1583–1584) is, as C. S. Lewis notes in his *English Literature in the Sixteenth Century, Excluding Drama* (1954), without equal before William Shakespeare. The two versions of the *Arcadia,* Sidney's most ambitious works, were written under the guiding spirit and often in the presence of Mary Sidney Herbert, his "dear Lady and sister, the Countess of Pembroke," herself a great patron of writers, to whom the two versions of the *Arcadia* are dedicated. Mary went on to serve as Sidney's literary executor after his death.

Nor can the benevolent influence of Sidney's mother, Lady Mary, be doubted. Lady-in-waiting to the queen, she contracted smallpox in October 1562 while caring for Elizabeth during her bout with the sickness. Her face severely disfigured, Lady Mary thereafter avoided appearing at court. According to Ben Jonson in the *Conversations with Drummond,* when Lady Mary could not avoid appearing in public she wore a mask. Four of Sidney's *Certain Sonnets* (8–11) that lament the damage done to a beautiful face by disease may owe something to his memory of his mother's ordeal. His portrait of the long-suffering Parthenia in the *New Arcadia,* whose lover, Argalus, marries her despite her ruined beauty, clearly echoes his mother's plight and his father's continuing devotion.

On 17 October 1564 Sir Henry enrolled the nine-year-old Philip in Shrewsbury School, the same day that Philip's lifelong friend and biographer, Fulke Greville, First Lord Brooke, was enrolled. Although far from Penshurst, Shrewsbury was a logical choice for Sidney's early education. The town was under Sir Henry's jurisdiction and boasted a fine grammar school under the direction of its headmaster, Thomas Ashton. The rigors of Elizabethan education – in winter students were at their studies from six o'clock in the morning until four-thirty in the afternoon – suited Sidney's precocity and his extraordinary self-discipline. The curriculum was almost entirely in Latin, though modern languages seem to have had some place at Shrewsbury. An account of Philip's expenses at school includes an entry "for two quires of paper, for example books, phrases and sentences in Latin and French." Another account records expenditures for a book of Virgil and a catechism of Calvin, testifying to the school's mix of classical and Puritan values. Philip may even have developed his taste and love for drama by acting in the didactic plays that were a staple of many Elizabethan grammar schools, including the one at Shrewsbury.

At school he demonstrated a remarkable mastery of academic subjects. Greville reports that "even his teachers found something in him to observe, and learn, above that which they had usually read, or taught." Greville may have appraised Sidney's accomplishments fairly accurately. The physician

Thomas Moffet, a friend of the Sidneys and another early biographer of Philip, notes his mastery of grammar, rhetoric, mathematics, Latin, French, and some Greek. But the remarkable trait of Sidney's mind was that he saw the aim of human life to be, as he said of poetry in *The Defence of Poetry* (1595), "well-doing, and not of well-knowing only." Though Moffet comments that Sidney neglected games and sports "for the sake of literary studies," he developed into a handsome young man with a natural grace and considerable athletic prowess. His excellent horsemanship would later make him, despite delicate health, a champion in tiltyards and tournaments. Greville's observation that Philip's "very play tend[ed] to enrich his mind" seems close to the mark. A similar desire to make all experience educational distinguishes the childhood of Pyrocles and Musidorus, the precocious hero-princes of the *Arcadia.*

Twice during his school days at Shrewsbury, Sidney traveled to Oxford for ceremonies over which Queen Elizabeth presided. On the first trip, in August 1566, he resided at Lincoln College and must have enjoyed a privileged view of the queen's activities, as he was in the company of his uncle, Robert Dudley, First Earl of Leicester and chancellor of the university. Sidney's servant, Thomas Marshall, recorded that on the return trip to Shrewsbury, his master gave twelve pence to a blind harper at Chipping Norton – a moment Sidney may have recalled years later in *The Defence of Poetry,* when he reflected on the pleasures of lyric: "I never heard the old song of Percy and Douglas that I found not my heart moved more than with a trumpet; and yet is it sung but by some blind crowder, with no rougher voice than rude style." The second trip to Oxford came early in 1568, just before Sidney completed his studies at Shrewsbury. On that occasion, according to his horoscope, he "delivered an oration before her most serene Highness that was both eloquent and elegant."

Shortly after his 1568 visit Sidney returned to Oxford as a student at Christ Church, where it seems he studied for three years. He soon established a reputation for excellence in public debate. Richard Carew recalls in his *Survey of Cornwall* (1602) an incident when "being a scholar in Oxford of fourteen years age, and three years standing, upon a wrong conceived opinion touching my sufficiency I was . . . called to dispute *ex tempore* (*impar congressus Achilli*) with the matchless Sir Philip Sidney, in presence of the Earls Leicester, Warwick, and other great personages."

Sidney's mother, Lady Mary Dudley

During his Oxford years a marriage was proposed between Philip and Anne Cecil, daughter of Sir William Cecil, that would have linked the Sidneys to one of the most powerful families of the realm. But when Sir William's investigations revealed that the Sidneys were relatively poor, his enthusiasm waned, and relations between the two families cooled. Anne later married Edward de Vere, Seventeenth Earl of Oxford.

Like most men of his rank Sidney left Oxford without taking a degree. After recovering from the plague in the spring of 1572, he may have spent a term at Cambridge. During this time his family was busy with preparations for his first tour of the Continent. A peace treaty between England and France, concluded in April, provided the opportunity. Late the following month he was given permission to travel to Paris as a member of the delegation accompanying Lord High Admiral Edward de Fiennes, Ninth Earl of Lincoln, with a license from Elizabeth for "her trusty and well-beloved Philip Sidney, Esquire, to go out of England into parts beyond the seas" for a period of two years. By her instructions he was to attain

knowledge of foreign languages. Leicester commended his nephew to Elizabeth's ambassador in Paris, Sir Francis Walsingham, who would become Sidney's friend, adviser, and father-in-law. Sidney was not yet eighteen years old.

Such trips were rare among Englishmen of Sidney's day. For him it was to be fateful, contributing deeply to his education and preparing him for a career in the service of the state. Traveling with Griffin Madox, his Welsh servant, and Lodowick Bryskett, a London-born gentleman of Italian parents, Sidney arrived in Paris in early June. There he participated in official ceremonies marking the Treaty of Blois. He and his companions remained in Paris for the summer, where Sidney cultivated the friendship – and earned the admiration – of an extraordinary variety of people, including Walsingham, the rhetorician Peter Ramus, the printer Andrew Wechel, and perhaps even the distinguished Huguenot Hubert Languet, his future mentor, whose friendship he cultivated later in Strasbourg. But Sidney impressed not only Protestant intellectuals. In early August 1572, King Charles IX created him "Baron de Sidenay" –

partly in recognition of his unusual personal appeal and partly in an effort to cultivate powerful English Protestants. Because Elizabeth disliked foreign titles, Sidney did not sign himself "Baron Sidney" in England, though his friends on the Continent regularly addressed him by that title.

This successful summer ended in horror. The marriage in late August of Charles IX's sister Margaret de Valois to the Huguenot King Henry III of Navarre was designed to end a decade of bloodshed between French Catholics and Protestants. Over the summer soberly dressed Huguenots from the provinces and splendidly attired Catholics of King Charles's family and the French nobility had flocked to Paris for the wedding. Rumors swelled that the Huguenots would attempt a coup d'état after the wedding. On the Catholic side, even before the wedding, Henri I de Lorraine, Duke of Guise (with the assent of Catherine de Médicis), had been plotting the assassination of Adm. Gaspard II de Coligny, the most able and powerful of Navarre's advisers.

Sidney witnessed many of the events of the week of 17–23 August 1572: secular and religious wedding ceremonies, important state meetings, and lavish evening entertainments. Festivities ended abruptly on Friday morning, when a sniper's bullet wounded Admiral de Coligny in the arm and finger. The Guise plot had been irrevocably launched. After a day of well-coordinated planning, the Saint Bartholomew's Day Massacre began in earnest just after midnight on Sunday, 23 August. All over Paris, Huguenot men, women, and children were rounded up and killed. The recuperating Coligny was murdered and his body thrown into the street. Peter Ramus was ambushed and butchered; his corpse was hurled from a window; and its entrails were dragged through the city. Languet himself barely escaped a gang of assassins. News of the violence spread beyond the city, and thousands more Protestants were dispatched in Lyons, Orléans, Bordeaux, and other regions.

How much of the slaughter Sidney witnessed in Paris is not known. Perhaps he was among the Englishmen who found refuge with Walsingham at the English embassy outside the city walls. Perhaps he was part of an English group taken to view the mutilated corpse of Coligny. He seems to have been in little danger; there is evidence that influential Catholics were careful to protect their English visitors. Nevertheless, when word of the violence reached England, the queen's council commanded Walsingham to secure Sidney's safe passage back to England. These instructions arrived too late, for Walsingham had already spirited Sidney away to Germany. He never returned to France.

Arriving in Frankfurt via Strasbourg, Sidney had the leisure over the following winter to establish his friendship with the fifty-four-year-old bachelor Hubert Languet, envoy of the elector of Saxony, with whom he was to exchange a voluminous and invaluable correspondence in Latin for more than a decade. The stately and erudite Languet, one of the leading Huguenot figures of Europe, took what now seems a more-than-fatherly interest in Sidney's personal well-being, the development of his scholarship, and the friendships he established on the Continent. He saw in the brilliant young Englishman a potential leader in an effort he himself regarded as essential: to interest England in an alliance for the protection of European Protestants.

After visiting Vienna for several months in 1573, Sidney set out in late August or early September on a brief trip into Hungary that extended into a three-month stay. His experience there is fondly remembered in *The Defence of Poetry* in a passage praising lyric songs: "In Hungary I have seen it the manner at all feasts, and other such meetings, to have the songs of their ancestors' valor, which that right soldierlike nation think one of the chiefest kindlers of brave courage." In his first letter to Sidney, dated September 1573, Languet chided him for not having revealed his plans: "When you left [Vienna] you said that you would not be gone for more than three days. But now, like a little bird that has forced its way through the bars of its cage, your delight makes you restless, flitting hither and yon, perhaps without a thought for your friends."

When Sidney announced his intention to visit Italy, Languet, envisioning an even longer and more dangerous separation from his protégé, could win from him only a promise that he would not visit Rome. Some of this anxiety was quite practical: the more tolerant cities of northern Italy were reasonably safe for Protestant travelers, but this was not the case farther south, where the Inquisition held sway. But Languet's letters reveal his fear that Sidney's youth and tolerant disposition would make him, despite events of the previous summer, susceptible to the persuasion of Catholics.

Because of their reputation for religious and intellectual tolerance, Venice and the university city of Padua were natural destinations for Englishmen who wanted to see Italy. Again traveling with

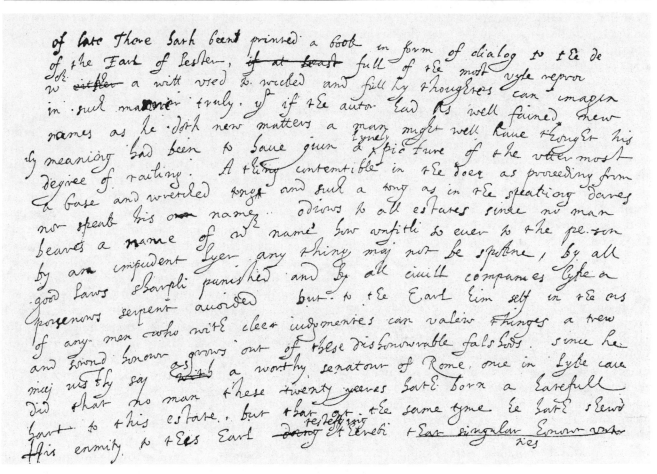

Opening of the manuscript for Sidney's defense of Robert Dudley, Earl of Leicester, written in reply to an anonymous 1584 pamphlet, A Dialogue between a Scholar, a Gentleman, and a Lawyer *(Bernard Quanitch catalogue, number 436, 1930)*

Bryskett and Madox, Sidney reached Venice in early November 1573. He spent most of the following year there and in Padua, with excursions to Genoa and Florence. In letters to Languet from Venice and Padua he recounted meeting his distant cousin Richard Shelley (an ancestor of the Romantic poet Percy Bysshe Shelley and a long-time resident of the city), an erudite man who was, in Sidney's phrase, "sadly addicted to Popery." In Venice he also met a variety of important Europeans.

Sidney immersed himself in Italian culture – so much so that in one letter Languet addressed him as "you Italians," and Walsingham began to be concerned that the young man was wavering in his faith. The philosopher Giordano Bruno, who later traveled to Oxford under Sidney's auspices and dedicated verses to him, recorded that Sidney enjoyed an excellent reputation during this visit. Yet one of Languet's replies to a now-missing letter suggests that Sidney was not overly smitten with Venice's fabled charms, and in a 1578 letter to his brother, Robert, Sidney roundly criticized the "tyrannous oppression" and "counterfeit learning" he observed in Italy, though he admitted to admiring Italian arms and horsemanship.

By February 1574 Sidney was sufficiently prominent in Venice to sit for a portrait (now lost) by the Venetian master Paolo Veronese. Languet seems to have found it indifferently pleasing. There are now extant only two primary likenesses of Sidney, neither painted *ad vivum:* the youthful Longleat portrait, dated 1578, and the Penshurst portrait executed for his brother, Robert, probably in the 1590s.

The renowned university at Padua, to which Sidney repaired in January 1574, provided a focus for his voluminous reading and improved his mastery of languages, particularly Latin. At Languet's suggestion he translated "Cicero into French, then from French into English, and then back into Latin again by an uninterrupted process." But he demurred at Languet's recommendation that he study German: "Of the German language I quite despair, for it has a certain harshness about it." He complained that at his age he had no hope of mastering it, "even so as to understand it." He seems also to have studied astronomy and geometry – the latter because he had "always had the impression that it is closely related to military science." His reading included a vast range of subjects. According to John Buxton, Sidney read works on Venetian government (considered the model of European nations), world history, a book on the Council of Trent, and collections of letters by Paolo Manzio, Bernardo Tasso, Pietro Bembo, and Lorenzo de' Medici – as well as several books on impresa, the emblematic device that he would put to great creative use in his life and writings.

Sidney also read widely in Italian poetry and criticism, which he chose not to mention to Languet. Like many of his contemporaries he held Italian literature in high esteem, and his work was significantly shaped by Italian influences. His reference in *The Defence of Poetry* to Dante's Beatrice (in the *Paradiso* rather than the *Vita nuova*) is the first by an Englishman. Jacopo Sannazaro, twice mentioned as an authority in *The Defence of Poetry,* through his *Arcadia* (1504) contributed to Sidney's understanding of pastoral romance. The valiant hero of Ludovico Ariosto's *Orlando Furioso* (1532), also twice mentioned in the *Defence,* helped shape the characters of Pyrocles and Musidorus in the *Arcadia.* Though he resists the influence of Petrarch and his followers in *Astrophil and Stella,* Sidney's awareness of Petrarchism is everywhere apparent.

In August 1574, after ten months in Italy, Sidney left Venice for Languet's house in Vienna, where he fell seriously ill. Nursed back to health by Languet, he spent the winter of 1574–1575 enjoying the friendship of that city's important men. His most intimate friend at the time was Edward Wotton, whom Walsingham had appointed to a post in Vienna. The friendship would last until Sidney's death. At the beginning of *The Defence of Poetry* he recalls how during his stay in Vienna he and "the right virtuous Edward Wotton" studied horsemanship under the famed John Pietro Pugliano, the Italian maestro of Emperor Maximilian II's stables:

> according to the fertileness of the Italian wit, [Pugliano] did not only afford us the demonstration of his practice, but sought to enrich our minds with the contemplations therein, which he thought most precious. . . . Nay, to so unbelieved a point he proceeded as that no earthly thing bred such wonder to a prince as to be a good

> horseman – skill of government was but a *pedanteria* in comparison. Then would he add certain praises, by telling what a peerless beast the horse was . . . that if I had not been a piece of a logician before I came to him, I think he would have persuaded me to have wished myself a horse.

Beneath the levity of this passage – part of the fun is that in its original Greek the name *Philip* (*phil-hippos*) denotes love of horses – is a tribute to an art that Sidney, like Wotton, practiced to excellence. That he chose to discourse upon the exercise of the "peerless beast" as an introduction to his work about the "peerless poet" may seem peculiar unless the reader realizes how highly he regarded horsemanship as an art of "well-doing" and not of "well-knowing" only. In sonnet 41 of *Astrophil and Stella* Sidney recalls the satisfaction of "Having this day my horse, my hand, my lance / Guided so well that I obtained the prize." In the *Arcadia* he explores the elements of horsemanship in greater detail, portraying the dynamics of control, the unspoken trust and communication between horse and rider, that makes of the two a single composite being.

Instructions from Leicester to hasten his return to England in the spring of 1575 altered Sidney's planned route through Burgundy and Paris. He followed Languet to Prague in early March, then joined Wotton in Dresden; after stops in Strasbourg and Frankfurt the company reached Antwerp at the beginning of May and arrived in England on the last day of the month – almost exactly three years after his departure.

He found his family well, though still mourning the death, in February 1574, of Philip's youngest sister, Ambrosia, at the age of ten. This event had prompted from the queen a letter of uncharacteristically intimate condolence, in view of her usually aloof and ambivalent treatment of the Sidneys. The same letter commanded Philip's sister Mary, not yet fourteen, to court. Sir Henry, who had resigned his post as lord deputy of Ireland in 1571, was happily employed as president of the Marches of Wales, but his wife was seriously depressed through bad health, bereavement, and financial problems.

Philip Sidney had left England "young and raw," in the words of his uncle Leicester; he returned in full manhood, having acquired a vast store of new experience and learning, a network of important Continental friends, and a knowledge of European political affairs that few Englishmen could match. Eager to enter the service of his country, he spent the next eighteen months in England, awaiting assignment. During his first summer at home he and his family witnessed the spectacular entertainments – pageants, speeches, hunts, tilts, games, animal baitings, and more – presented daily to the queen during her three-week visit to Kenilworth, Leicester's estate near Warwick.

Later that summer Sidney saw his father off to Ireland, where – much to Sir Henry's regret – he had been reappointed lord deputy. Neglecting his correspondence with his European friends, Philip spent the autumn and winter in London, where he gave himself over to the pleasures at court; Elizabeth made him her cupbearer. Letters from Languet and other friends on the Continent were addressed to him at Leicester House, and an edition of Ramus's *Commentaries* (1555) was dedicated to him. During this period Sidney enjoyed a deepening friendship with Walter Devereux, First Earl of Essex, Sir Henry's comrade in Ireland. The following summer Sidney accompanied Essex back to Ireland and was reunited with his father.

Essex soon fell victim to a plague of dysentery that swept Ireland, and he died on 22 September 1576 in Dublin. Sidney, who had received a letter summoning him to the earl's bedside, arrived too late. There he found a touching message, written during the earl's last days, in which he left Philip nothing except the wish that "if God do move both their hearts . . . he might match with my daughter." The earl continued, "he is so wise, so virtuous, so goodly; and if he go on in the course that he hath begun, he will be as famous and worthy a gentleman as ever England bred." This daughter, Penelope Devereux, would become the "Stella" of Sidney's *Astrophil and Stella.*

Although Essex's agent, Edward Waterhouse, repeated the hope that Philip and Penelope would marry, it is unlikely that Philip, much less his father or any of his mother's Dudley family, took this proposal seriously at the time. He was a man of twenty-one; Penelope a girl of twelve. Moreover, he longed for a political commission that would allow him to employ the knowledge and skills he had acquired during his three years on the Continent. If Astrophil is naively read as an undeflected representation of Sidney himself, he can be forgiven for his neglect of Penelope, though it is a neglect that he later regretted when she married Lord Robert Rich in 1581. In the second sonnet of *Astrophil and Stella,* Astrophil explains that his love for Stella was the result of a gradual process. In the thirty-third sonnet he blames himself for not hav-

ing taken advantage of opportunity when it presented itself:

> But to myself myself did give the blow,
> While too much wit (forsooth) so troubled me,
> That I respects for both our sakes must show:
> And yet could not by rising Morn foresee
> How fair a day was near, o punished eyes,
> That I had been more foolish or more wise.

When news of the death of Maximilian II of Austria reached England in late October 1576, Sidney seemed to Elizabeth's advisers the logical choice to lead a special embassy to extend her condolences to the emperor's family. Ostensibly, Sidney's mission would be strictly formal; its informal purpose was entirely political. Hard upon this news came the death of the staunch Calvinist Frederick III, elector of the Palatinate. Political uncertainty deepened when Spanish mercenaries in the Low Countries sacked and burned Antwerp as well as other smaller towns. While Sidney and his entourage visited the courts of Europe, he would use his audiences with heads of state to enlist their support for the creation of a Protestant League – a mission that seemed now more urgent and propitious than before.

After two months of preparations, Sidney's instructions were delivered on 7 February 1577, and he left for the Continent at the end of the month. Accompanying him were two experienced statesmen, Sir Henry Lee and Sir Jerome Bowes, among other career diplomats, and his personal friends Greville and Sir Edward Dyer, both of whom figure importantly in Sidney's literary career. At Louvain he charmed the Spanish governor, Don John, who (abetted by a group of English and Scottish exiles) was plotting to overthrow Elizabeth, free Mary, Queen of Scots, and marry her. From Brussels, Sidney's party traveled up the Rhine to Heidelberg, where he greeted Prince John Casimir, and then to Prague, where he accomplished his official mission of extending the queen's condolences to the family of Maximilian II.

In Prague Sidney also visited Edmund Campion, whom he must have known, if only casually, from their days at Oxford. To his tutor in Rome Campion described Sidney, mistakenly, as "a poor wavering soul" who might be amenable to conversion to the Roman Church. It is clear that his interest in Sidney was opportunistic. Yet Campion's words provide no basis for saying, as John Buxton has, that Sidney was cynically "using all his tact and charm to learn from Campion's own

Portrait of Sidney, sometimes attributed to Federico Zucarri (National Portrait Gallery, London)

lips how far conversion had led him on the path of disloyalty." Rather, though Sidney held Campion to be in "a full wrong divinity" – as he said of Orpheus, Amphion, and Homer in *The Defence of Poetry* – he probably admired the gifted and accomplished Jesuit, as many others did. Sidney genuinely sought "the prayers of all good men" and was happy to assist Catholics who would ease the suffering of the poor. The catalogue of the long-dispersed library at Penshurst, recently discovered by Germaine Warkentin, lists an edition of the *Conference in the Tower with Campion* (1581) published shortly after Campion's execution. If in fact this book belonged to Philip Sidney, perhaps he hoped to find in it evidence that Campion had discovered the true religion in the hours before his death.

On the return trip to England Sidney met with William I of Orange and discussed plans for a Protestant League. It is a testament to his growing inter-

national status – which S. K. Heninger Jr. believes was so great as to unsettle Elizabeth herself – that William offered him his daughter's hand in marriage. The promised dowry included the provinces of Holland and Zeeland. Of course, Elizabeth would never have tolerated the marriage of one of her most powerful courtiers to a foreign royal family, no matter how close the interests of England and Orange might be, and the proposal was not advanced.

In Ireland Sidney had witnessed firsthand Sir Henry's vigorous prosecution of the campaign against the Irish rebels. Returned from the Continent in the fall of 1577, he found himself obliged to defend his father's policies. To maintain the English garrison Sir Henry had ordered the imposition of a cess, or land tax, against certain lords living within the Pale. The Irish lords resisted the tax and through their effective spokesman, Thomas Butler, Tenth Earl of Ormonde, argued their case before Elizabeth and the queen's council. Sidney entered the debate with his "Discourse on Irish Affairs," which survives only in a holograph fragment.

To the modern reader Sidney's reasoning seems shockingly brutal, yet the repression he advocates is typical of English attitudes toward the Irish during Elizabeth's reign. He does argue that a tax that exempted no one would ease the suffering of the many, who had traditionally borne the brunt of taxation: "this touches the privileged . . . persons [who] be all the rich men of the Pale, the burden only lying upon the poor, who may groan, for their cry cannot be heard." But this argument seems ingenuous, for further on he advocates a policy of complete subjugation, saying that severe means are more justified in Ireland than lenity. In the end Sir Henry's fortunes in Ireland worsened, and he was recalled as lord deputy in February 1578.

In the years after 1577 Sidney's political career was frustrated by Elizabeth's interest in balancing the power of Spain against that of France, a balance she feared would be upset by the creation of a Protestant League. Thwarted in his political ambition, Sidney turned his attention briefly to exploration, investing in three New World voyages by Martin Frobisher. He also began, perhaps as early as 1578, what soon became an intensive writing career.

Among his first literary projects Sidney experimented with a type of drama that would reach its most sophisticated form in the seventeenth-century court masque. In 1578 or 1579, for the queen's visit to his uncle Leicester's new estate at Wanstead, he wrote the pastoral entertainment known as *The Lady of May*. The only published version, included in a 1598 edition of *Arcadia*, is not a text but rather a detailed transcription of the production, perhaps done at Sidney's request. Ostensibly a tribute to Elizabeth, it is a work of some literary merit and considerable political and propagandistic import.

The Lady of May, a young and beautiful maiden much pursued by country bachelors, faces an emblematic choice of marriage between two men she likes but does not love: the wealthy shepherd Espilus, a man "of very small deserts and no faults," and the pleasing but sometimes violent forester Theron, a man of "many deserts and many faults." The drama combines several elements that were to figure prominently as themes and issues in Sidney's later writings, especially *Astrophil and Stella* and the *Arcadia:* the Petrarchan stance of stylized veneration

of a lady by her lover, the pastoral mode of setting and plot, and some dramatized speculations about the uses and abuses of rhetoric. But like many of his contemporaries, Sidney adapts convention to topicality; and Elizabeth's own unmarried status together with her apparent pleasure at the courtship of François, Duke of Alençon and (after 1576) of Anjou are deeply implicated in this superficially innocuous entertainment. The action was designed to favor Theron the forester over Espilus the shepherd, in whose country blandness Sidney intended to reflect Alençon. But "it pleased her Majesty to judge that Espilus did the better deserve" the Lady of May. Although Sidney left open the way to such a resolution – the final verses of Espilus and Theron allow for either choice – Elizabeth's selection of Espilus over Theron illustrates the degree to which Sidney and his queen saw things differently.

Late in 1579 Sidney made his opposition to Alençon's suit explicit in an open letter to the queen. By that time the issue had focused the divided loyalties of English Protestants and Catholics. The queen had been considering Alençon's proposal of marriage for some time. Her childlessness invited a bitter struggle over succession, and many English Protestants feared a Catholic consort. Sidney's faction, which included his father and his powerful uncle Leicester, believed that a French marriage might lead to civil war.

To the modern reader this letter, "Written . . . to Queen Elizabeth, Touching Her Marriage with Monsieur," seems remarkably frank and fearless of the displeasure it might bring. Sidney addresses the queen forthrightly as a courtier whose function it is to advise his monarch. He reminds her that the peace of the land, no less than her own power, depends upon the confidence of her subjects, a confidence likely to be eroded by an unpopular marriage. Although he does not mention Alençon's famed ugliness, as others did, he does rehearse much about her prospective husband that she already knew and did not need to hear from one of her subjects: that Alençon was "a Frenchman, and a papist"; that his mother was the notorious Catherine de Médicis, "the Jezebel of our age" (though he does not directly say that she had engineered the massacre of Huguenots in 1572); that Alençon himself had sacked La Charité and Issoire "with fire and sword"; and that his race was afflicted with congenital "unhealthfulness." Sidney concludes with the warning that "if he do come hither, he must live here in far meaner reputation than his mind will well brook, having no other royalty to countenance him-

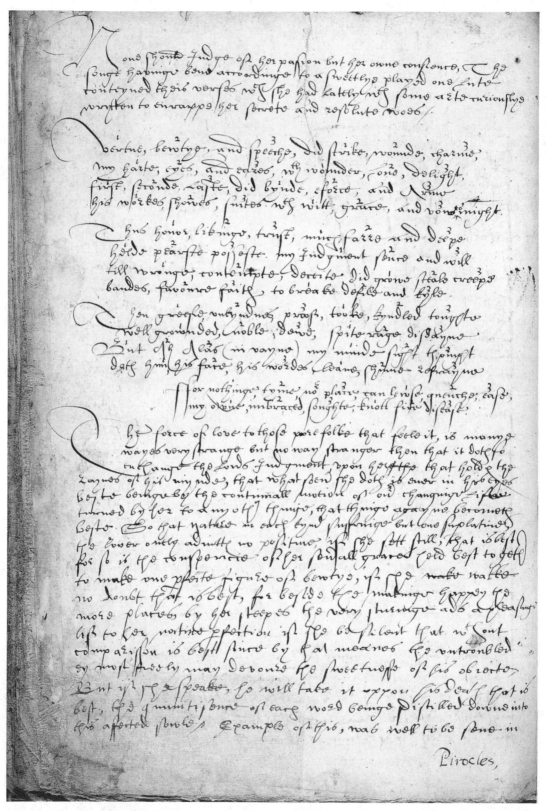

Pages from a manuscript for The Old Arcadia, *transcribed around 1580 in as many as five hands (Henry E. Huntington Library, HM 162; 116v and 154r)*

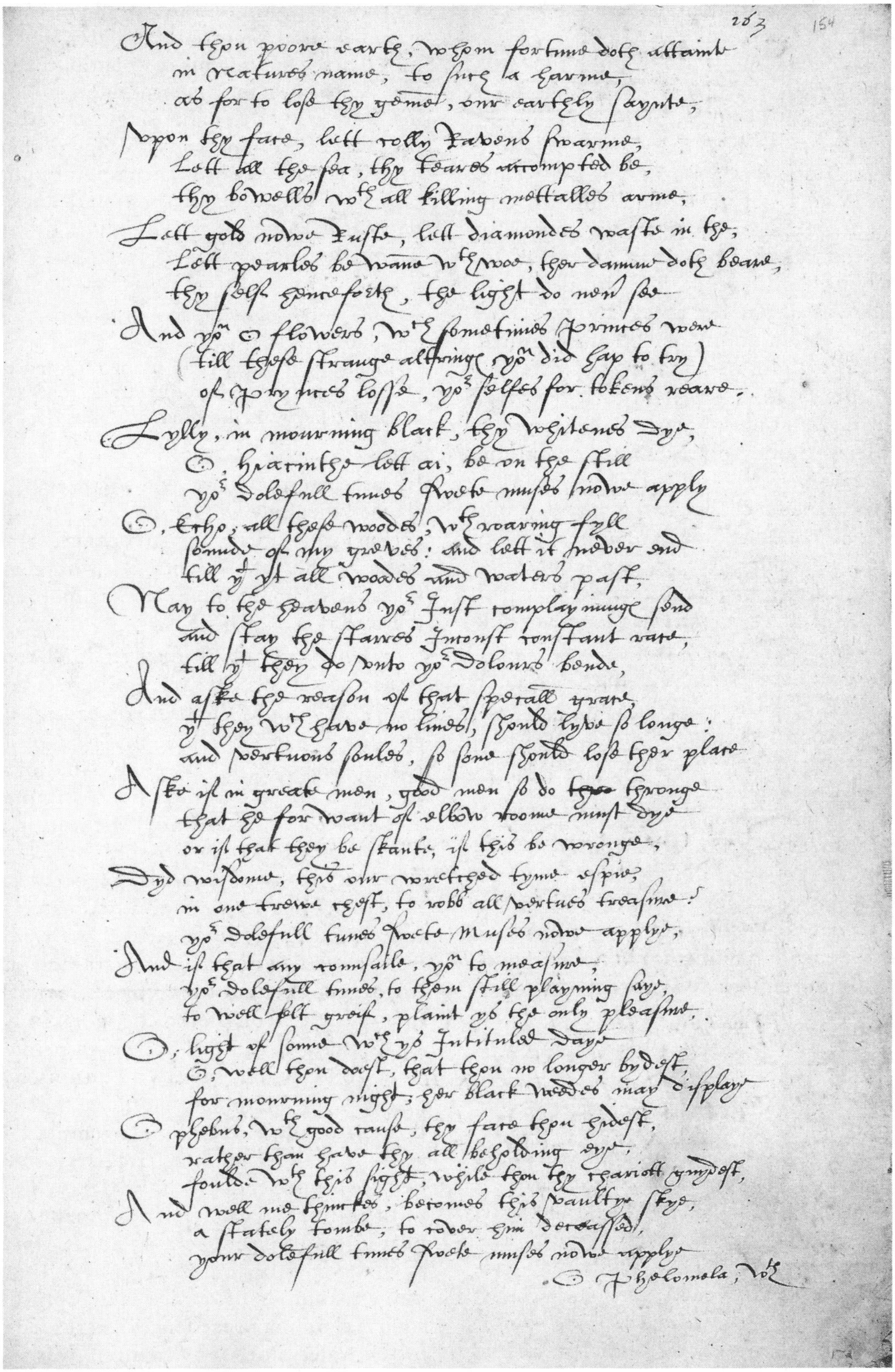

263   154

And thou poore earth, whom fortune doth attainte
in creatures name, to sure a harme,
as for to lose thy gemes, our earthly sayntes,

Upon thy face, lett rotty ravens swarme,
Lett all the sea, thy teares attempted be,
thy bowells with all killing mettalles arme,

Lett gold nowe ruste, lett diamondes waste in thee,
Lett pearles be wanne with woe, they damme doth beare,
thy self same forte, the light do not see

And you o flowers, with sometimes princes were
(till these strange althinge you did hap to try)
of your true losse, your selves for tokens weare.

Lilly, in mourning black, thy whitenes dye,
O, hyacinthe lett ai, be on thee still
your dolefull tunes swete muses nowe apply

O, Echo, all these woodes, with wayving fyll
sounde of my greves: and lett it never end
till that yt all woodes and waters past,

Nay to the heavens your iust complayninge send
and stay the starres inconstant constant race,
till that they do unto your dolours bende,

And aske the reason of that speciall grace,
yt they with have no limbs, should lyve so longe:
and vertuous soules, so sone should lose ther place

Aske if in greate men, good men so do thronge
that he for want of elbow roome must dye
or if that they be skantie, if this be wronge,

Did wisdome, thus our wretched tyme espie,
in one trewe right, to robb all vertues treasure?
your dolefull tunes swete muses nowe apply,

And if that any counsaile, you to measure,
your dolefull tunes, to them still playming says,
to well felt greif, plaint ys the only pleasure.

O, light of sonne with ys Intituled dayes
O well thou doest, that thou no longer bydest,
for mourning night; her black weedes may display

O phoebus, with good cause, thy face thou hidest,
rather than have they all beholding eye,
foule with this sight, while thou thy chariott gydest,

And well me thinkes, becomes this vaultye skye,
a stately tombe, to cover him decreased,
your dolefull tunes swete muses nowe apply

                            O Philomela, ye

self with; or else you must deliver him the keys of your kingdom, and live at his discretion."

There is no evidence that Elizabeth took umbrage at the letter, but it is difficult to imagine that it did anything to smooth the troubled relationship that persisted between the Sidney family and the queen throughout Philip's lifetime. Perhaps Sidney's tone in the letter owes something to a liminal resentment he felt because of her niggardly treatment of his father, who, as president of the Marches of Wales and twice as her lord deputy of Ireland, had been among her ablest subjects. Perhaps too it reflects on an incident that embroiled Sidney's politics with his personal dignity. Greville reports that sometime in 1579 Edward de Vere, Earl of Oxford, a staunch supporter of Alençon's suit, had ordered Sidney off a tennis court in the presence of the French delegation, calling Sidney "a puppy." Sidney issued a challenge the next day, but the queen herself intervened to prevent the duel and reminded him of his inferior status — a rebuke that may have recalled to him as well that de Vere had married Anne Cecil after her father had found the Sidney family unworthy.

Sidney was absent from the court the next year and probably spent much of the time at Wilton, his sister's home, composing the *Old Arcadia.* When he returned to court after a year in seclusion, Sidney presented Elizabeth with a 1581 New Year's gift of a "whip garnished with diamonds," signifying by this astonishing Petrarchan gesture his complete submission to the queen's will in the Alençon affair. That summer his personal fortunes received a blow when the countess of Leicester bore the earl a son, thereby depriving Sidney of both lands and title that he stood to inherit as Leicester's heir presumptive. On the following tilt day, Sidney bore the device *S-P-E-R-A-V-I* ("I hoped"), dashed through.

Around 1578 Sidney had begun writing poetry. It was an "unelected vocation," as he says in *The Defence of Poetry,* "in these my not old years and idlest times having slipped into the title of a poet." None of his works was published before 1590, four years after his death. This fact, together with the brevity and intensity of Sidney's writing career — no more than seven or eight years, during which he worked simultaneously on different texts — only complicates the problem of determining when his works were composed.

Among Sidney's earliest ventures, undertaken with his friends Greville and Dyer, were attempts at writing a new kind of English poetry, grounded not in accentual stress but in duration of syllables. The work was in progress by October 1579, when Edmund Spenser reported it in letters to Gabriel Harvey. These experiments in quantitative verse, examples of which Sidney incorporated into the *Old Arcadia,* were efforts to make English verse conform to the rules of Latin prosody. Although they never exerted a significant influence upon English metrics, they have long interested scholars and critics. The dactylic hexameters of *Old Arcadia* 13 are an example of what Sidney achieved:

> Lady, reserved by the heav'ns to do pastors' company honor
> Joining your sweet voice to the rural muse of a desert,
> Here you fully do find this strange operation of love,
> How to the woods love runs as well as rides to the palace.

In his correspondence with Harvey, Spenser also claimed that Sidney, Greville, and Dyer had formed an English Academy, or Areopagus, to advance the cause of the new metrics, a claim that has been investigated many times and is at present widely doubted.

The years 1579 through 1584 represent the peak of Sidney's literary activity. The winter of 1579–1580 seems the best conjectural date for his composition of *The Defence of Poetry,* probably written in response to Stephen Gosson's *School of Abuse,* which was printed in the summer of 1579 and dedicated to Sidney without permission. The connection with Gosson's work, along with a reference to Spenser's *Shepheardes Calender,* also published in 1579 and dedicated to Sidney, indicate that Sidney began *The Defence of Poetry* in that year, whereas the sustained intensity of his argument would seem to make it equally likely that he completed the work in a relatively short time. It did not appear in print, however, until 1595, which saw two editions by different printers. William Ponsonby, the established printer for the Sidney family, entered *The Defence of Poetry* in the Stationers' Register on 29 November 1594 but seems to have delayed publication until the next year. Before Ponsonby's text appeared, another edition, titled *An Apology for Poetry,* was published by Henry Olney. An unknown number of copies were sold before Ponsonby, claiming precedence, interceded and halted further sales. Ponsonby's edition was then printed and sold, and the title page of his edition was also fixed to some liberated copies of the Olney edition. The Ponsonby text and the De L'Isle manuscript at Penshurst form the basis of Jan van Dorsten and Katherine Duncan-Jones's definitive modern

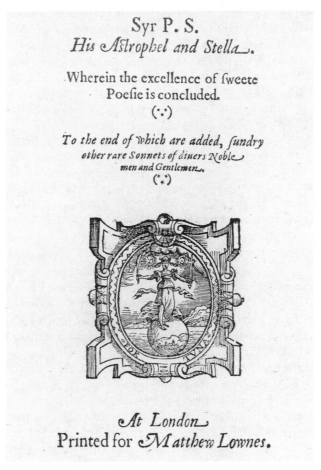

Syr P. S.
His Astrophel and Stella.

Wherein the excellence of sweete
Poesie is concluded.
(∵)

*To the end of which are added, sundry
other rare Sonnets of diuers Noble
men and Gentlemen.*
(∗)

At London
Printed for *Matthew Lownes.*

*Title page for Sidney's popular sonnet sequence, probably written
between 1581 and 1583 but not published until 1591*

edition in *Miscellaneous Prose of Sir Philip Sidney* (1973).

The Defence of Poetry is undoubtedly the most important critical treatise on poetry written by an Englishman during the Elizabethan period. It has achieved the status of a classical text. Although it reflects Sidney's Protestantism, it is nevertheless a worldly work. Drawing on an extraordinary range of classical and continental texts, Sidney sets out to defend "poor poetry" against its attackers and to argue positively that poetry, whose "final end is to lead and draw us to as high a perfection as our degenerate souls, made worse by their clayey lodgings, can be capable of," is the best vehicle for the "purifying of wit." He disposes his argument according to a traditional seven-part classical structure, beginning with an introduction, or exordium, and moving through the stages of proposition, division, examination, and refutation to a final peroration, and including, as custom permitted, a *digressio* on a related issue.

Sidney opens his argument by claiming that poetry gave rise to every other kind and division of learning. For this reason the Romans called the poet *vates,* "which is as much as a diviner, foreseer, or prophet," such as David revealed himself to be in his psalms. With equal reverence the Greeks called the poet a "maker," as do the English (from the Greek verb *poiein,* "to make"). In all cases true poetry makes things "either better than nature bringeth forth, or, quite anew, forms such as never were in nature." Nature's "world is brazen," Sidney argues; only the poets bring forth a golden one.

Sidney next explains that the poet is able to create this heightened fictive world by coupling an idea with an image: "the skill of each artificer standeth in that *idea* or fore-conceit of the work, and not in the work itself. And that the poet hath that *idea* is manifest, by delivering them forth in such excellency as he had imagined them." The union of fore-conceit and image results in a poetic event that has extraordinary "energaic" capacity, that is, the power to move the human will and, thus, to motivate its own reproduction. Xenophon's Cyrus is, then, a poetic creation so forceful that if readers comprehend the character, they will be prompted to reproduce its virtues in their own medium: "so far substantially it worketh, not only to make a Cyrus, which had been but a particular excellency as nature might have done, but to bestow a Cyrus upon the world to make many Cyruses, if [readers] will learn why and how that maker made him." It is the replicability of the poetic image among those who understand why and how it was created that distinguishes poetry from nature. The ongoing replication of poetic images is what enables our "erected wit" to mitigate against the effects of our "infected will."

Sidney concludes this narration by presenting his central proposition, the crucial definition of the process of encoding fore-conceits in images to create poetic constructs: "Poesy therefore is an art of imitation, for so Aristotle termeth it in the word *mimesis* — that is to say, a representing, counterfeiting, or figuring forth — to speak metaphorically, a speaking picture — with this end, to teach and delight." This definition — a tightly composed amalgam of ideas lifted from Aristotle ("mimesis"), Plutarch ("speaking picture"), and Horace ("teach and delight") — with its emphasis upon activity, informs all the theoretical matter of *The Defence of Poetry*.

In the section devoted to the divisions or kinds of mimetic poetry and their practitioners, Sidney conceives three types: divine poets who imitate the "unconceivable excellencies of God," of whom David, Solomon, and pagan poets — Orpheus, Amphion, and Homer, "though in a full wrong divinity" — are cited as examples; poets who imitate "matter philosophical," of which there are four subtypes (moral, natural, astronomical, and historical); and "right poets." Sidney is primarily concerned with the right poets: "these third be they which most properly do imitate to teach and delight, and to imitate borrow nothing of what is, has been, or shall be; but range, only reined with learned discretion, into the divine consideration of what may be and should be." They are arrayed in a hierarchy from "the most notable" heroic poets down to pastoral poets "and certain others, some of these being termed according to the matter they deal with, some by the sorts of verses they liked best to write in." But Sidney is quick to point out that verse is but "an ornament and no cause to poetry." Rather, the "feigning" of "notable images of virtues, vices, or what else,

with that delightful teaching . . . must be the right describing note to know a poet by."

The right poet is then set off against other masters of "earthly learning" who claim to lead men to "virtuous action," an ancient contest developed at length in Aristotle's *Poetics*. The poet's principal competitors are two: the moral philosopher, a figure of "sullen gravity . . . rudely clothed . . . casting largess . . . of definitions, divisions, and distinctions" before him; and the historian, "laden with old mouse-eaten records," who knows more about the past than his own age, who is "a wonder to young folks and a tyrant in table talk." The philosopher maintains that there is no better guide to virtue than he who "teacheth what virtue is; and teach it not only by delivering forth his very being, his causes and effects, but also by making known his enemy, vice, which must be destroyed, and his cumbersome servant, passion, which must be mastered." For his part the historian claims a significant advantage over the philosopher in that he teaches an "active" virtue rather than a "disputative" one. The philosopher delivers virtue "excellent in the dangerless Academy of Plato," but the historian "showeth forth [Virtue's] honorable face in . . . battles." The philosopher "teacheth virtue by certain abstract considerations," adds the historian, "but I only bid you follow the footing of them that have gone before you." Sidney can see no end to this tedious dispute and so interrupts it by noting only "that the one giveth the precept, and the other the example."

The poet, of course, stands "for the highest form in the school of learning" because he is the moderator between the philosopher and the historian. Through the art of mimesis the poet unites in one event the philosopher's precept and the historian's example. Rephrasing his earlier argument on fore-conceit and image, Sidney proclaims that the poet gives "a perfect picture" of something, "so as he coupleth the general notion with the particular example." He then lists exemplary precepts that poets encode in speaking pictures: anger, wisdom, temperance, valor, friendship, remorse, pride, cruelty, and ambition. But the greatest of these is "the most excellent determination of goodness," as in Xenophon's "feigning" of the prince in Cyrus, in Virgil's fashioning of a virtuous man in Aeneas, and in Sir Thomas More's representation of an entire commonwealth in his *Utopia* (1516). The reference to the Catholic More prompts a brief digression in which Sidney states a general tenet of mimesis he has not made before: if the poetic artifact is flawed, the fault lies with the poet, not with poetry. Having made this point, he caps his list by citing the practice of Jesus, who couched his teachings in lively stories.

Because of its forcefulness, the poet's "feigned example" has as much capacity as the "true example" for teaching what is to be shunned or followed. Moreover, Sidney remarks wryly, by reading a representation of, rather than actually duplicating, the strategy of Darius's faithful servant Zopyrus, who severed his own nose and ears to persuade the Babylonians that he was a traitor, "you shall save your nose by the bargain." Conversely, the poet's "moving is of a higher degree than [the philosopher's] teaching," for which he cites as his authority Aristotle's comments on *gnosis* (knowing) and *praxis* (acting, doing) in the *Ethics*.

The poet emerges from this examination transformed from moderator to monarch. "Either accompanied with, or prepared for, the well-enchanting skill of music," poetry has the capacity to transmute even horrors – "cruel battles, unnatural monsters" – into delightful experience. The effects of poetic invention are such that orators and prophets have employed it for their several purposes. Menenius Agrippa, Livy tells us, calmed the mutinous population of Rome not with "figurative speeches or cunning insinuations" but with a tale of the rebellious body attempting to starve the stomach and so hurting itself. Similarly, the prophet Nathan revealed to David a precept "most divinely true" by means of a feigned discourse.

In a second examination section of the *The Defence of Poetry,* Sidney considers the various subgenres in which poetry is arrayed, with a cautionary comment about overly rigid distinctions. At the outset he warns against overdetermining such matters, noting that "some poesies have coupled together two or three kinds, as the tragical and comical, whereupon is risen the tragi-comical." Anticipating the design of his *Arcadia*s, he recommends Jacob Sannazaro and Boethius, who "mingled prose and verse," and others who "mingled matters heroical and pastoral." If severed genres are good, he concludes, "the conjunction cannot be hurtful."

Sidney moves up the hierarchy of genres from the lowest to the highest, discussing pastoral, elegy, comedy, lyric, and epic or heroic, "whose very name (I think) should daunt all backbiters." Characteristically, he reserves his highest praise for the epic, whose champions – Achilles, Cyrus, Aeneas, Turnus, Tydeus, and Rinaldo – "not only teach and move to a truth, but teacheth and moveth to the most high and excellent truth."

Epic is, in short, "the best and most accomplished kind of poetry." He concludes this second examination with a summary of his major points: that poetry deals with universal considerations; that (unlike the historian and the philosopher) the poet is not confined to already delimited parameters of inquiry but brings his own "stuff" to the act of mimesis, so that he "doth not learn a conceit out of a matter, but maketh a matter out for conceit"; that poetry teaches goodness and delight; and that the Scriptures – indeed Christ himself – employed poetry. All this indicates that "the laurel crown appointed for triumphant captains doth worthily (of all other learnings) honor the poet's triumph."

Yet such reasoning is not likely to dissuade the *misomousoi,* the poet haters, who wrongly identify poetry with rhyming and versifying, although, Sidney concedes, poetry often employs verse because "verse far exceedeth prose in the knitting up of memory." But laying this complaint aside, Sidney begins his refutation with the claim that poetry and poets stand accused of four principal crimes: that they divert men from the pursuit of "other more fruitful knowledges"; that poetry "is the mother of lies"; that poetry "is the nurse of abuse, infecting us with many pestilent desires"; and that Plato banished poets from his ideal commonwealth in the *Republic*.

These charges are, of course, made by straw men whom Sidney will easily hew down. The first charge he has already demonstrated to be spurious, since of all learning poetry alone "teacheth and moveth to virtue." "I still and utterly deny," he writes, "that there is sprung out of the earth a more fruitful knowledge." The second charge, that poetry fosters lies, occasions a spirited rebuttal that anticipates several hallmark concepts of structuralist and poststructuralist assumptions about language, such as arbitrariness and difference. The confidence with which he addresses the third charge, that poetry fosters "not only love, but lust, but vanity, but (if they list [please]) scurrility," would seem to belie Astrophil's failed attempt to transmute his desire into spirituality. Nevertheless Sidney maintains that if love poetry leads man astray, one need "not say that poetry abuseth man's wit, but that man's wit abuseth poetry." Moreover, rather than enervating the spirit of warriors, implicit in the charge that it is the nurse of abuse, poetry is often "the companion of camps." Thus, Plutarch recounts, when Alexander went to war he left his teacher Aristotle behind but took Homer with him.

Of the four charges against poets issued by the poet haters, Sidney devotes the most space to refuting the final one, that Plato banned poets from his ideal republic. "But now indeed," he begins, "my burden is great; now Plato's name is laid upon me, whom, I must confess, of all philosophers I have ever esteemed most worthy of reverence," for Plato "is the most poetical." Yet if Plato would "defile the fountain out of which his flowing streams have proceeded," Sidney says, "let us boldly examine with what reasons he did it." He claims that philosophers have made a "school-art" out of the matter poets have conveyed "by a divine delightfulness" and then cast off their guides, "like ungrateful apprentices." Yet as Cicero noted, though many cities rejected philosophers, seven cities wished to claim Homer as a citizen. Simonides and Pindar made of the tyrant Hiero I a just king, while, and again Sidney follows Cicero, Plato was made the slave of Dionysius. For a clinching rhetorical effect Sidney, whose debt to Plato is everywhere apparent in *The Defence of Poetry*, reminds his readers that both Plato (in the *Symposium* and the *Phaedrus*) and Plutarch condoned the "abominable filthiness" of homosexuality.

Having thus exposed in Plato crimes far exceeding those of poets, Sidney rehabilitates his straw man. When he claims that in banning the poet from his republic Plato places the onus "upon the abuse, not upon poetry," one should remember that he began this passage by confessing that Plato was the most poetical of philosophers. Plato's strictures were directed toward practitioners of mimesis rather than mimesis itself: "Plato therefore . . . meant not in general of poets . . . but only meant to drive out those wrong opinions of the Deity (whereof now, without further law, Christianity hath taken away all the hurtful belief . . .) nourished by the then-esteemed poets" – as can be seen in the *Ion,* where Plato "giveth high and rightly divine commendation unto poetry." Indeed Plato, who "attributeth unto poesy more than myself do, namely, to be a very inspiring of a divine force," has been misread: witness Plato's mentor Socrates, who spent his old age turning Aesop's fables into verse, and Plato's student Aristotle, who wrote the *Poetics* – "and why, if it should not be written?" Nor should one forget Plutarch, who in writing philosophy and history "trimmeth both their garments with the guards of poesy."

Following this stirring refutation – actually a set piece with unanticipated ramifications for his own later work – Sidney considers, in a relevant digression, the lamentable condition of poetry in England, directing his criticism, characteristically, at poets rather than poetry. "Sweet poesy," he begins, "that hath anciently [claimed] kings, emperors, senators, great captains" and that had heretofore flourished in Britain, is in "idle England" now little more than flimflam, poets having "almost . . . the good reputation as the mountebanks at Venice." "Base men," he asserts, "with servile wits undertake it . . . as if all the Muses were got with child to bring forth bastard poets." Feigning as burdensome the task of defending poets and their work only to be "overmastered by some thoughts" and thus yielding "an inky tribute to them," he defers authority in the matter of poetry to those who practice it. Restating the hugely problematic conditions of mimesis he had already presented in the Cyrus passage, he concludes that "they that delight in poesy itself should seek to know what they do, and how they do and especially look in the unflattering glass of reason." For poetry must be led gently – or rather it must lead, as it cannot be acquired by human skill. "A poet no industry can make," Sidney claims in a reaffirmation of the poet as *vates*, "if his own genius be not carried into it."

Yet there are English poets who warrant commendation. Sidney is typical of his age in praising Geoffrey Chaucer's *Troilus and Criseyde* (circa 1385) but exceptional in acknowledging that Englishmen of his time had not mastered Chaucerian metrics: "I know not whether to marvel more, either that he in that misty time could see so clearly, or that we in this age go so stumblingly after him." He also approves of the brief tragedies gathered in the *Mirror for Magistrates* (1563) and commends the lyrics of Henry Howard, Earl of Surrey, who regularized the English sonnet form.

None of this material is controversial. However, Sidney's subsequent discussion of *The Shepheardes Calender* raises the question of how well, if at all, Sidney and Spenser were acquainted. He acknowledges that Spenser, who dedicated *The Shepheardes Calender* to him in 1579, "hath much poetry in his eclogues, indeed worthy of reading, if I be not deceived." In his correspondence with Gabriel Harvey, Spenser claimed to have had Sidney "in some use of familiarity." The two poets may have met at Leicester House, where Spenser was employed and where Sidney was a frequent guest at the time. Yet they were of vastly different social rank, Sidney being the earl's nephew and Spenser the earl's secretary. Sidney does not mention Spenser by name in his discussion of *The Shepheardes Calender* in *The Defence of Poetry*. Indeed, after praising its poetry, Sid-

THE

COVNTESSE

OF PEMBROKES

ARCADIA,

WRITTEN BY SIR PHILIPPE
SIDNEI.

LONDON
Printed for William Ponfonbie.
Anno Domini, 1590.

*Title page for the first published version of Sidney's influential
prose romance*

ney criticizes its author for the "framing of his style to an old rustic language." After his death in 1586, Sidney's influence upon Spenser was pervasive. Yet his only comments upon Spenser's work do not suggest the intimacy between them that Spenser claimed to enjoy.

It is noteworthy that Sidney devotes more of his survey of English literature to drama than to poetry. He possessed an instinctive sense of dramatic structure, as *The Lady of May* demonstrates. Readers since Thomas Nashe have been impressed by the dramatic character of *Astrophil and Stella,* and the first version of *Arcadia* is divided into acts. Yet although he offers here the first example of sustained dramatic criticism in English, Sidney's discussion utterly fails to anticipate the maverick forms of English theater that were to explode with such brilliance in the decade after his death. Except for Thomas Sackville and Thomas Norton's *Gorboduc* (1561), the first English tragedy in blank verse,

which he endorses with qualifications, and the tragedies of his friend George Buchanan, Sidney dismisses the rest of English drama he has seen as "observing rules neither of honest civility nor skillful poetry." He criticizes English playwrights for failing to observe the rigid program of unities (time, place, and action), a prescription generally attributed to Aristotle, and he praises ancient exemplars such as Terence (*Eunuchus*), Plautus (*Captivi* and *Amphitruo*), and Euripides (*Hecuba*).

Though he has claimed to see no harm in mixed poetic genres per se, he is especially harsh in his comments on English tragicomedy, which, he remarks, is guilty of promiscuously "mingling kings and clowns" and "hornpipes and funerals." English comedy also fails to make the necessary distinction between delight and laughter, a distinction he develops in considerable detail. He concludes that he has spent too much time on plays because "they are excelling parts of poesy" and because "none [other poetry is] so much used in England, and none can be more pitifully abused."

Just before his peroration Sidney returns to the subject of lyric poetry, "songs and sonnets," which poets should direct toward the Platonic end of "singing the praises of the immortal beauty: the immortal goodness of that God who giveth us hands to write and wits to conceive." In a passage rife with implications for *Astrophil and Stella,* he complains of the wooden language of so many love poets who, "if I were a mistress, would never persuade me they were in love." He attacks pseudo-Ciceronianism at some length, allowing himself to stray "from poetry to oratory." But he finally excuses the slip because it allows him to include penultimately a tribute to the ease, grace, and beauty of the English language, which "for the uttering sweetly and properly [of] the conceits of the mind . . . hath it equally with any other tongue in the world."

Apparently Sidney was serious in his private, concurrent hopes of introducing a quantitative metrics into English poetry, for he writes that of the two methods of versifying, by quantity and stress, "the English, before any vulgar language I know, is fit for both." Of other poetic qualities loosely grouped under the heading of rhyme, he argues that English is superior to other modern languages in its use of the caesura and in its ability to rhyme with masculine, feminine, and medial formations.

The brilliant peroration to *The Defence of Poetry* is a masterly composite of summary, exhortation, and admonition. Every praiseworthy poem is full of "virtue-breeding delightfulness" and possesses all traits of learning; the charges against it are "false or feeble," and bad poetry is produced by "poet-apes, not poets." The English language is "most fit to honor poesy, and to be honored by poesy." Then, in the name of the Nine Muses, Sidney enjoins the reader of his "ink-wasting toy" to believe with Aristotle that poets were the keepers of the Greek divinities; with Pietro Bembo that poets first brought civility to mankind; with Joseph Justus Scaliger that poetry will sooner make an honest man than philosophy; with the German Conrad Clauser that in fables poets communicated "all knowledge, logic, rhetoric, philosophy natural and moral, and *quid non*"; with Sidney himself "that there are many mysteries contained in poetry, which of purpose were written darkly"; and with Cristoforo Landino that poets are so loved by the gods that "whatsoever they write proceeds of a divine fury." Alluding wryly to the often ful-

some tone of dedications and patron-seeking prefaces, he reminds potential defenders of poetry that poets will make them "immortal by their verses," that their names "shall flourish in the printers' shops," and that poets shall make laymen "most fair, most rich, most wise," so that their souls shall dwell with Dante's Beatrice and Virgil's Anchises.

His concluding admonition, directed to anyone who might have "so earth-creeping a mind that it cannot lift itself up to look to the sky of poetry," is a masterpiece of tone, combining the witty with the deadly serious for an audience that knew both the triviality of much fashionable rhetoric and the crucial role of literature and language in resisting the monument-destroying power of mutability and relentless time. As for those who refuse to value poetry, in the name of all poets Sidney offers the malediction that "while you live, [may] you live in love, and never get favor for lacking skill of a sonnet; and when you die, your memory die from the earth for want of an epitaph."

The Defence of Poetry emerges today, in the hindsight of literary history, as a fulcrum in Sidney's career: gathering, organizing, and clarifying the critical energies developed in his early work (such as *The Lady of May* and the experiments in quantitative verse) and discharging these energies into the mature creations of the 1580s, *Astrophil and Stella* and the revised *Arcadia.* Sidney's attractiveness as a critic, like that of John Dryden in a later age, derives partly from his authority as a practicing poet who speaks as much from experience with what works and what does not as from familiarity with abstract notions of art. This is not to say, however, that his later works simply actualize conceptual blueprints from *The Defence of Poetry.* Rather, the mature writings are empirical tests whose results do not always confirm his theory. Indeed the sunny optimism of *The Defence of Poetry,* the blind faith in the ability of mimesis to overcome the obstacles presented by a realistic test of theory, is the first casualty of Sidney's praxis.

Astrophil and Stella provides a case in point. Written probably between 1581 and 1583 and circulated during Sidney's lifetime but not published until 1591, the 108 sonnets and 11 songs of this great sequence are freely experimental in technique and mark, according to William A. Ringler Jr., "an innovation in English poetry and in Sidney's own practice." Sidney employs Italian rather than English rhyme schemes and in six of the songs introduces a trochaic rhythm unknown in English before him. Descended from Dante through Petrarch and his imitators, the sonnet tradition, with its opposition of desire and reason, body and mind, heart and soul, offered the opportunity to experiment with a fictional lover-poet challenged with the task of transmuting physical love into spiritual love through the activity of mimesis. Thus, he might, as Sidney wrote in *The Defence of Poetry,* sing "the praises of immortal beauty," which is synonymous with the goodness of God.

Astrophil is a refracted version of Sidney himself; and, as the poems that pun on the word *rich* make clear (sonnets 24 and 37, for example), Stella is just as certainly a refracted version of Penelope Devereux, who married Lord Rich in 1581. The autobiographical dimensions of *Astrophil and Stella* remain of interest to scholars and critics. Yet it is as literary constructs that the lover and his beloved offer the most rewarding context for investigation. Both Astrophil and Stella are engaged in reading mimetic representations of each other. Stella, Astrophil hopes, will become a reader of his poetry in which his own painful love is written. He sketches this character-as-text metaphor in the opening sonnet:

> Loving in truth, and fain in verse my love to show,
> That the dear She might take some pleasure of my pain:
> Pleasure might cause her read, reading might make her know,
> Knowledge might pity win, and pity grace obtain,
> I sought fit words to paint the blackest face of woe.

This paradigm of persuasion, in which Stella is urged to read representations of Astrophil's suffering, reappears throughout the sequence (for example, sonnets 45, 57, 61, and 93). In sonnet 66 Astrophil observes that "Stella's eyes sent to me the beams of bliss, / Looking on me, while I looked other way." Belief that his woe has elicited Stella's pity fosters the hope celebrated in sonnet 67, which erupts into wild joy with the announcement in sonnet 69 that "Stella hath with words where faith doth shine, / Of her high heart given me the monarchy." He relishes the mere illusion of conquest: "I, I, oh I may say, that she is mine." Forgetting Stella's earlier caveats — that true love is not the slave of desire (61) and that she loves but with "a love not blind" (62) — Astrophil here scarcely pauses over the acknowledgment that Stella gives her heart "conditionally."

Astrophil is thus poised for a fall. The condition that Stella attaches to her love precludes expression of physical desire and points up the

misguided nature of Astrophil's attempt to persuade her to read him. Properly construed, the character-as-text metaphor, a metaphor dictated by the terms of mimesis presented in *The Defence of Poetry,* requires that Stella rather than Astrophil stand as the text to be read. Though he is blinded by desire, this necessity is not lost on Astrophil. In sonnet 71, at the structural center of the work, he reverses the paradigm, construing himself as the reader of Stella and so begins an ascent toward the "immortal beauty" that is synonymous with the "immortal goodness of God":

> Who will in fairest book of Nature know
> How Virtue may best lodged in beauty be,
> Let him but learn of Love to read in thee,
> Stella, those fair lines, which true goodness show.

Perceived as a representation of virtue, Stella's beauty has the capacity to rid Astrophil of tormenting desire that threatens to trap him in images of the flesh rather than free him in the reality of the spirit:

> There shall he find all vices' overthrow,
> Not by rude force, but sweetest sovereignty
> Of reason, from whose light those night-birds fly;
> That inward sun in thine eyes shineth so.

As Sidney repeatedly emphasizes in *The Defence of Poetry,* abstract knowledge is not the ultimate goal of mimesis but only an intermediate, preparatory condition that must yield action. Mimetic and didactic impulses properly complement each other when the literary creation serves to alter and improve the personality of the person exposed to it — in this case exposed both as reader and as author. Spenser discusses this in his letter to Sir Walter Ralegh affixed to *The Faerie Queene* of 1590, when he implies that a central purpose of the poem is to fashion its reader as well as its characters in "gentle and virtuous discipline." Thus, Sidney continues:

> And not content to be Perfection's heir
> Thyself, dost strive all minds that way to move,
> Who mark in thee what is in thee most fair.
> So while thy beauty draws the heart to love,
> As fast thy Virtue draws that love to good.

This is theory, however, not practice — the way things should be, not the way they are. In a single assertion of unconquerable appetite, the wrenching reversal of the ultimate line — "'But ah,' Desire still cries, 'give me some food'" — collapses the elegant ascent of the previous thirteen lines. Alimentary,

Sidney's funeral procession, 16 February 1587

gustatory, and instinctive, Desire devours Theory in sonnet 71 and so presages the stolen kiss of the Second Song, when Astrophil's failure to love properly, which is a precondition of mimetic poetry, becomes manifest.

Although readers as varied as Thomas Nashe in the sixteenth century and William A. Ringler Jr. and Alan Hager in the twentieth have detected a tragic design in *Astrophil and Stella,* such a view represents only a partial consensus of critical thought. There are cogent objections to it. For one thing, any tragic interpretation of the sequence assumes, perhaps untenably, that the order of the sonnets and songs is more or less accurate and deliberate, advanced in three more or less distinct stages. There is no evidence, however, that *Astrophil and Stella,* first published a decade after it was composed, presents the poems in Sidney's intended order. Indeed, Thomas Newman's pirated 1591 version of the work — the first to appear in print — grouped the songs together after the poems. Only in the first complete edition (1598) did its songs appear interspersed among its sonnets. Furthermore, none of the extant manuscripts of *Astrophil and Stella* seems to have been made during Sidney's lifetime.

A second weakness of the tragic reading may be that it takes the work too seriously, attributing a high degree of emotional and intellectual coherence to Sidney's persona where such is not the case. Richard A. Lanham denies both a necessary order to the work and, by implication, its tragic seriousness, arguing instead that *Astrophil and Stella* is an example of impure persuasion or applied poetry, wherein Astrophil's single aim is "to bed the girl." Sidney's persona is driven only by sexual frustration, and thus his organization is rhetorical rather than literary or logical. Pointing out that Sidney did not title the work, Lanham argues, as Donald V. Stump has since, that Astrophil is not a coherent character at all — that there really "is no Astrophil except in name." He concludes that the work "is a great poem, but not a philosophical one."

Readings that make only modest structural and intellectual claims for the sequence, while admitting the greatness and virtuosity of its poems, are a persistent strain of critical opinion, most recently taken up by Katherine Duncan-Jones, but by no means do such views represent a true consensus. Other influential studies — by A. C. Hamilton and Thomas P. Roche Jr., for example — trace astonishingly complex structural dynamics in the sequence and make for it claims of great ethical and artistic

acuity. In keeping with current theoretical interests, a growing number of scholar-critics are investigating equally complex political, social, and gender negotiations in *Astrophil and Stella.*

In numbers alone, though, the relationship between Sir Philip Sidney and Astrophil – that is, between history and fiction – is certainly the most fundamental and perennial subject of interest to Sidney scholars. It is a question that is impossible either to answer conclusively or to avoid. Unless unforeseen new documents from 1578 to 1582 bearing upon the relationship between Sidney and Penelope Devereux come to light, which is unlikely, every interpretation of *Astrophil and Stella* must grow from individual, and thus to some degree idiosyncratic, estimations of the Sidney/Astrophil identity.

Among the earliest examples of prose fiction in English, the two substantial versions of the *Arcadia* present an extraordinarily complex textual history. The original or *Old Arcadia* has five books or acts with poetic eclogues following Books 1 through 4. Sidney seems to have worked on this version at intervals from 1577 to 1582 (especially during his retirement at Wilton and Ivy Church from March to August 1580),

composing the work in the presence of his sister – and, Greville reports, at times on horseback.

Probably in 1582 Sidney undertook an extensive revision of the original work, which he broke off in midsentence, midway through Book 3 in 1584, the date of the Cambridge manuscript of the revised or *New Arcadia.* The first version to appear in print was the incomplete *New Arcadia,* titled *The Countess of Pembroke's Arcadia,* in 1590. Three years later appeared a second *Countess of Pembroke's Arcadia,* consisting of a republication of the 1590 version, a lengthy addition to Book 3, and the final two books of the *Old Arcadia.* This composite *Arcadia* of 1593 was the only version of the work read for the next three hundred years. Long suspected to exist, manuscripts of the original *Arcadia* were discovered by Bertram Dobell early in the twentieth century and first published by Albert Feuillerat in his edition of 1912–1926.

Both versions develop the same principal characters in a plot dictated by the terms of an oracle. Sidney models his work upon four Continental sources: the *Ethiopian History* of Heliodorus, a Greek romance of the third century; Jacob Sannazaro's pastoral *Arcadia* (1504); Jorge de Montemayor's

Spanish romance *Diana* (1559?); and a medieval book of chivalry, *Amadis of Gaul* (translated 1540). In the *Old Arcadia* the princes Pyrocles and Musidorus travel to Arcadia, where they fall in love with Philoclea and Pamela, daughters of the Arcadian king, Basilius, and his queen, Gynecia. To gain access to the princesses, Pyrocles and Musidorus disguise themselves as, respectively, a woman and a simple shepherd. The plot is complicated when both Basilius and Gynecia fall in love with Pyrocles, who is posing as an Amazon warrior under a nom de guerre (Cleophila in the *Old Arcadia,* Zelmane in the *New Arcadia*). Pyrocles pursues Philoclea while Basilius and Gynecia pursue him. Confusion reaches a crisis when Basilius is mistakenly given a sleeping potion. The plot to wed Philoclea and Pamela is discovered, and the princes are implicated in the apparent murder of the sleeping king. The judge at their trial is Euarchus, father of Musidorus and uncle to Pyrocles. Just before Euarchus delivers his verdict, the princes' true identities are revealed, and Euarchus faces the heavy responsibility of condemning his son and nephew to death. Basilius miraculously rises from his slumber, however, and the princes are absolved. Contrite, the king confesses his role in the plot and gives his daughters in marriage to Pyrocles and Musidorus. In a finale characteristic of pastoral romance, the *Old Arcadia* closes with the reconciliation of Basilius and Gynecia and the anticipated double wedding of their daughters and the princes.

In their thematic relations to the narrative as well as their remarkable variety and technical virtuosity, the four eclogues of the *Old Arcadia,* comprising twenty-seven poems in all, are of great interest. As textual boundaries demarcating the five prose books or "acts," the eclogues provide an alternative pastoral ethos in verse against which the reader interprets the dominant, often dialectically posed, romantic and ethical problems treated in the prose narrative. The stuff of the eclogues is drawn from the pastoral tradition from Theocritus through Sannazaro, the principal source for Sidney's original *Arcadia,* and beyond: the merits of public versus private experience, of the active versus contemplative life, of youth versus age, of reason versus desire. Because it is the most fundamental and sustained problem that Pyrocles and Musidorus confront in the prose narrative, the contest between reason and desire dominates all other matters of the eclogues, as the princes and the company of shepherds search, through poetic dialogue, for a way of living that, according to Rob-

ert E. Stillman, "merges the emphasis upon contentment in the Italianate [pastoral] tradition with the ethical concern of the Christian bucolic." In this concern with the ethics of contentment it is significant that, in the tradition of Virgil's Tityrus, Sannazaro's Sincero, and Spenser's Colin Clout, Sidney includes a version of himself in the eclogues as the love-stricken Philisides, the only shepherd to have poems in all four eclogues, whom Love has transformed into "Ruin's relique, care's web, and sorrow's food."

The extraordinary variety of poetic forms present in the eclogues mirrors the astonishing complexity and inclusiveness with which the *Old Arcadia* treats human problems associated with pastoralism. The eclogues contain thirteen of Sidney's experiments in quantitative verse – the prosodic rules for which appear in the marginalia of an *Old Arcadia* manuscript – and amply illustrate his mastery of an impressive range of poetic kinds. There are, for example, song contests, an emblematic poem, a love complaint, an echo poem, anacreonic verse, the first epithalamium in English, a versified beast fable, sestinas, and formal pastoral elegy. It is clear that Sidney meant to include eclogues in his revised version of the *Arcadia,* though when he abandoned that project in 1584 he left only the scantest indication of which poems he might have included and how the eclogues would have functioned vis-à-vis his new and vastly altered prose narrative.

More than twice as long, the unfinished *New Arcadia* covers less than half of the original plot. It contains substantial blocks of narrative transferred outright from the first two books of the old version, yet introduces entirely new adventures for the princes, with and against many new characters. Sidney also shifts the emphasis significantly: from pastoral romance to epic; from the influence of Sannazaro to that of Heliodorus and Montemayor. He opens his revision in medias res, disrupting the straightforward narrative of the original with many digressive episodes, and places a new emphasis upon the political dimension of represented experience. Nearly eliminating the role of his signature character, Philisides, Sidney moreover shifts the narrative from first-person to third-person point of view. Accompanying this shift in point of view is a dramatic increase in stylistic complexity and artificiality. Although the governing oracle, which remains essentially unchanged, implies that Sidney would have concluded the new version in basically the same fashion as the old, the *New Arcadia* is altogether a more ambitious work. As such, it offers complex implications for the theoretical program laid out in *The Defence of Poetry.*

Until recently, critics and scholars found the two versions of *Arcadia* of less interest than *Astrophil and Stella,* which has always been highly appreciated, yet among Sidney's contemporaries the *Arcadia* was remarkably influential. Puritans denounced its eroticism, but even in its cobbled-together composite form the work nevertheless quickly achieved the status of a manual of decorum and high sentiment. Abraham Fraunce pilfered from it many of the examples for his important *Arcadian Rhetoric* (1588), and many imitations, sequels, and expansions appeared through the middle of the next century. Ben Jonson mentioned the *Arcadia* in his *Every Man out of His Humor* (1600); William Shakespeare took the Gloucester subplot of *King Lear* (circa 1606) from it; and it provided the material for *Mucedorus* (1598), the most popular play of the age. In the seventeenth century the *Arcadia* was translated into French, Dutch, Italian, and German. Sidney, of course, did not live long enough to enjoy this success. In fact, except for a translation, or metaphrase, of forty-three of the Psalms, undertaken with his sister in 1584 or 1585, his writing career ended with the incomplete revision of the *Arcadia.*

Sidney's public career resumed in July 1585, when he was made master of the ordnance. In September he attempted to join the Sir Francis Drake expedition at Plymouth but was called back by the queen. In November 1585 Elizabeth compensated him with the governorship of Flushing, where, under his uncle Leicester, he served as second-in-command of the English expeditionary forces in the Low Countries. The brief remainder of Sidney's life was marked by struggle, loss, disaster, and death. Greatly respected by the Dutch, he maintained the Flushing garrison admirably but with much difficulty. Elizabeth, employing the same penurious strategy she had used with his father in Ireland, kept the garrison's finances at a barely minimal level. To add to Sidney's trials, his father died in the following May and his mother in August.

On 23 September 1586 Sidney participated with his uncle in an ill-advised ambush of Spanish troops near Zutphen; entering the skirmish without leg armor, he was fatally wounded in the thigh. Greville, who was not present, reported that as he was coming from the field Sidney offered his water bottle to a dying soldier with the words, "Thy necessity is yet greater than mine." He was removed from Zutphen to Arnhem, where he was joined by his wife, Frances (née Walsingham, whom he had married only the year before), his brother, other friends, and surgeons. For some days he seemed to recover. On 30 September he was sufficiently well to compose a will of several thousand words, so excessively generous that it would bankrupt his father-in-law and delay his burial for five months. The wound became septic, and Sidney's condition deteriorated rapidly. He died on 17 October. The physician George Gifford, a dubious source, reports that in his last hours Sidney spoke of Penelope Devereux, Lady Rich.

The legend of Sir Philip Sidney as the model of the Renaissance chivalric knight was conceived even before his writings appeared in print. After months of public mourning, his body was accorded what was tantamount to a state funeral on 17 February 1587. The procession was led by thirty-two poor people, signifying Sidney's thirty-two years, followed by his household, then two riderless horses, and the bier, carried by Thomas Dudley, Dyer, Greville, and Wotton. Then on horseback came high noblemen – Leicester, Huntingdon, Pembroke, and Essex – and a contingency of Dutch officials. The lord mayor and the aldermen, sheriffs, and civic guard of London closed the somber march up Ludgate Hill to the burial site in St. Paul's Cathedral.

Cherished to overripeness by nostalgic Victorians, the idealized portrait of Sidney the gentleman-warrior, a fulfillment of mythic aspirations, continued to obscure his merits as a poet and theorist well into the twentieth century. Like many legends, Sidney's betrays evidence of having been concocted at its origin. His sumptuous funeral followed by less than ten days the execution of Mary, Queen of Scots, and thus served to distract attention from that problematic event. Four years later, when the earl of Essex (the son of Philip's old friend), who had married Sidney's widow, appeared at the Ascension Day tilt carrying Sidney's best sword, the myth of Philisides the Shepherd Knight was being actively exploited. Jonson, who denies Sidney's fabled good looks in the *Conversations with Drummond* (1619), attempts to correct the legend, as does the seventeenth-century biographer John Aubrey, who claims that Sidney had died because he would not forgo sexual relations with his wife after being wounded. But counterlegend made little impact on a life destined for emblematic status. Only in the last half-century, as the armor of myth has been stripped away, has the more authentic and compelling figure emerged.

Letters:

The Correspondence of Sir Philip Sidney and Hubert Languet, translated and edited by Steuart A. Pears (London: W. Pickering, 1845).

Bibliographies:

William L. Godshalk, "Bibliography of Sidney Studies Since 1935," in *Sir Philip Sidney as a Literary Craftsman,* by Kenneth Orne Myrick (Lincoln: University of Nebraska Press, 1965), pp. 352–358;

Godshalk, "Recent Studies in Sidney, 1945–1969," *English Literary Renaissance,* 2 (Winter 1972): 148–164;

Godshalk and A. J. Colaianne, "Recent Studies in Sidney (1970–1977)," *English Literary Renaissance,* 8 (Spring 1978): 212–233;

Donald V. Stump, Jerome S. Dees, and C. Stuart Hunter, eds., *Sir Philip Sidney: Annotated Bibliography of Texts and Criticism, 1544–1984* (New York: G. K. Hall, 1994).

Biographies:

Fulke Greville, *The Life of Sir Philip Sidney,* edited by Nowell Smith (Oxford: Clarendon Press, 1907);

Thomas Moffet, *Nobilis, or A View of the Life and Death of a Sidney and Lessus Lugubris,* edited by Virgil B. Heltzel and Hoyt H. Hudson (San Marino, Cal.: Huntington Library, 1940);

Frederick S. Boas, *Sir Philip Sidney, Representative Elizabethan: His Life and Writings* (London: Staples, 1955);

James M. Osborn, *Young Philip Sidney 1572–1577,* published for the Elizabethan Club, series 5 (New Haven: Yale University Press, 1972);

A. C. Hamilton, *Sir Philip Sidney: A Study of His Life and Works* (Cambridge: Cambridge University Press, 1977);

John Buxton, *Sir Philip Sidney and the English Renaissance,* second edition (New York: St. Martin's Press, 1987);

Katherine Duncan-Jones, *Sir Philip Sidney: Courtier Poet* (New York & London: Yale University Press, 1991).

References:

Michael J. B. Allen and others, eds., *Sir Philip Sidney's Achievements* (New York: AMS Press, 1990);

John Aubrey, *Brief Lives,* edited by Oliver L. Dick (London: Secker, 1949);

Lorna Challis, "The Use of Oratory in Sidney's *Arcadia,*" *Studies in Philology,* 62 (July 1965): 561–576;

Dorothy Connell, *Sir Philip Sidney: The Maker's Mind* (Oxford: Clarendon Press, 1977);

Walter R. Davis, "A Map of Arcadia: Sidney's Romance in Its Tradition," *Yale Studies in English,* 158 (1965): 1–179;

Jan van Dorsten, Dominic Baker-Smith, and Arthur F. Kinney, eds., *Sir Philip Sidney: 1586 and the Creation of a Legend* (Leiden: Leiden University Press, 1986);

Katherine Duncan-Jones, "Philip Sidney's Toys," *Proceedings of the British Academy,* 66 (1980): 161–178;

Nona Fienberg, "The Emergence of Stella in *Astrophil and Stella,*" *Studies in English Literature 1500–1900,* 25 (Winter 1985): 5–19;

Reavley Gair, "Areopagus," in *The Spenser Encyclopedia,* edited by A. C. Hamilton and others (Toronto: University of Toronto Press, 1990);

John A. Galm, *Sidney's Arcadian Poems* (Salzburg: Institute for English Speech and Literature, 1973);

Stephen Greenblatt, "Sidney's *Arcadia* and the Mixed Mode," *Studies in Philology,* 70 (July 1973): 269–278;

Thelma Greenfield, *The Eye of Judgment: Reading the "New Arcadia"* (Lewisburg, Pa.: Bucknell University Press, 1982);

Alan Hager, *Dazzling Images: The Masks of Sir Philip Sidney* (Newark, N.J.: University of Delaware Press, 1991);

Hamilton, "Sidney's *Arcadia* as Prose Fiction: Its Relation to Its Sources," *English Literary Renaissance,* 2 (Winter 1972): 29–60;

Hamilton, "Sidney's *Astrophil and Stella* as a Sonnet Sequence," *English Literary History (ELH),* 36 (March 1969): 59–87;

S. K. Heninger Jr., *Sidney and Spenser: The Poet as Maker* (University Park: Pennsylvania State University Press, 1989);

Marvin Hunt, "Charactonymic Structures in Sidney's *Arcadias,*" *Studies in English Literature 1500–1900,* 33 (Winter 1993): 1–20;

Hunt, "'Of Lovers' Ruine some sad Tragedie': The *Hamartema* of *Astrophil and Stella,*" *Renaissance Papers* (Durham, N.C.: Southeastern Renaissance Conference, 1989), pp. 51–63;

Dennis Kay, ed., *Sir Philip Sidney: An Anthology of Modern Criticism* (Oxford: Clarendon Press, 1987);

Richard A. Lanham, "*Astrophil and Stella*: Pure and Impure Persuasion," *English Literary Renaissance,* 2 (Winter 1972): 100–115;

Nancy Lindheim, *The Structures of Sidney's "Arcadia"* (Toronto & Buffalo: University of Toronto Press, 1982);

Michael McCanles, *The Text of Sidney's Arcadian World* (Durham, N.C.: Duke University Press, 1989);

Richard C. McCoy, *Sir Philip Sidney: Rebellion in Arcadia* (New Brunswick, N.J.: Rutgers University Press, 1979);

Louis Adrian Montrose, "Celebration and Insinuation: Sir Philip Sidney and the Motives of Elizabethan Courtship," *Renaissance Drama,* new series 8 (1977): 3–35;

Morriss H. Partee, "Anti-Platonism in Sidney's *Defence,*" *English Miscellany,* 22 (1971): 7–29;

Thomas P. Roche Jr., "*Astrophil and Stella*: A Radical Reading," *Spenser Studies,* 3 (1982): 139–191;

James J. Scanlon, "Sidney's *Astrophil and Stella*: 'See what it is to Love' Sensually!," *Studies in English Literature 1500–1900,* 16 (Winter 1976): 65–74;

Alan Sinfield, "Sidney and Astrophil," *Studies in English Literature 1500–1900,* 20 (Winter 1980): 25–41;

Robert E. Stillman, *Sidney's Poetic Justice: "The Old Arcadia," Its Eclogues, and Renaissance Pastoral Traditions* (Lewisburg, Pa.: Bucknell University Press, 1986);

Donald V. Stump, "Sidney's Astrophil, Vanishing," *Renaissance Papers* (Durham, N.C.: Southeastern Renaissance Conference, 1988), pp. 1–13;

Germaine Warkentin, "Sidney's Authors," in *Sir Philip Sidney's Achievements,* edited by Allen and others (New York: AMS Press, 1990), pp. 69–89;

Andrew D. Weiner, *Sir Philip Sidney and the Poetics of Protestantism: A Study of Contexts* (Minneapolis: University of Minnesota Press, 1978).

Papers:

A fragment of Philip Sidney's "Discourse on Irish Affairs" (British Library) and a complete text of "Defence of the Earl of Leicester" (Pierpont Morgan Library, New York) exist in holograph. *Certain Sonnets* 6 (Cologny, Geneva) is the only literary work that survives in Sidney's hand. Copies of the *Old Arcadia* repose at Jesus and Queens Colleges, Oxford; at the Bodleian Library and British Museum; and at the Huntington and Folger Libraries in the United States. Manuscripts of the *New Arcadia* are housed at Cambridge University Library and Penshurst Place; manuscripts of *Astrophil and Stella* are located at the British Museum and the University of Edinburgh. A manuscript of *The Defence of Poetry* is part of the De L'Isle Collection at Penshurst Place; another is held by the Norwich Records Office.

Robert Southwell

(1561? – 21 February 1595)

F. W. Brownlow
Mount Holyoke College

BOOKS: *An Epistle of Comfort, to the Reuerend Priestes, & to the Laye Sort Restrayned in Durance* (London: Secretly printed, 1587);

Marie Magdalens Funeral Teares (London: Printed by John Wolfe for Gabriel Cawood, 1591);

Saint Peters Complaint, with Other Poemes (London: Printed by John Windet for John Wolfe, 1595);

Moeoniae. Or, Certaine Excellent Poems and Spirituall Hymnes: Omitted in the Last Impression of Peters Complaint (London: Printed by Valentine Sims for John Busbie, 1595);

The Triumphs over Death: or, a Consolatorie Epistle (London: Printed by Valentine Sims for John Busbie, 1595);

A Short Rule of Good Life. Newly Set Forth According to the Authours Direction before His Death (London?: Secretly printed, 1596–1597?) – includes "An Epistle of a Religious Priest Vnto His Father";

An Humble Supplication to Her Maiestie (London: Secretly printed, 1595 [i.e., 1600]).

Editions: *The Complete Poems of Robert Southwell,* edited by Alexander B. Grosart (London: Printed for private circulation by Robson & Sons, 1872);

The Triumphs over Death, edited by J. W. Trotman (London: Manresa Press, 1914);

Spiritual Exercises and Devotions, edited by J.-M. De Buck and translated by P. E. Hallett (London: Sheed & Ward, 1931);

An Humble Supplication to Her Majestie, edited by R. C. Bald (Cambridge: Cambridge University Press, 1953);

An Epistle of Comfort, edited by Margaret Waugh (Chicago: Loyola University Press, 1965);

The Poems of Robert Southwell, edited by James H. McDonald and Nancy Pollard Brown (Oxford: Clarendon Press, 1967);

Two Letters and Short Rules of a Good Life, edited by Brown (Charlottesville: University Press of Virginia, for the Folger Shakespeare Library, 1973).

Robert Southwell, a poet and prose writer of William Shakespeare and Ben Jonson's generation, spent his adolescence and early manhood in Italy. His brief literary career flourished during the years when he was an underground Jesuit priest in Protestant England. It is agreed that Southwell brought with him from Italy the themes and the aesthetics of militant Counter-Reformation piety, although there is disagreement over the terms used to describe the resulting style: *baroque, mannerist, metaphysical, meditative, Petrarchan,* and *contemplative* are among the adjectives proposed. There is also disagreement over Southwell's literary achievement and the extent and significance of his influence. What cannot be doubted is his extraordinary popularity during his brief English career and the forty years following it. Contemporary writers seem to have been impressed by his clear, precise English, by the beauty of its rhythms, and by Southwell's gift for combining passion with moral and intellectual analysis. There is a strong case to be made for his influence on his contemporaries, among them Thomas Nashe, Thomas Lodge, and Shakespeare.

Robert Southwell was born around 1561 at Horsham St. Faith, Norfolk, the youngest son and fifth child in a family of eight. The Southwells, a county family that had prospered from the dissolution of the monasteries, formed part of a network of wealthy, interrelated families that included the Wriothsleys, Howards, Bacons, and Cecils as well as recusants such as Vaux, Arden, and Copley. Southwell was a studious boy whose father liked to call him "Father Robert." In 1576 Southwell, like many other boys of his class, was sent overseas to be educated in the Jesuit school at Douai. He would not see England again for ten years. Between the ages of fifteen and seventeen he became convinced of his vocation to a religious life, and in 1578 he was admitted to the noviceship at Rome, where he embarked upon his formation as a Jesuit. In 1581 he transferred from the Roman to the English College, where he became tutor and

Robert Southwell; a Roman engraving alluding to his martyrdom

prefect of studies. He was ordained in 1584 and was sent on the English mission in 1586, landing secretly with his fellow Jesuit Henry Garnet somewhere between Dover and Folkestone in early July. He was about twenty-five years old.

Christopher Devlin estimated a Catholic priest's chance of survival in England in 1586 as one in three. Southwell led the active but disguised and secret life of a pastor for six years, working mostly in and around London except for some journeys into the Midlands. For much of this period he lived under the protection of Anne, countess of Arundel, whose husband, the earl, was a prisoner in the Tower of London. In June 1592 the notorious priest hunter Richard Topcliffe succeeded in capturing Southwell. Topcliffe, Elizabeth I's servant and favorite, "an atrocious psychopath," in Geoffrey Hill's words, was allowed to torture prisoners in his own house. Southwell was in this man's hands and then in the hands of Privy Council interrogators and torturers for a month; news of his transfer to solitary confinement in the Tower was a relief to his friends.

After more than two years' imprisonment he was moved to the notorious cell in Newgate called Limbo, and his trial took place on 20 February 1595 under the statute of 1585, which had made it treason to be a Catholic priest and administer the sacraments in England. He was found guilty and was executed the next day by hanging, drawing, and quartering. At his trial Southwell said that he had been tortured ten times and would rather have endured ten executions. Pierre Janelle, who quotes the records in detail, writes that Southwell made of his trial and execution "a work of art of supreme beauty." He was thirty-three at his death. Pope Paul VI canonized him on 25 October 1970 as one of the Forty Martyrs of England and Wales.

Southwell wrote most of his English works between the time of his return to England in 1586 and his capture in 1592. As a prisoner he had no access to writing materials. Janelle described his literary career as an "apostolate of letters" and thought that his superiors had instructed him to make writing a part of his missionary activity. This theory was perhaps based on the fact that Southwell and Garnet carried in their instructions permission to print "some small books for the defense of the faith and the edification of Catholics." Other critics have treated Southwell's work as versified doctrine, as religious propaganda, as a substitute for preaching, or as the outcome of his Jesuit training in religious faith and discipline by means of the *Spiritual Exercises* of Saint Ignatius of Loyola. Southwell states in the prefatory material to *Mary Magdalen's Funeral Tears* (1591) and to *Saint Peter's Complaint* (1595) that he wished to set an example of writing on religious themes in English, but nowhere does he say how or why he began to write.

His earliest works, dating from his Roman years, are Latin poems preserved at Stonyhurst. Brian Oxley has shown that these youthful poems share the mature Southwell's habits of thought as well as the verbal artistry found in his English work: "Southwell's sense of the artifice of holy things, and indeed, of the holiness of artifice, is central to his life and work." The Latin poems are evidence of a strong, probably irresistible vocation as a writer and poet.

Southwell's first full-length English work was the prose *An Epistle of Comfort* (1587), which originated as a series of pastoral letters written to his hostess's husband, the earl of Arundel, imprisoned in the Tower for his religion. Southwell published the book on a secret press supplied by the help of the countess — although it is unlikely that the press was actually in Arundel House, as some authorities suggest. Helen C. White has shown that the *Epistle of Comfort* — a letter written to encourage the persecuted, even to the point of martyrdom — is an example of an ancient Christian genre. It has sixteen chapters, the first eleven devoted to the various sources of comfort for the afflicted Catholics.

Southwell begins modestly and generally, pointing out that suffering is a sign that his readers are out of the devil's power, loved by God, and imitators of Christ. Suffering, he argues, is inseparable from human life and in most cases is no more than the sufferer deserves. Then, at midpoint, he turns to the peculiar situation of the recusants, beginning with the argument that there is comfort in suffering for the Catholic faith. He then presents a series of all-too-real possibilities, starting with general persecution and ascending through imprisonment and vi-

olent death to martyrdom itself. The concluding chapters deal with the unhappiness of the lapsed, the impossibility of martyrdom for the heretic, the glory that awaits the martyr, and, lastly, a warning to the persecutors. The content and the style are much influenced by the patristic authors whom Southwell quotes so deftly; the tone is measured, unyielding, even triumphant. In Southwell's mind, the Catholics' suffering is a direct consequence of the Protestant heresy, and that in turn is a manifestation of the perennial evil of earthly life. To bear its effects is an honor: "Let our adversaries therefore load us with the infamous titles of traitors, and rebels," he writes,

> as the *Arians* did in the persecution of the *Vandals,* and as the *Ethnics* were wont to call Christians *sarmentitios,* and *semasios,* because they were tied to halfpenny stakes, and burnt with shrubs: so let them draw us upon hurdles, hang us, unbowel us alive, mangle us, boil us, and set our quarters upon their gates, to be meat for the birds of the air, as they use to handle rebels: we will answer them as the Christians of former persecutions have done. *Hic est habitus victoriae nostrae, hec palmata vestis, tali curru triumphamus, merito itaque victis non placemus.* Such is the manner of our victory, such our conquerous garment, in such chariots do we triumph. What marvel therefore if our vanquished enemies mislike us?

The second of Southwell's prose works to appear in print was *Mary Magdalen's Funeral Tears.* It had been circulating in manuscript before Gabriel Cawood published it in late 1591 with an author's preface to the reader, and it, too, was written for one of the recusant circle: Dorothy Arundel, the daughter of Sir John Arundel of Lanherne; she later became a Benedictine nun. The work originated in a popular homily, usually attributed to Origen, on Saint John's account of Mary Magdalen's encounter with Christ on Easter morning. Southwell first read this homily in Italy, presumably in Italian and Latin (an Italian version survives in manuscript at Stonyhurst, attributed to Saint Bonaventura). In the Stonyhurst holograph there are fragments of Southwell's attempts at an English translation; they show how difficult he found English composition after speaking Latin and Italian for ten years. The homily was available in England, printed in Latin around 1504 and in English translation in 1565. There are signs that Southwell knew and used this translation. Some writers suggest that he may also have known Valvasone's poem *Le lagrime di S. Maria Maddalena,* but no clear evidence of this influence has been presented.

In Southwell's hands the little homily grows to a work three times as long. It used to be thought that the book originated as a sermon, but this theory was based on ignorance of the source. *Mary Magdalen's Funeral Tears* is a meditation on Mary's experience, cast largely in the form of a dialogue between Mary and the other persons present, the angels in the empty tomb, Christ, and the narrator. The homily provides the outline and some of the contents, but Southwell's tone is different from that of his source, partly owing to the intensity, detail, and accomplishment of his prose but mostly to his conception of the incident as a love story. Southwell's Mary is less the repentant sinner than the lover of Christ; she weeps tears of loss, not remorse. For her, Christ is the sum of all value, and in finding the empty tomb she experiences utter loss. All Mary's thoughts and actions proceed from her love, and as Southwell presents her, she is a heroic woman.

There is also an allegorical tendency in the work, which Southwell found in his source but which he develops according to his own preoccupations. Allegorically speaking, Mary is the Christian soul, separated from the living Christian truth that is her only happiness; more specifically, she is an English Catholic woman, and the violence that threatens her is that of contemporary England. The book has its *longeurs,* but it has passages of great power, among them the remarkable apostrophe on Mary's tears:

> Repentant eyes are the cellars of angels, and penitent tears their sweetest wines, which the savor of life perfumeth, the taste of grace sweeteneth, and the purest colors of returning innocency highly beautifieth. This dew of devotion never falleth, but the sun of justice draweth it up, and upon what face soever it droppeth it maketh it amiable in God's eye.... No, no, the angels must still bathe themselves in the pure streams of thy eyes, and thy face shall still be set with this liquid pearl, that as out of thy tears were stroken the first sparks of thy Lord's love, so thy tears may be the oil, to nourish and feed his flame. Till death dam up the springs, they shall never cease running: and then shall thy soul be ferried in them to the harbor of life, that as by them it was first passed from sin to grace, so in them it may be wafted from grace to glory.

Southwell also develops a real narrative intensity as he works out the logic of Mary's passion. It was his best-known and most influential prose work.

Southwell's next major prose work was *The Triumphs over Death* (1595), an elegy in epistolary form on Lady Margaret Sackville, written in September 1591 and addressed to her brother, Philip Howard, earl of Arundel. *The Triumphs* appears in three of the manuscript copies of Southwell's poems. It was published in late 1595, doubtless from a similar manuscript, by a minor poet called John Trussell, who provided prefatory poems and a dedication to Lady Margaret's children. Trussell describes himself as the work's "foster-sire"; his editorial comments present it as evidence of the quality of Southwell's mind and art and set it in the context of four lives and deaths: the subject's, the recipient's (Arundel died in August 1595), the author's, and the reader's. For its contemporary readers, therefore, *The Triumphs* became Southwell's last statement to death and to his own executioners, and this may be why it appears in the manuscripts with the poems. One sentence sums up its tone of absolute and exalted resignation: "Let God strip you to the skin, yea to the soul, so he stay with you himself."

Southwell's last major prose work, written in late 1591 or early 1592, is probably the most interesting from a historical and personal point of view. *An Humble Supplication* (1600) is a reply to the scurrilous royal proclamation of October 1591, which, besides stigmatizing the Catholic priests as unnatural subjects, baseborn, dissolute, and criminal ruffians, stated to the world that in England Catholics were punished solely for political, not religious, reasons. The *Supplication* is in the form of a petition to the queen, whom it exempts from direct knowledge of her ministers' behavior. It rebuts the proclamation, point by point, and asks for mercy for the Catholic minority on grounds of equity and right. It includes an extremely interesting and well-informed explanation of the Babington Plot as a "sting operation" practiced upon "green wits" by "Master Secretary's subtle and sifting wit," and there is a description of the atrocities suffered by Catholic prisoners in the hands of Elizabeth's legal officers that is a masterpiece of controlled indignation as well as a superb example of the power in controversy of the appeal to fact and reality:

> Divers have been thrown into unsavory and dark dungeons, and brought so near starving, that some for famine have licked the very moisture off the walls; some have so far been consumed that they were hardly recovered to life. What unsufferable agonies we have been put to upon the rack, it is not possible to express, the feeling so far exceedeth all speech. Some with instruments have been rolled up together like a ball, and so crushed that the blood sprouted out at divers parts of their bodies.

Southwell's minor works, *A Short Rule of Good Life* and the "Epistle to His Father" (published 1596–1597?), like the rest of his writings, circulated in manuscript before publication. *A Short Rule* is a small handbook for the layman who wishes to live a devout life. Like all of Southwell's prose, it draws upon the long tradition of Christian literature on its subject; and its style, plain and expository, is beautifully matched to its subject and purpose. Its adaptation to lay life of principles originally developed for conventual life is particularly interesting:

> After prayer, on working days, I must go presently about some work or exercise that may be of some profit, and of all other things take heed of idleness, the mother of all vices. Towards eleven (if company and other more weighty causes will permit) I may meditate a little and call to mind how I have spent the morning, asking God grace to spend the afternoon better.

Southwell's advice on running a household, bringing up children, looking after servants, and spending time wisely places him in the company of contemporaries such as the Calvinist William Perkins. *A Short Rule,* like Perkins's *Government of the Tongue,* is a founding document of Christian social and domestic life in the modern world. It is not surprising that *A Short Rule,* like Robert Persons's *Book of Resolution,* circulated in versions edited for Protestant use.

Unlike his prose, and with the exception of three topical poems (on Mary, Queen of Scots, on Philip Howard's condemnation, and on Lady Margaret Sackville's death), Southwell's poetry cannot be dated any more closely than within the six years of his English pastorate: 1586–1592. To judge from the dedicatory letter, "The Author to His Loving Cousin," Southwell prepared a collection of his short lyrics, but no example of this text exists. What survives are manuscript copies of a collection of fifty-two lyrics put together probably after Southwell's arrest by someone who was, in effect, a literary executor. One of these manuscripts includes a copy of the long poem *Saint Peter's Complaint,* which also exists in a copy made by a Catholic called Mowle. These manuscript copies were prepared by and circulated mostly, but not wholly, among Catholics. The poems became sufficiently well known to become a valuable literary property at the time of Southwell's death; hence the publication in 1595 of two volumes, *Saint Peter's Complaint* and *Moeoniae,* their contents undoubtedly derived from collections made by Catholic copyists but edited to remove os-

tentatiously Catholic material and arranged to suit the publishers.

When Southwell left England in 1576, the best poetry in print was Richard Tottell's *Songs and Sonnets* (1557); the *Mirror for Magistrates;* the work of such minor figures as Barnabe Googe, Thomas Churchyard, and Arthur Golding; and the recently published work of George Gascoigne. *The Paradise of Dainty Devices,* which replaced Tottell's anthology in popularity, appeared in 1576. When Southwell returned in 1586, the situation was different. With Sir Philip Sidney's poetry circulating in manuscript and Edmund Spenser's *The Shepheardes Calender* (1579) in print, the change in poetic style from "drab" to "golden" (C. S. Lewis's well-known terms) was well under way; but although Southwell enjoyed limited contact with English affairs through visitors and students in Rome, it is not surprising that the strongest English influences on his poetry should be Tottell, *The Paradise,* and Gascoigne – the sources of Southwell's English technique, syntax, stanzas, and meter.

On the other hand the strongest intellectual and aesthetic influences on Southwell's work are Continental and professional. *Saint Peter's Complaint,* written in the common six-line Tudor stanza, began as an imitation, even as a translation, of an early form of Luigi Tansillo's *Le Lagrime di San Pietro,* a once-popular exemplar of the literature of penitence and conversion characteristic of Counter-Reformation Italy. Mario Praz also thought that Southwell's "rich and gorgeous" sequence of sacred epigrams on the Blessed Virgin and Christ showed the influence of contemporary Italian poetry. The "professional" influence on Southwell emerges not merely in his continual use of patristic and biblical material in his conceits, but in his conceptions themselves. Many of his most extravagant looking passages, such as the stanza of *Saint Peter's Complaint* beginning "O Bethlehem cisterns, *David's* most desire," are the result of long familiarity with patristic Bible commentary. Some of the stylistic habits that earlier commentators attributed to the influence of Petrarch and John Lyly reflect Southwell's love of writers such as Saint Augustine and his favorite, Saint Bernard, whose works he asked for in the Tower. One last influence he shared with all his literate contemporaries (although, perhaps because of his priestly and academic training, its effect on his writing was unusual for the period): Southwell was a learned classicist who wrote in Latin before he wrote in English. Unlike his contemporaries, however, he did not Latinize his English; instead, he disciplined it to the standards of classical lucidity and precision.

The result of this blend of classical, sacred, secular, domestic, and Continental influences is a style so individual that Lewis, trying to place Southwell historically, asserts in *English Literature in the Sixteenth Century, Excluding Drama* (1954) that "His work sometimes recalls the past, sometimes anticipates the immediate future which he was unconsciously helping to create, and often seems to belong to no period at all."

Southwell's poetry is entirely religious. Like some of his Continental contemporaries, Southwell wished to turn poets' attention from the pagan, classical, often licentious subject matter typical of the period toward religious and moral themes. He explains this intention in four places: in the prefatory matter of *Mary Magdalen's Funeral Tears,* in the prose letter "to his loving cousin" accompanying his own (no longer extant) manuscript of his lyrics, and in the poems "To the Reader" prefacing the short poems and *Saint Peter's Complaint.* "Passions I allow, and loves I approve," he tells the dedicatee of the *Funeral Tears,* "only I would wish that men would alter their object and better their intent."

Such appeals are characteristic, for Southwell always strives to engage his reader in contemplation of the subject of the poem. He is not content simply to announce his intention; he so expresses it that his reader will be struck by its beauty, its charm, and even by its pathos. Joseph D. Scallon relates this aspect of Southwell's technique to the compositional structures of mannerist and baroque art "that draw the viewer into the scene depicted and demand that he share the emotions of the original situation." Louis L. Martz recognizes in Southwell's style the effects of a Jesuit's training in Ignatian meditation, especially that aspect of it called "the composition of place" or, as Ignatius wrote, "seeing in imagination the material place where the object is that we wish to contemplate." Martz demonstrates there are parallels between Ignatius's *Spiritual Exercises* and the structure of some of Southwell's poems. It seems more likely, however, that Ignatian meditation was a manifestation rather than a cause of a development that occurred more or less simultaneously in various fields of European activity. In Southwell's case his training would have systematized tendencies already present in him as a poet and writer.

The constant themes of Southwell's poetry are the absolute beauty and truth revealed in Christ and his mother and a correspondingly absolute necessity that humanity respond to revelation with contrition, repentance, and love. The circumstances of his mission in England, where state power required Catholics to deny their religion, invested his themes with extraordinary pathos and drama. *Saint Peter's Complaint* is about contrition and repentance, as Nancy Pollard Brown argues, but it is also about apostasy and betrayal. The best-known poem, "The Burning Babe," presents, as the prelude to Christmas, a vision of absolute love constant in rejection.

According to the Clarendon Press edition, fifty-seven short poems survive. The most impressive of them to twentieth-century taste is probably "A Vale of Tears," a *paysage moralisé* of the "troubled mind" based on the experience of traveling through the Alps. The Christmas hymns, "New Heaven, New War" and "New Prince, New Pomp," using a simple, ballad style for lofty, complex subject matter, have also been popular in this century. The gnomic poems such as "Times Go by Turns" or "Loss in Delays" are the least sympathetic to modern taste, but they were greatly admired by Southwell's first readers. The one long poem, *Saint Peter's Complaint,* is a complex study of a mind in the process of acknowledging that for almost no reason it has betrayed the person it loves most. The style, like that of Shakespeare's *Rape of Lucrece* (1594) — which it seems to have influenced — is elaborately, even extravagantly conceitist; but the conceits are functional rather than ornamental. They serve to locate the speaker's mind in a universe of reference and sympathetic relationship.

By 1636 nine editions of *Mary Magdalen's Funeral Tears* and fourteen editions of Southwell's poetry had been published in England. The cessation of the stream of editions after 1636 has been attributed to increasing Puritan sentiment; but since Shakespeare's narrative poems ceased publication at the same time, the change in taste signaled by the appearance of John Milton's *Poems* in 1645 is a more likely explanation. In modern times interest in Southwell has been almost wholly confined to his coreligionists, who naturally value his life more than his writings. In 1954 Martz's *Poetry of Meditation* placed Southwell in the mainstream of a meditative tradition in English poetry of the late sixteenth and seventeenth centuries and suggested that he was an important influence on George Herbert. The mainstream then fought back in reviews and articles, culminating in Barbara Kiefer Lewalski's *Protestant Poetics* (1979), which wrote Southwell out of the poetic tradition entirely. Lewis's assessment is more just, if patronizing: "Southwell's work is too small and too little varied for greatness: but it is very choice, very winning, and highly original."

There is no comparable assessment of Southwell's prose as a whole, but Geoffrey Hill's essay "The Absolute Reasonableness of Robert Southwell" (1984) lays down the basis of one. "For Southwell," he writes, " 'force of mind' is manifested in the power to remain unseduced and unterrified." The wonder of Southwell's short career is that he wrote so much and so well in such terrifying circumstances, and especially in the public medium of prose. Threatened with unspeakable violence and frivolity, he wrought in response, in his *Epistle of Comfort, Triumphs over Death,* and *Humble Supplication,* a lucid, reasonable, and humane style that places him among the greatest of English prose writers.

Letters:

"The Letters of Father Robert Southwell," in *Unpublished Documents Relating to the English Martyrs, Catholic Record Society Publications,* volume 5, edited by John Hungerford Pollen, S.J. (London: Catholic Record Society, 1908), pp. 293–333.

Bibliographies:

Peter Beal, "Robert Southwell," in *Index of English Literary Manuscripts,* volume 1, edited by P. J. Croft and others (London: Mansell, 1980), pp. 495–522;

John N. King, "Recent Studies in Southwell," *English Literary Renaissance,* 13 (Spring 1983): 221–227;

Vittorio F. Cavalli, "St. Robert Southwell, S.J.: A Selective Bibliographic Supplement to the Studies of Pierre Janelle and James H. McDonald," *Recusant History,* 21 (1993): 297–304.

Biography:

Christopher Devlin, *The Life of Robert Southwell, Poet and Martyr* (London: Longmans, Green, 1956).

References:

Nancy Pollard Brown, "Paperchase: The Dissemination of Catholic Texts in Elizabethan England," *English Manuscript Studies, 1100–1700,* 1 (1989): 120–143;

Brown, "The Structure of Southwell's 'Saint Peter's Complaint,' " *Modern Language Review,* 61 (January 1966): 3–11;

Peter M. Daly, "Southwell's 'Burning Babe' and the Emblematic Practice," *Wascana Review,* 3, no. 2 (1968): 29–44;

Louise Imogen Guiney, *Recusant Poets, with a Selection from Their Work: St. Thomas More to Ben Jonson* (New York: Sheed & Ward, 1939);

Andrew Harnack, "Robert Southwell's 'The Burning Babe' and the Typology of Christmastide," *Kentucky Philological Association Bulletin,* 4 (1977): 25–30;

Geoffrey Hill, "The Absolute Reasonableness of Robert Southwell," in his *The Lords of Limit: Essays on Literature and Ideas* (New York: Oxford University Press, 1984), pp. 19–37;

Pierre Janelle, *Robert Southwell the Writer: A Study in Religious Inspiration* (New York: Sheed & Ward, 1935);

Barbara Kiefer Lewalski, *Protestant Poetics and the Seventeenth-Century Religious Lyric* (Princeton, N.J.: Princeton University Press, 1979);

Louis L. Martz, *Poetry of Meditation,* revised edition (New Haven: Yale University Press, 1962);

James. H. McDonald, *The Poems and Prose Writings of Robert Southwell: A Bibliographical Study* (Oxford: Roxburghe Club, 1937);

Brian Oxley, "The Relation Between Robert Southwell's Neo-Latin and English Poetry," *Recusant History,* 17 (May 1985): 201–207;

Oxley, " 'Simples Are by Compounds Farre Exceld': Southwell's Longer Latin Poems and 'St Peters Complaint,' " *Recusant History,* 17 (1985): 330–340;

Mario Praz, "Robert Southwell's 'Saint Peter's Complaint' and Its Italian Source," *Modern Language Review,* 19 (1924): 273–290;

Anthony Raspa, *The Emotive Image: Jesuit Poetics in the English Renaissance* (Fort Worth: Texas Christian University Press, 1983);

J. R. Roberts, "The Influence of *The Spiritual Exercises* of St. Ignatius Loyola on the Nativity Poems of Robert Southwell," *Journal of English and Germanic Philology,* 59 (1960): 450–456;

Joseph D. Scallon, *The Poetry of Robert Southwell, S.J.* (Salzburg: Institut für Englische Sprache und Literatur, 1975);

Gregory O. Schweers, "Bernard of Clairvaux's Influence on English Recusant Letters: The Case of Robert Southwell, S.J.," *American Benedictine Review,* 41 (June 1990): 157–166;

L. J. Sundaram, "Robert Southwell's 'St. Peter's Complaint' – An Interpretation," in *Studies in Elizabethan Literature: Festschrift to Professor G. C. Bannerjee,* edited by P. S. Sastri (New Delhi: S. Chand, 1972), pp. 4–9;

Helen C. White, "The Contemplative Element in Robert Southwell," *Catholic Historical Review,* 48 (April 1962): 1–11;

White, "Southwell: Metaphysical and Baroque," *Modern Philology,* 61 (February 1964): 159–168;

White, *Tudor Books of Saints and Martyrs* (Madison: University of Wisconsin Press, 1963).

Papers:

All of Robert Southwell's work except *An Epistle of Comfort* and *Mary Magdalen's Funeral Tears* is preserved in manuscript copies. There are five MSS, substantially similar in contents, of the short poems. They are Stonyhurst MS A.v.27 (The Waldegrave MS), Bodleian MS Eng. poet. e. 113 (The Virtue and Cahill MS), British Library MS Addit. 10422, British Library MS Harleian 6921, and the Harmsworth manuscript, now at the Folger Shakespeare Library. *Saint Peter's Complaint* (in British Library MS Addit. 10422) is also preserved in a commonplace book compiled by Peter Mowle of Attleborough (Oscott College, Sutton Coldfield, Shelf RNN3). *The Triumphs over Death* and Southwell's "Epistle unto His Father" exist in the Waldegrave MS, in the Virtue and Cahill MS, and in MS Addit. 10422. The two latter MSS include two more prose letters. There are copies of *An Humble Supplication* at the Inner Temple Library (Petyt MS 538, vols. 10 and 36), the Huntington Library (MS EL 2089), the Folger Shakespeare Library (MS V.a.479), and the Pierpont Morgan Library (MA 291: incomplete). A few works survive solely in manuscript, including six of the English poems and the Latin *Exercitia et Devotiones.* A holograph collection of papers at Stonyhurst College (MS A.v.4) preserves draft translations of source materials for *Saint Peter's Complaint* and *Mary Magdalen's Funeral Tears,* as well as drafts and fragments of nine Latin poems and other Latin devotional materials.

Edmund Spenser
(circa 1552 – 13 January 1599)

Donald V. Stump
Saint Louis University

BOOKS: *The Shepheardes Calender Conteyning Twelue Æglogues Proportionable to the Twelue Monethes. Entitled to the Noble and Vertuous Gentleman Most Worthy of All Titles Both of Learning and Cheualrie M. Philip Sidney* (London: Printed by Hugh Singleton, 1579);

Three Proper and Wittie Familiar Letters: Lately Passed between Two Vniversity Men: Touching the Earthquake in April Last, and Our English Refourmed Versifying and *Two Other Very Commendable Letters of the Same Mens Writing: Both Touching the Foresaid Artificial Versifying, and Certain Other Particulars* (London: H. Bynneman, 1580);

The Faerie Qveene. Disposed into Twelue Books, Fashioning XII. Morall Vertues (London: Printed for William Ponsonby, 1590) – contains Books I–III;

Complaints. Containing Sundrie Small Poemes of the Worlds Vanitie. . . . By Ed. Sp. (London: Imprinted for William Ponsonby, 1591) – includes *The Rvines of Time, The Teares of the Mvses, Virgils Gnat, Prosopopoia: or Mother Hubberds Tale, Rvines of Rome: by Bellay, Mvoipotmos: or The Fate of the Bvtterflie, Visions of the Worlds Vanitie, The Visions of Bellay,* and *The Visions of Petrarch;*

Daphnaïda. An Elegie vpon the Death of the Noble and Vertuous Douglas Howard, Daughter and Heire of Henry Lord Howard, Viscount Byndon, and Wife of Arthure Gorges Esquier. Dedicated to the Right Honorable the Lady Helena, Marquesse of Northampton. By Ed. Sp. (London: Printed for William Ponsonby, 1591);

Colin Clovts Come Home Againe. By Ed. Sp. (London: Printed for William Ponsonby, 1595) – includes *Astrophell. A Pastorall Elegie vpon the Death of the Most Noble and Valorous Knight, Sir Philip Sidney;*

Amoretti and Epithalamion. Written Not Long Since by Edmunde Spenser (London: Printed for William Ponsonby, 1595);

The Faerie Qveene. Disposed into Twelue Bookes, Fashioning XII. Morall Vertues [Books I–VI, with revised ending to III] (London: Printed for William Ponsonby, 1596);

Fowre Hymns, Made by Edm. Spenser (London: Printed for William Ponsonby, 1596);

Prothalamion Or A Spousall Verse Made by Edm. Spenser. In Honovr of the Dovble Mariage of the Two Honorable & Vertuous Ladies, the Ladie Elizabeth and the Ladie Katherine Somerset, Daughters to the Right Honourable the Earle of Worcester and Espoused to the Two Worthie Gentlemen M. Henry Gilford, and M. William Peter Esquyers (London: Printed for William Ponsonby, 1596);

The Faerie Qveene, Disposed into XII. Bookes, Fashioning Twelue Morall Vertues, 2 volumes [Books I–VI and *Two Cantos of Mutabilitie* from Book VII](London: Printed by H[enry] L[ownes] for Mathew Lownes, 1609–1613);

A Vewe of the Present State of Ireland, in *The Historie of Ireland, Collected by Three Learned Avthors, viz. Meredith Hanmer . . . Edmvnd Campion . . . and Edmvnd Spenser, Esq.,* edited by Sir James Ware (Dublin: Printed by the Society of Stationers, 1633).

Editions and Collections: *Spenser's "Faerie Queene,"* 2 volumes, edited by J. C. Smith (Oxford: Clarendon Press, 1909);

Spenser's Minor Poems, edited by Ernest de Selincourt (Oxford: Clarendon Press, 1910);

Spenser: Poetical Works, edited by Smith and de Selincourt (Oxford: Clarendon Press, 1912);

The Works of Edmund Spenser: A Variorum Edition, 11 volumes, edited by Edwin Greenlaw, Charles Grosvenor Osgood, Frederick Morgan Padelford, and Ray Heffner (Baltimore: Johns Hopkins University Press, 1932–1957);

Books I and II of "The Faerie Queene," The Mutability Cantos, and Selections from the Minor Poetry, edited by Robert Kellogg and Oliver Steele (Indianapolis: Bobbs-Merrill, 1965);

The Mutabilitie Cantos, edited by S. P. Zitner (London: Nelson, 1968);

"The Faerie Queene" (1596), 2 volumes, edited by Graham Hough (Menston, Yorkshire: Scolar, 1976);

The Faerie Qveene, edited by A. C. Hamilton (London & New York: Longman, 1977);

The Faerie Queene, edited by Thomas P. Roche Jr. (Harmondsworth: Penguin, 1978);

Edmund Spenser: The Illustrated "Faerie Queene": A Modern Prose Adaptation, edited by Douglas Hill (New York: Newsweek, 1980);

The Yale Edition of the Shorter Poems of Edmund Spenser, edited by William A. Oram, Elinar Bjorvand, Ronald Bond, Thomas H. Cain, Alexander Dunlop, and Richard Schell (New Haven & London: Yale University Press, 1989);

Edmund Spenser's Poetry, third edition, Norton Critical Edition Series, edited by Hugh Maclean and Anne Lake Prescott (New York: Norton, 1993).

OTHER: "The Visions of Bellay" and "The Visions of Petrarch" in *A Theatre wherein Be Represented as Wel the Miseries & Calamities That Follow the Voluptuous Worldlings, As Also the Great Ioyes and Plesures Which the Faithfull Do Enioy.... Deuised by S. Iohn van-der Noodt* (London: Imprinted by Henry Bynneman, 1569).

To understand Edmund Spenser's place in the extraordinary literary renaissance that took place in England during the last two decades of the reign of Queen Elizabeth, it is helpful to begin with the remarks of the foremost literary critic of the age, Sir Philip Sidney. In *The Defence of Poetry* (1595), written in the early 1580s, Sidney looks back on the history of English literature and sees little to admire. He mentions the works of Geoffrey Chaucer and a few sonnets by Henry Howard, Earl of Surrey; occasional tragedies such as those printed in the 1560s in *A Mirror for Magistrates;* and one book of contemporary poetry, Spenser's *Shepheardes Calender* (1579). Although France and Italy and even lesser nations such as Scotland had their notable poets and held them in esteem, England, according to Sidney, had recently brought forth only "bastard poets" and "poet-apes," and, consequently, the art itself had "fallen to be the laughing-stock of children." Though one might quarrel with Sidney over his list of the best native writers, it is certainly true that England could boast of no early poet other than Chaucer comparable in stature to Dante, Petrarch, or Boccaccio. At the time Sidney was writing, moreover, England lacked altogether the sort of thriving literary culture that was so visible across the channel in France. Sidney himself set out to repair this deficiency, and with him the other most important writer of his generation, Edmund Spenser.

A glimpse of Spenser's audacious plan to help provide England with a great national literature appears in an appendix printed in the 1590 edition of the first three books of his most important work, *The Faerie Queene.* In a letter addressed to his neighbor Sir Walter Ralegh, Spenser sets out to explain the "general intention and meaning" of his richly elaborated epic. It is "an historicall fiction," written to glorify Queen Elizabeth I and "to fashion a gentleman or noble person in vertuous and gentle discipline." In pursuing this latter aim, the poet explains that he has followed the example of the greatest epic writers of the ancient and the modern worlds: Homer and Virgil, Ludovico Ariosto and Torquato Tasso. Now, to set out to depict the queen herself and to "fashion" members of her nobility in virtuous and well-bred discipline was certainly a bold undertaking for the son of a London weaver. For him to compare his work with the most exalted poetry of Italy, the glittering center of European culture in this period, must have seemed to many of his readers mere bravado or self-delusion.

The attempt to write a neoclassical epic in English was without precedent — unless, perhaps, one includes Sidney's *Arcadia* (1590), which was begun at about the same time. Among the heroic poets named in Spenser's "Letter to Ralegh" as worthy practitioners of the form, Virgil was generally regarded as the greatest, and Spenser, like Dante and Petrarch before him, seems to have taken Virgil as his personal mentor and guide. From the proem to Book I of *The Faerie Queene,* the reader may infer that Spenser sometimes thought of his entire career as a recapitulation of that of his illustrious Roman counterpart. He began, as Virgil had begun in his *Eclogues,* with pastoral poetry, which Spenser published in his first major work, *The Shepheardes Calender.* A decade later, in *The Faerie Queene,* he graduated to poetry on martial and political subjects, as Virgil had done when he wrote his great epic, the *Aeneid,* for the court of Caesar Augustus. Spenser's opening lines, which echo verses prefixed to the *Aeneid,* announce his intention to exchange his "Oaten reeds" (or shepherd's pipes) for "trumpets sterne." Although he transformed the traditional epic introduction to include an invocation to Cupid, the god of love, along with the more traditional address to the Muses and although the poem actually resembles the quasi-medieval romance epics of Ariosto and Tasso more closely than it does classical epics, the poet's claim to follow in the great line established by Homer and passed down by Virgil was altogether serious.

Conscious self-fashioning according to the practices of ancient poets, and also of more-recent ones on the Continent, was an essential part of Spenser's project — but only a part. With his eye fre-

quently turned to Chaucer and other English authors, he set out to create poetry that was distinctively English – in religion and politics, in history and custom, in setting and language. For example, he mentions in the "Letter to Ralegh" that he designed his epic to depict "twelve private morall vertues, as Aristotle hath devised." In reality, however, just three of the six books that he lived to complete revolve around virtues that Aristotle would have recognized, and even those three – temperance, friendship, and justice – were greatly altered by Spenser's Anglo-Protestant form of Christianity and by other elements in his English background. The other three – holiness, chastity, and courtesy – have little to do with Aristotle but much to do with England in the high Middle Ages. In the best sense Spenser's art is syncretistic, drawing together elements from many traditions. Its aim, however, was to enrich the culture of his native land.

The process by which he realized this aim was neither rapid nor predictable. Comparing Spenser with Sidney, C. S. Lewis has written that he was "a more ordinary man, less clever, less easily articulate," and he succeeded by working harder. For that very reason, perhaps – along with his understated humor, his deep understanding of human psychology, and his easy humanity and good sense – Spenser has been closer than Sidney to the hearts of many of his countrymen.

Edmund Spenser was born into the family of an obscure cloth maker named John Spenser, who belonged to the Merchant Taylors' Company and was married to a woman named Elizabeth, about whom almost nothing is known. Since parish records for the area of London where the poet grew up were destroyed in the Great Fire of 1666, his birth date is uncertain, though the dates of his schooling and a remark in one of his sonnets (*Amoretti* 60) lend credence to the date traditionally assigned, which is around 1552. Just which John Spenser was his father is also uncertain, since there were at least three men of that name working in London as weavers at this time. If the poet took his lineage from John Spenser of Hurstwood, then he derived from a well-established family that had lived in Lancashire since the thirteenth century. If he was the son of the John Spenser mentioned in John Stow's *Survey of London* (1603), then his father was a man of some prominence who in later years bought a house that had once belonged to Humphrey, Duke of Gloucester, and who was knighted in 1594 by Queen Elizabeth upon his election as lord mayor of London. In any case, the poem *Prothalamion* (1596) reveals that Spenser thought of himself as a descendant of "An house of auncient fame," namely the family of the Despencers. There is no evidence, however, that he could claim to be a gentleman, and that fact alone made his rise to prominence more difficult in a class-conscious age.

Spenser's parents took what may have been the most important step in advancing their son's fortunes by enrolling him in the Merchant Taylors' School in London. During the early 1560s, when Spenser began his studies there, it was under the able direction of a prominent humanist educator named Richard Mulcaster, who believed in thoroughly grounding his students in the classics and in Protestant Christianity and who seems to have encouraged such extracurricular activities as musical and dramatic performances. Mulcaster was also important to Spenser's career for purely pragmatic reasons, since he had good connections with the universities and sent students of modest means such as Spenser on to them with some regularity. The poet later expressed his gratitude to Mulcaster by depicting him as "A good olde shephearde, *Wrenock*" in the "December" eclogue of *The Shepheardes Calender* and by naming his first two children, Sylvanus and Katherine, after those of his master.

The only glimpse that survives of the young poet at school comes from financial records indicating that in 1569, when he was in his last year, he was one of six boys given a shilling and a new gown to attend the funeral of Robert Nowell, a prominent lawyer connected with the school. This connection with Nowell was to prove important to Spenser's later development, for the lawyer's estate helped support his subsequent education.

In 1569, at the usual age of sixteen or seventeen, Spenser left the Merchant Taylors' School for Cambridge, where he enrolled at Pembroke Hall. Even before he arrived, however, he was already composing poetry and attracting the attention of other writers. Per-

haps with the help of Mulcaster, who had friends in the Dutch immigrant community, he had recently arranged to publish thematically linked sets of epigrams and sonnets titled *The Visions of Petrarch* and *The Visions of Bellay,* which appeared in the collection commonly referred to as *A Theatre for Worldlings* (1569) by the Dutch poet Jan van der Noot. Even in his maturity Spenser seems to have thought well of these early translations of French and Italian poetry, for he revised and included them among his *Complaints* in 1591. Although not original, they nonetheless shed light on Spenser's interests at the time, which were directed toward poets of the Continent and had already settled on themes that would surface again in his later poetry, namely the tragic precariousness of life and the impermanence of things in the material world.

Such scraps of reliable information as are known about Spenser during his university days suggest that he served as a sizar (a scholar of limited means who does chores in return for room and board) and that he received his B.A. in 1573 and his M.A. in 1576 with no official marks of distinction as a scholar. He regarded the experience as vital to his development, however, as can be seen in his later reference to the university as "my mother Cambridge" in *The Faerie Queene* (IV.xi.34). Little is known of his friendships at Pembroke. He must have been acquainted with Lancelot Andrewes, two years his junior, who later became a bishop and was well known for his sermons and for his part in translating the King James Version of the Bible. Clearly, Spenser had also gained the confidence of the master of Pembroke, John Young, who later became Bishop of Rochester and gave the poet his first post as a personal secretary. Most important for Spenser's literary career, however, was his close friendship with Gabriel Harvey, a professor of rhetoric who served initially as his mentor and ultimately as his literary promoter. Spenser later celebrated their friendship in *The Shepheardes Calender,* in which he appears as Colin Clout and Harvey is represented as the wise shepherd Hobbinoll.

Though a lackluster poet himself, Harvey seems to have encouraged Spenser in many of the aspirations that later shaped his career. Harvey was characteristically effusive, for example, about the need to ground English poetry on the great models of Greco-Roman antiquity, both by shaping its versification on Latin principles and by undertaking classical genres that had not yet been attempted in English. In the late 1570s he composed a vernacular epic (now lost) and a work on the ancient Muses of poetry that is similar in outline to Spenser's *Teares of the Muses* (1591). At about the same time, he may

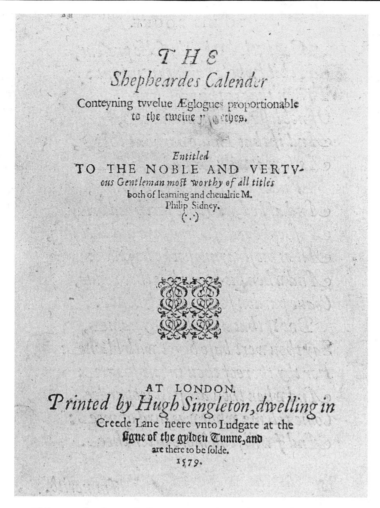

THE
Shepheardes Calender
Conteyning twelue Æglogues proportionable
to the twelue monethes.

Entitled
TO THE NOBLE AND VERTV-
ous Gentleman most worthy of all titles
both of learning and cheualrie M.
Philip Sidney.
(∴)

AT LONDON.
Printed by Hugh Singleton, dwelling in
Creede Lane neere vnto Ludgate at the
signe of the gylden Tunne, and
are there to be solde.
1579.

Title page for Spenser's first major work, a collection of eclogues that
signaled a turning point in the English literary renaissance

have played a part in introducing Spenser to Sidney and in securing for his friend a position in the London household of Robert Dudley, Earl of Leicester, who was a favorite of Queen Elizabeth as well as a key figure in the radical Protestant faction at court and one of the most powerful noblemen in the realm. The connections with Leicester and Sidney helped to launch Spenser's career, both as a poet and as a government official. Finally, in 1580, just before circumstances forced a separation between the two friends, Harvey gave Spenser's prominence as a writer a boost by publishing a set of five high-spirited letters that had passed between them, which helped to establish his friend's public image as England's "new poet."

In the letters Spenser and Harvey chat happily about their contacts with great men and their various works in progress, including Spenser's *Faerie Queene* and a surprising array of his other early works that were later lost – or perhaps silently incorporated into those that were published. These works included ten Latin comedies, several dream visions, an epithalamium celebrating the "marriage" of the rivers of England, and a work of literary criticism entitled *The English Poete*. The letters are even more interesting for their revelation that Spenser and Harvey had recently become involved in a literary circle gathered around Sidney. The group, which called itself the "Areopagus," was short-lived, and though it may have been formed with playful reference to the great literary academies of France and Italy, it seems to have been better known for its high spirits and good conversation than for its seriousness. The writers involved – including the learned diplomat Daniel Rogers, Sidney's friends Sir Edward Dyer and Fulke Greville, First Lord Brooke, and the academician Thomas Drant – seem to have occupied themselves primarily with experiments in Latin prosody, attempts at various genres of new poetry based on classical models, and the promotion of English as a literary language.

Rogers, however, also mentions grand discussions "of the law, of God, and of the good," which may have had some effect on the heroic works that occupied Sidney and Spenser in the years following.

Spenser's direct involvement with Sidney and his circle in 1579–1580 set him on a literary course that he would pursue for the rest of his life. Though the two men never saw one another again, they adopted remarkably similar literary agendas, writing mainly in genres that Sidney had encountered among prominent neoclassic and religious poets on the Continent. Both men, for example, wrote works of literary criticism addressing the current state of poetry in England, and both devoted most of their creative energies to pastoral poetry and romance epic, to sonnets and epithalamiums, and to religious hymns or psalms. Both also wrote political tracts about Ireland, where Sidney's father served for more than two decades and where Spenser was soon to become a government official. Expressions of admiration for the Sidneys and the Dudleys appear repeatedly in his works, from early poems such as his *Stemmata Dudleiana* (now lost) to late ones such as *The Ruines of Time* (1591), *Colin Clouts Come Home Againe* (1595), and *Astrophel* (1595).

Through his contact with men such as Sidney and Leicester, who were deeply involved in affairs of state, Spenser may have been emboldened to publish his *Shepeardes Calender,* which was dedicated to Sidney and dealt with sensitive political controversies of the day. Appearing in six editions before the end of the century, it became a milestone in the English literary renaissance because it was the first major published work of new poetry written along the neoclassic lines advocated by nationalistic poets such as those of the Areopagus. With a flair for self-promotion reminiscent of Harvey, Spenser – or perhaps his publisher – arranged to bring out the volume as if it were a venerable and ancient text. The archaic language of the poems, which Sidney impugned in his *Defence of Poetry,* may have been adopted in part to heighten this effect. Beautifully illustrated with woodcuts, the poems appeared from the outset already encrusted with learned prefatory matter and a running gloss by an unidentified scholar designated only as "E. K." Most likely, this was Spenser's friend Edward Kirke, whom he had known since their days together at Pembroke Hall in the early 1570s. Whoever he was, however, he shared Spenser's views that English poetry was in disarray and that it should be reestablished on "an eternall image of antiquitie" – an argument that is repeated in the eclogue for October. In his prefatory epistle to the volume, E. K. lauds Spenser as "this our new Poete," who will be "beloved of all, embraced of the most, and

wondred at of the best." If he had been writing of Virgil or Petrarch, rather than an obscure English poet, he could hardly have said more.

Spenser's skillful literary borrowings contributed to the volume's impressive effect. From the Italian poets Petrarch and Mantuan he adopted a variety of pastoral that conceals beneath its surface biting political allegories and topical allusions to prominent figures in the church and the state. From the more traditional *Edogues* of Virgil and from ancient writers such as Theocritus, Bion, and Moschus, he took other features, such as the curiously static sense of time characteristic of classical pastoral. His rustics debate and sing, love and despair, but there is no real narrative progression in the *Calender* and very little action. Variety is introduced in the subjects that the shepherds contemplate and in the poetic forms that they employ, which include amorous complaints, fables, singing matches and debates, an encomium, a funeral elegy, and a hymn to the god Pan.

Spenser also drew upon the visual arts of his day, particularly works known as "emblem books." These typically brought together three disparate elements: a series of pictures of a figurative or symbolic kind; "mottoes" or pithy sayings related to the pictures but phrased in enigmatic terms; and explanations in prose or verse that interpret the mottoes and pictures and draw a moral. Each of Spenser's twelve eclogues follows a more complicated version of this pattern. First comes a woodcut, which typically depicts the shepherd(s) in the eclogue and something from his songs or situations, with the sign of the zodiac appropriate to the month in question represented at the top. Then comes the poem itself, preceded by a brief "argument" or summary, which may have been added by E. K. After the eclogue comes one or more verbal "emblems," or mottoes, in various languages, which briefly sum up the nature or situation of the speakers and the themes of their songs but which often tease the imagination with alternative interpretations. And finally there is E. K.'s gloss, serving some of the same functions as the explanation beneath a conventional emblem.

Spenser also added important innovations to the traditional elements in the *Calender*. One involves poetic technique. In sheer variety of meter and form, his eclogues are without precedent in earlier pastoral poetry and provide an ample showcase for the experiments in prosody that so fascinated the poets of the Areopagus. Another conspicuous innovation is his organization of the poems into a seasonal progression. By following the cycle of the year, Spenser is able to employ the outer world of pasture and sheepfold as a way to depict the inner world of the young shepherd Colin Clout, whose unrequited love of Rosalind pro-

APRILL.

13

Aegloga quarta.

Emblem depicting Queen Elizabeth and her court, for the fourth eclogue of The Shepheardes Calender

vides a thread of unity through the entire volume. In the first poem, "January," Colin despairs, breaking his shepherd's pipe and, with it, the last source of pleasure that remains to him. In his eyes the land, the trees, and the flocks around him have themselves become emblems for the state of his soul. He complains, "Thou barrein ground, whome winters wrath hath wasted, / Art made a myrrhour, to behold my plight." Though not present or even mentioned in several of the eclogues, Colin provides a melancholy bass line over which all the other shepherds sing, setting their higher notes of anger and joy, debate and reflection, in poignant contrast to his listless desolation.

The emotional counterpoint is never more moving than in "April," where his good friend Hobbinoll sings one of Colin's old songs, written to celebrate the shepherdess Eliza in the springtime of an earlier and happier year. The inner world of the song continues to match the outward season in which it is sung, as all the songs in the *Calender* do; yet it also heightens the reader's sense of the dark winter of the soul in which Colin continues to suffer. At the midpoint of the cycle, in "June," he laments that Rosalind has left him for another shepherd named Menalcas. In

the final poem he sings weary complaints to the god Pan and feels premonitions of his imminent death, thus returning the sequence to a point resembling the one at which it began, though even more desolate.

Besides the revolving of the seasons, other cycles are involved in the work. As E. K.'s headnote to "December" reminds the reader, the passing of the year has traditionally served as an emblem for the stages of life. From the springtime of childhood to the summer of desire and love to the winter of loneliness and old age, Colin's life becomes an emblem for everyone's experience in this world. Interpreted in this way, the *Calender* returns to the themes of tragic uncertainty and relentless mutability expressed ten years earlier in Spenser's contributions to *A Theatre for Worldlings*.

These larger themes are, in turn, related to the political allegory that often lurks just below the surface of the poems. One of the implications of this allegory is that states, too, have their cycles of springtime and autumn. The celebration of "her Majestie" Eliza in "April," which is a thinly veiled encomium addressed to Queen Elizabeth, suggests that England is in the full flower of a new age. "Maye," "Julye," and "September," however, all turn on the controversy between Protestant reformers and Elizabeth's more conservative Catholic subjects, which was the greatest single threat to her ability to rule. The topical allegory in these eclogues suggests that, in 1579, strains in the body politic were a matter of particular concern to Spenser. The cause for his alarm was undoubtedly the marriage negotiations being carried out between Queen Elizabeth and a French Catholic prince, François, Duke of Alençon. The staunchly Protestant faction surrounding Leicester and Sidney took every opportunity to oppose such a marriage as a grave threat to the religious and political independence of England. If, as some critics suppose, Rosalind is a figure for Queen Elizabeth, and Colin for Spenser and his Protestant cause, then Rosalind's rejection of Colin for Menalcas may have to do with Queen Elizabeth's rejection of the Protestant faction in favor of the Catholic Alençon.

If this is so, then Colin's dejection at the end of the *Calender* may reflect Spenser's low political fortunes in late 1579 and early 1580, when the queen took harsh measures to silence critics of her plan for a French marriage. Sidney, for instance, was dismissed from court, most likely for addressing a letter to her on the subject. Spenser, too, seems to have feared the queen's displeasure, for he published his *Calender* under the pseudonym "Immeritô" and prefaced it with a poem to Sidney in which he speaks to the *Calender* itself, saying "when thou art past jeopardee, / Come tell me, what was sayd of mee / And I will send more after thee." It may be that the young poet's representation of delicate affairs of state had left him with few defenders and fewer prospects for advancement at court.

In any case, in July 1580 he accepted a post as a private secretary to Arthur Grey, the new Lord Deputy of Ireland. There is some evidence that when he set out for Dublin, he took with him a new wife named Machabyas Chylde, about whom little is known except that she married one "Edmounde Spenser" on 27 October 1579, that she apparently bore him two children named Sylvanus and Katherine, and that she died sometime before 1594. Most of the next twenty years of the poet's life were spent in Ireland, where he served in various governmental posts, from clerk of the Privy Council in Dublin in the early years to Queen's Justice and sheriff-designate for County Cork at the end of his life. His positions allowed him to acquire a considerable list of landholdings, including most prominently Kilcolman Castle with three thousand acres in County Cork, which served as his principal residence from 1588 until the year before his death in 1599. Such holdings were important, for they gave him the status of a landed gentle-

man, and thus eased his way in society, enabling him, for example, to make friends with Sir Walter Ralegh and to marry his second wife, Elizabeth Boyle, who came from an important landed family in Herefordshire.

References to Ireland appear frequently in Spenser's later poetry, and some of them reveal a good deal of gentle affection for the land and its people. Most memorable, perhaps, are the country wedding captured with such rustic beauty in his *Epithalamion* (1595) and the great judgment scene on Arlo Hill, a mountain near Kilcolman Castle, which occupies much of the *Mutabilitie Cantos* in Book VII of *The Faerie Queene*. Most of the poet's descriptions of Ireland, however, are colored by sorrow or disgust at the destitute state of its people or by resolute hostility toward its wily and elusive rebels, who harassed the English occupiers throughout the period. Spenser portrays the darker side of his experiences in Ireland, for example, in the attacks on the House of Alma in Book II of *The Faerie Queene* and in the savagery of the scurrilous, long-haired rebel Malengin in Book V.

The less submissive among the Irish had no reason to be any fonder of Spenser than he of them. In 1580, as a new official in the colonial administration, he was present when the English slaughtered papal troops at Smerwick, and he also witnessed the terrible famine in Munster that darkened the end of Desmond's rebellion. In fact, he wrote the official report on the battle of Smerwick and later described it and other incidents during the turbulent years of his colonial service in his only prose work, *A Vewe of the Present State of Ireland* (1633). This was written sometime before 1598 as a dialogue discussing the brutal measures needed to establish a stable colonial regime in the country, and parts of it may have been incorporated into an official report that he presented in London in 1598. In the late 1580s he had been responsible for settling English immigrants at Kilcolman on lands confiscated from the rebel Gerald Fitzgerald, fifteenth Earl of Desmond, and some of Spenser's other landholdings had come from the forced dissolution of Catholic monasteries in Ireland. It is not surprising, then, that his last years in Cork were ones of conflict, tumult, and loss.

Until the late 1590s, however, Ireland provided a living, a place to write, and even literary friends. During his years there, Spenser may have become acquainted with Barnabe Riche and Barnabe Googe, and he knew Sidney's close friend and occasional fellow poet Lodowick Bryskett, who turned two posts over to him before moving on. Most important, however, was Spenser's friendship with Ralegh, who was his neighbor on the former Desmond estates and who, in the summer and fall of 1589, came to see him at Kilcolman and took a personal interest in his poetry.

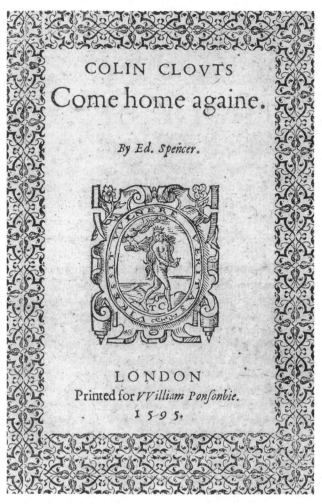

*Title page for Spenser's poem that includes an account of his
relationship with Sir Walter Ralegh*

Spenser later revealed the importance of his relationship with Ralegh by preserving a poetic account of it in *Colin Clouts Come Home Againe* and by writing the "Letter to Ralegh" and a dedicatory sonnet to him in *The Faerie Queene*. According to *Colin Clout*, it was Ralegh who arranged for Spenser to travel to London in 1590 to publish the first three books of his epic and to represent them in person to Queen Elizabeth, who was pleased and expressed a desire to hear it read to her "at timely houres." So pleased was she, in fact, that she granted the poet a pension of fifty pounds a year, which was more than the parsimonious queen granted to any other poet of the period. Spenser expressed his gratitude for Ralegh's patronage by writing a sympathetic allegory of the adventurer's often turbulent and romantically tinged relationship with the queen, which appears in the story of Timias and Belphoebe in Books III, IV, and VI of *The Faerie Queene*.

The best way to begin an examination of Spenser's epic is perhaps to come to it as Ralegh did, with

Spenser's prefatory letter in hand – though, admittedly, some of its intentions do not match the poem as the author actually wrote it. As the letter reveals, the six books (and two cantos of a seventh) that were ultimately published represent but a fraction of the plan, which was to extend to the traditional twelve books of an epic, one devoted to each of "the twelve private morall vertues." Another section of the poem, perhaps of equal length but never written, was to cover the public or "polliticke" virtues. Each book in this vast structure was to concentrate on a single habit of character, represented by one or more exemplary knights such as Britomart, the Knight of Chastity in Book III, and Sir Artegall, the Knight of Justice in Book V. It may be that, as time went on and Spenser realized the magnitude of the undertaking, he changed his mind and began to incorporate political virtues among the moral virtues of the first section. Certainly Book V, the Legend of Justice, involves a good deal of political allegory. In any case, the six books that he completed begin with virtues in a person's relations with God and self (holiness and temperance) and proceed to those involving relations with other people (chastity, friendship, justice, and courtesy). The entire scheme accords with the two great commandments of Christian tradition: "Thou shalt love the Lord thy God with all thy heart, and with all thy soul, and with all thy mind" and "Thou shalt love thy neighbor as thyself " (Matt. 22: 36–39).

The first twelve books were to be united by the presence of two dominant characters: Prince Arthur, mythical founder of the Round Table, who was to appear as a wandering knight in each of the books, and Gloriana, the Faerie Queene, who was to frame the action of the poem by holding an annual feast of twelve days, on which she assigned her knights twelve quests, each described in one book of the epic. At the end of the poem, it seems, Prince Arthur was to marry Gloriana, and since the poet postponed the wedding of other heroes in the individual books, there were doubtless to be other marriages in Book XII as well. Since Arthur represents the virtue of Magnificence, which comprehends within itself all the other active virtues, and since the Faerie Queene represents Glory, which was for Spenser the end of all earthly action, there is a tidy philosophy behind the entire structure.

As the poet concedes, the main difficulty for readers lies not in grasping the grand organization of the poem but in knowing how to interpret its allegory. He offers a clue, however, by calling the work a "continued" allegory, or "darke conceit." In his day, the term *conceit* could have carried at least two senses in this context, both of them helpful. First, it could have meant simply a thought or, in certain philosophical contexts, a form, or Idea, in something like the Platonic sense. Second, the term could have denoted an extended metaphor, that is, an implied comparison between the primary subject of the author's thought and something more easily visualized or grasped, which acts as a "figure" for that subject.

In interpreting Book I as such an extended metaphor, one might concentrate on the heroine, Una, the daughter of the "King of *Eden*," who sets out from her home to save her parents from a great dragon. To this end she travels to the court of the Faerie Queene and gains the help of the Red Crosse Knight, who, after various trials and wanderings, returns with her to her parents' city. There he defeats the dragon, is honored as a victor, and offers to marry Una once he has served his queen for six more years. Taking a clue from the Book of Revelation, which identifies Satan as a dragon that has enslaved human beings (the fallen descendants of Adam and Eve) and is the great enemy of the

Church, the reader might take Una as a "conceit" for the universal body of believers as it has acted through history. This, then, would be the metaphor "continued" through the whole of Book I. On this assumption, the reader might conclude that the meaning of the allegory is something like this: the Church, which is descended from sinful human beings, sets out to redeem them by releasing them from bondage to Satan. In this it requires the help of the individual Christian, who may lose his way for a time but, through the aid of the Church, will ultimately find the straight and narrow way again and will go on to defeat the forces of evil around him. Once he lives out his "six days" of life on earth, he will be united with the Church forever on the seventh, at rest on God's Sabbath Day in heaven (see VII.viii.2).

Such a reading, based on the assumption that the poem is a kind of code to be deciphered character by character, has something to be said for it. It reveals a point that is probably central to Spenser's attempt to "fashion a gentleman or noble person in vertuous and gentle discipline," namely that Christians tend to respond to the call of the Church enthusiastically enough in the beginning but often lose their zeal or fall away. Each stage in the wanderings of the Red Crosse Knight – his initial acceptance of lies about Una, his departure from her and his affair with another woman named Duessa, his drifting into the broad path of worldly fame and pleasure represented by the House of Pride, and finally his removal of his Christian armor, his defeat, and his overwhelming sense of failure at the Castle of Orgoglio and the Cave of Despair – represents a stage in the process by which an immature believer might fall away. A period of humility, instruction, and hard discipline (represented in the House of Holiness) is required before a young man like this can be of much use in helping others.

There are, however, problems with attempts to "decode" the poem in such a simplistic fashion. The most invidious, perhaps, is that once one has worked the puzzle, it loses its interest. In an 1831 issue of the *Edinburgh Review,* Thomas Macaulay, who must have read the poem in something like this way, complains that "even Spencer himself . . . could not succeed in the attempt to make allegory interesting. . . . One unpardonable fault, the fault of tediousness, pervades the whole of the *Fairy Queen.* We become sick of Cardinal Virtues and Deadly Sins, and long for the society of plain men and women." One wonders whether an attempt to decipher characters merely as clever signs for abstractions may not have been behind the tendency, notable throughout the nineteenth century, to discount Spenser's allegory and to concentrate instead on the beauties of his verse and imagery.

The Red Crosse Knight; woodcut from Spenser's The Faerie
Queene *(1590)*

The fault here lies more with Spenser's readers, however, than with the poet himself. There is nothing simple or boring about the allegory, which frequently manages to juggle several different meanings simultaneously. Along with "darke conceits" of a moral, political, and religious kind, Spenser also undertakes at least three other varieties. There are psychological allegories, which probe the faculties of the mind and their working in both normal and abnormal states; there are topical allegories, which glorify or satirize the actions of rulers and other prominent figures of Spenser's day; and there are historical allegories involving their personal or national pasts. Only by resolutely ignoring crucial details can one read the poem as a "continued" metaphor with a single pat "meaning."

Una, for instance, is not only the one true Church but also (as her name suggests) "oneness" itself. Spenser calls her simply "truth" and seems to have in mind the sense of oneness expounded by Renaissance Neoplatonic philosophers, who saw the world as a sometimes discordant multiplicity that emanates from the perfect unity and simplicity of the divine mind. To depart from Una is to lose sight of the truth apprehended by contemplating the eternal Ideas that inform everything in the material world. To take up with Duessa (duality, duplicity) is to depart from truth and break one's union with the one source of all that is good.

"Una" is also a name applied in this period to Queen Elizabeth, the one supreme governor of the Church of England, and Spenser's maiden lady is clearly one of many figures for her in the poem. Elizabeth lived under constant threat of military attack or assassination by the great Catholic princes on the Continent, who wanted to reverse the Protestant Reformation in England and to return the nation to the Catholic fold. In the historical allegory of the poem Duessa represents Mary, Queen of Scots, who had legal claims to the English crown and who vied with Elizabeth for the allegiance of the English people. In polemics of the day,

Mary was sometimes pictured as the "whore of Babylon" mentioned in the Book of Revelation, who rides on a beast with seven heads and is associated with Rome. In Canto viii Spenser employs this imagery when Duessa rides out on a "manyheaded beast" to attack the heroic representative of England, Prince Arthur, who defeats her and forces her to cast away her "golden cup" and "crowned mitre," which are symbols associated with the wealth and pride of the papacy.

Even the three quite different interpretations of Una discussed here may not exhaust the allegorical possibilities. Spenser was a master of compression and deep implication who recognized the multiplicity of meanings inherent in certain primal concepts and images, such as oneness and duality, and it is that multiplicity that lies at the heart of the fascination that *The Faerie Queene* has exerted over many of its readers. Rather than interpret the poet's "darke conceit" simply as an extended metaphor, one does better, particularly in analyzing the plots of the poem, to take it more broadly as a governing thought or form. Spenser's literary friend Sidney wrote in *The Defence of Poetry* that the poet begins with an "Idea, or fore-conceit," which he embodies in the matter of the poem – its stories, characters, and images. The reader then uses that matter as an "imaginative ground-plot of a profitable invention," comprehending the author's "conceit" by an act of mental re-creation. The richer the author's initial idea and the clearer the matter of his creation, the richer and more profitable the reader's own act of "invention" will be. So long as one remains true to the details of the matter, the possibilities for meaning are limited only to the extent that the primal forms or ideas are limited in their inherent implications.

In relation to Una, the Red Crosse Knight becomes an extraordinarily rich creation. As one learns in Canto x, he is Saint George, the patron saint of England. In many ways he is also the Everyman of medieval Christian tradition who, after a fall into sin and a recovery in the House of Holiness, imitates the life of Christ by fighting the dragon, falling in the battle, and being resurrected in victory on the morning of the third day. He also represents the English people at the time of the Protestant Reformation, defending the "one true church" against the late-medieval corruptions of Roman Catholicism. More particularly, he may represent Christian writers and intellectuals in sixteenth-century England who were prone to error and were in need of firmer doctrinal foundations. The knight begins his quest in Canto i with a battle against a lesser dragon named "Errour," which is associated with religious books and pamphlets, and only after he has been rescued from doctrinal error himself, represented in the false philosophy of Despair, can he fulfill his quest. After a period with the hermit Contemplation and other teachers in the House of Holiness, he fights a second and greater dragon, and this time, with God's grace, he prevails.

Even in the passages of Book I devoted to philosophical abstractions, such as the virtues and vices that bored Thomas Macaulay, Spenser invites more from his readers than a dry process of "decoding." His stories and pictorial descriptions are not simply means to convey philosophical insights. They are themselves the ends of the poet's labors, figures capable of transforming barren philosophy into what Sidney's friend Fulke Greville, first Lord Brooke, once called "pregnant images of life." It is one thing to know the definition of a particular vice but quite another to know how people afflicted with it might talk or act and to see how their sinful dispositions might harm them over a period of time. It is these latter points that most interested Spenser. In Canto iv of Book I, for example, Queen Lucifera and her "six wisards old" are readily identified as the Seven Deadly Sins of medieval Christian tradition. Yet it is the extraordinary detail with which the poet depicts them that matters, not simply what they represent. In a series of exquisitely painted miniatures, Spenser depicts each of the six counselors on one of the beasts that draw Lucifera's coach: Idleness on an ass, Gluttony on a pig, Lechery on a goat, Avarice on a camel, Envy on a wolf, and Wrath on a lion. Each detail in the imagery of coach and team – from the animals themselves to the clothing and behavior of their riders and the things that they bear in their hands – serves to characterize the six vices and Pride, their queen. Even the order of the riders is significant, for Spenser has dramatically altered the traditional Catholic sequence in order to place Idleness first as the "nourse of sin." Since Idleness is dressed "Like to an holy Monck," the change in order doubtless has to with what is now called the Protestant "work ethic" and with common complaints in the Renaissance that the Catholic monasteries were bastions of laziness and corruption.

It would, of course, be a mistake to suppose that every passage in the poem is as rich in meaning as the description of the House of Pride and its inhabitants, or that readers need understand everything that is lurking under the surface of the poem in order to enjoy it. Much of its appeal lies in plain sight, in its strange and marvelous stories and its colorful pageantry. In probing its deeper implications, however, it helps to begin with what are sometimes called the allegorical "cores," or "shrines," of the poem. In the great temples, palaces, noble houses, gardens, and caves that dominate the landscape, Spenser provides the

*Title page for the continuation of Spenser's most important work,
an epic poem that was widely recognized as the finest poetic
achievement of his generation*

main distinctions needed to comprehend the philosophical concepts that he is exploring, often revealing key points in the names of the characters and in the details of their appearance or their surroundings. Along with the House of Pride and the House of Holiness in Book I, major cores include the House of Alma, the Bower of Bliss, and the cave that contains the House of Mammon in Book II; the Garden of Adonis and the House of Busirane in Book III; the Temple of Venus in Book IV; the Temple of Isis and the Palace of Mercilla in Book V; Mount Acidale in Book VI; and Arlo Hill in the fragment of Book VII that Spenser left unpublished at his death. In the narratives that lead the main characters to and from such places of instruction, the poet often provides less-concentrated allegories in their actions, as in Una's wanderings after she is separated from the Red Crosse Knight. And finally, in the subsidiary stories and episodes constantly woven into the main lines of plot in each book, Spenser provides moral examples that further illustrate his main themes. An instance of such a tale in Book I is the story of Fraelissa and Fradubio, two lovers who are parted by Duessa in much the same way that the Red Crosse Knight is parted from Una.

In the sequence of allegorical cores within each book, Spenser tends to move from the simple to the complex, arriving only late in the action at a full picture of the virtue required of the hero. In Book II the first core leaves the impression that temperance is a "natural" virtue, that is, one that can be grasped without the divinely revealed truths of Scripture. Spenser offers portraits of three sisters: Elissa ("excess"), Perissa ("deficiency"), and Medina (the "golden mean"), and the Latin roots of their names call to mind the philosophy of Aristotle. One who is temperate, in Aristotle's view, has formed the habit of taking the mean between extremes, such as squandering and miserliness, foolhardiness and cowardice. The suitors courting Elissa and Perissa illustrate this point in a colorful way. Huddibras represents a "froward" nature that tends to draw back from others in arrogance or anger, and Sansloy represents a "forward" nature that draws toward others in uncontrolled desire. A temperate person would restrain impulses toward either of these extremes.

The House of Medina suggests that in Book II the reader has come into a new region of Spenser's fairyland, one different from the quasi-medieval religious landscape of Book I and more like the plain humanist schoolrooms of the Merchant Taylors' School that Spenser attended as a boy. To take its classical philosophy as his final word on temperance, however, would be a mistake. Guyon's attempt to put into practice the rational ideal embodied in Medina is successful, but only for a time. To be sure, he avoids the corruption inherent in characters such as Pyrochles and Cymochles, who allow themselves to be governed by excesses of the bodily fluids (or "humours") of choler and phlegm. The brothers provide emblems of the two great temptations of the book: irascibility, which is seen in the hotheaded characters of the early cantos, and concupiscence, which appears in lazy and self-indulgent figures later in the book. Guyon avoids both. Yet, as early as Canto iii, he makes a crucial blunder, allowing a buffoon named Braggadocchio to steal his horse and so becoming the only pedestrian hero in the poem. At the midpoint of the book, in Canto vi, he makes a second mistake in parting from his Christian counselor and friend, the Palmer. By accepting a boat ride from a languid and sensuous lady named Phaedria at Idle Lake and allowing the Palmer to go on by foot, Guyon needlessly subjects himself to temptation. He does so again in the next episode by voluntarily undertaking a traditional epic descent into the underworld, where he is tempted with every imaginable form of worldly excess. These are represented in three subterranean chambers: the treasure house of Mammon, god of money and possessions; the temple of Philotime, the goddess of honor and ambition; and the garden of Proserpina, the goddess of worldly pleasure and rest. The very sense of his own self-sufficiency that prompts the hero's needless descent into hell is a sign of danger, for, in Spenser's view, no one can long resist the sinful tendencies inherent in fallen human nature without the grace of God.

This point comes home in Canto vii, where, having emerged from Mammon's cave, Sir Guyon faints from exhaustion, falling prey to several of the enemies that he had earlier avoided, including Pyrochles and Cymochles. An angel is required to save him, and does so by fetching the Palmer, who stays with Guyon until Prince Arthur arrives to beat back the figures of intemperance attempting to despoil the hero of his armor. A stay in the House of Alma, which is the second important locus of instruction in the book, educates Guyon in the limits of his strength, presenting in the structure of the house an emblem of the human body and the human psyche for his instruction. It is a place besieged by assaults on the senses, which are represented in the attacks of lawless rebels outside the castle. Their leader, Maleger (who represents appetite and passion), has the ability to regain his strength simply by touching his mother, the earth. As Prince Arthur later discovers, Maleger can be defeated only when he is cast into the water.

This last point reveals the Christian conception of temperance that underlies the entire book. The water in which Maleger drowns is an emblem of baptism, and his defeat is related to the episode that first set Guyon forth on his quest. In Cantos i–ii he and the Palmer came upon the body of a knight, Sir Mortdant, who had been lured to his destruction by a false enchantress named Acrasia (whose name means both "badly mixed," referring perhaps to the bodily humors, and "incontinent," implying an inability to contain her desires). The knight's wife, Amavia, had stabbed herself in grief at his loss, and their baby, Ruddymane, had stained his hands in her blood. When Guyon attempted to wash the child's hand in an enchanted spring – one associated with pagan mythology and the goddess Nature – the stain would not wash away. It remained as an emblem of Original Sin, which can be cleansed only by the Christian sacrament of Holy Baptism. At the time, Guyon did not understand the meaning of this incident, but in the battle against Maleger the point comes home.

With his temperance now "fast setteled / On firme foundation," the hero departs on the last stage of his quest to avenge the death of Ruddymane's parents upon Acrasia. After a sea voyage on which he encounters fresh allegorical representations of the Seven Deadly Sins, he ruthlessly destroys Acrasia's Bower of Bliss, releasing the many men whom she has transformed to beasts and binding the witch herself.

From the analysis of inward psychological states in Book II, Spenser next turns to outward social relations in Book III. At the outset he pauses, as

Engraving of Spenser for George Vertue's Portraits of
Poets *(1727)*

he often does, to show the relation between the central virtues of adjoining books by having their heroes meet briefly in conversation and in feats of strength. Here, the superiority of the social virtue of chastity, represented by the heroine Britomart, over the personal virtue of temperance appears clearly in Britomart's defeat of Guyon in a joust. Other episodes suggest further contrasts between the books. In comparison with Acrasia's Bower of Bliss in Book II, Spenser portrays another garden in Book III that is also concerned with the fulfillment of bodily desires, but in healthier ways. Whereas the Bower had been a false paradise, apparently natural but actually created by self-indulgent art (see II.xii.58–59), the Garden of Adonis is a true Eden, where "All things, as they created were, doe grow" and obey God's first command "to increase and multiply" (III.vi.34). The two passages are linked by the classical myth of Adonis, presented first in a bad form in Acrasia's Bower and then in a good form in the Garden of Adonis.

Though the healthy garden embodies a philosophy of divine generation that is as rich and enigmatic as any other conceptual scheme in the poem, the place of the passage in the unfolding narrative is fairly straightforward. The chaotic inner forces of the psyche explored in Book II are here presented in ordered and temperate manifestations, with particular stress on healthy sexual desire. Whereas Acrasia is governed by an insatiable appetite for young men, the characters Amoret and Belphoebe, who were born and reared in the Garden of Adonis, seek higher goals. Amoret takes as her goals marriage and family, whereas Belphoebe chooses lifelong virginity and an active life outside the home.

The classical myths woven into these and other episodes in Book III do much to illuminate the characters. The myth of Cupid and Psyche, which is retold in the episode at the Garden of Adonis, shows the human mind brought into proper and fruitful union with the divine power. Britomart, the heroine of the book, best fulfills this ideal. She is not like the delicately beautiful Florimell, who is timid and inclined to flee from men. She is not like Belphoebe, who seems contemptuous of affairs of the heart. Nor is she like Amoret, who lives for such experiences. Britomart combines the best qualities of all three women, drawing them toward a golden mean. She shares, for example, Florimell's determination to leave the comforts of courtly life and search through the world for the man whom she is destined to marry. She matches Belphoebe in mental prowess, courage, and skill in manly pursuits such as hunting and jousting. Yet she also shares Amoret's capacity for warmth and nurturing.

It is tempting to take Britomart as a figure for Queen Elizabeth, but it seems likely that she is something far more complex. The "Letter to Ralegh," which identifies major figures for the queen in the poem, makes no mention of Britomart in this regard. As the wise magician Merlin reveals in Canto iii, she is actually an ancestor of the English queen, though one who displays a close family resemblance. Britomart is, in fact, a far more glorious figure than either of the other main embodiments of Elizabeth: the noble but somewhat icy Belphoebe, who represents the queen in her private life, and the magnificent but absent Gloriana, who represents Elizabeth in her public role as a ruler but who appears only in the dreams of Prince Arthur (I.vii) and in brief references in the proems and elsewhere, but never in the action itself. Some scholars see Britomart's quest for her future husband, Artegall – which begins with a vision of him in a crystal ball and is destined to end in marriage, joint rule over England, and a long line of glorious offspring – as a reference to Elizabeth's often-stated desire to marry no suitor but England itself. This way of reading the poem makes a good deal of sense of later passages in Book V, where the character Radigund represents Mary, Queen of Scots; Britomart resembles Elizabeth; and Artegall suggests some of Elizabeth's most powerful noblemen at court, who were torn in their allegiances between the two queens. When Britomart rescues Artegall from captivity in Radigund's city of Amazons, there is reason to believe that the incident represents Elizabeth's salvation of England from the threat of Catholic domination under Mary. Yet the potentially fruitful Britomart stands in notable contrast to the virginal and childless Belphoebe, and it may be that one of Spenser's points in the poem was to criticize Elizabeth for not marrying and providing England with a proper heir.

In any case, Britomart stands in glorious contrast to two degraded types of womanhood in Book III, both defined once again with the help of classical mythology. The first is Malecasta in Canto i, who represents the tradition of courtly love. She leads men on by the gradual stages of courtship represented in the six knights who fight on her behalf: Gardante ("brief glances"), Parlante ("enticing words"), Iocante ("courtly play"), Basciante ("kissing"), Bacchante ("wine drinking"), and Noctante ("spending the night"). Once Malecasta has conquered a man, she makes him a slave to her whims and desires. She represents woman as predator. The tapestries depicting Venus and Adonis that hang in her castle link her with the more classical figure of Acrasia in Book II. The second example of unchastity in Book III is Hellenore, who represents the tradition of Ovidian love. Like Helen of Troy, she yields to the seductions of a guest (named, appropriately, Paridell) and allows herself to be carried away from her aged and jealous husband, Malbecco, only to be discarded by her new lover and left to satisfy the lusts of forest satyrs. She represents woman as prey.

Both she and Malecasta are medieval embodiments of ancient types, and their presence helps to extend the moral allegory of the poem to include glimpses of the history of Western culture. For Spenser, lines of dynastic descent are important, as they had been for earlier epic poets such as those mentioned in his "Letter to Ralegh." Here, he glorifies Britain through the ancestry of its representative, Britomart. Like Paridell (and Virgil's Aeneas), she traces her ancestry back to the old stock of Troy. Unlike Paridell, however, she descends from the worthy hero Brutus, the founder of Troynovant (or London), not from the lustful and irresponsible Paris (III.ix.32–46). Through passages such as this – along with depictions of legendary English heroes throughout the poem and accounts of early English history, such as those that Arthur reads at Alma's castle and Britomart hears in Merlin's cave – Spenser establishes himself as a writer of "an historicall fiction" on which England may establish a sense of its national heritage.

In the climactic episode of Book III, when Britomart rescues Amoret from the evil enchanter Busirane, Spenser briefly sketches the history of relations between the sexes in Western culture, tying his account to the current difficulties that Amoret has suffered in marrying the aggressive young knight Scudamour. As the reader subsequently learns in Canto i of Book IV, she was kidnapped by Busirane during a ribald entertainment, or "masque," performed on the night of her wedding,

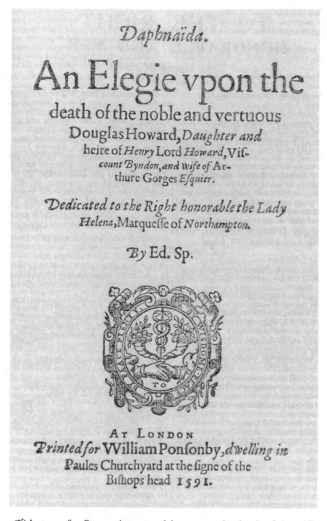

Title page for Spenser's pastoral lament on the death of the wife of his friend Arthur Gorges

and clues in various rooms of the enchanter's house suggest that he represents the power of poetry and the visual arts to shape the attitudes of one gender toward the other. At least one of Amoret's problems on that night was a clash of cultural expectations.

In the first room, rich tapestries illustrate the dominance of men over women that characterized the myths of ancient Greece and Rome. In the second room, golden ornaments suggest the dominance of women over men found in the tradition of Courtly Love in the late Middle Ages. In the third room, where Amoret herself appears, the reader finds what seems to be a Renaissance confusion of masculine and feminine dominance, fostered by an attempt to combine classical and medieval erotic ideals. As the reader learns in Book IV, Amoret's husband, Scudamour, sees himself as a domineering male of the classical sort, who bears the sign of triumphant Cupid on his shield (see III.xi.7 and IV.x). Amoret, however, sees herself as a "recluse virgin,"

whose education at the Temple of Venus has elevated her to a station much like that enjoyed by women in the medieval tradition of Courtly Love (see IV.x). If the reader may assume that Amoret's mental state following the night of her marriage is represented in the nightmarish procession known as the Masque of Cupid that appears in Busirane's third room, then the lady is not only suffering from a virgin's fears of the bridal night but also from confusion over her proper role as a wife. The allegorical figures surrounding her in the masque represent the course of her relationship with Scudamour. It begins happily enough with Ease, Fancy, and Desire but eventually graduates to more-turbulent emotions such as Fear and Hope, Grief and Fury, and ends with feelings of Cruelty and Despight. Following these personifications comes the cause of her distress, depicted as Cupid riding on a lion. This figure reminds us of Scudamour's shield and probably represents his aggressive desire to dominate. Although

Scudamour has attempted to release his bride from Busirane, only a third party such as Britomart, who understands the problem from a woman's point of view, can subdue the enchanter and dispel Amoret's fears.

In the second edition of the poem, which was printed in 1596, the problem of Scudamour and Amoret is never satisfactorily resolved. In Book IV she transfers her affections to her new friend Britomart, is captured by a lustful giant and rescued by Timias, and passes through a series of painful adventures ending in the Castle of Corflambo (or "burning heart"), from which she can be saved only by the intervention of Prince Arthur himself. Meanwhile, Scudamour mistakes the armed Britomart for a man and, after she goes off with Amoret, suffers a fit of jealousy in the Cave of Care. Not until Canto vi, in which he attacks Britomart, does he discover her gender and his own folly. After these incidents, the reader hears little more of him or of Amoret. In the first edition of the poem published in 1590, however, Spenser fully resolved the tensions between the newlyweds. Upon Amoret's release from captivity to Busirane, she and Scudamour embrace and fuse with one another in a single hermaphroditic form, which seems to symbolize not only sexual union but also a golden mean between masculine and feminine forms of dominance and the consummation of an ideal Christian marriage.

By now it should be obvious that, as Spenser moves from the inward virtues of holiness and temperance in Books I and II to the more outward ones of chastity and friendship in Books III and IV, he adopts a far more complicated method of plotting. The first two books follow a fairly straightforward and self-contained pattern: the hero sets forth on his quest, suffers a disastrous fall, is rescued by Arthur in Canto viii, joins forces with the prince for a time, undergoes a process of reeducation, and finally completes his quest with a victory in Canto xii. In Books III and IV, however, events are far more chaotic. This may be the case because the god Cupid has come into the picture. Among the epic invocations at the beginning of the poem, Spenser adds something not found in Virgil or Homer, a prayer to the "most dreaded impe of highest Jove, / Faire Venus sonne," and Cupid's enormous power over earthly events is manifested in the social disorder of Books III and IV.

In the opening canto of Book III, for example, Spenser demonstrates love's power by drawing together all the major heroes of the poem so far, only to have Cupid divide and scatter them. Arthur appears with his squire Timias; Guyon with the Palmer; Britomart with her nurse, Glauce – and,

not far away from them, the women also encounter the Red Crosse Knight. Almost as soon as the heroes meet, however, Florimell rides by, fleeing a forester who intends to rape her, and the men in the party ride off in hot pursuit. Guyon and Arthur pursue the lady more, it seems, for her beauty than for her safety, and they soon become separated and lost. Timias nobly rides off to subdue the forester but afterward falls in love with Belphoebe, forgetting about Arthur and eventually becoming entangled in a romantic scandal involving Belphoebe and Amoret that drives him to despair and turns him into a hermit. Even the Red Crosse Knight loses his head in Book III, requiring assistance from Britomart in turning back Malecasta's six knights. Thereafter, hardly a male in the poem can guide his own affairs sensibly until a semblance of order has been restored in Book V. The point seems to be that, in matters of love and friendship, women do better than men, and no one does very well. The beauty of a woman such as Florimell is like a comet, an astrological sign that "importunes death and dolefull drerihed" (III.i.16).

One of the governing aims of Books III and IV is to harmonize love with friendship. In the Renaissance many took from antiquity the view that bonds between two men were nobler than those between a man and a woman or between two women. Spenser undercuts this view by exalting marriage over friendship and also by idealizing amicable relationships between women and between members of the opposite sexes. In the first episode of Book IV Britomart and Amoret arrive at a castle where no knight may enter without a lady. Britomart's solution is to exploit her disguise as a knight in order to enter as Amoret's champion, thus raising interesting issues of homoerotic attraction between the two ladies but also exalting the importance of their friendship. Later, Prince Arthur saves Amoret at the Castle of Corflambo, acting magnanimously as her male friend rather than as a potential lover.

Spenser's emblem of the social ideal is a foursome of two men and two women, all bound in complex interrelationships of erotic attraction and friendship. This pattern is seen most clearly in the main heroes of Book IV, Campbell and Triamond, and in the ladies whom they love. Before Campbell will allow anyone to marry his sister Canacee, he requires that they first defeat him in battle. Triamond's two brothers, Priamond and Diamond, try and fail. Because, however, their mother, Agape (or "love"), has made a pact with the Destinies that Triamond should inherit the spirits and the strengths of his brothers, he is able to succeed where they failed.

Later, Campbell marries Triamond's sister Cambina, and the four become fast friends.

A second foursome, that of Paridell and Blandamour and their ladies, Duessa and Ate, acts as a false parody of the first. Since the men are altogether faithless to one another and to their ladies, they quarrel over a third woman, a demonic copy of Florimell created by a witch in Book III. Once they have gone after this new "comet" of beauty in Canto ii, discord erupts among all four members of the group.

The primary destructive force in Book IV is represented in the hag Ate, the "mother of debate / And all dissention, which doth dayly grow / Amongst fraile men" (IV.i.19). Her power can be seen most dramatically in the central incident of the book, the Tournament of Satyrane. There, ladies compete for the "glorie vaine" of owning a magic girdle of "chast love / and wivehood true" that once belonged to Florimell. This prize is to be given to the most beautiful among them, and the knights are to do battle for the hand of the winner. Ironically, at the end of the violent turmoil and strife represented in the tournament, the girdle is awarded to the false Florimell, who represents the beautiful but cruel mistress idealized in Petrarchan love sonnets of the period. Victory on the field is awarded to Satyrane, one of the Knights of Maidenhead (who, in the historical allegory of the episode, are associated with the virgin queen Elizabeth). The false Florimell, however, insists on choosing a mate to her own liking and selects one as shallow as she is, namely the impostor Braggadocchio. The folly of Petrarchan love conventions, which Spenser will take up again in the episode of Serena among the cannibals in Book VI and in his sonnet sequence Amoretti, is amusingly satirized in this outcome.

Yet even amid the discord and delusions of Book IV, the "fatall purpose of divine foresight" is nonetheless at work, guiding lovers to mates destined to them by higher powers from the foundation of the world (see III.iii.1–2). At Satyrane's tournament, Britomart encounters and defeats her long-sought future husband, Artegall, though without recognizing him in his disguise as the Salvage Knight. In Canto vi he attempts to avenge this dishonor on her, but when her helmet falls off in battle, he falls in love with her instead. After a brief period of courtship, he plights his troth to marry her. Similarly, the true Florimell, who had been taken captive by the sea-god Proteus in Book III, finds her Marinell in the closing cantos of Book IV and is subsequently betrothed to him, as prophecies had foretold. Though confusion still reigns late in the book — as the brawl in Canto ix involving Britomart and Scudamour,

Blandamour and Paridell, and Prince Arthur and others reveals — images of harmony begin to appear, like sunlight after a storm. Most notable is the image of Concord celebrated in the Temple of Venus. Spenser says of her, "Of litle much, of foes she maketh frends, / And to afflicted minds sweet rest and quiet sends" (IV.x.34).

Many of the discords of Book IV are resolved in Book V, which recounts the Legend of Justice. Florimell marries Marinell at another great tournament, and in this contest the outcome is more just. Braggadocchio is revealed as a coward and a fraud; the false Florimell is revealed as a demonic illusion; and Guyon, who had long ago lost his horse to Braggadocchio, reclaims it again. Yet both the proem and the opening canto of the book remind us of the deeply fallen state of the world, where even the stars and planets no longer follow their ancient courses, and the goddess of justice, Astraea, has departed from the earth. Spenser here invokes Ovid's myth of the Four Ages of Mankind, which began with the Golden Age of Saturn and has since declined from the Age of Silver toward those of Brass and Stone.

The allegory of Book V focuses on the last period in this decline, stressing the corruption and injustice of England's enemies in Spenser's own day. Nearly everything in the main plot is related to Queen Elizabeth's struggle to preserve the independence of the English church and state against the Catholic forces arrayed against her in Scotland and Ireland, France and Spain. The main quest of the book is Artegall's attempt to rescue Irena from the tyrant Grantorto, which represents the English attempt to free Ireland from Catholic domination in the 1580s and 1590s. The incident in which Artegall encounters the Amazons and Queen Radigund is an account of the actions of Mary, Queen of Scots, beginning in 1558 and ending in 1571, when Elizabeth imprisoned her in England. Her execution in 1587 is later portrayed in the death of Duessa in Canto ix. The incident in which Prince Arthur and Artegall defeat the Souldan in Canto viii represents England's repulse of the sea invasion mounted by the Spanish Armada in 1588, and Arthur's rescue of Belgae from Geryoneo in Cantos x–xi represents England's intervention to free the Netherlands from Spanish forces in the 1580s, in which Sidney died and Leicester came to grief.

Against these forces, the hero of the book proves — like the Red Crosse Knight and Guyon before him — an inexperienced and sometimes inadequate hero. When Artegall first appears in the Tournament of Satyrane in Book IV, he is armed as the Salvage Knight, and some of his untamed

Title page for Spenser's collection of nine poems on the themes of mutability and the vanity of earthly desires

roughness carries over into Book V. Although he is successful in the early episodes, overthrowing Munera (or "bribery") and settling property disputes between the likes of Amidas and Bracidas, he seems incapable of conceiving of justice in any but harsh, inflexible, legalistic terms. His limitations appear most clearly in the brutality of his servant Talus and in his own submission to the Amazonian tyrant Radigund, who manages to lure him into agreeing to a foolish contract with her concerning their private combat in Canto v. What Artegall requires is a sounder philosophy of justice that will allow him to avoid such errors and to moderate his severity. Spenser provides him with one in the figure of his future wife, Britomart, who rescues him from Radigund.

Britomart represents a form of justice known as "equity," which allows a judge or public official to mitigate the severity of punishments or to adjust the application of the law whenever the case involves unusual circumstances that could not have been foreseen when the written legal code was drafted. In following normal procedures of equity, the judge returns to the philosophical principles on which the code was originally based and infers the proper way to handle the case at hand. Such moderating procedures are allegorized at the Temple of Isis in Canto vii, where Britomart learns to temper Artegall's sternness with clemency and his rigid adherence to the legal code with wisdom. After she has rescued him from Radigund, he serves an apprenticeship under Prince Arthur and receives his final education in the Palace of Mercilla.

The queen of that house represents the Christian virtue of mercy, which is different from the equitable justice allegorized in Britomart. Whereas equity returns to philosophical principles in order to ensure that the defendant receives his proper due, mercy offers freely to redeem offenders who sincerely repent their crimes. Artegall's education thus leads him from legal justice through classical equity to Christian mercy, symbolized respectively in the iron man Talus, the mostly silver idol of Isis, and the gold-bedecked queen Mercilla. By this progression the poet seems to point the way to reclaim Ovid's lost Age of Gold, and indeed, with Artegall's liberation of Belgae in Canto xii, nearly all the disorders of Books III–V have been resolved.

As often happens in *The Faerie Queene,* however, moments of victory and harmony prove short-lived. At the end of Book V, Artegall encounters a new threat, the Blatant Beast, whose name means both "prattling," or "babbling," and "hurtful." The monster, which Spenser describes as a "hellish Dog," represents slander, backbiting, and other forms of verbal abuse that tend to disrupt in private the social harmony that Artegall has been working so hard to establish in public. The monster may seem a minor threat in comparison with the more imposing enemies of justice in Book V – such as the Giant with Scales in Canto ii, who advocates the overthrow of the aristocracy in favor of an egalitarian form of government, or Grantorto in Canto xii, who represents political and religious tyranny. Yet because of the widespread and covert nature of its abuses, the Blatant Beast is more difficult to subdue. Throughout Book VI it appears unexpectedly, attacking with poisoned teeth and a "thousand tongues" and then disappearing again before anyone can bring it to bay. It is first set on by Envy and Detraction (V.xii.35–37) and is later employed by Despetto ("malice"), Decetto ("deceit"), and Defetto ("detraction"), who succeed in provoking the Beast to wound Timias, a figure identified by his name with "honor" (VI.v). The two major strands of plot in Book VI – those involving Calidore's quest to bind the Beast and Calepine's search for Serena – both include episodes illustrating the power of the tongue.

The line of plot in which Serena (or "tranquillity") is ravaged by the Blatant Beast suggests the loss of reputation and the subsequent shunning and abuse that aristocratic women of Spenser's day sometimes suffered because of rumors that they had been unchaste. In Serena's case, the Beast attacks soon after she is discovered in a secluded forest glade with her lover, Calepine, who has violated the social conventions of aristocratic courtship by removing his armor "To solace with his lady in delight" (VI.iii.20). The inward torments that she suffers in consequence of this tryst appear in her gradual decline into illness, which is brought on by the festering bites of the Beast (Cantos v–vi). The social degradations to which she is subjected are allegorized in her subsequent capture by the "Salvage Nation," a band of cannibals who are prevented from sacrificing her naked body on a forest altar only by the timely arrival

of Calepine (Canto viii). The threat of similarly violent social repercussions hangs over Priscilla and her less nobly born lover, Aladine, in Canto ii, where they are also found dallying in the woods and are immediately attacked by a lustful knight.

The story of Serena among the cannibals involves more, however, than issues of reputation and the abuse of young lovers who overstep the bounds of custom. The language of the episode suggests the Petrarchan love poetry of Spenser's day, in which the woman is depicted as alluringly beautiful but cold and unattainable, and her lover is expected to vacillate endlessly between abject adoration and frustrated erotic desire. That such poetry should degrade an entire "Nation" to the level of savages, worshiping feminine beauty in a leering and cannibalistic religion of love, raises serious questions about the proper role of literature in shaping the social order. The more refined and pragmatic lover Calepine, whose name means "gracious speech," offers a contrasting ideal, in which love is mutual and courtship progresses naturally toward "solace" and "delight."

The chivalric code of the Middle Ages – in which men have a duty to honor and protect women, and women have an obligation to provide patterns of morality and images of "grace" to temper masculine aggressiveness – lies behind much of Spenser's thought about love and courtesy in Book VI. The opening episode, for example, involves an inversion of this ideal. In it the proud knight Crudor entices the lady Briana to serve him by forcing knights and ladies who pass her castle to shave their beards or their hair. By this means she hopes to win Crudor's love by lining a mantle with hair, as he has demanded. The chivalric ideal is at least partially reasserted when Calidor intervenes on behalf of Briana, forcing her cruel knight to marry her. Crudor must also promise to behave better toward errant knights and to assist ladies "in every stead and stound" (VI.i.42). The Knight of Courtesy later confronts ethical dilemmas posed by this chivalric ideal. In Canto iii, for example, he violates his knightly duty to tell the truth in order to conceal Priscilla's secret meetings with Aladine from her father. In Cantos ix–xi, Calidore is tempted to discard his armor and to abandon his quest altogether in order to court the shepherdess Pastorella.

This last incident reveals a conflict between personal fulfillment and social responsibility that is an underlying theme of Book VI. Spenser identifies the virtue responsible for maintaining a proper balance between the two as courtesy, which he sees broadly as "the ground, / And roote of civill conversation" (VI.i.1). In its original sense, courtesy was simply the pattern of conduct acceptable at a prince's court. By

Spenser's day, however, it had come to imply a rather lengthy list of personal traits and abilities: noble birth and elegant manners, comely appearance and cultivated speech, athletic skill and martial prowess. All these traits were combined in a man such as Sir Philip Sidney, who is sometimes regarded as the Elizabethan knight on whom Sir Calidore was modeled. In the initial description of the Knight of Courtesy, Spenser depicts him as a marvel of courtly refinement. He is one

> In whom it seemes, that gentlenesse of spright
> And manners mylde were planted naturall;
> To which he adding comely guize withall,
> And gracious speach, did steale mens hearts away.
> Nathlesse thereto he was full stout and tall,
> And well approv'd in batteilous affray. (VI.i.2)

Only certain parts of this description, however, actually involve things that Calidore has "added" at court. The first qualities mentioned are the "naturall" elements of courtesy: "gentlenesse of spright" and "manners mylde," and these subsequently receive special attention.

Perhaps because Spenser was distressed by the extravagant artificialities and corruptions common in the royal courts of his day, he laid his greatest stress on the natural roots of courtesy. His most idealized depictions of the virtue are set in the partly civilized yet predominantly natural settings of the pastoral countryside. The sheepfolds of Pastorella and her foster father, Meliboe, in Cantos ix–xi provide a refuge both from the savagery of uncivilized nature (represented by the brigands who live in nearby forests and caves) and from the follies and extravagances of aristocratic life (depicted at the castles of Briana and Aldus). The fruitful interplay between the natural and the cultivated, the wild and the civilized, is depicted emblematically in Calepine's rescue of an infant from a wild bear in Canto iv. Afterward, he gives the orphan to the barren Lady Matilde and her husband, Sir Bruin, so that their aristocratic house may have a suitable heir.

In the central episode involving Turpine (or "baseness") and his wife, Blandina (or "flattery"), in Cantos vi–vii, Spenser explores the two extremes represented in the symbolic forests and castles of the book. Both characters have the trappings, but not the substance, of true civility. When Calepine attempts to find shelter for the wounded Serena in Turpine's castle, he is repulsed and forced to spend the night with his lady in the forest, where he is gravely wounded by Turpine on the next day. From the forest, however, comes a wild and apparently "Salvage" man, who is actually more courteous than Turpine and his wife. That the wild man risks his life to rescue Calepine and his lady and carefully tends the knight's wounds sug-

gests something of the inherent goodness of human nature. That he succeeds in curing only Calepine's injuries and not those of Serena, however, suggests the limitations of that nature when it is not cultivated by civil custom and informed by religion. A pious hermit who had once been a great knight is the only one who can save Serena.

In Calidore's quest to subdue the Blatant Beast, Spenser presents a further exploration of the relationship between the civil and the natural. The knight first finds the Beast in Gloriana's city of Cleopolis, which in one of its allegorical senses stands for Elizabethan London. The knight then pursues the monster from smaller towns past outlying castles to the sheepfolds of Pastorella and Meliboe, which are associated with Spenser's own rural home in Ireland. So much more courteous are the simple shepherd and his daughter than those whom Calidore has left behind in "civil" society that he abandons his life as a knight and takes up that of a shepherd, hoping to win the heart of Pastorella. His most exalted moment comes in Canto x, when he is immersed in the beauties of nature, far from the court of his queen. Walking on Mount Acidale, he comes upon the shepherd Colin Clout, whose name associates him with Spenser and *The Shepheardes Calender*. Colin is playing his pipes, and all before him are "An hundred naked maidens lilly white," dancing in a ring about the three Graces of classical mythology. The Graces, in turn, are dancing about Colin's beloved, who represents Spenser's second wife, Elizabeth Boyle. Though the poet might have placed Queen Elizabeth in the midst of the rings, portraying her as the central emblem of grace and courtesy in Book VI, he pointedly avoids doing so, beseeching his monarch to give him leave to place his own Elizabeth there instead. His own natural bonds with his wife take precedence over his civil bonds with his queen.

This curious detail is sometimes interpreted as a sign that Spenser, like his hero Calidore, had turned away from Gloriana's court, abandoning in disillusionment his great project of glorifying Queen Elizabeth in *The Faerie Queene*. Apparently he composed very little more of the poem after he finished the pastoral cantos of Book VI, which were the last episodes published in his own lifetime. Yet the poet's gesture toward his wife need not be taken as a slight to the queen. After all, he had only recently remarried and therefore had special reason to request leave of his monarch "To make one [brief passage] of thy poore handmayd, / And underneath thy feete to place her prayse" (VI.x.28). It seems clear, moreover, that he did not entirely endorse Calidore's "truancy" among the shepherds. By adopting their life of pleasure and contemplation, the knight has acted irresponsibly, as subsequent events reveal.

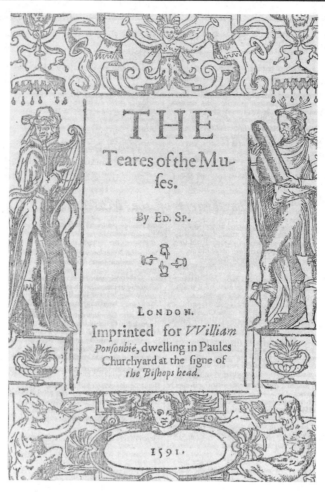

*Title page for Spenser's book lamenting the status of poets
in England*

Not only has he left the Blatant Beast free to do further harm, which is described in Canto xii, but he has also left Pastorella and her father undefended from other evils in the surrounding forest. A band of brigands soon sweeps down on them, killing Meliboe and several other shepherds and binding Pastorella in a cave in hopes of selling her into slavery. To rescue her, Calidore is forced to rearm himself, and after he has scattered the brigands, he is compelled to seek shelter for his beloved at a nearby castle. In a fallen world, the natural life divorced from the civil is no more sustainable than the civil divorced from the natural.

Even Calidore's idealization of the shepherds has been based partly on a mistake, for as he discovers in Canto xii, Pastorella is actually a child of the aristocracy, born to Sir Bellamour and Lady Claribell in a secret love affair like those examined elsewhere in Book VI. She was abandoned among the shepherds to conceal her parents' shame. At the climax of the book, this noble child reared by common shepherds

returns in joy to her parents as an emblem of the ideal union of the natural with the civilized. Whatever Spenser's personal attitudes toward Elizabeth and her court may have been when he wrote this part of the poem, the passage hardly endorses a radical reappraisal of the prevailing social order or a renunciation of the poet's lifelong project. At the end of Book VI, Calidore resumes his quest, captures the Blatant Beast, and leads it captive through Faerie Land.

When Books I–III of *The Faerie Queene* were first published in 1590, Queen Elizabeth was not the only one to admire them, and by 1596, when Books IV–VI appeared, her grant of a royal pension was not the only reward that its author had received. The poem won immediate recognition as the finest poetic achievement of its generation, and further works by the poet were evidently in demand. In 1591 he returned to London to print two other works, *Daphnaïda* and the *Complaints.* Just four years later, three more of his works were published; *Colin Clouts Come Home Againe,* and the sonnet sequence titled *Amoretti* with his widely admired *Epithalamion*. These were followed in 1596 by the last works published during his lifetime, *Fowre Hymnes* and the *Prothalamion*.

Daphnaïda is a dreary and somewhat overly expansive pastoral lament written soon after the death of the wife of Spenser's friend Arthur Gorges, a minor poet and translator. Based on Chaucer's *Book of the Duchess* (circa 1370), it is partly an experiment in patterning poetry according to symbolic numbers (here multiples of seven, the number associated with divine judgment and rest from sorrows), and it may have helped to prepare the way for the wonderfully detailed and suggestive number symbolism of the *Epithalamion*.

More successful were the *Complaints,* nine lengthy poems on the general themes of mutability and the vanity of earthly desires. The volume looks back to Spenser's earliest work, reprinting revised versions of his two dream visions from the 1569 volume *A Theatre for Worldings* and adding a similar poem titled *Visions of the Worlds Vanitie.* These three show a side of Spenser that would later appeal to writers of the Romantic period, namely his sense of the poet as a prophet, speaking inspired truths against the follies of his age. The volume also includes an imitation of the French poet Joachim du Bellay's *Antiquitez de Rome* (1558), which is a meditation on the tragic impermanence of even the greatest works of human ambition, epitomized in the ancient city of Rome.

The *Complaints* continue the experiments in poetic technique characteristic of *The Shepheardes Calender,* and they also explore some of the same literary forms and themes. Like "October," for example, *The Teares of the Muses* laments the current low esteem of poets in England. Like "Maye" and "September," *Mother Hubberds Tale* employs a beast fable for satiric purposes, presenting four stories about a fox and an ape that warn of abuses among the three traditional estates of English society: commoners, clergy, and nobility. The dedication preceding the poem calls it "the raw conceipt" of the poet's youth, and since topical allusions tie it to political affairs in the years 1579–1580, it is probably work of the same period as the *Calender.*

Mingled with early materials such as these, however, are poems that have more to do with the major works of Spenser's maturity. *Miuopotmos,* for example, resembles "February" in its use of a beast fable to expound a moral point. Its primary affiliation, however, is with *The Faerie Queene.* It is a mock epic about a vain butterfly caught by an envious spider and may have been written as a light interlude in the serious business of composing the longer poem. In Clarion, the butterfly, it depicts a diminutive hero who, like the human

characters in Spenser's epic, was born under the biblical injunction "to be Lord of all the workes of Nature" yet is also bound by the will of "the heavens in their secret doome" (lines 211, 225). In the rhetorical questions of the three central stanzas of the poem, just before the butterfly becomes ensnared in the webs of its tragic antagonist, Arachne, Spenser echoes one of the great themes of *The Faerie Queene,* the contrast between human folly and shortsightedness and "The fatall purpose of divine foresight" (III.iii.2).

As a counter to the dominant theme of the *Complaints,* which is the transience of earthly things, Spenser turns to poetry as one of the few means that human beings have to resist the depredations of time. The volume begins with *The Ruines of Time,* a poem that contrasts a depiction of the great but forgotten city of Verulame with an elegy for Sidney, who had died of wounds suffered in battle in the Netherlands in 1586. By means of this contrast Spenser celebrates the power of poetry to confer on Sidney a kind of glory that will outlast empires. The pastoral poem *Astrophel* and the six elegies and epitaphs for Sidney by other authors that Spenser gathered four years later at the end of *Colin Clouts Come Home Againe* reiterate this theme and offer a belated though impressive tribute to the dead poet-hero who had served as Spenser's early mentor.

Sidney's impact on Spenser did not end with the tributes printed in the *Complaints* and *Colin Clouts.* Along with the mingling of pastoral and epic in Book VI of *The Faerie Queene,* which resembles the same blending in Sidney's *Arcadia* (1590, 1593), the deceased poet's influence also appears in the *Amoretti,* a series of sonnets published with the *Epithalamion* in 1595. Spenser's volume reads as if it were designed as a reply to Sidney's dazzling sonnet sequence, *Astrophil and Stella,* which was printed in London in 1591 by Spenser's own publisher, William Ponsonby, and which began a vogue for English sonnets that lasted more than a decade.

The contrasts between the two sequences are illuminating. Whereas Sidney's poems follow continental models in depicting the love of a distant and unattainable woman, Spenser's sonnets go against this widespread Petrarchan convention by celebrating a successful courtship, which culminates in the joyous wedding ceremony depicted in the *Epithalamion.* Both sequences seem to have been, at least in part, autobiographical, with Sidney's reflecting his love of Lady Penelope Rich and Spenser's his courtship of his second wife, Elizabeth Boyle, who later bore him a son named Peregrine. Yet, whereas Sidney depicts love with another man's wife and describes a gradual process by which passion conquers reason and religious principle, Spenser moves

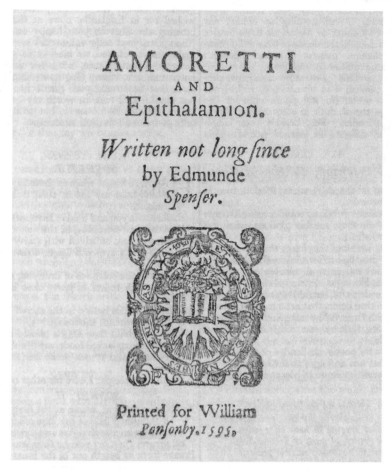

AMORETTI
AND
Epithalamion.

*Written not long since
by Edmunde
Spenser.*

Printed for William
Ponsonby. 1595.

*Title page for the sonnet sequence in which Spenser eschews Petrarchan
convention by celebrating a successful courtship*

from such passion early in his sequence toward an eventual restoration of Christian piety and self-control. His address to the *Amoretti* themselves in Sonnet 1 sets a tone for the entire sequence that is lighter and less turbulent than that of *Astrophil and Stella:* "Happy ye leaves when as those lilly hands, . . . Shall handle you." Though the poems that follow show the influence of various earlier sonneteers – including Petrarch and Philippe Desportes, Tasso and du Bellay – Spenser never departs from his own vision of healthy courtship, which progresses from the follies and excesses of infatuation toward the stability and fruitfulness of Christian marriage.

The organizing principle of the *Amoretti* and the *Epithalamion* is, as in *The Shepheardes Calender,* the passage of time. The poet's wooing of Elizabeth Boyle initially seems an endless endeavor. Like Petrarch's love of Laura, it drives the poet to exclaim in Sonnet 25, "How long shall this lyke dying lyfe endure . . . [?]" Yet, even as he says this, an important phase in the courtship has already begun that will eventually lead to the resolution that he desires. As Alexander Dunlop and other scholars have pointed out, in Sonnet 22 he mentions the beginning of Lent, "This holy season fit to fast and pray." If one sonnet is counted for each day between Ash Wednesday and Easter, then the celebration of Christ's Resurrection would be expected in Sonnet 68, and that is where it appears. Sonnet 67 announces the end of the lover's "hunt" for his "gentle deare," in which the lady has been "fyrmely tyde" and "goodly wonne." In Sonnet 68 the poet prays to Christ: "This joyous day, deare Lord, with joy begin, / and grant that we for whom thou diddest dye / being with thy deare blood clene washt from sin, / may live for ever in felicity." Before the Lenten section there are twenty-one sonnets of preparation, and after the Easter sonnet there are again twenty-one in the denouement. These eighty-nine, plus the four short mythological poems known as anacreontics that come between the Amoretti and the Epithalamion, make a total of ninety-three, which is the number of days in the season of spring. That the central sonnets of the sequence are meant to be read as a depiction of springtime courtship is suggested in Sonnets 19 and 70, which fall just before and after the Lenten sonnets.

The *Epithalamion* continues this elaborately patterned sequence of symbolic seasons and times. Spenser's wedding took place on Saint Barnabas's Day, 11 June 1594, which was, by Elizabethan reckoning, the longest day of the year. As A. Kent Hieatt has shown, the twenty-four stanzas of the poem represent the hours of that particular day, beginning with the groom's preparations before dawn and ending at the same hushed hour on the following morning. So precise is the temporal sequence that the coming of night is announced in the fourth line of stanza 17, just as Irish almanacs of the period set the hour of sunset at sixteen and a fraction hours after sunrise. All the stanzas leading up to this long-awaited moment contain a refrain that rejoices in the happy sounds of the day, from the singing of the birds at the bride's awakening to the joyous ringing of the church bells after the ceremony is over. All the stanzas after nightfall, however, call for silence: "Ne let the woods us answere, nor our Eccho ring."

As in *The Shepheardes Calender,* where the passing of the months becomes a metaphor for the entire span of Colin's life, so here the hours are connected with the larger cycles of the year and of life itself. Perhaps to magnify the significance of the wedding day, it is represented as if it had lasted a year, as the reader can see from the fact that the poem contains 365 long lines (while the 68 shorter lines total the number of weeks, months, and seasons). At the end, as Spenser and his bride lie in bed in the darkness before the dawn, he thinks of the whole course of their coming life together, looking forward to their final rest and that of their children in "heavenly tabernacles." Along with this God-given way to escape from time, the wedding poem itself provides another, becoming, as the last line suggests, "for short time an endlesse moniment."

Throughout the *Epithalamion* Spenser maintains a delicate balance between the heavenly and the earthly, the classical and the Christian. The poem begins with invocations to the Muses and to the forest, river, and sea nymphs of antiquity, who, along with Hymen and the Graces and the greater gods Bacchus and Venus, Cynthia and Juno, rule over mundane affairs in the poem. The poet, acting as a genial (though sometimes fretful) master of ceremonies, seems to invite the entire creation to join in celebrating his wedding day. He begins by depicting the sun as it rises, proceeds through the fish in the river and the beasts and birds in the forest, and continues up the Great Chain of Being to village children and the musicians hired to play for the wedding. This progression leads finally to his bride, who comes forth like a goddess among less comely "merchants daughters." At the beginning of stanzas 12 and 13, which lie at the formal and conceptual center of the poem, the poet sings, "Open the temple gates unto my love," and this turns the reader's attention from the world outside the church to the Christian ceremony of Holy Matrimony that is to be celebrated within. The musicians then raise a great crescendo to heaven, and the priest unites the couple before the altar, invoking the authority of a God who stands far above the pagan deities in the natural world of the poem. At the metrical center of the central line, Spenser places the words *endlesse matrimony.* After the ceremony comes feasting with bells and carols and wine poured out "by the belly full." The wedding party gradually disperses, leaving the poet alone with his bride, and the final image that lingers at the end is of Spenser lying awake beside her in the silence just before dawn, thinking of children to come and the joys of heaven. This image is perhaps his most telling response to the fruitless idolatry and the frustrated earthly desire that are the subjects of Sidney's *Astrophil and Stella.*

A similar, though more puzzling, blend of the classical with the Christian appears in Spenser's next volume, the *Fowre Hymnes.* The first two hymns, which are meditations on earthly love and beauty, invoke the pagan gods Cupid and Venus as their reigning deities. The second two, which deal with heavenly love and heavenly beauty, are addressed to Christ and Sapience (or Christian wisdom). Though hymns modeled on the work of Pindar and other pagan poets of antiquity had recently been revived on the Continent, Spenser's book is unusual in setting such poems side by side with more-traditional Christian material. To be sure, the pagan hymns follow a Platonic "ladder of love" in which the speaker progresses from love of the body to love of the soul, but there is no way to reconcile their essentially worldly and self-centered philosophy with that depicted in the second pair of poems. Whereas the pagan hymns celebrate an altogether human form of love that aims to conquer and possess the beloved for its own self-fulfillment, the Christian hymns celebrate a divine love that aims to free others from bondage to sin by undertaking selfless acts of personal sacrifice.

The difficulty in resolving such contradictions has led some critics to accept at face value comments in the poet's letter of dedication to the volume, which suggest that the first pair was written "in the greener times of my youth" and the second was offered by way of a retraction. Other scholars have noted, however, internal evidence suggesting that the pagan hymns were written – or at least revised – in the same period as the Christian ones and therefore that they are not

*Title page for Spenser's work that blends classical and
Christian elements*

likely to represent the mere errors of Spenser's youth. Perhaps the most likely explanation is that the poet was simply repeating a pedagogical device employed frequently in *The Faerie Queene.* First, he presents a widely respected view from antiquity, and then he offers a far richer Christian view of the same subject, leaving his readers to puzzle out the differences and choose for themselves.

The *Prothalamion,* which was the last of Spenser's poems to be published during his lifetime, also involves unresolved tensions, though of a darker sort than those found in the *Fowre Hymnes.* The poem was written to celebrate a double betrothal ceremony for the two daughters of Edward Somerset, Earl of Worcester. It took place during Spenser's journey to London in the latter half of 1596, which he apparently undertook in order to seek a government position in England. Like *The Shepheardes Calender,* the poem begins with notes of weariness and despair. As the poet wanders along the bank of the river Thames, thinking about his own "long fruitlesse stay / In Princes Court" and seeking to ease

his "payne," he sees two lovely swans floating on the water, with river nymphs gathering about them. These, of course, represent the prospective brides and their attendants. The counterpoint between the poet's sadness and the rising tones of joy in the betrothal ceremony is caught most movingly in a song of blessing sung to the swans by one of the nymphs. Only two years earlier, Spenser had sung a wedding song of his own, but sorrows have since crowded in upon him. In coming from a turbulent world beyond the security of London, he cannot see the peaceful scene before him without thinking of faraway wars, glimpsed briefly at the end of the poem in a stanza glorifying the recent English burning of the Spanish fleet at Cadiz under the direction of Elizabeth's young favorite, Robert Devereux, second Earl of Essex. The refrain in the poem, which invokes the river to "runne softly, till I end my Song," suggests that the river may not always run softly, and the lingering impression of the poem is one of fragile beauty and transient joy.

The tone of dejection in Spenser's *Prothalamion* appears in other of his works published in 1596. It may reflect the worsening situation in Ireland, where Tyrone's Rebellion would soon uproot the English colonists and, with them, Spenser's family. It may also have arisen from Spenser's belief that he was being slandered at the English court and that old enemies were preventing him from gaining a better and safer position there. Both concerns stand out prominently in the last three cantos of Book VI of *The Faerie Queene*. There, shepherds associated with Spenser's literary persona, Colin Clout, are attacked by lawless brigands, and the poet's final words are a complaint that the Blatant Beast has escaped and "raungeth through the world againe . . . Ne spareth he the gentle Poets rime, / But rends without regard of person or of time." This passage probably refers to William Cecil, Baron Burghley, Elizabeth's powerful counselor, who had censured Spenser's epic for dealing too much with themes of erotic love (see *The Faerie Queene*, IV. Proem).

The poet's last work, the *Mutabilitie Cantos,* published posthumously in 1609, reflects once again on the old themes of time and the sorrows and uncertainties of life. The cantos were apparently written as the main allegorical "core" for an otherwise unfinished book of *The Faerie Queene,* which a headnote by the printer identifies as "the legend of *Constancie.*" Appropriately set amid the turbulence of the Irish countryside, the cantos place the local and the immediate problems threatening Spenser and his family within a universal context, reflecting on the role of mutability in God's creation. Once again using classical myth to explore issues that deeply touched his Christian view of the world, Spenser tells the story of the goddess Mutabilitie, a daughter of the Titans who long ago rebelled against Jove. Longing to be admired like her sisters Hecate and Bellona, Mutabilitie sets out in the world's first innocence to ravage "all which nature had establisht first" and all the laws of civil society, thereby bringing death into the world. She then mounts up to the circle of the moon, attempting to drag from her throne the goddess Cynthia (who, in one of her allegorical references, stands for Queen Elizabeth). Ascending higher, Mutabilitie then challenges Jove himself, putting forth her case that she is the rightful ruler of the universe. In order to resolve her dispute with Jove, she appeals to the highest judge of all, Dame Nature, who assembles all the gods on Arlo Hill to hear her judgment.

Within this larger framework Spenser tells the story of Faunus, who bribes the Irish river nymph Molanna to place him near Diana's favored haunts on Arlo Hill, where he may see the goddess bathing. When the satyr betrays himself by laughing, he is captured by Diana's nymphs, covered with a deer skin, and set upon by hounds. He manages to escape, but Diana thereafter abandons Arlo Hill, cursing it as a haunt for wolves and thieves. Through the Irish setting of the story and its depiction of a humiliation offered to the moon goddess Diana, the poet links the account of Faunus to Mutabilitie's attack on Cynthia and her subsequent trial by Dame Nature. The inner story raises, however, an important issue not so clearly presented in the outer story, namely the role of erotic desire in bringing discord into the world.

The *Mutabilitie Cantos* represent the perfection of Spenser's art, combining almost effortlessly the strains of moral, psychological, and historical allegory that run through the entire poem. The poet's description of the great trial on Arlo Hill brings forth all his poetic powers, providing opportunities for dramatic word paintings of Mutabilitie's effects upon the heavens and the earth, but also for more delicate passages, such as the color miniatures of the seasons, months, and hours that parade before Dame Nature as evidence of endless change. Many of the dominant themes and images of Spenser's other works, from the earliest vision poems and The Shepheardes Calender to the Complaints and the Prothalamion, come together here.

The closing stanzas of the *Mutabilitie Cantos* offer Spenser's last word on the problem that had preoccupied him throughout his life, and, like the mottoes in the *Calender,* that word is enigmatic. Addressing Mutability, Dame Nature says only,

I well consider all that ye have sayd,
And find that all things stedfastnes doe hate
And changed be: yet being rightly wayd
They are not changed from their first estate;
But by their change their being doe dilate:
And turning to themselves at length againe,
Doe work their owne perfection so by fate:
Then over them Change doth not rule and raigne;
But they raigne over change, and doe their states maintaine.
(VII.vii.58)

Characteristically, Spenser leaves his readers to bring light to this "darke conceit," offering afterward only another equally mysterious solution to the problem of mutability, a Christian one that lies beyond the earthly wisdom of Dame Nature:

. . . all that moveth, doth in *Change* delight:
But thence-forth all shall rest eternally
With Him that is the God of Sabbaoth hight:

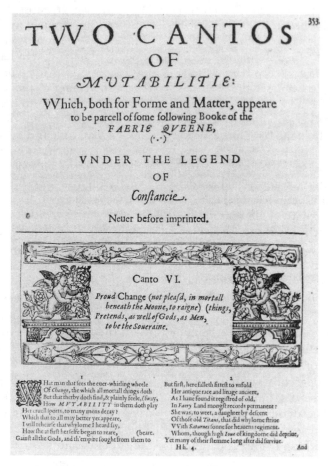

Page from the first folio edition (1609) of The Faerie
Queene, *the first edition to include the two cantos*
from the incomplete Book VII

o that great Sabbaoth God, graunt me that Sabaoths sight.
(VII.viii.2)

It may be that this prayer for rest in another world was the last line of poetry that Spenser ever wrote, for after it the fragmentary third canto of *Mutabilitie* breaks off. Certainly, the last two years of his life allowed him little leisure to write. In 1598 rebels attacked and burned Kilcolman Castle, forcing Spenser and his family to flee to Cork. In December he returned to England, where he delivered a report on the Irish crisis at Whitehall on Christmas Eve. Three weeks later, on 13 January 1599, he died, perhaps of illness brought on by exhaustion. He was buried soon after in the south transept of Westminster Abbey in Poets' Corner.

Twenty years after Spenser's death, Anne Clifford, Countess of Dorset, erected at his tomb a monument on which is engraved, "Heare lyes (expecting the Second comming of our Saviour Christ Jesus) the body of Edmond Spencer, the Prince of Poets in his tyme." If there is partiality here, shown in the surprising preference of Spenser over Shakespeare, the inscription is for that reason revealing because it suggests the strong devotion that the poet has so often aroused in his readers. Although his impact in the twentieth century has not been great by the standards of Chaucer, Shakespeare, or Milton, in earlier periods he exerted an influence on English culture that rivaled that of any poet in the language. Much of this influence was exerted through other poets, who have frequently turned to him as a teacher, incorporating his thought or his poetic methods into their own works. It is not without reason that Spenser is called the "poet's poet."

This may, in some measure, have been true even during Spenser's lifetime. In describing his funeral, the contemporary historian William Camden records that his body was placed "neere *Chawcer* . . . all Poets carrying his body to Church, and casting their dolefull Verses, and Pens too into his grave." Already, contemporaries such as Michael Drayton, Samuel Daniel, and Thomas Lodge were beginning to imitate *The Faerie*

Queene and *The Shepheardes Calender.* His influence continued to grow among writers of the seventeenth century, including William Browne of Tavistock, Giles and Phineas Fletcher, and Sir William Davenant. Ben Jonson, who once remarked about *The Faerie Queene* that "Spencers stanzas pleased him not, nor the matter," elsewhere calls the poem "*Spenser's* noble booke" and lists him, sometimes rather grumpily, among the great writers in the language. Milton was more consistent in his praise, depicting Spenser in the masque *Comus* (1637) as the wise shepherd Meliboeus and calling him in *Areopagitica* (1644) "our sage and serious poet *Spencer,* whom I dare be known to think a better teacher than *Scotus* or *Aquinas.*" Dryden confirms the autobiographical importance of this statement, reporting in *Fables, Ancient and Modern* (1700) that "*Milton* has acknowledg'd to me that *Spencer* was his Original."

Even more striking, however, is the response of writers in the eighteenth century, when scores of poets produced literally hundreds of imitations, adaptations, and continuations of Spenser's works. No other English poet except Milton can claim a greater following among the writers of that period. So pervasive was his influence, in fact, that Samuel Johnson felt obliged to write an essay in *Rambler* no. 20 opposing the publication of any more imitations, remarking with some exasperation that "they appeal not to reason or passion, but to memory, and pre-suppose an accidental or artificial state of mind." Johnson was right, of course; most of these imitations have since been forgotten. Yet some — by writers of ability such as James Thomson, James Beattie, Samuel Croxall, Moses Mendez, and Robert Burns — retain much of their original force, if not their original popularity.

By the nineteenth century the flood of imitations in England had narrowed, but it had also grown deeper. Along with Chaucer, Shakespeare, and Milton, Spenser stood as one of the great English sources of inspiration for the Romantic Age, providing in *The Faerie Queene* the quasi-medieval setting, the romance form, the stanzaic and metrical patterns, the archaic language, and the mingling of the natural with the artful and the supernatural that became the very stuff of Romanticism. Every one of the major Romantic poets was a serious reader of his works. William Wordsworth, who had memorized long swatches of his poetry as a boy and who frequently adapted and imitated his poetic effects, describes him in *The Prelude* (1850) as "Sweet Spenser, moving through his clouded heaven / With the moon's beauty and the moon's soft pace." Samuel Taylor Coleridge revealed his indebtedness in the archaic language of the *Rime of the Ancient Mariner* (1798) and the forested realms of chivalry and enchantment in *Christabel* (1816). John Keats, in turn, was so delighted by Spenser's language and prosody (and by *Christabel*) that he composed his *Eve of Saint Agnes* (1820) and four other poems (including his first and his last) in Spenserian stanzas. During his last illness he passed the time marking favorite passages in Spenser for the young Fanny Brawne, whom he had hoped to marry. Percy Bysshe Shelley looked to his Renaissance predecessor for models of multifaceted allegory, attempting in *Laon and Cythna* (1818) the longest of the Romantic poems in Spenserian stanzas and composing *Adonais* (1821) in response to Spenser's funeral elegy *Astrophel.* Even George Gordon, Lord Byron, was affected, fashioning his Childe Harold after the knights of *The Faerie Queene* and composing much of his early poetry in Spenserian stanzas, which he called "the measure most after my own heart."

Though most writers of the nineteenth century looked to Spenser for his metrical forms and his language, for his setting and his "atmospherics," there were some who admired him for the thought embodied in his poetry. William Butler Yeats incorporated Spenser's Platonism in his early Rose Poems and pondered, in his edition of the *Poems of Spenser,* the moving interplay between the delights of the senses and the stern moral allegories of *The Faerie Queene.* Widespread reaction against such allegory throughout the century, however, inevitably meant that influential writers other than practicing poets gradually came to read him less and less. There were, however, notable exceptions. In England prose writers such as Sir Walter Scott, Charles Lamb, and George MacDonald were deeply touched by Spenser's work, and in America, where religious sympathies were perhaps closer to Spenser's devout brand of Anglo-Protestantism, Nathaniel Hawthorne and Herman Melville turned to *The Faerie Queene* for its moral allegory and for its rich abundance of narrative models.

At the beginning of the twentieth century, just when Spenser's poetry was finally losing its place on the writing tables of practicing poets, it was rapidly finding its way onto the desks of professional scholars. In 1912 J. C. Smith and Ernest de Selincourt prepared the way for systematic study of his poems by bringing out a definitive edition (based on their Oxford English Text volumes of 1909 and 1910). During the next two decades, works of scholarship appeared with increasing frequency. In 1932 a group of Americans headed by Edwin Greenlaw at Johns Hopkins University brought out the first volume of the most important work on Spenser published during the first half of the century: the *Variorum Edition* of his collected works. Published over a period of twenty-five years, this vast compilation spans more than three centuries of published commentary and research. It also includes the only full-length biography of the poet ever written, Alexander C.

Spenser's tomb in Westminster Abbey

Judson's *The Life of Edmund Spenser* (1945; now notably outdated). In the period from the 1930s to the 1950s, the work of other scholars of international stature, such as C. S. Lewis at Cambridge University and A. S. P. Woodhouse at the University of Toronto, contributed significantly to the surge in interest that was gaining ground in the United States.

Even as the last volume of the *Variorum* was being published in 1957, however, critical fashions were changing. The scholars who had dominated Anglo-American studies of English literature earlier in the century had tended to divide their interests among biographical studies, investigations of obscure phrases and learned allusions, and the sort of historical research that attempts to place a writer such as Spenser in the larger social, philosophical, political, and literary traditions of his age. In consequence, relatively little systematic attention had been paid to the inner patterns of genre, sound, language, and rhetoric that are the most immediately perceptible features of a poet's work. By the late 1950s, however, biographical and historical research was gradually giving way to close exegesis, particularly the detailed analysis of genre, structure, and inner dynamics that became known as the "New Criticism." Works by scholars trained in the elegant pattern-tracing that is the hallmark of this school – Paul J. Alpers, Harry Berger Jr., Donald Cheney, A. C. Hamilton, A. Kent Hieatt, William Nelson, Thomas P. Roche Jr., Humphrey Tonkin, Kathleen Williams, and others – set in motion a new wave of interest in Spenser that swelled dramatically in the 1960s and 1970s. Although the expanding production of scholarly books and articles on the poet may be attributed, in part, to requirements for publication among a rapidly increasing population of university professors in the United States and Canada, Spenser received more than his share of their attention because he proved an ideal subject for the critical methods in which they had been trained. He rewarded nearly every kind of investigation favored by the New Critics – except, perhaps, the study of complex characterization. Not only were his poems elaborately patterned and structured but they were also rich in irony and ambiguity, tangled with multiple meanings, dense with allegorical plotting and symbolic imagery, laced through with delicate motifs, subtle in their humor, and ingenious in narrative technique. In consequence, Spenser attracted much more scholarly attention during twenty years of the New Criticism than he had in the preceding sixty years of historical and biographical scholarship.

Beginning in the 1980s, a second wave of changes in methodology swept through English departments in North America and the British Isles, challenging the assumptions of the New Criticism much as the New Critics had challenged the assumptions of their less analytical predecessors. The preoccupation with generic form and inner structure came under increasing fire because it tended to draw attention away from matters thought to be of more consequence, such as the political, cultural, and psychological forces at work in the poet and his contemporaries. The New Criticism was also criticized for having idealized – or at least exempted from ethical or ideological scrutiny – the works that it had so painstakingly analyzed. The tendency to explicate a work like *The Faerie Queene* without offering any sort of evaluation of its social or political effects seemed irresponsible to a generation of North American scholars taught by the upheavals of the 1960s to be suspicious of most cultural productions, particularly those with ties to powerful political or economic institutions and those implicated in patterns of discrimination based on class, gender, or ethnicity. With the advent of a series of critical methods loosely grouped under the heading "poststructuralist theory," or simply "theory," there has been a rapid diversification in critical approaches to Spenser's works. To be sure, the aims of the New Criticism, as well as those of traditional biographical and historical scholarship, continue to inform much of the work that is currently published, including recent efforts (by Judith H. Anderson, Donald Cheney, David A. Richardson, and others) to expand knowledge of Spenser's life and its immediate circumstances. Increasingly, however, less traditional approaches – derived from disciplines such as linguistics, philosophy, psychology, and the social sciences – are altering the scholarly agenda.

Among the approaches associated with the vague term *poststructuralism*, Marxist criticism has proved the slowest to attract attention, though Simon Shepherd has published a book on the entire corpus of Spenser's works based on cultural materialist aims and assumptions. More prevalent are instances of reader-response criticism (nicely illustrated in some of Thomas H. Cain's work), psychoanalytic criticism (explored by critics such as Benjamin G. Lockerd Jr. and David Lee Miller), and deconstructive criticism (notable in the work of Elizabeth Bellamy). Most influential of all have been approaches that stress the cultural, political, or psychological forces at work in shaping Spenser's thought and language. Jonathan Goldberg, for example, has adapted a theoretical scheme proposed by Roland Barthes to explain Spenser's resistance to closure in designing the complex plots and structures of *The Faerie Queene*. New Historicist critics such as Stephen Greenblatt, Louis A. Montrose, and Richard Helgerson have examined the poet's ideological stances in relation to the bases of political and social power in Elizabethan society. Finally, feminist critics such as Pamela Joseph Benson, Sheila T. Cavanagh, and Susanne Woods have undertaken a reevaluation of the poet's attitudes toward traditional gender roles, particularly the tension between his view that women are "borne to base humilitie, / Unlesse the heavens them lift to lawfull soveraintie" (*The Faerie Queene,* V.v.25) and his lofty praise for their abilities in such traditional areas of male dominance as warfare, the arts, and public policy (III.ii.1–3).

Such critical approaches have led to various judgments of the poet and his work. To some commentators, he was the conscious or unconscious purveyor of cultural biases designed to preserve and extend the privileges of a ruling class. To others, he was a subtly subversive figure, one who concealed criticism of Queen Elizabeth and her court within the elaborate encomiums of *The Faerie Queene*. To some, he was a willing instrument of a brutally repressive colonial regime in Ireland. To others, he was a dissatisfied – though more or less loyal – critic of government policy. To some, he was an early and remarkably enlightened spokesman for the movement to expand opportunities for women. To others, he was a social conservative, conceding the possibility of extraordinary attainments in a few public figures such as Queen Elizabeth but regarding most women as properly confined to their traditional duties at home. It seems fair to say that, in contemporary criticism, there is no longer one Spenser but many Spensers. Clearly, however, the controversies surrounding the poet have done nothing to diminish his appeal. If the annual bibliographies are to be believed, he has been studied more intensively in academic circles during the last fifteen years than in any previous period.

The extraordinary strength of Spenser's appeal over the centuries can perhaps be most clearly revealed by comparing him with Sidney. Initially, the poet of *Astrophil and Stella* and *Arcadia* was far more important than Spenser, exerting an influence on the Renaissance that was arguably broader and greater than that of any other author of the Elizabethan period. By the time Milton had published the final version of *Paradise Lost* (1674), however, Sidney's impact upon the world of letters was diminishing rapidly, and his reputation as a poet did not rebound to any great extent until the late nineteenth century.

Spenser, on the other hand, grew in importance during the same periods when Sidney suffered his greatest decline. Only in the twentieth century has his influence on the literary culture of the English-speaking world diminished. The qualities in his work that earlier ages valued – his fondness for things time-worn and venerable, his deeply religious cast of mind, his subordination of his own delicate appreciation of the delights of the senses to the nobler aims of ethical and political action, and his endless fascination with the complexities of literary form – have proved liabilities in a culture shaped by spare and skeptical modernism and by forms of entertainment more immediately striking to the senses than poetry. His decline as a major force among poets and writers of other forms of literature, however, has not necessarily meant a decline in the size of his broader audience, since he probably delights more readers today in college and university classrooms throughout the world than he ever did in the middle- and upper-class parlors of England during the periods of his greatest influence.

Bibliographies:

Frederick Ives Carpenter, *A Reference Guide to Edmund Spenser* (Chicago: University of Chicago Press, 1923);

Francis R. Johnson, *A Critical Bibliography of the Works of Edmund Spenser Printed before 1700* (Baltimore: Johns Hopkins University Press, 1933);

Jewell Wurtsbaugh, *Two Centuries of Spenserian Scholarship (1609–1805)* (Baltimore: Johns Hopkins University Press, 1936);

Dorothy R. Atkinson, *Edmund Spenser: A Bibliographical Supplement* (Baltimore: Johns Hopkins University Press, 1937) – covers the period 1923–1937;

A. C. Hamilton, "Edmund Spenser," in *The New Cambridge Bibliography of English Literature,* volume 1, edited by George Watson (Cambridge: Cambridge University Press, 1974), cols. 1029–1047;

Waldo F. McNeir and Foster Provost, *Edmund Spenser: An Annotated Bibliography 1937–72* (Pittsburgh: Duquesne University Press, 1975);

William L. Sipple and Bernard Vondersmith, *Edmund Spenser 1900–1936: A Reference Guide* (Boston: G. K. Hall, 1984).

Biographies:

Alexander C. Judson, *The Life of Edmund Spenser* (Baltimore: Johns Hopkins University Press, 1945);

Willy Maley, *A Spenser Chronology* (Totowa, N.J.: Barnes & Noble, 1994).

References:

Paul J. Alpers, *The Poetry of "The Faerie Queene"* (Princeton: Princeton University Press, 1967);

Alpers, "Spenser's Late Pastorals," *English Literary History (ELH),* 56 (Winter 1989): 797–816;

Alpers, ed., *Edmund Spenser: A Critical Anthology* (Baltimore: Penguin, 1969);

Judith H. Anderson, " 'In liuing colours and right hew': The Queen of Spenser's Central Books," in *Poetic Traditions of the English Renaissance,* edited by Maynard Mack and George de Forest Lord (New Haven: Yale University Press, 1982), pp. 47–66;

Anderson, Donald Cheney, and David A. Richardson, eds., *Spenser and the Subject of Biography* (Amherst: University of Massachusetts Press, 1996);

Jane Aptekar, *Icons of Justice: Iconography and Thematic Imagery in Book V of "The Faerie Queene"* (New York: Columbia University Press, 1969);

Mark A. Archer, "The Meaning of 'Grace' and 'Courtesy': Book VI of *The Faerie Queene,*" *Studies in English Literature,* 27 (Winter 1987): 17–34;

Peter Bayley, ed., *Spenser: "The Faerie Queene": A Casebook* (London: Macmillan, 1977);

John B. Bender, *Spenser and Literary Pictorialism* (Princeton: Princeton University Press, 1972);

Pamela Joseph Benson, *The Invention of the Renaissance Woman: The Challenge of Female Independence in the Literature and Thought of Italy and England* (University Park: Pennsylvania State University Press, 1992);

Harry Berger Jr., *The Allegorical Temper: Vision and Reality in Book II of Spenser's "Faerie Queene"* (New Haven: Yale University Press, 1957);

Berger, *Revisionary Play: Studies in the Spenserian Dynamics* (Berkeley: University of California Press, 1988);

Berger, ed., *Spenser: A Collection of Critical Essays* (Englewood Cliffs, N.J.: Prentice-Hall, 1968);

John D. Bernard, *Ceremonies of Innocence: Pastoralism in the Poetry of Edmund Spenser* (Cambridge: Cambridge University Press, 1989);

Philippa Berry, *Of Chastity and Power: Elizabethan Literature and the Unmarried Queen* (London: Routledge, 1989), pp. 153–165;

Harold Bloom, ed., *Modern Critical Views: Edmund Spenser* (New York: Chelsea, 1986);

Kenneth Borris, *Spenser's Poetics of Prophecy in "The Faerie Queene" V, English Literary Studies,* Monograph Series No. 52 (Victoria, B.C.: University of Victoria, 1991);

Brendan Bradshaw, Andrew Hadfield, and Willy Maley, eds., *Representing Ireland: Literature and the Origins of Conflict, 1534–1660* (Cambridge: Cambridge University Press, 1993);

Douglas Brooks-Davies, *Spenser's "Faerie Queene": A Critical Commentary on Books I and II* (Manchester: Manchester University Press, 1977);

Thomas H. Cain, *Praise in "The Faerie Queene"* (Lincoln: University of Nebraska Press, 1978);

Sheila T. Cavanagh, *Wanton Eyes and Chaste Desires: Female Sexuality in "The Faerie Queene"* (Bloomington: University of Indiana Press, 1994);

Donald Cheney, *Spenser's Image of Nature: Wild Man and Shepherd in "The Faerie Queene"* (New Haven: Yale University Press, 1966);

Patrick Cheney, "The Old Poet Presents Himself: *Prothalamion* as a Defense of Spenser's Career," *Spenser Studies,* 8 (1987): 211–238;

Patrick Cheney, *Spenser's Famous Flight: A Renaissance Idea of a Literary Career* (Toronto: University of Toronto Press, 1993);

Terry Comito, "A Dialectic of Images in Spenser's *Fowre Hymnes,*" *Studies in Philology,* 74 (July 1977): 301–321;

Patricia Coughlin, ed., *Spenser and Ireland: An Interdisciplinary Perspective,* with an introduction by Nicholas Canny (Cork: Cork University Press, 1989);

Martha Craig, "The Secret Wit of Spenser's Language," in *Elizabethan Poetry: Essays in Criticism,* edited by Paul J. Alpers (New York: Oxford University Press, 1967), pp. 447–472;

Critical Essays on Spenser from "ELH" (Baltimore: Johns Hopkins University Press, 1970);

R. M. Cummings, *Spenser: The Critical Heritage* (Totowa, N.J.: Barnes & Noble, 1971);

Judith Dundas, *Pencils Rhetorique: Renaissance Poets and the Art of Painting* (Toronto & London: Associated University Presses, 1993);

Dundas, *The Spider and the Bee: The Artistry of Spenser's "Faerie Queene"* (Urbana: University of Illinois Press, 1985);

Alexander Dunlop, "The Unity of Spenser's *Amoretti,*" in *Silent Poetry: Essays in Numerological Analysis,* edited by Alastair Fowler (London: Routledge & Kegan Paul, 1970), pp. 153–169;

T. K. Dunseath, *Spenser's Allegory of Justice in Book Five of "The Faerie Queene"* (Princeton: Princeton University Press, 1968);

Calvin Edwards, *Spenser and the Ovidian Tradition,* dissertation, Yale University, 1958;

John R. Elliott Jr., ed., *The Prince of Poets: Essays on Edmund Spenser* (New York: New York University Press, 1968);

Robert Ellrodt, *Neoplatonism in the Poetry of Edmund Spenser* (Geneva: E. Droz, 1960);

Maurice Evans, *Spenser's Anatomy of Heroism: A Commentary on "The Faerie Queene"* (Cambridge: Cambridge University Press, 1970);

Rosemary Freeman, *"The Faerie Queene": A Companion for Readers* (Berkeley: University of California Press, 1970);

Richard C. Frushell and Bernard J. Vondersmith, eds., *Contemporary Thought on Edmund Spenser* (Carbondale: University of Southern Illinois Press, 1975);

Lila Geller, "Venus and the Three Graces: A Neoplatonic Paradigm for Book III of *The Faerie Queene,*" *Journal of English and Germanic Philology,* 75 (January/April 1976): 56–74;

A. Bartlett Giamatti, *Play of Double Senses: Spenser's "Faerie Queene"* (Englewood Cliffs, N.J.: Prentice-Hall, 1975);

Jonathan Goldberg, *Endlesse Worke: Spenser and the Structures of Discourse* (Baltimore: Johns Hopkins University Press, 1981);

Stephen Greenblatt, *Renaissance Self-Fashioning: From More to Shakespeare* (Chicago: University of Chicago Press, 1980), pp. 157–192;

Gladys D. Haase, *Spenser's Orthography: An Examination of a Poet's Use of the Variant Pronunciations of Elizabethan English,* dissertation, Columbia University, 1952;

A. C. Hamilton, " 'Like Race to Runne': The Parallel Structure of *The Faerie Queene,* Books I and II," *Publications of the Modern Language Association,* 73 (September 1958): 327–334;

Hamilton, *The Structure of Allegory in "The Faerie Queene"* (Oxford: Clarendon Press, 1961);

Hamilton, ed., *Essential Articles for the Study of Edmund Spenser* (Hamden, Conn.: Archon, 1972);

Hamilton, Donald Cheney, W. F. Blissett, David A. Richardson, and William W. Barker, eds., *The Spenser Encyclopedia* (Toronto: University of Toronto Press, 1990);

John Erskine Hankins, *Source and Meaning in Spenser's Allegory: A Study of "The Faerie Queene"* (Oxford: Clarendon Press, 1971);

Elizabeth Heale, *"The Faerie Queene": A Study Guide* (Cambridge: Cambridge University Press, 1987);

Richard Helgerson, *Self-Crowned Laureates: Spenser, Jonson, Milton and the Literary System* (Berkeley: University of California Press, 1983);

S. K. Heninger Jr., *Sidney and Spenser: The Poet as Maker* (University Park: Pennsylvania State University Press, 1989);

A. Kent Hieatt, *Chaucer, Spenser, Milton: Mythopoetic Continuities and Transformations* (Montreal: McGill-Queen's University Press, 1975);

Hieatt, "The Genesis of Shakespeare's Sonnets: Spenser's *Ruines of Rome: by Bellay*," *Publications of the Modern Language Association,* 98 (October 1983): 800–814;

Hieatt, *Short Time's Endless Monument: The Symbolism of the Numbers in Edmund Spenser's "Epithalamion"* (New York: Columbia University Press, 1960);

Robert Hoopes, " 'God Guide Thee, Guyon': Nature and Grace Reconciled in *The Faerie Queene,* Book II," *Review of English Studies,* new series 5, no. 17 (1954): 14–24;

Ronald A. Horton, *The Unity of "The Faerie Queene"* (Athens:.University of Georgia Press, 1978);

Graham Hough, *A Preface to "The Faerie Queene"* (London: Duckworth, 1962);

Merritt Y. Hughes, *Virgil and Spenser* (Berkeley: University of California Press, 1929);

Clark Hulse, "Spenser and the Myth of Power," *Studies in Philology,* 85 (Summer 1988): 378–389;

Anthea Hume, *Edmund Spenser: Protestant Poet* (Cambridge: Cambridge University Press, 1984);

Lynn Staley Johnson, *"The Shepheardes Calender": An Introduction* (University Park: Pennsylvania State University Press, 1990);

Carol V. Kaske, "Spenser's *Amoretti* and *Epithalamion* of 1595: Structure, Genre, and Numerology," *English Literary Renaissance,* 8 (Autumn 1978): 271–295;

Judith M. Kennedy and James A. Reither, eds., *A Theatre for Spenserians* (Toronto: University of Toronto Press, 1973);

John N. King, *Spenser's Poetry and the Reformation Tradition* (Princeton: Princeton University Press, 1990);

Theresa M. Krier, *Gazing on Secret Sights: Spenser, Classical Imitation, and the Decorum of Vision* (Ithaca: Cornell University Press, 1990);

Robert Lane, *Shepheards Devises: Edmund Spenser's "Shepheardes Calender" and the Institutions of Elizabethan Society* (Athens & London: University of Georgia Press, 1993);

Michael Leslie, *Spenser's "Fierce Warres and Faithfull Loves": Martial and Chivalric Symbolism in "The Faerie Queene"* (Cambridge: D. S. Brewer, 1983);

C. S. Lewis, *The Allegory of Love* (Oxford: Clarendon Press, 1936), pp. 297–360;

Lewis, "Sidney and Spenser," in his *English Literature in the Sixteenth Century, Excluding Drama* (Oxford: Clarendon Press, 1954), pp. 318–393;

Benjamin G. Lockerd Jr., *The Sacred Marriage: Psychic Integration in "The Faerie Queene"* (Lewisburg, Pa.: Bucknell University Press, 1987);

Isabel G. MacCaffrey, *Spenser's Allegory: The Anatomy of Imagination* (Princeton: Princeton University Press, 1976);

Richard A. McCabe, *The Pillars of Eternity: Time and Providence in "The Faerie Queene,"* Dublin Series in Medieval and Renaissance Literature (Dublin: Irish Academic Press, 1989);

Russell J. Meyer, *"The Faerie Queene": Educating the Reader* (Boston: Twayne, 1991);

David Lee Miller, *The Poem's Two Bodies: The Poetics of the 1590 "Faerie Queene"* (Princeton: Princeton University Press, 1988);

Miller and Dunlop, eds., *Approaches to Teaching Spenser's "Faerie Queene"* (New York: Modern Language Association, 1994);

Charles Bowie Millican, *Spenser and the Table Round: A Study in the Contemporaneous Background for Spenser's Use of the Arthurian Legend* (Cambridge, Mass.: Harvard University Press, 1932);

Louis A. Montrose, "The Elizabethan Subject and the Spenserian Text," in *Literary Theory/Renaissance Texts,* edited by Patricia Parker and David Quint (Baltimore: Johns Hopkins University Press, 1986), pp. 303–340;

William R. Mueller, *Spenser's Critics: Changing Currents in Literary Taste* (Syracuse: Syracuse University Press, 1959);

William Nelson, *The Poetry of Edmund Spenser: A Study* (New York: Columbia University Press, 1963);

Nelson, ed., *Form and Convention in the Poetry of Edmund Spenser* (New York: Columbia University Press, 1961);

Richard Neuse, "Book VI as Conclusion to *The Faerie Queene,*" *English Literary History (ELH),* 35 (September 1968): 329–353;

James Nohrnberg, *The Analogy of "The Faerie Queene"* (Princeton: Princeton University Press, 1976);

Michael O'Connell, *Mirror and Veil: The Historical Dimension of Spenser's "Faerie Queene"* (Chapel Hill: University of North Carolina Press, 1977);

William A. Oram, "Elizabethan Fact and Spenserian Fiction," *Spenser Studies,* 4 (1983): 33–47;

Charles Grosvenor Osgood, *A Concordance to the Poems of Edmund Spenser* (Washington, D.C.: Carnegie Institution of Washington, 1915);

Camille Paglia, *Sexual Personae: Art and Decadence from Nefertiti to Emily Dickinson* (New Haven: Yale University Press, 1990), pp. 170–193;

Annabel Patterson, *Reading Between the Lines* (Madison: University of Wisconsin Press, 1993);

Richard Rambuss, *Spenser's Secret Career* (Cambridge: Cambridge University Press, 1993);

W. L. Renwick, *Edmund Spenser: An Essay on Renaissance Poetry* (London: Edward Arnold, 1925);

Herbert David Rix, *Rhetoric in Spenser's Poetry* (University Park: Pennsylvania State University Press, 1940);

Gareth Roberts, *The Faerie Queene* (Buckingham & Philadelphia: Open University Press, 1992);

Thomas P. Roche Jr., *The Kindly Flame: A Study of the Third and Fourth Books of Spenser's "Faerie Queene"* (Princeton: Princeton University Press, 1964);

Mark Rose, *Spenser's Art: A Companion to Book One of "The Faerie Queene"* (Cambridge, Mass.: Harvard University Press, 1975);

Roger Sale, *Reading Spenser: An Introduction to "The Faerie Queene"* (New York: Random House, 1968);

Naseeb Shaheen, *Biblical References in "The Faerie Queene"* (Memphis, Tenn.: Memphis State University Press, 1977);

Simon Shepherd, *Spenser* (Atlantic Highlands, N.J.: Humanities Press International, 1989);

Helena Shire, *A Preface to Spenser* (London & New York: Longman, 1978);

David R. Shore, *Spenser and the Poetics of Pastoral: A Study of the World of Colin Clout* (Kingston, Ont.: McGill-Queen's University Press, 1985);

Lauren Silberman, "Singing Unsung Heroines: Androgynous Discourse in Book 3 of *The Faerie Queene*," in *Rewriting the Renaissance: The Discourses of Sexual Difference in Early Modern Europe,* edited by Margaret W. Ferguson, Maureen Quilligan, and Nancy J. Vickers (Chicago: University of Chicago Press, 1986), pp. 259–271;

Silberman, *Transforming Desire: Erotic Knowledge in Books III and IV of "The Faerie Queene"* (Berkeley: University of California Press, 1995);

Charles G. Smith, *Spenser's Proverb Lore* (Cambridge, Mass.: Harvard University Press, 1970);

Hallett Smith, *Elizabethan Poetry: A Study in Conventions, Meaning, and Expression* (Cambridge, Mass.: Harvard University Press, 1952);

Spenser Newsletter (1969–);

Spenser Studies: A Renaissance Poetry Annual (1980–);

Donald V. Stump, "Isis versus Mercilla: The Allegorical Shrines in Spenser's Legend of Justice," *Spenser Studies,* 3 (1983): 87–98;

Herbert W. Sugden, *The Grammar of Spenser's "Faerie Queene"* (Philadelphia: Linguistic Society of America, 1936);

Humphrey Tonkin, *The Faerie Queene* (London: Unwin, 1989);

Tonkin, *Spenser's Courteous Pastoral: Book VI of "The Faerie Queene"* (Oxford: Clarendon Press, 1972);

Gary Waller, *Edmund Spenser: A Literary Life* (New York: St. Martin's Press, 1994);

John Watkins, *The Specter of Dido: Spenser and the Virgilian Epic* (New Haven: Yale University Press, 1995);

Harold L. Weatherby, *Mirrors of Celestial Grace: Patristic Theology in Spenser's Allegory* (Toronto: University of Toronto Press, 1994);

Robin Headlam Wells, *Spenser's "Faerie Queene" and the Cult of Elizabeth* (Totowa, N.J.: Barnes & Noble, 1983);

William Wells, ed., *Spenser Allusions in the Sixteenth and Seventeenth Centuries,* 2 volumes, *Studies in Philology,* Texts and Studies 78–79 (1971–1972);

Virgil K. Whitaker, *The Religious Basis of Spenser's Thought* (Stanford, Cal.: Stanford University Press, 1950);

Charles Huntington Whitman, *A Subject Index to the Poems of Edmund Spenser* (New Haven: Yale University Press, 1918);

Arnold Williams, *Flower on a Lowly Stalk: The Sixth Book of the "Faerie Queene"* (Lansing: Michigan State University Press, 1967);

Kathleen Williams, *Spenser's "Faerie Queene": The World of Glass* (Berkeley: University of California Press, 1966);

Susanne Lindgren Wofford, *The Choice of Achilles: The Ideology of Figure in the Epic* (Stanford, Cal.: Stanford University Press, 1992), pp. 215–371;

A. S. P. Woodhouse, "Nature and Grace in *The Faerie Queene*," *English Literary History* (*ELH*), 16 (September 1949): 194–228;

Susanne Woods, "Spenser and the Problem of Women's Rule," *Huntington Library Quarterly,* 48 (Spring 1985): 141–158.

Papers:

More than one hundred autograph items by Edmund Spenser survive. Unfortunately, however, none are of his literary or political works. The majority are official letters and documents that he prepared as secretary to Arthur, Lord Grey, and later to Sir John Norris in Ireland, and the rest are addresses, endorsements, receipts, and legal documents relating to his landholdings and other matters. The only literary items are his transcriptions of two Latin poems by Lotichius and a Latin letter on poetry by Erhardus Stibarus. Most of his papers are among the State Papers of Ireland in the Public Record Office, the Additional and Cotton Manuscripts in the British Library, and the Cecil Papers at Hatfield House. A complete listing may be found in Anthony G. Petti's article on Spenser's handwriting in *The Spenser Encyclopedia.*

Appendix I

Author-Printers, 1476–1599

Author-Printers, 1476–1599

Sheila Ahern
Victoria University of Wellington, New Zealand

See also the William Baldwin entry in *DLB 132: Sixteenth-Century British Nondramatic Writers, First Series*; the Henry Chettle entry in *DLB 136: Sixteenth-Century British Nondramatic Writers, Second Series*; the Robert Copland entry in *DLB 136: Sixteenth-Century British Nondramatic Writers, Second Series*; the Anthony Munday entry in *DLB 62: Elizabethan Dramatists*; and the John Rastell entry in *DLB 136: Sixteenth-Century British Nondramatic Writers, Second Series*.

Printers are to be found among the writers of all kinds of early printed literature. Their craft opened exciting possibilities to shape and direct the thoughts and attitudes of society, and many of the first printers were learned humanist scholars eager to promote the common good by educating the ignorant. The invention of the printing press enabled literary and educational aims to be set and achieved in accord with the new secular humanist view of society. Making knowledge accessible invariably meant translating Latin works or writing new works in the vernacular language, and many printers did both. Their prefaces show the pride taken in offering good works, good texts, and good authors to a public that might well have been satisfied with less.

As authors, they furthered the development of English prose, wrote works of literature, contributed to the writing of history, wrote legal and medical treatises, increased scientific knowledge, and spread new religious ideas. Through their role as editors they helped to preserve the nation's literary heritage, and as translators they popularized hitherto specialized areas of knowledge such as medicine, law, and local government. If some of the literature that printers wrote was not very good (such as John Awdeley's or Robert Crowley's metrical verses), it was, nevertheless, written to influence public opinion and was typically readable and popular. Although the history of English literature must deal with great writers, theirs is not the only literature to be taken seriously. Booksellers' stalls were always full of lesser writings, many written by the printers themselves, that influenced popular opinion. Indeed, this seemingly tasteless literature often

had the greater immediate significance in contemporary sixteenth-century society.

In the opening years of the sixteenth century, London printers were few in number. They lived in close proximity to one another and as a direct result of the establishment of their trade in Fleet Street began the legendary association of London's best-known thoroughfare with the new art of printing. A well-established and flourishing international trade in books already existed, with presses set up in some two hundred European cities, so that for books of quality it was customary for English buyers to look to the Continental market. The production of vernacular works, however, became a self-imposed duty and a matter of pride for the first English printers, who set themselves goals of a common language and a national literature.

William Caxton (circa 1422–1491) established England's first printing press in 1476 at the Red Pale in Westminster where he printed the first edition of Geoffrey Chaucer's *Canterbury Tales* (circa 1375–1400), several romances, and books of English poetry. Caxton wrote original works in English, but a third of the works he published were his translations, bearing prefaces and epilogues that describe his difficulties with the unpolished English language. A love of literature and a dedication to the common good led him to translate and print books for those who were read to or could read English themselves, with the laudable aim of their improvement and education. In the prologue to his 1484 translation of Cato, he states his purpose to be "the erudition and learning of them that be ignorant that they may thereby profit and be the better."

Caxton's successor, Wynkyn de Worde (flourished 1494–1535) from Worth in Lorraine, followed his lead but depended upon an English assistant, Robert Copland, for literary advice. In 1500 de Worde moved the press to Fleet Street, which was already becoming a printing center through the residence and commercial activities there of three other printers, all of whom, like de Worde, were foreign-born: John Lettou; William de Machlina; and Julian Notary.

In 1509 de Worde opened a bookseller's booth among the shops in St. Paul's Churchyard, where he sold his own editions, including new romances such as the anonymous *Apollonius of Tyre* (1510) and La Coudrette's *Melusine* (1510?). Like Fleet Street, St. Paul's Churchyard became another center for printers, and there, at midcentury, Stationers' Hall was built. Yet at no time during the century was the number of printers very great: even in 1582, when Christopher Barker wrote his account of the London printers, he recorded only twenty-two printing-houses, although this number did not include secret presses operating undercover.

Although detailed knowledge of the background and education of many early printers is lacking, it is clear that printing was an occupation calling for a reasonably high level of literacy and learning, since it was usual for the additional functions of writer, editor, translator, and selector of texts to be undertaken by the printer. At the advent of printing, books were extremely expensive and highly esteemed as possessions, so it was natural in its early days that printing should attract the attention of the learned, the interest of the literary, and the favor of the great. By the end of the sixteenth century, many well-known writers had once worked as printers' apprentices and assistants, the most notable being William Baldwin (circa 1515–1563), Henry Chettle (circa 1560–circa 1603), Raphael Holinshed (died 1580), Anthony Munday (1560–1633), and Thomas Proctor (flourished 1578–1584).

John W. Martin's statement that printing was "the new trade by which energetic artisans made money and gained status" is far from accurate, however, and the suggestion that Richard Day (1552–1607) and Robert Crowley (1518–1588) gave up printing and took holy orders because of "a Tudor equivalent of Victorian society's taboo against gentlemen engaging in trade" is misleading. It was, in fact, advantageous for English printers to be men of some substance with sufficient capital to establish a new craft. Caxton, for example, was a wealthy merchant and man of learning, as were Richard Grafton (died 1573), Edward Whitchurch (died 1562), and John Mayler (flourished 1539–1545). The lawyer John Rastell (1475?–1536) was educated at Oxford, then at Lincoln's Inn, and successfully practiced law for several years before he became a printer. His son, William Rastell (1508?–1565), was also a lawyer and printer, and John Butler (flourished 1529), another Fleet Street printer, was a judge of common pleas.

Several printers were notable scholars, such as Richard Jugge (flourished 1548–1577) from King's College; Thomas Gibson (died 1562), compiler and printer in 1535 of the first concordance of the New Testament in English; and Thomas Raynalde (flourished 1539–1552), a printer, scholar, and physician. When Phillip Luckombe recorded in 1771 that John Rastell took up the employ of printing after attending Oxford, he added that it "at that time was esteemed a profession for a scholar." The extent of Rastell's learning, therefore, carried more weight with him than the fact that Rastell was a gentleman and the brother-in-law of Sir Thomas More. Unquestionably, in the early days printing was a prestigious occupation, and its practitioners entered into negotiations with wealthy patrons and entertained learned writers in their homes. Individual members of the Stationers' Company had influential friends at court and in the church hierarchy, and the status of the Stationers' Company is undoubtedly reflected by the fact that the queen's secretary, Sir Thomas Smith, sought admission to the Company by redemption.

For the first three decades of the sixteenth century, the book trade in England was dominated by foreign printers and booksellers. Wynkyn de Worde from Worth and Richard Pynson (flourished 1490–1529) from Normandy printed between them during the first twenty years of the new century more than 70 percent of the total book production. They catered largely to the traditional market in Latin texts for clergy and students, while making some provision for the increasing demand for works in the vernacular.

The first English-born printers after Caxton, John Rastell and Robert Copland (1470?–1548), deliberately worked toward extending that market by encouraging learned authors to write in the vulgar tongue. They were consciously following Caxton's example of increasing the number of available English texts by undertaking translations from Latin and French and by writing and printing their own English works.

Their enthusiasm for useful works in English was shared by Thomas Berthelet (flourished 1517–1555), who worked as Pynson's English assistant before he established himself as a London printer in 1530. Berthelet was eager to promote English humanism and to this end wrote prefatory verses that tried to break down the contemporary prejudice shown by the learned against low or commonplace subjects. His prefatory letter to a 1523 edition of John Fitzherbert's *Book of Surveying* printed by Pynson explains Berthelet's conviction that contempt for ordinary matters was neither in the true classical tradition nor in the nation's best interests:

The worthy Cato, that excellent Roman
Columella, Varro, and Vergilius
Of husbandry to write, had in no disdain
Nor many other, eloquent and famous,
Thought it not a thing inglorious
Such matter to write, whereby they might advance
The commonwealth and their country enhance.
But in our days, some are blinded so with folly
That they count husbandry but a thing right vile.

Most contemporary printers added their own prefatory verses to their publications in Latin and in English, but Rastell and Copland were author-printers who deserve to be ranked alongside Caxton as the earliest promoters of printed English literature. Although other printers were also authors of broadsides, pamphlets, and news sheets, through catering for the popular taste by writing and printing entertaining tales that would sell, both Rastell and Copland personally made notable contributions to the jest literature of the age. However, they were also determined to make use of the printing press as a way of educating their fellow citizens, as the prologues to their works invariably state.

Rastell's dramatic works, historical writing, and law treatises were intended to enhance the English language while conveying a powerful humanist message of social justice and civic responsibility. Moreover, Rastell appears to have been the only Englishman in the first half of the sixteenth century to have written on exploration. In his play *Four Elements* (1525?), he reminds the learned of their duty to write serious works in English for the benefit of the ignorant, and he uses the work to instruct his audience in a proper appreciation of science and geography. He declares it would be a wonderful thing if Englishmen were the first to take possession of land in the New World and raise buildings there as "a memory perpetual." However, his purpose is also to provoke a humanitarian concern for primitive people in need of religion and education: "And what a great meritorious deed / It were to have the people instructed." In fact, he had earlier embarked on an unsuccessful voyage to the New World in 1517 accompanied by Berthelet, apparently with the intention of educating the populace through introducing the art of printing there.

Although Rastell began his printing and writing career in the hope of creating lay interest in good law and government, he ultimately became involved with religious writing. In 1530 he wrote *A New Book of Purgatory,* but in the ensuing debate with the reformer John Frith, Rastell was won over to the new faith. His last years, before he died in prison in 1536, were spent writing reformist religious works, referred to in his correspondence with Thomas Cromwell and mentioned by John Bale, which do not seem to have survived. Their existence is, however, supported by opposition to his writings from Catholic rebels in the Pilgrimage of Grace – the rising of 1536 against the closure of monasteries. Rastell had better success with his plays, which led Frederick S. Boas to label him an "early Tudor Bernard Shaw" for his reformist intentions. These ideals included promotion of the English language and advocacy of serious thought and social responsibility in a manner acceptable to the public.

From 1514 to 1548 Copland worked at the Rose Garland in Fleet Street. In 1547 Andrew Boorde, whose work Copland was then printing, described him as "the eldest printer in England" (*The Principles of Astronomy*). Copland was a prolific writer, translator, and printer whose name was associated with the London trade for almost fifty years. He had been an apprentice to Caxton and to de Worde, and his influence is believed to be the reason behind de Worde's commercial success. Copland's interests were primarily literary, but he was also interested in developing and standardizing the English language and its spelling. His printing is significant for his choice of texts and for an interest in punctuation that brought about the introduction of the comma in its modern form into England.

It was Copland's constant complaint that the man in the street preferred to buy jest-books, ballads, and similar cheap trifles. His verses prefacing Chaucer's *Parliament of Fowls* (1530) lament that "Trifles and toys they be the things so sought," while he, the meritorious printer, struggles to raise literary standards by offering the works of Chaucer, John Lydgate, and John Gower to a reluctant public: "Their books you lay up till that the leather moulds / But yet for your minds this book I will impress." Copland made an important contribution to English literature with his own verse satires, most notably *The Highway to the Spital-House* (1536), which raised the problems of poverty and destitution in Tudor society in a revealing yet entertaining way.

As the sixteenth century progressed, the number of English printers increased and the percentage of books printed in the vernacular language rose to exceed the production of Latin works. At the same time the contents of many books became more secular. However, providing vernacular works for a new class of lay readers created some resentment from certain scholars. Richard Tottel's printer's preface to his *Miscellany* (1557) condemns these critics as "ungentle hoarders" who withheld "treasure" from society. In his opinion, printers who publish in English both enrich the English language and accomplish a good deed for the community.

Civic and ecclesiastical authorities, however, were naturally alarmed by the tremendous sphere of influence that printing offered authors and printers. Nowhere was it more obvious than in the production of religious works that certain printers had deliberately chosen the profession as a means of shaping public beliefs. Thomas Gibson (died 1562), for example, was a physician and reformist scholar who compiled and printed the first concordance of the *New Testament* in English in 1535. In the four years that he practiced the trade, he printed five books, four of which were religious. During Mary's reign he was compelled to live abroad along with other English religious exiles.

Between 1539 and 1555 Thomas Raynalde, like Gibson a physician as well as a printer, printed thirty-four books, thirty of which were religious — a clear indication that he used his press to promote religious reform. Raynalde's brief printing career is distinguished by the fact that he was the first copperplate printer in England. In the medical work that he enlarged, *The Birth of Mankind* (1545), his prologue daringly recommends the Bible in English to all women, stating, "The most holy and sacred Bible teaches nothing but holiness and virtuous living, charity to God and to our neighbor, reformation of our wicked living, and briefly the highway to God." This was, in fact, contrary to Henry VIII's 1543 Act for the Advancement of True Religion, which expressly forbade reading of the Bible for women below the rank of gentlewomen; the act was not repealed until 1547, two years after the appearance of Raynalde's book. In his dedication Raynalde praises books written in "vulgar English" as a way of "enriching our mother tongue" to the great profit of all who used the language. During Mary's reign, he printed two primers and then ceased printing altogether. He thus did not become a member of the Stationers' Company when it was incorporated with a charter from Mary, who intended to tighten control over what was being printed. Several other printers with known Protestant sympathies did not join as founder-members, among them Richard Grafton and Edward Whitchurch.

Another advocate of lay literacy and of reading the Scriptures in English at the end of Henry VIII's reign was Richard Taverner (1505?–1575), who was actively involved with Richard Bankes's press. Taverner's preface to his *Postils on Epistles and Gospels* (1540) avows:

> Forasmuch as, good Christian reader, at the present time, according to our Lord's word, the harvest is great and plenteous, but the laborers are few (I mean as thus, that the people be very desirous and greedy to receive God's Word, if they had plenty of sober, modest, sincere teachers; whereas now for scarcity of such in some places they be destitute and scattered abroad even as sheep lacking faithful shepherds), I was instantly required . . . by this means [to] thrust forth his laborers into the harvest.

Taverner had associated with the Reformers while he was a student at Oxford and had been in trouble over the circulation of Tyndale's *New Testament*. He was the author of several religious works, and in the more permissive days of Edward VI he obtained a special license to preach in order to influence as wide an audience as possible.

The movement for social reform that many Protestant preachers championed during Edward VI's reign was ably supported by the writings of a group of printers that included Humphrey Powell (flourished 1548–1566), who, after working in London between 1547 and 1551, went to Ireland in 1551. There he made printing history by setting up the first Irish printing press. In addition to printing only the works of Protestant reformers, Powell wrote and published his satiric *Will of the Devil* (1550), which mocked Catholic practices. His theme was that the strife and turbulence of the times were bequests of the devil, who was anxious to disrupt the good work of reformation. Whereas Jesus Christ was called the devil's "most deadly enemy," Stephen Gardiner was called one of the devil's good, special, and trusty friends. In simple but satiric language, Powell shows that images and crucifixes belong to the devil, who showers them on private papists for secret worship.

One of the most outspoken social critics during Edward VI's reign was Robert Crowley, a scholar and preacher who began a lifetime association with the book trade after being compelled to resign from a fellowship at Magdalen College, Oxford, in 1545. He worked as a proofreader for John Day, who probably encouraged him to take up the art of printing in 1548 in order to increase the output of Protestant literature. Through the medium of print, Crowley waged a crusade for social justice and religious reform, including the first printed edition of *Piers Plowman* (1550), as well as tracts of his own authorship.

His message was a forthright condemnation of the abuses in society that could be eradicated if the populace reformed. In verse and in prose he recorded the disillusionment of many of his contemporaries, caused mainly by the fact that the poor had in no way benefited from the appropriation of monastic foundations. In a little-known allegorical fable, *Philargyry of Great Britain* (1551), Crowley describes rampant oppression caused by Avarice's domination of Britain. The blame for this he lays squarely on the shoulders of self-seeking parliamentarians and merchants. He claims that their actions were responsible for provoking the peasant risings of 1549 in Norfolk, Cornwall, and Devon. His analysis blames the despairing peasants less for the social unrest than it does a new class of profiteers then coming into dominance in England. Crowley believed that greed and self-interest were destroying the fabric of society, but his writings show that he failed to appreciate that his age was one of social and religious transition. This explanation of the underlying cause of social distress was, however, also the theme of *Robin Conscience and His Father,* written and printed in 1560 by John Awdeley (flourished 1559–1577). Awdeley's interest in analyzing the problems of contemporary society led to his writing another social commentary, *The Fraternity of Vagabonds* (1565).

Many of the reformist printers were forced into exile during Mary's reign, Crowley among them. Nevertheless, among the founder-members of the Stationers' Company in 1556 appeared several printers and stationers who had been questioned or arrested by the authorities at various times, one of the most famous being the Protestant printer John Day (flourished 1546–1584), respected as the friend of John Foxe and later publisher of Foxe's *Book of Martyrs* (1563). Foxe paid tribute to Day in his preface to *The Whole Works of W. Tyndall, J. Frith, and Dr Barnes* (1572–1573):

> The printer of this book has diligently collected and in one volume together enclosed the works I mean of William Tyndall, John Frith, and Robert Barnes. . . . Wherein as we have much to praise God for such good books left to the Church, and also for such printers in preserving by their industry and charges such books from perishing.

Day's son, Richard, was a scholar at King's College, Cambridge, before he became a printer, translator, and writer in 1576. When he printed Peter Baro's *De Fide Ejusque Ortu* (1580) in Latin, he wrote a letter to the reader that attempts to allay doubts about the printer's scholarly ability to make changes from the author's manuscript:

> I thought it would be in my interests, O reader, to warn you at the beginning that I received only the bare manuscript from the author, and that it was copied out not in his own hand but in someone else's. If then the external appearance of the book should seem too presumptuous, and the chapters of each of the treatises should seem to promise too much, the blame for this ought to be placed on my shoulders, because I decided to embellish the book with these headings. It's not a case of the printer failing to stick to his last, since he became a printer after having previously been a scholar.

Richard Day, like other well-educated men who had been through the universities, wrote several prefaces declaring he had been drawn to printing as an occupation in the service of God. This was in the tradition of the *Book of Martyrs,* where Foxe extolled the new art of printing as God's tool for bringing enlightenment to the populace and success to the Reformation movement. Day wrote several good verses in Latin and English, among them a rhyming couplet from *A Book of Christian Prayers* (1578), in which he reflects upon the immortality of the printed word: "We printers wrote with Wisdom's pen. / She lives for aye, we die as men."

Printing was, however, to play an important role in the development of Tudor literary historiography at a time when universities made no provision for the needs of historians. Although the humanist view of society engendered an enthusiasm for history, no chair of history was founded in England until 1623. History was a source from which the humanist could draw examples pertinent to the secular life of the community, as John Rastell showed, but it could also be used in the Reformation to provide an English tradition of national sovereignty. Consequently, the reformers also showed a strong interest in reinterpreting history as a means of furthering the Reformation.

Printers such as John Mychell (flourished 1530–1547), Richard Grafton, Reginald Wolfe (1500–1573), and Raphael Holinshed adopted a more secular and Protestant approach to the writing of history. Mychell, printing in Canterbury, appealed to the London printers not to pirate his work in *A Breviat Chronicle* (1551): "suffer me quietly to enjoy the benefit of these my own labors, and to have the advantage of my own invention as I shall gladly suffer every one of them to enjoy the commodities of his and that we shall brotherlike live in concord." His appeal apparently fell on deaf ears, for between 1555 and 1561 six new editions of his history were put out by the London presses. Crowley saw the propaganda value of history when in 1559 he added to *Lanquet's Chronicle* a highly dramatic and emotive account of the savage persecutions of Mary's reign. The same year, Crowley's friend, the author and printer John Awdeley, wrote and printed a brief verse history, *The Wonders of England,* with a similar message and written in the same popular racy style:

The sun thus quietened, and day made dark,
And cocks in coops from crowing kept,
Then straight these devils began to work,
And to the churches fiercely leapt.

Rastell, Copland, Crowley, and Awdeley are well known for writing popular verse tracts, and no doubt the many other printers who tried their hands at poetry helped make versifying a popular and widespread pastime in the sixteenth century. Richard Tottel, however, published the first printed collection of poems in his *Miscellany* (1557), for which he wrote an interesting preface praising the poetic styles of Henry Howard, earl of Surrey, and Sir Thomas Wyatt. He admonished that if the superiority of Wyatt and Surrey were not obvious to readers, then they must take steps to improve their literary perception and "by reading to learn to be more skillful and to purge that swinelike grossness." It is to Tottel's credit that he appreciated the new poetry and in doing so helped to initiate a new direction for English poetry.

In an age of religious upheavals, it was inevitable that religious works should make up the greater part of popular reading matter, and printers such as Day, Crowley, Powell, and Rastell chose to use their presses to spread Reformist ideas. Moreover, printers contributed by their writings and translations to all kinds of works of instruction and exposition: to the writing of history, legal works, moral books, and scientific and social studies. Francis Seager and Robert Crowley wrote on manners and behavior for children in *The School of Virtue* (1557), and William Baldwin was editor of *A Mirror for Magistrates* (1559), which proved to be a popular and influential work of historical example and moral guidance. Despite its contemporary fame and literary influence, *A Mirror for Magistrates* had no lasting effect; but it is worth noting that it was an important pioneering attempt to transfer political teaching from the historian to the poet. *A Mirror for Magistrates* was the work of a group of well-known learned men, so to find three printers – Baldwin, Holinshed, and Seager – among its ten contributors is a reflection of the pioneering and literary predilections of Tudor printers.

In an age noted for its belief in portents, miracles, charms, and magic, printers took a share in debunking such frivolous notions. Some did this through writing works of Christian guidance, but others – such as Copland in *The Highway to the Spital-House* (1536?), Awdeley in *The Fraternity of Vagabonds* (1565), and Baldwin in *Beware the Cat* (1570) – made a direct contribution to a literature of exposure and enlightenment. In taking a stand against ignorance and mistaken beliefs, printers attempted to impose higher social standards on their community as well as broaden their literary base.

Through the anonymity of news sheets and ballads, several printers added their weight to the controversial issues of their day, sometimes avoiding discovery by the use of fictitious imprints. Heretical works banned during Henry VIII's reign were openly read in Edward VI's time; what was acceptable in Edward's reign was, in turn, publicly burned in Mary's; and books acceptable to Mary were forbidden by Elizabeth, so that an eagerness was created to obtain as well as produce new religious works. In all this the loss of books attributable to the ecclesiastical authorities was great, but perhaps the greatest loss was occasioned by the Dissolution of the Monasteries, when whole shiploads of books were dispatched abroad.

The writing and printing of religious tracts frequently brought printers into conflict with the authorities, and Robert Waldegrave, Thomas Orwin, and John Hodgkins took grave risks through their involvement in a series of pro-Presbyterian pamphlets known as the Martin Marprelate tracts. There were, of course, printers who remained attached to the old faith, and in Elizabeth's reign the Catholic printer William Carter was executed on a charge of treason. More infamous, however, because of his involvement in the Gunpowder Plot, was Henry Garnet, who set up a secret recusant press in 1592, mainly to publish his own works and translations.

Londoners in particular were noted for their Protestant sympathies in the sixteenth century, and the return from exile of many of the radical printers after Mary's death clearly met with their approbation. In fact, the lead that many printers continued to take in religious reform drew a favorable response from the City, so that the reformer John Day was unofficially appointed City Printer in Elizabeth's reign and received one of the City Gates as a residence. The Corporation, moreover, ordered all the London Companies to purchase and display a copy of Day's 1570 edition of Foxe's *Acts and Monuments*.

Even when reformist printers conflicted with the Elizabethan authorities, they did not lose favor with the City, which was the case with the two well-known Marian exiles Robert Crowley and Hugh Singleton. After Crowley had become vicar of St. Giles, Cripplegate, he was suspended in 1565 for writing and preaching against the wearing of vestments by Archbishop Parker. When he was reinstated, he was invited by the civic authorities to preach the first City sermon ever printed for general distribution. Hugh Singleton came close to losing his right hand for printing John Stubbs's *Discovery of a Gaping Gulf* (1583), which criticized Elizabeth's betrothal to the French king's brother, but the next year was given the distinction of becoming London's first officially appointed City Printer. The City apparently shared as well as admired the religious convictions that caused printers to place their business and their liberty at risk.

Printing held particular appeal for those with literary, educational, and social interests, and the concept of the meritorious printer serving his fellow countrymen was an ideal shared by many practitioners of the trade. Aware of the power of the printed word, these printers seized upon the opportunity to educate and to mold public opinion by their own writings as well as by the selection of what they considered to be profitable texts. Printers' prefaces invariably speak of educational and literary goals or show a professional pride in the printers' accomplishments by extolling the service rendered to society by their trade. There is no good reason for disbelieving printers who declared that they had given greater thought to the common good than to consideration of their own profit and self-interest when any new departure clearly involved a commercial risk.

Printers wrote about the major social questions of their day and wielded a powerful influence upon contemporary society. Examination of their productions and study of the motives and intentions described in printers' prefaces and dedications provide an important clue to the literary taste and culture of the time. No discussion of the development of the English language and the spread of literacy can afford to ignore the printers' contribution. Without doubt, current knowledge of the way in which English culture developed in the sixteenth century will be greatly increased by further study of the wider implications of printing.

References:

Edward Arber, *A Transcript of the Registers of the Company of Stationers of London 1557–1640*, 5 volumes (London & Birmingham: Privately printed, 1875–1894);

Frederick Compton Avis, *Printers of Fleet Street and Saint Paul's Churchyard in the 16th Century* (London: F. C. Avis, 1964);

Henry S. Bennett, *English Books and Readers 1475–1557* (Cambridge: Cambridge University Press, 1952);

Bennett, *English Books and Readers 1558–1603* (Cambridge: Cambridge University Press, 1965);

Norman Francis Blake, *Caxton: England's First Publisher* (London: Osprey, 1976);

Peter Blayney, *The Bookshops in Paul's Cross Churchyard* (London: Bibliographical Society, 1990);

Frederick Samuel Boas, *An Introduction to Tudor Drama* (Oxford: Oxford University Press, 1953);

David Richard Carlson, *English Humanist Books: Writers and Patrons, Manuscripts and Print, 1475–1525* (Toronto: University of Toronto Press, 1993);

Richard Deacon, *A Biography of William Caxton: The First English Editor* (London: Muller, 1976);

E. Gordon Duff, *A Century of the Book Trade* (Philadelphia: Folcroft Library Edition, 1972);

F. Smith Fussner, *Tudor History and the Historians* (New York: Basic Books, 1970);

John N. King, *English Reformation Literature* (Princeton: Princeton University Press, 1982);

Philip Luckombe, *The History and Art of Printing* (London: Gregg Press, 1965);

John W. Martin, "The Publishing Career of Crowley, Robert — A Sidelight on the Tudor Book Trade," *Publishing History,* 14 (Autumn 1983): 85–98;

Ronald B. McKerrow, *Printers' & Publishers' Devices in England & Scotland 1485–1640* (London: Bibliographical Society, 1949);

Christopher Lewis Oastler, *John Day, the Elizabethan Printer* (Oxford: Bodleian Library, 1975);

William Kaye Sessions, *John Mychell, Canterbury's First Printer* (York: Ebor, 1983);

Charles Welch, "The City Printers," *Transactions of the Bibliographical Society,* 14 (1915–1917): 175–241.

Appendix II

Documents on Sixteenth-Century Literature

Documents on Sixteenth-Century Literature

Richard Tottel, "The Printer to the Reader," from *Songes and Sonettes, written by the Ryght Honorable Lorde Henry Haward Late Earle of Surrey, and Other* (London: R. Tottel, 1557).

That to haue wel written in verse, yea & in small parcelles, deserueth great praise, the workes of diuers Latines, Italians, and other, doe proue sufficiently. That our tong is able in that kynde to do as praiseworthely as ye rest, the honorable stile of the noble earle of Surrey, and the weightinesse of the depewitted sir Thomas Wyat the elders verse, with seuerall graces in sondry good Englishe writers, doe show abundantly. It resteth nowe (gentle reder) that thou thinke it not euill doon, to publish, to the honor of the Englishe tong, and for profit of the studious of Englishe eloquence, those workes which the vngentle horders vp of such treasure haue heretofore enuied thee. And for this point (good reder) thine own profit and pleasure, in these presently, and in moe hereafter, shal answere for my defence. If parhappes some mislike the statelinesse of stile remoued from the rude skill of common eares: I aske help of the learned to defend their learned frendes, the authors of this work: And I exhort the vnlearned, by reding to learne to be more skilfull, and to purge that swinelike grossenesse, that maketh the swete maierome not to smell to their delight.

Edmund Spenser, "To His Booke," from *The Shepheardes Calender* (1579).

> Goe little booke: thy selfe present,
> As child whose parent is vnkent:
> To him that is the president
> Of noblesse and of ckeualree,
> And if that Enuie barke at thee,
> As sure it will, for succoure flee
>   Vnder the shadow of his wing,
> And asked, who thee forth did bring,
> A shepheards swaine saye did thee sing,
> All as his straying flocke he fedde:
> And when his honor has thee redde,
> Craue pardon for my hardyhedde.

> But if that any aske thy name,
> Say thou wert base begot with blame:
> For thy thereof thou takest shame.
> And when thou art past ieopardee,
> Come tell me, what was sayd of mee:
> And I will send more after thee.

> *— Immeritô.*

Spenser, "To the Most Excellent and Learned Both Orator and Poete, Mayster Gabriell Haruey, His Verie Special and Singular Good Frend E. K. Commendeth the Good Lyking of This His Labour, and the Patronage of the New Poete," from *The Shepheardes Calender*.

Vncovthe Vnkiste, Sayde the olde famous Poete Chaucer: whom for his excellencie and wonderfull skil in making, his scholler Lidgate, a worthy scholler of so excellent a maister, calleth the Loadestarre of our Language: and whom our Colin clout in his Æglogue calleth Tityrus the God of shepheards, comparing hym to the worthines of the Roman Tityrus Virgile. Which prouerbe, myne owne good friend Ma. Haruey, as in that good old Poete it serued well Pandares purpose, for the bolstering of his baudy brocage, so very well taketh place in this our new Poete, who for that he is vncouthe (as said Chaucer) is vnkist, and vnknown to most men, is regarded but of few. But I dout not, so soone as his name shall come into the knowledg of men, and his worthines be sounded in the tromp of fame, but that he shall be not onely kiste, but also beloued of all, embraced of the most, and wondred at of the best. No lesse I thinke, deserueth his wittinesse in deuising, his pithinesse in vttering, his complaints of loue so louely, his discourses of pleasure so pleasantly, his pastorall rudenesse, his morall wisenesse, his dewe obseruing of Decorum euerye where, in personages, in seasons, in matter, in speach, and generally in al seemely simplycitie of handeling his matter, and framing his words: the which of many thinges which in him be straunge, I know will seeme the straungest, the words them selues being so auncient, the knitting of them so

277

short and intricate, and the whole Periode and compasse of speache so delightsome for the roundnesse, and so graue for the straungenesse. And firste of the wordes to speake, I graunt they be something hard, and of most men vnused, yet both English, and also vsed of most excellent Authors and most famous Poetes. In whom whenas this our Poet hath bene much traueiled and throughly redd, how could it be, (as that worthy Oratour sayde) but that walking in the sonne although for other cause he walked, yet needes he mought be sunburnt; and hauing the sound of those auncient Poetes still ringing in his eares, he mought needes in singing hit out some of theyr tunes. But whether he vseth them by such casualtye and custome, or of set purpose and choyse, as thinking them fittest for such rusticall rudenesse of shepheards, eyther for that theyr rough sounde would make his rymes more ragged and rustical, or els because such olde and obsolete wordes are most used of country folke, sure I think, and think I think not amisse, that they bring great grace and, as one would say, auctoritie to the verse. For albe amongst many other faultes it specially be obiected of Valla against Liuie, and of other against Saluste, that with ouer much studie they affect antiquitie, as coueting thereby credence and honor of elder yeeres, yet I am of opinion, and eke the best learned are of the lyke, that those auncient solemne wordes are a great ornament both in the one and in the other; the one labouring to set forth in hys worke an eternall image of antiquitie, and the other carefully discoursing matters of grauitie and importaunce. For if my memory fayle not, Tullie in that booke, wherein he endeuoureth to set forth the paterne of a perfect Oratour, sayth that ofttimes an auncient worde maketh the style seeme graue, and as it were reuerend: no otherwise then we honour and reuerence gray heares for a certein religious regard, which we haue of old age. Yet nether euery where must old words be stuffed in, nor the commen Dialecte and maner of speaking so corrupted therby, that as in old buildings it seme disorderly and ruinous. But all as in most exquisite pictures they vse to blaze and portraict not onely the daintie lineaments of beautye, but also rounde about it to shadow the rude thickets and craggy clifts, that by the basenesse of such parts, more excellency may accrew to the principall; for oftimes we fynde ourselues, I knowe not how, singularly delighted with the shewe of such naturall rudenesse, and take great pleasure in that disorderly order. Euen so doe those rough and harsh termes enlumine and make more clearly to appeare the brightnesse of braue and glorious words. So oftentimes a dischorde in

Musick maketh a comely concordaunce: so great delight tooke the worthy Poete Alceus to behold a blemish in the ioynt of a wel shaped body. But if any will rashly blame such his purpose in choyse of old and vnwonted words, him may I more iustly blame and condemne, or of witlesse headinesse in iudging, or of heedelesse hardinesse in condemning for not marking the compasse of hys bent, he wil iudge of the length of his cast. For in my opinion it is one special prayse, of many whych are dew to this Poete, that he hath laboured to restore, as to theyr rightfull heritage such good and naturall English words, as haue ben long time out of vse and almost cleane disherited. Which is the onely cause, that our Mother tonge, which truely of it self is both ful enough for prose and stately enough for verse, hath long time ben counted most bare and barrein of both. Which default when as some endeuoured to salue and recure, they patched vp the holes with peces and rags of other languages, borrowing here of the french, there of the Italian, euery where of the Latine, not weighing how il, those tongues accorde with themselues, but much worse with ours: So now they haue made our English tongue, a gallimaufray or hodgepodge of al other speches. Other some not so wel seene in the English tonge as perhaps in other languages, if they happen to here an olde word albeit very naturall and significant, crye out streight way, that we speak no English, but gibbrish, or rather such, as in old time Euanders mother spake. Whose first shame is, that they are not ashamed, in their own mother tonge straungers to be counted and alienes. The second shame no lesse then the first, that what so they vnderstand not, they streight way deeme to be sencelesse, and not at al to be vnderstode. Much like to the Mole in Æesopes fable, that being blynd her selfe, would in no wise be perswaded, that any beast could see. The last more shameful then both, that of their owne country and natural speach, which together with their Nources milk they sucked, they haue so base regard and bastard iudgement, that they will not onely themselues not labor to garnish and beautifie it, but also repine, that of other it shold be embellished. Like to the dogge in the maunger, that him selfe can eate no hay, and yet barketh at the hungry bullock, that so faine would feede: whose currish kind though it cannot be kept from barking, yet I conne them thanke that they refrain from byting.

Now for the knitting of sentences, whych they call the ioynts and members therof, and for al the compasse of the speach, it is round without roughnesse, and learned wythout hardnes, such indeede as may be perceiued of the leaste, vnderstoode of the moste, but iudged onely of the learned. For what in most English wryters vseth to be loose, and as it were vngyrt, in this Authour is well grounded, finely framed, and strongly trussed vp together. In regard wherof, I scorne and spue out the rakehellye route of our ragged rymers (for so themselues vse to hunt the letter) which without learning boste, without iudgement iangle, without reason rage and fome, as if some instinct of Poeticall spirite had newly rauished them aboue the meanenesse of commen capacitie. And being in the middest of all theyr brauery, sodenly eyther for want of matter, or of ryme, or hauing forgotten theyr former conceipt, they seeme to be so pained and traueiled in theyr remembrance, as it were a woman in childbirth or as that same Pythia, when the traunce came vpon her.

Os rabidum fera corda domans &c.

Nethelesse let them a Gods name feede on theyr owne folly, so they seeke not to darken the beames of others glory. As for Colin, vnder whose person the Author selfe is shadowed, how furre he is from such vaunted titles and glorious shewes, both him selfe sheweth, where he sayth.

Of Muses Hobbin. I conne no skill. And,
Enough is me to paint out my vnrest, &c.

And also appeareth by the basenesse of the name, wherein, it semeth, he chose rather to vnfold great matter of argument couertly, then professing it, not suffice thereto accordingly. Which moued him rather in Æglogues, then other wise to write, doubting perhaps his habilitie, which he little needed, or mynding to furnish our tongue with this kinde, wherein it faulteth, or following the example of the best and most auncient Poetes, which deuised this kind of wryting, begin both so base for the matter, and homely for the manner, at the first to trye theyr habilities: and as young birdes, that be newly crept out of the nest, by little first to proue theyr tender wyngs, before they make a greater flyght. So flew Theocritus, as you may perceiue he was all ready full fledged. So flew Virgile, as not yet well feeling his winges. So flew Mantuane, as being not full somd. So Petrarque. So Boccace; So Marot, Sanazarus, and also diuers other excellent both Italian and French Poetes, whose foting this Author euery where followeth, yet so as few, but they be wel sented can trace him out. So finally flyeth this our new Poete, as a bird, whose principals be scarce

growen out, but yet as that in time shall be hable to keepe wing with the best.

Now as touching the generall dryft and purpose of his Æglogues, I mind not to say much, him selfe labouring to conceale it. Onely this appeareth, that his vnstayed yougth had long wandred in the common Labyrinth of Loue, in which time to mitigate and allay the heate of his passion, or els to warne (as he sayth) the young shepheards as his equalls and companions of his vnfortunate folly, he compiled these xij. Æglogues, which for that they be proportioned to the state of the xij. monethes, he termeth the SHEPHEARDS CALENDAR, applying an olde name to a new worke. Hereunto haue I added a certain Glosse or scholion for thexposition of old wordes and harder phrases: which maner of glosing and commenting, well I wote, wil seeme straunge and rare in our tongue: yet for somuch as I knew many excellent and proper deuises both in wordes and matter would passe in the speedy course of reading, either as vnknowen, or as not marked, and that in this kind, as in other we might be equal to the learned of other nations, I thought good to take the paines vpon me, the rather for that by meanes of some familiar acquaintaunce I was made priuie to his counsell and secret meaning in them, as also in sundry other works of his. Which albeit I know he nothing so much hateth, as to promulgate, yet thus much haue I aduentured vpon his frendship, him selfe being for long time furre estraunged, hoping that this will the rather occasion him, to put forth diuers other excellent works of his, which slepe in silence, as his Dreames, his Legendes, his Court of Cupide, and sondry others; whose commendations to set out, were verye vayne; the thinges though worthy of many, yet being knowen to few. These my present paynes if to any they be pleasurable or profitable, be you iudge, mine own good Maister Haruey, to whom I haue both in respect of your worthinesse generally, and otherwyse vpon some particular and special considerations voued this my labour, and the maydenhead of this our commen frends Poetrie, himselfe hauing already in the beginning dedicated it to the Noble and worthy Gentleman, the right worshipfull Ma. Phi. Sidney, a special fauourer and maintainer of all kind of learning. Whose cause I pray you Sir, yf Enuie shall stur vp any wrongful accusasion, defend with your mighty Rhetorick and other your rare gifts of learning, as you can, and shield with your good wil, as you ought, against the malice and outrage of so many enemies, as I know wilbe set on fire with the sparks of his kindled glory. And thus recommending the Author vnto you, as vnto his most special good frend, and my selfe vnto you both, as one making singuler account of two so very good and so choise frends, I bid you both most hartely farwel, and commit you and your most commendable studies to the tuicion of the greatest.

— *Your owne assuredly to*
be commaunded E. K.

Post scr

Now I trust M. Haruey, that vpon sight of your speciall frends and fellow Poets doings, or els for enuie of so many vnworthy Quidams, which catch at the garlond, which to you alone is dewe, you will be perswaded to pluck out of the hateful darknesse, those so many excellent English poemes of yours, which lye hid, and bring them forth to eternall light. Trust me you doe both them great wrong, in depriuing them of the desired sonne, and also yourselfe, in smoothering your deserued prayses, and all men generally, in withholding from them so diuine pleasures, which they might conceiue of your gallant English verses, as they haue already doen of your Latine Poemes, which in my opinion both for inuention and Elocution are very delicate, and superexcellent. And thus againe, I take my leaue of my good Mayster Haruey. From my lodging at London thys IO. of Aprill. 1579.

Spenser, "The Generall Argument of the Whole Booke," from *The Shepheardes Calender.*

Little I hope, needeth me at large to discourse the first Originall of Æglogues, hauing alreadie touched the same. But for the word Æglogues I know is vnknowen to most, and also mistaken of some the best learned (as they think) I wyll say somewhat thereof, being not at all impertinent to my present purpose.

They were first of the Greekes the inuentours of them called Æglogaj as it were αἴγον or αιγονομων. λόγοι. that is Goteheards tales. For although in Virgile and others the speakers be more shepheards, then Goteheards, yet Theocritus in whom is more ground of authoritie, then in Virgile, this specially from that deriuing, as from the first head and welspring the whole Inuention of his Æglogues, maketh Goteheards the persons and authors of his tales. This being, who seeth not the grossenesse of such as by colour of learning would make vs beleeue that they are more rightly termed Eclogai, as they would say, extraordinary discourses of vnnecessarie matter, which difinition albe in substaunce and meaning it agree with the nature of the thing, yet no whit answereth with the αναλυσιδ and interpretation of the word. For they be not termed Eclogues, but Æglogues. Which sentence this authour very well obseruing, vpon good iudgement, though indeede few Goteheards haue to doe herein, nethelesse doubteth not to cal them by the vsed and best knowen name. Other curious discourses hereof I reserue to greater occasion. These xij. Æclogues euery where answering to the seasons of the twelue monthes may be well deuided into three formes or ranckes. For eyther they be Plaintiue, as the first, the sixt, the eleuenth, and the twelfth, or recreatiue, such as al those be, which conceiue matter of loue, or commendation of special personages, or Moral: which for the most part be mixed with some Satyrical bitternesse, namely the second of reuerence dewe to old age, the fift of coloured deceipt, the seuenth and ninth of dissolute shepheards and pastours, the tenth of contempt of Poetrie and pleasaunt wits. And to this diuision may euery thing herein be reasonably applyed: A few onely except, whose speciall purpose and meaning I am not priuie to. And thus much generally of these xij. Æclogues. Now will we speake particularly of all, and first of the first. Which he calleth by the first monethes name Ianuarie: wherein to some he may seeme fowly to haue faulted, in that he erroniously beginneth with that moneth, which beginneth not the yeare. For it is wel known, and stoutely mainteyned with stronge reasons of the learned, that the yeare beginneth in March. For then the sonne reneweth his finished course, and the seasonable spring refresheth the earth, and the plesaunce thereof being buried in the sadnesse of the dead winter now worne away, reliueth. This opinion maynteine the olde Astrologers and Philosophers, namely the reuerend Andalo, and Macrobius in his holydayes of Saturne, which accoumpt also was generally obserued both of Grecians and Romans. But sauing the leaue of such learned heads, we maintaine a custome of coumpting the seasons from the moneth Ianuary, vpon a more speciall cause, then the heathen Philosophers euer coulde conceiue, that is, for the incarnation of our mighty Sauiour and eternall redeemer the L. Christ, who as then renewing the state of the decayed world, and returning the compasse of expired yeres to theyr former date and first commencement, left to vs his heires a memoriall of his birth in the ende of the last yeere and beginning of the next. Which reckoning, beside that eternall monument of our saluation, leaneth also vppon good proofe of special iudgement. For albeit that in elder times, when as yet the coumpt of the yere was not perfected, as afterwarde it was by Iulius Cæsar, they began to tel the monethes from Marches beginning, and according to the same God (as is sayd in Scripture) comaunded the people of the Iewes to count the moneth Abib, that which we call March, for the first moneth, in remembraunce that in that moneth he brought them out of the land of Ægipt: yet according to tradition of latter times it hath bene otherwise obserued, both in gouernment of the church, and rule of Mightiest Realmes. For from Iulius Cæsar who first obserued the leape yeere which he called Bissextilem Annum, and brought in to a more certain course the odde wandring dayes which of the Greekes were called υπερβαινοντε. Of the Romanes intercalares (for in such matter of learning I am forced to vse the termes of the learned) the monethes haue bene nombred xij. which in the first ordinaunce of Romulus were but tenne, counting but CCCiiij. dayes in euery yeare, and beginning with March. But Numa Pompilius, who was the father of al the Romain ceremonies and religion, seeing that reckoning to agree neither with the course of the sonne, nor of the Moone, therevnto added two monethes, Ianuary and February: wherin it seemeth, that wise king minded vpon good reason to begin the yeare at Ianuarie, of him therefore so called tanquam Ianua anni the gate and entraunce of the yere, or of the name of the god Ianus, to which god for that the old Paynims attributed the byrth and beginning of all creatures new comming into the worlde, it seemeth that he therfore to him assigned the beginning and first entraunce of the yeare. Which account for the most part hath hetherto continued. Notwithstanding that the Ægiptians beginne theyr yeare at September, for that according to the opinion of the best Rabbins, and very purpose of the scripture selfe, God made the worlde in that Moneth, that is called of them Tisri. And therefore he commaunded them, to keepe the feast of Pauilions in the end of the yeare, in the xv. day of the seuenth moneth, which before that time was the first.

But our Authour respecting nether the subtiltie of thone parte, nor the antiquitie of thother, thinketh it fittest according to the simplicitie of commen vnderstanding, to begin with Ianuarie, wening it perhaps no decorum, that Shepheard should be seene in matter of so deepe insight, or canuase a case of so doubtful iudgment. So therefore beginneth he, and so continueth he throughout.

Spenser, Envoy from *The Shepheardes Calender*.

Loe I haue made a Calender for euery yeare,
That steele in strength, and time in durance shall out-
    weare:
And if I marked well the starres reuolution,
    It shall continewe till the worlds dissolution.
To teach the ruder shepheard how to feede his sheepe,
And from the falsers fraud his folded flocke to keepe.
    Goe lyttle Calender, thou hast a free passeporte,
Goe but a lowly gate emongste the meaner sorte.
Dare not to match thy pype with Tityrus hys style,
    Nor with the Pilgrim that the Ploughman playde a
    whyle:
But followe them farre off, and their high steppes
    adore,
The better please, the worse despise, I aske nomore.

Merce non mercede.

Spenser, "A Letter of the Authors Expounding His Whole Intention in the Course of this Worke: Which for that It Giueth Great Light to the Reader, for the Better Vnderstanding Is Hereunto Annexed," from *The Faerie Qveene* (1590).

To the Right noble, and Valorous, Sir Walter Raleigh knight, Lo. Wardein of the Stanneryes, and her Maiesties liefetenaunt of the County of Cornewayll.

Sir knowing how doubtfully all Allegories may be construed, and this booke of mine, which I haue entituled the Faery Queene, being a continued Allegory, or darke conceit, I haue thought good aswell for auoyding of gealous opinions and misconstructions, as also for your better light in reading therof, (being so by you commanded,) to discouer vnto you the general intention and meaning, which in the whole course thereof I haue fashioned, without expressing of any particular purposes or by-accidents therein occasioned. The generall end therefore of all the booke is to fashion a gentleman or noble person in vertuous and gentle discipline: Which for that I conceiued shoulde be most plausible and pleasing, being coloured with an historicall fiction, the which the most part of men delight to read, rather for variety of matter, then for profite of the ensample: I chose the historye of king Arthure, as most fitte for the excellency of his person, being made famous by many mens former workes and also furthest from the daunger of enuy, and suspition of present time. In which I haue ollowed all the antique Poets historicall, first Homere, who in the Persons of Agamemnon and Vlysses hath ensampled a good gouernour and a vertuous man, the one in his Ilias, the other in his Odysseis: then Virgil, whose like intention was to doe in the person of Aeneas: after him Ariosto comprised them both in his Orlando: and lately Tasso disseuered them againe, and formed both parts in two persons, namely that part which they in Philosophy call Ethice, or vertues of a priuate man, coloured in his Rinaldo: The other named Politice in his Godfredo. By ensample of which excellente Poets, I labour to pourtraict in Arthure, before he was king, the image of a braue knight, perfected in the twelue priuate morall vertues, as Aristotle hath deuised, the which is the purpose of these first twelue bookes: which if I finde to be well accepted, I may be perhaps encoraged, to frame the other part of polliticke vertues in his person, after that hee came to be king. To some I know this Methode will seeme displeasaunt, which had rather haue good discipline deliuered plainly in way of precepts, or sermoned at large, as they vse, then thus clowdily enwrapped in Allegoricall deuises. But such, me seeme, should be satisfide with the vse of these dayes, seeing all things accounted by their showes, and nothing esteemed of, that is not delightfull and pleasing to commune sence. For this cause is Xenophon preferred before Plato, for that the one in the exquisite depth of his iudgement, formed a Commune welth such as it should be, but the other in the person of Cyrus and the Persians fashioned a gouernement such as might best be: So much more profitable and gratious is doctrine by ensample, then by rule. So haue I laboured to doe in the person of Arthure: whome I conceiue after his long education by Timon, to whom he was by Merlin deliuered to be brought vp, so soone as he was borne of the Lady Igrayne, to haue seene in a dream or vision the Faery Queen, with whose excellent beauty rauished, he awaking resolued to seeke her out, and so being by Merlin armed, and by Timon throughly instructed, he went to seeke her forth in Faerye land. In that Faery Queene I meane glory in my generall intention, but in my particular I conceiue the most excellent and glorious person of our soueraine the Queene, and her kingdome in Faery land. And yet in some places els, I doe otherwise shadow her. For considering she beareth two persons, the one of a most royall Queene or Empresse, the other of a most vertuous and beautifull Lady, this latter part in some places I doe expresse in

Belphœbe, fashioning her name according to your owne excellent conceipt of Cynthia, (Phœbe and Cynthia being both names of Diana.) So in the person of Prince Arthure I sette forth magnificence in particular, which vertue for that (according to Aristotle and the rest) it is the perfection of all the rest, and conteineth in it them all, therefore in the whole course I mention the deedes of Arthure applyable to that vertue, which I write of in that booke. But of the xii. other vertues, I make xii. other knights the patrones, for the more variety of the history: Of which these three bookes contayne three, The first of the knight of the Redcrosse, in whome I expresse Holynes: The seconde of Sir Guyon, in whome I sette forth Temperaunce: The third of Britomartis a Lady knight, in whome I picture Chastity. But because the beginning of the whole worke seemeth abrupte and as depending vpon other antecedents, it needs that ye know the occasion of these three knights seuerall aduentures. For the Methode of a Poet historical is not such, as of an Historiographer. For an Historiographer discourseth of affayres orderly as they were donne, accounting as well the times as the actions, but a Poet thrusteth into the middest, euen where it most concerneth him, and there recoursing to the thinges forepaste, and diuining of thinges to come, maketh a pleasing Analysis of all. The beginning therefore of my history, if it were to be told by an Historiographer, should be the twelfth booke, which is the last, where I deuise that the Faery Queene kept her Annuall feaste xii. dayes, vppon which xii. seuerall dayes, the occasions of the xii. seuerall aduentures hapned, which being vndertaken by xii. seuerall knights, are in these xii books seuerally handled and discoursed. The first was this. In the beginning of the feast, there presented him selfe a tall clownishe younge man, who falling before the Queen of Faries desired a boone (as the manner then was) which during that feast she might not refuse: which was that hee might haue the atchieuement of any aduenture, which during that feaste should happen, that being graunted, he rested him on the floore, vnfitte through his rusticity for a better place. Soone after entred a faire Ladye in mourning weedes, riding on a white Asse, with a dwarfe behind her leading a warlike steed, that bore the Armes of a knight, and his speare in the dwarfes hand. Shee falling before the Queene of Faeries, complayned that her father and mother an ancient King and Queene, had bene by an huge dragon many years shut vp in a brasen Castle, who thence suffred them not to yssew: and therefore besought the Faery Queene to assygne her some one of her knights to take on him that exployt. Presently that clownish person vpstarting, desired that aduenture: whereat the Queene much wondering, and the Lady much gainesaying, yet he earnestly importuned his desire. In the end the Lady told him that vnlesse that armour which she brought, would serue him (that is the armour of a Christian man specified by Saint Paul v. Ephes.) that he could not succeed in that enterprise, which being forthwith put vpon him with dewe furnitures thereunto, he seemed the goodliest man in al that company, and was well liked of the Lady. And eftesoones taking on him knighthood, and mounting on that straunge Courser, he went forth with her on that aduenture: where beginneth the first booke, vz.

A gentle knight was pricking on the playne. &c.

The second day ther came in a Palmer bearing an Infant with bloody hands, whose Parents he complained to haue bene slayn by an Enchaunteresse called Acrasia: and therfore craued of the Faery Queene, to appoint him some knight, to performe that aduenture, which being assigned to Sir Guyon, he presently went forth with that same Palmer: which is the beginning of the second booke and the whole subiect thereof. The third day there came in, a Groome who complained before the Faery Queene, that a vile Enchaunter called Busirane had in hand a most faire lady called Amoretta, whom he kept in most grieuous torment, because she would not yield him the pleasure of her body. Whereupon Sir Scudamour the louer of that Lady presently tooke on him that aduenture. But being vnable to performe it by reason of the hard Enchauntments, after long sorrow, in the end met with Britomartis, who succoured him, and reskewed his loue.

But by occasion hereof, many other aduentures are intermedled, but rather as Accidents, then intendments. As the loue of Britomart, the ouerthrow of Marinell, the misery of Florimell, the vertuousnes of Belphœbe, the lasciuiousnes of Hellenora, and many the like.

Thus much Sir, I haue briefly ouerronne to direct your vnderstanding to the wel-head of the History, that from thence gathering the whole intention of the conceit, yet may as in a handfull gripe al the discourse, which otherwise may happily seeme tedious and confused. So humbly crauing the continuaunce of your honorable fauour towards me, and th'eternall establishment of your happines, I humbly take leaue.

23. Ianuary. 1589.
Yours most humbly affectionate.
Ed. Spenser.

Sir Philip Sidney, *An Apologie for Poetrie* (the Olney edition, 1595, of *Defence of Poesie*).

Exordium.

When the right vertuous *Edward Wotton* and I were at the Emperors Court together, wee gave our selves to learne horsemanship of *Iohn Pietro Pugliano;* one that with great commendation had the place of an Esquire in his stable. And hee, according to the fertilnes of the Italian wit, did not onely afoord us the demonstration of his practise, but sought to enrich our mindes with the contemplations therein, which hee thought most precious. But with none I remember mine eares were at any time more loden, then when (either angred with slowe paiment, or mooved with our learner-like admiration) he exercised his speech in the prayse of his facultie. Hee sayd, Souldiours were the noblest estate of mankinde, and horsemen the noblest of Souldiours. Hee sayde, they were the Maisters of warre, and ornaments of peace: speedy goers, and strong abiders: triumphers both in Camps and Courts. Nay, to so unbeleeved a poynt hee proceeded, as that no earthly thing bred such wonder to a Prince, as to be a good horseman. Skill of government was but a *Pedanteria* in comparison. Then would hee adde certain prayses, by telling what a peerlesse beast a horse was: the onely serviceable Courtier without flattery, the beast of most beutie, faithfulnes, courage; and such more, that, if I had not beene a peece of a Logician before I came to him, I think he would have perswaded mee to have wished my selfe a horse. But thus much at least with his no fewe words hee drave into me, that selfe-love is better then any guilding to make that seeme gorgious wherein our selves are parties. Wherein, if *Pugliano* his strong affection and weake argument will not satisfie you, I wil give you a neerer example of my selfe, who (I knowe not by what mischance) in these my not old yeres and idlest times, having slipt into the title of a Poet, am provoked to say somthing unto you in the defence of that my unelected vocation; which if I handle with more good will than good reasons, beare with me, sith the scholler is to be pardoned that foloweth the steppes of his Maister. And yet I must say, that as I have iust cause to make a pittiful defence of poore Poetry, which, from almost the highest estimation of learning, is fallen to be the laughing-stocke of children; so have I need to bring some more availeable proofes: sith the former is by no man barred of his deserved credite, the silly latter hath had even the names of Philosophers used to the defacing of it, with great danger of civill war among the Muses.

Narration.

And first, truly to al them that professing learning inveigh against Poetry may iustly be obiected, that they goe very neer to ungratfulnes, to seek to deface that, which in the noblest nations and languages that are knowne, hath been the first light-giver to ignorance, and first Nurse, whose milk by little and little enabled them to feed afterwards of tougher knowledges: and will they now play the Hedghog, that being received into the den, drave out his host? or rather the Vipers, that with theyr birth kill their Parents? Let learned Greece, in any of her manifold Sciences, be able to shew me one booke before *Musaeus, Homer,* and *Hesiodus:* all three nothing els but Poets. Nay, let any historie be brought, that can say any Writers were there before them, if they were not men of the same skil, as *Orpheus, Linus,* and some others are named: who, having beene the first of that Country that made pens deliverers of their knowledge to their posterity, may iustly challenge to bee called their Fathers in learning: for not only in time they had this priority (although in it self antiquity be venerable), but went before them as causes, to drawe with their charming sweetnes the wild untamed wits to an admiration of knowledge. So as *Amphion* was sayde to move stones with his Poetrie to build Thebes; and *Orpheus* to be listened to by beastes, indeed stony and beastly people: so among the Romans were *Liuius Andronicus,* and *Ennius;* so in the Italian language, the first that made it aspire to be a Treasure-house of Science were the Poets *Dante, Boccace,* and *Petrarch;* so in our English were *Gower* and *Chawcer.*

After whom, encouraged and delighted with theyr excellent fore-going, others have followed, to beautifie our mother tongue, as wel in the same kinde as in other Arts. This did so notably shewe it selfe, that the Philosophers of Greece durst not a long time appeare to the worlde but under the masks of Poets. So *Thales, Empedocles, Parmenides* sange their naturall Philosophie in verses: so did *Pythagoras* and *Phocilides* their morrall counsells: so did *Tirteus* in war matters, and *Solon* in matters of policie: or rather, they beeing Poets dyd exercise their delightful vaine in those points of highest knowledge, which before them lay hid to the world. For that wise *Solon* was directly a Poet it is manifest, having written in verse the notable fable of the Atlantick Iland, which was continued by *Plato.*

And truely, even *Plato,* whosoever well considereth, shall find, that in the body of his work, though the inside and strength were Philosophy, the skinne as it were and beautie depended most of Poetrie: for all standeth upon Dialogues, wherein he faineth many honest Burgesses of Athens to speake of such matters, that, if they had been sette on the racke, they would never have confessed them. Besides, his poetical describing the circumstances of their meetings, as the well ordering of a banquet, the delicacie of a walke, with enterlacing meere tales, as *Giges* Ring, and others, which who knoweth not to be flowers of Poetrie did never walke into Apollo's Garden.

And even Historiographers, although theyr lippes sounde of things doone, and veritie be written in theyr fore-heads, have been glad to borrow both fashion, and perchance weight of Poets. So *Herodotus* entituled his Historie by the name of the nine Muses: and both he, and all the rest that followed him, either stole or usurped of Poetrie their passionate describing of passions; the many particularities of battailes which no man could affirme; or, if that be denied me, long Orations put in the mouthes of great Kings and Captaines, which it is certaine they never pronounced. So that truely, neyther Philosopher nor Historiographer coulde at the first have entred into the gates of populer iudgements, if they had not taken a great pasport of Poetry, which in all Nations at this day, wher learning florisheth not, is plaine to be seene: in all which they have some feeling of Poetry. In Turky, besides their lawe-giving Divines, they have no other Writers but Poets. In our neighbour Countrey Ireland, where truelie learning goeth very bare, yet are theyr Poets held in a devoute reverence. Even among the most barbarous and simple Indians where no writing is, yet have they their Poets, who make and sing songs which they call *Areytos,* both of theyr Auncestors deedes, and praises of theyr Gods: a sufficient probabilitie, that, if ever learning come among them, it must be by having theyr hard dull wits softened and sharpened with the sweete delights of Poetrie. For untill they find a pleasure in the exercises of the minde, great promises of much knowledge will little perswade them that knowe not the fruites of knowledge. In Wales, the true remnant of the auncient Brittons, as there are good authorities to shewe the long time they had Poets which they called *Bardes;* so thorough all the conquests of Romaines, Saxons, Danes, and Normans, some of whom did seeke to ruine all memory of learning from among them, yet doo their Poets even to this day last: so as it is not more notable in soone beginning then in long continuing. But since the Authors of most of our Sciences were the Romans, and before them the Greekes, let us a little stand upon their authorities, but even so farre as to see what names they have given unto this now scorned skill.

Among the Romans a Poet was called *Vates,* which is as much as a Diviner, Fore-seer, or Prophet, as by his conioyned wordes *Vaticinium* and *Vaticinari* is manifest: so heavenly a title did that excellent people bestow upon this hart-ravishing knowledge. And so farre were they carried into the admiration thereof, that they thought in the chaunceable hitting upon any such verses great fore-tokens of their following fortunes were placed. Whereupon grew the worde of *Sortes Virgilianae,* when by suddaine opening *Virgils* booke, they lighted upon any verse of hys making: whereof the histories of the Emperors lives are full: As of *Albinus* the Governour of our Iland, who in his childehoode mette with this verse *"Arma amens capio nec sat rationis in armis":* and in his age performed it. Which although it were a very vaine and godles superstition, as also it was to think that spirits were commaunded by such verses, – whereupon this word charmes, derived of *Carmina* commeth, – so yet serveth it to shew the great reverence those wits were helde in. And altogether not without ground, since both the Oracles of *Delphos* and *Sibillas* prophecies were wholy delivered in verses. For that same exquisite observing of number and measure in words, and that high flying liberty of conceit proper to the Poet, did seeme to have some dyvine force in it.

And may not I presume a little further, to shew the reasonablenes of this worde *Vates?* And say that the holy *Davids* Psalmes are a divine Poem? If I doo, I shall not do it without the testimonie of great learned men, both auncient and moderne. But even the name Psalmes will speake for mee, which, being interpreted, is nothing but songes: then that it is fully written in meeter, as all learned Hebricians agree, although the rules be not yet fully found: lastly and principally, his handeling his prophecy, which is meerely poetical. For what els is the awaking his musicall instruments; the often and free changing of persons; his notable *Prosopopeias,* when he maketh you as it were, see God comming in his Maiestie; his telling of the Beastes ioyfulnes, and hills leaping, but a heavenlie poesie, wherein almost hee sheweth himselfe a passionate lover of that unspeakable and everlasting beautie to be seene by the eyes of the minde, onely cleered by fayth? But truely nowe having named him, I feare mee I seeme to prophane that holy name, applying it to Poetrie, which is among us throwne downe to so ridiculous an estimation: but they that with quiet iudgements will looke a little deeper into it, shall finde the end and working of it such, as, beeing rightly applyed, deserveth not to bee scourged out of the Church of God.

But now, let us see how the Greekes named it, and howe they deemed of it. The Greekes called him a Poet, which name hath, as the most excellent, gone thorough other Languages. It commeth of this word *Poiein,* which is to make: wherein I know not, whether by lucke or wisedome, wee Englishmen have mette with the Greekes in calling him a maker: which name, how high and incomparable a title it is, I had rather were knowne by marking the scope of other Sciences, then by my partiall allegation.

There is no Arte delivered to mankinde, that hath not the workes of Nature for his principall obiect, without which they could not consist, and on which they so depend, as they become Actors and Players, as it were, of what Nature will have set foorth. So doth the Astronomer looke upon the starres, and by that he seeth setteth downe what order Nature hath taken therein. So doe the Geometrician, and Arithmetician, in their diverse sorts of quantities. So doth the Musitian in times tel you which by nature agree, which not. The naturall Philosopher thereon hath his name, and the Morrall Philosopher standeth upon the naturall vertues, vices, and passions of man: 'and followe Nature' (saith hee) 'therein, and thou shalt not erre.' The Lawyer sayth what men have determined. The Historian what men have done. The Grammarian speaketh onely of the rules of speech: and the Rethorician, and Logitian, considering what in Nature will soonest prove and perswade, thereon give artificiall rules, which still are compassed within the circle of a question, according to the proposed matter. The Phisition waigheth the nature of a mans bodie, and the nature of things helpeful or hurtefull unto it. And the Metaphisick, though it be in the seconde and abstract notions, and therefore be counted supernaturall, yet doth hee indeede builde upon the depth of Nature. Onely the Poet, disdayning to be tied to any such subiection, lifted up with the vigor of his owne invention, dooth growe in effect into another nature, in making things either better than Nature bringeth forth, or, quite anewe, formes such as never were in Nature, as the *Heroes, Demigods, Cyclops, Chimeras, Furies,* and such like: so as hee goeth hand in hand with Nature, not inclosed within the narrow warrant of her guifts, but freely ranging onely within the Zodiack of his owne wit.

Nature never set forth the earth in so rich tapistry, as divers Poets have done, neither with so plesant rivers, fruitful trees, sweet smelling flowers, nor whatsoever els may make the too much loved earth more lovely. Her world is brasen, the Poets only deliver a golden. But let those things alone and goe to man, for whom as the other things are, so it seemeth in him her uttermost cunning is imployed, and knowe whether shee have brought foorth so true a lover as *Theagines,* so constant a friende as *Pilades,* so valiant a man as *Orlando,* so right a Prince as *Xenophons Cyrus,* so excellent a man every way as *Virgils Aeneas:* neither let this be iestingly conceived, because the works of the one be essensiall, the other, in imitation or fiction: for any understanding knoweth the skil of the Artificer standeth in that *Idea* or fore-conceite of the work, and not in the work it selfe. And that the Poet hath that *Idea,* is manifest, by delivering them forth in such excellencie as hee hath imagined them. Which delivering forth also, is not wholie imaginative, as we are wont to say by them that build Castles in the ayre: but so farre substantially it worketh, not onely to make a *Cyrus,* which had been but a particuler excellencie as Nature might have done, but to bestow a *Cyrus* upon the worlde, to make many *Cyrus's,* if they wil learne aright why and how that Maker made him.

Neyther let it be deemed too sawcie a comparison to ballance the highest poynt of mans wit with the efficacie of Nature: but rather give right honor to the heavenly Maker of that maker; who having made man to his owne likenes, set him beyond and over all the workes of that second nature: which in nothing hee sheweth so much as in Poetrie; when, with the force of a divine breath, he bringeth things forth far surpassing her dooings, with no small argument to the incredulous of that first accursed fall of *Adam:* sith our erected wit maketh us know what perfection is, and yet our infected will keepeth us from reaching unto it. But these arguments wil by fewe be understood, and by fewer granted. Thus much (I hope) will be given me, that the Greekes, with some probabilitie of reason, gave him the name above all names of learning. Now let us goe to a more ordinary opening of him, that the trueth may be more palpable: and so I hope, though we get not so unmatched a praise as the Etimologie of his names wil grant, yet his very description, which no man will denie, shall not iustly be barred from a principall commendation.

Proposition.

Poesie therefore is an arte of imitation, for so *Aristotle* termeth it in his word *Mimesis,* that is to say, a representing, counterfetting, or figuring foorth: to speake metaphorically, a speaking picture: with this end, to teach and delight; of this have beene three severall kindes.

Divisions.

The chiefe both in antiquitie and excellencie, were they that did imitate the inconceivable excellencies of GOD. Such were, *David* in his Psalmes, *Salomon* in his song of Songs, in his Ecclesiastes, and Proverbs: *Moses* and *Debora* in theyr Hymnes, and the writer of *Iob;* which beside other, the learned *Emanuell Tremilius* and *Franciscus Iunius,* doe entitle the poeticall part of the Scripture. Against these none will speak that hath the holie Ghost in due holy reverence. In this kinde, though in a full wrong divinitie, were *Orpheus, Amphion, Homer* in his hymnes, and many other, both Greekes and Romaines: and this Poesie must be used, by whosoever will follow *S. Iames* his counsell, in singing Psalmes when they are merry: and I knowe is used with the fruite of comfort by some, when, in sorrowfull pangs of their death-bringing sinnes, they find the consolation of the never-leaving goodnesse.

The second kinde is of them that deale with matters Philosophicall; eyther morrall, as *Tirteus, Phocilides* and *Cato:* or naturall, as *Lucretius* and *Virgils Georgicks:* or Astronomicall, as *Manilius,* and *Pontanus:* or historical, as *Lucan:* which who mislike, the faulte is in their iugdements quite out of taste, and not in the sweet foode of sweetly uttered knowledge.

But because thys second sorte is wrapped within the folde of the proposed subiect, and takes not the course of his owne invention, whether they properly be Poets or no, let Gramarians dispute: and goe to the thyrd, indeed right Poets, of whom chiefly this question ariseth; betwixt whom, and these second is such a kinde of difference, as betwixt the meaner sort of Painters (who counterfet onely such faces as are sette before them) and the more excellent, who having no law but wit, bestow that in cullours upon you which is fittest for the eye to see: as the constant though lamenting looke of *Lucrecia,* when she punished in her selfe an others fault. Wherein he painted not *Lucrecia,* whom he never sawe, but painteth the outwarde beauty of such a vertue. For these third be they which most properly do imitate to teach and delight, and to imitate, borrow nothing of what is, hath been, or shall be: but range, onely rayned with learned discretion, into the divine consideration of what may be and should be. These bee they, that, as the first and most noble sorte may iustly bee termed *Vates,* so these are waited on in the excellentest languages and best understandings with the fore described name of Poets. For these indeede doo meerely make to imitate; and imitate both to delight and teach; and delight to move men to take that goodnes in hande, which without delight they would flye as from a stranger; and teach, to make them know that goodnes whereunto they are mooved: which being the noblest scope to which ever any learning was directed, yet want there not idle tongues to barke at them.

These be subdivided into sundry more speciall denominations. The most notable bee the *Heroick, Lirick, Tragick, Comick, Satirick, Iambick, Elegiack, Pastorall,* and certaine others. Some of these being termed according to the matter they deale with, some by the sorts of verses they liked best to write in, for indeede the greatest part of Poets have apparelled their poeticall inventions in that numbrous kinde of writing which is called verse: indeed but apparelled, verse being but an ornament and no cause to Poetry; sith there have beene many most excellent Poets that never versified, and now swarme many versifiers that neede never aunswere to the name of Poets. For *Xenophon,* who did imitate so excellently as to give us *effigiem iusti imperij,* the portraiture of a iust Empire, under the name of *Cyrus* (as *Cicero* sayth of him), made therein an absolute heroicall Poem. So did *Heliodorus* in his sugred invention of that picture of love in *Theagines* and *Cariclea.* And yet both these writ in Prose: which I speak to shew, that it is not riming and versing that maketh a Poet, no more then a long gowne maketh an Advocate; who though he pleaded in armor should be an Advocate and no Souldier. But it is that fayning notable images of vertues, vices, or what els, with that delightfull teaching, which must be the right describing note to know a Poet by. Although indeed the Senate of Poets have chosen verse as their fittest rayment, meaning, as in matter they passed all in all, so in maner to goe beyond them: not speaking (table talke fashion, or like men in a dreame,) words as they chanceably fall from the mouth, but peyzing each sillable of each worde by iust proportion according to the dignitie of the subiect.

Examination 1.

Nowe therefore it shall not bee amisse first to waigh this latter sort of Poetrie by his works, and then by his partes; and if in neyther of these Anato-

mies hee be condemnable, I hope wee shall obtaine a more favourable sentence. This purifing of wit, this enritching of memory, enabling of iudgment, and enlarging of conceyt, which commonly we call learning, under what name soever it com forth, or to what immediat end soever it be directed, the final end is, to lead and draw us to as high a perfection, as our degenerate soules, made worse by theyr clayey lodgings, can be capable of. This, according to the inclination of the man, bred many formed impressions: for some that thought this felicity principally to be gotten by knowledge, and no knowledge to be so high and heavenly as acquaintance with the starres, gave themselves to Astronomie; others, perswading themselves to be *Demigods* if they knewe the causes of things, became naturall and supernaturall Philosophers; some an admirable delight drew to Musicke; and some the certainty of demonstration to the Mathematickes. But all, one and other, having this scope — to knowe, and by knowledge to lift up the mind from the dungeon of the body to the enioying his owne divine essence. But when, by the ballance of experience, it was found that the Astronomer looking to the starres might fall into a ditch, that the enquiring Philosopher might be blinde in himselfe, and the Mathematician might draw foorth a straight line with a crooked hart: then loe, did proofe, the over ruler of opinions, make manifest that all these are but serving Sciences, which as they have each a private end in themselves, so yet are they all directed to the highest end of the mistres Knowledge, by the Greekes called *Arkitecktonike,* which stands (as I thinke) in the knowledge of a mans selfe, in the Ethicke and politick consideration, with the end of well dooing and not of well knowing onely: even as the Sadlers next end is to make a good saddle, but his farther end to serve a nobler facultie, which is horsemanship: so the horsemans to souldiery, and the Souldier not onely to have the skill, but to performe the practice of a Souldier: so that, the ending end of all earthly learning being vertuous action, those skilles that most serve to bring forth that have a most iust title to bee Princes over all the rest: wherein wee can shewe the Poets noblenes, by setting him before his other Competitors.

Among whom as principall challengers step forth the morrall Philosophers: whom, me thinketh, I see comming towards me with a sullen gravity, as though they could not abide vice by day light; rudely clothed for to witnes outwardly their contempt of outward things; with bookes in their hands agaynst glory, whereto they sette theyr names; sophistically speaking against subtility; and angry with any man in whom they see the foule fault of anger. These men casting larges as they goe of Definitions, Divisions, and Distinctions, with a scornefull interogative doe soberly aske, whether it bee possible to finde any path so ready to leade a man to vertue, as that which teacheth what vertue is? and teacheth it not onely by delivering forth his very being, his causes, and effects; but also, by making known his enemie vice, which must be destroyed, and his combersome servant Passion, which must be maistered; by shewing the generalities that contayneth it, and the specialities that are derived from it. Lastly, by playne setting downe how it extendeth it selfe, out of the limits of a mans own little world, to the government of families, and maintayning of publique societies.

The Historian, scarcely giveth leysure to the Moralist to say so much, but that he, – loden with old Mouse-eaten records, authorising himselfe (for the most part) upon other histories, whose greatest authorities are built upon the notable foundation of Heare-say, having much a-doe to accord differing Writers, and to pick trueth out of partiality; better acquainted with a thousande yeeres a goe, then with the present age, and yet better knowing how this world goeth, then how his owne wit runneth; curious for antiquities, and inquisitive of novelties; a wonder to young folkes, and a tyrant in table talke, – denieth in a great chafe, that any man for teaching of vertue, and vertuous actions, is comparable to him. I am *Lux vitæ, Temporum Magistra, Vita memoriæ, Nuncia vetustatis. &c.* 'The philosopher' (sayth hee) 'teacheth a disputative vertue, but I doe an active; his vertue is excellent in the dangerlesse Academie of *Plato,* but mine sheweth foorth her honorable face, in the battailes of *Marathon, Pharsalia, Poitiers,* and *Agincourt.* Hee teacheth vertue by certaine abstract considerations, but I onely bid you follow the footing of them that have gone before you. Olde-aged experience goeth beyond the fine-witted Philosopher, but I give the experience of many ages. Lastly, if he make the Song-booke, I put the learners hande to the Lute: and if hee be the guide, I am the light.' Then woulde hee alledge you innumerable examples, confirming storie by storie, how much the wisest Senatours and Princes have beene directed by the credite of history, as *Brutus, Alphonsus* of *Aragon,* and who not, if need bee? At length, the long lyne of theyr disputation maketh a poynt in thys, that the one giveth the precept, and the other the example.

Nowe, whom shall wee finde (sith the question standeth for the highest forme in the Schoole of learning) to bee Moderator? Trulie, as me seemeth, the Poet; and if not a Moderator, even the man that ought to carrie the title from them both, and much more from all other serving Sciences. Therefore compare we the Poet with the Historian, and with the Morrall Philosopher, and, if hee goe beyond them both, no other humaine skill can match him. For as for the Divine, with all reverence it is ever to be excepted, not only for having his scope as far beyonde any of these, as eternitie exceedeth a moment, but even for passing each of these in themselves. And for the Lawyer, though *Ius* bee the Daughter of Iustice, and Iustice the chiefe of Vertues; yet because hee seeketh to make men good rather *Formidine pænæ,* then *Virtutis amore,* or, to say righter, dooth not indevour to make men good, but that their evill hurt not others, – having no care, so hee be a good Cittizen, how bad a man he be: therefore, as our wickednesse maketh him necessarie, and necessitie maketh him honorable, so is hee not in the deepest trueth to stande in rancke with these; who all indevour to take naughtines away, and plant goodnesse even in the secretest cabinet of our soules. And these foure are all that any way deale in that consideration of mens manners, which beeing the supreme knowledge, they that best breed it deserve the best commendation.

The Philosopher therfore and the Historian are they which would win the gole: the one by precept, the other by example. But both not having both, doe both halte. For the Philosopher, setting downe with thorny argument the bare rule, is so hard of utterance, and so mistie to bee conceived, that one that hath no other guide but him shall wade in him till hee be olde, before he shall finde sufficient cause to bee honest: for his knowledge standeth so upon the abstract and generall, that happie is that man who may understande him, and more happie that can applye what hee dooth understand. On the other side, the Historian, wanting the precept, is so tyed, not to what shoulde bee, but to what is; to the particuler truth of things, and not to the general reason of things; that hys example draweth no necessary consequence, and therefore a lesse fruitfull doctrine.

Nowe dooth the peerelesse Poet performe both: for whatsoever the Philosopher sayth shoulde be doone, hee giveth a perfect picture of it in some one, by whom he presupposeth it was done. So as hee coupleth the generall notion with the particuler example. A perfect picture I say, for hee yeeldeth to the powers of the minde an image of that whereof the Philosopher bestoweth but a woordish description: which dooth neyther strike, pierce, nor possesse the sight of the soule so much as that other dooth. For as in outward things, to a man that had never seene an Elephant or a Rinoceros, who should tell him most exquisitely all theyr shapes, cullour, bignesse, and perticular markes; or of a gorgeous Pallace an Architecture, with declaring the full beauties might well make the hearer able to repeate as it were by rote all hee had heard, yet should never satisfie his inward conceits with being witnes to it selfe of a true lively knowledge. But the same man, as soone as hee might see those beasts well painted, or the house wel in moddel, should straightwaies grow, without need of any description, to a iudicial comprehending of them. So no doubt the Philosopher with his learned definition, bee it of vertue, vices, matters of publick policie, or privat government, replenisheth the memory with many infallible grounds of wisdom; which, notwithstanding, lye darke before the imaginative and iudging powre, if they bee not illuminated or figured foorth by the speaking picture of Poesie.

Tullie taketh much paynes, and many times not without poeticall helpes, to make us knowe the force love of our Countrey hath in us. Let us but heare old *Anchises* speaking in the middest of Troyes flames, or see *Ulisses,* in the fulnes of all *Calipso's* delights, bewayle his absence from barraine and beggerly *Ithaca.* Anger the *Stoicks* say, was a short maddnes: let but *Sophocles* bring you *Aiax* on a stage, killing and whipping Sheepe and Oxen, thinking them the Army of Greeks with theyr Chiefetaines *Agamemnon* and *Menelaus:* and tell mee if you have not a more familiar insight into anger, then finding in the Schoolemen his *Genus* and *difference?* See whether wisdome and temperance in *Ulisses* and *Diomedes,* valure in *Achilles,* friendship in *Nisus* and *Eurialus,* even to an ignoraunt man, carry not an apparent shyning; and contrarily, the remorse of conscience in *Oedipus,* the soone repenting pride of *Agamemnon,* the selfe-devouring crueltie in his Father *Atreus,* the violence of ambition in the two *Theban* brothers, the sowre-sweetnes of revenge in *Medæa;* and, to fall lower, the *Terentian Gnato,* and our *Chaucers* Pandar, so exprest, that we nowe use their names to signifie their trades. And finally, all vertues, vices, and passions, so in their own naturall seates layd to the viewe, that wee seeme not to heare of them, but cleerely to see through them. But even in the most excellent determination of goodnes, what Philosophers counsell can so redily direct a Prince, as the fayned *Cyrus* in *Xenophon?* or a vertuous man in all fortunes, as *Aeneas* in *Virgill?* or a whole Common-wealth, as the way of Sir *Thomas Moore's Eutopia?* I say the way, because where Sir *Thomas Moore* erred, it was the fault of the man and

not of the Poet, for that way of patterning a Commonwealth was most absolute, though hee perchaunce hath not so absolutely perfourmed it. For the question is, whether the fayned image of Poesie, or the regular instruction of Philosophy, hath the more force in teaching: wherein, if the Philosophers have more rightly shewed themselves Philosophers then the Poets have attained to the high top of their profession, as in truth,

> *Mediocribus esse poetis,*
> *Non Di, non homines, non concessere Columnæ:*

it is I say againe, not the fault of the Art, but that by fewe men that Arte can bee accomplished. Certainly, even our Saviour Christ could as well have given the morrall common places of uncharitablenes and humblenes, as the divine narration of *Dives* and *Lazarus:* or of disobedience and mercy, as that heavenly discourse of the lost Child and the gratious Father; but that hys through-searching wisdom knewe the estate of *Dives* burning in hell, and of *Lazarus* being in *Abrahams* bosome, would more constantly (as it were) inhabit both the memory and iudgment. Truly, for my selfe, mee seemes I see before my eyes the lost Childes disdainefull prodigality, turned to envie a Swines dinner: which by the learned Divines are thought not historicall acts, but instructing Parables. For conclusion, I say the Philosopher teacheth, but he teacheth obscurely, so as the learned onely can understande him; that is to say, he teacheth them that are already taught: but the Poet is the foode for the tenderest stomacks, the Poet is indeed the right Popular Philosopher, whereof *Esops* tales give good proofe; whose pretty Allegories, stealing under the formall tales of Beastes, make many, more beastly then Beasts, begin to heare the sound of vertue from these dumbe speakers.

But now may it be alledged, that if this imagining of matters be so fitte for the imagination, then must the Historian needs surpasse, who bringeth you images of true matters, such as indeede were doone, and not such as fantastically or falsely may be suggested to have been doone. Truely *Aristotle* himselfe in his discourse of Poesie, plainely determineth this question, saying, that Poetry is *Philosophoteron* and *Spoudaioteron,* that is to say, it is more Philosophicall, and more studiously serious, then history. His reason is, because Poesie dealeth with *Katholou,* that is to say, with the universall consideration; and the history with *Kathekaston,* the perticuler; 'nowe' sayth he, 'the universall wayes what is fit to bee sayd or done, eyther in likelihood or necessity, (which the Poesie considereth in his imposed names); and the perticuler onely marks, whether *Alcibiades* did or suffered this or that.' Thus farre *Aristotle:* which reason of his (as all his) is most full of reason. For indeed, if the question were whether it were better to have a perticular acte truly or falsly set down, there is no doubt which is to be chosen; no more then whether you had rather have *Vespasians* picture right as hee was, or at the Painters pleasure nothing resembling. But if the question be for your owne use and learning, whether it be better to have it set downe as it should be, or as it was: then certainely is more doctrinable the fained Cyrus of *Xenophon* then the true *Cyrus* in *Iustine:* and the fayned *Aeneas* in *Virgil,* then the right *Aeneas* in *Dares Phrygius.* As to a Lady that desired to fashion her countenance to the best grace, a Painter should more benefite her to portraite a most sweet face, wryting *Canidia* upon it, then to paynt *Canidia* as she was, who *Horace* sweareth was foule and ill favoured.

If the Poet doe his part aright, he will shew you in *Tantalus, Atreus,* and such like, nothing that is not to be shunned: in *Cyrus, Aeneas, Ulisses,* each thing to be followed; where the Historian, bound to tell things as things were, cannot be liberall (without hee will be poeticall) of a perfect patterne; but, as in *Alexander* or *Scipio* himselfe, shew dooings, some to be liked, some to be misliked. And then how will you discerne what to followe but by your owne discretion, which you had without reading *Quintus Curtius?* And whereas a man may say, though in universall consideration of doctrine the Poet prevaileth; yet that the historie, in his saying such a thing was doone, doth warrant a man more in that hee shall follow. The aunswere is manifest, that if hee stande upon that was; as if hee should argue, because it rayned yesterday, therefore it shoulde rayne to day, then indeede it hath some advantage to a grose conceite. But if he know an example onlie, informes a coniectured likelihood, and so goe by reason, the Poet dooth so farre exceede him, as hee is to frame his example to that which is most reasonable, be it in warlike, politick, or private matters; where the Historian in his bare *Was,* hath many times that which wee call fortune to over-rule the best wisedome. Manie times, he must tell events, whereof he can yeelde no cause: or, if hee doe, it must be poeticall.

For that a fayned example hath asmuch force to teach, as a true example (for as for to moove, it is cleere, sith the fayned may bee tuned to the highest key of passion) let us take one example, wherein a Poet and a Historian doe concur. *Herodotus* and *Iust-*

ine do both testifie that *Zopirus,* King *Darius* faithful servaunt, seeing his Maister long resisted by the rebellious *Babilonians,* fayned himselfe in extreame disgrace of his King: for verifying of which, he caused his own nose and eares to be cut off, and so flying to the *Babylonians,* was received: and for his knowne valour so far credited, that hee did finde meanes to deliver them over to *Darius.* Much like matter doth *Livie* record of *Tarquinius* and his sonne. *Xenophon* excellently faineth such another stratageme, performed by *Abradates* in *Cyrus* behalfe. Now would I fayne know, if occasion bee presented unto you, to serve your Prince by such an honest dissimulation, why you doe not as well learne it of *Xenophons* fiction as of the others verity: and truely so much the better, as you shall save your nose by the bargaine; for *Abradates* did not counterfet so far. So then the best of the Historian is subiect to the Poet; for whatsoever action, or faction, whatsoever counsell, pollicy, or warre stratagem the Historian is bound to recite, that may the Poet (if he list) with his imitation make his own; beautifying it both for further teaching, and more delighting, as it pleaseth him: having all, from *Dante,* his heaven to hys hell, under the authoritie of his penne. Which if I be asked what Poets have done so, as I might well name some, yet say I, and say againe, I speak of the Arte, and not of the Artificer.

Nowe, to that which commonly is attributed to the prayse of histories, in respect of the notable learning is gotten by marking the successe, as though therein a man should see vertue exalted, and vice punished. Truly that commendation is peculiar to Poetrie, and farre of from History. For indeede Poetrie ever setteth vertue so out in her best cullours, making Fortune her wel-wayting hand-mayd, that one must needs be enamored of her. Well may you see *Ulisses* in a storme, and in other hard plights; but they are but exercises of patience and magnanimitie, to make them shine the more in the neere-following prosperitie. And of the contrarie part, if evill men come to the stage, they ever goe out (as the Tragedie Writer answered to one that misliked the shew of such persons) so manacled, as they little animate folkes to followe them. But the Historian, beeing captived to the trueth of a foolish world, is many times a terror from well dooing, and an incouragement to unbrideled wickednes. For, see wee not valiant *Milciades* rot in his fetters? The iust *Phocion,* and the accomplished *Socrates,* put to death like Traytors? The cruell *Severus* live prosperously? The excellent *Severus* miserably murthered? *Sylla* and *Marius* dying in theyr beddes? *Pompey* and *Cicero* slaine then, when they would have thought exile a happinesse? See wee not vertuous *Cato* driven to kyll himselfe? and rebell *Cæsar* so advaunced, that his name yet, after 1600 yeares, lasteth in the highest honor? And marke but even *Cæsars* own words of the fore-named *Sylla*, (who in that onely did honestly, to put downe his dishonest tyrannie,) *Literas nescivit:* as if want of learning caused him to doe well. Hee meant it not by Poetrie, which not content with earthly plagues, deviseth new punishments in hel for Tyrants: nor yet by Philosophie, which teacheth *Occidendos esse:* but no doubt by skill in Historie; for that indeede can affoord your *Cipselus, Periander, Phalaris, Dionisius,* and I know not how many more of the same kennell, that speede well enough in theyr abhominable uniustice or usurpation.

I conclude therefore, that hee excelleth Historie, not onely in furnishing the minde with knowledge, but in setting it forward, to that which deserveth to be called and accounted good: which setting forward, and mooving to well dooing, indeed setteth the Lawrell crowne upon the Poet as victorious, not onely of the Historian, but over the Philosopher: howsoever in teaching it may bee questionable. For suppose it be granted (that which I suppose with great reason may be denied) that the Philosopher, in respect of his methodical proceeding, doth teach more perfectly then the Poet: yet do I thinke that no man is so much *Philophilosophos,* as to compare the Philosopher in mooving with the Poet. And that mooving is of a higher degree then teaching, it may by his appeare, that it is wel nigh the cause and the effect of teaching. For who will be taught, if hee bee not mooved with desire to be taught? and what so much good doth that teaching bring forth (I speake still of morrall doctrine), as that it mooveth one to doe that which it dooth teach? for as *Aristotle* sayth, it is not *Gnosis,* but *Praxis* must be the fruit. And howe *Praxis* cannot be, without being mooved to practise, it is no hard matter to consider.

The Philosopher sheweth you the way, hee informeth you of the particularities, as well of the tediousnes of the way, as of the pleasant lodging you shall have when your iourney is ended, as of the many by-turnings that may divert you from your way. But this is to no man but to him that will read him, and read him with attentive studious painfulnes. Which constant desire, whosoever hath in him, hath already past halfe the hardnes of the way, and therefore is beholding to the Philosopher but for the other halfe. Nay truely, learned men have learnedly thought, that, where once reason hath so much over-mastred passion as that the minde hath a free desire to doe well, the inward light each minde hath in it selfe, is as good as a Philosophers booke; seeing in nature we know it is wel to doe well, and what is well and what is evill, although not in the words of Arte which Philosophers bestowe upon us; for out of naturall conceit, the Philosophers drew it: but to be moved to doe that which we know, or to be mooved with desire to knowe, *Hoc opus: Hic labor est.*

Nowe therein of all Sciences (I speak still of humane, and according to the humane conceits) is our Poet the Monarch. For he dooth not only shew the way, but giveth so sweete a prospect into the way, as will intice any man to enter into it. Nay, he dooth, as if your iourney should lye through a fayre Vineyard, at the first give you a cluster of Grapes; that, full of that taste, you may long to passe further. He beginneth not with obscure definitions, which must blur the margent with interpretations, and load the memory with doubtfulnesse: but hee commeth to you with words set in delightfull proportion, either accompanied with, or prepared for the well inchaunting skill of Musicke; and with a tale forsooth he commeth unto you, with a tale which holdeth chidren from play, and old men from the chimney corner; and, pretending no more, doth intende the winning of the mind from wickednesse to vertue: even as the childe is often brought to take most wholsom things, by hiding them in such other as have a pleasant tast: which, if one should beginne to tell them the nature of *Aloes* or *Rubarb* they shoulde receive, woulde sooner take their Phisicke at their eares then at their mouth. So is it in men (most of which are childish in the best things, till they bee cradled in their graves,) glad they will be to heare the tales of *Hercules, Achilles, Cyrus,* and *Aeneas:* and hearing them, must needs heare the right description of wisdom, valure, and iustice; which, if they had been barely, that is to say, Philosophically set out, they would sweare they bee brought to schoole againe.

That imitation, wherof Poetry is, hath the most conveniency to Nature of all other: in somuch that, as *Aristotle* sayth, those things which in themselves are horrible, as cruell battailes, unnaturall Monsters, are made in poeticall imitation delightfull. Truely I have knowen men, that even with reading *Amadis de Gaule,* (which God knoweth wanteth much of a perfect Poesie) have found their harts mooved to the exercise of courtesie, liberalitie, and especially courage. Who readeth *Aeneas* carrying olde *Anchises* on his back, that wisheth not it were his fortune to perfourme so excellent an acte? Whom doe not the words of *Turnus* moove? (the tale of *Turnus* having planted his image in the imagination,)

> *Fugientem hæc terra videbit?*
> *Usque adeone mori miserum est?*

Where the Philosophers, as they scorne to delight, so must they bee content little to moove: saving wrangling whether Vertue bee the chiefe of the onely good: whether the contemplative or the active life doe excell. Which *Plato* and *Boethius* well knew; and therefore made Mistres Philosophy very often borrow the masking rayment of Poesie. For even those harde harted evill men, who thinke vertue a schoole name, and knowe no other good but *indulgere genio,* and therefore despise the austere admonitions of the Philosopher, and feele not the inward reason they stand upon, yet will be content to be delighted; which is al the good felow Poet seemeth to promise: and so steale to see the forme of goodnes (which seene they cannot but love) ere themselves be aware, as if they tooke a medicine of Cherries.

Infinite proofes of the strange effects of this poeticall invention might be alledged, onely two shall serve, which are so often remembred, as I thinke all men knowe them. The one of *Menenius Agrippa,* who, when the whole people of Rome had resolutely devided themselves from the Senate, with apparant shew of utter ruine, though hee were (for that time) an excellent Oratour, came not among them upon trust of figurative speeches, or cunning insinuations: and much lesse, with farre fet *Maximes* of Philosophie, which (especially if they were *Platonick*) they must have learned Geometric before they could well have conceived: but forsooth he behaves himselfe, like a homely, and familiar Poet. Hee telleth them a tale, that there was a time, when all the parts of the body made a mutinous conspiracie against the belly, which they thought devoured the fruits of each others labour: they concluded they would let so unprofitable a spender starve. In the end, to be short, (for the tale is notorious, and as notorious that it was a tale,) with punishing the belly they plagued themselves. This applied by him wrought such effect in the people, as I never read that ever words brought forth but then so suddaine and so good an alteration; for, upon reasonable conditions, a perfect reconcilement ensued. The other is of *Nathan* the Prophet, who when the holie *David* had so far forsaken God, as to confirme adulterie with murther: when hee was to doe the tenderest office of a friende, in laying his owne shame before his eyes, sent by God to call againe so

chosen a servant: how doth he it? but by telling of a man, whose beloved Lambe was ungratefullie taken from his bosome: the applycation most divinely true, but the discourse it selfe, fayned: which made *David,* (I speake of the second and instrumental cause) as in a glasse, to see his own filthines, as that heavenly Psalme of mercie wel testifieth.

By these therefore examples and reasons, I think it may be manifest, that the Poet with that same hand of delight doth draw the mind more effectually then any other Arte dooth: and so a conclusion not unfitlie ensueth, that as vertue is the most excellent resting place for all worldlie learning to make his end of: so Poetrie, beeing the most familiar to teach it, and most princelie to move towards it, in the most excellent work is the most excellent workman.

Examination 2.

But I am content, not onely to decipher him by his workes, (although works, in commendation or disprayse, must ever holde an high authority) but more narrowly will examine his parts: so that (as in a man) though all together may carry a presence ful of maiestie and beautie, perchance in some one defectious peece, we may find a blemish: now in his parts, kindes, or *Species* (as you list to terme them) it is to be noted, that some Poesies have coupled together two or three kindes, as Tragicall and Comicall, wher-upon is risen the Tragi-comicall. Some in the like manner have mingled Prose and Verse, as *Sanazzar* and *Boetius.* Some have mingled matters Heroicall and Pastorall. But that commeth all to one in this question, for, if severed they be good, the coniunction cannot be hurtfull. Therefore perchaunce forgetting some, and leaving some as needlesse to be remembred, it shall not be amisse in a worde to cite the speciall kindes, to see what faults may be found in the right use of them.

Is it then the Pastorall Poem which is misliked? (for perchance, where the hedge is lowest they will soonest leape over.) Is the poore pype disdained, which sometime out of *Melibeus* mouth can shewe the miserie of people under hard Lords or ravening Souldiours? And again, by *Titirus,* what blessednes is derived to them that lye lowest from the goodnesse of them that sit highest? Sometimes, under the prettie tales of Wolves and Sheepe, can include the whole considerations of wrong dooing and patience; sometimes shew, that contention for trifles can get but a trifling victorie. Where pechaunce a man may see, that even *Alexander* and *Darius,* when they strave who should be Cocke of thys worlds dunghill, the benefit they got was, that the after-livers may say,

Hæc memini et victum frustra contendere Thirsin:
Ex illo Coridon Coridon est tempore nobis.

Or is it the lamenting Elegiack, which in a kinde hart would moove rather pitty then blame, who bewailes, with the great Philosopher *Heraclitus,* the weakenes of man-kind and the wretchednes of the world: who surely is to be praysed, either for compassionate accompanying iust causes of lamentation, or for rightly paynting out how weake be the passions of wofulnesse. Is it the bitter but wholsome Iambick, which rubs the galled minde, in making shame the trumpet of villanie, with bolde and open crying out against naughtines; or the Satirick, who *"omne vafer vitium ridenti tangit amico?"* Who sportingly never leaveth, until hee make a man laugh at folly, and at length ashamed to laugh at himselfe; which he cannot avoyd, without avoyding the follie. Who while *"circum praecordia ludit"* giveth us to feele, how many head-aches a passionate life bringeth us to: how, when all is done, *"Est Ulubris, animus si nos non deficit æquus."* No perchance it is the Comick, whom naughtie Play-makers and Stage-keepers have iustly made odious. To the argument of abuse I will answer after. Onely thus much now is to be said, that the Comedy is an imitation of the common errors of our life, which he representeth in the most ridiculous and scornefull sort that may be; so as it is impossible that any beholder can be content to be such a one. Now, as in Geometry, the oblique must bee knowne as wel as the right; and in Arithmetick, the odde aswell as the even: so, in the actions of our life, who seeth not the filthines of evil wanteth a great foile to perceive the beauty of vertue. This doth the Comedy handle so in our private and domestical matters, as with hearing it we get, as it were, an experience what is to be looked for of a nigardly *Demea:* of a crafty *Davus:* of a flattering *Gnato:* of a vaine glorious *Thraso:* and not onely to know what effects are to be expected, but to know who be such, by the signifying badge given them by the Comedian. And little reason hath any man to say, that men learne evill by seeing it so set out: sith, as I sayd before, there is no man living but, by the force trueth hath in nature, no sooner seeth these men play their parts, but wisheth them in *Pistrinum:* although perchance the sack of his owne faults lye so behinde hys back, that he seeth not himselfe daunce the same measure: whereto yet nothing can more open his eyes, then to finde his own actions contemptibly set forth.

So that the right use of Comedy will (I thinke) by no body be blamed, and much lesse of the high and excellent Tragedy, that openeth the greatest wounds, and sheweth forth the Ulcers that are covered with Tissue; that maketh Kinges feare to be Tyrants, and Tyrants manifest their tirannicall humors; that with stirring the affects of admiration and commiseration, teacheth the uncertainety of this world, and upon how weake foundations guilden roofes are builded. That maketh us knowe,

Qui sceptra saevus duro imperio regit,
Timet timentes, metus in aucthorem redit.

But how much it can moove, *Plutarch* yeeldeth a notable testimonie of the abhominable Tyrant *Alexander Pheraeus;* from whose eyes a Tragedy, wel made and represented, drewe aboundance of teares: who without all pitty, had murthered infinite numbers, and some of his owne blood. So as he, that was not ashamed to make matters for Tragedies, yet coulde not resist the sweet violence of a Tragedie. And if it wrought no further good in him, it was that he, in despight of himselfe, withdrewe himselfe from harkening to that, which might mollifie his hardened heart. But it is not the Tragedy they doe mislike: For it were too absurd to cast out so excellent a representation of whatsoever is most worthy to be learned.

Is it the Lyricke that most displeaseth, who with his tuned Lyre, and wel accorded voyce, giveth praise, the reward of vertue, to vertuous acts; who gives morrall precepts, and naturall Problemes; who sometimes rayseth up his voice to the height of the heavens, in singing the laudes of the immortall God? Certainly I must confesse my own barbarousnes, I never heard the olde song of *Percy* and *Duglas,* that I found not my heart mooved more then with a Trumpet: and yet is it sung but by some blinde Crouder, with no rougher voyce then rude stile: which being so evill apparrelled in the dust and cobwebbes of that uncivill age, what would it worke trymmed in the gorgeous eloquence of *Pindar?* In *Hungary* I have seene it the manner at all Feasts, and other such meetings, to have songes of their Auncestours valour; which that right Souldier-like Nation thinks the chiefest kindlers of brave courage. The incomparable *Lacedemonians* did not only carry that kinde of Musicke ever with them to the field; but even at home, as such songs were made, so were they all content to bee the singers of them, when the lusty men were to tell what they dyd, the olde men what they had done, and the young men what they wold doe. And where a man may say, that *Pindar* many times prayseth highly victories of small moment, matters rather of sport then vertue: as it may be aunswered, it was the fault of the Poet, and not of the Poetry; so indeede the chiefe fault was in the tyme and custome of the Greekes, who set those toyes at so high a price, that *Phillip* of *Macedon* reckoned a horserace wonne at *Olympus* among hys three fearefull felicities. But as the unimitable *Pindar* often did, so is that kinde most capable and most fit to awake the thoughts from the sleep of idlenes, to imbrace honorable enterprises.

There rests the Heroicall, whose very name (I thinke) should daunt all back-biters; for by what conceit can a tongue be directed to speake evill of that, which draweth with it, no lesse Champions then *Achilles, Cyrus, Aeneas, Turnus, Tydeus,* and *Rinaldo?* who doth not onely teach and move to a truth, but teacheth and mooveth to the most high and excellent truth. Who maketh magnanimity and iustice shine, throughout all misty fearefulnes and foggy desires. Who, if the saying of *Plato* and *Tullie* bee true, that who could see Vertue would be wonderfully ravished with the love of her beauty: this man sets her out to make her more lovely in her holyday apparell to the eye of any that will daine not to disdaine, untill they understand. But if any thing be already sayd in the defence of sweete Poetry, all concurreth to the maintaining the Heroicall, which is not onely a kinde, but the best and most accomplished kinde of Poetry. For as the image of each action stirreth and instructeth the mind, so the loftie image of such Worthies most inflameth the mind with desire to be worthy, and informes with counsel how to be worthy. Only let *Aeneas* be worne in the tablet of your memory; how he governeth himselfe in the ruine of his Country; in the preserving his old Father, and carrying away his religious ceremonies; in obeying the Gods commandement to leave *Dido,* though not onely all passionate kindenes, but even the humane consideration of vertuous gratefulnes, would have craved other of him; how in storms; howe in sports; howe in warre; how in peace; how a fugitive; how victorious; how besiedged; how besiedging; howe to strangers; howe to allyes; how to enemies; howe to his owne: lastly, how in his inward selfe, and how in his outward government. And I thinke, in a minde not preiudiced with a preiudicating humor, hee will be found in excellencie fruitefull: yea, even as *Horace* sayth *"melius Chrisippo et Crantore."* But truely I imagine, it falleth out with these Poetwhyppers, as with some good women, who often are sicke, but in fayth they cannot tel where. So the

name of Poetrie is odious to them, but neither his cause nor effects, neither the sum that containes him, nor the particularities descending from him, give any fast handle to their carping disprayse.

Sith then Poetrie is of all humane learning the most auncient, and of most fatherly antiquitie, as from whence other learnings have taken theyr beginnings: sith it is so universall, that no learned Nation dooth despise it, nor no barbarous Nation is without it: sith both Roman and Greek gave divine names unto it, the one of prophecying, the other of making: and that indeede, that name of making is fit for him; considering, that, whereas other Arts retaine themselves within their subiect, and receive as it were their beeing from it, the Poet onely bringeth his owne stuffe, and dooth not learne a conceite out of a matter, but maketh matter for a conceite: Sith neither his description nor his ende contayneth any evill, the thing described cannot be evill: Sith his effects be so good as to teach goodnes and to delight the learners: Sith therein (namely in morrall doctrine, the chiefe of all knowledges) hee dooth not onely farre passe the Historian, but, for instructing, is well nigh comparable to the Philosopher; and, for moving, leaves him behind him: Sith the holy scripture (wherein there is no uncleannes) hath whole parts in it poeticall, and that even our Saviour Christ vouchsafed to use the flowers of it: Sith all his kindes are not onlie in their united formes, but in their severed dissections fully commendable; I think (and think I thinke rightly) the Lawrell crowne, appointed for triumphing Captaines, doth worthilie (of al other learnings) honor the Poets triumph.

Refutation.

But because wee have eares aswell as tongues, and that the lightest reasons that may be will seeme to weigh greatly, if nothing be put in the counterballance: let us heare, and, aswell as wee can, ponder, what obiections may bee made against this Arte, which may be worthy eyther of yeelding, or answering.

First truely I note, not onely in these *Misomousoi* Poet-haters, but in all that kinde of people, who seek a prayse by dispraysing others, that they doe prodigally spend a great many wandering wordes in quips and scoffes; carping and taunting at each thing, which by stirring the Spleene, may stay the braine from a through beholding the worthines of the subiect. Those kinde of obiections, as they are full of very idle easines, sith there is nothing of so sacred a maiestie, but that an itching tongue may rubbe it selfe upon it: so deserve they no other answer, but, in steed of laughing at the iest, to laugh at the iester. Wee know a playing wit can prayse the discretion of an Asse; the comfortablenes of being in debt; and the iolly commoditie of beeing sick of the plague. So of the contrary side, if we will turne *Ovids* verse, *"Ut lateat virtus proximitate mali,"* that good lye hid in neerenesse of the evill: *Agrippa* will be as merry in shewing the vanitie of Science, as *Erasmus* was in commending of follie. Neyther shall any man or matter escape some touch of these smyling raylers. But for *Erasmus* and *Agrippa,* they had another foundation then the superficiall part would promise. Mary, these other pleasant Fault-finders, who wil correct the Verbe, before they under stande the Noune, and confute others knowledge before they confirme theyr owne: I would have them only remember, that scoffing commeth not of wisedom. So as the best title in English they gette with their merriments, is to be called good fooles: for so have our grave Fore-fathers ever termed that humorous kinde of iesters: but that which gyveth greatest scope to their scorning humors, is ryming and versing. It is already sayde (and, as I think, trulie sayde) it is not ryming and versing that maketh Poesie. One may bee a Poet without versing, and a versifier without Poetry. But yet, presuppose it were inseparable (as indeede it seemeth *Scaliger* iudgeth) truelie it were an inseparable commendation. For if *Oratio,* next to *Ratio,* Speech next to Reason, bee the greatest gyft bestowed upon mortalitie: that can not be praiselesse, which dooth most pollish that blessing of speech, which considers each word, not only (as a man may say) by his forcible qualitie, but by his best measured quantitie, carrying even in themselves, a Harmonie (without perchaunce Number, Measure, Order, Proportion, be in our time growne odious.) But lay a side the iust prayse it hath, by beeing the onely fit speech for Musick (Musick, I say, the most divine striker of the sences), thus much is undoubtedly true, that if reading bee foolish without remembering, memorie being the onely treasurer of knowledge, those words which are fittest for memory, are likewise most convenient for knowledge.

Now, that Verse farre exceedeth Prose in the knitting up of the memory, the reason is manifest. The words, besides theyr delight (which hath a great affinitie to memory), beeing so set, as one word cannot be lost, but the whole worke failes: which accuseth it selfe, calleth the remembrance backe to it selfe, and so most strongly confirmeth it; besides, one word so as it were begetting another, as, be it in ryme or measured verse, by the former man shall have a neere gesse to the follower: lastly,

even they that have taught the Art of memory, have shewed nothing so apt for it, as a certaine roome devided into many places well and throughly knowne. Now, that hath the verse in effect perfectly: every word having his naturall seate, which seate, must needes make the words remembred. But what needeth more in a thing so knowne to all men? who is it that ever was a scholler, that doth not carry away some verses of *Virgill, Horace,* or *Cato,* which in his youth he learned, and even to his old age serve him for howrely lessons? But the fitnes it hath for memory, is notably proved by all delivery of Arts: wherein for the most part, from Grammer, to Logick, Mathematick, Phisick, and the rest, the rules chiefely necessary to bee borne away, are compiled in verses. So that, verse being in it selfe sweete and orderly, and beeing best for memory, the onely handle of knowledge, it must be in iest that any man can speake against it.

Nowe then goe wee to the most important imputations laid to the poore Poets. For ought I can yet learne, they are these: first, that there beeing many other more fruitefull knowledges, a man might better spend this tyme in them, then in this. Secondly, that it is the mother of lyes. Thirdly, that it is the Nurse of abuse, infecting us with many pestilent desires: with a Syrens sweetnes, drawing the mind to the Serpents tayle of sinfull fancy: − and heerein especially, Comedies give the largest field to ere, as *Chaucer* sayth: − howe both in other Nations and in ours, before Poets did soften us, we were full of courage, given to martiall exercises; the pillers of manlyke liberty, and not lulled a sleepe in shady idlenes with Poets pastimes. And lastly, and chiefely, they cry out with an open mouth, as if they out shot *Robin Hood,* that *Plato* banished them out of hys Commonwealth. Truely, this is much, if there be much truth in it.

First to the FIRST: that a man might better spend his tyme, is a reason indeede: but it doth (as they say) but *Petere principium:* for if it be as I affirme, that no learning is so good, as that which teacheth and mooveth to vertue; and that none can both teach and move thereto so much as Poetry: then is the conclusion manifest, that Incke and Paper cannot be to a more profitable purpose employed. And certainly, though a man should graunt their first assumption, it should followe (me thinkes) very unwillingly, that good is not good, because better is better. But I still and utterly denye, that there is sprong out of earth a more fruitefull knowledge. To the SECOND therefore, that they should be the principall lyars; I aunswere paradoxically, but, truely, I thinke truely; that of all Writers under the sunne, the Poet is the least lier: and though he would, as a Poet can scarcely be a lyer, the Astronomer, with his cosen the Geometrician, can hardly escape, when they take upon them to measure the height of the starres. How often, thinke you, doe the Phisitians lye, when they aver things good for sicknesses, which afterwards send *Charon* a great nomber of soules drowned in a potion before they come to his Ferry. And no lesse of the rest, which take upon them to affirme. Now, for the Poet, he nothing affirmes, and therefore never lyeth. For, as I take it, to lye is to affirme that to be true which is false. So as the other Artists, and especially the Historian, affirming many things, can in the cloudy knowledge of mankinde hardly escape from many lyes. But the Poet (as I sayd before) never affirmeth. The Poet never maketh any circles about your imagination, to coniure you to beleeve for true what he writes. Hee citeth not authorities of other Histories, but even for hys entry called the sweete Muses to inspire into him a good invention: in troth, not labouring to tell you what is, or is not, but what should or should not be: and therefore, though he recount things not true, yet because hee telleth them not for true, he lyeth not, without we will say that *Nathan* lyed in his speech before alledged to *David.* Which as a wicked man durst scarce say, so think I none so simple would say that *Esope* lyed in the tales of his beasts: for who thinks that *Esope* writ it for actually true were well worthy to have his name chronicled among the beastes hee writeth of. What childe is there, that comming to a Play, and seeing *Thebes* written in great Letters upon an olde doore, doth beleeve that it is *Thebes?* If, then, a man can arrive at that childs age to know that the Poets persons and dooings are but pictures what should be, and not stories what have beene, they will never give the lye to things not affirmatively, but allegorically and figurativelie written. And therefore, as in Historie, looking for trueth, they goe away full fraught with falshood: so in Poesie, looking for fiction, they shal use the narration but as an imagination groundplot of a profitable invention.

But heereto is replyed, that the Poets gyve names to men they write of, which argueth a conceite of an actuall truth, and so, not being true, prooves a falshood. And doth the Lawyer lye then, when under the names of *Iohn a stile* and *Iohn a noakes,* hee puts his case? But that is easily answered. Theyr naming of men, is but to make theyr picture the more lively, and not to builde any historie. Paynting men, they cannot leave men namelesse. We see we cannot play at Chesse, but

that wee must give names to our Chessemen; and yet, mee thinks, hee were a very partiall Champion of truth, that would say we lyed for giving a peece of wood the reverend title of a Bishop. The Poet nameth *Cyrus* or *Aeneas* no other way, then to shewe what men of theyr fames, fortunes, and estates, should doe.

Their THIRD is, how much it abuseth mens wit, trayning it to wanton sinfulnes, and lustfull love: for indeed that is the principall, if not the onely abuse I can heare alledged. They say, the Comedies rather teach, then reprehend, amorous conceits. They say, the Lirick is larded with passionate Sonnets. The Elegiack weepes the want of his mistresse. And that even to the Heroical *Cupid* hath ambitiously climed. Alas Love, I would thou couldest as well defende thy selfe, as thou canst offende others! I would those, on whom thou doost attend, could eyther put thee away, or yeelde good reason why they keepe thee! But grant love of beautie to be a beastlie fault, (although it be very hard, sith onely man, and no beast, hath that gyft to discerne beauty.) Grant, that lovely name of Love to deserve all hatefull reproches: (although even some of my Maisters the Philosophers, spent a good deale of theyr Lamp-oyle, in setting foorth the excellencie of it.) Grant, I say, what soever they wil have granted; that not onely love, but lust, but vanitie, but (if they list) scurrilitie, possesseth many leaves of the Poets bookes: yet thinke I, when this is granted, they will finde theyr sentence may, with good manners, put the last words foremost: and not say, that Poetrie abuseth mans wit, but that mans wit abuseth Poetrie. For I will not denie, but that mans wit may make Poesie, which should be *Eikastike* (which some learned have defined, figuring foorth good things,) to be *Phantastike:* which doth, contrariwise, infect the fancie with unworthy obiects. As the Painter, that shoulde give to the eye eyther some excellent perspective, or some fine picture, fit for building or fortification: or contayning in it some notable example, as *Abraham,* sacrificing his Sonne *Isaack, Iudith* killing *Holofernes, David* fighting with *Goliah,* may leave those, and please an ill-pleased eye with wanton shewes of better hidden matters.

But what! shall the abuse of a thing make the right use odious? Nay truely, though I yeeld, that Poesie may not onely be abused, but that beeing abused, by the reason of his sweete charming force, it can doe more hurt then any other Armie of words: yet shall it be so far from concluding, that the abuse should give reproch to the abused, that contrariwise it is a good reason, that whatsoever being abused dooth most harme, beeing rightly used (and upon the right use each thing conceiveth his title) doth most good.

Doe wee not see the skill of Phisick (the best rampire to our often-assaulted bodies), beeing abused, teach poyson the most violent destroyer? Dooth not knowledge of Law, whose end is to even and right all things, being abused, grow the crooked fosterer of horrible iniuries? Doth not (to goe to the highest) Gods word abused breed heresie? and his Name abused become blasphemie? Truely, a needle cannot doe much hurt, and as truely (with leave of Ladies be it spoken) it cannot doe much good. With a sword, thou maist kill thy Father, and with a sword thou maist defende thy Prince and Country. So that, as in their calling Poets the Fathers of lyes, they say nothing: so in this theyr argument of abuse, they proove the commendation.

They alledge heere-with, that before Poets beganne to be in price, our Nation hath set their harts delight upon action, and not upon imagination: rather doing things worthy to bee written, then writing things fitte to be done. What that before tyme was I thinke scarcely *Sphinx* can tell: sith no memory is so auncient, that hath the precedence of Poetrie. And certaine it is, that in our plainest homelines, yet never was the *Albion* Nation without Poetrie. Mary, thys argument, though it bee leaveld against Poetrie, yet is it indeed a chaine-shot against all learning or bookishnes, as they commonly tearme it. Of such minde were certaine *Gothes,* of whom it is written, that having in the spoile of a famous Citie taken a fayre librarie, one hangman (bee like fitte to execute the fruites of their wits who had murthered a great number of bodies) would have set fire on it: 'no' sayde another very gravely, 'take heed what you doe, for whyle they are busie about these toyes, wee shall with more leysure conquer their Countries.' This indeede is the ordinary doctrine of ignorance, and many wordes sometymes I have heard spent in it: but because this reason is generally against all learning, aswell as Poetrie; or rather, all learning but Poetry: because it were too large a digression to handle, or at least too superfluous, (sith it is manifest, that all government of action is to be gotten by knowledg, and knowledge best by gathering many knowledges, which is reading,) I onely with, *Horace,* to him that is of that opinion, *"Iubeo stultum esse libenter":* for as for Poetrie it selfe, it is the freest from thys obiection; for Poetrie is the companion of the Campes.

I dare undertake, *Orlando Furioso,* or honest King *Arthur,* will never displease a Souldier: but the quiddity of *Ens* and *Prima materia,* will hardely agree with a Corslet: and therefore, as I said in the beginning, even Turks and Tartares are delighted with Poets. *Homer,* a Greek, florished before Greece florished: and if to a slight coniecture a coniecture may be opposed, truly it may seeme, that as by him their learned men tooke almost their first light of knowledge, so their active men received their first motions of courage. Onlie *Alexanders* example may serve, who by *Plutarch* is accounted of such vertue, that Fortune was not his guide but his foote-stoole: whose acts speake for him, though *Plutarch* did not, indeede the Phœnix of warlike Princes. This *Alexander* left his Schoolemaister, living *Aristotle,* behinde him, but tooke deade *Homer* with him: he put the Philosopher *Calisthenes* to death for his seeming philosophicall, indeed mutinous stubburnnes; but the chiefe thing he ever was heard to wish for, was, that *Homer* had been alive. He well found he received more braverie of minde bye the patterne of *Achilles,* then by hearing the definition of Fortitude: and therefore, if *Cato* misliked *Fulvius,* for carying *Ennius* with him to the fielde; it may be aunswered, that if *Cato* misliked it, the noble *Fulvius* liked it, or els he had not doone it: for it was not the excellent *Cato Uticensis,* (whose authority I would much more have reverenced), but it was the former; in truth a bitter punisher of faults, but else a man that had never wel sacrificed to the Graces. Hee misliked and cryed out upon all Greeke learning, and yet being 80 yeeres olde began to learne it; be-like fearing that *Pluto* understood not Latine. Indeede, the Romaine lawes allowed no person to be carried to the warres, but hee that was in the Souldiers role: and therefore, though *Cato* misliked his unmustered person, hee misliked not his worke. And if hee had, *Scipio Nasica,* iudged by common consent the best Romaine, loved him. Both the other *Scipio* Brothers, who had by their vertues no lesse surnames, then of *Asia* and *Affrick,* so loved him, that they caused his body to be buried in their Sepulcher. So as *Cato,* his authoritie being but against his person, and that aunswered with so farre greater then himselfe, is heerein of no validitie.

But now indeede my burthen is great; now *Plato* his name is layde upon mee, whom I must confesse, of all Philosophers, I have ever esteemed most worthy of reverence; and with great reason, sith of all Philosophers he is the most poeticall. Yet if he will defile the Fountaine, out of which his flowing streames have proceeded, let us boldly examine with what reasons hee did it.

First truly, a man might maliciously obiect, that *Plato,* being a Philosopher, was a naturall enemie of Poets: for indeede, after the Philosophers had picked out of the sweete misteries of Poetrie the right discerning true points of knowledge, they forthwith, putting it in method, and making a Schoole-arte of that which the Poets did onely teach by a divine delightfulnes, beginning to spurne at their guides, like ungratefull Prentises, were not content to set up shops for themselves, but sought by all meanes to discredit their Maisters; which by the force of delight beeing barred them, the lesse they could overthrow them, the more they hated them. For indeede, they found for *Homer* seven Cities strove who sould have him for their Citizen: where many Citties banished Philosophers, as not fitte members to live among them. For onely repeating certaine of *Euripides* verses, many *Athenians* had their lyves saved of the *Syracusians:* when the *Athenians* themselves thought many Philosophers unwoorthie to live. Certaine Poets, as *Simonides,* and *Pindarus* had so prevailed with *Hiero* the first, that of a Tirant they made him a iust King, where *Plato* could do so little with *Dionisius,* that he himselfe, of a Philosopher, was made a slave. But who should doe thus, I confesse, should requite the obiections made against Poets, with like cavillation against Philosophers, as likewise one should doe, that should bid one read *Phædrus,* or *Symposium* in *Plato,* or the discourse of love in *Plutarch,* and see whether any Poet doe authorize abhominable filthines, as they doe. Againe, a man might aske out of what Common-wealth *Plato* did banish them? insooth, thence where he himselfe alloweth communitie of women. So as belike, this banishment grewe not for effeminate wantonnes, sith little should poeticall Sonnets be hurtfull, when a man might have what woman he listed. But I honor philosophicall instructions, and blesse the wits which bred them, so as they be not abused: which is likewise stretched to Poetrie.

S. *Paule* himselfe (who yet for the credite of Poets alledgeth twise two Poets, and one of them by the name of a Prophet) setteth a watch-word upon Philosophy, indeede upon the abuse. So dooth *Plato* upon the abuse, not upon Poetrie. *Plato* found fault, that the Poets of his time filled the worlde with wrong opinons of the Gods, making light tale of that unspotted essence; and therefore would not have the youth depraved with such opinons. Heerin may much be said. Let this suffice: the Poets did not induce such opinions, but dyd imitate those opinions already induced. For all the Greek stories can well testifie, that the very religion of that time stoode upon many and many-fashioned Gods, not taught so by the Poets, but followed according to their nature of imitation. Who list, may reade in *Plutarch* the discourses of *Isis* and *Osiris,* of the cause

why Oracles ceased, of the divine providence: and see whether the Theologie of that nation stood not upon such dreames, which the Poets indeed supersticiously observed, and truly (sith they had not the light of Christ) did much better in it then the Philosophers, who, shaking off superstition, brought in Atheisme.

Plato therefore, (whose authoritie I had much rather iustly conster then uniustly resist) meant not in general of Poets, in those words of which *Iulius Scaliger* saith: *Qua authoritate barbari quidam atque hispidi abuti velint ad Poetas e republica exigendos:* but only meant, to drive out those wrong opinions of the Deitie (whereof now, without further law, Christianity hath taken away all the hurtful beliefe) perchance, as he thought, norished by the then esteemed Poets. And a man need goe no furhter then to *Plato* himselfe to know his meaning; who in his Dialogue called *Ion* giveth high and rightly divine commendation to Poetrie. So as *Plato,* banishing the abuse not the thing, not banishing it but giving due honor unto it, shall be our Patron and not our adversarie. For indeed I had much rather (sith truly I may doe it) shew theyr mistaking of *Plato,* under whose Lyons skin they would make an Asse-like braying against Poesie, then goe about to overthrow his authority, whom the wiser a man is, the more iust cause he shall find to have in admiration: especially, sith he attributeth unto Poesie more then my selfe doe; namely, to be a very inspiring of a divine force, farre above mans wit, as in the afore-named Dialogue is apparant.

Of the other side, who wold shew the honors have been by the best sort of iudgements granted them, a whole Sea of examples woulde present themselves. *Alexanders, Cæsars, Scipios* al favorers of Poets. *Lelius,* called the Romane *Socrates,* himselfe a Poet; so as part of *Heautontimorumenon* in *Terence,* was supposed to be made by him. And even the Greek *Socrates,* whom *Apollo* confirmed to be the onely wise man, is sayde to have spent part of his old tyme in putting *Esops* fables into verses. And therefore, full evill should it become his scholler *Plato* to put such words in his Maisters mouth against Poets. But what need more? *Aristotle* writes the Arte of Poesie: and why if it should not be written? *Plutarch* teacheth the use to be gathered of them, and how if they should not be read? And who reades *Plutarchs* eyther historie or philosophy shall finde hee trymmeth both theyr garments with gards of Poesie.

But I list not to defend Poesie with the helpe of her underling, Historiography. Let it suffise, that it is a fit soyle for prayse to dwell upon: and what dispraise may set upon it is eyther easily over-come, or transformed into iust commendation. So that, sith the excellencies of it may be so easily and so iustly confirmed, and the low-creeping obiections so soone troden downe; it not being an Art of lyes, but of true doctrine: not of effeminatenes, but of notable stirring of courage: not of abusing mans witte, but of strengthning mans wit: not banished, but honored by *Plato:* let us rather plant more Laurels, for to engarland our Poets heads, (which honor of beeing laureat, as besides them onely triumphant Captaines weare, is a sufficient authority to shewe the price they ought to be had in,) then suffer the ill-favouring breath of such wrong-speakers once to blowe upon the cleere springs of Posie.

Digression.

But sith I have runne so long a careere in this matter, me thinks, before I give my penne a full stop, it shalbe but a little more lost time, to inquire, why England (the Mother of excellent mindes) should bee growne so hard a step-mother to Poets, who certainly in wit ought to passe all other: sith all onely proceedeth from their wit, being indeede makers of themselves, not takers of others. How can I but exclaime, *"Musa mihi causas memora, quo numine læso."* Sweete Poesie, that hath aunciently had Kings, Emperors, Senators, great Captaines, such, as besides a thousand others, *David, Adrian, Sophocles, Germanicus,* not onely to favour Poets, but to be Poets. And of our neerer times, can present for her Patrons, a *Robert,* king of Sicil, the great king *Francis* of France, King *Iames* of Scotland. Such Cardinals as *Bembus* and *Bibiena.* Such famous Preachers and Teachers, as *Beza* and *Melancthon.* So learned Philosophers, as *Fracastorius* and *Scaliger.* So great Orators, as *Pontanus* and *Muretus.* So piercing wits, as *George Buchanan.* So grave Counsellors, as besides many, but before all, that *Hospitall* of Fraunce: then whom (I thinke) that Realme never brought forth a more accomplished iudgement, more firmely builded upon vertue. I say these, with numbers of others, not onely to read others Poesies, but to poetise for others reading. That Poesie, thus embraced in all other places, should only finde in our time a hard welcome in England, I thinke the very earth lamenteth it, and therefore decketh our Soyle with fewer Laurels then it was accustomed. For heertofore Poets have in England also florished; and, which is to be noted, even in those times when the trumpet of *Mars* did sounde loudest. And now, that an over-faint quietnes should seeme to strew the house for Poets, they are almost in as good reputation, as the *Mountibancks* at *Venice.*

Truly even that, as of the one side it giveth great praise to Poesie, which like *Venus* (but to better purpose) hath rather be troubled in the net with *Mars,* then enioy the homelie quiet of *Vulcan:* so serves it for a peece of a reason, why they are lesse gratefull to idle England, which nowe can scarce endure the payne of a pen.

Upon this necessarily followeth, that base men with servile wits undertake it; who think it inough if they can be rewarded of the Printer. And so, as *Epaminondas* is sayd with the honor of his vertue to have made an office, by his exercising it, which before was contemptible to become highly respected: so these, no more but setting their names to it, by their owne disgracefulnes disgrace the most gracefull Poesie. For now, as if all the Muses were gotte with childe to bring foorth bastard Poets, without any commission they doe poste over the banckes of *Helicon,* tyll they make the readers more weary then Post-horses: while in the mean tyme, they *"Queis meliore luto finxit præcordia Titan,"* are better content, to suppresse the out-flowing of their wit, then by publishing them to bee accounted Knights of the same order. But I that, before ever I durst aspire unto the dignitie, am admitted into the company of the Paper-blurrers, doe finde the very true cause of our wanting estimation is want of desert: taking upon us to be Poets in despight of *Pallas.* Nowe, wherein we want desert were a thanke-worthy labour to expresse: but if I knew, I should have mended my selfe. But I, as I never desired the title, so have I neglected the meanes to come by it. Onely, over-mastred by some thoughts, I yeelded an inckie tribute unto them. Mary, they that delight in Poesie it selfe should seeke to knowe what they doe, and how they doe; and, especially, looke themselves in an unflattering Glasse of reason, if they bee inclinable unto it.

For Poesie, must not be drawne by the eares, it must bee gently led, or, rather, it must lead. Which was partly the cause, that made the auncient-learned affirme, it was a divine gift, and no humaine skill: sith all other knowledges lie ready for any that hath strength of witte; a Poet no industrie can make, if his owne *Genius* bee not carried unto it; and therefore is it an old Proverbe, *Orator fit, Poeta nascitur.* Yet confesse I alwayes that, as the firtilest ground must bee manured, so must the highest flying wit have a *Dedalus* to guide him. That *Dedalus,* they say, both in this and in other, hath three wings to beare it selfe up into the ayre of due commendation: that is, Arte, Imitation, and Exercise. But these, neyther artificiall rules nor imitative patternes, we much cumber our selves withall. Exercise indecde wee doe, but that very fore-back-wardly: for where we should exercise to know, wee exercise as having knowne: and so is oure braine delivered of much matter which never was begotten by knowledge. For, there being two principal parts, matter to be expressed by wordes, and words to expresse the matter, in nether wee use Arte or Imitation rightly. Our matter is *Quodlibet* indeed, though wrongly perfourming *Ovids* verse *"Quicquid conabar dicere versus erat"*: never marshalling it into an assured rancke, that almost the readers cannot tell where to finde themselves.

Chaucer undoubtedly did excellently in hys *Troylus* and *Cresseid;* of whom, truly I know not, whether to mervaile more, either that he, in that mistie time, could see so clearly, or that wee, in this cleare age, walke so stumblingly after him. Yet had he great wants, fitte to be forgiven in so reverent antiquity. I account the *Mirrour of Magistrates* meetely furnished of beautiful parts; and in the Earle of Surries *Liricks* many things tasting of a noble birth, and worthy of a noble minde. The *Sheapheards Kalender* hath much Poetrie in his Eglogues: indeede worthy the readng if I be not deceived. That same framing of his stile to an old rustick language I dare not alowe, sith neyther *Theocritus* in Greeke, *Virgill* in Latine, nor *Sanazar* in Italian, did affect it. Besides these, doe I not remember to have seene but fewe (to speake boldely) printed, that have poeticall sinnewes in them. For proofe whereof let but most of the verses bee put in Prose, and then aske the meaning; and it will be found, that one verse did but beget another, without ordering at the first what should be at the last: which becomes a confused masses of words, with a tingling sound of ryme, barely accompanied with reason.

Our Tragedies, and Comedies (not without cause cried out against) observing rules neyther of honest civilitie nor of skilfull Poetrie, excepting *Gorboduck* (againe, I say, of those that I have seene,) which notwithstanding, as it is full of stately speeches and well sounding Phrases, clyming to the height of *Seneca* his stile, and as full of notable moralitie, which it doth most delightfully teach, and so obtayne the very end of Poesie; yet in troth it is very defectious in the circumstances: which greeveth mee, because it might not remaine as an exact model of all Tragedies. For it is faulty both in place and time, the two necessary companions of all corporall actions. For where the stage should alwaies represent but one place, and the uttermost time presupposed in it should be, both by *Aristotles* precept and common reason, but one day: there is both many dayes, and many places, inartificially im-agined. But if it be so in *Gorboduck,* how much more in al the rest? where you shal have *Asia* of the one side, and *Affrick* of the other, and so many other under-kingdoms, that the Player, when he commeth in, must ever begin with telling where he is; or els, the tale wil not be conceived. Now ye shal have three Ladies walke to gather flowers, and then we must beleeve the stage to be a Garden. By and by, we heare newes of shipwracke in the same place, and then wee are to blame, if we accept it not for a Rock. Upon the backe of that, comes out a hidious Monster, with fire and smoke, and then the miserable beholders are bounde to take it for a Cave. While in the mean-time, two Armies flye in, represented with foure swords and bucklers, and then what harde heart will not receive it for a pitched fielde?

Now, of time they are much more liberall. For ordinary it is that two young Princes fall in love: after many traverces, she is got with childe, delivered of a faire boy; he is lost, groweth a man, falls in love, and is ready to get another child, and all this in two hours space: which how absurd it is in sense, even sense may imagine, and Arte hath taught, and all auncient examples iustified: and at this day, the ordinary Players in Italie wil not erre in. Yet wil some bring in an example of *Eunuchus* in *Terence,* that containeth matter of two dayes, yet far short of twenty yeeres. True it is, and so was it to be playd in two daies, and so fitted to the time it set forth. And though *Plautus* hath in one place done amisse, let us hit with him, and not misse with him.

But they wil say, how then shal we set forth a story, which containeth both many places, and many times? And doe they not knowe, that a Tragedie is tied to the lawes of Poesie, and not of Historie? not bound to follow the storie, but having liberty, either to faine a quite newe matter, or to frame the history to the most tragicall conveniencie. Againe, many things may be told which cannot be shewed, if they knowe the difference betwixt reporting and representing. As for example, I may speake (though I am heere) of *Peru,* and in speech digresse from that to the description of *Calicut:* but in action, I cannot represent it without *Pacolets* horse: and so was the manner the Auncients tooke, by some *Nuncius* to recount thinges done in former time, or other place.

Lastly, if they wil represent an history, they must not (as *Horace* saith) beginne *Ab ovo:* but they must come to the principall poynt of that one action, which they wil represent. By example this wil be best expressed. I have a story of young *Polidorus* delivered for safeties sake, with great riches, by his

Father *Priamus* to *Polimnestor* king of *Thrace,* in the Troyan war time. Hee after some yeeres, hearing the over-throwe of *Priamus,* for to make the treasure his owne, murthereth the child: the body of the child is taken up by *Hecuba;* shee the same day findeth a slight to bee revenged most cruelly of the Tyrant. Where nowe would one of our Tragedy writers begin, but with the delivery of the childe? Then should he sayle over into *Thrace,* and so spend I know not how many yeeres and travaile numbers of places. But where dooth *Euripides?* Even with the finding of the body, leaving the rest to be tolde by the spirit of *Polidorus.* This need no further to be inlarged, the dullest wit may conceive it.

But besides these grosse absurdities, how all theyr Playes be neither right Tragedies, nor right Comedies: mingling Kings and Clownes, not because the matter so carrieth it: but thrust in Clownes by head and shoulders, to play a part in maiesticall matters, with neither decencie nor discretion. So as neither the admiration and commiseration, nor the right sportfulnes, is by their mungrell Tragy-comedie obtained. I know *Apuleius* did somewhat so, but that is a thing recounted with space of time, not represented in one moment: and I knowe, the Aunciants have one or two examples of Tragycomedies, as *Plautus* hath *Amphitrio.* But if we marke them well, we shall find that they never, or very daintily, match Horn-pypes and Funeralls. So falleth it out, that, having indeed no right Comedy, in that comicall part of our Tragedy we have nothing but scurrility, unwoorthy of any chast eares: or some extreame shew of doltishnes, indeed fit to lift up a loude laughter and nothing els: where the whole tract of a Comedy shoulde be full of delight, as the Tragedy shoulde be still maintained in a well raised admiration.

But our Comedians thinke there is no delight without laughter: which is very wrong, for though laughter may come with delight, yet commeth is not of delight, as though delight should be the cause of laughter. But well may one thing breed both together. Nay, rather in themselves they have as it were a kind of contrarietie: for delight we scarcely doe, but in things that have a conveniencie to our selves or to the generall nature: laughter almost ever commeth of things most disproportioned to our selves and nature. Delight hath a ioy in it, either permanent or present. Laughter hath onely a scornful tickling. For example, we are ravished with delight to see a faire woman, and yet are far from being moved to laughter. We laugh at deformed creatures, wherein certainely we cannot delight. We delight in good chaunces, we laugh at mischaunces;

we delight to heare the happines of our friends or Country, at which he were worthy to be laughed at, that would laugh; wee shall contrarily laugh sometimes, to finde a matter quite mistaken and goe downe the hill agaynst the byas, in the mouth of some such men, as for the respect of them, one shalbe hartely sorry, yet he cannot chuse but laugh; and so is rather pained, then delight without laughter. Yet deny I not, but that they may goe well together; for as in *Alexanders* picture well set out, wee delight without laughter, and in twenty mad Anticks we laugh without delight: so in *Hercules,* painted with his great beard and furious countenance, in womans attire, spinning at *Omphales* commaundement, it breedeth both delight and laughter. For the representing of so strange a power in love procureth delight: and the scornefulnes of the action stirreth laughter.

But I speake to this purpose, that all the end of the comicall part bee not upon such scornefull matters, as stirreth laughter onely: but, mixt with it, that delightful teaching which is the end of Poesie. And the great fault even in that point of laughter, and forbidden plainely by *Aristotle,* is, that they styrre laughter in sinfull things; which are rather execrable then ridiculous: or in miserable, which are rather to be pittied than scorned. For what is it to make folkes gape at a wretched Begger, or a beggerly Clowne; or, against lawe of hospitality, to iest at straungers, because they speake not English so well as wee doe? What do we learne? Sith it is certaine

Nil habet infelix paupertas durius in se,
Quam quod ridiculos homines facit.

But rather a busy loving Courtier, a hartles threatening *Thraso;* a selfe-wise-seeming schoolemaster; a awry-transformed Traveller: these if we sawe walke in stage names, which wee play naturally, therein were delightfull laughter, and teaching delightfulnes: as in the other, the Tragedies of *Buchanan* doe iustly bring forth a divine admiration. But I have lavished out too many wordes of this play matter. I doe it because, as they are excelling parts of Poesie, so is there none so much used in England, and none can be more pittifully abused. Which like an unmannerly Daughter, shewing a bad education, causeth her mother Poesies honesty to bee called in question.

Other sorts of Poetry almost have we none, but that Lyricall kind of Songs and Sonnets: which, Lord, if he gave us so good mindes, how well it might be imployed, and with howe heavenly fruite, both private and publique, in singing the prayses of the immortall beauty, the immortall goodnes of that God, who gyveth us hands to write, and wits to conceive! of which we might well want words, but never matter; of which we could turne our eies to nothing but we should ever have a new budding occasions. But truely many of such writings, as come under the banner of unresistable love, if I were a Mistres, would never perswade mee they were in love: so coldely they apply fiery speeches, as men that had rather red Lovers writings, and so caught up certaine swelling phrases, which hang together, like a man which once tolde mee, the winde was at North West, and by South, because he would be sure to name windes enowe, – then that in truth they feele those passions: which easily (as I think) may be bewrayed by that same forciblenes or *Energia* (as the Greekes cal it) of the writer. But let this bee a sufficient, though short note, that wee misse the right use of the materiall point of Poesie.

Now, for the out-side of it, which is words, or (as I may tearme it) *Diction,* is is even well worse. So is that honny-flowing Matron Eloquence apparelled, or rather disguised, in a Curtizan-like painted affectation: one time with so farre fette words, they may seeme Monsters, but must seeme straungers, to any poore English man; another tyme, with coursing of a Letter, as if they were bound to followe the method of a Dictionary: an other tyme, with figures and flowers, extreamelie winter-starved. But I would this fault were only peculier to Versifiers, and had not as large possession among Prose-printers; and (which is to be mervailed) among many Schollers; and (which is to be pittied) among some Preachers. Truly I could wish, if at least I might be so bold to wish in a thing beyond the reach of my capacity, the diligent imitators of *Tullie* and *Demosthenes* (most worthy to be imitated) did not so much keep *Nizolian* Paper-bookes of their figures and phrases, as by attentive translation (as it were) devoure them whole, and make them wholly theirs. For nowe they cast Sugar and Spice upon every dish that is served to the table; like those Indians, not content to weare eare-rings at the fit and naturall place of the eares, but they will thrust Iewels through their nose and lippes, because they will be sure to be fine. *Tullie,* when he was to drive out *Cateline,* as it were with a Thunder-bolt of eloquence, often used that figure of repitition, *Vivit vivit? imo in Senatum venit &c.* Indeed, inflamed with a well-grounded rage, hee would have his words (as it were) double out of his mouth: and so doe that artificially, which we see men doe in choller naturally. And wee, having noted the grace of those words,

hale them in sometime to a familier Epistle, when it were to too much choller to be chollerick.

Now for similitudes, in certaine printed discourses, I thinke all Herbarists, all stories of Beasts, Foules, and Fishes, are rifled up, that they come in multitudes to waite upon any of our conceits; which certainly is as absurd a surfet to the eares, as is possible. For the force of a similitude, not being to proove anything to a contrary Disputer, but onely to explane to a willing hearer, when that is done, the rest is a most tedious pratling: rather over-swaying the memory from the purpose whereto they were applied, then any whit informing the iudgement, already eyther satisfied, or by similitudes not to be satisfied. For my part, I doe not doubt, when *Antonius* and *Crassus,* the great forefathers of *Cicero* in eloquence, the one (as *Cicero* testifieth of them) pretended not to know Arte, the other not to set by it: because with a playne sensiblenes they might win credit of popular eares; which credit is the neerest step to perswasion: which perswasion is the chiefe marke of Oratory; – I doe not doubt (I say) but that they used these knacks very sparingly, which who doth generally use, any man may see doth daunce to his owne musick: and so be noted by the audience, more carefull to speake curiously, then to speake truly.

Undoubtedly (at least to my opinion undoubtedly) I have found in divers smally learned Courtiers, a more sounde stile, then in some professors of learning: of which I can gesse no other cause, but that the Courtier following that which by practise hee findeth fittest to nature, therein (though he know it not) doth according to Art, though not by Art: where the other, using Art to shew Art, and not to hide Art (as in these cases he should doe), flyeth from nature, and indeede abuseth Art.

But what? me thinkes I deserve to be pounded, for straying from Poetrie to Oratorie: but both have such an affinity in this wordish consideration, that I thinke this digression will make my meaning receive the fuller understanding: which is not to take upon me to teach Poets howe they should doe, but onely finding my selfe sick among the rest, to shewe some one or two spots of the common infection, growne among the most part of Writers: that acknowledging our selves somewhat awry, we may bend to the right use both of matter and manner; whereto our language gyveth us great occasion, beeing indeed capable of any excellent exercising of it. I know, some will say it is a mingled language. And why not so much the better, taking the best of both the other? Another will say it wanteth Grammer. Nay truly, it hath that prayse, that it wanteth not Grammer: for Grammer it might have, but it needes it not; beeing so easie of it selfe, and so voyd of those cumbersome differences of Cases, Genders, Moodes, and Tenses, which I thinke was a peece of the Tower of *Babilons* curse, that a man should be put to schoole to learne his mother-tongue. But for the uttering sweetly and properly the conceits of the minde, which is the end of speech, that hath it equally with any other tongue in the world: and is particulerly happy in compositions of two or three words together, neere the Greeke, far beyond the Latine: which is one of the greatest beauties can be in a language.

Now, of versifying there are two sorts, the one Auncient, the other Moderne: the Auncient marked the quantitie of each silable, and according to that, framed his verse: the Moderne, observing onely number (with some regarde of the accent), the chiefe life of it standeth in that lyke sounding of the words, which wee call Ryme. Whether of these be the most excellent, would beare many speeches. The Auncient (no doubt) more fit for Musick, both words and tune observing quantity, and more fit lively to expresse divers passions, by the low and lofty sounde of the well-weyed silable. The latter likewise, with hys Ryme, striketh a certaine musick to the eare: and in fine, sith it dooth delight, though by another way, it obtaines the same purpose: there beeing in eyther sweetnes, and wanting in neither maiestie. Truely the English, before any other vulgar language I know, is fit for both sorts: for, for the Ancient, the Italian is so full of Vowels, that it must ever be cumbred with *Elisions.* The Dutch, so of the other side with Consonants, that they cannot yeeld the sweet slyding, fit for a Verse. The French, in his whole language, hath not one word, that hath his accent in the last silable saving two, called *Antepenultima;* and little more hath the Spanish: and therefore, very gracelesly may they use *Dactiles.* The English is subiect to none of these defects.

Nowe, for the ryme, though wee doe not observe quantity, yet wee observe the accent very precisely; which other languages, eyther cannot doe, or will not doe so absolutely. That *Cæsura,* or breathing place in the middest of the verse, neither Italian nor Spanish have, the French and we never almost fayle of. Lastly, even the very ryme it selfe the Italian cannot put in the last silable, by the French named the Masculine ryme, but still in the next to the last, which the French call the Female; or the next before that, which the Italians terme *Sdrucciola.* The example of the former, is *Buono, Suono,* of the *Sdrucciola, Femina, Semina.* The French, of the other side, hath both the Male, as *Bon, Son,* and the Female, as *Plaise, Taise.* But the *Sdrucciola* hee hath not: where the English hath all three, as *Due, True, Father, Rather, Motion, Potion;* with much more which might be sayd, but that I finde already the triflingnes of this discourse is much too much enlarged.

Peroration.

So that sith the ever-praise-worthy Poesie, is full of vertue-breeding delightfulnes, and voyde of no gyfte, that ought to be in the noble name of learning: sith the blames laid against it are either false or feeble: sith the cause why it is not esteemed in Englande is the fault of Poet-apes, not Poets: sith lastly, our tongue is most fit to honor Poesie, and to bee honored by Poesie, I coniure you all, that have had the evill lucke to read this incke-wasting toy of mine, even in the name of the nyne Muses, no more to scorne the sacred mysteries of Poesie: no more to laugh at the name of Poets, as though they were next inheritours to Fooles: no more to iest at the reverent title of a Rymer. But to beleeve with *Aristotle,* that they were the auncient Treasurers of the Græcians Divinity. To beleeve with *Bembus,* that they were first bringers in of all civilitie. To beleeve with *Scaliger,* that no Philosophers precepts can sooner make you an honest man, then the reading of *Virgill.* To beleeve with *Clauserus,* the Translator of *Cornutus,* that it pleased the heavenly Deitie, by *Hesiod* and *Homer,* under the vayle of fables, to give us all knowledge, Logick, Rethorick, Philosophy naturall and morall; and *Quid non?* To beleeve with me, that there are many mysteries contained in Poetrie, which of purpose were written darkely, least by prophane wits it should bee abused. To beleeve with *Landin,* that they are so beloved of the Gods, that whatsoever they write proceeds of a divine fury. Lastly, to beleeve themselves, when they tell you they will make you immortall by their verses.

Thus doing, your name shal florish in the Printers shoppes; thus doing, you shall bee of kinne to many a poeticall Preface; thus doing, you shall be most fayre, most ritch, most wise, most all. You shall dwell upon Superlatives. Thus dooing, though you be *Libertino patre natus,* you shall suddenly grow *Herculea proles* "*Si quid mea carmina possunt.*" Thus doing, your soule shal be placed with *Dantes Beatrix,* or *Virgils Anchises.* But if (fie of such a but) you be borne so neere the dull making *Cataract* of *Nilus,* that you cannot heare the Plannet-like Musick of Poetrie; if you have so earth-creeping a mind, that it cannot lift it selfe up to looke to the sky of Poetry; or rather, by a certaine rusticall disdaine, will become such a Mome, as to be a *Momus* of Poetry: then, though I will not wish unto you the Asses eares of *Midas,* nor to bee driven by a Poets verses (as *Bubonax* was) to hang himselfe, nor to be rimed to death, as is sayd to be doone in Ireland: yet thus much curse I must send you in the behalfe of all Poets, that while you live, you live in love, and never get favour for lacking skill of a *Sonnet:* and when you die, your memory die from the earth for want of an *Epitaph.*

FINIS.

Checklist of Further Readings

Bibliographies and other reference materials:

Arber, Edward, ed. *A Transcript of the Registers of the Company of Stationers of London, 1554–1640 [Stationers' Register]*, 5 volumes. London, 1875–1894.

Bietenholz, Peter G., and Thomas B. Deutscher, eds., *Contemporaries of Erasmus: A Biographical Register of the Renaissance and Reformation*, 3 volumes. Toronto & Buffalo, N.Y.: University of Toronto Press, 1984–1987.

Eccles, Mark. "Brief Lives: Tudor and Stuart Authors," *Studies in Philology: Texts and Studies 1982*, 79 (Fall 1982): 1–135.

"English Literature/1500–1599," *MLA Bibliography of Books and Articles on the Modern Languages and Literatures*. New York: Modern Language Association, annually.

Fédération international des sociétés et instituts pour l'étude de la Renaissance. *Bibliographie internationale de l'humanisme et de la Renaissance*. Geneva: Droz, annually.

Hamilton, A. C., gen. ed. *The Spenser Encyclopedia*. Toronto: University of Toronto Press, 1990.

Hardin, Richard F. "Recent Studies in Neo-Latin Literature." *English Literary Renaissance*, 24 (Autumn 1994): 660–698.

Harner, James L. *English Renaissance Prose Fiction, 1500–1660: An Annotated Bibliography of Criticism*. Boston: G. K. Hall, 1978.

Harner. *English Renaissance Prose Fiction, 1500–1660: An Annotated Bibliography of Criticism, 1976–1983*. New York: G. K. Hall, 1985.

Harner. *English Renaissance Prose Fiction, 1500–1660: An Annotated Bibliography of Criticism, 1984–1990*. New York: G. K. Hall, 1992.

Hogrefe, Pearl. *Women of Action in Tudor England: Nine Biographical Sketches*. Ames: Iowa State University Press, 1977.

Ijsewijn, Jozef. *Companion to Neo-Latin Studies*. Amsterdam: North-Holland, 1977.

Lanham, Richard A. *A Handlist of Rhetorical Terms*, second edition. Berkeley: University of California Press, 1991.

Lievsay, John L., ed. *The Sixteenth Century: Skelton Through Hooker*, Goldentree Bibliographies. New York: Appleton-Century-Crofts, 1968.

Marcuse, Michael J. "Literature of the Renaissance and Earlier Seventeenth Century," section O in *A Reference Guide for English Studies*. Berkeley: University of California Press, 1990, pp. 323–338.

O'Dell, Sterg, ed. *A Chronological List of Prose Fiction in English Printed in England and Other Countries, 1475–1640*. Cambridge, Mass.: MIT Press, 1954.

Ousby, Ian, cd. *The Cambridge Guide to English Literature*. Cambridge: Cambridge University Press, 1988.

Pollard, A. W., and G. R. Redgrave, eds. *A Short-Title of Catalogue of Books Printed in England, Scotland, and Ireland, and of English Books Printed Abroad, 1475–1640 [STC]*, 3 volumes. London: Bibliographical Society, 1926; revised and enlarged by W. A. Jackson, F. S. Ferguson, and Katharine F. Pantzer, London: Bibliographical Society, 1976–1991.

Preminger, Alex, and T. V. F. Brogan, eds. *The New Princeton Encyclopedia of Poetry and Poetics*. Princeton: Princeton University Press, 1993.

"Recent Studies in the English Renaissance," *Studies in English Literature, 1500–1900*. Annually, Winter.

Ruoff, James E. *Crowell's Handbook of Elizabethan and Stuart Literature*. New York: Crowell, 1975.

Schweitzer, Frederick M., and Harry E. Wedeck, eds. *Dictionary of the Renaissance*. New York: Philosophical Library, 1967.

The State of Renaissance Studies: A Special Twenty-fifth Anniversary Symposium in Honor of Dan S. Collins. English Literary Renaissance, 25 (Autumn 1995).

Stephen, Leslie, and Sidney Lee, eds. *The Dictionary of National Biography from the Earliest Times to 1900 [DNB]*. London: Oxford University Press, 1885–1900; reprinted with supplements, 1967–1968.

Watson, George, ed. *The New Cambridge Bibliography of English Literature [NCBEL]*, volume 1: *600–1600*. Cambridge: Cambridge University Press, 1974.

Ziegler, Georgianna M. "Recent Studies in Women Writers of Tudor England, 1485–1603 (1990 to mid-1993)." *English Literary Renaissance*, 24 (Winter 1994): 229–242.

Anthologies, collections:

Alexander, Nigel, ed. *Elizabethan Narrative Verse*. Cambridge, Mass.: Harvard University Press, 1968.

Byrne, Muriel St. Clare, ed. *The Lisle Letters*, 6 volumes. Chicago: University of Chicago Press, 1981.

Dodd, A. H., ed. *Life in Elizabethan England*. New York: Putnam, 1961.

Donno, Elizabeth Story, ed. *Elizabethan Minor Epics*. New York: Columbia University Press, 1963.

Ferguson, Moira, ed. *First Feminists: British Women Writers, 1578–1799*. Bloomington: Indiana University Press / Old Westbury, N.Y.: Feminist Press, 1985.

Henderson, Katherine Usher, and Barbara F. McManus, eds. *Half Humankind: Contexts and Texts of the Controversy about Women in England, 1540–1640*. Urbana: University of Illinois Press, 1985.

Hurstfield, Joel, and Alan G. R. Smith, eds. *Elizabethan People: State and Society*. New York: St. Martin's Press, 1972.

Mahl, Mary R., and Helene Koon, eds. *The Female Spectator: English Women Writers before 1800*. Bloomington: Indiana University Press / Old Westbury, N.Y.: Feminist Press, 1977.

Manley, Lawrence, ed. *London in the Age of Shakespeare: An Anthology*. London: Croom Helm, 1986.

May Steven W., ed. *The Elizabethan Courtier Poets: The Poems and Their Contexts*. Columbia: University of Missouri Press, 1991.

Millward, J. W., ed. *Portraits and Documents: Sixteenth Century*. London: Hutchinson, 1961.

Myers, James P. Jr., ed. *Elizabethan Ireland: A Selection of Writings by Elizabethan Writers on Ireland*. Hamden, Conn.: Archon, 1983.

Otten, Charlotte F., ed. *English Women's Voices, 1540–1700*. Miami: Florida International University Press, 1992.

Rollins, Hyder E., and Herschell Baker, eds. *The Renaissance in England: Non-dramatic Prose and Verse of the Sixteenth Century*. Lexington, Mass.: Heath, 1954; reprinted, Prospect Heights, Ill.: Waveland, 1992.

Shepherd, Simon, ed. *The Women's Sharp Revenge: Five Women Pamphleteers from the Renaissance*. New York: St. Martin's Press, 1985; republished as *The Women's Sharp Revenge: Five Women's Pamphlets from the Renaissance*. London: Fourth Estate, 1985.

Smith, G. Gregory, ed. *Elizabethan Critical Essays*, 2 volumes. Oxford: Oxford University Press, 1904.

Travitsky, Betty, ed. *The Paradise of Women: Writings by Englishwomen of the Renaissance*. Westport, Conn.: Greenwood Press, 1981; revised edition, New York: Columbia University Press, 1989.

Williams, Penry, ed. *Life in Tudor England*. New York: Putnam, 1964.

Wilson, Katharina M., ed. *Women Writers of the Renaissance and Reformation*. Athens: University of Georgia Press, 1987.

H. R. Woudhuysen, ed. *The Penguin Book of Renaissance Verse, 1509–1659,* selected by David Norbrook. London: Penguin, 1992.

Recommended works:

Allen, Don Cameron. *Mysterious Meant: The Rediscovery of Pagan Symbolism and Allegorical Interpretation in the Renaissance*. Baltimore: Johns Hopkins University Press, 1970.

Alpers, Paul J., ed. *Elizabethan Poetry: Modern Essays in Criticism*. New York: Oxford University Press, 1967.

Anderson, Judith H. *Biographical Truth: The Representation of Historical Persons in Tudor-Stuart Writing*. New Haven: Yale University Press, 1984.

Bainton, Roland H. *The Reformation of the Sixteenth Century*. Boston: Beacon, 1952.

Bakhtin, Mikhail M. *Rabelais and His World,* translated by Hélène Iswolsky. Cambridge, Mass.: MIT Press, 1984.

Beilin, Elaine V. *Redeeming Eve: Women Writers of the English Renaissance*. Princeton: Princeton University Press, 1987.

Benson, Pamela Joseph. *The Invention of the Renaissance Woman: The Challenge of Female Independence in the Literature and Thought of Italy and England*. University Park: Pennsylvania State University Press, 1992.

Binns, J. W. *Intellectual Culture in Elizabethan and Jacobean England: The Latin Writings of the Age*. Leeds: Cairns, 1990.

Black, J. B. *The Reign of Elizabeth, 1558–1603,* second edition, volume 8 of *The Oxford History of England*, edited by George Clark. Oxford: Clarendon Press, 1959.

Booty, John E., and others, eds. *The Godly Kingdom of Tudor England: Great Books of the English Reformation.* Wilton, Conn.: Morehouse-Barlow, 1981.

Bradner, Leicester. *Musae Anglicanae: A History of Anglo-Latin Poetry, 1500–1925.* New York: Modern Language Association, 1940; republished with supplement in *Library,* fifth series 22 (1967): 93–103.

Briggs, Julia. *This State-Play World: English Literature and Its Background, 1580–1625.* Oxford: Oxford University Press, 1983.

Brooke, Tucker, and Matthias A. Shaaber. *The Renaissance (1500–1600),* book 2 of *A Literary History of England,* second edition, edited by Albert C. Baugh. New York: Appleton-Century-Crofts, 1967.

Burckhardt, Jacob. *The Civilization of the Renaissance in Italy,* translated by S. G. C. Middlemore. Oxford: Oxford University Press, 1944.

Bush, Douglas. *Mythology and the Renaissance Tradition in English Poetry,* revised edition. New York: Norton, 1963.

Bush. *Prefaces to Renaissance Literature.* Cambridge, Mass.: Harvard University Press, 1965.

Bush. *The Renaissance and English Humanism.* Toronto: University of Toronto Press, 1939.

Camden, Charles Carroll. *The Elizabethan Woman.* Houston: Elsevier Press, 1952.

Campbell, Lily B. *Divine Poetry and Drama in Sixteenth-Century England.* Berkeley: University of California Press, 1959.

Carlson, David R. *English Humanist Books: Writers and Patrons, Manuscripts and Print, 1475–1525.* Toronto: University of Toronto Press, 1993.

Colie, Rosalie L. *The Resources of Kind: Genre-Theory in the Renaissance,* edited by Barbara K. Lewalski. Berkeley: University of California Press, 1973.

Craig, Hardin. *The Enchanted Glass: The Elizabethan Mind in Literature.* Oxford: Blackwell, 1966.

Dobson, Eric John. *English Pronunciation: 1500–1700,* second edition, 2 volumes. Oxford: Clarendon Press, 1968.

Dowling, Maria. *Humanism in the Age of Henry VIII.* London & Dover, N.H.: Croom Helm, 1986.

Dubrow, Heather, and Richard Strier, eds. *Historical Renaissance: New Essays on Tudor and Stuart Culture.* Chicago: University of Chicago Press, 1988.

Eccles, Mark. "A Biographical Dictionary of Elizabethan Authors," *Huntington Library Quarterly,* 5 (April 1942): 281–302.

Ferguson, Margaret, and others, eds. *Rewriting the Renaissance: The Discourse of Sexual Difference in Early Modern Europe.* Chicago: University of Chicago Press, 1986.

Ferry, Anne. *The "Inward" Language: Sonnets of Wyatt, Sidney, Shakespeare, Donne.* Chicago: University of Chicago Press, 1983.

Ford, Boris, ed. *Renaissance and Reformation,* volume 3 of *The Cambridge Guide to the Arts in Britain.* Cambridge: Cambridge University Press, 1989; republished as *Sixteenth-century Britain,* volume 3 of *The Cambridge Cultural History of Britian.* Cambridge: Cambridge University Press, 1992.

Foucault, Michel. "What Is an Author?," translated by Josué V. Harari, in *The Foucault Reader,* edited by Paul Rabinow. New York: Pantheon, 1984, pp. 101–120.

Fox, Alistair. *Politics and Literature in the Reigns of Henry VII and Henry VIII.* Oxford: Blackwell, 1989.

Fox and John Guy. *Reassessing the Henrician Age: Humanism, Politics and Reform, 1500–1550.* Oxford: Blackwell, 1986.

Fraser, Russell. *The War against Poetry.* Princeton: Princeton University Press, 1970.

Fraser. *The Dark Ages and the Age of Gold.* Princeton: Princeton University Press, 1973.

Grant, Leonard. *Neo-Latin Literature and the Pastoral.* Chapel Hill: University of North Carolina Press, 1965.

Greenblatt, Stephen Jay. *Renaissance Self-Fashioning from More to Shakespeare.* Chicago: University of Chicago Press, 1980.

Greene, Thomas M. *Light in Troy: Imitation and Discovery in Renaissance Poetry.* New Haven: Yale University Press, 1982.

Guy. *Tudor England.* New York: Oxford University Press, 1988.

Hannay, Margaret P., ed. *Silent but for the Word: Tudor Women as Patrons, Translators, and Writers of Religious Works.* Kent, Ohio: Kent State University Press, 1985.

Haselkorn, Anne M., and Betty S. Travitsky, eds. *The Renaissance English Woman in Print: Counterbalancing the Canon.* Amherst: University of Massachusetts Press, 1990.

Haugaard, William P. "The Preface," in *The Folger Library Edition of the Works of Richard Hooker,* volume 6, part 1. Binghamton, N.Y.: Medieval and Renaissance Texts and Studies, 1993, pp. 1–80.

Helgerson, Richard. *Self-Crowned Laureates: Spenser, Jonson, Milton, and the Literary System.* Berkeley: University of California Press, 1983.

Heninger, S. K. Jr. *Touches of Sweet Harmony: Pythagorean Cosmology and Renaissance Poetics.* San Marino, Cal.: Huntington Library, 1974.

Hoffmann, Ann. *Lives of the Tudor Age, 1485–1603.* London: Osprey, 1977; New York: Barnes & Noble, 1977.

Hogrefe, Pearl. *Tudor Women: Commoners and Queens.* Ames: Iowa State University Press, 1975.

Howell, Wilbur Samuel. *Logic and Rhetoric in England, 1500–1700.* Princeton: Princeton University Press, 1956.

Hull, Suzanne W. *Chaste, Silent, and Obedient: English Books for Women, 1475–1640.* San Marino, Cal.: Huntington Library, 1982.

Javitch, Daniel. *Poetry and Courtliness in Renaissance England.* Princeton: Princeton University Press, 1978.

Kay, Dennis. *Melodious Tears: The English Funeral Elegy from Spenser to Milton.* Oxford: Clarendon Press, 1990.

Keach, William. *Elizabethan Erotic Narrative: Irony and Pathos in the Ovidian Poetry of Shakespeare, Marlowe, and Their Contemporaries.* New Brunswick, N.J.: Rutgers University Press, 1977.

Kelley, Donald R. "The Theory of History," in *The Cambridge History of Renaissance Philosophy,* edited by Charles B. Schmitt and others. Cambridge: Cambridge University Press, 1988, pp. 746–761.

Kernan, Alvin. *The Cankered Muse: Satire of the English Renaissance.* Yale Studies in English 142. New Haven: Yale University Press, 1959.

Kerrigan, William, and Gordon Braden. *The Idea of the Renaissance.* Baltimore & London: Johns Hopkins University Press, 1989.

King, John N. *English Reformation Literature: The Tudor Origins of the Protestant Tradition.* Princeton: Princeton University Press, 1982.

Kökeritz, Helge. *Shakespeare's Pronunciation.* New Haven: Yale University Press, 1953.

Kristeller, Paul Otto. "Humanism," in *The Cambridge History of Renaissance Philosophy,* pp. 113–137.

Lathrop, Henry Burrowes. *Translations from the Classics into English from Caxton to Chapman, 1477–1620.* University of Wisconsin Studies in Language and Literature, no. 35. Madison: University of Wisconsin Press 1933; New York: Octagon, 1967.

Levao, Ronald. *Renaissance Minds and Their Fictions: Cusanus, Sidney, Shakespeare.* Berkeley: University of California Press, 1985.

Levin, Carole, and Patricia A. Sullivan, eds. *Political Rhetoric, Power, and Renaissance Women.* Albany: State University of New York Press, 1995.

Levin, Harry T. *The Myth of the Golden Age in the Renaissance.* Bloomington: Indiana University Press, 1969.

Lewis, C. S. *The Discarded Image: An Introduction to Medieval and Renaissance Literature.* Cambridge: Cambridge University Press, 1964.

Lewis. *English Literature in the Sixteenth Century, Excluding Drama,* volume 3 of *The Oxford History of English Literature,* edited by F. P. Wilson and Bonamy Dobrée. Oxford: Clarendon Press, 1954.

Lovejoy, Arthur O. *The Great Chain of Being: A Study of the History of an Idea.* Cambridge, Mass.: Harvard University Press, 1936.

Mackie, J. D. *The Earlier Tudors, 1485–1558,* volume 7 of *The Oxford History of England,* edited by George Clark. Oxford: Clarendon Press, 1978.

Marcus, Leah S. "Renaissance / Early Modern Studies," in *Redrawing the Boundaries: The Transformation of English and American Literary Studies,* edited by Greenblatt and Giles Gunn. New York: Modern Language Association of America, 1992, pp. 41–63.

Mason, H. A. *Humanism and Poetry in the Early Tudor Period: An Essay.* London: Routledge & Kegan Paul, 1959.

Matthiessen, F. O. *Translation: An Elizabethan Art.* Cambridge, Mass.: Harvard University Press, 1931.

May, Steven W. *The Elizabethan Courtier Poets: The Poems and Their Contexts.* Columbia: University of Missouri Press, 1991.

Maynard, Winifred. *Elizabethan Lyric Poetry and Its Music*. Oxford: Clarendon Press, 1986.

Mayer, Thomas F., and D. R. Woolf, eds. *The Rhetorics of Life-Writing in Early Modern Europe: Forms of Biography from Cassandra Fedele to Louis XIV*. Ann Arbor: University of Michigan Press, 1995.

Mazzaro, Jerome. *Transformations in the Renaissance English Lyric*. Ithaca: Cornell University Press, 1970.

McLean, Antonia. *Humanism and the Rise of Science in Tudor England*. London: Heinemann Educational, 1972; New York: Watson Academic, 1972.

Mueller, Janel M. *The Native Tongue and the Word: Developments in English Prose Style, 1380–1580*. Chicago: University of Chicago Press, 1984.

Norbrook, David. Introduction to *The Penguin Book of Renaissance Verse, 1509–1659,* selected by Norbrook, edited by H. R. Woudhuysen. London: Penguin, 1992, pp. 1–67.

Norbrook. *Poetry and Politics of the English Renaissance*. London: Routledge & Kegan Paul, 1984.

Parker, Patricia A. *Literary Fat Ladies: Rhetoric, Gender, Property*. Berkeley: University of California Press, 1987.

Parker and David Quint, eds. *Literary Theory / Renaissance Texts*. Baltimore: Johns Hopkins University Press, 1986.

Patrides, C. A., and Joseph Wittreich, eds. *The Apocalypse in English Renaissance Thought and Literature: Patterns, Antecedents and Repercussions*. Ithaca: Cornell University Press, 1984.

Patterson, Annabel. *Censorship and Interpretation: The Conditions of Writing and Reading in Early Modern England*. Madison: University of Wisconsin Press, 1984.

Pearcey, Lee T. *The Mediated Muse: English Translations of Ovid, 1560–1700*. Hamden, Conn.: Archon, 1984.

Peterson, Douglas L. *The English Lyric from Wyatt to Donne: A History of the Plain and Eloquent Styles,* second edition. Princeton: Princeton University Press, 1990.

Pitcher, John. "Tudor Literature (1485–1603)," in *The Oxford Illustrated History of English Literature,* edited by Pat Rogers. Oxford: Oxford University Press, 1987, pp. 59–111.

Relihan, Constance C. *Fashioning Authority: The Development of Elizabethan Novelistic Discourse*. Kent, Ohio: Kent State University Press, 1994.

Ricks, Christopher, ed. *English Poetry and Prose, 1540–1674,* revised edition, volume 2 of *[Sphere] History of Literature in the English Language*. London: Barrie & Jenkins, 1986.

Rivers, Isabel. *Classical and Christian Ideas in English Renaissance Poetry: A Students' Guide*. London: Allen & Unwin, 1979.

Rose, Mary Beth, ed. *Women in the Middle Ages and the Renaissance: Literary and Historical Perspectives*. Syracuse, N.Y.: Syracuse University Press, 1986.

Rubel, Veré L. *Poetic Diction in the English Renaissance from Skelton through Spenser*. New York: Modern Language Association, 1941.

Salzman, Paul. *English Prose Fiction, 1558–1700: A Critical History*. Oxford: Clarendon Press, 1985.

Schmitt, Charles B., and others, eds. *The Cambridge History of Renaissance Philosophy*. Cambridge: Cambridge University Press, 1988.

Sloan, Thomas O., and Raymond B. Waddington, eds. *Rhetoric of Renaissance Poetry from Wyatt to Milton*. Berkeley: University of California Press, 1974.

Smith, Hallett. *Elizabethan Poetry: A Study in Conventions, Meaning, and Expression*. Cambridge, Mass.: Harvard University Press, 1952.

Southall, Raymond. *The Courtly Maker: An Essay on the Poetry of Wyatt and His Contemporaries*. Oxford: Blackwell, 1964.

Stauffer, Donald A. *English Biography before 1700*. Cambridge, Mass.: Harvard University Press, 1930.

Stevens, John. *Music and Poetry in the Early Tudor Court*. London: Methuen, 1961.

Stone, Lawrence. *The Crisis of the Aristocracy, 1558–1641*. Oxford: Clarendon Press, 1965.

Stone. *The Family, Sex and Marriage in England, 1500–1800*. New York: Harper & Row, 1977.

Tayler, Edward Williams. *Nature and Art in Renaissance Literature*. New York: Columbia University Press, 1964.

Thomas, Keith. *Religion and the Decline of Magic*. New York: Scribners, 1971.

Tillyard, E. M. W. *The Elizabethan World Picture*. New York: Macmillan, 1944.

Travitsky, Betty S., and Adele F. Seeff, eds. *Attending to Women in Early Modern England*. Newark: University of Delaware Press, 1994.

Trinkaus, Charles. *The Scope of Renaissance Humanism*. Ann Arbor: University of Michigan Press, 1983.

Tuve, Rosemund. *Allegorical Imagery: Some Medieval Books and Their Posterity*. Princeton: Princeton University Press, 1966.

Tuve. *Elizabethan and Metaphysical Imagery: Renaissance Poetics and Twentieth-Century Critics*. Chicago: University of Chicago Press, 1947.

Vickers, Brian. *In Defence of Rhetoric*. Oxford: Clarendon Press, 1988.

Vickers, "Rhetoric and Poetics," in *The Cambridge History of Renaissance Philosophy,* pp. 715–745.

Waller, Gary. *English Poetry of the Sixteenth Century*. London: Longman, 1986.

Warnicke, Retha M. *Women of the English Renaissance and Reformation,* Contributions in Women's Studies, no. 38. Westport, Conn.: Greenwood Press, 1983.

Whigham, Frank. *Ambition and Privilege: The Social Tropes of Elizabethan Courtesy Literature*. Berkeley: University of California Press, 1984.

Wilson, K. J. *Incomplete Fictions: The Formation of English Renaissance Dialogue*. Washington, D.C.: Catholic University of America Press, 1985.

Wilson, Katharina A., ed. *Women Writers of the Renaissance and Reformation.* Athens: University of Georgia Press, 1987.

Winters, Yvor. "The 16th Century Lyric in England: A Critical and Historical Reinterpretation," in his *Forms of Discovery: Critical and Historical Essays on the Forms of the Short Poem in English.* Chicago: Swallow, 1967, pp. 1–120; reprinted in Alpers, ed., *Elizabethan Poetry: Modern Essays in Criticism,* pp. 93–125.

Woodbridge, Linda. *Women and the English Renaissance: Literature and the Nature of Womankind, 1540–1640.* Urbana: University of Illinois Press, 1984.

Wright, Louis B. *Middle-Class Culture in Elizabethan England.* Chapel Hill: University of North Carolina Press, 1935.

Zocca, Louis R. *Elizabethan Narrative Poetry.* New Brunswick, N.J.: Rutgers University Press, 1950.

Contributors

Sheila Ahern .... *Victoria University of Wellington, New Zealand*
Derek B. Alwes .... *Clark University*
Reid Barbour .... *University of North Carolina*
William Barker .... *Memorial University of Newfoundland*
Kenneth R. Bartlett .... *Victoria College, University of Toronto*
F. W. Brownlow .... *Mount Holyoke College*
Sandra Clark .... *Birkbeck College, University of London*
Richard Y. Duerden .... *Brigham Young University*
Wayne Erickson .... *Georgia State University*
Alexandra Halasz .... *Dartmouth College*
Margaret P. Hannay .... *Siena College*
Peter C. Herman .... *San Diego State University*
Marvin Hunt .... *North Carolina State University*
Frederick Kiefer .... *University of Arizona*
Elizabeth McCutcheon .... *University of Hawaii*
Peter E. Medine .... *University of Arizona*
David Parkinson .... *University of Saskatchewan*
Richard Rambuss .... *Emory University*
James Robertson .... *University of the West Indies, Mona*
Carolyn F. Scott .... *Fu Jen University, Taiwan*
M. Rick Smith .... *Wichita State University*
Emily E. Stockard .... *Florida Atlantic University*
Donald V. Stump .... *Saint Louis University*
Charles Whitworth .... *University of Montpellier*

315

Cumulative Index

Dictionary of Literary Biography, Volumes 1-167
Dictionary of Literary Biography Yearbook, 1980-1995
Dictionary of Literary Biography Documentary Series, Volumes 1-13

Cumulative Index

DLB before number: *Dictionary of Literary Biography,* Volumes 1-167
Y before number: *Dictionary of Literary Biography Yearbook,* 1980-1995
DS before number: *Dictionary of Literary Biography Documentary Series,* Volumes 1-13

A

Abbey Press DLB-49

The Abbey Theatre and Irish Drama,
1900-1945 ....DLB-10

Abbot, Willis J. 1863-1934 ....DLB-29

Abbott, Jacob 1803-1879 ....DLB-1

Abbott, Lee K. 1947- DLB-130

Abbott, Lyman 1835-1922 ....DLB-79

Abbott, Robert S. 1868-1940 ....DLB-29, 91

Abelard, Peter circa 1079-1142 .....DLB-115

Abelard-Schuman DLB-46

Abell, Arunah S. 1806-1888 ....DLB-43

Abercrombie, Lascelles 1881-1938 ...DLB-19

Aberdeen University Press
Limited DLB-106

Abish, Walter 1931- DLB-130

Ablesimov, Aleksandr Onisimovich
1742-1783 ....DLB-150

Abrahams, Peter 1919- DLB-117

Abrams, M. H. 1912- DLB-67

Abrogans circa 790-800 ....DLB-148

Abse, Dannie 1923- DLB-27

Academy Chicago Publishers DLB-46

Accrocca, Elio Filippo 1923- DLB-128

Ace Books DLB-46

Achebe, Chinua 1930- DLB-117

Achtenberg, Herbert 1938- DLB-124

Ackerman, Diane 1948- DLB-120

Ackroyd, Peter 1949- DLB-155

Acorn, Milton 1923-1986 ....DLB-53

Acosta, Oscar Zeta 1935?- DLB-82

Actors Theatre of Louisville DLB-7

Adair, James 1709?-1783? DLB-30

Adam, Graeme Mercer 1839-1912 ...DLB-99

Adame, Leonard 1947- DLB-82

Adamic, Louis 1898-1951 ....DLB-9

Adams, Alice 1926- Y-86

Adams, Brooks 1848-1927 ....DLB-47

Adams, Charles Francis, Jr.
1835-1915 ....DLB-47

Adams, Douglas 1952- Y-83

Adams, Franklin P. 1881-1960 ......DLB-29

Adams, Henry 1838-1918 ....DLB-12, 47

Adams, Herbert Baxter 1850-1901 ...DLB-47

Adams, J. S. and C.
[publishing house] DLB-49

Adams, James Truslow 1878-1949 ...DLB-17

Adams, John 1735-1826 ....DLB-31

Adams, John Quincy 1767-1848 .....DLB-37

Adams, Léonie 1899-1988 ....DLB-48

Adams, Levi 1802-1832 ....DLB-99

Adams, Samuel 1722-1803 ......DLB-31, 43

Adams, Thomas
1582 or 1583-1652 ....DLB-151

Adams, William Taylor 1822-1897 ..DLB-42

Adamson, Sir John 1867-1950 ......DLB-98

Adcock, Arthur St. John
1864-1930 ....DLB-135

Adcock, Betty 1938- DLB-105

Adcock, Betty, Certain Gifts DLB-105

Adcock, Fleur 1934- DLB-40

Addison, Joseph 1672-1719 ....DLB-101

Ade, George 1866-1944 ....DLB-11, 25

Adeler, Max (see Clark, Charles Heber)

Adonias Filho 1915-1990 ....DLB-145

Advance Publishing Company DLB-49

AE 1867-1935 ....DLB-19

Ælfric circa 955-circa 1010 ....DLB-146

Aesthetic Poetry (1873), by
Walter Pater DLB-35

After Dinner Opera Company Y-92

Afro-American Literary Critics:
An Introduction DLB-33

Agassiz, Jean Louis Rodolphe
1807-1873 ....DLB-1

Agee, James 1909-1955 ....DLB-2, 26, 152

The Agee Legacy: A Conference at
the University of Tennessee
at Knoxville...................Y-89

Aguilera Malta, Demetrio
1909-1981 ....DLB-145

Ai 1947- DLB-120

Aichinger, Ilse 1921- DLB-85

Aidoo, Ama Ata 1942- DLB-117

Aiken, Conrad 1889-1973 ....DLB-9, 45, 102

Aiken, Joan 1924- DLB-161

Aikin, Lucy 1781-1864 ....DLB-144, 163

Ainsworth, William Harrison
1805-1882 ....DLB-21

Aitken, George A. 1860-1917 ......DLB-149

Aitken, Robert [publishing house] ...DLB-49

Akenside, Mark 1721-1770 ....DLB-109

Akins, Zoë 1886-1958 ....DLB-26

Alabaster, William 1568-1640 ......DLB-132

Alain-Fournier 1886-1914 ....DLB-65

Alarcón, Francisco X. 1954- DLB-122

Alba, Nanina 1915-1968 ....DLB-41

Albee, Edward 1928- DLB-7

Albert the Great circa 1200-1280 ...DLB-115

Alberti, Rafael 1902- DLB-108

Albertinus, Aegidius
circa 1560-1620 ....DLB-164

Alcott, Amos Bronson 1799-1888 .....DLB-1

Alcott, Louisa May
1832-1888 ....DLB-1, 42, 79

Alcott, William Andrus 1798-1859 ....DLB-1

Alcuin circa 732-804 ....DLB-148

Alden, Henry Mills 1836-1919 ......DLB-79

Alden, Isabella 1841-1930 ....DLB-42

Alden, John B. [publishing house] DLB-49

Alden, Beardsley and Company DLB-49

Aldington, Richard
1892-1962 . . . . DLB-20, 36, 100, 149

Aldis, Dorothy 1896-1966 . . . . DLB-22

Aldiss, Brian W. 1925- DLB-14

Aldrich, Thomas Bailey
1836-1907 . . . . DLB-42, 71, 74, 79

Alegría, Ciro 1909-1967 . . . . DLB-113

Alegría, Claribel 1924- DLB-145

Aleixandre, Vicente 1898-1984 . . . . DLB-108

Aleramo, Sibilla 1876-1960 . . . . DLB-114

Alexander, Charles 1868-1923 . . . . . . DLB-91

Alexander, Charles Wesley
[publishing house] DLB-49

Alexander, James 1691-1756 . . . . DLB-24

Alexander, Lloyd 1924- DLB-52

Alexander, Sir William, Earl of Stirling
1577?-1640 . . . . DLB-121

Alexis, Willibald 1798-1871 . . . . DLB-133

Alfred, King 849-899 . . . . DLB-146

Alger, Horatio, Jr. 1832-1899 . . . . DLB-42

Algonquin Books of Chapel Hill DLB-46

Algren, Nelson
1909-1981 . . . . DLB-9; Y-81, 82

Allan, Andrew 1907-1974 . . . . DLB-88

Allan, Ted 1916- DLB-68

Allbeury, Ted 1917- DLB-87

Alldritt, Keith 1935- DLB-14

Allen, Ethan 1738-1789 . . . . DLB-31

Allen, Frederick Lewis 1890-1954 . . DLB-137

Allen, Gay Wilson
1903-1995 . . . . DLB-103; Y-95

Allen, George 1808-1876 . . . . DLB-59

Allen, George [publishing house] . . . DLB-106

Allen, George, and Unwin
Limited DLB-112

Allen, Grant 1848-1899 . . . . DLB-70, 92

Allen, Henry W. 1912- Y-85

Allen, Hervey 1889-1949 . . . . DLB-9, 45

Allen, James 1739-1808 . . . . DLB-31

Allen, James Lane 1849-1925 . . . . DLB-71

Allen, Jay Presson 1922- DLB-26

Allen, John, and Company DLB-49

Allen, Samuel W. 1917- DLB-41

Allen, Woody 1935- DLB-44

Allende, Isabel 1942- DLB-145

Alline, Henry 1748-1784 . . . . DLB-99

Allingham, Margery 1904-1966 . . . . . DLB-77

Allingham, William 1824-1889 . . . . . . DLB-35

Allison, W. L. [publishing house] DLB-49

The Alliterative Morte Arthure and
the Stanzaic Morte Arthur
circa 1350-1400 . . . . DLB-146

Allott, Kenneth 1912-1973 . . . . DLB-20

Allston, Washington 1779-1843 . . . . . . DLB-1

Almon, John [publishing house] DLB-154

Alonzo, Dámaso 1898-1990 . . . . DLB-108

Alsop, George 1636-post 1673 . . . . DLB-24

Alsop, Richard 1761-1815 . . . . DLB-37

Altemus, Henry, and Company DLB-49

Altenberg, Peter 1885-1919 . . . . DLB-81

Altolaguirre, Manuel 1905-1959 . . . . DLB-108

Aluko, T. M. 1918- DLB-117

Alurista 1947- DLB-82

Alvarez, A. 1929- DLB-14, 40

Amadi, Elechi 1934- DLB-117

Amado, Jorge 1912- DLB-113

Ambler, Eric 1909- DLB-77

America: or, a Poem on the Settlement of the
British Colonies (1780?), by Timothy
Dwight DLB-37

American Conservatory Theatre DLB-7

American Fiction and the 1930s DLB-9

American Humor: A Historical Survey
East and Northeast
South and Southwest
Midwest
West DLB-11

The American Library in Paris Y-93

American News Company DLB-49

The American Poets' Corner: The First
Three Years (1983-1986) Y-86

American Proletarian Culture:
The 1930s DS-11

American Publishing Company DLB-49

American Stationers' Company DLB-49

American Sunday-School Union DLB-49

American Temperance Union DLB-49

American Tract Society DLB-49

The American Writers Congress
(9-12 October 1981) Y-81

The American Writers Congress: A Report
on Continuing Business Y-81

Ames, Fisher 1758-1808 . . . . DLB-37

Ames, Mary Clemmer 1831-1884 . . . . DLB-23

Amini, Johari M. 1935- DLB-41

Amis, Kingsley 1922-
. . . . DLB-15, 27, 100, 139

Amis, Martin 1949- DLB-14

Ammons, A. R. 1926- DLB-5, 165

Amory, Thomas 1691?-1788 . . . . .DLB-39

Anaya, Rudolfo A. 1937- DLB-82

Ancrene Riwle circa 1200-1225 . . . . . . .DLB-146

Andersch, Alfred 1914-1980 . . . . .DLB-69

Anderson, Margaret 1886-1973 . . . DLB-4, 91

Anderson, Maxwell 1888-1959 . . . . . . .DLB-7

Anderson, Patrick 1915-1979 . . . . . . .DLB-68

Anderson, Paul Y. 1893-1938 . . . . . . .DLB-29

Anderson, Poul 1926- DLB-8

Anderson, Robert 1750-1830 . . . . . . .DLB-142

Anderson, Robert 1917- DLB-7

Anderson, Sherwood
1876-1941 . . . . DLB-4, 9, 86; DS-1

Andreae, Johann Valentin
1586-1654 . . . . .DLB-164

Andreas-Salomé, Lou 1861-1937 . . . .DLB-66

Andres, Stefan 1906-1970 . . . . .DLB-69

Andreu, Blanca 1959- DLB-134

Andrewes, Lancelot 1555-1626 . . . . .DLB-151

Andrews, Charles M. 1863-1943 . . . . .DLB-17

Andrews, Miles Peter ?-1814 . . . . .DLB-89

Andrian, Leopold von 1875-1951 . . . .DLB-81

Andrić, Ivo 1892-1975 . . . . .DLB-147

Andrieux, Louis (see Aragon, Louis)

Andrus, Silas, and Son DLB-49

Angell, James Burrill 1829-1916 . . . . .DLB-64

Angelou, Maya 1928- DLB-38

Anger, Jane flourished 1589 . . . . .DLB-136

Angers, Félicité (see Conan, Laure)

Anglo-Norman Literature in the Development
of Middle English Literature DLB-146

The Anglo-Saxon Chronicle
circa 890-1154 . . . . .DLB-146

The "Angry Young Men" DLB-15

Angus and Robertson (UK)
Limited DLB-112

Anhalt, Edward 1914- DLB-26

Anners, Henry F. [publishing house] . . .DLB-49

Annolied between 1077 and 1081 . . . .DLB-148

Anselm of Canterbury 1033-1109 . . .DLB-115

Anstey, F. 1856-1934 . . . . .DLB-141

Anthony, Michael 1932- DLB-125

Anthony, Piers 1934- DLB-8

Anthony Burgess's *99 Novels:*
An Opinion Poll Y-84

Antin, Mary 1881-1949 . . . . Y-84

Antschel, Paul (see Celan, Paul)

Anyidoho, Kofi 1947- DLB-157

Anzaldúa, Gloria 1942- DLB-122

Anzengruber, Ludwig 1839-1889 . . . DLB-129

Apodaca, Rudy S. 1939- DLB-82

Apple, Max 1941- DLB-130

Appleton, D., and Company DLB-49

Appleton-Century-Crofts DLB-46

Applewhite, James 1935- DLB-105

Apple-wood Books DLB-46

Aquin, Hubert 1929-1977 . . . . DLB-53

Aquinas, Thomas 1224 or
1225-1274 . . . . DLB-115

Aragon, Louis 1897-1982 . . . . DLB-72

Arbor House Publishing
Company DLB-46

Arbuthnot, John 1667-1735 . . . . DLB-101

Arcadia House DLB-46

Arce, Julio G. (see Ulica, Jorge)

Archer, William 1856-1924 . . . . DLB-10

The Archpoet circa 1130?-? DLB-148

Archpriest Avvakum (Petrovich)
1620?-1682 . . . . DLB-150

Arden, John 1930- DLB-13

Arden of Faversham DLB-62

Ardis Publishers Y-89

Ardizzone, Edward 1900-1979 . . . . . . DLB-160

Arellano, Juan Estevan 1947- DLB-122

The Arena Publishing Company DLB-49

Arena Stage DLB-7

Arenas, Reinaldo 1943-1990 . . . . DLB-145

Arensberg, Ann 1937- Y-82

Arguedas, José María 1911-1969 . . . . DLB-113

Argueta, Manlio 1936- DLB-145

Arias, Ron 1941- DLB-82

Arland, Marcel 1899-1986 . . . . DLB-72

Arlen, Michael 1895-1956 . . DLB-36, 77, 162

Armah, Ayi Kwei 1939- DLB-117

Der arme Hartmann
?-after 1150 . . . . DLB-148

Armed Services Editions DLB-46

Armstrong, Richard 1903- DLB-160

Arndt, Ernst Moritz 1769-1860 . . . . . DLB-90

Arnim, Achim von 1781-1831 . . . . . . DLB-90

Arnim, Bettina von 1785-1859 . . . . . . DLB-90

Arno Press DLB-46

Arnold, Edwin 1832-1904 . . . . DLB-35

Arnold, Matthew 1822-1888 . . . . . DLB-32, 57

Arnold, Thomas 1795-1842 . . . . DLB-55

Arnold, Edward
[publishing house] DLB-112

Arnow, Harriette Simpson
1908-1986 . . . . DLB-6

Arp, Bill (see Smith, Charles Henry)

Arreola, Juan José 1918- DLB-113

Arrowsmith, J. W.
[publishing house] DLB-106

Arthur, Timothy Shay
1809-1885 . . . . DLB-3, 42, 79; DS-13

The Arthurian Tradition and Its European
Context DLB-138

Artmann, H. C. 1921- DLB-85

Arvin, Newton 1900-1963 . . . . DLB-103

As I See It, by Carolyn Cassady DLB-16

Asch, Nathan 1902-1964 . . . . DLB-4, 28

Ash, John 1948- DLB-40

Ashbery, John 1927- DLB-5, 165; Y-81

Ashendene Press DLB-112

Asher, Sandy 1942- Y-83

Ashton, Winifred (see Dane, Clemence)

Asimov, Isaac 1920-1992 . . . . DLB-8; Y-92

Askew, Anne circa 1521-1546 . . . . . . DLB-136

Asselin, Olivar 1874-1937 . . . . DLB-92

Asturias, Miguel Angel
1899-1974 . . . . DLB-113

Atheneum Publishers DLB-46

Atherton, Gertrude 1857-1948 . . . . DLB-9, 78

Athlone Press DLB-112

Atkins, Josiah circa 1755-1781 . . . . . DLB-31

Atkins, Russell 1926- DLB-41

The Atlantic Monthly Press DLB-46

Attaway, William 1911-1986 . . . . DLB-76

Atwood, Margaret 1939- DLB-53

Aubert, Alvin 1930- DLB-41

Aubert de Gaspé, Phillipe-Ignace-François
1814-1841 . . . . DLB-99

Aubert de Gaspé, Phillipe-Joseph
1786-1871 . . . . DLB-99

Aubin, Napoléon 1812-1890 . . . . DLB-99

Aubin, Penelope 1685-circa 1731 . . . . DLB-39

Aubrey-Fletcher, Henry Lancelot
(see Wade, Henry)

Auchincloss, Louis 1917- DLB-2; Y-80

Auden, W. H. 1907-1973 . . . . DLB-10, 20

Audio Art in America: A Personal
Memoir Y-85

Auerbach, Berthold 1812-1882 . . . . . DLB-133

Auernheimer, Raoul 1876-1948 . . . . . DLB-81

Augustine 354-430 . . . . DLB-115

Austen, Jane 1775-1817 . . . . DLB-116

Austin, Alfred 1835-1913 . . . . DLB-35

Austin, Mary 1868-1934 . . . . DLB-9, 78

Austin, William 1778-1841 . . . . DLB-74

Author-Printers, 1476–1599 . . . . DLB-167

The Author's Apology for His Book
(1684), by John Bunyan DLB-39

An Author's Response, by
Ronald Sukenick Y-82

Authors and Newspapers
Association DLB-46

Authors' Publishing Company DLB-49

Avalon Books DLB-46

Avancini, Nicolaus 1611-1686 . . . . . DLB-164

Avendaño, Fausto 1941- DLB-82

Averroës 1126-1198 . . . . DLB-115

Avery, Gillian 1926- DLB-161

Avicenna 980-1037 . . . . DLB-115

Avison, Margaret 1918- DLB-53

Avon Books DLB-46

Awdry, Wilbert Vere 1911- DLB-160

Awoonor, Kofi 1935- DLB-117

Ayckbourn, Alan 1939- DLB-13

Aymé, Marcel 1902-1967 . . . . DLB-72

Aytoun, Sir Robert 1570-1638 . . . . . DLB-121

Aytoun, William Edmondstoune
1813-1865 . . . . DLB-32, 159

B

B. V. (see Thomson, James)

Babbitt, Irving 1865-1933 . . . . DLB-63

Babbitt, Natalie 1932- DLB-52

Babcock, John [publishing house] . . . DLB-49

Baca, Jimmy Santiago 1952- DLB-122

Bache, Benjamin Franklin
1769-1798 . . . . DLB-43

Bachmann, Ingeborg 1926-1973 ..... DLB-85

Bacon, Delia 1811-1859 ....DLB-1

Bacon, Francis 1561-1626 .... DLB-151

Bacon, Roger circa
1214/1220-1292 .... DLB-115

Bacon, Sir Nicholas
circa 1510-1579 .... DLB-132

Bacon, Thomas circa 1700-1768 .... DLB-31

Badger, Richard G.,
and Company DLB-49

Bage, Robert 1728-1801 .... DLB-39

Bagehot, Walter 1826-1877 .... DLB-55

Bagley, Desmond 1923-1983 .... DLB-87

Bagnold, Enid 1889-1981 ...... DLB-13, 160

Bagryana, Elisaveta 1893-1991 ..... DLB-147

Bahr, Hermann 1863-1934 ..... DLB-81, 118

Bailey, Alfred Goldsworthy
1905- DLB-68

Bailey, Francis [publishing house] ... DLB-49

Bailey, H. C. 1878-1961 .... DLB-77

Bailey, Jacob 1731-1808 .... DLB-99

Bailey, Paul 1937- DLB-14

Bailey, Philip James 1816-1902 ..... DLB-32

Baillargeon, Pierre 1916-1967 .... DLB-88

Baillie, Hugh 1890-1966 .... DLB-29

Baillie, Joanna 1762-1851 .... DLB-93

Bailyn, Bernard 1922- DLB-17

Bainbridge, Beryl 1933- DLB-14

Baird, Irene 1901-1981 .... DLB-68

Baker, Augustine 1575-1641 .... DLB-151

Baker, Carlos 1909-1987 .... DLB-103

Baker, David 1954- DLB-120

Baker, Herschel C. 1914-1990 ..... DLB-111

Baker, Houston A., Jr. 1943- DLB-67

Baker, Samuel White 1821-1893 ... DLB-166

Baker, Walter H., Company
("Baker's Plays") DLB-49

The Baker and Taylor Company DLB-49

Balaban, John 1943- DLB-120

Bald, Wambly 1902- DLB-4

Balde, Jacob 1604-1668 .... DLB-164

Balderston, John 1889-1954 .... DLB-26

Baldwin, James
1924-1987 .... DLB-2, 7, 33; Y-87

Baldwin, Joseph Glover
1815-1864 .... DLB-3, 11

Baldwin, William
circa 1515-1563 .... DLB-132

Bale, John 1495-1563 .... DLB-132

Balestrini, Nanni 1935- DLB-128

Ballantine Books DLB-46

Ballantyne, R. M. 1825-1894 ...... DLB-163

Ballard, J. G. 1930- DLB-14

Ballerini, Luigi 1940- DLB-128

Ballou, Maturin Murray
1820-1895 .... DLB-79

Ballou, Robert O.
[publishing house] DLB-46

Balzac, Honoré de 1799-1855 ...... DLB-119

Bambara, Toni Cade 1939- DLB-38

Bancroft, A. L., and
Company DLB-49

Bancroft, George
1800-1891 ....DLB-1, 30, 59

Bancroft, Hubert Howe
1832-1918 ....DLB-47, 140

Bangs, John Kendrick
1862-1922 ....DLB-11, 79

Banim, John 1798-1842 ...DLB-116, 158, 159

Banim, Michael 1796-1874 ....DLB-158, 159

Banks, John circa 1653-1706 .... DLB-80

Banks, Russell 1940- DLB-130

Bannerman, Helen 1862-1946 ..... DLB-141

Bantam Books DLB-46

Banville, John 1945- DLB-14

Baraka, Amiri
1934- DLB-5, 7, 16, 38; DS-8

Barbauld, Anna Laetitia
1743-1825 ...... DLB-107, 109, 142, 158

Barbeau, Marius 1883-1969 .... DLB-92

Barber, John Warner 1798-1885 ..... DLB-30

Bàrberi Squarotti, Giorgio
1929- DLB-128

Barbey d'Aurevilly, Jules-Amédée
1808-1889 .... DLB-119

Barbour, John circa 1316-1395 ..... DLB-146

Barbour, Ralph Henry
1870-1944 .... DLB-22

Barbusse, Henri 1873-1935 .... DLB-65

Barclay, Alexander
circa 1475-1552 .... DLB-132

Barclay, E. E., and Company DLB-49

Bardeen, C. W.
[publishing house] DLB-49

Barham, Richard Harris
1788-1845 .... DLB-159

Baring, Maurice 1874-1945 .... DLB-34

Baring-Gould, Sabine 1834-1924 ....DLB-156

Barker, A. L. 1918- DLB-14, 139

Barker, George 1913-1991 .... DLB-20

Barker, Harley Granville
1877-1946 ....DLB-10

Barker, Howard 1946- DLB-13

Barker, James Nelson 1784-1858 .....DLB-37

Barker, Jane 1652-1727 .... DLB-39, 131

Barker, Lady Mary Anne
1831-1911 ....DLB-166

Barker, William
circa 1520-after 1576 ....DLB-132

Barker, Arthur, Limited DLB-112

Barkov, Ivan Semenovich
1732-1768 ....DLB-150

Barks, Coleman 1937- DLB-5

Barlach, Ernst 1870-1938 ...... DLB-56, 118

Barlow, Joel 1754-1812 ....DLB-37

Barnard, John 1681-1770 ....DLB-24

Barne, Kitty (Mary Catherine Barne)
1883-1957 ....DLB-160

Barnes, Barnabe 1571-1609 ....DLB-132

Barnes, Djuna 1892-1982 ...... DLB-4, 9, 45

Barnes, Julian 1946- Y-93

Barnes, Margaret Ayer 1886-1967 .....DLB-9

Barnes, Peter 1931- DLB-13

Barnes, William 1801-1886 ....DLB-32

Barnes, A. S., and Company DLB-49

Barnes and Noble Books DLB-46

Barnet, Miguel 1940- DLB-145

Barney, Natalie 1876-1972 ....DLB-4

Baron, Richard W.,
Publishing Company DLB-46

Barr, Robert 1850-1912 .... DLB-70, 92

Barral, Carlos 1928-1989 ....DLB-134

Barrax, Gerald William
1933- DLB-41, 120

Barrès, Maurice 1862-1923 ....DLB-123

Barrett, Eaton Stannard
1786-1820 ....DLB-116

Barrie, J. M. 1860-1937 .... DLB-10, 141, 156

Barrie and Jenkins DLB-112

Barrio, Raymond 1921- DLB-82

Barrios, Gregg 1945- DLB-122

Barry, Philip 1896-1949 ....DLB-7

Barry, Robertine (see Françoise)

Barse and Hopkins DLB-46

Barstow, Stan 1928- DLB-14, 139

Barth, John 1930- DLB-2

Barthelme, Donald
1931-1989 ....DLB-2; Y-80, 89

Barthelme, Frederick 1943- Y-85

Bartholomew, Frank 1898-1985 ....DLB-127

Bartlett, John 1820-1905 ....DLB-1

Bartol, Cyrus Augustus 1813-1900 ....DLB-1

Barton, Bernard 1784-1849 ....DLB-96

Barton, Thomas Pennant
1803-1869 ....DLB-140

Bartram, John 1699-1777 ....DLB-31

Bartram, William 1739-1823 ....DLB-37

Basic Books DLB-46

Basille, Theodore (see Becon, Thomas)

Bass, T. J. 1932- Y-81

Bassani, Giorgio 1916- DLB-128

Basse, William circa 1583-1653 .....DLB-121

Bassett, John Spencer 1867-1928 .....DLB-17

Bassler, Thomas Joseph (see Bass, T. J.)

Bate, Walter Jackson 1918- DLB-67, 103

Bateman, Stephen
circa 1510-1584 ....DLB-136

Bates, H. E. 1905-1974 ....DLB-162

Bates, Katharine Lee 1859-1929 .....DLB-71

Batsford, B. T.
[publishing house] DLB-106

Battiscombe, Georgina 1905- DLB-155

The Battle of Maldon circa 1000 ......DLB-146

Bauer, Bruno 1809-1882 ....DLB-133

Bauer, Wolfgang 1941- DLB-124

Baum, L. Frank 1856-1919 ....DLB-22

Baum, Vicki 1888-1960 ....DLB-85

Baumbach, Jonathan 1933- Y-80

Bausch, Richard 1945- DLB-130

Bawden, Nina 1925- DLB-14, 161

Bax, Clifford 1886-1962 ....DLB-10, 100

Baxter, Charles 1947- DLB-130

Bayer, Eleanor (see Perry, Eleanor)

Bayer, Konrad 1932-1964 ....DLB-85

Baynes, Pauline 1922- DLB-160

Bazin, Hervé 1911- DLB-83

Beach, Sylvia 1887-1962 ....DLB-4

Beacon Press DLB-49

Beadle and Adams DLB-49

Beagle, Peter S. 1939- Y-80

Beal, M. F. 1937- Y-81

Beale, Howard K. 1899-1959 ....DLB-17

Beard, Charles A. 1874-1948 ......DLB-17

A Beat Chronology: The First Twenty-five
Years, 1944-1969 ....DLB-16

Beattie, Ann 1947- Y-82

Beattie, James 1735-1803 ....DLB-109

Beauchemin, Nérée 1850-1931 ......DLB-92

Beauchemin, Yves 1941- DLB-60

Beaugrand, Honoré 1848-1906 ......DLB-99

Beaulieu, Victor-Lévy 1945- DLB-53

Beaumont, Francis circa 1584-1616
and Fletcher, John 1579-1625 ...DLB-58

Beaumont, Sir John 1583?-1627 ....DLB-121

Beaumont, Joseph 1616–1699 ......DLB-126

Beauvoir, Simone de
1908-1986 ....DLB-72; Y-86

Becher, Ulrich 1910- DLB-69

Becker, Carl 1873-1945 ....DLB-17

Becker, Jurek 1937- DLB-75

Becker, Jurgen 1932- DLB-75

Beckett, Samuel
1906-1989 ....DLB-13, 15; Y-90

Beckford, William 1760-1844 ....DLB-39

Beckham, Barry 1944- DLB-33

Becon, Thomas circa 1512-1567 ....DLB-136

Beddoes, Thomas 1760-1808 ......DLB-158

Beddoes, Thomas Lovell
1803-1849 ....DLB-96

Bede circa 673-735 ....DLB-146

Beecher, Catharine Esther
1800-1878 ....DLB-1

Beecher, Henry Ward
1813-1887 ....DLB-3, 43

Beer, George L. 1872-1920 ....DLB-47

Beer, Patricia 1919- DLB-40

Beerbohm, Max 1872-1956 .....DLB-34, 100

Beer-Hofmann, Richard
1866-1945 ....DLB-81

Beers, Henry A. 1847-1926 ....DLB-71

Beeton, S. O. [publishing house] ...DLB-106

Bégon, Elisabeth 1696-1755 ....DLB-99

Behan, Brendan 1923-1964 ....DLB-13

Behn, Aphra 1640?-1689 ....DLB-39, 80, 131

Behn, Harry 1898-1973 ....DLB-61

Behrman, S. N. 1893-1973 ....DLB-7, 44

Belaney, Archibald Stansfeld (see Grey Owl)

Belasco, David 1853-1931 ....DLB-7

Belford, Clarke and Company DLB-49

Belitt, Ben 1911- DLB-5

Belknap, Jeremy 1744-1798 ......DLB-30, 37

Bell, Clive 1881-1964 ....DS-10

Bell, James Madison 1826-1902 ......DLB-50

Bell, Marvin 1937- DLB-5

Bell, Millicent 1919- DLB-111

Bell, Quentin 1910- DLB-155

Bell, Vanessa 1879-1961 ....DS-10

Bell, George, and Sons DLB-106

Bell, Robert [publishing house] DLB-49

Bellamy, Edward 1850-1898 ....DLB-12

Bellamy, Joseph 1719-1790 ....DLB-31

Bellezza, Dario 1944- DLB-128

La Belle Assemblée 1806-1837 ....DLB-110

Belloc, Hilaire
1870-1953 ....DLB-19, 100, 141

Bellow, Saul
1915- DLB-2, 28; Y-82; DS-3

Belmont Productions DLB-46

Bemelmans, Ludwig 1898-1962 ......DLB-22

Bemis, Samuel Flagg 1891-1973 .....DLB-17

Bemrose, William
[publishing house] DLB-106

Benchley, Robert 1889-1945 ....DLB-11

Benedetti, Mario 1920- DLB-113

Benedictus, David 1938- DLB-14

Benedikt, Michael 1935- DLB-5

Benét, Stephen Vincent
1898-1943 ....DLB-4, 48, 102

Benét, William Rose 1886-1950 .....DLB-45

Benford, Gregory 1941- Y-82

Benjamin, Park 1809-1864 .....DLB-3, 59, 73

Benlowes, Edward 1602-1676 ......DLB-126

Benn, Gottfried 1886-1956 ....DLB-56

Benn Brothers Limited DLB-106

Bennett, Arnold
1867-1931 ....DLB-10, 34, 98, 135

Bennett, Charles 1899- DLB-44

Bennett, Gwendolyn 1902- DLB-51

Bennett, Hal 1930- DLB-33

Bennett, James Gordon 1795-1872 ...DLB-43

Bennett, James Gordon, Jr.
1841-1918 . . . . DLB-23

Bennett, John 1865-1956 . . . . DLB-42

Bennett, Louise 1919- DLB-117

Benoit, Jacques 1941- DLB-60

Benson, A. C. 1862-1925 . . . . DLB-98

Benson, E. F. 1867-1940 . . . . . . DLB-135, 153

Benson, Jackson J. 1930- DLB-111

Benson, Robert Hugh 1871-1914 . . . DLB-153

Benson, Stella 1892-1933 . . . . . . DLB-36, 162

Bentham, Jeremy 1748-1832 . . . DLB-107, 158

Bentley, E. C. 1875-1956 . . . . DLB-70

Bentley, Richard
[publishing house] DLB-106

Benton, Robert 1932- and Newman,
David 1937- DLB-44

Benziger Brothers DLB-49

Beowulf circa 900-1000
or 790-825 . . . . DLB-146

Beresford, Anne 1929- DLB-40

Beresford, John Davys
1873-1947 . . . . DLB-162

Beresford-Howe, Constance
1922- DLB-88

Berford, R. G., Company DLB-49

Berg, Stephen 1934- DLB-5

Bergengruen, Werner 1892-1964 . . . . DLB-56

Berger, John 1926- DLB-14

Berger, Meyer 1898-1959 . . . . DLB-29

Berger, Thomas 1924- DLB-2; Y-80

Berkeley, Anthony 1893-1971 . . . . . . DLB-77

Berkeley, George 1685-1753 . . . . DLB-31, 101

The Berkley Publishing
Corporation DLB-46

Berlin, Lucia 1936- DLB-130

Bernal, Vicente J. 1888-1915 . . . . DLB-82

Bernanos, Georges 1888-1948 . . . . . . DLB-72

Bernard, Harry 1898-1979 . . . . DLB-92

Bernard, John 1756-1828 . . . . DLB-37

Bernard of Chartres
circa 1060-1124? DLB-115

Bernhard, Thomas
1931-1989 . . . . DLB-85, 124

Berriault, Gina 1926- DLB-130

Berrigan, Daniel 1921- DLB-5

Berrigan, Ted 1934-1983 . . . . .DLB-5

Berry, Wendell 1934- DLB-5, 6

Berryman, John 1914-1972 . . . . DLB-48

Bersianik, Louky 1930- DLB-60

Bertolucci, Attilio 1911- DLB-128

Berton, Pierre 1920- DLB-68

Besant, Sir Walter 1836-1901 . . . . . . DLB-135

Bessette, Gerard 1920- DLB-53

Bessie, Alvah 1904-1985 . . . . DLB-26

Bester, Alfred 1913-1987 . . . . DLB-8

The Bestseller Lists: An Assessment Y-84

Betjeman, John 1906-1984 . . . . . DLB-20; Y-84

Betocchi, Carlo 1899-1986 . . . . DLB-128

Bettarini, Mariella 1942- DLB-128

Betts, Doris 1932- Y-82

Beveridge, Albert J. 1862-1927 . . . . . . DLB-17

Beverley, Robert
circa 1673-1722 . . . . DLB-24, 30

Beyle, Marie-Henri (see Stendhal)

Bianco, Margery Williams
1881-1944 . . . . DLB-160

Bibaud, Adèle 1854-1941 . . . . DLB-92

Bibaud, Michel 1782-1857 . . . . DLB-99

Bibliographical and Textual Scholarship
Since World War II Y-89

The Bicentennial of James Fenimore
Cooper: An International
Celebration Y-89

Bichsel, Peter 1935- DLB-75

Bickerstaff, Isaac John
1733-circa 1808 . . . . DLB-89

Biddle, Drexel [publishing house] DLB-49

Bidermann, Jacob
1577 or 1578-1639 . . . . DLB-164

Bidwell, Walter Hilliard
1798-1881 . . . . DLB-79

Bienek, Horst 1930- DLB-75

Bierbaum, Otto Julius 1865-1910 . . . . DLB-66

Bierce, Ambrose
1842-1914? DLB-11, 12, 23, 71, 74

Bigelow, William F. 1879-1966 . . . . . . DLB-91

Biggle, Lloyd, Jr. 1923- DLB-8

Biglow, Hosea (see Lowell, James Russell)

Bigongiari, Piero 1914- DLB-128

Billinger, Richard 1890-1965 . . . . DLB-124

Billings, John Shaw 1898-1975 . . . . . DLB-137

Billings, Josh (see Shaw, Henry Wheeler)

Binding, Rudolf G. 1867-1938 . . . . . . DLB-66

Bingham, Caleb 1757-1817 . . . . DLB-42

Bingham, George Barry
1906-1988 . . . . .DLB-127

Bingley, William
[publishing house] DLB-154

Binyon, Laurence 1869-1943 . . . . . . .DLB-19

Biographia Brittanica DLB-142

Biographical Documents I Y-84

Biographical Documents II Y-85

Bioren, John [publishing house] DLB-49

Bioy Casares, Adolfo 1914- DLB-113

Bird, Isabella Lucy 1831-1904 . . . . . .DLB-166

Bird, William 1888-1963 . . . . .DLB-4

Birken, Sigmund von 1626-1681 . . . .DLB-164

Birney, Earle 1904- DLB-88

Birrell, Augustine 1850-1933 . . . . . . .DLB-98

Bishop, Elizabeth 1911-1979 . . . . .DLB-5

Bishop, John Peale 1892-1944 . . DLB-4, 9, 45

Bismarck, Otto von 1815-1898 . . . . .DLB-129

Bisset, Robert 1759-1805 . . . . .DLB-142

Bissett, Bill 1939- DLB-53

Bitzius, Albert (see Gotthelf, Jeremias)

Black, David (D. M.) 1941- DLB-40

Black, Winifred 1863-1936 . . . . .DLB-25

Black, Walter J.
[publishing house] DLB-46

The Black Aesthetic: Background DS-8

The Black Arts Movement, by
Larry Neal DLB-38

Black Theaters and Theater Organizations in
America, 1961-1982:
A Research List DLB-38

Black Theatre: A Forum
[excerpts] DLB-38

Blackamore, Arthur 1679-? DLB-24, 39

Blackburn, Alexander L. 1929- Y-85

Blackburn, Paul 1926-1971 . . . . DLB-16; Y-81

Blackburn, Thomas 1916-1977 . . . . . .DLB-27

Blackmore, R. D. 1825-1900 . . . . . . .DLB-18

Blackmore, Sir Richard
1654-1729 . . . . .DLB-131

Blackmur, R. P. 1904-1965 . . . . .DLB-63

Blackwell, Basil, Publisher DLB-106

Blackwood, Algernon Henry
1869-1951 . . . . DLB-153, 156

Blackwood, Caroline 1931- DLB-14

Blackwood, William, and
Sons, Ltd. DLB-154

Blackwood's Edinburgh Magazine
    1817-1980 ....DLB-110

Blair, Eric Arthur (see Orwell, George)

Blair, Francis Preston 1791-1876 .....DLB-43

Blair, James circa 1655-1743 ....DLB-24

Blair, John Durburrow 1759-1823 ....DLB-37

Blais, Marie-Claire 1939- DLB-53

Blaise, Clark 1940- DLB-53

Blake, Nicholas 1904-1972 ....DLB-77
    (see Day Lewis, C.)

Blake, William
    1757-1827 .... DLB-93, 154, 163

The Blakiston Company DLB-49

Blanchot, Maurice 1907- DLB-72

Blanckenburg, Christian Friedrich von
    1744-1796 ....DLB-94

Blaser, Robin 1925- DLB-165

Bledsoe, Albert Taylor
    1809-1877 ....DLB-3, 79

Blelock and Company DLB-49

Blennerhassett, Margaret Agnew
    1773-1842 ....DLB-99

Bles, Geoffrey
    [publishing house] DLB-112

Blessington, Marguerite, Countess of
    1789-1849 ....DLB-166

The Blickling Homilies
    circa 971 ....DLB-146

Blish, James 1921-1975 ....DLB-8

Bliss, E., and E. White
    [publishing house] DLB-49

Bliven, Bruce 1889-1977 ....DLB-137

Bloch, Robert 1917-1994 ....DLB-44

Block, Rudolph (see Lessing, Bruno)

Blondal, Patricia 1926-1959 ....DLB-88

Bloom, Harold 1930- DLB-67

Bloomer, Amelia 1818-1894 ....DLB-79

Bloomfield, Robert 1766-1823 ....DLB-93

Bloomsbury Group DS-10

Blotner, Joseph 1923- DLB-111

Bloy, Léon 1846-1917 ....DLB-123

Blume, Judy 1938- DLB-52

Blunck, Hans Friedrich 1888-1961 ...DLB-66

Blunden, Edmund
    1896-1974 .... DLB-20, 100, 155

Blunt, Wilfrid Scawen 1840-1922 ....DLB-19

Bly, Nellie (see Cochrane, Elizabeth)

Bly, Robert 1926- DLB-5

Blyton, Enid 1897-1968 ....DLB-160

Boaden, James 1762-1839 ....DLB-89

Boas, Frederick S. 1862-1957 ......DLB-149

The Bobbs-Merrill Archive at the
    Lilly Library, Indiana University ... Y-90

The Bobbs-Merrill Company DLB-46

Bobrov, Semen Sergeevich
    1763?-1810 ....DLB-150

Bobrowski, Johannes 1917-1965 .....DLB-75

Bodenheim, Maxwell 1892-1954 .. DLB-9, 45

Bodenstedt, Friedrich von
    1819-1892 ....DLB-129

Bodini, Vittorio 1914-1970 ....DLB-128

Bodkin, M. McDonnell
    1850-1933 ....DLB-70

Bodley Head DLB-112

Bodmer, Johann Jakob 1698-1783 ...DLB-97

Bodmershof, Imma von 1895-1982 .. DLB-85

Bodsworth, Fred 1918- DLB-68

Boehm, Sydney 1908- DLB-44

Boer, Charles 1939- DLB-5

Boethius circa 480-circa 524 ....DLB-115

Boethius of Dacia circa 1240-? DLB-115

Bogan, Louise 1897-1970 ....DLB-45

Bogarde, Dirk 1921- DLB-14

Bogdanovich, Ippolit Fedorovich
    circa 1743-1803 ....DLB-150

Bogue, David [publishing house] ... DLB-106

Böhme, Jakob 1575-1624 ....DLB-164

Bohn, H. G. [publishing house] DLB-106

Boie, Heinrich Christian
    1744-1806 ....DLB-94

Bok, Edward W. 1863-1930 ....DLB-91

Boland, Eavan 1944- DLB-40

Bolingbroke, Henry St. John, Viscount
    1678-1751 ....DLB-101

Böll, Heinrich 1917-1985 ..... Y-85, DLB-69

Bolling, Robert 1738-1775 ....DLB-31

Bolotov, Andrei Timofeevich
    1738-1833 ....DLB-150

Bolt, Carol 1941- DLB-60

Bolt, Robert 1924- DLB-13

Bolton, Herbert E. 1870-1953 ....DLB-17

Bonaventura DLB-90

Bonaventure circa 1217-1274 ......DLB-115

Bond, Edward 1934- DLB-13

Bond, Michael 1926- DLB-161

Boni, Albert and Charles
    [publishing house] DLB-46

Boni and Liveright DLB-46

Robert Bonner's Sons DLB-49

Bontemps, Arna 1902-1973 ......DLB-48, 51

The Book League of America DLB-46

Book Reviewing in America: I Y-87

Book Reviewing in America: II Y-88

Book Reviewing in America: III Y-89

Book Reviewing in America: IV Y-90

Book Reviewing in America: V Y-91

Book Reviewing in America: VI Y-92

Book Reviewing in America: VII Y-93

Book Reviewing in America: VIII Y-94

Book Reviewing in America and the
    Literary Scene Y-95

Book Supply Company DLB-49

The Book Trade History Group Y-93

The Booker Prize
    Address by Anthony Thwaite,
    Chairman of the Booker Prize Judges
    Comments from Former Booker
    Prize Winners Y-86

Boorde, Andrew circa 1490-1549 ...DLB-136

Boorstin, Daniel J. 1914- DLB-17

Booth, Mary L. 1831-1889 ....DLB-79

Booth, Philip 1925- Y-82

Booth, Wayne C. 1921- DLB-67

Borchardt, Rudolf 1877-1945 ....DLB-66

Borchert, Wolfgang
    1921-1947 ....DLB-69, 124

Borel, Pétrus 1809-1859 ....DLB-119

Borges, Jorge Luis
    1899-1986 ....DLB-113; Y-86

Börne, Ludwig 1786-1837 ....DLB-90

Borrow, George
    1803-1881 .... DLB-21, 55, 166

Bosch, Juan 1909- DLB-145

Bosco, Henri 1888-1976 ....DLB-72

Bosco, Monique 1927- DLB-53

Boston, Lucy M. 1892-1990 ....DLB-161

Boswell, James 1740-1795 .....DLB-104, 142

Botev, Khristo 1847-1876 ....DLB-147

Botta, Anne C. Lynch 1815-1891 .....DLB-3

Bottomley, Gordon 1874-1948 ......DLB-10

Bottoms, David 1949- DLB-120; Y-83

Bottrall, Ronald 1906- DLB-20

Boucher, Anthony 1911-1968 ....DLB-8

Boucher, Jonathan 1738-1804 .... DLB-31

Boucher de Boucherville, George
1814-1894 .... DLB-99

Boudreau, Daniel (see Coste, Donat)

Bourassa, Napoléon 1827-1916 ..... DLB-99

Bourget, Paul 1852-1935 .... DLB-123

Bourinot, John George 1837-1902 ... DLB-99

Bourjaily, Vance 1922- DLB-2, 143

Bourne, Edward Gaylord
1860-1908 .... DLB-47

Bourne, Randolph 1886-1918 .... DLB-63

Bousoño, Carlos 1923- DLB-108

Bousquet, Joë 1897-1950 .... DLB-72

Bova, Ben 1932- Y-81

Bovard, Oliver K. 1872-1945 .... DLB-25

Bove, Emmanuel 1898-1945 .... DLB-72

Bowen, Elizabeth 1899-1973 .... DLB-15, 162

Bowen, Francis 1811-1890 .... DLB-1, 59

Bowen, John 1924- DLB-13

Bowen, Marjorie 1886-1952 .... DLB-153

Bowen-Merrill Company DLB-49

Bowering, George 1935- DLB-53

Bowers, Claude G. 1878-1958 ...... DLB-17

Bowers, Edgar 1924- DLB-5

Bowers, Fredson Thayer
1905-1991 .... DLB-140; Y-91

Bowles, Paul 1910- DLB-5, 6

Bowles, Samuel III 1826-1878 ...... DLB-43

Bowles, William Lisles 1762-1850 ... DLB-93

Bowman, Louise Morey
1882-1944 .... DLB-68

Boyd, James 1888-1944 ....DLB-9

Boyd, John 1919- DLB-8

Boyd, Thomas 1898-1935 ....DLB-9

Boyesen, Hjalmar Hjorth
1848-1895 ....DLB-12, 71; DS-13

Boyle, Kay
1902-1992 ....DLB-4, 9, 48, 86; Y-93

Boyle, Roger, Earl of Orrery
1621-1679 .... DLB-80

Boyle, T. Coraghessan 1948- Y-86

Brackenbury, Alison 1953- DLB-40

Brackenridge, Hugh Henry
1748-1816 .... DLB-11, 37

Brackett, Charles 1892-1969 .... DLB-26

Brackett, Leigh 1915-1978 ...... DLB-8, 26

Bradburn, John
[publishing house] DLB-49

Bradbury, Malcolm 1932- DLB-14

Bradbury, Ray 1920- DLB-2, 8

Bradbury and Evans DLB-106

Braddon, Mary Elizabeth
1835-1915 ....DLB-18, 70, 156

Bradford, Andrew 1686-1742 .... DLB-43, 73

Bradford, Gamaliel 1863-1932 ...... DLB-17

Bradford, John 1749-1830 .... DLB-43

Bradford, Roark 1896-1948 .... DLB-86

Bradford, William 1590-1657 .... DLB-24, 30

Bradford, William III
1719-1791 ....DLB-43, 73

Bradlaugh, Charles 1833-1891 ...... DLB-57

Bradley, David 1950- DLB-33

Bradley, Marion Zimmer 1930- DLB-8

Bradley, William Aspenwall
1878-1939 .... DLB-4

Bradley, Ira, and Company DLB-49

Bradley, J. W., and Company DLB-49

Bradstreet, Anne
1612 or 1613-1672 .... DLB-24

Bradwardine, Thomas circa
1295-1349 .... DLB-115

Brady, Frank 1924-1986 .... DLB-111

Brady, Frederic A.
[publishing house] DLB-49

Bragg, Melvyn 1939- DLB-14

Brainard, Charles H.
[publishing house] DLB-49

Braine, John 1922-1986 ....DLB-15; Y-86

Braithwait, Richard 1588-1673 ..... DLB-151

Braithwaite, William Stanley
1878-1962 ....DLB-50, 54

Braker, Ulrich 1735-1798 .... DLB-94

Bramah, Ernest 1868-1942 .... DLB-70

Branagan, Thomas 1774-1843 .... DLB-37

Branch, William Blackwell
1927- DLB-76

Branden Press DLB-46

Brassey, Lady Annie (Allnutt)
1839-1887 .... DLB-166

Brathwaite, Edward Kamau
1930- DLB-125

Brault, Jacques 1933- DLB-53

Braun, Volker 1939- DLB-75

Brautigan, Richard
1935-1984 .... DLB-2, 5; Y-80, 84

Braxton, Joanne M. 1950- DLB-41

Bray, Anne Eliza 1790-1883 ....DLB-116

Bray, Thomas 1656-1730 ....DLB-24

Braziller, George
[publishing house] DLB-46

The Bread Loaf Writers'
Conference 1983 .... Y-84

The Break-Up of the Novel (1922),
by John Middleton Murry DLB-36

Breasted, James Henry 1865-1935 ....DLB-47

Brecht, Bertolt 1898-1956 ...... DLB-56, 124

Bredel, Willi 1901-1964 ....DLB-56

Breitinger, Johann Jakob
1701-1776 ....DLB-97

Bremser, Bonnie 1939- DLB-16

Bremser, Ray 1934- DLB-16

Brentano, Bernard von
1901-1964 ....DLB-56

Brentano, Clemens 1778-1842 ....DLB-90

Brentano's DLB-49

Brenton, Howard 1942- DLB-13

Breton, André 1896-1966 ....DLB-65

Breton, Nicholas
circa 1555-circa 1626 ....DLB-136

The Breton Lays
1300-early fifteenth century DLB-146

Brewer, Warren and Putnam DLB-46

Brewster, Elizabeth 1922- DLB-60

Bridgers, Sue Ellen 1942- DLB-52

Bridges, Robert 1844-1930 ...... DLB-19, 98

Bridie, James 1888-1951 ....DLB-10

Briggs, Charles Frederick
1804-1877 ....DLB-3

Brighouse, Harold 1882-1958 ....DLB-10

Bright, Mary Chavelita Dunne
(see Egerton, George)

Brimmer, B. J., Company DLB-46

Brines, Francisco 1932- DLB-134

Brinley, George, Jr. 1817-1875 ......DLB-140

Brinnin, John Malcolm 1916- DLB-48

Brisbane, Albert 1809-1890 ....DLB-3

Brisbane, Arthur 1864-1936 ....DLB-25

British Academy DLB-112

The British Library and the Regular
Readers' Group Y-91

The British Critic 1793-1843 ....DLB-110

*The British Review and London
Critical Journal* 1811-1825 ....DLB-110

Brito, Aristeo 1942- DLB-122

Broadway Publishing Company DLB-46

Broch, Hermann 1886-1951 .....DLB-85, 124

Brochu, André 1942- DLB-53

Brock, Edwin 1927- DLB-40

Brod, Max 1884-1968 ....DLB-81

Brodber, Erna 1940- DLB-157

Brodhead, John R. 1814-1873 ....DLB-30

Brodkey, Harold 1930- DLB-130

Brome, Richard circa 1590-1652 .....DLB-58

Brome, Vincent 1910- DLB-155

Bromfield, Louis 1896-1956 .... DLB-4, 9, 86

Broner, E. M. 1930- DLB-28

Bronk, William 1918- DLB-165

Bronnen, Arnolt 1895-1959 ....DLB-124

Brontë, Anne 1820-1849 ....DLB-21

Brontë, Charlotte 1816-1855 ....DLB-21, 159

Brontë, Emily 1818-1848 ....DLB-21, 32

Brooke, Frances 1724-1789 ......DLB-39, 99

Brooke, Henry 1703?-1783 ....DLB-39

Brooke, L. Leslie 1862-1940 ....DLB-141

Brooke, Rupert 1887-1915 ....DLB-19

Brooker, Bertram 1888-1955 ....DLB-88

Brooke-Rose, Christine 1926- DLB-14

Brookner, Anita 1928- Y-87

Brooks, Charles Timothy
1813-1883 ....DLB-1

Brooks, Cleanth 1906-1994 ....DLB-63; Y-94

Brooks, Gwendolyn
1917- DLB-5, 76, 165

Brooks, Jeremy 1926- DLB-14

Brooks, Mel 1926- DLB-26

Brooks, Noah 1830-1903 .... DLB-42; DS-13

Brooks, Richard 1912-1992 ....DLB-44

Brooks, Van Wyck
1886-1963 .... DLB-45, 63, 103

Brophy, Brigid 1929- DLB-14

Brossard, Chandler 1922-1993 ......DLB-16

Brossard, Nicole 1943- DLB-53

Broster, Dorothy Kathleen
1877-1950 ....DLB-160

Brother Antoninus (see Everson, William)

Brougham and Vaux, Henry Peter
Brougham, Baron
1778-1868 ....DLB-110, 158

Brougham, John 1810-1880 ....DLB-11

Broughton, James 1913- DLB-5

Broughton, Rhoda 1840-1920 ....DLB-18

Broun, Heywood 1888-1939 ....DLB-29

Brown, Alice 1856-1948 ....DLB-78

Brown, Bob 1886-1959 ....DLB-4, 45

Brown, Cecil 1943- DLB-33

Brown, Charles Brockden
1771-1810 ....DLB-37, 59, 73

Brown, Christy 1932-1981 ....DLB-14

Brown, Dee 1908- Y-80

Brown, Frank London 1927-1962 ... DLB-76

Brown, Fredric 1906-1972 ....DLB-8

Brown, George Mackay
1921- DLB-14, 27, 139

Brown, Harry 1917-1986 ....DLB-26

Brown, Marcia 1918- DLB-61

Brown, Margaret Wise
1910-1952 ....DLB-22

Brown, Morna Doris (see Ferrars, Elizabeth)

Brown, Oliver Madox
1855-1874 ....DLB-21

Brown, Sterling
1901-1989 ....DLB-48, 51, 63

Brown, T. E. 1830-1897 ....DLB-35

Brown, William Hill 1765-1793 .....DLB-37

Brown, William Wells
1814-1884 ....DLB-3, 50

Browne, Charles Farrar
1834-1867 ....DLB-11

Browne, Francis Fisher
1843-1913 ....DLB-79

Browne, Michael Dennis
1940- DLB-40

Browne, Sir Thomas 1605-1682 .... DLB-151

Browne, William, of Tavistock
1590-1645 ....DLB-121

Browne, Wynyard 1911-1964 ....DLB-13

Browne and Nolan DLB-106

Brownell, W. C. 1851-1928 ....DLB-71

Browning, Elizabeth Barrett
1806-1861 ....DLB-32

Browning, Robert
1812-1889 ....DLB-32, 163

Brownjohn, Allan 1931- DLB-40

Brownson, Orestes Augustus
1803-1876 ....DLB-1, 59, 73

Bruccoli, Matthew J. 1931- DLB-103

Bruce, Charles 1906-1971 ....DLB-68

Bruce, Leo 1903-1979 ....DLB-77

Bruce, Philip Alexander
1856-1933 ....DLB-47

Bruce Humphries
[publishing house] DLB-46

Bruce-Novoa, Juan 1944- DLB-82

Bruckman, Clyde 1894-1955 ....DLB-26

Bruckner, Ferdinand 1891-1958 ....DLB-118

Brundage, John Herbert (see Herbert, John)

Brutus, Dennis 1924- DLB-117

Bryant, Arthur 1899-1985 ....DLB-149

Bryant, William Cullen
1794-1878 ....DLB-3, 43, 59

Bryce Echenique, Alfredo
1939- DLB-145

Bryce, James 1838-1922 ....DLB-166

Brydges, Sir Samuel Egerton
1762-1837 ....DLB-107

Bryskett, Lodowick 1546?-1612 ....DLB-167

Buchan, John 1875-1940 ... DLB-34, 70, 156

Buchanan, George 1506-1582 ......DLB-132

Buchanan, Robert 1841-1901 ....DLB-18, 35

Buchman, Sidney 1902-1975 ....DLB-26

Buchner, Augustus 1591-1661 ......DLB-164

Büchner, Georg 1813-1837 ....DLB-133

Buck, Pearl S. 1892-1973 ....DLB-9, 102

Bucke, Charles 1781-1846 ....DLB-110

Bucke, Richard Maurice
1837-1902 ....DLB-99

Buckingham, Joseph Tinker 1779-1861 and
Buckingham, Edwin
1810-1833 ....DLB-73

Buckler, Ernest 1908-1984 ....DLB-68

Buckley, William F., Jr.
1925- DLB-137; Y-80

Buckminster, Joseph Stevens
1784-1812 ....DLB-37

Buckner, Robert 1906- DLB-26

Budd, Thomas ?-1698 ....DLB-24

Budrys, A. J. 1931- DLB-8

Buechner, Frederick 1926- Y-80

Buell, John 1927- DLB-53

Buffum, Job [publishing house] DLB-49

Bugnet, Georges 1879-1981 ....DLB-92

Buies, Arthur 1840-1901 ....DLB-99

Building the New British Library
at St Pancras Y-94

Bukowski, Charles 1920-1994 ....DLB-5, 130

Bullein, William
between 1520 and 1530-1576 ...DLB-167

Bullins, Ed 1935- DLB-7, 38

Bulwer-Lytton, Edward (also Edward Bulwer)
1803-1873 .... DLB-21

Bumpus, Jerry 1937- Y-81

Bunce and Brother DLB-49

Bunner, H. C. 1855-1896 ...... DLB-78, 79

Bunting, Basil 1900-1985 .... DLB-20

Bunyan, John 1628-1688 .... DLB-39

Burch, Robert 1925- DLB-52

Burciaga, José Antonio 1940- DLB-82

Bürger, Gottfried August
1747-1794 .... DLB-94

Burgess, Anthony 1917-1993 .... DLB-14

Burgess, Gelett 1866-1951 .... DLB-11

Burgess, John W. 1844-1931 .... DLB-47

Burgess, Thornton W.
1874-1965 .... DLB-22

Burgess, Stringer and Company DLB-49

Burk, John Daly circa 1772-1808 .... DLB-37

Burke, Edmund 1729?-1797 .... DLB-104

Burke, Kenneth 1897-1993 ...... DLB-45, 63

Burlingame, Edward Livermore
1848-1922 .... DLB-79

Burnet, Gilbert 1643-1715 .... DLB-101

Burnett, Frances Hodgson
1849-1924 ....DLB-42, 141; DS-13

Burnett, W. R. 1899-1982 ....DLB-9

Burnett, Whit 1899-1973 and
Martha Foley 1897-1977 .... DLB-137

Burney, Fanny 1752-1840 .... DLB-39

Burns, Alan 1929- DLB-14

Burns, John Horne 1916-1953 .... Y-85

Burns, Robert 1759-1796 .... DLB-109

Burns and Oates DLB-106

Burnshaw, Stanley 1906- DLB-48

Burr, C. Chauncey 1815?-1883 ..... DLB-79

Burroughs, Edgar Rice 1875-1950 .....DLB-8

Burroughs, John 1837-1921 .... DLB-64

Burroughs, Margaret T. G.
1917- DLB-41

Burroughs, William S., Jr.
1947-1981 .... DLB-16

Burroughs, William Seward
1914- DLB-2, 8, 16, 152; Y-81

Burroway, Janet 1936- DLB-6

Burt, Maxwell S. 1882-1954 .... DLB-86

Burt, A. L., and Company DLB-49

Burton, Hester 1913- DLB-161

Burton, Isabel Arundell
1831-1896 .... DLB-166

Burton, Miles (see Rhode, John)

Burton, Richard Francis
1821-1890 ....:..DLB-55, 166

Burton, Robert 1577-1640 .... DLB-151

Burton, Virginia Lee 1909-1968 ..... DLB-22

Burton, William Evans
1804-1860 .... DLB-73

Burwell, Adam Hood 1790-1849 ..... DLB-99

Bury, Lady Charlotte
1775-1861 .... DLB-116

Busch, Frederick 1941- DLB-6

Busch, Niven 1903-1991 .... DLB-44

Bushnell, Horace 1802-1876 ....DS-13

Bussieres, Arthur de 1877-1913 ..... DLB-92

Butler, Juan 1942-1981 .... DLB-53

Butler, Octavia E. 1947- DLB-33

Butler, Samuel 1613-1680 .....DLB-101, 126

Butler, Samuel 1835-1902 ....DLB-18, 57

Butler, William Francis
1838-1910 .... DLB-166

Butler, E. H., and Company DLB-49

Butor, Michel 1926- DLB-83

Butterworth, Hezekiah 1839-1905 ... DLB-42

Buttitta, Ignazio 1899- DLB-114

Byars, Betsy 1928- DLB-52

Byatt, A. S. 1936- DLB-14

Byles, Mather 1707-1788 .... DLB-24

Bynner, Witter 1881-1968 .... DLB-54

Byrd, William II 1674-1744 .....DLB-24, 140

Byrne, John Keyes (see Leonard, Hugh)

Byron, George Gordon, Lord
1788-1824 ....DLB-96, 110

C

Caballero Bonald, José Manuel
1926- DLB-108

Cabañero, Eladio 1930- DLB-134

Cabell, James Branch
1879-1958 ....DLB-9, 78

Cabeza de Baca, Manuel
1853-1915 ....DLB-122

Cabeza de Baca Gilbert, Fabiola
1898- DLB-122

Cable, George Washington
1844-1925 .... DLB-12, 74; DS-13

Cabrera, Lydia 1900-1991 ....DLB-145

Cabrera Infante, Guillermo
1929- DLB-113

Cadell [publishing house] DLB-154

Cady, Edwin H. 1917- DLB-103

Caedmon flourished 658-680 ......DLB-146

Caedmon School circa 660-899 .....DLB-146

Cahan, Abraham
1860-1951 .... DLB-9, 25, 28

Cain, George 1943- DLB-33

Caldecott, Randolph 1846-1886 .....DLB-163

Calder, John
(Publishers), Limited DLB-112

Caldwell, Ben 1937- DLB-38

Caldwell, Erskine 1903-1987 ..... DLB-9, 86

Caldwell, H. M., Company DLB-49

Calhoun, John C. 1782-1850 ....DLB-3

Calisher, Hortense 1911- DLB-2

A Call to Letters and an Invitation
to the Electric Chair,
by Siegfried Mandel DLB-75

Callaghan, Morley 1903-1990 ....DLB-68

Callaloo Y-87

Calmer, Edgar 1907- DLB-4

Calverley, C. S. 1831-1884 ....DLB-35

Calvert, George Henry
1803-1889 .... DLB-1, 64

Cambridge Press DLB-49

Cambridge Songs (Carmina Cantabrigensia)
circa 1050 ....DLB-148

Camden House: An Interview with
James Hardin Y-92

Cameron, Eleanor 1912- DLB-52

Cameron, George Frederick
1854-1885 ....DLB-99

Cameron, Lucy Lyttelton
1781-1858 ....DLB-163

Cameron, William Bleasdell
1862-1951 ....DLB-99

Camm, John 1718-1778 ....DLB-31

Campana, Dino 1885-1932 ....DLB-114

Campbell, Gabrielle Margaret Vere
(see Shearing, Joseph, and Bowen, Marjorie)

Campbell, James Dykes
1838-1895 ....DLB-144

Campbell, James Edwin
1867-1896 ....DLB-50

Campbell, John 1653-1728 ....DLB-43

Campbell, John W., Jr.
1910-1971 ....DLB-8

Campbell, Roy 1901-1957 ....DLB-20

Campbell, Thomas
1777-1844 ....DLB-93, 144

Campbell, William Wilfred
1858-1918 ....DLB-92

Campion, Edmund 1539-1581 ......DLB-167

Campion, Thomas 1567-1620 ......DLB-58

Camus, Albert 1913-1960 ....DLB-72

Canby, Henry Seidel 1878-1961 .....DLB-91

Candelaria, Cordelia 1943- DLB-82

Candelaria, Nash 1928- DLB-82

Candour in English Fiction (1890),
by Thomas Hardy DLB-18

Canetti, Elias 1905-1994 ....DLB-85, 124

Canham, Erwin Dain
1904-1982 ....DLB-127

Cankar, Ivan 1876-1918 ....DLB-147

Cannan, Gilbert 1884-1955 ....DLB-10

Cannell, Kathleen 1891-1974 ....DLB-4

Cannell, Skipwith 1887-1957 ....DLB-45

Canning, George 1770-1827 ....DLB-158

Cantwell, Robert 1908-1978 ....DLB-9

Cape, Jonathan, and Harrison Smith
[publishing house] DLB-46

Cape, Jonathan, Limited DLB-112

Capen, Joseph 1658-1725 ....DLB-24

Capes, Bernard 1854-1918 ....DLB-156

Capote, Truman
1924-1984 .... DLB-2; Y-80, 84

Caproni, Giorgio 1912-1990 ......DLB-128

Cardarelli, Vincenzo 1887-1959 ....DLB-114

Cárdenas, Reyes 1948- DLB-122

Cardinal, Marie 1929- DLB-83

Carew, Jan 1920- DLB-157

Carew, Thomas
1594 or 1595-1640 ....DLB-126

Carey, Henry
circa 1687-1689-1743 ....DLB-84

Carey, Mathew 1760-1839 ....DLB-37, 73

Carey and Hart DLB-49

Carey, M., and Company DLB-49

Carlell, Lodowick 1602-1675 ....DLB-58

Carleton, William 1794-1869 ......DLB-159

Carleton, G. W.
[publishing house] DLB-49

Carlile, Richard 1790-1843 ....DLB-110, 158

Carlyle, Jane Welsh 1801-1866 ......DLB-55

Carlyle, Thomas 1795-1881 .... DLB-55, 144

Carman, Bliss 1861-1929 ....DLB-92

Carmina Burana circa 1230 ....DLB-138

Carnero, Guillermo 1947- DLB-108

Carossa, Hans 1878-1956 ....DLB-66

Carpenter, Humphrey 1946- DLB-155

Carpenter, Stephen Cullen
?-1820? DLB-73

Carpentier, Alejo 1904-1980 ....DLB-113

Carrier, Roch 1937- DLB-53

Carrillo, Adolfo 1855-1926 ....DLB-122

Carroll, Gladys Hasty 1904- DLB-9

Carroll, John 1735-1815 ....DLB-37

Carroll, John 1809-1884 ....DLB-99

Carroll, Lewis 1832-1898 ..... DLB-18, 163

Carroll, Paul 1927- DLB-16

Carroll, Paul Vincent 1900-1968 ....DLB-10

Carroll and Graf Publishers DLB-46

Carruth, Hayden 1921- DLB-5, 165

Carryl, Charles E. 1841-1920 ....DLB-42

Carswell, Catherine 1879-1946 .....DLB-36

Carter, Angela 1940-1992 ....DLB-14

Carter, Elizabeth 1717-1806 ....DLB-109

Carter, Henry (see Leslie, Frank)

Carter, Hodding, Jr. 1907-1972 .... DLB-127

Carter, Landon 1710-1778 ....DLB-31

Carter, Lin 1930- Y-81

Carter, Martin 1927- DLB-117

Carter and Hendee DLB-49

Carter, Robert, and Brothers DLB-49

Cartwright, John 1740-1824 ....DLB-158

Cartwright, William circa
1611-1643 ....DLB-126

Caruthers, William Alexander
1802-1846 ....DLB-3

Carver, Jonathan 1710-1780 ....DLB-31

Carver, Raymond
1938-1988 ....DLB-130; Y-84, 88

Cary, Joyce 1888-1957 ....DLB-15, 100

Cary, Patrick 1623?-1657 ....DLB-131

Casey, Juanita 1925- DLB-14

Casey, Michael 1947- DLB-5

Cassady, Carolyn 1923- DLB-16

Cassady, Neal 1926-1968 ....DLB-16

Cassell and Company DLB-106

Cassell Publishing Company DLB-49

Cassill, R. V. 1919- DLB-6

Cassity, Turner 1929- DLB-105

The Castle of Perseverance
circa 1400-1425 ....DLB-146

Castellano, Olivia 1944- DLB-122

Castellanos, Rosario 1925-1974 ....DLB-113

Castillo, Ana 1953- DLB-122

Castlemon, Harry (see Fosdick, Charles Austin)

Caswall, Edward 1814-1878 ....DLB-32

Catacalos, Rosemary 1944- DLB-122

Cather, Willa
1873-1947 .... DLB-9, 54, 78; DS-1

Catherine II (Ekaterina Alekseevna), "The
Great," Empress of Russia
1729-1796 ....DLB-150

Catherwood, Mary Hartwell
1847-1902 ....DLB-78

Catledge, Turner 1901-1983 ....DLB-127

Cattafi, Bartolo 1922-1979 ....DLB-128

Catton, Bruce 1899-1978 ....DLB-17

Causley, Charles 1917- DLB-27

Caute, David 1936- DLB-14

Cavendish, Duchess of Newcastle,
Margaret Lucas 1623-1673 .....DLB-131

Cawein, Madison 1865-1914 ....DLB-54

The Caxton Printers, Limited DLB-46

Cayrol, Jean 1911- DLB-83

Cecil, Lord David 1902-1986 ......DLB-155

Celan, Paul 1920-1970 ....DLB-69

Celaya, Gabriel 1911-1991 ....DLB-108

Céline, Louis-Ferdinand
1894-1961 ....DLB-72

The Celtic Background to Medieval English
Literature DLB-146

Center for Bibliographical Studies and
Research at the University of
California, Riverside Y-91

The Center for the Book in the Library
of Congress Y-93

Center for the Book Research Y-84

Centlivre, Susanna 1669?-1723 ......DLB-84

The Century Company DLB-49

Cernuda, Luis 1902-1963 ....DLB-134

Cervantes, Lorna Dee 1954- DLB-82

Chacel, Rosa 1898- DLB-134

Chacón, Eusebio 1869-1948 ....DLB-82

Chacón, Felipe Maximiliano
1873-? DLB-82

Chadwyck-Healey's Full-Text Literary Databases: Editing Commercial Databases of Primary Literary Texts Y-95

Challans, Eileen Mary (see Renault, Mary)

Chalmers, George 1742-1825 .... DLB-30

Chaloner, Sir Thomas 1520-1565 .... DLB-167

Chamberlain, Samuel S. 1851-1916 .... DLB-25

Chamberland, Paul 1939- DLB-60

Chamberlin, William Henry 1897-1969 .... DLB-29

Chambers, Charles Haddon 1860-1921 .... DLB-10

Chambers, W. and R. [publishing house] DLB-106

Chamisso, Albert von 1781-1838 .... DLB-90

Champfleury 1821-1889 .... DLB-119

Chandler, Harry 1864-1944 .... DLB-29

Chandler, Norman 1899-1973 ..... DLB-127

Chandler, Otis 1927- DLB-127

Chandler, Raymond 1888-1959 .... DS-6

Channing, Edward 1856-1931 ..... DLB-17

Channing, Edward Tyrrell 1790-1856 .... DLB-1, 59

Channing, William Ellery 1780-1842 .... DLB-1, 59

Channing, William Ellery, II 1817-1901 ....DLB-1

Channing, William Henry 1810-1884 .... DLB-1, 59

Chaplin, Charlie 1889-1977 .... DLB-44

Chapman, George 1559 or 1560 - 1634 .... DLB-62, 121

Chapman, John DLB-106

Chapman, William 1850-1917 ...... DLB-99

Chapman and Hall DLB-106

Chappell, Fred 1936- DLB-6, 105

Chappell, Fred, A Detail in a Poem DLB-105

Charbonneau, Jean 1875-1960 ...... DLB-92

Charbonneau, Robert 1911-1967 .... DLB-68

Charles, Gerda 1914- DLB-14

Charles, William [publishing house] DLB-49

The Charles Wood Affair: A Playwright Revived Y-83

Charlotte Forten: Pages from her Diary DLB-50

Charteris, Leslie 1907-1993 .... DLB-77

Charyn, Jerome 1937- Y-83

Chase, Borden 1900-1971 .... DLB-26

Chase, Edna Woolman 1877-1957 .... DLB-91

Chase-Riboud, Barbara 1936- DLB-33

Chateaubriand, François-René de 1768-1848 .... DLB-119

Chatterton, Thomas 1752-1770 .... DLB-109

Chatto and Windus DLB-106

Chaucer, Geoffrey 1340?-1400 ..... DLB-146

Chauncy, Charles 1705-1787 .... DLB-24

Chauveau, Pierre-Joseph-Olivier 1820-1890 .... DLB-99

Chávez, Denise 1948- DLB-122

Chávez, Fray Angélico 1910- DLB-82

Chayefsky, Paddy 1923-1981 ....DLB-7, 44; Y-81

Cheever, Ezekiel 1615-1708 .... DLB-24

Cheever, George Barrell 1807-1890 .... DLB-59

Cheever, John 1912-1982 .... DLB-2, 102; Y-80, 82

Cheever, Susan 1943- Y-82

Cheke, Sir John 1514-1557 .... DLB-132

Chelsea House DLB-46

Cheney, Ednah Dow (Littlehale) 1824-1904 .... DLB-1

Cheney, Harriet Vaughn 1796-1889 .... DLB-99

Cherry, Kelly 1940 .... Y-83

Cherryh, C. J. 1942- Y-80

Chesnutt, Charles Waddell 1858-1932 ....DLB-12, 50, 78

Chester, Alfred 1928-1971 .... DLB-130

Chester, George Randolph 1869-1924 .... DLB-78

The Chester Plays circa 1505-1532; revisions until 1575 .... DLB-146

Chesterfield, Philip Dormer Stanhope, Fourth Earl of 1694-1773 ...... DLB-104

Chesterton, G. K. 1874-1936 ... DLB-10, 19, 34, 70, 98, 149

Chettle, Henry circa 1560-circa 1607 .... DLB-136

Chew, Ada Nield 1870-1945 .... DLB-135

Cheyney, Edward P. 1861-1947 ..... DLB-47

Chicano History DLB-82

Chicano Language DLB-82

Child, Francis James 1825-1896 .... DLB-1, 64

Child, Lydia Maria 1802-1880 .... DLB-1, 74

Child, Philip 1898-1978 ....DLB-68

Childers, Erskine 1870-1922 ....DLB-70

Children's Book Awards and Prizes DLB-61

Children's Illustrators, 1800-1880 .... DLB-163

Childress, Alice 1920-1994 .... DLB-7, 38

Childs, George W. 1829-1894 ....DLB-23

Chilton Book Company DLB-46

Chinweizu 1943- DLB-157

Chitham, Edward 1932- DLB-155

Chittenden, Hiram Martin 1858-1917 ....DLB-47

Chivers, Thomas Holley 1809-1858 ....DLB-3

Chopin, Kate 1850-1904 .... DLB-12, 78

Chopin, Rene 1885-1953 ....DLB-92

Choquette, Adrienne 1915-1973 .....DLB-68

Choquette, Robert 1905- DLB-68

The Christian Publishing Company DLB-49

Christie, Agatha 1890-1976 ..... DLB-13, 77

Christus und die Samariterin circa 950 ....DLB-148

Chulkov, Mikhail Dmitrievich 1743?-1792 ....DLB-150

Church, Benjamin 1734-1778 ....DLB-31

Church, Francis Pharcellus 1839-1906 ....DLB-79

Church, William Conant 1836-1917 ....DLB-79

Churchill, Caryl 1938- DLB-13

Churchill, Charles 1731-1764 ......DLB-109

Churchill, Sir Winston 1874-1965 ....DLB-100

Churchyard, Thomas 1520?-1604 ....DLB-132

Churton, E., and Company DLB-106

Chute, Marchette 1909-1994 ....DLB-103

Ciardi, John 1916-1986 .... DLB-5; Y-86

Cibber, Colley 1671-1757 ....DLB-84

Cima, Annalisa 1941- DLB-128

Cirese, Eugenio 1884-1955 ....DLB-114

Cisneros, Sandra 1954- DLB-122, 152

City Lights Books DLB-46

Cixous, Hélène 1937- DLB-83

Clampitt, Amy 1920-1994 ....DLB-105

Clapper, Raymond 1892-1944 . . . . DLB-29

Clare, John 1793-1864 . . . . DLB-55, 96

Clarendon, Edward Hyde, Earl of
1609-1674 . . . . DLB-101

Clark, Alfred Alexander Gordon
(see Hare, Cyril)

Clark, Ann Nolan 1896- DLB-52

Clark, Catherine Anthony
1892-1977 . . . . DLB-68

Clark, Charles Heber
1841-1915 . . . . DLB-11

Clark, Davis Wasgatt 1812-1871 . . . . . DLB-79

Clark, Eleanor 1913- DLB-6

Clark, J. P. 1935- DLB-117

Clark, Lewis Gaylord
1808-1873 . . . . DLB-3, 64, 73

Clark, Walter Van Tilburg
1909-1971 . . . . DLB-9

Clark, C. M., Publishing
Company DLB-46

Clarke, Austin 1896-1974 . . . . DLB-10, 20

Clarke, Austin C. 1934- DLB-53, 125

Clarke, Gillian 1937- DLB-40

Clarke, James Freeman
1810-1888 . . . . DLB-1, 59

Clarke, Pauline 1921- DLB-161

Clarke, Rebecca Sophia
1833-1906 . . . . DLB-42

Clarke, Robert, and Company DLB-49

Clarkson, Thomas 1760-1846 . . . . . . DLB-158

Claudius, Matthias 1740-1815 . . . . . . DLB-97

Clausen, Andy 1943- DLB-16

Claxton, Remsen and
Haffelfinger DLB-49

Clay, Cassius Marcellus
1810-1903 . . . . DLB-43

Cleary, Beverly 1916- DLB-52

Cleaver, Vera 1919- and
Cleaver, Bill 1920-1981 . . . . DLB-52

Cleland, John 1710-1789 . . . . DLB-39

Clemens, Samuel Langhorne
1835-1910 . . . . DLB-11, 12, 23, 64, 74

Clement, Hal 1922- DLB-8

Clemo, Jack 1916- DLB-27

Cleveland, John 1613-1658 . . . . DLB-126

Cliff, Michelle 1946- DLB-157

Clifford, Lady Anne 1590-1676 . . . . . DLB-151

Clifford, James L. 1901-1978 . . . . . . DLB-103

Clifford, Lucy 1853?-1929 . . . . DLB-135, 141

Clifton, Lucille 1936- DLB-5, 41

Clode, Edward J.
[publishing house] DLB-46

Clough, Arthur Hugh 1819-1861 . . . . DLB-32

Cloutier, Cécile 1930- DLB-60

Clutton-Brock, Arthur
1868-1924 . . . . DLB-98

Coates, Robert M.
1897-1973 . . . . DLB-4, 9, 102

Coatsworth, Elizabeth 1893- DLB-22

Cobb, Charles E., Jr. 1943- DLB-41

Cobb, Frank I. 1869-1923 . . . . DLB-25

Cobb, Irvin S.
1876-1944 . . . . DLB-11, 25, 86

Cobbett, William 1763-1835 . . . . DLB-43, 107

Cochran, Thomas C. 1902- DLB-17

Cochrane, Elizabeth 1867-1922 . . . . . DLB-25

Cockerill, John A. 1845-1896 . . . . . . DLB-23

Cocteau, Jean 1889-1963 . . . . DLB-65

Coderre, Emile (see Jean Narrache)

Coffee, Lenore J. 1900?-1984 . . . . . . DLB-44

Coffin, Robert P. Tristram
1892-1955 . . . . DLB-45

Cogswell, Fred 1917- DLB-60

Cogswell, Mason Fitch
1761-1830 . . . . DLB-37

Cohen, Arthur A. 1928-1986 . . . . . . DLB-28

Cohen, Leonard 1934- DLB-53

Cohen, Matt 1942- DLB-53

Colden, Cadwallader
1688-1776 . . . . DLB-24, 30

Cole, Barry 1936- DLB-14

Cole, George Watson
1850-1939 . . . . DLB-140

Colegate, Isabel 1931- DLB-14

Coleman, Emily Holmes
1899-1974 . . . . DLB-4

Coleman, Wanda 1946- DLB-130

Coleridge, Hartley 1796-1849 . . . . . . DLB-96

Coleridge, Mary 1861-1907 . . . . . DLB-19, 98

Coleridge, Samuel Taylor
1772-1834 . . . . DLB-93, 107

Colet, John 1467-1519 . . . . DLB-132

Colette 1873-1954 . . . . DLB-65

Colette, Sidonie Gabrielle (see Colette)

Colinas, Antonio 1946- DLB-134

Collier, John 1901-1980 . . . . DLB-77

Collier, Mary 1690-1762 . . . . DLB-95

Collier, Robert J. 1876-1918 . . . . DLB-91

Collier, P. F. [publishing house] DLB-49

Collin and Small DLB-49

Collingwood, W. G. 1854-1932 . . . . DLB-149

Collins, An floruit circa 1653 . . . . . . DLB-131

Collins, Merle 1950- DLB-157

Collins, Mortimer 1827-1876 . . . . DLB-21, 35

Collins, Wilkie 1824-1889 . . DLB-18, 70, 159

Collins, William 1721-1759 . . . . DLB-109

Collins, William, Sons and
Company DLB-154

Collins, Isaac [publishing house] DLB-49

Collyer, Mary 1716?-1763? DLB-39

Colman, Benjamin 1673-1747 . . . . . . DLB-24

Colman, George, the Elder
1732-1794 . . . . DLB-89

Colman, George, the Younger
1762-1836 . . . . DLB-89

Colman, S. [publishing house] DLB-49

Colombo, John Robert 1936- DLB-53

Colquhoun, Patrick 1745-1820 . . . . . DLB-158

Colter, Cyrus 1910- DLB-33

Colum, Padraic 1881-1972 . . . . DLB-19

Colvin, Sir Sidney 1845-1927 . . . . . . DLB-149

Colwin, Laurie 1944-1992 . . . . Y-80

Comden, Betty 1919- and Green,
Adolph 1918- DLB-44

Comi, Girolamo 1890-1968 . . . . DLB-114

The Comic Tradition Continued
[in the British Novel] DLB-15

Commager, Henry Steele
1902- DLB-17

The Commercialization of the Image of
Revolt, by Kenneth Rexroth DLB-16

Community and Commentators: Black
Theatre and Its Critics DLB-38

Compton-Burnett, Ivy
1884?-1969 . . . . DLB-36

Conan, Laure 1845-1924 . . . . DLB-99

Conde, Carmen 1901- DLB-108

Conference on Modern Biography Y-85

Congreve, William
1670-1729 . . . . DLB-39, 84

Conkey, W. B., Company DLB-49

Connell, Evan S., Jr. 1924- . . . DLB-2; Y-81

Connelly, Marc 1890-1980 . . . . . . DLB-7; Y-80

Connolly, Cyril 1903-1974 . . . . DLB-98

Connolly, James B. 1868-1957 . . . . . . DLB-78

Connor, Ralph 1860-1937 .... DLB-92

Connor, Tony 1930- DLB-40

Conquest, Robert 1917- DLB-27

Conrad, Joseph
1857-1924 ....DLB-10, 34, 98, 156

Conrad, John, and Company DLB-49

Conroy, Jack 1899-1990 .... Y-81

Conroy, Pat 1945- DLB-6

The Consolidation of Opinion: Critical
Responses to the Modernists DLB-36

Constable, Henry 1562-1613 ...... DLB-136

Constable and Company
Limited DLB-112

Constable, Archibald, and
Company DLB-154

Constant, Benjamin 1767-1830 .... DLB-119

Constant de Rebecque, Henri-Benjamin de
(see Constant, Benjamin)

Constantine, David 1944- DLB-40

Constantin-Weyer, Maurice
1881-1964 .... DLB-92

Contempo Caravan: Kites in
a Windstorm Y-85

A Contemporary Flourescence of Chicano
Literature Y-84

The Continental Publishing
Company DLB-49

A Conversation with Chaim Potok Y-84

Conversations with Editors Y-95

Conversations with Publishers I: An Interview
with Patrick O'Connor Y-84

Conversations with Publishers II: An Interview
with Charles Scribner III Y-94

Conversations with Publishers III: An Interview
with Donald Lamm Y-95

Conversations with Rare Book Dealers I: An
Interview with Glenn Horowitz Y-90

Conversations with Rare Book Dealers II: An
Interview with Ralph Sipper Y-94

The Conversion of an Unpolitical Man,
by W. H. Bruford DLB-66

Conway, Moncure Daniel
1832-1907 ....DLB-1

Cook, Ebenezer
circa 1667-circa 1732 .... DLB-24

Cook, Edward Tyas 1857-1919 .... DLB-149

Cook, Michael 1933- DLB-53

Cook, David C., Publishing
Company DLB-49

Cooke, George Willis 1848-1923 .... DLB-71

Cooke, Increase, and Company DLB-49

Cooke, John Esten 1830-1886 .... DLB-3

Cooke, Philip Pendleton
1816-1850 ....DLB-3, 59

Cooke, Rose Terry
1827-1892 ....DLB-12, 74

Coolbrith, Ina 1841-1928 .... DLB-54

Cooley, Peter 1940- DLB-105

Cooley, Peter, Into the Mirror DLB-105

Coolidge, Susan (see Woolsey, Sarah Chauncy)

Coolidge, George
[publishing house] DLB-49

Cooper, Giles 1918-1966 .... DLB-13

Cooper, James Fenimore 1789-1851 ... DLB-3

Cooper, Kent 1880-1965 .... DLB-29

Cooper, Susan 1935- DLB-161

Coote, J. [publishing house] DLB-154

Coover, Robert 1932- DLB-2; Y-81

Copeland and Day DLB-49

Copland, Robert 1470?-1548 ...... DLB-136

Coppard, A. E. 1878-1957 ....DLB-162

Coppel, Alfred 1921- Y-83

Coppola, Francis Ford 1939- DLB-44

Corazzini, Sergio 1886-1907 ....DLB-114

Corbett, Richard 1582-1635 ....DLB-121

Corcoran, Barbara 1911- DLB-52

Corelli, Marie 1855-1924 ....DLB-34, 156

Corle, Edwin 1906-1956 ....Y-85

Corman, Cid 1924- DLB-5

Cormier, Robert 1925- DLB-52

Corn, Alfred 1943- DLB-120; Y-80

Cornish, Sam 1935- DLB-41

Cornish, William
circa 1465-circa 1524 .... DLB-132

Cornwall, Barry (see Procter, Bryan Waller)

Cornwallis, Sir William, the Younger
circa 1579-1614 .... DLB-151

Cornwell, David John Moore
(see le Carré, John)

Corpi, Lucha 1945- DLB-82

Corrington, John William 1932- DLB-6

Corrothers, James D. 1869-1917 ..... DLB-50

Corso, Gregory 1930- DLB-5, 16

Cortázar, Julio 1914-1984 .... DLB-113

Cortez, Jayne 1936- DLB-41

Corvo, Baron (see Rolfe, Frederick William)

Cory, Annie Sophie (see Cross, Victoria)

Cory, William Johnson
1823-1892 ....DLB-35

Coryate, Thomas 1577?-1617 ......DLB-151

Cosin, John 1595-1672 ....DLB-151

Cosmopolitan Book Corporation DLB-46

Costain, Thomas B. 1885-1965 ....DLB-9

Coste, Donat 1912-1957 ....DLB-88

Costello, Louisa Stuart 1799-1870 ...DLB-166

Cota-Cárdenas, Margarita
1941- DLB-122

Cotter, Joseph Seamon, Sr.
1861-1949 ....DLB-50

Cotter, Joseph Seamon, Jr.
1895-1919 ....DLB-50

Cottle, Joseph [publishing house] DLB-154

Cotton, Charles 1630-1687 ....DLB-131

Cotton, John 1584-1652 ....DLB-24

Coulter, John 1888-1980 ....DLB-68

Cournos, John 1881-1966 ....DLB-54

Cousins, Margaret 1905- DLB-137

Cousins, Norman 1915-1990 ....DLB-137

Coventry, Francis 1725-1754 ....DLB-39

Coverdale, Miles
1487 or 1488-1569 ....DLB-167

Coverly, N. [publishing house] DLB-49

Covici-Friede DLB-46

Coward, Noel 1899-1973 ....DLB-10

Coward, McCann and
Geoghegan DLB-46

Cowles, Gardner 1861-1946 ....DLB-29

Cowles, Gardner ("Mike"), Jr.
1903-1985 .... DLB-127, 137

Cowley, Abraham
1618-1667 .... DLB-131, 151

Cowley, Hannah 1743-1809 ....DLB-89

Cowley, Malcolm
1898-1989 .... DLB-4, 48; Y-81, 89

Cowper, William 1731-1800 ... DLB-104, 109

Cox, A. B. (see Berkeley, Anthony)

Cox, James McMahon
1903-1974 ....DLB-127

Cox, James Middleton
1870-1957 ....DLB-127

Cox, Palmer 1840-1924 ....DLB-42

Coxe, Louis 1918-1993 ....DLB-5

Coxe, Tench 1755-1824 ....DLB-37

Cozzens, James Gould
1903-1978 .... DLB-9; Y-84; DS-2

Crabbe, George 1754-1832 ....DLB-93

Crackanthorpe, Hubert
1870-1896 ....DLB-135

Craddock, Charles Egbert
(see Murfree, Mary N.)

Cradock, Thomas 1718-1770 ....DLB-31

Craig, Daniel H. 1811-1895 ....DLB-43

Craik, Dinah Maria
1826-1887 ....DLB-35, 136

Cranch, Christopher Pearse
1813-1892 ....DLB-1, 42

Crane, Hart 1899-1932 ....DLB-4, 48

Crane, R. S. 1886-1967 ....DLB-63

Crane, Stephen 1871-1900 ... DLB-12, 54, 78

Crane, Walter 1845-1915 ....DLB-163

Cranmer, Thomas 1489-1556 ......DLB-132

Crapsey, Adelaide 1878-1914 ....DLB-54

Crashaw, Richard
1612 or 1613-1649 ....DLB-126

Craven, Avery 1885-1980 ....DLB-17

Crawford, Charles
1752-circa 1815 ....DLB-31

Crawford, F. Marion 1854-1909 .....DLB-71

Crawford, Isabel Valancy
1850-1887 ....DLB-92

Crawley, Alan 1887-1975 ....DLB-68

Crayon, Geoffrey (see Irving, Washington)

Creasey, John 1908-1973 ....DLB-77

Creative Age Press DLB-46

Creech, William
[publishing house] DLB-154

Creel, George 1876-1953 ....DLB-25

Creeley, Robert 1926- DLB-5, 16

Creelman, James 1859-1915 ....DLB-23

Cregan, David 1931- DLB-13

Creighton, Donald Grant
1902-1979 ....DLB-88

Cremazie, Octave 1827-1879 ....DLB-99

Crémer, Victoriano 1909?- DLB-108

Crescas, Hasdai
circa 1340-1412? DLB-115

Crespo, Angel 1926- DLB-134

Cresset Press DLB-112

Cresswell, Helen 1934- DLB-161

Crèvecoeur, Michel Guillaume Jean de
1735-1813 ....DLB-37

Crews, Harry 1935- DLB-6, 143

Crichton, Michael 1942- Y-81

A Crisis of Culture: The Changing Role
of Religion in the New Republic
.... DLB-37

Crispin, Edmund 1921-1978 .... DLB-87

Cristofer, Michael 1946- DLB-7

"The Critic as Artist" (1891), by
Oscar Wilde DLB-57

"Criticism In Relation To Novels" (1863),
by G. H. Lewes DLB-21

Crnjanski, Miloš 1893-1977 .... DLB-147

Crockett, David (Davy)
1786-1836 .... DLB-3, 11

Croft-Cooke, Rupert (see Bruce, Leo)

Crofts, Freeman Wills
1879-1957 .... DLB-77

Croker, John Wilson 1780-1857 .... DLB-110

Croly, George 1780-1860 .... DLB-159

Croly, Herbert 1869-1930 .... DLB-91

Croly, Jane Cunningham
1829-1901 .... DLB-23

Crompton, Richmal 1890-1969 .... DLB-160

Crosby, Caresse 1892-1970 .... DLB-48

Crosby, Caresse 1892-1970 and Crosby,
Harry 1898-1929 .... DLB-4

Crosby, Harry 1898-1929 .... DLB-48

Cross, Gillian 1945- DLB-161

Cross, Victoria 1868-1952 .... DLB-135

Crossley-Holland, Kevin
1941- DLB-40, 161

Crothers, Rachel 1878-1958 .... DLB-7

Crowell, Thomas Y., Company DLB-49

Crowley, John 1942- Y-82

Crowley, Mart 1935- DLB-7

Crown Publishers DLB-46

Crowne, John 1641-1712 .... DLB-80

Crowninshield, Edward Augustus
1817-1859 .... DLB-140

Crowninshield, Frank 1872-1947 .... DLB-91

Croy, Homer 1883-1965 .... DLB-4

Crumley, James 1939- Y-84

Cruz, Victor Hernández 1949- DLB-41

Csokor, Franz Theodor
1885-1969 .... DLB-81

Cuala Press DLB-112

Cullen, Countee 1903-1946 ... DLB-4, 48, 51

Culler, Jonathan D. 1944- DLB-67

The Cult of Biography
Excerpts from the Second Folio Debate:
"Biographies are generally a disease of
English Literature" — Germaine Greer,
Victoria Glendinning, Auberon Waugh,
and Richard Holmes Y-86

Cumberland, Richard 1732-1811 ....DLB-89

Cummings, E. E. 1894-1962 ......DLB-4, 48

Cummings, Ray 1887-1957 ....DLB-8

Cummings and Hilliard DLB-49

Cummins, Maria Susanna
1827-1866 ....DLB-42

Cundall, Joseph
[publishing house] DLB-106

Cuney, Waring 1906-1976 ....DLB-51

Cuney-Hare, Maude 1874-1936 .....DLB-52

Cunningham, Allan
1784-1842 ....DLB-116, 144

Cunningham, J. V. 1911- DLB-5

Cunningham, Peter F.
[publishing house] DLB-49

Cunquiero, Alvaro 1911-1981 ......DLB-134

Cuomo, George 1929- Y-80

Cupples and Leon DLB-46

Cupples, Upham and Company DLB-49

Cuppy, Will 1884-1949 ....DLB-11

Curll, Edmund
[publishing house] DLB-154

Currie, James 1756-1805 ....DLB-142

Currie, Mary Montgomerie Lamb Singleton,
Lady Currie (see Fane, Violet)

Cursor Mundi circa 1300 ....DLB-146

Curti, Merle E. 1897- DLB-17

Curtis, Anthony 1926- DLB-155

Curtis, Cyrus H. K. 1850-1933 ......DLB-91

Curtis, George William
1824-1892 ....DLB-1, 43

Curzon, Robert 1810-1873 ....DLB-166

Curzon, Sarah Anne 1833-1898 .....DLB-99

Cynewulf circa 770-840 ....DLB-146

Czepko, Daniel 1605-1660 ....DLB-164

D

D. M. Thomas: The Plagiarism
Controversy Y-82

Dabit, Eugène 1898-1936 ....DLB-65

Daborne, Robert circa 1580-1628 ....DLB-58

Dacey, Philip 1939- DLB-105

Dacey, Philip, Eyes Across Centuries: Contemporary Poetry and "That Vision Thing" DLB-105

Dach, Simon 1605-1659 .... DLB-164

Daggett, Rollin M. 1831-1901 ...... DLB-79

D'Aguiar, Fred 1960- DLB-157

Dahl, Roald 1916-1990 .... DLB-139

Dahlberg, Edward 1900-1977 .... DLB-48

Dahn, Felix 1834-1912 .... DLB-129

Dale, Peter 1938- DLB-40

Dall, Caroline Wells (Healey) 1822-1912 ....DLB-1

Dallas, E. S. 1828-1879 .... DLB-55

The Dallas Theater Center DLB-7

D'Alton, Louis 1900-1951 .... DLB-10

Daly, T. A. 1871-1948 .... DLB-11

Damon, S. Foster 1893-1971 .... DLB-45

Damrell, William S. [publishing house] DLB-49

Dana, Charles A. 1819-1897 ...... DLB-3, 23

Dana, Richard Henry, Jr 1815-1882 ....DLB-1

Dandridge, Ray Garfield DLB-51

Dane, Clemence 1887-1965 .... DLB-10

Danforth, John 1660-1730 .... DLB-24

Danforth, Samuel, I 1626-1674 ..... DLB-24

Danforth, Samuel, II 1666-1727 ..... DLB-24

Dangerous Years: London Theater, 1939-1945 .... DLB-10

Daniel, John M. 1825-1865 .... DLB-43

Daniel, Samuel 1562 or 1563-1619 .... DLB-62

Daniel Press DLB-106

Daniells, Roy 1902-1979 .... DLB-68

Daniels, Jim 1956- DLB-120

Daniels, Jonathan 1902-1981 ...... DLB-127

Daniels, Josephus 1862-1948 .... DLB-29

Dannay, Frederic 1905-1982 and Manfred B. Lee 1905-1971 ..... DLB-137

Danner, Margaret Esse 1915- DLB-41

Dantin, Louis 1865-1945 .... DLB-92

D'Arcy, Ella circa 1857-1937 ...... DLB-135

Darley, George 1795-1846 .... DLB-96

Darwin, Charles 1809-1882 .... DLB-57, 166

Darwin, Erasmus 1731-1802 .... DLB-93

Daryush, Elizabeth 1887-1977 ...... DLB-20

Dashkova, Ekaterina Romanovna (née Vorontsova) 1743-1810 .... DLB-150

Dashwood, Edmée Elizabeth Monica de la Pasture (see Delafield, E. M.)

Daudet, Alphonse 1840-1897 ...... DLB-123

d'Aulaire, Edgar Parin 1898- and d'Aulaire, Ingri 1904- DLB-22

Davenant, Sir William 1606-1668 ....DLB-58, 126

Davenport, Guy 1927- DLB-130

Davenport, Robert ?-? DLB-58

Daves, Delmer 1904-1977 .... DLB-26

Davey, Frank 1940- DLB-53

Davidson, Avram 1923-1993 .... DLB-8

Davidson, Donald 1893-1968 .... DLB-45

Davidson, John 1857-1909 .... DLB-19

Davidson, Lionel 1922- DLB-14

Davie, Donald 1922- DLB-27

Davie, Elspeth 1919- DLB-139

Davies, John, of Hereford 1565?-1618 .... DLB-121

Davies, Rhys 1901-1978 .... DLB-139

Davies, Robertson 1913- DLB-68

Davies, Samuel 1723-1761 .... DLB-31

Davies, Thomas 1712?-1785 ...DLB-142, 154

Davies, W. H. 1871-1940 .... DLB-19

Davies, Peter, Limited DLB-112

Daviot, Gordon 1896?-1952 .... DLB-10 (see also Tey, Josephine)

Davis, Charles A. 1795-1867 .... DLB-11

Davis, Clyde Brion 1894-1962 .... DLB-9

Davis, Dick 1945- DLB-40

Davis, Frank Marshall 1905-? DLB-51

Davis, H. L. 1894-1960 .... DLB-9

Davis, John 1774-1854 .... DLB-37

Davis, Lydia 1947- DLB-130

Davis, Margaret Thomson 1926- ... DLB-14

Davis, Ossie 1917- DLB-7, 38

Davis, Paxton 1925-1994 ....Y-94

Davis, Rebecca Harding 1831-1910 .... DLB-74

Davis, Richard Harding 1864-1916 .... DLB-12, 23, 78, 79; DS-13

Davis, Samuel Cole 1764-1809 ...... DLB-37

Davison, Peter 1928- DLB-5

Davys, Mary 1674-1732 .... DLB-39

DAW Books DLB-46

Dawson, Ernest 1882-1947 ....DLB-140

Dawson, Fielding 1930- DLB-130

Dawson, William 1704-1752 ....DLB-31

Day, Angel flourished 1586 ....DLB-167

Day, Benjamin Henry 1810-1889 ....DLB-43

Day, Clarence 1874-1935 ....DLB-11

Day, Dorothy 1897-1980 ....DLB-29

Day, Frank Parker 1881-1950 ....DLB-92

Day, John circa 1574-circa 1640 .....DLB-62

Day Lewis, C. 1904-1972 .... DLB-15, 20 (see also Blake, Nicholas)

Day, Thomas 1748-1789 ....DLB-39

Day, The John, Company DLB-46

Day, Mahlon [publishing house] DLB-49

Deacon, William Arthur 1890-1977 ....DLB-68

Deal, Borden 1922-1985 ....DLB-6

de Angeli, Marguerite 1889-1987 .....DLB-22

De Angelis, Milo 1951- DLB-128

De Bow, James Dunwoody Brownson 1820-1867 .... DLB-3, 79

de Bruyn, Günter 1926- DLB-75

de Camp, L. Sprague 1907- DLB-8

The Decay of Lying (1889), by Oscar Wilde [excerpt] DLB-18

Dedication, Ferdinand Count Fathom (1753), by Tobias Smollett DLB-39

Dedication, The History of Pompey the Little (1751), by Francis Coventry DLB-39

Dedication, Lasselia (1723), by Eliza Haywood [excerpt] DLB-39

Dedication, The Wanderer (1814), by Fanny Burney DLB-39

Dee, John 1527-1609 ....DLB-136

Deeping, George Warwick 1877-1950 .... DLB 153

Defense of Amelia (1752), by Henry Fielding DLB-39

Defoe, Daniel 1660-1731 .... DLB-39, 95, 101

de Fontaine, Felix Gregory 1834-1896 ....DLB-43

De Forest, John William 1826-1906 ....DLB-12

DeFrees, Madeline 1919- DLB-105

DeFrees, Madeline, The Poet's Kaleidoscope: The Element of Surprise in the Making of the Poem DLB-105

de Graff, Robert 1895-1981 .... Y-81

de Graft, Joe 1924-1978 ....DLB-117

De Heinrico circa 980? DLB-148

Deighton, Len 1929- DLB-87

DeJong, Meindert 1906-1991 ....DLB-52

Dekker, Thomas circa 1572-1632 ....DLB-62

Delacorte, Jr., George T.
   1894-1991 ....DLB-91

Delafield, E. M. 1890-1943 ....DLB-34

Delahaye, Guy 1888-1969 ....DLB-92

de la Mare, Walter
   1873-1956 .... DLB-19, 153, 162

Deland, Margaret 1857-1945 ....DLB-78

Delaney, Shelagh 1939- DLB-13

Delany, Martin Robinson
   1812-1885 ....DLB-50

Delany, Samuel R. 1942- DLB-8, 33

de la Roche, Mazo 1879-1961 ....DLB-68

Delbanco, Nicholas 1942- DLB-6

De León, Nephtal 1945- DLB-82

Delgado, Abelardo Barrientos
   1931- DLB-82

De Libero, Libero 1906-1981 ....DLB-114

DeLillo, Don 1936- DLB-6

de Lisser H. G. 1878-1944 ....DLB-117

Dell, Floyd 1887-1969 ....DLB-9

Dell Publishing Company DLB-46

delle Grazie, Marie Eugene
   1864-1931 ....DLB-81

Deloney, Thomas died 1600 ....DLB-167

del Rey, Lester 1915-1993 ....DLB-8

Del Vecchio, John M. 1947- DS-9

de Man, Paul 1919-1983 ....DLB-67

Demby, William 1922- DLB-33

Deming, Philander 1829-1915 ....DLB-74

Demorest, William Jennings
   1822-1895 ....DLB-79

De Morgan, William 1839-1917 ....DLB-153

Denham, Sir John
   1615-1669 ....DLB-58, 126

Denison, Merrill 1893-1975 ....DLB-92

Denison, T. S., and Company DLB-49

Dennie, Joseph
   1768-1812 .... DLB-37, 43, 59, 73

Dennis, John 1658-1734 ....DLB-101

Dennis, Nigel 1912-1989 ....DLB-13, 15

Dent, Tom 1932- DLB-38

Dent, J. M., and Sons DLB-112

Denton, Daniel circa 1626-1703 .....DLB-24

DePaola, Tomie 1934- DLB-61

De Quincey, Thomas
   1785-1859 .... DLB-110, 144

Derby, George Horatio
   1823-1861 .... DLB-11

Derby, J. C., and Company DLB-49

Derby and Miller DLB-49

Derleth, August 1909-1971 .... DLB-9

The Derrydale Press DLB-46

Derzhavin, Gavriil Romanovich
   1743-1816 .... DLB-150

Desaulniers, Gonsalve
   1863-1934 .... DLB-92

Desbiens, Jean-Paul 1927- DLB-53

des Forêts, Louis-Rene 1918- DLB-83

DesRochers, Alfred 1901-1978 ..... DLB-68

Desrosiers, Léo-Paul 1896-1967 ..... DLB-68

Destouches, Louis-Ferdinand
   (see Céline, Louis-Ferdinand)

De Tabley, Lord 1835-1895 .... DLB-35

Deutsch, Babette 1895-1982 .... DLB-45

Deutsch, André, Limited DLB-112

Deveaux, Alexis 1948- DLB-38

The Development of the Author's Copyright
   in Britain DLB-154

The Development of Lighting in the Staging
   of Drama, 1900-1945 .... DLB-10

de Vere, Aubrey 1814-1902 .... DLB-35

Devereux, second Earl of Essex, Robert
   1565-1601 .... DLB-136

The Devin-Adair Company DLB-46

De Voto, Bernard 1897-1955 .... DLB-9

De Vries, Peter 1910-1993 ..... DLB-6; Y-82

Dewdney, Christopher 1951- DLB-60

Dewdney, Selwyn 1909-1979 .... DLB-68

DeWitt, Robert M., Publisher DLB-49

DeWolfe, Fiske and Company DLB-49

Dexter, Colin 1930- DLB-87

de Young, M. H. 1849-1925 .... DLB-25

Dhlomo, H. I. E. 1903-1956 .... DLB-157

Dhuoda circa 803-after 843 .... DLB-148

The Dial Press DLB-46

Diamond, I. A. L. 1920-1988 ..... DLB-26

Di Cicco, Pier Giorgio 1949- DLB-60

Dick, Philip K. 1928-1982 .... DLB-8

Dick and Fitzgerald DLB-49

Dickens, Charles
   1812-1870 ..... DLB-21, 55, 70, 159, 166

Dickinson, Peter 1927- DLB-161

Dickey, James
   1923- DLB-5; Y-82, 93; DS-7

Dickey, William 1928-1994 ....DLB-5

Dickinson, Emily 1830-1886 ....DLB-1

Dickinson, John 1732-1808 ....DLB-31

Dickinson, Jonathan 1688-1747 ......DLB-24

Dickinson, Patric 1914- DLB-27

Dickinson, Peter 1927- DLB-87

Dicks, John [publishing house] DLB-106

Dickson, Gordon R. 1923- DLB-8

*Dictionary of Literary Biography
Yearbook* Awards Y-92, 93

The Dictionary of National Biography
   ....DLB-144

Didion, Joan 1934- DLB-2; Y-81, 86

Di Donato, Pietro 1911- DLB-9

Diego, Gerardo 1896-1987 ....DLB-134

Digges, Thomas circa 1546-1595 ...DLB-136

Dillard, Annie 1945- Y-80

Dillard, R. H. W. 1937- DLB-5

Dillingham, Charles T.,
   Company DLB-49

The Dillingham, G. W.,
   Company DLB-49

Dilly, Edward and Charles
   [publishing house] DLB-154

Dilthey, Wilhelm 1833-1911 ....DLB-129

Dingelstedt, Franz von
   1814-1881 ....DLB-133

Dintenfass, Mark 1941- Y-84

Diogenes, Jr. (see Brougham, John)

DiPrima, Diane 1934- DLB-5, 16

Disch, Thomas M. 1940- DLB-8

Disney, Walt 1901-1966 ....DLB-22

Disraeli, Benjamin 1804-1881 ....DLB-21, 55

D'Israeli, Isaac 1766-1848 ....DLB-107

Ditzen, Rudolf (see Fallada, Hans)

Dix, Dorothea Lynde 1802-1887 ......DLB-1

Dix, Dorothy (see Gilmer,
   Elizabeth Meriwether)

Dix, Edwards and Company DLB-49

Dixon, Paige (see Corcoran, Barbara)

Dixon, Richard Watson
   1833-1900 ....DLB-19

Dixon, Stephen 1936- DLB-130

Dmitriev, Ivan Ivanovich
  1760-1837 .... DLB-150

Dobell, Sydney 1824-1874 .... DLB-32

Döblin, Alfred 1878-1957 .... DLB-66

Dobson, Austin
  1840-1921 .... DLB-35, 144

Doctorow, E. L. 1931- DLB-2, 28; Y-80

Documents on Sixteenth-Century
  Literature DLB-167

Dodd, William E. 1869-1940 .... DLB-17

Dodd, Anne [publishing house] DLB-154

Dodd, Mead and Company DLB-49

Doderer, Heimito von 1896-1968 ... DLB-85

Dodge, Mary Mapes
  1831?-1905 .... DLB-42, 79; DS-13

Dodge, B. W., and Company DLB-46

Dodge Publishing Company DLB-49

Dodgson, Charles Lutwidge
  (see Carroll, Lewis)

Dodsley, Robert 1703-1764 .... DLB-95

Dodsley, R. [publishing house] DLB-154

Dodson, Owen 1914-1983 .... DLB-76

Doesticks, Q. K. Philander, P. B.
  (see Thomson, Mortimer)

Doheny, Carrie Estelle
  1875-1958 .... DLB-140

Domínguez, Sylvia Maida
  1935- DLB-122

Donahoe, Patrick
  [publishing house] DLB-49

Donald, David H. 1920- DLB-17

Donaldson, Scott 1928- DLB-111

Donleavy, J. P. 1926- DLB-6

Donnadieu, Marguerite (see Duras,
  Marguerite)

Donne, John 1572-1631 .... DLB-121, 151

Donnelley, R. R., and Sons
  Company DLB-49

Donnelly, Ignatius 1831-1901 .... DLB-12

Donohue and Henneberry DLB-49

Donoso, José 1924- DLB-113

Doolady, M. [publishing house] DLB-49

Dooley, Ebon (see Ebon)

Doolittle, Hilda 1886-1961 .... DLB-4, 45

Doplicher, Fabio 1938- DLB-128

Dor, Milo 1923- DLB-85

Doran, George H., Company DLB-46

Dorgelès, Roland 1886-1973 .... DLB-65

Dorn, Edward 1929- DLB-5

Dorr, Rheta Childe 1866-1948 ...... DLB-25

Dorset and Middlesex, Charles Sackville,
  Lord Buckhurst,
  Earl of 1643-1706 .... DLB-131

Dorst, Tankred 1925- DLB-75, 124

Dos Passos, John
  1896-1970 .... DLB-4, 9; DS-1

Doubleday and Company DLB-49

Dougall, Lily 1858-1923 .... DLB-92

Doughty, Charles M.
  1843-1926 .... DLB-19, 57

Douglas, Gavin 1476-1522 .... DLB-132

Douglas, Keith 1920-1944 .... DLB-27

Douglas, Norman 1868-1952 .... DLB-34

Douglass, Frederick
  1817?-1895 .... DLB-1, 43, 50, 79

Douglass, William circa
  1691-1752 .... DLB-24

Dourado, Autran 1926- DLB-145

Dove, Rita 1952- DLB-120

Dover Publications DLB-46

Doves Press DLB-112

Dowden, Edward 1843-1913 .... DLB-35, 149

Dowell, Coleman 1925-1985 ...... DLB-130

Downes, Gwladys 1915- DLB-88

Downing, J., Major (see Davis, Charles A.)

Downing, Major Jack (see Smith, Seba)

Dowson, Ernest 1867-1900 ..... DLB-19, 135

Doxey, William
  [publishing house] DLB-49

Doyle, Sir Arthur Conan
  1859-1930 .... DLB-18, 70, 156

Doyle, Kirby 1932- DLB-16

Drabble, Margaret 1939- DLB-14, 155

Drach, Albert 1902- DLB-85

The Dramatic Publishing
  Company DLB-49

Dramatists Play Service DLB-46

Drant, Thomas
  early 1540s?-1578 .... DLB-167

Draper, John W. 1811-1882 .... DLB-30

Draper, Lyman C. 1815-1891 .... DLB-30

Drayton, Michael 1563-1631 .... DLB-121

Dreiser, Theodore
  1871-1945 .... DLB-9, 12, 102, 137; DS-1

Drewitz, Ingeborg 1923-1986 .... DLB-75

Drieu La Rochelle, Pierre
  1893-1945 .... DLB-72

Drinkwater, John 1882-1937
  .... DLB-10, 19, 149

Droste-Hülshoff, Annette von
  1797-1848 .... DLB-133

The Drue Heinz Literature Prize
  Excerpt from "Excerpts from a Report
  of the Commission," in David
  Bosworth's *The Death of Descartes*
  An Interview with David
  Bosworth Y-82

Drummond, William Henry
  1854-1907 .... DLB-92

Drummond, William, of Hawthornden
  1585-1649 .... DLB-121

Dryden, John 1631-1700 ... DLB-80, 101, 131

Držić, Marin circa 1508-1567 .... DLB-147

Duane, William 1760-1835 .... DLB-43

Dubé, Marcel 1930- DLB-53

Dubé, Rodolphe (see Hertel, François)

Dubie, Norman 1945- DLB-120

Du Bois, W. E. B.
  1868-1963 .... DLB-47, 50, 91

Du Bois, William Pène 1916- DLB-61

Dubus, Andre 1936- DLB-130

Ducharme, Réjean 1941- DLB-60

Dučić, Jovan 1871-1943 .... DLB-147

Duck, Stephen 1705?-1756 .... DLB-95

Duckworth, Gerald, and
  Company Limited DLB-112

Dudek, Louis 1918- DLB-88

Duell, Sloan and Pearce DLB-46

Duff Gordon, Lucie 1821-1869 ..... DLB-166

Duffield and Green DLB-46

Duffy, Maureen 1933- DLB-14

Dugan, Alan 1923- DLB-5

Dugas, Marcel 1883-1947 .... DLB-92

Dugdale, William
  [publishing house] DLB-106

Duhamel, Georges 1884-1966 .... DLB-65

Dujardin, Edouard 1861-1949 ..... DLB-123

Dukes, Ashley 1885-1959 .... DLB-10

Du Maurier, George 1834-1896 .... DLB-153

Dumas, Alexandre, *père*
  1802-1870 .... DLB-119

Dumas, Henry 1934-1968 .... DLB-41

Dunbar, Paul Laurence
  1872-1906 .... DLB-50, 54, 78

Dunbar, William
  circa 1460-circa 1522 ..... DLB-132, 146

Duncan, Norman 1871-1916 .... DLB-92

Duncan, Quince 1940- DLB-145

Duncan, Robert 1919-1988 ....DLB-5, 16

Duncan, Ronald 1914-1982 ....DLB-13

Duncan, Sara Jeannette
1861-1922 ....DLB-92

Dunigan, Edward, and Brother DLB-49

Dunlap, John 1747-1812 ....DLB-43

Dunlap, William
1766-1839 .... DLB-30, 37, 59

Dunn, Douglas 1942- DLB-40

Dunn, Stephen 1939- DLB-105

Dunn, Stephen, The Good,
The Not So Good DLB-105

Dunne, Finley Peter
1867-1936 ....DLB-11, 23

Dunne, John Gregory 1932- Y-80

Dunne, Philip 1908-1992 ....DLB-26

Dunning, Ralph Cheever
1878-1930 ....DLB-4

Dunning, William A. 1857-1922 .....DLB-17

Duns Scotus, John
circa 1266-1308 ....DLB-115

Dunsany, Lord (Edward John Moreton
Drax Plunkett, Baron Dunsany)
1878-1957 .... DLB-10, 77, 153, 156

Dupin, Amantine-Aurore-Lucile (see Sand,
George)

Durand, Lucile (see Bersianik, Louky)

Duranty, Walter 1884-1957 ....DLB-29

Duras, Marguerite 1914- DLB-83

Durfey, Thomas 1653-1723 ....DLB-80

Durrell, Lawrence
1912-1990 .... DLB-15, 27; Y-90

Durrell, William
[publishing house] DLB-49

Dürrenmatt, Friedrich
1921-1990 ....DLB-69, 124

Dutton, E. P., and Company DLB-49

Duvoisin, Roger 1904-1980 ....DLB-61

Duyckinck, Evert Augustus
1816-1878 ....DLB-3, 64

Duyckinck, George L. 1823-1863 .....DLB-3

Duyckinck and Company DLB-49

Dwight, John Sullivan 1813-1893 .....DLB-1

Dwight, Timothy 1752-1817 ....DLB-37

Dybek, Stuart 1942- DLB-130

Dyer, Charles 1928- DLB-13

Dyer, George 1755-1841 ....DLB-93

Dyer, John 1699-1757 ....DLB-95

Dyer, Sir Edward 1543-1607 ......DLB-136

Dylan, Bob 1941- DLB-16

E

Eager, Edward 1911-1964 ....DLB-22

Eames, Wilberforce 1855-1937 .....DLB-140

Earle, James H., and Company DLB-49

Earle, John 1600 or 1601-1665 .....DLB-151

Early American Book Illustration,
by Sinclair Hamilton DLB-49

Eastlake, William 1917- DLB-6

Eastman, Carol ?- DLB-44

Eastman, Max 1883-1969 ....DLB-91

Eaton, Daniel Isaac 1753-1814 .....DLB-158

Eberhart, Richard 1904- DLB-48

Ebner, Jeannie 1918- DLB-85

Ebner-Eschenbach, Marie von
1830-1916 ....DLB-81

Ebon 1942- DLB-41

Ecbasis Captivi circa 1045 ....DLB-148

Ecco Press DLB-46

Eckhart, Meister
circa 1260-circa 1328 ....DLB-115

The Eclectic Review 1805-1868 ....DLB-110

Edel, Leon 1907- DLB-103

Edes, Benjamin 1732-1803 ....DLB-43

Edgar, David 1948- DLB-13

Edgeworth, Maria
1768-1849 ....DLB-116, 159, 163

The Edinburgh Review 1802-1929 ....DLB-110

Edinburgh University Press DLB-112

The Editor Publishing Company DLB-49

Editorial Statements DLB-137

Edmonds, Randolph 1900- DLB-51

Edmonds, Walter D. 1903- DLB-9

Edschmid, Kasimir 1890-1966 ......DLB-56

Edwards, Jonathan 1703-1758 ......DLB-24

Edwards, Jonathan, Jr. 1745-1801 ... DLB-37

Edwards, Junius 1929- DLB-33

Edwards, Richard 1524-1566 ....DLB-62

Edwards, James
[publishing house] DLB-154

Effinger, George Alec 1947- DLB-8

Egerton, George 1859-1945 ....DLB-135

Eggleston, Edward 1837-1902 ......DLB-12

Eggleston, Wilfred 1901-1986 ......DLB-92

Ehrenstein, Albert 1886-1950 ....DLB-81

Ehrhart, W. D. 1948- DS-9

Eich, Günter 1907-1972 ....DLB-69, 124

Eichendorff, Joseph Freiherr von
1788-1857 ....DLB-90

1873 Publishers' Catalogues DLB-49

Eighteenth-Century Aesthetic
Theories DLB-31

Eighteenth-Century Philosophical
Background DLB-31

Eigner, Larry 1927- DLB-5

Eikon Basilike 1649 ....DLB-151

Eilhart von Oberge
circa 1140-circa 1195 ....DLB-148

Einhard circa 770-840 ....DLB-148

Eisenreich, Herbert 1925-1986 ......DLB-85

Eisner, Kurt 1867-1919 ....DLB-66

Eklund, Gordon 1945- Y-83

Ekwensi, Cyprian 1921- DLB-117

Elder, Lonne III 1931- DLB-7, 38, 44

Elder, Paul, and Company DLB-49

Elements of Rhetoric (1828; revised, 1846),
by Richard Whately [excerpt] DLB-57

Elie, Robert 1915-1973 ....DLB-88

Elin Pelin 1877-1949 ....DLB-147

Eliot, George 1819-1880 .....DLB-21, 35, 55

Eliot, John 1604-1690 ....DLB-24

Eliot, T. S. 1888-1965 ..... DLB-7, 10, 45, 63

Elizabeth I 1533-1603 ....DLB-136

Elizondo, Salvador 1932- DLB-145

Elizondo, Sergio 1930- DLB-82

Elkin, Stanley 1930- DLB-2, 28; Y-80

Elles, Dora Amy (see Wentworth, Patricia)

Ellet, Elizabeth F. 1818?-1877 ....DLB-30

Elliot, Ebenezer 1781-1849 ....DLB-96

Elliot, Frances Minto (Dickinson)
1820-1898 ....DLB-166

Elliott, George 1923- DLB-68

Elliott, Janice 1931- DLB-14

Elliott, William 1788-1863 ....DLB-3

Elliott, Thomes and Talbot DLB-49

Ellis, Edward S. 1840-1916 ....DLB-42

Ellis, Frederick Staridge
[publishing house] DLB-106

The George H. Ellis Company DLB-49

Ellison, Harlan 1934- DLB-8

Ellison, Ralph Waldo
1914-1994 . . . . DLB-2, 76; Y-94

Ellmann, Richard
1918-1987 . . . . DLB-103; Y-87

The Elmer Holmes Bobst Awards in Arts
and Letters Y-87

Elyot, Thomas 1490?-1546 . . . . DLB-136

Emanuel, James Andrew 1921- DLB-41

Emecheta, Buchi 1944- DLB-117

The Emergence of Black Women
Writers DS-8

Emerson, Ralph Waldo
1803-1882 . . . . DLB-1, 59, 73

Emerson, William 1769-1811 . . . . DLB-37

Emin, Fedor Aleksandrovich
circa 1735-1770 . . . . DLB-150

Empson, William 1906-1984 . . . . DLB-20

The End of English Stage Censorship,
1945-1968 . . . . DLB-13

Ende, Michael 1929- DLB-75

Engel, Marian 1933-1985 . . . . DLB-53

Engels, Friedrich 1820-1895 . . . . DLB-129

Engle, Paul 1908- DLB-48

English Composition and Rhetoric (1866),
by Alexander Bain [excerpt] DLB-57

The English Language:
410 to 1500 . . . . DLB-146

The English Renaissance of Art (1908),
by Oscar Wilde DLB-35

Enright, D. J. 1920- DLB-27

Enright, Elizabeth 1909-1968 . . . . . . DLB-22

L'Envoi (1882), by Oscar Wilde DLB-35

Epps, Bernard 1936- DLB-53

Epstein, Julius 1909- and
Epstein, Philip 1909-1952 . . . . DLB-26

Equiano, Olaudah
circa 1745-1797 . . . . DLB-37, 50

Eragny Press DLB-112

Erasmus, Desiderius 1467-1536 . . . . DLB-136

Erba, Luciano 1922- DLB-128

Erdrich, Louise 1954- DLB-152

Erichsen-Brown, Gwethalyn Graham
(see Graham, Gwethalyn)

Eriugena, John Scottus
circa 810-877 . . . . DLB-115

Ernest Hemingway's Toronto Journalism
Revisited: With Three Previously
Unrecorded Stories Y-92

Ernst, Paul 1866-1933 . . . . DLB-66, 118

Erskine, Albert 1911-1993 . . . . Y-93

Erskine, John 1879-1951 . . . . DLB-9, 102

Ervine, St. John Greer 1883-1971 . . . . DLB-10

Eschenburg, Johann Joachim
1743-1820 . . . . DLB-97

Escoto, Julio 1944- DLB-145

Eshleman, Clayton 1935- DLB-5

Espriu, Salvador 1913-1985 . . . . DLB-134

Ess Ess Publishing Company DLB-49

Essay on Chatterton (1842), by
Robert Browning DLB-32

Essex House Press DLB-112

Estes, Eleanor 1906-1988 . . . . DLB-22

Estes and Lauriat DLB-49

Etherege, George 1636-circa 1692 . . . . DLB-80

Ethridge, Mark, Sr. 1896-1981 . . . . DLB-127

Ets, Marie Hall 1893- DLB-22

Etter, David 1928- DLB-105

Eudora Welty: Eye of the Storyteller Y-87

Eugene O'Neill Memorial Theater
Center DLB-7

Eugene O'Neill's Letters: A Review Y-88

Eupolemius
flourished circa 1095 . . . . DLB-148

Evans, Caradoc 1878-1945 . . . . DLB-162

Evans, Donald 1884-1921 . . . . DLB-54

Evans, George Henry 1805-1856 . . . . DLB-43

Evans, Hubert 1892-1986 . . . . DLB-92

Evans, Mari 1923- DLB-41

Evans, Mary Ann (see Eliot, George)

Evans, Nathaniel 1742-1767 . . . . DLB-31

Evans, Sebastian 1830-1909 . . . . DLB-35

Evans, M., and Company DLB-46

Everett, Alexander Hill
790-1847 . . . . DLB-59

Everett, Edward 1794-1865 . . . . . . DLB-1, 59

Everson, R. G. 1903- DLB-88

Everson, William 1912-1994 . . . . . . DLB-5, 16

Every Man His Own Poet; or, The
Inspired Singer's Recipe Book (1877),
by W. H. Mallock DLB-35

Ewart, Gavin 1916- DLB-40

Ewing, Juliana Horatia
1841-1885 . . . . DLB-21, 163

The Examiner 1808-1881 . . . . DLB-110

Exley, Frederick
1929-1992 . . . . DLB-143; Y-81

Experiment in the Novel (1929),
by John D. Beresford DLB-36

Erskine, John 1879-1951 . . . . DLB-9, 102

Eyre and Spottiswoode DLB-106

Ezzo ?-after 1065 . . . . DLB-148

F

"F. Scott Fitzgerald: St. Paul's Native Son
and Distinguished American Writer":
University of Minnesota Conference,
29-31 October 1982 . . . . Y-82

Faber, Frederick William
1814-1863 . . . . DLB-32

Faber and Faber Limited DLB-112

Faccio, Rena (see Aleramo, Sibilla)

Fagundo, Ana María 1938- DLB-134

Fair, Ronald L. 1932- DLB-33

Fairfax, Beatrice (see Manning, Marie)

Fairlie, Gerard 1899-1983 . . . . DLB-77

Fallada, Hans 1893-1947 . . . . DLB-56

Fancher, Betsy 1928- Y-83

Fane, Violet 1843-1905 . . . . DLB-35

Fanfrolico Press DLB-112

Fanning, Katherine 1927 . . . . DLB-127

Fanshawe, Sir Richard
1608-1666 . . . . DLB-126

Fantasy Press Publishers DLB-46

Fante, John 1909-1983 . . . . DLB-130; Y-83

Al-Farabi circa 870-950 . . . . DLB-115

Farah, Nuruddin 1945- DLB-125

Farber, Norma 1909-1984 . . . . DLB-61

Farigoule, Louis (see Romains, Jules)

Farjeon, Eleanor 1881-1965 . . . . DLB-160

Farley, Walter 1920-1989 . . . . DLB-22

Farmer, Penelope 1939- DLB-161

Farmer, Philip José 1918- DLB-8

Farquhar, George circa 1677-1707 . . . . DLB-84

Farquharson, Martha (see Finley, Martha)

Farrar, Frederic William
1831-1903 . . . . DLB-163

Farrar and Rinehart DLB-46

Farrar, Straus and Giroux DLB-46

Farrell, James T.
1904-1979 . . . . DLB-4, 9, 86; DS-2

Farrell, J. G. 1935-1979 . . . . DLB-14

Fast, Howard 1914- DLB-9

Faulkner, William 1897-1962
. . . . DLB-9, 11, 44, 102; DS-2; Y-86

Faulkner, George
[publishing house] DLB-154

Fauset, Jessie Redmon 1882-1961 . . . . DLB-51

Faust, Irvin 1924- DLB-2, 28; Y-80

Fawcett Books DLB-46

Fearing, Kenneth 1902-1961 . . . . DLB-9

Federal Writers' Project DLB-46

Federman, Raymond 1928- Y-80

Feiffer, Jules 1929- DLB-7, 44

Feinberg, Charles E. 1899-1988 . . . . Y-88

Feinstein, Elaine 1930- DLB-14, 40

Felipe, Léon 1884-1968 . . . . DLB-108

Fell, Frederick, Publishers DLB-46

Felltham, Owen 1602?-1668 . . . DLB-126, 151

Fels, Ludwig 1946- DLB-75

Felton, Cornelius Conway
1807-1862 . . . . DLB-1

Fennario, David 1947- DLB-60

Fenno, John 1751-1798 . . . . DLB-43

Fenno, R. F., and Company DLB-49

Fenton, Geoffrey 1539?-1608 . . . . DLB-136

Fenton, James 1949- DLB-40

Ferber, Edna 1885-1968 . . . . . . DLB-9, 28, 86

Ferdinand, Vallery III (see Salaam, Kalamu ya)

Ferguson, Sir Samuel 1810-1886 . . . . . DLB-32

Ferguson, William Scott
1875-1954 . . . . DLB-47

Fergusson, Robert 1750-1774 . . . . . . DLB-109

Ferland, Albert 1872-1943 . . . . DLB-92

Ferlinghetti, Lawrence 1919- DLB-5, 16

Fern, Fanny (see Parton, Sara Payson Willis)

Ferrars, Elizabeth 1907- DLB-87

Ferré, Rosario 1942- DLB-145

Ferret, E., and Company DLB-49

Ferrier, Susan 1782-1854 . . . . DLB-116

Ferrini, Vincent 1913- DLB-48

Ferron, Jacques 1921-1985 . . . . DLB-60

Ferron, Madeleine 1922- DLB-53

Fetridge and Company DLB-49

Feuchtersleben, Ernst Freiherr von
1806-1849 . . . . DLB-133

Feuchtwanger, Lion 1884-1958 . . . . . . DLB-66

Feuerbach, Ludwig 1804-1872 . . . . . . DLB-133

Fichte, Johann Gottlieb
1762-1814 . . . . DLB-90

Ficke, Arthur Davison 1883-1945 . . . . DLB-54

Fiction Best-Sellers, 1910-1945 . . . . . . DLB-9

Fiction into Film, 1928-1975: A List of Movies
Based on the Works of Authors in
British Novelists, 1930-1959 . . . . . . DLB-15

Fiedler, Leslie A. 1917- DLB-28, 67

Field, Edward 1924- DLB-105

Field, Edward, The Poetry File DLB-105

Field, Eugene
1850-1895 . . . . DLB-23, 42, 140; DS-13

Field, John 1545?-1588 . . . . DLB-167

Field, Marshall, III 1893-1956 . . . . . DLB-127

Field, Marshall, IV 1916-1965 . . . . . DLB-127

Field, Marshall, V 1941- DLB-127

Field, Nathan 1587-1619 or 1620 . . . . DLB-58

Field, Rachel 1894-1942 . . . . DLB-9, 22

A Field Guide to Recent Schools of American
Poetry Y-86

Fielding, Henry
1707-1754 . . . . DLB-39, 84, 101

Fielding, Sarah 1710-1768 . . . . DLB-39

Fields, James Thomas 1817-1881 . . . . . DLB-1

Fields, Julia 1938- DLB-41

Fields, W. C. 1880-1946 . . . . DLB-44

Fields, Osgood and Company DLB-49

Fifty Penguin Years Y-85

Figes, Eva 1932- DLB-14

Figuera, Angela 1902-1984 . . . . DLB-108

Filmer, Sir Robert 1586-1653 . . . . . . DLB-151

Filson, John circa 1753-1788 . . . . DLB-37

Finch, Anne, Countess of Winchilsea
1661-1720 . . . . DLB-95

Finch, Robert 1900- DLB-88

Findley, Timothy 1930- DLB-53

Finlay, Ian Hamilton 1925- DLB-40

Finley, Martha 1828-1909 . . . . DLB-42

Finn, Elizabeth Anne (McCaul)
1825-1921 . . . . DLB-166

Finney, Jack 1911- DLB-8

Finney, Walter Braden (see Finney, Jack)

Firbank, Ronald 1886-1926 . . . . DLB-36

Firmin, Giles 1615-1697 . . . . DLB-24

First Edition Library/Collectors'
Reprints, Inc. Y-91

First International F. Scott Fitzgerald
Conference Y-92

First Strauss "Livings" Awarded to Cynthia
Ozick and Raymond Carver
An Interview with Cynthia Ozick
An Interview with Raymond
Carver Y-83

Fischer, Karoline Auguste Fernandine
1764-1842 . . . . DLB-94

Fish, Stanley 1938- DLB-67

Fishacre, Richard 1205-1248 . . . . DLB-115

Fisher, Clay (see Allen, Henry W.)

Fisher, Dorothy Canfield
1879-1958 . . . . DLB-9, 102

Fisher, Leonard Everett 1924- DLB-61

Fisher, Roy 1930- DLB-40

Fisher, Rudolph 1897-1934 . . . . DLB-51, 102

Fisher, Sydney George 1856-1927 . . . . DLB-47

Fisher, Vardis 1895-1968 . . . . DLB-9

Fiske, John 1608-1677 . . . . DLB-24

Fiske, John 1842-1901 . . . . DLB-47, 64

Fitch, Thomas circa 1700-1774 . . . . . DLB-31

Fitch, William Clyde 1865-1909 . . . . . DLB-7

FitzGerald, Edward 1809-1883 . . . . . DLB-32

Fitzgerald, F. Scott
1896-1940 . . . . . DLB-4, 9, 86; Y-81; DS-1

Fitzgerald, Penelope 1916- DLB-14

Fitzgerald, Robert 1910-1985 . . . . Y-80

Fitzgerald, Thomas 1819-1891 . . . . . . DLB-23

Fitzgerald, Zelda Sayre 1900-1948 . . . . . . Y-84

Fitzhugh, Louise 1928-1974 . . . . DLB-52

Fitzhugh, William
circa 1651-1701 . . . . DLB-24

Flanagan, Thomas 1923- Y-80

Flanner, Hildegarde 1899-1987 . . . . . DLB-48

Flanner, Janet 1892-1978 . . . . DLB-4

Flaubert, Gustave 1821-1880 . . . . . . DLB-119

Flavin, Martin 1883-1967 . . . . DLB-9

Fleck, Konrad (flourished circa 1220)
. . . . DLB-138

Flecker, James Elroy 1884-1915 . . DLB-10, 19

Fleeson, Doris 1901-1970 . . . . DLB-29

Fleißer, Marieluise 1901-1974 . . . DLB-56, 124

Fleming, Ian 1908-1964 . . . . DLB-87

Fleming, Paul 1609-1640 . . . . DLB-164

The Fleshly School of Poetry and Other
Phenomena of the Day (1872), by Robert
Buchanan DLB-35

The Fleshly School of Poetry: Mr. D. G.
Rossetti (1871), by Thomas Maitland
(Robert Buchanan) DLB-35

Fletcher, Giles, the Elder
1546-1611 . . . . DLB-136

Fletcher, Giles, the Younger
1585 or 1586-1623 . . . . DLB-121

Cumulative Index

Fletcher, J. S. 1863-1935 .... DLB-70

Fletcher, John (see Beaumont, Francis)

Fletcher, John Gould 1886-1950 .. DLB-4, 45

Fletcher, Phineas 1582-1650 .... DLB-121

Flieg, Helmut (see Heym, Stefan)

Flint, F. S. 1885-1960 .... DLB-19

Flint, Timothy 1780-1840 .... DLB-734

Foix, J. V. 1893-1987 .... DLB-134

Foley, Martha (see Burnett, Whit, and
    Martha Foley)

Folger, Henry Clay 1857-1930 ..... DLB-140

Folio Society DLB-112

Follen, Eliza Lee (Cabot) 1787-1860 ...DLB-1

Follett, Ken 1949- Y-81, DLB-87

Follett Publishing Company DLB-46

Folsom, John West
    [publishing house] DLB-49

Fontane, Theodor 1819-1898 ...... DLB-129

Fonvisin, Denis Ivanovich
    1744 or 1745-1792 .... DLB-150

Foote, Horton 1916- DLB-26

Foote, Samuel 1721-1777 .... DLB-89

Foote, Shelby 1916- DLB-2, 17

Forbes, Calvin 1945- DLB-41

Forbes, Ester 1891-1967 .... DLB-22

Forbes and Company DLB-49

Force, Peter 1790-1868 .... DLB-30

Forché, Carolyn 1950- DLB-5

Ford, Charles Henri 1913- DLB-4, 48

Ford, Corey 1902-1969 .... DLB-11

Ford, Ford Madox
    1873-1939 .... DLB-34, 98, 162

Ford, Jesse Hill 1928- DLB-6

Ford, John 1586-? DLB-58

Ford, R. A. D. 1915- DLB-88

Ford, Worthington C. 1858-1941 ... DLB-47

Ford, J. B., and Company DLB-49

Fords, Howard, and Hulbert DLB-49

Foreman, Carl 1914-1984 .... DLB-26

Forester, Frank (see Herbert, Henry William)

Fornés, María Irene 1930- DLB-7

Forrest, Leon 1937- DLB-33

Forster, E. M.
    1879-1970 ....DLB-34, 98, 162; DS-10

Forster, Georg 1754-1794 .... DLB-94

Forster, John 1812-1876 .... DLB-144

Forster, Margaret 1938- DLB-155

Forsyth, Frederick 1938- DLB-87

Forten, Charlotte L. 1837-1914 ..... DLB-50

Fortini, Franco 1917- DLB-128

Fortune, T. Thomas 1856-1928 ..... DLB-23

Fosdick, Charles Austin
    1842-1915 .... DLB-42

Foster, Genevieve 1893-1979 .... DLB-61

Foster, Hannah Webster
    1758-1840 .... DLB-37

Foster, John 1648-1681 .... DLB-24

Foster, Michael 1904-1956 .... DLB-9

Foulis, Robert and Andrew / R. and A.
    [publishing house] DLB-154

Fouqué, Caroline de la Motte
    1774-1831 .... DLB-90

Fouqué, Friedrich de la Motte
    1777-1843 .... DLB-90

Four Essays on the Beat Generation,
    by John Clellon Holmes DLB-16

Four Seas Company DLB-46

Four Winds Press DLB-46

Fournier, Henri Alban (see Alain-Fournier)

Fowler and Wells Company DLB-49

Fowles, John 1926- DLB-14, 139

Fox, John, Jr. 1862 or
    1863-1919 ....DLB-9; DS-13

Fox, Paula 1923- DLB-52

Fox, Richard Kyle 1846-1922 .... DLB-79

Fox, William Price 1926- DLB-2; Y-81

Fox, Richard K.
    [publishing house] DLB-49

Foxe, John 1517-1587 .... DLB-132

Fraenkel, Michael 1896-1957 .... DLB-4

France, Anatole 1844-1924 .... DLB-123

France, Richard 1938- DLB-7

Francis, Convers 1795-1863 .... DLB-1

Francis, Dick 1920- DLB-87

Francis, Jeffrey, Lord 1773-1850 .... DLB-107

Francis, C. S. [publishing house] DLB-49

François 1863-1910 .... DLB-92

François, Louise von 1817-1893 .... DLB-129

Francke, Kuno 1855-1930 .... DLB-71

Frank, Bruno 1887-1945 .... DLB-118

Frank, Leonhard 1882-1961 ....DLB-56, 118

Frank, Melvin (see Panama, Norman)

Frank, Waldo 1889-1967 ....DLB-9, 63

Franken, Rose 1895?-1988 .... Y-84

Franklin, Benjamin
    1706-1790 .... DLB-24, 43, 73

Franklin, James 1697-1735 ....DLB-43

Franklin Library DLB-46

Frantz, Ralph Jules 1902-1979 ....DLB-4

Franzos, Karl Emil 1848-1904 ..... DLB-129

Fraser, G. S. 1915-1980 ....DLB-27

Frattini, Alberto 1922- DLB-128

Frau Ava ?-1127 ....DLB-148

Frayn, Michael 1933- DLB-13, 14

Frederic, Harold
    1856-1898 ....DLB-12, 23; DS-13

Freeling, Nicolas 1927- DLB-87

Freeman, Douglas Southall
    1886-1953 ....DLB-17

Freeman, Legh Richmond
    1842-1915 ....DLB-23

Freeman, Mary E. Wilkins
    1852-1930 .... DLB-12, 78

Freeman, R. Austin 1862-1943 ....DLB-70

Freidank circa 1170-circa 1233 .....DLB-138

Freiligrath, Ferdinand 1810-1876 ....DLB-133

French, Alice 1850-1934 ..... DLB-74; DS-13

French, David 1939- DLB-53

French, James [publishing house] DLB-49

French, Samuel [publishing house] ...DLB-49

Samuel French, Limited DLB-106

Freneau, Philip 1752-1832 ...... DLB-37, 43

Freni, Melo 1934- DLB-128

Freytag, Gustav 1816-1895 ....DLB-129

Fried, Erich 1921-1988 ....DLB-85

Friedman, Bruce Jay 1930- DLB-2, 28

Friedrich von Hausen
    circa 1171-1190 ....DLB-138

Friel, Brian 1929- DLB-13

Friend, Krebs 1895?-1967? DLB-4

Fries, Fritz Rudolf 1935- DLB-75

Fringe and Alternative Theater
    in Great Britain DLB-13

Frisch, Max 1911-1991 .... DLB-69, 124

Frischmuth, Barbara 1941- DLB-85

Fritz, Jean 1915- DLB-52

Fromentin, Eugene 1820-1876 ......DLB-123

From The Gay Science, by
    E. S. Dallas DLB-21

Frost, A. B. 1851-1928 ....DS-13

Frost, Robert 1874-1963 . . . . . . DLB-54; DS-7

Frothingham, Octavius Brooks
 1822-1895 . . . . DLB-1

Froude, James Anthony
 1818-1894 . . . . DLB-18, 57, 144

Fry, Christopher 1907- DLB-13

Fry, Roger 1866-1934 . . . . DS-10

Frye, Northrop 1912-1991 . . . . DLB-67, 68

Fuchs, Daniel
 1909-1993 . . . . DLB-9, 26, 28; Y-93

Fuentes, Carlos 1928- DLB-113

Fuertes, Gloria 1918- DLB-108

The Fugitives and the Agrarians:
 The First Exhibition Y-85

Fuller, Charles H., Jr. 1939- DLB-38

Fuller, Henry Blake 1857-1929 . . . . . . DLB-12

Fuller, John 1937- DLB-40

Fuller, Roy 1912-1991 . . . . DLB-15, 20

Fuller, Samuel 1912- DLB-26

Fuller, Sarah Margaret, Marchesa
 D'Ossoli 1810-1850 . . . . . . DLB-1, 59, 73

Fuller, Thomas 1608-1661 . . . . DLB-151

Fulton, Len 1934- Y-86

Fulton, Robin 1937- DLB-40

Furbank, P. N. 1920- DLB-155

Furman, Laura 1945- Y-86

Furness, Horace Howard
 1833-1912 . . . . DLB-64

Furness, William Henry 1802-1896 . . . DLB-1

Furthman, Jules 1888-1966 . . . . DLB-26

The Future of the Novel (1899), by
 Henry James DLB-18

Fyleman, Rose 1877-1957 . . . . DLB-160

G

The G. Ross Roy Scottish Poetry
 Collection at the University of
 South Carolina Y-89

Gaddis, William 1922- DLB-2

Gág, Wanda 1893-1946 . . . . DLB-22

Gagnon, Madeleine 1938- DLB-60

Gaine, Hugh 1726-1807 . . . . DLB-43

Gaine, Hugh [publishing house] DLB-49

Gaines, Ernest J.
 1933- DLB-2, 33, 152; Y-80

Gaiser, Gerd 1908-1976 . . . . DLB-69

Galarza, Ernesto 1905-1984 . . . . DLB-122

Galaxy Science Fiction Novels DLB-46

Gale, Zona 1874-1938 . . . . DLB-9, 78

Gall, Louise von 1815-1855 . . . . DLB-133

Gallagher, Tess 1943- DLB-120

Gallagher, Wes 1911- DLB-127

Gallagher, William Davis
 1808-1894 . . . . DLB-73

Gallant, Mavis 1922- DLB-53

Gallico, Paul 1897-1976 . . . . DLB-9

Galsworthy, John
 1867-1933 . . . . DLB-10, 34, 98, 162

Galt, John 1779-1839 . . . . DLB-99, 116

Galton, Sir Francis 1822-1911 . . . . . DLB-166

Galvin, Brendan 1938- DLB-5

Gambit DLB-46

Gamboa, Reymundo 1948- DLB-122

Gammer Gurton's Needle DLB-62

Gannett, Frank E. 1876-1957 . . . . . . DLB-29

Gaos, Vicente 1919-1980 . . . . DLB-134

García, Lionel G. 1935- DLB-82

García Lorca, Federico
 1898-1936 . . . . DLB-108

García Márquez, Gabriel
 1928- DLB-113

Gardam, Jane 1928- DLB-14, 161

Garden, Alexander
 circa 1685-1756 . . . . DLB-31

Gardiner, Margaret Power Farmer (see
 Blessington, Marguerite, Countess of)

Gardner, John 1933-1982 . . . . . . DLB-2; Y-82

Garfield, Leon 1921- DLB-161

Garis, Howard R. 1873-1962 . . . . . . DLB-22

Garland, Hamlin
 1860-1940 . . . . DLB-12, 71, 78

Garneau, Francis-Xavier
 1809-1866 . . . . DLB-99

Garneau, Hector de Saint-Denys
 1912-1943 . . . . DLB-88

Garneau, Michel 1939- DLB-53

Garner, Alan 1934- DLB-161

Garner, Hugh 1913-1979 . . . . DLB-68

Garnett, David 1892-1981 . . . . DLB-34

Garnett, Eve 1900-1991 . . . . DLB-160

Garraty, John A. 1920- DLB-17

Garrett, George
 1929- DLB-2, 5, 130, 152; Y-83

Garrick, David 1717-1779 . . . . DLB-84

Garrison, William Lloyd
 1805-1879 . . . . DLB-1, 43

Garro, Elena 1920- DLB-145

Garth, Samuel 1661-1719 . . . . DLB-95

Garve, Andrew 1908- DLB-87

Gary, Romain 1914-1980 . . . . DLB-83

Gascoigne, George 1539?-1577 . . . . . DLB-136

Gascoyne, David 1916- DLB-20

Gaskell, Elizabeth Cleghorn
 1810-1865 . . . . DLB-21, 144, 159

Gaspey, Thomas 1788-1871 . . . . DLB-116

Gass, William Howard 1924- DLB-2

Gates, Doris 1901- DLB-22

Gates, Henry Louis, Jr. 1950- DLB-67

Gates, Lewis E. 1860-1924 . . . . DLB-71

Gatto, Alfonso 1909-1976 . . . . DLB-114

Gautier, Théophile 1811-1872 . . . . . DLB-119

Gauvreau, Claude 1925-1971 . . . . . . DLB-88

The Gawain-Poet
 flourished circa 1350-1400 . . . . . DLB-146

Gay, Ebenezer 1696-1787 . . . . DLB-24

Gay, John 1685-1732 . . . . DLB-84, 95

The Gay Science (1866), by E. S. Dallas
 [excerpt] DLB-21

Gayarré, Charles E. A. 1805-1895 . . . DLB-30

Gaylord, Edward King
 1873-1974 . . . . DLB-127

Gaylord, Edward Lewis 1919- DLB-127

Gaylord, Charles
 [publishing house] DLB-49

Geddes, Gary 1940- DLB-60

Geddes, Virgil 1897- DLB-4

Gedeon (Georgii Andreevich Krinovsky)
 circa 1730-1763 . . . . DLB-150

Geibel, Emanuel 1815-1884 . . . . DLB-129

Geis, Bernard, Associates DLB-46

Geisel, Theodor Seuss
 1904-1991 . . . . DLB-61; Y-91

Gelb, Arthur 1924- DLB-103

Gelb, Barbara 1926- DLB-103

Gelber, Jack 1932- DLB-7

Gelinas, Gratien 1909- DLB-88

Gellert, Christian Füerchtegott
 1715-1769 . . . . DLB-97

Gellhorn, Martha 1908- Y-82

Gems, Pam 1925- DLB-13

A General Idea of the College of Mirania (1753),
 by William Smith [excerpts] DLB-31

Genet, Jean 1910-1986 . . . . DLB-72; Y-86

Genevoix, Maurice 1890-1980 . . . . . . DLB-65

Genovese, Eugene D. 1930- DLB-17

Gent, Peter 1942- Y-82

Geoffrey of Monmouth
circa 1100-1155 . . . . DLB-146

George, Henry 1839-1897 . . . . DLB-23

George, Jean Craighead 1919- DLB-52

Georgslied 896? DLB-148

Gerhardie, William 1895-1977 . . . . . . DLB-36

Gerhardt, Paul 1607-1676 . . . . DLB-164

Gérin, Winifred 1901-1981 . . . . DLB-155

Gérin-Lajoie, Antoine 1824-1882 . . . . DLB-99

German Drama 800-1280 . . . . DLB-138

German Drama from Naturalism
to Fascism: 1889-1933 . . . . DLB-118

German Literature and Culture from
Charlemagne to the Early Courtly
Period DLB-148

German Radio Play, The DLB-124

German Transformation from the Baroque
to the Enlightenment, The DLB-97

The Germanic Epic and Old English Heroic
Poetry: *Widseth, Waldere,* and *The
Fight at Finnsburg* DLB-146

Germanophilism, by Hans Kohn DLB-66

Gernsback, Hugo 1884-1967 . . . . DLB-8, 137

Gerould, Katharine Fullerton
1879-1944 . . . . DLB-78

Gerrish, Samuel [publishing house] . . DLB-49

Gerrold, David 1944- DLB-8

Gersonides 1288-1344 . . . . DLB-115

Gerstäcker, Friedrich 1816-1872 . . . DLB-129

Gerstenberg, Heinrich Wilhelm von
1737-1823 . . . . DLB-97

Gervinus, Georg Gottfried
1805-1871 . . . . DLB-133

Geßner, Salomon 1730-1788 . . . . DLB-97

Geston, Mark S. 1946- DLB-8

Al-Ghazali 1058-1111 . . . . DLB-115

Gibbon, Edward 1737-1794 . . . . DLB-104

Gibbon, John Murray 1875-1952 . . . . DLB-92

Gibbon, Lewis Grassic (see Mitchell,
James Leslie)

Gibbons, Floyd 1887-1939 . . . . DLB-25

Gibbons, Reginald 1947- DLB-120

Gibbons, William ?-? DLB-73

Gibson, Charles Dana 1867-1944 . . . . .DS-13

Gibson, Charles Dana 1867-1944 . . . . .DS-13

Gibson, Graeme 1934- DLB-53

Gibson, Margaret 1944- DLB-120

Gibson, Wilfrid 1878-1962 . . . . DLB-19

Gibson, William 1914- DLB-7

Gide, André 1869-1951 . . . . DLB-65

Giguère, Diane 1937- DLB-53

Giguère, Roland 1929- DLB-60

Gil de Biedma, Jaime 1929-1990 . . . . DLB-108

Gil-Albert, Juan 1906- DLB-134

Gilbert, Anthony 1899-1973 . . . . DLB-77

Gilbert, Michael 1912- DLB-87

Gilbert, Sandra M. 1936- DLB-120

Gilbert, Sir Humphrey
1537-1583 . . . . DLB-136

Gilchrist, Alexander
1828-1861 . . . . DLB-144

Gilchrist, Ellen 1935- DLB-130

Gilder, Jeannette L. 1849-1916 . . . . . . DLB-79

Gilder, Richard Watson
1844-1909 . . . . DLB-64, 79

Gildersleeve, Basil 1831-1924 . . . . DLB-71

Giles, Henry 1809-1882 . . . . DLB-64

Giles of Rome circa 1243-1316 . . . . . DLB-115

Gilfillan, George 1813-1878 . . . . DLB-144

Gill, Eric 1882-1940 . . . . DLB-98

Gill, William F., Company DLB-49

Gillespie, A. Lincoln, Jr.
1895-1950 . . . . DLB-4

Gilliam, Florence ?-? DLB-4

Gilliatt, Penelope 1932-1993 . . . . DLB-14

Gillott, Jacky 1939-1980 . . . . DLB-14

Gilman, Caroline H. 1794-1888 . . . DLB-3, 73

Gilman, W. and J.
[publishing house] DLB-49

Gilmer, Elizabeth Meriwether
1861-1951 . . . . DLB-29

Gilmer, Francis Walker
1790-1826 . . . . DLB-37

Gilroy, Frank D. 1925- DLB-7

Gimferrer, Pere (Pedro) 1945- DLB-134

Gingrich, Arnold 1903-1976 . . . . DLB-137

Ginsberg, Allen 1926- DLB-5, 16

Ginzkey, Franz Karl 1871-1963 . . . . . . DLB-81

Gioia, Dana 1950- DLB-120

Giono, Jean 1895-1970 . . . . DLB-72

Giotti, Virgilio 1885-1957 . . . . DLB-114

Giovanni, Nikki 1943- DLB-5, 41

Gipson, Lawrence Henry
1880-1971 . . . . .DLB-17

Girard, Rodolphe 1879-1956 . . . . . . .DLB-92

Giraudoux, Jean 1882-1944 . . . . .DLB-65

Gissing, George 1857-1903 . . . . . DLB-18, 135

Giudici, Giovanni 1924- DLB-128

Giuliani, Alfredo 1924- DLB-128

Gladstone, William Ewart
1809-1898 . . . . .DLB-57

Glaeser, Ernst 1902-1963 . . . . .DLB-69

Glanville, Brian 1931- DLB-15, 139

Glapthorne, Henry 1610-1643? DLB-58

Glasgow, Ellen 1873-1945 . . . . DLB-9, 12

Glaspell, Susan 1876-1948 . . . . . DLB-7, 9, 78

Glass, Montague 1877-1934 . . . . .DLB-11

Glassco, John 1909-1981 . . . . .DLB-68

Glauser, Friedrich 1896-1938 . . . . . . .DLB-56

F. Gleason's Publishing Hall DLB-49

Gleim, Johann Wilhelm Ludwig
1719-1803 . . . . .DLB-97

Glendinning, Victoria 1937- DLB-155

Glover, Richard 1712-1785 . . . . .DLB-95

Glück, Louise 1943- DLB-5

Glyn, Elinor 1864-1943 . . . . .DLB-153

Gobineau, Joseph-Arthur de
1816-1882 . . . . .DLB-123

Godbout, Jacques 1933- DLB-53

Goddard, Morrill 1865-1937 . . . . . . .DLB-25

Goddard, William 1740-1817 . . . . . . .DLB-43

Godden, Rumer 1907- DLB-161

Godey, Louis A. 1804-1878 . . . . .DLB-73

Godey and McMichael DLB-49

Godfrey, Dave 1938- DLB-60

Godfrey, Thomas 1736-1763 . . . . . . .DLB-31

Godine, David R., Publisher DLB-46

Godkin, E. L. 1831-1902 . . . . .DLB-79

Godolphin, Sidney 1610-1643 . . . . . .DLB-126

Godwin, Gail 1937- DLB-6

Godwin, Mary Jane Clairmont
1766-1841 . . . . .DLB-163

Godwin, Parke 1816-1904 . . . . DLB-3, 64

Godwin, William
1756-1836 . . . .DLB-39, 104, 142, 158, 163

Godwin, M. J., and Company DLB-154

Goering, Reinhard 1887-1936 . . . . . .DLB-118

Goes, Albrecht 1908-　..........DLB-69

Goethe, Johann Wolfgang von
1749-1832　..................DLB-94

Goetz, Curt 1888-1960　...........DLB-124

Goffe, Thomas circa 1592-1629　......DLB-58

Goffstein, M. B. 1940-　...........DLB-61

Gogarty, Oliver St. John
1878-1957　................DLB-15, 19

Goines, Donald 1937-1974　.........DLB-33

Gold, Herbert 1924-　........DLB-2; Y-81

Gold, Michael 1893-1967　........DLB-9, 28

Goldbarth, Albert 1948-　........DLB-120

Goldberg, Dick 1947-　............DLB-7

Golden Cockerel Press　...........DLB-112

Golding, Arthur 1536-1606　.......DLB-136

Golding, William 1911-1993　....DLB-15, 100

Goldman, William 1931-　........DLB-44

Goldsmith, Oliver
1730?-1774　...DLB-39, 89, 104, 109, 142

Goldsmith, Oliver 1794-1861　.......DLB-99

Goldsmith Publishing Company　.....DLB-46

Gollancz, Victor, Limited　.........DLB-112

Gómez-Quiñones, Juan 1942-　.....DLB-122

Gomme, Laurence James
[publishing house]　.............DLB-46

Goncourt, Edmond de 1822-1896　...DLB-123

Goncourt, Jules de 1830-1870　......DLB-123

Gonzales, Rodolfo "Corky"
1928-　.....................DLB-122

González, Angel 1925-　..........DLB-108

Gonzalez, Genaro 1949-　........DLB-122

Gonzalez, Ray 1952-　...........DLB-122

González de Mireles, Jovita
1899-1983　.................DLB-122

González-T., César A. 1931-　......DLB-82

Goodbye, Gutenberg? A Lecture at
the New York Public Library,
18 April 1995　.................Y-95

Goodison, Lorna 1947-　.........DLB-157

Goodman, Paul 1911-1972　........DLB-130

The Goodman Theatre　...........DLB-7

Goodrich, Frances 1891-1984 and
Hackett, Albert 1900-　........DLB-26

Goodrich, Samuel Griswold
1793-1860　.............DLB-1, 42, 73

Goodrich, S. G. [publishing house]　...DLB-49

Goodspeed, C. E., and Company　....DLB-49

Goodwin, Stephen 1943-　.........Y-82

Googe, Barnabe 1540-1594　.......DLB-132

Gookin, Daniel 1612-1687　........DLB-24

Gordon, Caroline
1895-1981　.........DLB-4, 9, 102; Y-81

Gordon, Giles 1940-　........DLB-14, 139

Gordon, Lyndall 1941-　.........DLB-155

Gordon, Mary 1949-　........DLB-6; Y-81

Gordone, Charles 1925-　..........DLB-7

Gore, Catherine 1800-1861　.......DLB-116

Gorey, Edward 1925-　...........DLB-61

Görres, Joseph 1776-1848　.........DLB-90

Gosse, Edmund 1849-1928　.....DLB-57, 144

Gotlieb, Phyllis 1926-　...........DLB-88

Gottfried von Straßburg
died before 1230　.............DLB-138

Gotthelf, Jeremias 1797-1854　......DLB-133

Gottschalk circa 804/808-869　......DLB-148

Gottsched, Johann Christoph
1700-1766　..................DLB-97

Götz, Johann Nikolaus
1721-1781　..................DLB-97

Gould, Wallace 1882-1940　........DLB-54

Govoni, Corrado 1884-1965　.......DLB-114

Gower, John circa 1330-1408　....:.DLB-146

Goyen, William 1915-1983　.....DLB-2; Y-83

Goytisolo, José Augustín 1928-　...DLB-134

Gozzano, Guido 1883-1916　.......DLB-114

Grabbe, Christian Dietrich
1801-1836　..................DLB-133

Gracq, Julien 1910-　...........DLB-83

Grady, Henry W. 1850-1889　.......DLB-23

Graf, Oskar Maria 1894-1967　.......DLB-56

Graf Rudolf between circa 1170
and circa 1185　..............DLB-148

Graham, George Rex 1813-1894　....DLB-73

Graham, Gwethalyn 1913-1965　.....DLB-88

Graham, Jorie 1951-　...........DLB-120

Graham, Katharine 1917-　.......DLB-127

Graham, Lorenz 1902-1989　........DLB-76

Graham, Philip 1915-1963　........DLB-127

Graham, R. B. Cunninghame
1852-1936　...............DLB-98, 135

Graham, Shirley 1896-1977　.......DLB-76

Graham, W. S. 1918-　...........DLB-20

Graham, William H.
[publishing house]　............DLB-49

Graham, Winston 1910-　........DLB-77

Grahame, Kenneth
1859-1932　...............DLB-34, 141

Grainger, Martin Allerdale
1874-1941　..................DLB-92

Gramatky, Hardie 1907-1979　.......DLB-22

Grand, Sarah 1854-1943　..........DLB-135

Grandbois, Alain 1900-1975　........DLB-92

Grange, John circa 1556-?　........DLB-136

Granich, Irwin (see Gold, Michael)

Grant, Duncan 1885-1978　...........DS-10

Grant, George 1918-1988　..........DLB-88

Grant, George Monro 1835-1902　....DLB-99

Grant, Harry J. 1881-1963　.........DLB-29

Grant, James Edward 1905-1966　.....DLB-26

Grass, Günter 1927-　........DLB-75, 124

Grasty, Charles H. 1863-1924　.......DLB-25

Grau, Shirley Ann 1929-　..........DLB-2

Graves, John 1920-　.................Y-83

Graves, Richard 1715-1804　.........DLB-39

Graves, Robert
1895-1985　..........DLB-20, 100; Y-85

Gray, Asa 1810-1888　..............DLB-1

Gray, David 1838-1861　............DLB-32

Gray, Simon 1936-　..............DLB-13

Gray, Thomas 1716-1771　.........DLB-109

Grayson, William J. 1788-1863　....DLB-3, 64

The Great Bibliographers Series　........Y-93

The Great War and the Theater, 1914-1918
[Great Britain]　.................DLB-10

Greeley, Horace 1811-1872　.......DLB-3, 43

Green, Adolph (see Comden, Betty)

Green, Duff 1791-1875　............DLB-43

Green, Gerald 1922-　............DLB-28

Green, Henry 1905-1973　..........DLB-15

Green, Jonas 1712-1767　..........DLB-31

Green, Joseph 1706-1780　.........DLB-31

Green, Julien 1900-　...........DLB-4, 72

Green, Paul 1894-1981　.......DLB-7, 9; Y-81

Green, T. and S.
[publishing house]　...........DLB-49

Green, Timothy
[publishing house]　...........DLB-49

Greenaway, Kate 1846-1901　.......DLB-141

Greenberg: Publisher　.............DLB-46

Green Tiger Press　................DLB-46

Greene, Asa 1789-1838　...........DLB-11

Greene, Benjamin H.
[publishing house] DLB-49

Greene, Graham 1904-1991
. . . . DLB-13, 15, 77, 100, 162; Y-85, Y-91

Greene, Robert 1558-1592 . . . . . DLB-62, 167

Greenhow, Robert 1800-1854 . . . . DLB-30

Greenough, Horatio 1805-1852 . . . . . . .DLB-1

Greenwell, Dora 1821-1882 . . . . DLB-35

Greenwillow Books DLB-46

Greenwood, Grace (see Lippincott, Sara Jane
Clarke)

Greenwood, Walter 1903-1974 . . . . . DLB-10

Greer, Ben 1948- DLB-6

Greflinger, Georg 1620?-1677 . . . . . DLB-164

Greg, W. R. 1809-1881 . . . . DLB-55

Gregg Press DLB-46

Gregory, Isabella Augusta
Persse, Lady 1852-1932 . . . . DLB-10

Gregory, Horace 1898-1982 . . . . DLB-48

Gregory of Rimini
circa 1300-1358 . . . . DLB-115

Gregynog Press DLB-112

Grenfell, Wilfred Thomason
1865-1940 . . . . DLB-92

Greve, Felix Paul (see Grove, Frederick Philip)

Greville, Fulke, First Lord Brooke
1554-1628 . . . . DLB-62

Grey, Lady Jane 1537-1554 . . . . DLB-132

Grey Owl 1888-1938 . . . . DLB-92

Grey, Zane 1872-1939 . . . . .DLB-9

Grey Walls Press DLB-112

Grier, Eldon 1917- DLB-88

Grieve, C. M. (see MacDiarmid, Hugh)

Griffin, Gerald 1803-1840 . . . . DLB-159

Griffith, Elizabeth 1727?-1793 . . . DLB-39, 89

Griffiths, Trevor 1935- DLB-13

Griffiths, Ralph
[publishing house] DLB-154

Griggs, S. C., and Company DLB-49

Griggs, Sutton Elbert 1872-1930 . . . . DLB-50

Grignon, Claude-Henri 1894-1976 . . DLB-68

Grigson, Geoffrey 1905- DLB-27

Grillparzer, Franz 1791-1872 . . . . . . DLB-133

Grimald, Nicholas
circa 1519-circa 1562 . . . . DLB-136

Grimké, Angelina Weld
1880-1958 . . . . DLB-50, 54

Grimm, Hans 1875-1959 . . . . DLB-66

Grimm, Jacob 1785-1863 . . . . DLB-90

Grimm, Wilhelm 1786-1859 . . . . DLB-90

Grindal, Edmund
1519 or 1520-1583 . . . . DLB-132

Griswold, Rufus Wilmot
1815-1857 . . . . DLB-3, 59

Gross, Milt 1895-1953 . . . . DLB-11

Grosset and Dunlap DLB-49

Grossman Publishers DLB-46

Grosseteste, Robert
circa 1160-1253 . . . . DLB-115

Grosvenor, Gilbert H. 1875-1966 . . . . DLB-91

Groth, Klaus 1819-1899 . . . . DLB-129

Groulx, Lionel 1878-1967 . . . . DLB-68

Grove, Frederick Philip 1879-1949 . . . DLB-92

Grove Press DLB-46

Grubb, Davis 1919-1980 . . . . DLB-6

Gruelle, Johnny 1880-1938 . . . . DLB-22

Grymeston, Elizabeth
before 1563-before 1604 . . . . DLB-136

Gryphius, Andreas 1616-1664 . . . . . . DLB-164

Guare, John 1938- DLB-7

Guerra, Tonino 1920- DLB-128

Guest, Barbara 1920- DLB-5

Guèvremont, Germaine
1893-1968 . . . . DLB-68

Guidacci, Margherita 1921-1992 . . . . DLB-128

Guide to the Archives of Publishers, Journals,
and Literary Agents in North American
Libraries .Y-93

Guillén, Jorge 1893-1984 . . . . DLB-108

Guilloux, Louis 1899-1980 . . . . DLB-72

Guilpin, Everard
circa 1572-after 1608? DLB-136

Guiney, Louise Imogen 1861-1920 . . . DLB-54

Guiterman, Arthur 1871-1943 . . . . . . DLB-11

Günderrode, Caroline von
1780-1806 . . . . DLB-90

Gundulić, Ivan 1589-1638 . . . . DLB-147

Gunn, Bill 1934-1989 . . . . DLB-38

Gunn, James E. 1923- DLB-8

Gunn, Neil M. 1891-1973 . . . . DLB-15

Gunn, Thom 1929- DLB-27

Gunnars, Kristjana 1948- DLB-60

Gurik, Robert 1932- DLB-60

Gustafson, Ralph 1909- DLB-88

Gütersloh, Albert Paris 1887-1973 . . . DLB-81

Guthrie, A. B., Jr. 1901- DLB-6

Guthrie, Ramon 1896-1973 . . . . .DLB-4

The Guthrie Theater DLB-7

Gutzkow, Karl 1811-1878 . . . . .DLB-133

Guy, Ray 1939- DLB-60

Guy, Rosa 1925- DLB-33

Guyot, Arnold 1807-1884 . . . . DS-13

Gwynne, Erskine 1898-1948 . . . . .DLB-4

Gyles, John 1680-1755 . . . . .DLB-99

Gysin, Brion 1916- DLB-16

H

H. D. (see Doolittle, Hilda)

Habington, William 1605-1654 . . . . .DLB-126

Hacker, Marilyn 1942- DLB-120

Hackett, Albert (see Goodrich, Frances)

Hacks, Peter 1928- DLB-124

Hadas, Rachel 1948- DLB-120

Hadden, Briton 1898-1929 . . . . .DLB-91

Hagelstange, Rudolf 1912-1984 . . . . . .DLB-69

Haggard, H. Rider 1856-1925 . . . .DLB-70, 156

Haggard, William 1907-1993 . . . . Y-93

Hahn-Hahn, Ida Gräfin von
1805-1880 . . . . .DLB-133

Haig-Brown, Roderick 1908-1976 . . . .DLB-88

Haight, Gordon S. 1901-1985 . . . . . . .DLB-103

Hailey, Arthur 1920- DLB-88; Y-82

Haines, John 1924- DLB-5

Hake, Edward
flourished 1566-1604 . . . . .DLB-136

Hake, Thomas Gordon 1809-1895 . . .DLB-32

Hakluyt, Richard 1552?-1616 . . . . . .DLB-136

Halbe, Max 1865-1944 . . . . .DLB-118

Haldane, J. B. S. 1892-1964 . . . . . . .DLB-160

Haldeman, Joe 1943- DLB-8

Haldeman-Julius Company DLB-46

Hale, E. J., and Son DLB-49

Hale, Edward Everett
1822-1909 . . . . DLB-1, 42, 74

Hale, Kathleen 1898- DLB-160

Hale, Leo Thomas (see Ebon)

Hale, Lucretia Peabody
1820-1900 . . . . .DLB-42

Hale, Nancy 1908-1988 . . . . DLB-86; Y-80, 88

Hale, Sarah Josepha (Buell)
1788-1879 . . . . DLB-1, 42, 73

Hales, John 1584-1656 ....DLB-151

Haley, Alex 1921-1992 ....DLB-38

Haliburton, Thomas Chandler
1796-1865 ....DLB-11, 99

Hall, Anna Maria 1800-1881 ....DLB-159

Hall, Donald 1928- DLB-5

Hall, Edward 1497-1547 ....DLB-132

Hall, James 1793-1868 ....DLB-73, 74

Hall, Joseph 1574-1656 ....DLB-121, 151

Hall, Samuel [publishing house] DLB-49

Hallam, Arthur Henry 1811-1833 ....DLB-32

Halleck, Fitz-Greene 1790-1867 ....DLB-3

Hallmark Editions DLB-46

Halper, Albert 1904-1984 ....DLB-9

Halperin, John William 1941- DLB-111

Halstead, Murat 1829-1908 ....DLB-23

Hamann, Johann Georg 1730-1788 ...DLB-97

Hamburger, Michael 1924- DLB-27

Hamilton, Alexander 1712-1756 .....DLB-31

Hamilton, Alexander 1755?-1804 ....DLB-37

Hamilton, Cicely 1872-1952 ....DLB-10

Hamilton, Edmond 1904-1977 ....DLB-8

Hamilton, Elizabeth
1758-1816 ....DLB-116, 158

Hamilton, Gail (see Corcoran, Barbara)

Hamilton, Ian 1938- DLB-40, 155

Hamilton, Patrick 1904-1962 ....DLB-10

Hamilton, Virginia 1936- DLB-33, 52

Hamilton, Hamish, Limited DLB-112

Hammett, Dashiell 1894-1961 .... DS-6

Dashiell Hammett:
An Appeal in *TAC* Y-91

Hammon, Jupiter 1711-died between
1790 and 1806 ....DLB-31, 50

Hammond, John ?-1663 ....DLB-24

Hamner, Earl 1923- DLB-6

Hampton, Christopher 1946- DLB-13

Handel-Mazzetti, Enrica von
1871-1955 ....DLB-81

Handke, Peter 1942- DLB-85, 124

Handlin, Oscar 1915- DLB-17

Hankin, St. John 1869-1909 ....DLB-10

Hanley, Clifford 1922- DLB-14

Hannah, Barry 1942- DLB-6

Hannay, James 1827-1873 ....DLB-21

Hansberry, Lorraine 1930-1965 ...DLB-7, 38

Hapgood, Norman 1868-1937 ...... DLB-91

Harcourt Brace Jovanovich DLB-46

Hardenberg, Friedrich von (see Novalis)

Harding, Walter 1917- DLB-111

Hardwick, Elizabeth 1916- DLB-6

Hardy, Thomas 1840-1928 ... DLB-18, 19, 135

Hare, Cyril 1900-1958 .... DLB-77

Hare, David 1947- DLB-13

Hargrove, Marion 1919- DLB-11

Häring, Georg Wilhelm Heinrich (see Alexis,
Willibald)

Harington, Donald 1935- DLB-152

Harington, Sir John 1560-1612 ..... DLB-136

Harjo, Joy 1951- DLB-120

Harlow, Robert 1923- DLB-60

Harman, Thomas
flourished 1566-1573 .... DLB-136

Harness, Charles L. 1915- DLB-8

Harnett, Cynthia 1893-1981 .... DLB-161

Harper, Fletcher 1806-1877 .... DLB-79

Harper, Frances Ellen Watkins
1825-1911 .... DLB-50

Harper, Michael S. 1938- DLB-41

Harper and Brothers DLB-49

Harraden, Beatrice 1864-1943 ..... DLB-153

Harrap, George G., and Company
Limited DLB-112

Harriot, Thomas 1560-1621 .... DLB-136

Harris, Benjamin ?-circa 1720 .... DLB-42, 43

Harris, Christie 1907- DLB-88

Harris, Frank 1856-1931 .... DLB-156

Harris, George Washington
1814-1869 .... DLB-3, 11

Harris, Joel Chandler
1848-1908 ....DLB-11, 23, 42, 78, 91

Harris, Mark 1922- DLB-2; Y-80

Harris, Wilson 1921- DLB-117

Harrison, Charles Yale
1898-1954 .... DLB-68

Harrison, Frederic 1831-1923 .... DLB-57

Harrison, Harry 1925- DLB-8

Harrison, Jim 1937- Y-82

Harrison, Mary St. Leger Kingsley (see Malet,
Lucas)

Harrison, Paul Carter 1936- DLB-38

Harrison, Susan Frances
1859-1935 .... DLB-99

Harrison, Tony 1937- DLB-40

Harrison, William 1535-1593 ......DLB-136

Harrison, James P., Company DLB-49

Harrisse, Henry 1829-1910 ....DLB-47

Harsdörffer, Georg Philipp
1607-1658 ....DLB-164

Harsent, David 1942- DLB-40

Hart, Albert Bushnell 1854-1943 .....DLB-17

Hart, Julia Catherine 1796-1867 .....DLB-99

The Lorenz Hart Centenary Y-95

Hart, Moss 1904-1961 ....DLB-7

Hart, Oliver 1723-1795 ....DLB-31

Hart-Davis, Rupert, Limited DLB-112

Harte, Bret 1836-1902 ... DLB-12, 64, 74, 79

Harte, Edward Holmead 1922- ...DLB-127

Harte, Houston Harriman
1927- DLB-127

Hartlaub, Felix 1913-1945 ....DLB-56

Hartlebon, Otto Erich
1864-1905 ....DLB-118

Hartley, L. P. 1895-1972 ....DLB-15, 139

Hartley, Marsden 1877-1943 ....DLB-54

Hartling, Peter 1933- DLB-75

Hartman, Geoffrey H. 1929- DLB-67

Hartmann, Sadakichi 1867-1944 .....DLB-54

Hartmann von Aue
circa 1160-circa 1205 ....DLB-138

Harvey, Gabriel 1550?-1631 ....DLB-167

Harvey, Jean-Charles 1891-1967 .....DLB-88

Harvill Press Limited DLB-112

Harwood, Lee 1939- DLB-40

Harwood, Ronald 1934- DLB-13

Haskins, Charles Homer
1870-1937 ....DLB-47

Hass, Robert 1941- DLB-105

The Hatch-Billops Collection DLB-76

Hathaway, William 1944- DLB-120

Hauff, Wilhelm 1802-1827 ....DLB-90

A Haughty and Proud Generation (1922),
by Ford Madox Hueffer DLB-36

Hauptmann, Carl
1858-1921 ....DLB-66, 118

Hauptmann, Gerhart
1862-1946 ....DLB-66, 118

Hauser, Marianne 1910- Y-83

Hawes, Stephen
1475?-before 1529 ....DLB-132

Hawker, Robert Stephen 1803-1875 .... DLB-32

Hawkes, John 1925- DLB-2, 7; Y-80

Hawkesworth, John 1720-1773 .... DLB-142

Hawkins, Sir Anthony Hope (see Hope, Anthony)

Hawkins, Sir John 1719-1789 .... DLB-104, 142

Hawkins, Walter Everette 1883-? ... DLB-50

Hawthorne, Nathaniel 1804-1864 .... DLB-1, 74

Hay, John 1838-1905 .... DLB-12, 47

Hayden, Robert 1913-1980 .... DLB-5, 76

Haydon, Benjamin Robert 1786-1846 .... DLB-110

Hayes, John Michael 1919- DLB-26

Hayley, William 1745-1820 .... DLB-93, 142

Haym, Rudolf 1821-1901 .... DLB-129

Hayman, Robert 1575-1629 .... DLB-99

Hayman, Ronald 1932- DLB-155

Hayne, Paul Hamilton 1830-1886 .... DLB-3, 64, 79

Hays, Mary 1760-1843 .... DLB-142, 158

Haywood, Eliza 1693?-1756 .... DLB-39

Hazard, Willis P. [publishing house] ...DLB-49

Hazlitt, William 1778-1830 .... DLB-110, 158

Hazzard, Shirley 1931- Y-82

Head, Bessie 1937-1986 .... DLB-117

Headley, Joel T. 1813-1897 .. DLB-30; DS-13

Heaney, Seamus 1939- DLB-40

Heard, Nathan C. 1936- DLB-33

Hearn, Lafcadio 1850-1904 ...... DLB-12, 78

Hearne, John 1926- DLB-117

Hearne, Samuel 1745-1792 .... DLB-99

Hearst, William Randolph 1863-1951 .... DLB-25

Hearst, William Randolph, Jr 1908-1993 .... DLB-127

Heath, Catherine 1924- DLB-14

Heath, Roy A. K. 1926- DLB-117

Heath-Stubbs, John 1918- DLB-27

Heavysege, Charles 1816-1876 ...... DLB-99

Hebbel, Friedrich 1813-1863 ...... DLB-129

Hebel, Johann Peter 1760-1826 ..... DLB-90

Hébert, Anne 1916- DLB-68

Hébert, Jacques 1923- DLB-53

Hecht, Anthony 1923- DLB-5

Hecht, Ben 1894-1964 .... DLB-7, 9, 25, 26, 28, 86

Hecker, Isaac Thomas 1819-1888 ..... DLB-1

Hedge, Frederic Henry 1805-1890 ....DLB-1, 59

Hefner, Hugh M. 1926- DLB-137

Hegel, Georg Wilhelm Friedrich 1770-1831 .... DLB-90

Heidish, Marcy 1947- Y-82

Heißenbüttel 1921- DLB-75

Hein, Christoph 1944- DLB-124

Heine, Heinrich 1797-1856 .... DLB-90

Heinemann, Larry 1944- DS-9

Heinemann, William, Limited DLB-112

Heinlein, Robert A. 1907-1988 .... DLB-8

Heinrich Julius of Brunswick 1564-1613 .... DLB-164

Heinrich von dem Türlîn flourished circa 1230 .... DLB-138

Heinrich von Melk flourished after 1160 .... DLB-148

Heinrich von Veldeke circa 1145-circa 1190 .... DLB-138

Heinrich, Willi 1920- DLB-75

Heiskell, John 1872-1972 .... DLB-127

Heinse, Wilhelm 1746-1803 .... DLB-94

Hejinian, Lyn 1941- DLB-165

Heliand circa 850 .... DLB-148

Heller, Joseph 1923- DLB-2, 28; Y-80

Heller, Michael 1937- DLB-165

Hellman, Lillian 1906-1984 ..... DLB-7; Y-84

Hellwig, Johann 1609-1674 .... DLB-164

Helprin, Mark 1947- Y-85

Helwig, David 1938- DLB-60

Hemans, Felicia 1793-1835 .... DLB-96

Hemingway, Ernest 1899-1961 ....DLB-4, 9, 102; Y-81, 87; DS-1

Hemingway: Twenty-Five Years Later Y-85

Hémon, Louis 1880-1913 .... DLB-92

Hemphill, Paul 1936- Y-87

Hénault, Gilles 1920- DLB-88

Henchman, Daniel 1689-1761 .... DLB-24

Henderson, Alice Corbin 1881-1949 .... DLB-54

Henderson, Archibald 1877-1963 .... DLB-103

Henderson, David 1942- DLB-41

Henderson, George Wylie 1904- DLB-51

Henderson, Zenna 1917-1983 .... DLB-8

Henisch, Peter 1943- DLB-85

Henley, Beth 1952- Y-86

Henley, William Ernest 1849-1903 .... DLB-19

Henniker, Florence 1855-1923 ..... DLB-135

Henry, Alexander 1739-1824 .... DLB-99

Henry, Buck 1930- DLB-26

Henry VIII of England 1491-1547 .... DLB-132

Henry, Marguerite 1902- DLB-22

Henry, O. (see Porter, William Sydney)

Henry of Ghent circa 1217-1229 - 1293 .... DLB-115

Henry, Robert Selph 1889-1970 ..... DLB-17

Henry, Will (see Allen, Henry W.)

Henryson, Robert 1420s or 1430s-circa 1505 ...... DLB-146

Henschke, Alfred (see Klabund)

Hensley, Sophie Almon 1866-1946 ...DLB-99

Henty, G. A. 1832?-1902 ...... DLB-18, 141

Hentz, Caroline Lee 1800-1856 ....DLB-3

Herbert, Alan Patrick 1890-1971 .....DLB-10

Herbert, Edward, Lord, of Cherbury 1582-1648 .... DLB-121, 151

Herbert, Frank 1920-1986 ....DLB-8

Herbert, George 1593-1633 ....DLB-126

Herbert, Henry William 1807-1858 .... DLB-3, 73

Herbert, John 1926- DLB-53

Herbert, Mary Sidney, Countess of Pembroke (see Sidney, Mary)

Herbst, Josephine 1892-1969 ....DLB-9

Herburger, Gunter 1932- DLB-75, 124

Hercules, Frank E. M. 1917- DLB-33

Herder, Johann Gottfried 1744-1803 .... DLB-97

Herder, B., Book Company DLB-49

Herford, Charles Harold 1853-1931 .... DLB-149

Hergesheimer, Joseph 1880-1954 .... DLB-9, 102

Heritage Press DLB-46

Hermann the Lame 1013-1054 ..... DLB-148

Hermes, Johann Timotheus 1738-1821 .... DLB-97

Hermlin, Stephan 1915- DLB-69

Hernández, Alfonso C. 1938- DLB-122

Hernández, Inés 1947- DLB-122

Hernández, Miguel 1910-1942 ......DLB-134

Hernton, Calvin C. 1932- DLB-38

"The Hero as Man of Letters: Johnson,
Rousseau, Burns" (1841), by Thomas
Carlyle [excerpt] DLB-57

The Hero as Poet. Dante; Shakspeare (1841),
by Thomas Carlyle DLB-32

Heron, Robert 1764-1807 ....DLB-142

Herrera, Juan Felipe 1948- DLB-122

Herrick, Robert 1591-1674 ....DLB-126

Herrick, Robert 1868-1938 .... DLB-9, 12, 78

Herrick, William 1915- Y-83

Herrick, E. R., and Company DLB-49

Herrmann, John 1900-1959 ....DLB-4

Hersey, John 1914-1993 ....DLB-6

Hertel, François 1905-1985 ....DLB-68

Hervé-Bazin, Jean Pierre Marie (see Bazin,
Hervé)

Hervey, John, Lord 1696-1743 .....DLB-101

Herwig, Georg 1817-1875 ....DLB-133

Herzog, Emile Salomon Wilhelm (see Maurois,
André)

Hesse, Hermann 1877-1962 ....DLB-66

Hewat, Alexander
circa 1743-circa 1824 ....DLB-30

Hewitt, John 1907- DLB-27

Hewlett, Maurice 1861-1923 ....DLB-34, 156

Heyen, William 1940- DLB-5

Heyer, Georgette 1902-1974 ....DLB-77

Heym, Stefan 1913- DLB-69

Heyse, Paul 1830-1914 ....DLB-129

Heytesbury, William
circa 1310-1372 or 1373 ....DLB-115

Heyward, Dorothy 1890-1961 ....DLB-7

Heyward, DuBose
1885-1940 .... DLB-7, 9, 45

Heywood, John 1497?-1580? DLB-136

Heywood, Thomas
1573 or 1574-1641 ....DLB-62

Hibbs, Ben 1901-1975 ....DLB-137

Hichens, Robert S. 1864-1950 ......DLB-153

Hickman, William Albert
1877-1957 ....DLB-92

Hidalgo, José Luis 1919-1947 ......DLB-108

Hiebert, Paul 1892-1987 ....DLB-68

Hierro, José 1922- DLB-108

Higgins, Aidan 1927- DLB-14

Higgins, Colin 1941-1988 ....DLB-26

Higgins, George V. 1939- DLB-2; Y-81

Higginson, Thomas Wentworth
1823-1911 .... DLB-1, 64

Highwater, Jamake 1942?- ... DLB-52; Y-85

Hijuelos, Oscar 1951- DLB-145

Hildegard von Bingen
1098-1179 .... DLB-148

Das Hildesbrandslied circa 820 .... DLB-148

Hildesheimer, Wolfgang
1916-1991 .... DLB-69, 124

Hildreth, Richard
1807-1865 .... DLB-1, 30, 59

Hill, Aaron 1685-1750 .... DLB-84

Hill, Geoffrey 1932- DLB-40

Hill, "Sir" John 1714?-1775 .... DLB-39

Hill, Leslie 1880-1960 .... DLB-51

Hill, Susan 1942- DLB-14, 139

Hill, Walter 1942- DLB-44

Hill and Wang DLB-46

Hill, George M., Company DLB-49

Hill, Lawrence, and Company,
Publishers DLB-46

Hillberry, Conrad 1928- DLB-120

Hilliard, Gray and Company DLB-49

Hills, Lee 1906- DLB-127

Hillyer, Robert 1895-1961 .... DLB-54

Hilton, James 1900-1954 .... DLB-34, 77

Hilton, Walter died 1396 .... DLB-146

Hilton and Company DLB-49

Himes, Chester
1909-1984 .... DLB-2, 76, 143

Hine, Daryl 1936- DLB-60

Hingley, Ronald 1920- DLB-155

Hinojosa-Smith, Rolando
1929- DLB-82

Hippel, Theodor Gottlieb von
1741-1796 .... DLB-97

Hirsch, E. D., Jr. 1928- DLB-67

Hirsch, Edward 1950- DLB-120

The History of the Adventures of Joseph Andrews
(1742), by Henry Fielding
[excerpt] DLB-39

Hoagland, Edward 1932- DLB-6

Hoagland, Everett H., III 1942- ... DLB-41

Hoban, Russell 1925- DLB-52

Hobbes, Thomas 1588-1679 .... DLB-151

Hobby, Oveta 1905- DLB-127

Hobby, William 1878-1964 ....DLB-127

Hobsbaum, Philip 1932- DLB-40

Hobson, Laura Z. 1900- DLB-28

Hoby, Thomas 1530-1566 ....DLB-132

Hoccleve, Thomas
circa 1368-circa 1437 ....DLB-146

Hochhuth, Rolf 1931- DLB-124

Hochman, Sandra 1936- DLB-5

Hodder and Stoughton, Limited DLB-106

Hodgins, Jack 1938- DLB-60

Hodgman, Helen 1945- DLB-14

Hodgskin, Thomas 1787-1869 ......DLB-158

Hodgson, Ralph 1871-1962 ....DLB-19

Hodgson, William Hope
1877-1918 .... DLB-70, 153, 156

Hoffenstein, Samuel 1890-1947 ......DLB-11

Hoffman, Charles Fenno
1806-1884 ....DLB-3

Hoffman, Daniel 1923- DLB-5

Hoffmann, E. T. A. 1776-1822 ......DLB-90

Hofmann, Michael 1957- DLB-40

Hofmannsthal, Hugo von
1874-1929 ....DLB-81, 118

Hofstadter, Richard 1916-1970 ......DLB-17

Hogan, Desmond 1950- DLB-14

Hogan and Thompson DLB-49

Hogarth Press DLB-112

Hogg, James 1770-1835 ... DLB-93, 116, 159

Hohl, Ludwig 1904-1980 ....DLB-56

Holbrook, David 1923- DLB-14, 40

Holcroft, Thomas
1745-1809 .... DLB-39, 89, 158

Holden, Jonathan 1941- DLB-105

Holden, Jonathan, Contemporary
Verse Story-telling DLB-105

Holden, Molly 1927-1981 ....DLB-40

Hölderlin, Friedrich 1770-1843 ......DLB-90

Holiday House DLB-46

Holinshed, Raphael died 1580 .....DLB-167

Holland, J. G. 1819-1881 .... DS-13

Holland, Norman N. 1927- DLB-67

Hollander, John 1929- DLB-5

Holley, Marietta 1836-1926 ....DLB-11

Hollingsworth, Margaret 1940- DLB-60

Hollo, Anselm 1934- DLB-40

Holloway, Emory 1885-1977 ...... DLB-103

Holloway, John 1920- DLB-27

Holloway House Publishing
Company DLB-46

Holme, Constance 1880-1955 .... DLB-34

Holmes, Abraham S. 1821?-1908 .... DLB-99

Holmes, John Clellon 1926-1988 .... DLB-16

Holmes, Oliver Wendell
1809-1894 ....DLB-1

Holmes, Richard 1945- DLB-155

Holroyd, Michael 1935- DLB-155

Holst, Hermann E. von
1841-1904 .... DLB-47

Holt, John 1721-1784 .... DLB-43

Holt, Henry, and Company DLB-49

Holt, Rinehart and Winston DLB-46

Holthusen, Hans Egon 1913- DLB-69

Hölty, Ludwig Christoph Heinrich
1748-1776 .... DLB-94

Holz, Arno 1863-1929 .... DLB-118

Home, Henry, Lord Kames (see Kames, Henry
Home, Lord)

Home, John 1722-1808 .... DLB-84

Home, William Douglas 1912- DLB-13

Home Publishing Company DLB-49

Homes, Geoffrey (see Mainwaring, Daniel)

Honan, Park 1928- DLB-111

Hone, William 1780-1842 ..... DLB-110, 158

Hongo, Garrett Kaoru 1951- DLB-120

Honig, Edwin 1919- DLB-5

Hood, Hugh 1928- DLB-53

Hood, Thomas 1799-1845 .... DLB-96

Hook, Theodore 1788-1841 .... DLB-116

Hooker, Jeremy 1941- DLB-40

Hooker, Richard 1554-1600 .... DLB-132

Hooker, Thomas 1586-1647 .... DLB-24

Hooper, Johnson Jones
1815-1862 .... DLB-3, 11

Hope, Anthony 1863-1933 .... DLB-153, 156

Hopkins, Gerard Manley
1844-1889 .... DLB-35, 57

Hopkins, John (see Sternhold, Thomas)

Hopkins, Lemuel 1750-1801 .... DLB-37

Hopkins, Pauline Elizabeth
1859-1930 .... DLB-50

Hopkins, Samuel 1721-1803 .... DLB-31

Hopkins, John H., and Son DLB-46

Hopkinson, Francis 1737-1791 ...... DLB-31

Horgan, Paul 1903- DLB-102; Y-85

Horizon Press DLB-46

Horne, Frank 1899-1974 .... DLB-51

Horne, Richard Henry (Hengist)
1802 or 1803-1884 .... DLB-32

Hornung, E. W. 1866-1921 .... DLB-70

Horovitz, Israel 1939- DLB-7

Horton, George Moses
1797?-1883? DLB-50

Horváth, Ödön von
1901-1938 ....DLB-85, 124

Horwood, Harold 1923- DLB-60

Hosford, E. and E.
[publishing house] DLB-49

Hoskyns, John 1566-1638 .... DLB-121

Hotchkiss and Company DLB-49

Hough, Emerson 1857-1923 .... DLB-9

Houghton Mifflin Company DLB-49

Houghton, Stanley 1881-1913 .... DLB-10

Household, Geoffrey 1900-1988 ..... DLB-87

Housman, A. E. 1859-1936 .... DLB-19

Housman, Laurence 1865-1959 ..... DLB-10

Houwald, Ernst von 1778-1845 ..... DLB-90

Hovey, Richard 1864-1900 .... DLB-54

Howard, Donald R. 1927-1987 ..... DLB-111

Howard, Maureen 1930- Y-83

Howard, Richard 1929- DLB-5

Howard, Roy W. 1883-1964 .... DLB-29

Howard, Sidney 1891-1939 ......DLB-7, 26

Howe, E. W. 1853-1937 ....DLB-12, 25

Howe, Henry 1816-1893 .... DLB-30

Howe, Irving 1920-1993 .... DLB-67

Howe, Joseph 1804-1873 .... DLB-99

Howe, Julia Ward 1819-1910 .... DLB-1

Howe, Percival Presland
1886-1944 .... DLB-149

Howe, Susan 1937- DLB-120

Howell, Clark, Sr. 1863-1936 .... DLB-25

Howell, Evan P. 1839-1905 .... DLB-23

Howell, James 1594?-1666 .... DLB-151

Howell, Warren Richardson
1912-1984 .... DLB-140

Howell, Soskin and Company DLB-46

Howells, William Dean
1837-1920 .... DLB-12, 64, 74, 79

Howitt, William 1792-1879 and
Howitt, Mary 1799-1888 ....DLB-110

Hoyem, Andrew 1935- DLB-5

Hoyers, Anna Ovena 1584-1655 ....DLB-164

Hoyos, Angela de 1940- DLB-82

Hoyt, Palmer 1897-1979 ....DLB-127

Hoyt, Henry [publishing house]......DLB-49

Hrabanus Maurus 776?-856 ....DLB-148

Hrotsvit of Gandersheim
circa 935-circa 1000 ....DLB-148

Hubbard, Elbert 1856-1915 ....DLB-91

Hubbard, Kin 1868-1930 ....DLB-11

Hubbard, William circa 1621-1704 ...DLB-24

Huber, Therese 1764-1829 ....DLB-90

Huch, Friedrich 1873-1913 ....DLB-66

Huch, Ricarda 1864-1947 ....DLB-66

Huck at 100: How Old Is
Huckleberry Finn? Y-85

Huddle, David 1942- DLB-130

Hudgins, Andrew 1951- DLB-120

Hudson, Henry Norman
1814-1886 ....DLB-64

Hudson, W. H. 1841-1922 ..... DLB-98, 153

Hudson and Goodwin DLB-49

Huebsch, B. W.
[publishing house] DLB-46

Hughes, David 1930- DLB-14

Hughes, John 1677-1720 ....DLB-84

Hughes, Langston
1902-1967 ....DLB-4, 7, 48, 51, 86

Hughes, Richard 1900-1976 .... DLB-15, 161

Hughes, Ted 1930- DLB-40, 161

Hughes, Thomas 1822-1896 .... DLB-18, 163

Hugo, Richard 1923-1982 ....DLB-5

Hugo, Victor 1802-1885 ....DLB-119

Hugo Awards and Nebula Awards DLB-8

Hull, Richard 1896-1973 ....DLB-77

Hulme, T. E. 1883-1917 ....DLB-19

Humboldt, Alexander von
1769-1859 ....DLB-90

Humboldt, Wilhelm von
1767-1835 ....DLB-90

Hume, David 1711-1776 ....DLB-104

Hume, Fergus 1859-1932 ....DLB-70

Hummer, T. R. 1950- DLB-120

Humorous Book Illustration DLB-11

Humphrey, William 1924- DLB-6

Humphreys, David 1752-1818 . . . . . . .DLB-37

Humphreys, Emyr 1919- DLB-15

Huncke, Herbert 1915- DLB-16

Huneker, James Gibbons
1857-1921 . . . . .DLB-71

Hunt, Irene 1907- DLB-52

Hunt, Leigh 1784-1859 . . . . DLB-96, 110, 144

Hunt, Violet 1862-1942 . . . . .DLB-162

Hunt, William Gibbes 1791-1833 . . . .DLB-73

Hunter, Evan 1926- Y-82

Hunter, Jim 1939- DLB-14

Hunter, Kristin 1931- DLB-33

Hunter, Mollie 1922- DLB-161

Hunter, N. C. 1908-1971 . . . . .DLB-10

Hunter-Duvar, John 1821-1899 . . . . .DLB-99

Huntington, Henry E.
1850-1927 . . . . .DLB-140

Hurd and Houghton DLB-49

Hurst, Fannie 1889-1968 . . . . .DLB-86

Hurst and Blackett DLB-106

Hurst and Company DLB-49

Hurston, Zora Neale
1901?-1960 . . . . .DLB-51, 86

Husson, Jules-François-Félix (see Champfleury)

Huston, John 1906-1987 . . . . .DLB-26

Hutcheson, Francis 1694-1746 . . . . . . .DLB-31

Hutchinson, Thomas
1711-1780 . . . . .DLB-30, 31

Hutchinson and Company
(Publishers) Limited DLB-112

Hutton, Richard Holt 1826-1897 . . . .DLB-57

Huxley, Aldous
1894-1963 . . . . DLB-36, 100, 162

Huxley, Elspeth Josceline 1907- DLB-77

Huxley, T. H. 1825-1895 . . . . .DLB-57

Huyghue, Douglas Smith
1816-1891 . . . . .DLB-99

Huysmans, Joris-Karl 1848-1907 . . . .DLB-123

Hyman, Trina Schart 1939- DLB-61

I

Iavorsky, Stefan 1658-1722 . . . . .DLB-150

Ibn Bajja circa 1077-1138 . . . . .DLB-115

Ibn Gabirol, Solomon
circa 1021-circa 1058 . . . . .DLB-115

The Iconography of Science-Fiction
Art DLB-8

Iffland, August Wilhelm
1759-1814 . . . . .DLB-94

Ignatow, David 1914- DLB-5

Ike, Chukwuemeka 1931- DLB-157

Iles, Francis (see Berkeley, Anthony)

The Illustration of Early German
Literary Manuscripts,
circa 1150-circa 1300 . . . . .DLB-148

Imbs, Bravig 1904-1946 . . . . .DLB-4

Imbuga, Francis D. 1947- DLB-157

Immermann, Karl 1796-1840 . . . . . .DLB-133

Inchbald, Elizabeth 1753-1821 . . .DLB-39, 89

Inge, William 1913-1973 . . . . .DLB-7

Ingelow, Jean 1820-1897 . . . . . . .DLB-35, 163

Ingersoll, Ralph 1900-1985 . . . . .DLB-127

The Ingersoll Prizes Y-84

Ingoldsby, Thomas (see Barham, Richard
Harris)

Ingraham, Joseph Holt 1809-1860 . . . .DLB-3

Inman, John 1805-1850 . . . . .DLB-73

Innerhofer, Franz 1944- DLB-85

Innis, Harold Adams 1894-1952 . . . . .DLB-88

Innis, Mary Quayle 1899-1972 . . . . . .DLB-88

International Publishers Company . .DLB-46

An Interview with David Rabe Y-91

An Interview with George Greenfield,
Literary Agent Y-91

An Interview with James Ellroy Y-91

An Interview with Peter S. Prescott Y-86

An Interview with Russell Hoban Y-90

An Interview with Tom Jenks Y-86

Introduction to Paul Laurence Dunbar,
Lyrics of Lowly Life (1896),
by William Dean Howells DLB-50

Introductory Essay: *Letters of Percy Bysshe
Shelley* (1852), by Robert
Browning DLB-32

Introductory Letters from the Second Edition
of *Pamela* (1741), by Samuel
Richardson DLB-39

Irving, John 1942- DLB-6; Y-82

Irving, Washington
1783-1859 . . . . .DLB-3, 11, 30, 59, 73, 74

Irwin, Grace 1907- DLB-68

Irwin, Will 1873-1948 . . . . .DLB-25

Isherwood, Christopher
1904-1986 . . . . .DLB-15; Y-86

The Island Trees Case: A Symposium on
School Library Censorship
An Interview with Judith Krug
An Interview with Phyllis Schlafly
An Interview with Edward B. Jenkinson
An Interview with Lamarr Mooneyham
An Interview with Harriet
Bernstein Y-82

Islas, Arturo 1938-1991 . . . . .DLB-122

Ivers, M. J., and Company DLB-49

Iyayi, Festus 1947- DLB-157

J

Jackmon, Marvin E. (see Marvin X)

Jacks, L. P. 1860-1955 . . . . .DLB-135

Jackson, Angela 1951- DLB-41

Jackson, Helen Hunt
1830-1885 . . . . .DLB-42, 47

Jackson, Holbrook 1874-1948 . . . . . . .DLB-98

Jackson, Laura Riding 1901-1991 . . . .DLB-48

Jackson, Shirley 1919-1965 . . . . .DLB-6

Jacob, Piers Anthony Dillingham (see Anthony,
Piers)

Jacobi, Friedrich Heinrich
1743-1819 . . . . .DLB-94

Jacobi, Johann Georg 1740-1841 . . . . .DLB-97

Jacobs, Joseph 1854-1916 . . . . .DLB-141

Jacobs, W. W. 1863-1943 . . . . .DLB-135

Jacobs, George W., and Company . . .DLB-49

Jacobson, Dan 1929- DLB-14

Jahier, Piero 1884-1966 . . . . .DLB-114

Jahnn, Hans Henny
1894-1959 . . . . .DLB-56, 124

Jakes, John 1932- Y-83

James, C. L. R. 1901-1989 . . . . .DLB-125

James, George P. R. 1801-1860 . . . . .DLB-116

James, Henry
1843-1916 . . . . . . .DLB-12, 71, 74; DS-13

James, John circa 1633-1729 . . . . .DLB-24

The James Jones Society Y-92

James, M. R. 1862-1936 . . . . .DLB-156

James, P. D. 1920- DLB-87

James Joyce Centenary: Dublin, 1982 . . .Y-82

James Joyce Conference Y-85

James VI of Scotland, I of England
1566-1625 . . . . .DLB-151

James, U. P. [publishing house] DLB-49

Jameson, Anna 1794-1860 . . . . . .DLB-99, 166

Jameson, Fredric 1934- DLB-67

Jameson, J. Franklin 1859-1937 ..... DLB-17

Jameson, Storm 1891-1986 .... DLB-36

Janés, Clara 1940- DLB-134

Jaramillo, Cleofas M. 1878-1956 ... DLB-122

Jarman, Mark 1952- DLB-120

Jarrell, Randall 1914-1965 ...... DLB-48, 52

Jarrold and Sons DLB-106

Jasmin, Claude 1930- DLB-60

Jay, John 1745-1829 .... DLB-31

Jefferies, Richard 1848-1887 .... DLB-98, 141

Jeffers, Lance 1919-1985 .... DLB-41

Jeffers, Robinson 1887-1962 .... DLB-45

Jefferson, Thomas 1743-1826 .... DLB-31

Jelinek, Elfriede 1946- DLB-85

Jellicoe, Ann 1927- DLB-13

Jenkins, Elizabeth 1905- DLB-155

Jenkins, Robin 1912- DLB-14

Jenkins, William Fitzgerald (see Leinster, Murray)

Jenkins, Herbert, Limited DLB-112

Jennings, Elizabeth 1926- DLB-27

Jens, Walter 1923- DLB-69

Jensen, Merrill 1905-1980 .... DLB-17

Jephson, Robert 1736-1803 .... DLB-89

Jerome, Jerome K. 1859-1927 .... DLB-10, 34, 135

Jerome, Judson 1927-1991 .... DLB-105

Jerome, Judson, Reflections: After a Tornado DLB-105

Jerrold, Douglas 1803-1857 ... DLB-158, 159

Jesse, F. Tennyson 1888-1958 ...... DLB-77

Jewett, Sarah Orne 1849-1909 ... DLB-12, 74

Jewett, John P., and Company DLB-49

The Jewish Publication Society DLB-49

Jewitt, John Rodgers 1783-1821 ..... DLB-99

Jewsbury, Geraldine 1812-1880 ..... DLB-21

Jhabvala, Ruth Prawer 1927- DLB-139

Jiménez, Juan Ramón 1881-1958 ... DLB-134

Joans, Ted 1928- DLB-16, 41

John, Eugenie (see Marlitt, E.)

John of Dumbleton circa 1310-circa 1349 .... DLB-115

John Edward Bruce: Three Documents DLB-50

John O'Hara's Pottsville Journalism Y-88

John Steinbeck Research Center Y-85

John Webster: The Melbourne Manuscript Y-86

Johns, Captain W. E. 1893-1968 .... DLB-160

Johnson, B. S. 1933-1973 .... DLB-14, 40

Johnson, Charles 1679-1748 .... DLB-84

Johnson, Charles R. 1948- DLB-33

Johnson, Charles S. 1893-1956 ... DLB-51, 91

Johnson, Denis 1949- DLB-120

Johnson, Diane 1934- Y-80

Johnson, Edgar 1901- DLB-103

Johnson, Edward 1598-1672 .... DLB-24

Johnson, Fenton 1888-1958 ...... DLB-45, 50

Johnson, Georgia Douglas 1886-1966 .... DLB-51

Johnson, Gerald W. 1890-1980 ...... DLB-29

Johnson, Helene 1907- DLB-51

Johnson, James Weldon 1871-1938 .... DLB-51

Johnson, John H. 1918- DLB-137

Johnson, Linton Kwesi 1952- DLB-157

Johnson, Lionel 1867-1902 .... DLB-19

Johnson, Nunnally 1897-1977 ...... DLB-26

Johnson, Owen 1878-1952 .... Y-87

Johnson, Pamela Hansford 1912- DLB-15

Johnson, Pauline 1861-1913 .... DLB-92

Johnson, Samuel 1696-1772 .... DLB-24

Johnson, Samuel 1709-1784 .... DLB-39, 95, 104, 142

Johnson, Samuel 1822-1882 .... DLB-1

Johnson, Uwe 1934-1984 .... DLB-75

Johnson, Benjamin [publishing house] DLB-49

Johnson, Benjamin, Jacob, and Robert [publishing house] DLB-49

Johnson, Jacob, and Company DLB-49

Johnson, Joseph [publishing house] ... DLB-154

Johnston, Annie Fellows 1863-1931 .. DLB-42

Johnston, Basil H. 1929- DLB-60

Johnston, Denis 1901-1984 .... DLB-10

Johnston, George 1913- DLB-88

Johnston, Jennifer 1930- DLB-14

Johnston, Mary 1870-1936 .... DLB-9

Johnston, Richard Malcolm 1822-1898 .... DLB-74

Johnstone, Charles 1719?-1800? DLB-39

Johst, Hanns 1890-1978 .... DLB-124

Jolas, Eugene 1894-1952 .... DLB-4, 45

Jones, Alice C. 1853-1933 .... DLB-92

Jones, Charles C., Jr. 1831-1893 .....DLB-30

Jones, D. G. 1929- DLB-53

Jones, David 1895-1974 .... DLB-20, 100

Jones, Diana Wynne 1934- DLB-161

Jones, Ebenezer 1820-1860 ....DLB-32

Jones, Ernest 1819-1868 ....DLB-32

Jones, Gayl 1949- DLB-33

Jones, Glyn 1905- DLB-15

Jones, Gwyn 1907- DLB-15, 139

Jones, Henry Arthur 1851-1929 ......DLB-10

Jones, Hugh circa 1692-1760 ....DLB-24

Jones, James 1921-1977 .... DLB-2, 143

Jones, Jenkin Lloyd 1911- DLB-127

Jones, LeRoi (see Baraka, Amiri)

Jones, Lewis 1897-1939 ....DLB-15

Jones, Madison 1925- DLB-152

Jones, Major Joseph (see Thompson, William Tappan)

Jones, Preston 1936-1979 ....DLB-7

Jones, Rodney 1950- DLB-120

Jones, Sir William 1746-1794 ....DLB-109

Jones, William Alfred 1817-1900 .....DLB-59

Jones's Publishing House DLB-49

Jong, Erica 1942- DLB-2, 5, 28, 152

Jonke, Gert F. 1946- DLB-85

Jonson, Ben 1572?-1637 .... DLB-62, 121

Jordan, June 1936- DLB-38

Joseph, Jenny 1932- DLB-40

Joseph, Michael, Limited DLB-112

Josephson, Matthew 1899-1978 ....DLB-4

Josiah Allen's Wife (see Holley, Marietta)

Josipovici, Gabriel 1940- DLB-14

Josselyn, John ?-1675 ....DLB-24

Joudry, Patricia 1921- DLB-88

Jovine, Giuseppe 1922- DLB-128

Joyaux, Philippe (see Sollers, Philippe)

Joyce, Adrien (see Eastman, Carol)

Joyce, James 1882-1941 ....DLB-10, 19, 36, 162

Judd, Sylvester 1813-1853 ....DLB-1

Judd, Orange, Publishing Company DLB-49

Judith circa 930 ....DLB-146

Julian of Norwich
1342-circa 1420 . . . . .DLB-1146

Julian Symons at Eighty Y-92

June, Jennie (see Croly, Jane Cunningham)

Jung, Franz 1888-1963 . . . . .DLB-118

Jünger, Ernst 1895- DLB-56

Der jüngere Titurel circa 1275 . . . . . . .DLB-138

Jung-Stilling, Johann Heinrich
1740-1817 . . . . .DLB-94

Justice, Donald 1925- Y-83

The Juvenile Library (see Godwin, M. J., and
Company)

K

Kacew, Romain (see Gary, Romain)

Kafka, Franz 1883-1924 . . . . .DLB-81

Kaiser, Georg 1878-1945 . . . . .DLB-124

Kaiserchronik circca 1147 . . . . .DLB-148

Kalechofsky, Roberta 1931- DLB-28

Kaler, James Otis 1848-1912 . . . . . . .DLB-12

Kames, Henry Home, Lord
1696-1782 . . . . .DLB-31, 104

Kandel, Lenore 1932- DLB-16

Kanin, Garson 1912- DLB-7

Kant, Hermann 1926- DLB-75

Kant, Immanuel 1724-1804 . . . . .DLB-94

Kantemir, Antiokh Dmitrievich
1708-1744 . . . . .DLB-150

Kantor, Mackinlay 1904-1977 . . . .DLB-9, 102

Kaplan, Fred 1937- DLB-111

Kaplan, Johanna 1942- DLB-28

Kaplan, Justin 1925- DLB-111

Kapnist, Vasilii Vasilevich
1758?-1823 . . . . .DLB-150

Karadžić, Vuk Stefanović
1787-1864 . . . . .DLB-147

Karamzin, Nikolai Mikhailovich
1766-1826 . . . . .DLB-150

Karsch, Anna Louisa 1722-1791 . . . . .DLB-97

Kasack, Hermann 1896-1966 . . . . . . .DLB-69

Kaschnitz, Marie Luise 1901-1974 . . .DLB-69

Kaštelan, Jure 1919-1990 . . . . .DLB-147

Kästner, Erich 1899-1974 . . . . .DLB-56

Kattan, Naim 1928- DLB-53

Katz, Steve 1935- Y-83

Kauffman, Janet 1945- Y-86

Kauffmann, Samuel 1898-1971 . . . . .DLB-127

Kaufman, Bob 1925- DLB-16, 41

Kaufman, George S. 1889-1961 . . . . . .DLB-7

Kavanagh, P. J. 1931- DLB-40

Kavanagh, Patrick 1904-1967 . . . .DLB-15, 20

Kaye-Smith, Sheila 1887-1956 . . . . . .DLB-36

Kazin, Alfred 1915- DLB-67

Keane, John B. 1928- DLB-13

Keary, Annie 1825-1879 . . . . DLB-163

Keating, H. R. F. 1926- DLB-87

Keats, Ezra Jack 1916-1983 . . . . DLB-61

Keats, John 1795-1821 . . . . DLB-96, 110

Keble, John 1792-1866 . . . . DLB-32, 55

Keeble, John 1944- Y-83

Keeffe, Barrie 1945- DLB-13

Keeley, James 1867-1934 . . . . DLB-25

W. B. Keen, Cooke
and Company DLB-49

Keillor, Garrison 1942- Y-87

Keith, Marian 1874?-1961 . . . . DLB-92

Keller, Gary D. 1943- DLB-82

Keller, Gottfried 1819-1890 . . . . DLB-129

Kelley, Edith Summers 1884-1956 . . . . DLB-9

Kelley, William Melvin 1937- DLB-33

Kellogg, Ansel Nash 1832-1886 . . . . . DLB-23

Kellogg, Steven 1941- DLB-61

Kelly, George 1887-1974 . . . . DLB-7

Kelly, Hugh 1739-1777 . . . . DLB-89

Kelly, Robert 1935- DLB-5, 130, 165

Kelly, Piet and Company DLB-49

Kelmscott Press DLB-112

Kemble, Fanny 1809-1893 . . . . DLB-32

Kemelman, Harry 1908- DLB-28

Kempe, Margery
circa 1373-1438 . . . . DLB-146

Kempner, Friederike 1836-1904 . . . . DLB-129

Kempowski, Walter 1929- DLB-75

Kendall, Claude
[publishing company] DLB-46

Kendell, George 1809-1867 . . . . DLB-43

Kenedy, P. J., and Sons DLB-49

Kennedy, Adrienne 1931- DLB-38

Kennedy, John Pendleton 1795-1870 . . . DLB-3

Kennedy, Leo 1907- DLB-88

Kennedy, Margaret 1896-1967 . . . . . DLB-36

Kennedy, Patrick 1801-1873 . . . . DLB-159

Kennedy, Richard S. 1920- DLB-111

Kennedy, William 1928- DLB-143; Y-85

Kennedy, X. J. 1929- DLB-5

Kennelly, Brendan 1936- DLB-40

Kenner, Hugh 1923- DLB-67

Kennerley, Mitchell
[publishing house] DLB-46

Kent, Frank R. 1877-1958 . . . . .DLB-29

Kenyon, Jane 1947- DLB-120

Keppler and Schwartzmann DLB-49

Kerner, Justinus 1776-1862 . . . . .DLB-90

Kerouac, Jack 1922-1969 . . . DLB-2, 16; DS-3

The Jack Kerouac Revival Y-95

Kerouac, Jan 1952- DLB-16

Kerr, Orpheus C. (see Newell, Robert Henry)

Kerr, Charles H., and Company DLB-49

Kesey, Ken 1935- DLB-2, 16

Kessel, Joseph 1898-1979 . . . . .DLB-72

Kessel, Martin 1901- DLB-56

Kesten, Hermann 1900- DLB-56

Keun, Irmgard 1905-1982 . . . . .DLB-69

Key and Biddle DLB-49

Keynes, John Maynard 1883-1946 . . . . DS-10

Keyserling, Eduard von 1855-1918 . . .DLB-66

Khan, Ismith 1925- DLB-125

Khemnitser, Ivan Ivanovich
1745-1784 . . . . .DLB-150

Kheraskov, Mikhail Matveevich
1733-1807 . . . . .DLB-150

Khvostov, Dmitrii Ivanovich
1757-1835 . . . . .DLB-150

Kidd, Adam 1802?-1831 . . . . .DLB-99

Kidd, William
[publishing house] DLB-106

Kiely, Benedict 1919- DLB-15

Kiggins and Kellogg DLB-49

Kiley, Jed 1889-1962 . . . . .DLB-4

Kilgore, Bernard 1908-1967 . . . . .DLB-127

Killens, John Oliver 1916- DLB-33

Killigrew, Anne 1660-1685 . . . . .DLB-131

Killigrew, Thomas 1612-1683 . . . . . . .DLB-58

Kilmer, Joyce 1886-1918 . . . . .DLB-45

Kilwardby, Robert
circa 1215-1279 . . . . .DLB-115

Kincaid, Jamaica 1949- DLB-157

King, Clarence 1842-1901 . . . . .DLB-12

King, Florence 1936 . . . . Y-85

King, Francis 1923- DLB-15, 139

King, Grace 1852-1932 . . . . DLB-12, 78

King, Henry 1592-1669 . . . . DLB-126

King, Stephen 1947- DLB-143; Y-80

King, Woodie, Jr. 1937- DLB-38

King, Solomon [publishing house] . . . DLB-49

Kinglake, Alexander William
1809-1891 . . . . DLB-55, 166

Kingsley, Charles
1819-1875 . . . . DLB-21, 32, 163

Kingsley, Henry 1830-1876 . . . . DLB-21

Kingsley, Sidney 1906- DLB-7

Kingsmill, Hugh 1889-1949 . . . . DLB-149

Kingston, Maxine Hong 1940- Y-80

Kingston, William Henry Giles
1814-1880 . . . . DLB-163

Kinnell, Galway 1927- DLB-5; Y-87

Kinsella, Thomas 1928- DLB-27

Kipling, Rudyard
1865-1936 . . . . DLB-19, 34, 141, 156

Kipphardt, Heinar 1922-1982 . . . . . . DLB-124

Kirby, William 1817-1906 . . . . DLB-99

Kircher, Athanasius 1602-1680 . . . . DLB-164

Kirk, John Foster 1824-1904 . . . . DLB-79

Kirkconnell, Watson 1895-1977 . . . . . DLB-68

Kirkland, Caroline M.
1801-1864 . . . . DLB-3, 73, 74; DS-13

Kirkland, Joseph 1830-1893 . . . . DLB-12

Kirkpatrick, Clayton 1915- DLB-127

Kirkup, James 1918- DLB-27

Kirouac, Conrad (see Marie-Victorin, Frère)

Kirsch, Sarah 1935- DLB-75

Kirst, Hans Hellmut 1914-1989 . . . . . DLB-69

Kitcat, Mabel Greenhow
1859-1922 . . . . .DLB-135

Kitchin, C. H. B. 1895-1967 . . . . DLB-77

Kizer, Carolyn 1925- DLB-5

Klabund 1890-1928 . . . . DLB-66

Klaj, Johann 1616-1656 . . . . DLB-164

Klappert, Peter 1942- DLB-5

Klass, Philip (see Tenn, William)

Klein, A. M. 1909-1972 . . . . DLB-68

Kleist, Ewald von 1715-1759 . . . . DLB-97

Kleist, Heinrich von 1777-1811 . . . . . DLB-90

Klinger, Friedrich Maximilian
1752-1831 . . . . DLB-94

Klopstock, Friedrich Gottlieb
1724-1803 . . . . DLB-97

Klopstock, Meta 1728-1758 . . . . DLB-97

Kluge, Alexander 1932- DLB-75

Knapp, Joseph Palmer 1864-1951 . . . . DLB-91

Knapp, Samuel Lorenzo
1783-1838 . . . . DLB-59

Knapton, J. J. and P.
[publishing house] DLB-154

Kniazhnin, Iakov Borisovich
1740-1791 . . . . DLB-150

Knickerbocker, Diedrich (see Irving,
Washington)

Knigge, Adolph Franz Friedrich Ludwig,
Freiherr von 1752-1796 . . . . DLB-94

Knight, Damon 1922- DLB-8

Knight, Etheridge 1931-1992 . . . . DLB-41

Knight, John S. 1894-1981 . . . . DLB-29

Knight, Sarah Kemble 1666-1727 . . . . DLB-24

Knight, Charles, and Company DLB-106

Knister, Raymond 1899-1932 . . . . . . DLB-68

Knoblock, Edward 1874-1945 . . . . DLB-10

Knopf, Alfred A. 1892-1984 . . . . .Y-84

Knopf, Alfred A.
[publishing house] DLB-46

Knowles, John 1926- DLB-6

Knox, Frank 1874-1944 . . . . DLB-29

Knox, John circa 1514-1572 . . . . DLB-132

Knox, John Armoy 1850-1906 . . . . . . DLB-23

Knox, Ronald Arbuthnott
1888-1957 . . . . DLB-77

Kober, Arthur 1900-1975 . . . . DLB-11

Kocbek, Edvard 1904-1981 . . . . DLB-147

Koch, Howard 1902- DLB-26

Koch, Kenneth 1925- DLB-5

Koenigsberg, Moses 1879-1945 . . . . . . DLB-25

Koeppen, Wolfgang 1906- DLB-69

Koertge, Ronald 1940- DLB-105

Koestler, Arthur 1905-1983 . . . . .Y-83

Kokoschka, Oskar 1886-1980 . . . . . . DLB-124

Kolb, Annette 1870-1967 . . . . DLB-66

Kolbenheyer, Erwin Guido
1878-1962 . . . . DLB-66, 124

Kolleritsch, Alfred 1931- DLB-85

Kolodny, Annette 1941- DLB-67

Komarov, Matvei
circa 1730-1812 . . . . DLB-150

Komroff, Manuel 1890-1974 . . . . DLB-4

Komunyakaa, Yusef 1947- DLB-120

Konigsburg, E. L. 1930- DLB-52

Konrad von Würzburg
circa 1230-1287 . . . . .DLB-138

Konstantinov, Aleko 1863-1897 . . . .DLB-147

Kooser, Ted 1939- DLB-105

Kopit, Arthur 1937- DLB-7

Kops, Bernard 1926?- DLB-13

Kornbluth, C. M. 1923-1958 . . . . .DLB-8

Körner, Theodor 1791-1813 . . . . .DLB-90

Kornfeld, Paul 1889-1942 . . . . .DLB-118

Kosinski, Jerzy 1933-1991 . . . . . . DLB-2; Y-82

Kosovel, Srečko 1904-1926 . . . . .DLB-147

Kostrov, Ermil Ivanovich
1755-1796 . . . . .DLB-150

Kotzebue, August von 1761-1819 . . . .DLB-94

Kovačić, Ante 1854-1889 . . . . .DLB-147

Kraf, Elaine 1946- Y-81

Kranjčević, Silvije Strahimir
1865-1908 . . . . .DLB-147

Krasna, Norman 1909-1984 . . . . .DLB-26

Kraus, Karl 1874-1936 . . . . .DLB-118

Krauss, Ruth 1911-1993 . . . . .DLB-52

Kreisel, Henry 1922- DLB-88

Kreuder, Ernst 1903-1972 . . . . .DLB-69

Kreymborg, Alfred 1883-1966 . . . . DLB-4, 54

Krieger, Murray 1923- DLB-67

Krim, Seymour 1922-1989 . . . . .DLB-16

Krleža, Miroslav 1893-1981 . . . . . . .DLB-147

Krock, Arthur 1886-1974 . . . . .DLB-29

Kroetsch, Robert 1927- DLB-53

Krutch, Joseph Wood 1893-1970 . . . . .DLB-63

Krylov, Ivan Andreevich
1769-1844 . . . . .DLB-150

Kubin, Alfred 1877-1959 . . . . .DLB-81

Kubrick, Stanley 1928- DLB-26

Kudrun circa 1230-1240 . . . . .DLB-138

Kuffstein, Hans Ludwig von
1582-1656 . . . . .DLB-164

Kumin, Maxine 1925- DLB-5

Kunene, Mazisi 1930- DLB-117

Kunitz, Stanley 1905- DLB-48

Kunjufu, Johari M. (see Amini, Johari M.)

Kunnert, Gunter 1929- DLB-75

Kunze, Reiner 1933- DLB-75

Kupferberg, Tuli 1923- DLB-16

Kürnberger, Ferdinand
  1821-1879 ....DLB-129

Kurz, Isolde 1853-1944 ....DLB-66

Kusenberg, Kurt 1904-1983 ....DLB-69

Kuttner, Henry 1915-1958 ....DLB-8

Kyd, Thomas 1558-1594 ....DLB-62

Kyffin, Maurice
  circa 1560?-1598 ....DLB-136

Kyger, Joanne 1934- DLB-16

Kyne, Peter B. 1880-1957 ....DLB-78

L

L. E. L. (see Landon, Letitia Elizabeth)

Laberge, Albert 1871-1960 ....DLB-68

Laberge, Marie 1950- DLB-60

Lacombe, Patrice (see Trullier-Lacombe,
  Joseph Patrice)

Lacretelle, Jacques de 1888-1985 .....DLB-65

Ladd, Joseph Brown 1764-1786 ......DLB-37

La Farge, Oliver 1901-1963 ....DLB-9

Lafferty, R. A. 1914- DLB-8

La Guma, Alex 1925-1985 ....DLB-117

Lahaise, Guillaume (see Delahaye, Guy)

Lahontan, Louis-Armand de Lom d'Arce,
  Baron de 1666-1715? DLB-99

Laing, Kojo 1946- DLB-157

Laird, Carobeth 1895- Y-82

Laird and Lee DLB-49

Lalonde, Michèle 1937- DLB-60

Lamantia, Philip 1927- DLB-16

Lamb, Charles
  1775-1834 .... DLB-93, 107, 163

Lamb, Lady Caroline 1785-1828 ....DLB-116

Lamb, Mary 1764-1874 ....DLB-163

Lambert, Betty 1933-1983 ....DLB-60

Lamming, George 1927- DLB-125

L'Amour, Louis 1908?- Y-80

Lampman, Archibald 1861-1899 .....DLB-92

Lamson, Wolffe and Company DLB-49

Lancer Books DLB-46

Landesman, Jay 1919- and
  Landesman, Fran 1927- DLB-16

Landon, Letitia Elizabeth 1802-1838 .DLB-96

Landor, Walter Savage
  1775-1864 ....DLB-93, 107

Landry, Napoléon-P. 1884-1956 ....DLB-92

Lane, Charles 1800-1870 ....DLB-1

Lane, Laurence W. 1890-1967 ......DLB-91

Lane, M. Travis 1934- DLB-60

Lane, Patrick 1939- DLB-53

Lane, Pinkie Gordon 1923- DLB-41

Lane, John, Company DLB-49

Laney, Al 1896- DLB-4

Lang, Andrew 1844-1912 ......DLB-98, 141

Langevin, André 1927- DLB-60

Langgässer, Elisabeth 1899-1950 ....DLB-69

Langhorne, John 1735-1779 ....DLB-109

Langland, William
  circa 1330-circa 1400 ....DLB-146

Langton, Anna 1804-1893 ....DLB-99

Lanham, Edwin 1904-1979 ....DLB-4

Lanier, Sidney 1842-1881 ....DLB-64; DS-13

Lanyer, Aemilia 1569-1645 ....DLB-121

Lapointe, Gatien 1931-1983 ....DLB-88

Lapointe, Paul-Marie 1929- DLB-88

Lardner, Ring 1885-1933 ....DLB-11, 25, 86

Lardner, Ring, Jr. 1915- DLB-26

Lardner 100: Ring Lardner
  Centennial Symposium Y-85

Larkin, Philip 1922-1985 ....DLB-27

La Roche, Sophie von 1730-1807 ....DLB-94

La Rocque, Gilbert 1943-1984 ......DLB-60

Laroque de Roquebrune, Robert (see Roquebrune, Robert de)

Larrick, Nancy 1910- DLB-61

Larsen, Nella 1893-1964 ....DLB-51

Lasker-Schüler, Else
  1869-1945 ....DLB-66, 124

Lasnier, Rina 1915- DLB-88

Lassalle, Ferdinand 1825-1864 .....DLB-129

Lathrop, Dorothy P. 1891-1980 .....DLB-22

Lathrop, George Parsons
  1851-1898 ....DLB-71

Lathrop, John, Jr. 1772-1820 ....DLB-37

Latimer, Hugh 1492?-1555 ....DLB-136

Latimore, Jewel Christine McLawler
  (see Amini, Johari M.)

Latymer, William 1498-1583 ......DLB-132

Laube, Heinrich 1806-1884 ....DLB-133

Laughlin, James 1914- DLB-48

Laumer, Keith 1925- DLB-8

Lauremberg, Johann 1590-1658 ....DLB-164

Laurence, Margaret 1926-1987 ......DLB-53

Laurents, Arthur 1918- DLB-26

Laurie, Annie (see Black, Winifred)

Laut, Agnes Christiana 1871-1936 ...DLB-92

Lavater, Johann Kaspar 1741-1801 ...DLB-97

Lavin, Mary 1912- DLB-15

Lawes, Henry 1596-1662 ....DLB-126

Lawless, Anthony (see MacDonald, Philip)

Lawrence, D. H.
  1885-1930 ...... DLB-10, 19, 36, 98, 162

Lawrence, David 1888-1973 ....DLB-29

Lawrence, Seymour 1926-1994 ....Y-94

Lawson, John ?-1711 ....DLB-24

Lawson, Robert 1892-1957 ....DLB-22

Lawson, Victor F. 1850-1925 ....DLB-25

Layard, Sir Austen Henry
  1817-1894 ....DLB-166

Layton, Irving 1912- DLB-88

LaZamon flourished circa 1200 .....DLB-146

Lazarević, Laza K. 1851-1890 ......DLB-147

Lea, Henry Charles 1825-1909 ......DLB-47

Lea, Sydney 1942- DLB-120

Lea, Tom 1907- DLB-6

Leacock, John 1729-1802 ....DLB-31

Leacock, Stephen 1869-1944 ....DLB-92

Lead, Jane Ward 1623-1704 ....DLB-131

Leadenhall Press DLB-106

Leapor, Mary 1722-1746 ....DLB-109

Lear, Edward 1812-1888 .. DLB-32, 163, 166

Leary, Timothy 1920-1996 ....DLB-16

Leary, W. A., and Company DLB-49

Léautaud, Paul 1872-1956 ....DLB-65

Leavitt, David 1961- DLB-130

Leavitt and Allen DLB-49

le Carré, John 1931- DLB-87

Lécavelé, Roland (see Dorgeles, Roland)

Lechlitner, Ruth 1901- DLB-48

Leclerc, Félix 1914- DLB-60

Le Clézio, J. M. G. 1940- DLB-83

Lectures on Rhetoric and Belles Lettres (1783),
  by Hugh Blair [excerpts] DLB-31

Leder, Rudolf (see Hermlin, Stephan)

Lederer, Charles 1910-1976 ....DLB-26

Ledwidge, Francis 1887-1917 ....DLB-20

Lee, Dennis 1939- DLB-53

Lee, Don L. (see Madhubuti, Haki R.)

Lee, George W. 1894-1976 . . . . DLB-51

Lee, Harper 1926- DLB-6

Lee, Harriet (1757-1851) and
Lee, Sophia (1750-1824) DLB-39

Lee, Laurie 1914- DLB-27

Lee, Li-Young 1957- DLB-165

Lee, Manfred B. (see Dannay, Frederic, and
Manfred B. Lee)

Lee, Nathaniel circa 1645 - 1692 . . . . DLB-80

Lee, Sir Sidney 1859-1926 . . . . DLB-149

Lee, Sir Sidney, "Principles of Biography," in
Elizabethan and Other Essays DLB-149

Lee, Vernon 1856-1935 . . . . DLB-57, 153, 156

Lee and Shepard DLB-49

Le Fanu, Joseph Sheridan
1814-1873 . . . . DLB-21, 70, 159

Leffland, Ella 1931- Y-84

le Fort, Gertrud von 1876-1971 . . . . . DLB-66

Le Gallienne, Richard 1866-1947 . . . . . .DLB-4

Legaré, Hugh Swinton
1797-1843 . . . . DLB-3, 59, 73

Legaré, James M. 1823-1859 . . . . .DLB-3

The Legends of the Saints and a Medieval
Christian Worldview DLB-148

Léger, Antoine-J. 1880-1950 . . . . DLB-88

Le Guin, Ursula K. 1929- DLB-8, 52

Lehman, Ernest 1920- DLB-44

Lehmann, John 1907- DLB-27, 100

Lehmann, Rosamond 1901-1990 . . . . DLB-15

Lehmann, Wilhelm 1882-1968 . . . . . . DLB-56

Lehmann, John, Limited DLB-112

Leiber, Fritz 1910-1992 . . . . .DLB-8

Leicester University Press DLB-112

Leinster, Murray 1896-1975 . . . . .DLB-8

Leisewitz, Johann Anton
1752-1806 . . . . DLB-94

Leitch, Maurice 1933- DLB-14

Leithauser, Brad 1943- DLB-120

Leland, Charles G. 1824-1903 . . . . . . DLB-11

Leland, John 1503?-1552 . . . . DLB-136

Lemay, Pamphile 1837-1918 . . . . DLB-99

Lemelin, Roger 1919- DLB-88

Lemon, Mark 1809-1870 . . . . DLB-163

Le Moine, James MacPherson
1825-1912 . . . . DLB-99

Le Moyne, Jean 1913- DLB-88

L'Engle, Madeleine 1918- DLB-52

Lennart, Isobel 1915-1971 . . . . DLB-44

Lennox, Charlotte
1729 or 1730-1804 . . . . DLB-39

Lenox, James 1800-1880 . . . . DLB-140

Lenski, Lois 1893-1974 . . . . DLB-22

Lenz, Hermann 1913- DLB-69

Lenz, J. M. R. 1751-1792 . . . . DLB-94

Lenz, Siegfried 1926- DLB-75

Leonard, Hugh 1926- DLB-13

Leonard, William Ellery
1876-1944 . . . . DLB-54

Leonowens, Anna 1834-1914 . . .DLB-99, 166

LePan, Douglas 1914- DLB-88

Leprohon, Rosanna Eleanor
1829-1879 . . . . DLB-99

Le Queux, William 1864-1927 . . . . . . DLB-70

Lerner, Max 1902-1992 . . . . DLB-29

Lernet-Holenia, Alexander
1897-1976 . . . . DLB-85

Le Rossignol, James 1866-1969 . . . . . DLB-92

Lescarbot, Marc circa 1570-1642 . . . . DLB-99

LeSeur, William Dawson
1840-1917 . . . . DLB-92

LeSieg, Theo. (see Geisel, Theodor Seuss)

Leslie, Frank 1821-1880 . . . . DLB-43, 79

Leslie, Frank, Publishing House DLB-49

Lesperance, John 1835?-1891 . . . . . . DLB-99

Lessing, Bruno 1870-1940 . . . . DLB-28

Lessing, Doris 1919- DLB-15, 139; Y-85

Lessing, Gotthold Ephraim
1729-1781 . . . . DLB-97

Lettau, Reinhard 1929- DLB-75

Letter from Japan Y-94

Letter to [Samuel] Richardson on *Clarissa*
(1748), by Henry Fielding DLB-39

Lever, Charles 1806-1872 . . . . DLB-21

Leverson, Ada 1862-1933 . . . . DLB-153

Levertov, Denise 1923- DLB-5, 165

Levi, Peter 1931- DLB-40

Levien, Sonya 1888-1960 . . . . DLB-44

Levin, Meyer 1905-1981 . . . .DLB-9, 28; Y-81

Levine, Norman 1923- DLB-88

Levine, Philip 1928- DLB-5

Levis, Larry 1946- DLB-120

Levy, Amy 1861-1889 . . . . DLB-156

Levy, Benn Wolfe
1900-1973 . . . . DLB-13; Y-81

Lewald, Fanny 1811-1889 . . . . .DLB-129

Lewes, George Henry
1817-1878 . . . . DLB-55, 144

Lewis, Alfred H. 1857-1914 . . . . .DLB-25

Lewis, Alun 1915-1944 . . . . DLB-20, 162

Lewis, C. Day (see Day Lewis, C.)

Lewis, C. S. 1898-1963 . . . . DLB-15, 100, 160

Lewis, Charles B. 1842-1924 . . . . . . .DLB-11

Lewis, Henry Clay 1825-1850 . . . . . . .DLB-3

Lewis, Janet 1899- Y-87

Lewis, Matthew Gregory
1775-1818 . . . . DLB-39, 158

Lewis, R. W. B. 1917- DLB-111

Lewis, Richard circa 1700-1734 . . . . . .DLB-24

Lewis, Sinclair
1885-1951 . . . . DLB-9, 102; DS-1

Lewis, Wilmarth Sheldon
1895-1979 . . . . .DLB-140

Lewis, Wyndham 1882-1957 . . . . . . .DLB-15

Lewisohn, Ludwig
1882-1955 . . . . DLB-4, 9, 28, 102

Lezama Lima, José 1910-1976 . . . . . .DLB-113

The Library of America DLB-46

The Licensing Act of 1737 . . . . .DLB-84

Lichtenberg, Georg Christoph
1742-1799 . . . . .DLB-94

Liebling, A. J. 1904-1963 . . . . .DLB-4

Lieutenant Murray (see Ballou, Maturin
Murray)

Lighthall, William Douw
1857-1954 . . . . .DLB-92

Lilar, Françoise (see Mallet-Joris, Françoise)

Lillo, George 1691-1739 . . . . .DLB-84

Lilly, J. K., Jr. 1893-1966 . . . . .DLB-140

Lilly, Wait and Company DLB-49

Lily, William circa 1468-1522 . . . . . .DLB-132

Limited Editions Club DLB-46

Lincoln and Edmands DLB-49

Lindsay, Jack 1900- Y-84

Lindsay, Sir David
circa 1485-1555 . . . . .DLB-132

Lindsay, Vachel 1879-1931 . . . . .DLB-54

Linebarger, Paul Myron Anthony (see Smith,
Cordwainer)

Link, Arthur S. 1920- DLB-17

Linn, John Blair 1777-1804 . . . . .DLB-37

Lins, Osman 1924-1978 . . . . .DLB-145

Linton, Eliza Lynn 1822-1898 . . . . . .DLB-18

Linton, William James 1812-1897 . . . . DLB-32

Lion Books DLB-46

Lionni, Leo 1910- DLB-61

Lippincott, Sara Jane Clarke
1823-1904 . . . . DLB-43

Lippincott, J. B., Company DLB-49

Lippmann, Walter 1889-1974 . . . . . . DLB-29

Lipton, Lawrence 1898-1975 . . . . DLB-16

Liscow, Christian Ludwig
1701-1760 . . . . DLB-97

Lish, Gordon 1934- DLB-130

Lispector, Clarice 1925-1977 . . . . . . DLB-113

The Literary Chronicle and Weekly Review
1819-1828 . . . . DLB-110

Literary Documents: William Faulkner
and the People-to-People
Program Y-86

Literary Documents II: *Library Journal*
Statements and Questionnaires from
First Novelists Y-87

Literary Effects of World War II
[British novel] DLB-15

Literary Prizes [British] DLB-15

Literary Research Archives: The Humanities
Research Center, University of
Texas Y-82

Literary Research Archives II: Berg
Collection of English and American
Literature of the New York Public
Library Y-83

Literary Research Archives III:
The Lilly Library Y-84

Literary Research Archives IV:
The John Carter Brown Library Y-85

Literary Research Archives V:
Kent State Special Collections Y-86

Literary Research Archives VI: The Modern
Literary Manuscripts Collection in the
Special Collections of the Washington
University Libraries Y-87

Literary Research Archives VII:
The University of Virginia
Libraries Y-91

Literary Research Archives VIII:
The Henry E. Huntington
Library Y-92

"Literary Style" (1857), by William
Forsyth [excerpt] DLB-57

Literatura Chicanesca: The View From
Without DLB-82

Literature at Nurse, or Circulating Morals (1885),
by George Moore DLB-18

Littell, Eliakim 1797-1870 . . . . DLB-79

Littell, Robert S. 1831-1896 . . . . DLB-79

Little, Brown and Company DLB-49

Littlewood, Joan 1914- DLB-13

Lively, Penelope 1933- DLB-14, 161

Liverpool University Press DLB-112

The Lives of the Poets DLB-142

Livesay, Dorothy 1909- DLB-68

Livesay, Florence Randal
1874-1953 . . . . DLB-92

Livings, Henry 1929- DLB-13

Livingston, Anne Howe
1763-1841 . . . . DLB-37

Livingston, Myra Cohn 1926- DLB-61

Livingston, William 1723-1790 . . . . . DLB-31

Livingstone, David 1813-1873 . . . . . DLB-166

Liyong, Taban lo (see Taban lo Liyong)

Lizárraga, Sylvia S. 1925- DLB-82

Llewellyn, Richard 1906-1983 . . . . . . DLB-15

Lloyd, Edward
[publishing house] DLB-106

Lobel, Arnold 1933- DLB-61

Lochridge, Betsy Hopkins (see Fancher, Betsy)

Locke, David Ross 1833-1888 . . . DLB-11, 23

Locke, John 1632-1704 . . . . DLB-31, 101

Locke, Richard Adams 1800-1871 . . . DLB-43

Locker-Lampson, Frederick
1821-1895 . . . . DLB-35

Lockhart, John Gibson
1794-1854 . . . . DLB-110, 116 144

Lockridge, Ross, Jr.
1914-1948 . . . . DLB-143; Y-80

Locrine and *Selimus* DLB-62

Lodge, David 1935- DLB-14

Lodge, George Cabot 1873-1909 . . . . DLB-54

Lodge, Henry Cabot 1850-1924 . . . . . DLB-47

Loeb, Harold 1891-1974 . . . . DLB-4

Loeb, William 1905-1981 . . . . DLB-127

Lofting, Hugh 1886-1947 . . . . DLB-160

Logan, James 1674-1751 . . . . DLB-24, 140

Logan, John 1923- DLB-5

Logan, William 1950- DLB-120

Logau, Friedrich von 1605-1655 . . . DLB-164

Logue, Christopher 1926- DLB-27

Lomonosov, Mikhail Vasil'evich
1711-1765 . . . . DLB-150

London, Jack 1876-1916 . . . . . . DLB-8, 12, 78

The London Magazine 1820-1829 . . . . . DLB-110

Long, Haniel 1888-1956 . . . . DLB-45

Long, Ray 1878-1935 . . . . DLB-137

Long, H., and Brother DLB-49

Longfellow, Henry Wadsworth
1807-1882 . . . . DLB-1, 59

Longfellow, Samuel 1819-1892 . . . . . . DLB-1

Longford, Elizabeth 1906- DLB-155

Longley, Michael 1939- DLB-40

Longman, T. [publishing house] DLB-154

Longmans, Green and Company DLB-49

Longmore, George 1793?-1867 . . . . . . DLB-99

Longstreet, Augustus Baldwin
1790-1870 . . . . DLB-3, 11, 74

Longworth, D. [publishing house] . . . DLB-49

Lonsdale, Frederick 1881-1954 . . . . . . DLB-10

A Look at the Contemporary Black Theatre
Movement DLB-38

Loos, Anita 1893-1981 . . . . . DLB-11, 26; Y-81

Lopate, Phillip 1943- Y-80

López, Diana (see Isabella, Ríos)

Loranger, Jean-Aubert 1896-1942 . . . . DLB-92

Lorca, Federico García 1898-1936 . . DLB-108

Lord, John Keast 1818-1872 . . . . DLB-99

The Lord Chamberlain's Office and Stage
Censorship in England DLB-10

Lorde, Audre 1934-1992 . . . . DLB-41

Lorimer, George Horace
1867-1939 . . . . DLB-91

Loring, A. K. [publishing house] DLB-49

Loring and Mussey DLB-46

Lossing, Benson J. 1813-1891 . . . . DLB-30

Lothar, Ernst 1890-1974 . . . . DLB-81

Lothrop, Harriet M. 1844-1924 . . . . . DLB-42

Lothrop, D., and Company DLB-49

Loti, Pierre 1850-1923 . . . . DLB-123

Lott, Emeline ?-? DLB-166

The Lounger, no. 20 (1785), by Henry
Mackenzie DLB-39

Lounsbury, Thomas R. 1838-1915 . . . DLB-71

Louÿs, Pierre 1870-1925 . . . . DLB-123

Lovelace, Earl 1935- DLB-125

Lovelace, Richard 1618-1657 . . . . . . DLB-131

Lovell, Coryell and Company DLB-49

Lovell, John W., Company DLB-49

Lover, Samuel 1797-1868 . . . . DLB-159

Lovesey, Peter 1936- DLB-87

Lovingood, Sut (see Harris,
George Washington)

Low, Samuel 1765-? DLB-37

Lowell, Amy 1874-1925 .... DLB-54, 140

Lowell, James Russell
1819-1891 .... DLB-1, 11, 64, 79

Lowell, Robert 1917-1977 .... DLB-5

Lowenfels, Walter 1897-1976 .... DLB-4

Lowndes, Marie Belloc 1868-1947 ... DLB-70

Lowry, Lois 1937- DLB-52

Lowry, Malcolm 1909-1957 .... DLB-15

Lowther, Pat 1935-1975 .... DLB-53

Loy, Mina 1882-1966 .... DLB-4, 54

Lozeau, Albert 1878-1924 .... DLB-92

Lubbock, Percy 1879-1965 .... DLB-149

Lucas, E. V. 1868-1938 .... DLB-98, 149, 153

Lucas, Fielding, Jr.
[publishing house] DLB-49

Luce, Henry R. 1898-1967 .... DLB-91

Luce, John W., and Company DLB-46

Lucie-Smith, Edward 1933- DLB-40

Lucini, Gian Pietro 1867-1914 ..... DLB-114

Ludlum, Robert 1927- Y-82

Ludus de Antichristo circa 1160 ...... DLB-148

Ludvigson, Susan 1942- DLB-120

Ludwig, Jack 1922- DLB-60

Ludwig, Otto 1813-1865 .... DLB-129

Ludwigslied 881 or 882 .... DLB-148

Luera, Yolanda 1953- DLB-122

Luft, Lya 1938- DLB-145

Luke, Peter 1919- DLB-13

Lupton, F. M., Company DLB-49

Lupus of Ferrières
circa 805-circa 862 .... DLB-148

Lurie, Alison 1926- DLB-2

Luzi, Mario 1914- DLB-128

L'vov, Nikolai Aleksandrovich
1751-1803 .... DLB-150

Lyall, Gavin 1932- DLB-87

Lydgate, John circa 1370-1450 ..... DLB-146

Lyly, John circa 1554-1606 ..... DLB-62, 167

Lynch, Patricia 1898-1972 ..... DLB-160

Lynd, Robert 1879-1949 .... DLB-98

Lyon, Matthew 1749-1822 .... DLB-43

Lytle, Andrew 1902-1995 ...... DLB-6; Y-95

Lytton, Edward (see Bulwer-Lytton, Edward)

Lytton, Edward Robert Bulwer
1831-1891 .... DLB-32

M

Maass, Joachim 1901-1972 .... DLB-69

Mabie, Hamilton Wright
1845-1916 .... DLB-71

Mac A'Ghobhainn, Iain (see Smith, Iain
Crichton)

MacArthur, Charles
1895-1956 ....DLB-7, 25, 44

Macaulay, Catherine 1731-1791 .... DLB-104

Macaulay, David 1945- DLB-61

Macaulay, Rose 1881-1958 .... DLB-36

Macaulay, Thomas Babington
1800-1859 ....DLB-32, 55

Macaulay Company DLB-46

MacBeth, George 1932- DLB-40

Macbeth, Madge 1880-1965 .... DLB-92

MacCaig, Norman 1910- DLB-27

MacDiarmid, Hugh 1892-1978 ...... DLB-20

MacDonald, Cynthia 1928- DLB-105

MacDonald, George
1824-1905 ....DLB-18, 163

MacDonald, John D.
1916-1986 ....DLB-8; Y-86

MacDonald, Philip 1899?-1980 ...... DLB-77

Macdonald, Ross (see Millar, Kenneth)

MacDonald, Wilson 1880-1967 ...... DLB-92

Macdonald and Company
(Publishers) DLB-112

MacEwen, Gwendolyn 1941- DLB-53

Macfadden, Bernarr
1868-1955 ....DLB-25, 91

MacGregor, John 1825-1892 ...... DLB-166

MacGregor, Mary Esther (see Keith, Marian)

Machado, Antonio 1875-1939 ...... DLB-108

Machado, Manuel 1874-1947 ...... DLB-108

Machar, Agnes Maule 1837-1927 .... DLB-92

Machen, Arthur Llewelyn Jones
1863-1947 ....DLB-36, 156

MacInnes, Colin 1914-1976 .... DLB-14

MacInnes, Helen 1907-1985 .... DLB-87

Mack, Maynard 1909- DLB-111

Mackall, Leonard L. 1879-1937 .... DLB-140

MacKaye, Percy 1875-1956 .... DLB-54

Macken, Walter 1915-1967 .... DLB-13

Mackenzie, Alexander 1763-1820 .... DLB-99

Mackenzie, Compton
1883-1972 ....DLB-34, 100

Mackenzie, Henry 1745-1831 .... DLB-39

Mackey, William Wellington
1937- DLB-38

Mackintosh, Elizabeth (see Tey, Josephine)

Mackintosh, Sir James
1765-1832 .... DLB-158

Maclaren, Ian (see Watson, John)

Macklin, Charles 1699-1797 .... DLB-89

MacLean, Katherine Anne 1925- DLB-8

MacLeish, Archibald
1892-1982 .... DLB-4, 7, 45; Y-82

MacLennan, Hugh 1907-1990 .... DLB-68

Macleod, Fiona (see Sharp, William)

MacLeod, Alistair 1936- DLB-60

Macleod, Norman 1906-1985 .... DLB-4

Macmillan and Company DLB-106

The Macmillan Company DLB-49

Macmillan's English Men of Letters,
First Series (1878-1892) DLB-144

MacNamara, Brinsley 1890-1963 .... DLB-10

MacNeice, Louis 1907-1963 ..... DLB-10, 20

MacPhail, Andrew 1864-1938 .... DLB-92

Macpherson, James 1736-1796 ...... DLB-109

Macpherson, Jay 1931- DLB-53

Macpherson, Jeanie 1884-1946 ...... DLB-44

Macrae Smith Company DLB-46

Macrone, John
[publishing house] DLB-106

MacShane, Frank 1927- DLB-111

Macy-Masius DLB-46

Madden, David 1933- DLB-6

Maddow, Ben 1909-1992 .... DLB-44

Maddux, Rachel 1912-1983 .... Y-93

Madgett, Naomi Long 1923- DLB-76

Madhubuti, Haki R.
1942- DLB-5, 41; DS-8

Madison, James 1751-1836 .... DLB-37

Maginn, William 1794-1842 ... DLB-110, 159

Mahan, Alfred Thayer 1840-1914 ....DLB-47

Maheux-Forcier, Louise 1929- DLB-60

Mahin, John Lee 1902-1984 .... DLB-44

Mahon, Derek 1941- DLB-40

Maikov, Vasilii Ivanovich
1728-1778 .... DLB-150

Mailer, Norman
1923- ... DLB-2, 16, 28; Y-80, 83; DS-3

Maillet, Adrienne 1885-1963 .... DLB-68

Maimonides, Moses 1138-1204 .... DLB-115

Maillet, Antonine 1929- DLB-60

Maillu, David G. 1939- DLB-157

Main Selections of the Book-of-the-Month Club, 1926-1945 ....DLB-9

Main Trends in Twentieth-Century Book Clubs DLB-46

Mainwaring, Daniel 1902-1977 ......DLB-44

Mair, Charles 1838-1927 ....DLB-99

Mais, Roger 1905-1955 ....DLB-125

Major, Andre 1942- DLB-60

Major, Clarence 1936- DLB-33

Major, Kevin 1949- DLB-60

Major Books DLB-46

Makemie, Francis circa 1658-1708 ...DLB-24

The Making of a People, by J. M. Ritchie DLB-66

Maksimović, Desanka 1898-1993 ...DLB-147

Malamud, Bernard 1914-1986 .....DLB-2, 28, 152; Y-80, 86

Malet, Lucas 1852-1931 ....DLB-153

Malleson, Lucy Beatrice (see Gilbert, Anthony)

Mallet-Joris, Françoise 1930- DLB-83

Mallock, W. H. 1849-1923 ....DLB-18, 57

Malone, Dumas 1892-1986 ....DLB-17

Malone, Edmond 1741-1812 ....DLB-142

Malory, Sir Thomas circa 1400-1410 - 1471 ....DLB-146

Malraux, André 1901-1976 ....DLB-72

Malthus, Thomas Robert 1766-1834 ....DLB-107, 158

Maltz, Albert 1908-1985 ....DLB-102

Malzberg, Barry N. 1939- DLB-8

Mamet, David 1947- DLB-7

Manaka, Matsemela 1956- DLB-157

Manchester University Press DLB-112

Mandel, Eli 1922- DLB-53

Mandeville, Bernard 1670-1733 ....DLB-101

Mandeville, Sir John mid fourteenth century DLB-146

Mandiargues, André Pieyre de 1909- DLB-83

Manfred, Frederick 1912-1994 ....DLB-6

Mangan, Sherry 1904-1961 ....DLB-4

Mankiewicz, Herman 1897-1953 .....DLB-26

Mankiewicz, Joseph L. 1909-1993 ....DLB-44

Mankowitz, Wolf 1924- DLB-15

Manley, Delarivière 1672?-1724 ....DLB-39, 80

Mann, Abby 1927- DLB-44

Mann, Heinrich 1871-1950 .....DLB-66, 118

Mann, Horace 1796-1859 ....DLB-1

Mann, Klaus 1906-1949 ....DLB-56

Mann, Thomas 1875-1955 ....DLB-66

Mann, William D'Alton 1839-1920 ....DLB-137

Manning, Marie 1873?-1945 ....DLB-29

Manning and Loring DLB-49

Mannyng, Robert flourished 1303-1338 ....DLB-146

Mano, D. Keith 1942- DLB-6

Manor Books DLB-46

Mansfield, Katherine 1888-1923 ....DLB-162

Mapanje, Jack 1944- DLB-157

March, William 1893-1954 ....DLB-9, 86

Marchand, Leslie A. 1900- DLB-103

Marchant, Bessie 1862-1941 ....DLB-160

Marchessault, Jovette 1938- DLB-60

Marcus, Frank 1928- DLB-13

Marden, Orison Swett 1850-1924 ....DLB-137

Marechera, Dambudzo 1952-1987 ....DLB-157

Marek, Richard, Books DLB-46

Mares, E. A. 1938- DLB-122

Mariani, Paul 1940- DLB-111

Marie-Victorin, Frère 1885-1944 ....DLB-92

Marin, Biagio 1891-1985 ....DLB-128

Marincović, Ranko 1913- DLB-147

Marinetti, Filippo Tommaso 1876-1944 ....DLB-114

Marion, Frances 1886-1973 ....DLB-44

Marius, Richard C. 1933- Y-85

The Mark Taper Forum DLB-7

Mark Twain on Perpetual Copyright ...Y-92

Markfield, Wallace 1926- DLB-2, 28

Markham, Edwin 1852-1940 ....DLB-54

Markle, Fletcher 1921-1991 ...DLB-68; Y-91

Marlatt, Daphne 1942- DLB-60

Marlitt, E. 1825-1887 ....DLB-129

Marlowe, Christopher 1564-1593 ...DLB-62

Marlyn, John 1912- DLB-88

Marmion, Shakerley 1603-1639 .....DLB-58

Der Marner before 1230-circa 1287 ....DLB-138

The *Marprelate Tracts* 1588-1589 ....DLB-132

Marquand, John P. 1893-1960 ....DLB-9, 102

Marqués, René 1919-1979 ....DLB-113

Marquis, Don 1878-1937 ....DLB-11, 25

Marriott, Anne 1913- DLB-68

Marryat, Frederick 1792-1848 ...DLB-21, 163

Marsh, George Perkins 1801-1882 ....DLB-1, 64

Marsh, James 1794-1842 ....DLB-1, 59

Marsh, Capen, Lyon and Webb DLB-49

Marsh, Ngaio 1899-1982 ....DLB-77

Marshall, Edison 1894-1967 ....DLB-102

Marshall, Edward 1932- DLB-16

Marshall, Emma 1828-1899 ....DLB-163

Marshall, James 1942-1992 ....DLB-61

Marshall, Joyce 1913- DLB-88

Marshall, Paule 1929- DLB-33, 157

Marshall, Tom 1938- DLB-60

Marsilius of Padua circa 1275-circa 1342 ....DLB-115

Marson, Una 1905-1965 ....DLB-157

Marston, John 1576-1634 ....DLB-58

Marston, Philip Bourke 1850-1887 ...DLB-35

Martens, Kurt 1870-1945 ....DLB-66

Martien, William S. [publishing house] DLB-49

Martin, Abe (see Hubbard, Kin)

Martin, Charles 1942- DLB-120

Martin, Claire 1914- DLB-60

Martin, Jay 1935- DLB-111

Martin, Violet Florence (see Ross, Martin)

Martin du Gard, Roger 1881-1958 ...DLB-65

Martineau, Harriet 1802-1876 ....DLB-21, 55, 159, 163, 166

Martínez, Eliud 1935- DLB-122

Martínez, Max 1943- DLB-82

Martyn, Edward 1859-1923 ....DLB-10

Marvell, Andrew 1621-1678 ....DLB-131

Marvin X 1944- DLB-38

Marx, Karl 1818-1883 ....DLB-129

Marzials, Theo 1850-1920 ....DLB-35

Masefield, John 1878-1967 ....DLB-10, 19, 153, 160

Mason, A. E. W. 1865-1948 ....DLB-70

Mason, Bobbie Ann 1940- Y-87

Mason, William 1725-1797 .... DLB-142

Mason Brothers DLB-49

Massey, Gerald 1828-1907 .... DLB-32

Massinger, Philip 1583-1640 .... DLB-58

Masson, David 1822-1907 .... DLB-144

Masters, Edgar Lee 1868-1950 ...... DLB-54

Mather, Cotton
1663-1728 .... DLB-24, 30, 140

Mather, Increase 1639-1723 .... DLB-24

Mather, Richard 1596-1669 .... DLB-24

Matheson, Richard 1926- DLB-8, 44

Matheus, John F. 1887- DLB-51

Mathews, Cornelius
1817?-1889 .... DLB-3, 64

Mathews, Elkin
[publishing house] DLB-112

Mathias, Roland 1915- DLB-27

Mathis, June 1892-1927 .... DLB-44

Mathis, Sharon Bell 1937- DLB-33

Matoš, Antun Gustav 1873-1914 ... DLB-147

The Matter of England
1240-1400 .... DLB-146

The Matter of Rome
early twelfth to late fifteenth
century DLB-146

Matthews, Brander
1852-1929 .... DLB-71, 78; DS-13

Matthews, Jack 1925- DLB-6

Matthews, William 1942- DLB-5

Matthiessen, F. O. 1902-1950 .... DLB-63

Matthiessen, Peter 1927- DLB-6

Maugham, W. Somerset
1874-1965 ...... DLB-10, 36, 77, 100, 162

Maupassant, Guy de 1850-1893 .... DLB-123

Mauriac, Claude 1914- DLB-83

Mauriac, François 1885-1970 .... DLB-65

Maurice, Frederick Denison
1805-1872 .... DLB-55

Maurois, André 1885-1967 .... DLB-65

Maury, James 1718-1769 .... DLB-31

Mavor, Elizabeth 1927- DLB-14

Mavor, Osborne Henry (see Bridie, James)

Maxwell, H. [publishing house] DLB-49

Maxwell, John [publishing house] .. DLB-106

Maxwell, William 1908- Y-80

May, Elaine 1932- DLB-44

May, Karl 1842-1912 .... DLB-129

May, Thomas 1595 or 1596-1650 .... DLB-58

Mayer, Bernadette 1945- DLB-165

Mayer, Mercer 1943- DLB-61

Mayer, O. B. 1818-1891 .... DLB-3

Mayes, Herbert R. 1900-1987 ...... DLB-137

Mayes, Wendell 1919-1992 .... DLB-26

Mayfield, Julian 1928-1984 .... DLB-33; Y-84

Mayhew, Henry 1812-1887 ...... DLB-18, 55

Mayhew, Jonathan 1720-1766 ...... DLB-31

Mayne, Jasper 1604-1672 .... DLB-126

Mayne, Seymour 1944- DLB-60

Mayor, Flora Macdonald
1872-1932 .... DLB-36

Mayrocker, Friederike 1924- DLB-85

Mazrui, Ali A. 1933- DLB-125

Mažuranić, Ivan 1814-1890 .... DLB-147

Mazursky, Paul 1930- DLB-44

McAlmon, Robert 1896-1956 ..... DLB-4, 45

McArthur, Peter 1866-1924 .... DLB-92

McBride, Robert M., and
Company DLB-46

McCaffrey, Anne 1926- DLB-8

McCarthy, Cormac 1933- DLB-6, 143

McCarthy, Mary 1912-1989 .... DLB-2; Y-81

McCay, Winsor 1871-1934 .... DLB-22

McClatchy, C. K. 1858-1936 .... DLB-25

McClellan, George Marion
1860-1934 .... DLB-50

McCloskey, Robert 1914- DLB-22

McClung, Nellie Letitia 1873-1951 ... DLB-92

McClure, Joanna 1930- DLB-16

McClure, Michael 1932- DLB-16

McClure, Phillips and Company DLB-46

McClure, S. S. 1857-1949 .... DLB-91

McClurg, A. C., and Company DLB-49

McCluskey, John A., Jr. 1944- DLB-33

McCollum, Michael A. 1946 .... Y-87

McConnell, William C. 1917- DLB-88

McCord, David 1897- DLB-61

McCorkle, Jill 1958- Y-87

McCorkle, Samuel Eusebius
1746-1811 .... DLB-37

McCormick, Anne O'Hare
1880-1954 .... DLB-29

McCormick, Robert R. 1880-1955 ... DLB-29

McCourt, Edward 1907-1972 ....DLB-88

McCoy, Horace 1897-1955 ....DLB-9

McCrae, John 1872-1918 ....DLB-92

McCullagh, Joseph B. 1842-1896 .....DLB-23

McCullers, Carson 1917-1967 ..... DLB-2, 7

McCulloch, Thomas 1776-1843 ......DLB-99

McDonald, Forrest 1927- DLB-17

McDonald, Walter
1934- DLB-105, DS-9

McDonald, Walter, Getting Started:
Accepting the Regions You Own–
or Which Own You DLB-105

McDougall, Colin 1917-1984 ....DLB-68

McDowell, Obolensky DLB-46

McEwan, Ian 1948- DLB-14

McFadden, David 1940- DLB-60

McFall, Frances Elizabeth Clarke
(see Grand, Sarah)

McFarlane, Leslie 1902-1977 ....DLB-88

McFee, William 1881-1966 ....DLB-153

McGahern, John 1934- DLB-14

McGee, Thomas D'Arcy
1825-1868 ....DLB-99

McGeehan, W. O. 1879-1933 ....DLB-25

McGill, Ralph 1898-1969 ....DLB-29

McGinley, Phyllis 1905-1978 .... DLB-11, 48

McGirt, James E. 1874-1930 ....DLB-50

McGlashan and Gill DLB-106

McGough, Roger 1937- DLB-40

McGraw-Hill DLB-46

McGuane, Thomas 1939- DLB-2; Y-80

McGuckian, Medbh 1950- DLB-40

McGuffey, William Holmes
1800-1873 ....DLB-42

McIlvanney, William 1936- DLB-14

McIlwraith, Jean Newton
1859-1938 ....DLB-92

McIntyre, James 1827-1906 ....DLB-99

McIntyre, O. O. 1884-1938 ....DLB-25

McKay, Claude
1889-1948 .... DLB-4, 45, 51, 117

The David McKay Company DLB-49

McKean, William V. 1820-1903 .....DLB-23

McKinley, Robin 1952- DLB-52

McLachlan, Alexander 1818-1896 ....DLB-99

McLaren, Floris Clark 1904-1978 ....DLB-68

McLaverty, Michael 1907- DLB-15

McLean, John R. 1848-1916 .... DLB-23

McLean, William L. 1852-1931 ...... DLB-25

McLennan, William 1856-1904 ...... DLB-92

McLoughlin Brothers DLB-49

McLuhan, Marshall 1911-1980 ...... DLB-88

McMaster, John Bach 1852-1932 ..... DLB-47

McMurtry, Larry
1936- DLB-2, 143; Y-80, 87

McNally, Terrence 1939- DLB-7

McNeil, Florence 1937- DLB-60

McNeile, Herman Cyril
1888-1937 .... DLB-77

McPherson, James Alan 1943- DLB-38

McPherson, Sandra 1943- Y-86

McWhirter, George 1939- DLB-60

McWilliams, Carey 1905-1980 .... DLB-137

Mead, L. T. 1844-1914 .... DLB-141

Mead, Matthew 1924- DLB-40

Mead, Taylor ?- DLB-16

Mechthild von Magdeburg
circa 1207-circa 1282 .... DLB-138

Medill, Joseph 1823-1899 .... DLB-43

Medoff, Mark 1940- DLB-7

Meek, Alexander Beaufort
1814-1865 .... DLB-3

Meeke, Mary ?-1816? DLB-116

Meinke, Peter 1932- DLB-5

Mejia Vallejo, Manuel 1923- DLB-113

Melançon, Robert 1947- DLB-60

Mell, Max 1882-1971 .... DLB-81, 124

Mellow, James R. 1926- DLB-111

Meltzer, David 1937- DLB-16

Meltzer, Milton 1915- DLB-61

Melville, Herman 1819-1891 ...... DLB-3, 74

Memoirs of Life and Literature (1920),
by W. H. Mallock [excerpt] DLB-57

Mencken, H. L.
1880-1956 .... DLB-11, 29, 63, 137

Mencken and Nietzsche: An Unpublished
Excerpt from H. L. Mencken's *My Life
as Author and Editor* Y-93

Mendelssohn, Moses 1729-1786 ..... DLB-97

Méndez M., Miguel 1930- DLB-82

Mercer, Cecil William (see Yates, Dornford)

Mercer, David 1928-1980 .... DLB-13

Mercer, John 1704-1768 .... DLB-31

Meredith, George
1828-1909 .... DLB-18, 35, 57, 159

Meredith, Louisa Anne
1812-1895 .... DLB-166

Meredith, Owen (see Lytton, Edward Robert
Bulwer)

Meredith, William 1919- DLB-5

Mérimée, Prosper 1803-1870 ...... DLB-119

Merivale, John Herman
1779-1844 .... DLB-96

Meriwether, Louise 1923- DLB-33

Merlin Press DLB-112

Merriam, Eve 1916-1992 .... DLB-61

The Merriam Company DLB-49

Merrill, James
1926-1995 .... DLB-5, 165; Y-85

Merrill and Baker DLB-49

The Mershon Company DLB-49

Merton, Thomas 1915-1968 ... DLB-48; Y-81

Merwin, W. S. 1927- DLB-5

Messner, Julian [publishing house] ... DLB-46

Metcalf, J. [publishing house] DLB-49

Metcalf, John 1938- DLB-60

The Methodist Book Concern DLB-49

Methuen and Company DLB-112

Mew, Charlotte 1869-1928 ..... DLB-19, 135

Mewshaw, Michael 1943- Y-80

Meyer, Conrad Ferdinand
1825-1898 .... DLB-129

Meyer, E. Y. 1946- DLB-75

Meyer, Eugene 1875-1959 .... DLB-29

Meyer, Michael 1921- DLB-155

Meyers, Jeffrey 1939- DLB-111

Meynell, Alice
1847-1922 .... DLB-19, 98

Meynell, Viola 1885-1956 .... DLB-153

Meyrink, Gustav 1868-1932 .... DLB-81

Michaels, Leonard 1933- DLB-130

Micheaux, Oscar 1884-1951 .... DLB-50

Michel of Northgate, Dan
circa 1265-circa 1340 .... DLB-146

Micheline, Jack 1929- DLB-16

Michener, James A. 1907?- DLB-6

Micklejohn, George
circa 1717-1818 .... DLB-31

Middle English Literature:
An Introduction DLB-146

The Middle English Lyric DLB-146

Middle Hill Press DLB-106

Middleton, Christopher 1926- DLB-40

Middleton, Richard 1882-1911 ..... DLB-156

Middleton, Stanley 1919- DLB-14

Middleton, Thomas 1580-1627 ...... DLB-58

Miegel, Agnes 1879-1964 .... DLB-56

Miles, Josephine 1911-1985 .... DLB-48

Milius, John 1944- DLB-44

Mill, James 1773-1836 .... DLB-107, 158

Mill, John Stuart 1806-1873 .... DLB-55

Millar, Kenneth
1915-1983 .... DLB-2; Y-83; DS-6

Millar, Andrew
[publishing house] DLB-154

Millay, Edna St. Vincent
1892-1950 .... DLB-45

Miller, Arthur 1915- DLB-7

Miller, Caroline 1903-1992 .... DLB-9

Miller, Eugene Ethelbert 1950- DLB-41

Miller, Heather Ross 1939- DLB-120

Miller, Henry 1891-1980 ..... DLB-4, 9; Y-80

Miller, J. Hillis 1928- DLB-67

Miller, James [publishing house] DLB-49

Miller, Jason 1939- DLB-7

Miller, May 1899- DLB-41

Miller, Paul 1906-1991 .... DLB-127

Miller, Perry 1905-1963 .... DLB-17, 63

Miller, Sue 1943- DLB-143

Miller, Walter M., Jr. 1923- DLB-8

Miller, Webb 1892-1940 .... DLB-29

Millhauser, Steven 1943- DLB-2

Millican, Arthenia J. Bates
1920- DLB-38

Mills and Boon DLB-112

Milman, Henry Hart 1796-1868 ..... DLB-96

Milne, A. A.
1882-1956 .... DLB-10, 77, 100, 160

Milner, Ron 1938- DLB-38

Milner, William
[publishing house] DLB-106

Milnes, Richard Monckton (Lord Houghton)
1809-1885 .... DLB-32

Milton, John 1608-1674 .... DLB-131, 151

The Minerva Press DLB-154

Minnesang circa 1150-1280 .... DLB-138

Minns, Susan 1839-1938 .... DLB-140

Minor Illustrators, 1880-1914 ...... DLB-141

Minor Poets of the Earlier Seventeenth
Century DLB-121

Minton, Balch and Company DLB-46

Mirbeau, Octave 1848-1917 .... DLB-123

Mirk, John died after 1414? DLB-146

Miron, Gaston 1928- DLB-60

A Mirror for Magistrates DLB-167

Mitchel, Jonathan 1624-1668 .... DLB-24

Mitchell, Adrian 1932- DLB-40

Mitchell, Donald Grant
1822-1908 .... DLB-1; DS-13

Mitchell, Gladys 1901-1983 .... DLB-77

Mitchell, James Leslie 1901-1935 .... DLB-15

Mitchell, John (see Slater, Patrick)

Mitchell, John Ames 1845-1918 ..... DLB-79

Mitchell, Julian 1935- DLB-14

Mitchell, Ken 1940- DLB-60

Mitchell, Langdon 1862-1935 .... DLB-7

Mitchell, Loften 1919- DLB-38

Mitchell, Margaret 1900-1949 .... DLB-9

Mitchell, W. O. 1914- DLB-88

Mitchison, Naomi Margaret (Haldane)
1897- DLB-160

Mitford, Mary Russell
1787-1855 .... DLB-110, 116

Mittelholzer, Edgar 1909-1965 ..... DLB-117

Mitterer, Erika 1906- DLB-85

Mitterer, Felix 1948- DLB-124

Mizener, Arthur 1907-1988 .... DLB-103

Modern Age Books DLB-46

"Modern English Prose" (1876),
by George Saintsbury DLB-57

The Modern Language Association of America
Celebrates Its Centennial Y-84

The Modern Library DLB-46

"Modern Novelists – Great and Small" (1855),
by Margaret Oliphant DLB-21

"Modern Style" (1857), by Cockburn
Thomson [excerpt] DLB-57

The Modernists (1932), by Joseph Warren
Beach DLB-36

Modiano, Patrick 1945- DLB-83

Moffat, Yard and Company DLB-46

Moffet, Thomas 1553-1604 .... DLB-136

Mohr, Nicholasa 1938- DLB-145

Moix, Ana María 1947- DLB-134

Molesworth, Louisa 1839-1921 .... DLB-135

Möllhausen, Balduin 1825-1905 .... DLB-129

Momaday, N. Scott 1934- DLB-143

Monkhouse, Allan 1858-1936 .... DLB-10

Monro, Harold 1879-1932 .... DLB-19

Monroe, Harriet 1860-1936 ...... DLB-54, 91

Monsarrat, Nicholas 1910-1979 ..... DLB-15

Montagu, Lady Mary Wortley
1689-1762 .... DLB-95, 101

Montague, John 1929- DLB-40

Montale, Eugenio 1896-1981 .... DLB-114

Monterroso, Augusto 1921- DLB-145

Montgomerie, Alexander
circa 1550?-1598 .... DLB-167

Montgomery, James
1771-1854 .... DLB-93, 158

Montgomery, John 1919- DLB-16

Montgomery, Lucy Maud
1874-1942 .... DLB-92

Montgomery, Marion 1925- DLB-6

Montgomery, Robert Bruce (see Crispin,
Edmund)

Montherlant, Henry de 1896-1972 ... DLB-72

The Monthly Review 1749-1844 ...... DLB-110

Montigny, Louvigny de 1876-1955 ... DLB-92

Montoya, José 1932- DLB-122

Moodie, John Wedderburn Dunbar
1797-1869 .... DLB-99

Moodie, Susanna 1803-1885 .... DLB-99

Moody, Joshua circa 1633-1697 ..... DLB-24

Moody, William Vaughn
1869-1910 .... DLB-7, 54

Moorcock, Michael 1939- DLB-14

Moore, Catherine L. 1911- DLB-8

Moore, Clement Clarke 1779-1863 .. DLB-42

Moore, Dora Mavor 1888-1979 ..... DLB-92

Moore, George
1852-1933 .... DLB-10, 18, 57, 135

Moore, Marianne
1887-1972 .... DLB-45; DS-7

Moore, Mavor 1919- DLB-88

Moore, Richard 1927- DLB-105

Moore, Richard, The No Self, the Little Self,
and the Poets DLB-105

Moore, T. Sturge 1870-1944 .... DLB-19

Moore, Thomas 1779-1852 ..... DLB-96, 144

Moore, Ward 1903-1978 .... DLB-8

Moore, Wilstach, Keys and
Company DLB-49

The Moorland-Spingarn Research
Center DLB-76

Moorman, Mary C. 1905-1994 ..... DLB-155

Moraga, Cherríe 1952- DLB-82

Morales, Alejandro 1944- DLB-82

Morales, Mario Roberto 1947- DLB-145

Morales, Rafael 1919- DLB-108

Morality Plays: *Mankind* circa 1450-1500 and
Everyman circa 1500 .... DLB-146

More, Hannah
1745-1833 .... DLB-107, 109, 116, 158

More, Henry 1614-1687 .... DLB-126

More, Sir Thomas
1477 or 1478-1535 .... DLB-136

Moreno, Dorinda 1939- DLB-122

Morency, Pierre 1942- DLB-60

Moretti, Marino 1885-1979 .... DLB-114

Morgan, Berry 1919- DLB-6

Morgan, Charles 1894-1958 .... DLB-34, 100

Morgan, Edmund S. 1916- DLB-17

Morgan, Edwin 1920- DLB-27

Morgan, John Pierpont
1837-1913 .... DLB-140

Morgan, John Pierpont, Jr.
1867-1943 .... DLB-140

Morgan, Robert 1944- DLB-120

Morgan, Sydney Owenson, Lady
1776?-1859 .... DLB-116, 158

Morgner, Irmtraud 1933- DLB-75

Morhof, Daniel Georg
1639-1691 .... DLB-164

Morier, James Justinian
1782 or 1783?-1849 .... DLB-116

Mörike, Eduard 1804-1875 .... DLB-133

Morin, Paul 1889-1963 .... DLB-92

Morison, Richard 1514?-1556 ...... DLB-136

Morison, Samuel Eliot 1887-1976 .... DLB-17

Moritz, Karl Philipp 1756-1793 ...... DLB-94

Moriz von Craûn
circa 1220-1230 .... DLB-138

Morley, Christopher 1890-1957 .... DLB-9

Morley, John 1838-1923 .... DLB-57, 144

Morris, George Pope 1802-1864 ..... DLB-73

Morris, Lewis 1833-1907 .... DLB-35

Morris, Richard B. 1904-1989 .... DLB-17

Morris, William
1834-1896 .... DLB-18, 35, 57, 156

Morris, Willie 1934- Y-80

Morris, Wright 1910- DLB-2; Y-81

Morrison, Arthur 1863-1945 ....DLB-70, 135

Morrison, Charles Clayton
1874-1966 ....DLB-91

Morrison, Toni
1931- DLB-6, 33, 143; Y-81

Morrow, William, and Company DLB-46

Morse, James Herbert 1841-1923 ....DLB-71

Morse, Jedidiah 1761-1826 ....DLB-37

Morse, John T., Jr. 1840-1937 ....DLB-47

Mortimer, Favell Lee 1802-1878 ....DLB-163

Mortimer, John 1923- DLB-13

Morton, Carlos 1942- DLB-122

Morton, John P., and Company DLB-49

Morton, Nathaniel 1613-1685 ....DLB-24

Morton, Sarah Wentworth
1759-1846 ....DLB-37

Morton, Thomas
circa 1579-circa 1647 ....DLB-24

Moscherosch, Johann Michael
1601-1669 ....DLB-164

Möser, Justus 1720-1794 ....DLB-97

Mosley, Nicholas 1923- DLB-14

Moss, Arthur 1889-1969 ....DLB-4

Moss, Howard 1922-1987 ....DLB-5

Moss, Thylias 1954- DLB-120

The Most Powerful Book Review in America
[*New York Times Book Review*] Y-82

Motion, Andrew 1952- DLB-40

Motley, John Lothrop
1814-1877 .... DLB-1, 30, 59

Motley, Willard 1909-1965 .....DLB-76, 143

Motte, Benjamin Jr.
[publishing house] DLB-154

Motteux, Peter Anthony
1663-1718 ....DLB-80

Mottram, R. H. 1883-1971 ....DLB-36

Mouré, Erin 1955- DLB-60

Movies from Books, 1920-1974 ......DLB-9

Mowat, Farley 1921- DLB-68

Mowbray, A. R., and Company,
Limited DLB-106

Mowrer, Edgar Ansel 1892-1977 .....DLB-29

Mowrer, Paul Scott 1887-1971 ......DLB-29

Moxon, Edward
[publishing house] DLB-106

Mphahlele, Es'kia (Ezekiel)
1919- DLB-125

Mtshali, Oswald Mbuyiseni
1940- DLB-125

Mucedorus DLB-62

Mudford, William 1782-1848 ...... DLB-159

Mueller, Lisel 1924- DLB-105

Muhajir, El (see Marvin X)

Muhajir, Nazzam Al Fitnah (see Marvin X)

Mühlbach, Luise 1814-1873 .... DLB-133

Muir, Edwin 1887-1959 .... DLB-20, 100

Muir, Helen 1937- DLB-14

Mukherjee, Bharati 1940- DLB-60

Mulcaster, Richard
1531 or 1532-1611 .... DLB-167

Muldoon, Paul 1951- DLB-40

Müller, Friedrich (see Müller, Maler)

Müller, Heiner 1929- DLB-124

Müller, Maler 1749-1825 .... DLB-94

Müller, Wilhelm 1794-1827 .... DLB-90

Mumford, Lewis 1895-1990 .... DLB-63

Munby, Arthur Joseph 1828-1910 ... DLB-35

Munday, Anthony 1560-1633 ...... DLB-62

Mundt, Clara (see Mühlbach, Luise)

Mundt, Theodore 1808-1861 ...... DLB-133

Munford, Robert circa 1737-1783 ... DLB-31

Mungoshi, Charles 1947- DLB-157

Munonye, John 1929- DLB-117

Munro, Alice 1931- DLB-53

Munro, H. H. 1870-1916 ...... DLB-34, 162

Munro, Neil 1864-1930 .... DLB-156

Munro, George
[publishing house] DLB-49

Munro, Norman L.
[publishing house] DLB-49

Munroe, James, and Company DLB-49

Munroe, Kirk 1850-1930 .... DLB-42

Munroe and Francis DLB-49

Munsell, Joel [publishing house] DLB-49

Munsey, Frank A. 1854-1925 .... DLB-25, 91

Munsey, Frank A., and
Company DLB-49

Murav'ev, Mikhail Nikitich
1757-1807 .... DLB-150

Murdoch, Iris 1919- DLB-14

Murdoch, Rupert 1931- DLB-127

Murfree, Mary N. 1850-1922 .... DLB-12, 74

Murger, Henry 1822-1861 .... DLB-119

Murger, Louis-Henri (see Murger, Henry)

Muro, Amado 1915-1971 ....DLB-82

Murphy, Arthur 1727-1805 .....DLB-89, 142

Murphy, Beatrice M. 1908- DLB-76

Murphy, Emily 1868-1933 ....DLB-99

Murphy, John H., III 1916- DLB-127

Murphy, John, and Company DLB-49

Murphy, Richard 1927-1993 ....DLB-40

Murray, Albert L. 1916- DLB-38

Murray, Gilbert 1866-1957 ....DLB-10

Murray, Judith Sargent 1751-1820 ...DLB-37

Murray, Pauli 1910-1985 ....DLB-41

Murray, John [publishing house] DLB-154

Murry, John Middleton
1889-1957 ....DLB-149

Musäus, Johann Karl August
1735-1787 ....DLB-97

Muschg, Adolf 1934- DLB-75

The Music of *Minnesang* DLB-138

Musil, Robert 1880-1942 ....DLB-81, 124

Muspilli circa 790-circa 850 ....DLB-148

Mussey, Benjamin B., and
Company DLB-49

Mwangi, Meja 1948- DLB-125

Myers, Gustavus 1872-1942 ....DLB-47

Myers, L. H. 1881-1944 ....DLB-15

Myers, Walter Dean 1937- DLB-33

N

Nabbes, Thomas circa 1605-1641 ....DLB-58

Nabl, Franz 1883-1974 ....DLB-81

Nabokov, Vladimir
1899-1977 ..... DLB-2; Y-80, Y-91; DS-3

Nabokov Festival at Cornell Y-83

The Vladimir Nabokov Archive
in the Berg Collection Y-91

Nafis and Cornish DLB-49

Naipaul, Shiva 1945-1985 ....DLB-157; Y-85

Naipaul, V. S. 1932- DLB-125; Y-85

Nancrede, Joseph
[publishing house] DLB-49

Naranjo, Carmen 1930- DLB-145

Narrache, Jean 1893-1970 ....DLB-92

Nasby, Petroleum Vesuvius (see Locke, David
Ross)

Nash, Ogden 1902-1971 ....DLB-11

Nash, Eveleigh
[publishing house] DLB-112

Nashe, Thomas 1567-1601? DLB-167

Nast, Conde 1873-1942 .... DLB-91

Nastasijević, Momčilo 1894-1938 ... DLB-147

Nathan, George Jean 1882-1958 .... DLB-137

Nathan, Robert 1894-1985 .... DLB-9

The National Jewish Book Awards Y-85

The National Theatre and the Royal
Shakespeare Company: The
National Companies DLB-13

Naughton, Bill 1910- DLB-13

Nazor, Vladimir 1876-1949 .... DLB-147

Ndebele, Njabulo 1948- DLB-157

Neagoe, Peter 1881-1960 .... DLB-4

Neal, John 1793-1876 .... DLB-1, 59

Neal, Joseph C. 1807-1847 .... DLB-11

Neal, Larry 1937-1981 .... DLB-38

The Neale Publishing Company DLB-49

Neely, F. Tennyson
[publishing house] DLB-49

Negri, Ada 1870-1945 .... DLB-114

"The Negro as a Writer," by
G. M. McClellan DLB-50

"Negro Poets and Their Poetry," by
Wallace Thurman DLB-50

Neidhart von Reuental
circa 1185-circa 1240 .... DLB-138

Neihardt, John G. 1881-1973 ..... DLB-9, 54

Neledinsky-Meletsky, Iurii Aleksandrovich
1752-1828 .... DLB-150

Nelligan, Emile 1879-1941 .... DLB-92

Nelson, Alice Moore Dunbar
1875-1935 .... DLB-50

Nelson, Thomas, and Sons [U.S.] ... DLB-49

Nelson, Thomas, and Sons [U.K.] .. DLB-106

Nelson, William 1908-1978 .... DLB-103

Nelson, William Rockhill
1841-1915 .... DLB-23

Nemerov, Howard 1920-1991 ... DLB-5, 6; Y-83

Nesbit, E. 1858-1924 .... DLB-141, 153

Ness, Evaline 1911-1986 .... DLB-61

Nestroy, Johann 1801-1862 .... DLB-133

Neugeboren, Jay 1938- DLB-28

Neumann, Alfred 1895-1952 .... DLB-56

Neumark, Georg 1621-1681 .... DLB-164

Nevins, Allan 1890-1971 .... DLB-17

Nevinson, Henry Woodd
1856-1941 .... DLB-135

The New American Library DLB-46

New Approaches to Biography: Challenges
from Critical Theory, USC Conference
on Literary Studies, 1990 .... Y-90

New Directions Publishing
Corporation DLB-46

A New Edition of Huck Finn Y-85

New Forces at Work in the American Theatre:
1915-1925 .... DLB-7

New Literary Periodicals:
A Report for 1987 .... Y-87

New Literary Periodicals:
A Report for 1988 .... Y-88

New Literary Periodicals:
A Report for 1989 .... Y-89

New Literary Periodicals:
A Report for 1990 .... Y-90

New Literary Periodicals:
A Report for 1991 .... Y-91

New Literary Periodicals:
A Report for 1992 .... Y-92

New Literary Periodicals:
A Report for 1993 .... Y-93

The New Monthly Magazine
1814-1884 .... DLB-110

The New Ulysses Y-84

The New Variorum Shakespeare Y-85

A New Voice: The Center for the Book's First
Five Years Y-83

The New Wave [Science Fiction] DLB-8

New York City Bookshops in the 1930s and
1940s: The Recollections of Walter
Goldwater Y-93

Newbery, John
[publishing house] DLB-154

Newbolt, Henry 1862-1938 .... DLB-19

Newbound, Bernard Slade (see Slade, Bernard)

Newby, P. H. 1918- DLB-15

Newby, Thomas Cautley
[publishing house] DLB-106

Newcomb, Charles King 1820-1894 ... DLB-1

Newell, Peter 1862-1924 .... DLB-42

Newell, Robert Henry 1836-1901 .... DLB-11

Newhouse, Samuel I. 1895-1979 .... DLB-127

Newman, Cecil Earl 1903-1976 ..... DLB-127

Newman, David (see Benton, Robert)

Newman, Frances 1883-1928 .... Y-80

Newman, John Henry
1801-1890 .... DLB-18, 32, 55

Newman, Mark [publishing house] ... DLB-49

Newnes, George, Limited DLB-112

Newsome, Effie Lee 1885-1979 ...... DLB-76

Newspaper Syndication of American
Humor DLB-11

Newton, A. Edward 1864-1940 ..... DLB-140

Ngugi wa Thiong'o 1938- DLB-125

The Nibelungenlied and the Klage
circa 1200 .... DLB-138

Nichol, B. P. 1944- DLB-53

Nicholas of Cusa 1401-1464 .... DLB-115

Nichols, Dudley 1895-1960 .... DLB-26

Nichols, Grace 1950- DLB-157

Nichols, John 1940- Y-82

Nichols, Mary Sargeant (Neal) Gove 1810-
1884 .... DLB-1

Nichols, Peter 1927- DLB-13

Nichols, Roy F. 1896-1973 .... DLB-17

Nichols, Ruth 1948- DLB-60

Nicholson, Norman 1914- DLB-27

Nicholson, William 1872-1949 ..... DLB-141

Ní Chuilleanáin, Eiléan 1942- DLB-40

Nicol, Eric 1919- DLB-68

Nicolai, Friedrich 1733-1811 .... DLB-97

Nicolay, John G. 1832-1901 and
Hay, John 1838-1905 .... DLB-47

Nicolson, Harold 1886-1968 ... DLB-100, 149

Nicolson, Nigel 1917- DLB-155

Niebuhr, Reinhold 1892-1971 .... DLB-17

Niedecker, Lorine 1903-1970 .... DLB-48

Nieman, Lucius W. 1857-1935 .... DLB-25

Nietzsche, Friedrich 1844-1900 ..... DLB-129

Niggli, Josefina 1910- Y-80

Nightingale, Florence 1820-1910 .... DLB-166

Nikolev, Nikolai Petrovich
1758-1815 .... DLB-150

Niles, Hezekiah 1777-1839 .... DLB-43

Nims, John Frederick 1913- DLB-5

Nin, Anaïs 1903-1977 .... DLB-2, 4, 152

1985: The Year of the Mystery:
A Symposium Y-85

Nissenson, Hugh 1933- DLB-28

Niven, Frederick John 1878-1944 .... DLB-92

Niven, Larry 1938- DLB-8

Nizan, Paul 1905-1940 .... DLB-72

Njegoš, Petar II Petrović
1813-1851 .... DLB-147

Nkosi, Lewis 1936- DLB-157

Nobel Peace Prize
The 1986 Nobel Peace Prize
    Nobel Lecture 1986: Hope, Despair   and
    Memory
    Tributes from Abraham Bernstein,
    Norman Lamm, and
    John R. Silber Y-86

The Nobel Prize and Literary Politics ...Y-86

Nobel Prize in Literature
The 1982 Nobel Prize in Literature
    Announcement by the Swedish Academy
    of the Nobel Prize Nobel Lecture 1982:
    The Solitude of Latin America Excerpt
    from *One Hundred Years of Solitude* The
    Magical World of Macondo A Tribute
    to Gabriel García Márquez Y-82

The 1983 Nobel Prize in Literature
    Announcement by the Swedish Academy
    Nobel Lecture 1983 The Stature of
    William Golding Y-83

The 1984 Nobel Prize in Literature
    Announcement by the Swedish Academy
    Jaroslav Seifert Through the Eyes of the
    English-Speaking Reader
    Three Poems by Jaroslav Seifert Y-84

The 1985 Nobel Prize in Literature
    Announcement by the Swedish Academy
    Nobel Lecture 1985 ....Y-85

The 1986 Nobel Prize in Literature
    Nobel Lecture 1986: This Past Must
    Address Its Present Y-86

The 1987 Nobel Prize in Literature
    Nobel Lecture 1987 ....Y-87

The 1988 Nobel Prize in Literature
    Nobel Lecture 1988 ....Y-88

The 1989 Nobel Prize in Literature
    Nobel Lecture 1989 ....Y-89

The 1990 Nobel Prize in Literature
    Nobel Lecture 1990 ....Y-90

The 1991 Nobel Prize in Literature
    Nobel Lecture 1991 ....Y-91

The 1992 Nobel Prize in Literature
    Nobel Lecture 1992 ....Y-92

The 1993 Nobel Prize in Literature
    Nobel Lecture 1993 ....Y-93

The 1994 Nobel Prize in Literature
    Nobel Lecture 1994 ....Y-94

The 1995 Nobel Prize in Literature
    Nobel Lecture 1995 ....Y-95

Nodier, Charles 1780-1844 ....DLB-119

Noel, Roden 1834-1894 ....DLB-35

Nolan, William F. 1928- DLB-8

Noland, C. F. M. 1810?-1858 ....DLB-11

Nonesuch Press DLB-112

Noonday Press DLB-46

Noone, John 1936- DLB-14

Nora, Eugenio de 1923- DLB-134

Nordhoff, Charles 1887-1947 .... DLB-9

Norman, Charles 1904- DLB-111

Norman, Marsha 1947- Y-84

Norris, Charles G. 1881-1945 .... DLB-9

Norris, Frank 1870-1902 .... DLB-12

Norris, Leslie 1921- DLB-27

Norse, Harold 1916- DLB-16

North Point Press DLB-46

Nortje, Arthur 1942-1970 .... DLB-125

Norton, Alice Mary (see Norton, Andre)

Norton, Andre 1912- DLB-8, 52

Norton, Andrews 1786-1853 .... DLB-1

Norton, Caroline 1808-1877 .... DLB-21, 159

Norton, Charles Eliot 1827-1908 .. DLB-1, 64

Norton, John 1606-1663 .... DLB-24

Norton, Mary 1903-1992 .... DLB-160

Norton, Thomas (see Sackville, Thomas)

Norton, W. W., and Company DLB-46

Norwood, Robert 1874-1932 .... DLB-92

Nossack, Hans Erich 1901-1977 ..... DLB-69

Notker Balbulus circa 840-912 ..... DLB-148

Notker III of Saint Gall
    circa 950-1022 .... DLB-148

Notker von Zweifalten ?-1095 ..... DLB-148

A Note on Technique (1926), by
    Elizabeth A. Drew [excerpts] DLB-36

Nourse, Alan E. 1928- DLB-8

Novak, Vjenceslav 1859-1905 ...... DLB-147

Novalis 1772-1801 .... DLB-90

Novaro, Mario 1868-1944 .... DLB-114

Novás Calvo, Lino 1903-1983 ..... DLB-145

"The Novel in [Robert Browning's] 'The Ring
    and the Book' " (1912), by
    Henry James DLB-32

The Novel of Impressionism,
    by Jethro Bithell DLB-66

Novel-Reading: *The Works of Charles Dickens,*
    The Works of W. Makepeace Thackeray (1879),
    by Anthony Trollope DLB-21

The Novels of Dorothy Richardson (1918), by
    May Sinclair DLB-36

Novels with a Purpose (1864), by Justin
    M'Carthy DLB-21

Noventa, Giacomo 1898-1960 ..... DLB-114

Novikov, Nikolai Ivanovich
    1744-1818 .... DLB-150

Nowlan, Alden 1933-1983 .... DLB-53

Noyes, Alfred 1880-1958 ....DLB-20

Noyes, Crosby S. 1825-1908 ....DLB-23

Noyes, Nicholas 1647-1717 ....DLB-24

Noyes, Theodore W. 1858-1946 .....DLB-29

N-Town Plays
    circa 1468 to early sixteenth
    century DLB-146

Nugent, Frank 1908-1965 ....DLB-44

Nusic, Branislav 1864-1938 ....DLB-147

Nutt, David [publishing house] DLB-106

Nwapa, Flora 1931- DLB-125

Nye, Edgar Wilson (Bill)
    1850-1896 ....DLB-11, 23

Nye, Naomi Shihab 1952- DLB-120

Nye, Robert 1939- DLB-14

O

Oakes, Urian circa 1631-1681 ....DLB-24

Oates, Joyce Carol
    1938- DLB-2, 5, 130; Y-81

Ober, William 1920-1993 ....Y-93

Oberholtzer, Ellis Paxson
    1868-1936 ....DLB-47

Obradović, Dositej 1740?-1811 .....DLB-147

O'Brien, Edna 1932- DLB-14

O'Brien, Fitz-James 1828-1862 ......DLB-74

O'Brien, Kate 1897-1974 ....DLB-15

O'Brien, Tim
    1946- DLB-152; Y-80; DS-9

O'Casey, Sean 1880-1964 ....DLB-10

Ochs, Adolph S. 1858-1935 ....DLB-25

Ochs-Oakes, George Washington
    1861-1931 ....DLB-137

O'Connor, Flannery
    1925-1964 ..... DLB-2, 152; Y-80; DS-12

O'Connor, Frank 1903-1966 ....DLB-162

Octopus Publishing Group DLB-112

Odell, Jonathan 1737-1818 ....DLB-31, 99

O'Dell, Scott 1903-1989 ....DLB-52

Odets, Clifford 1906-1963 ....DLB-7, 26

Odhams Press Limited DLB-112

O'Donnell, Peter 1920- DLB-87

O'Donovan, Michael (see O'Connor, Frank)

O'Faolain, Julia 1932- DLB-14

O'Faolain, Sean 1900- DLB-15, 162

Off Broadway and Off-Off Broadway . DLB-7

Off-Loop Theatres DLB-7

Offord, Carl Ruthven 1910- DLB-76

O'Flaherty, Liam
1896-1984 .... DLB-36, 162; Y-84

Ogilvie, J. S., and Company DLB-49

Ogot, Grace 1930- DLB-125

O'Grady, Desmond 1935- DLB-40

Ogunyemi, Wale 1939- DLB-157

O'Hagan, Howard 1902-1982 ...... DLB-68

O'Hara, Frank 1926-1966 .... DLB-5, 16

O'Hara, John 1905-1970 .... DLB-9, 86; DS-2

Okara, Gabriel 1921- DLB-125

O'Keeffe, John 1747-1833 .... DLB-89

Okigbo, Christopher 1930-1967 .... DLB-125

Okot p'Bitek 1931-1982 .... DLB-125

Okpewho, Isidore 1941- DLB-157

Okri, Ben 1959- DLB-157

Olaudah Equiano and Unfinished Journeys:
The Slave-Narrative Tradition and
Twentieth-Century Continuities, by
Paul Edwards and Pauline T.
Wangman DLB-117

Old English Literature:
An Introduction DLB-146

Old English Riddles
eighth to tenth centuries DLB-146

Old Franklin Publishing House DLB-49

Old German Genesis and *Old German Exodus*
circa 1050-circa 1130 .... DLB-148

Old High German Charms and
Blessings DLB-148

The *Old High German Isidor*
circa 790-800 .... DLB-148

Older, Fremont 1856-1935 .... DLB-25

Oldham, John 1653-1683 .... DLB-131

Olds, Sharon 1942- DLB-120

Olearius, Adam 1599-1671 .... DLB-164

Oliphant, Laurence
1829?-1888 .... DLB-18, 166

Oliphant, Margaret 1828-1897 ...... DLB-18

Oliver, Chad 1928- DLB-8

Oliver, Mary 1935- DLB-5

Ollier, Claude 1922- DLB-83

Olsen, Tillie 1913?- DLB-28; Y-80

Olson, Charles 1910-1970 .... DLB-5, 16

Olson, Elder 1909- DLB-48, 63

Omotoso, Kole 1943- DLB-125

"On Art in Fiction "(1838),
by Edward Bulwer DLB-21

On Learning to Write Y-88

On Some of the Characteristics of Modern
Poetry and On the Lyrical Poems of
Alfred Tennyson (1831), by Arthur
Henry Hallam DLB-32

"On Style in English Prose" (1898), by
Frederic Harrison DLB-57

"On Style in Literature: Its Technical
Elements" (1885), by Robert Louis
Stevenson DLB-57

"On the Writing of Essays" (1862),
by Alexander Smith DLB-57

Ondaatje, Michael 1943- DLB-60

O'Neill, Eugene 1888-1953 .... DLB-7

Onetti, Juan Carlos 1909-1994 ..... DLB-113

Onions, George Oliver
1872-1961 .... DLB-153

Onofri, Arturo 1885-1928 .... DLB-114

Opie, Amelia 1769-1853 ....DLB-116, 159

Opitz, Martin 1597-1639 .... DLB-164

Oppen, George 1908-1984 ......DLB-5, 165

Oppenheim, E. Phillips 1866-1946 ... DLB-70

Oppenheim, James 1882-1932 .... DLB-28

Oppenheimer, Joel 1930- DLB-5

Optic, Oliver (see Adams, William Taylor)

Orczy, Emma, Baroness
1865-1947 .... DLB-70

Origo, Iris 1902-1988 .... DLB-155

Orlovitz, Gil 1918-1973 .... DLB-2, 5

Orlovsky, Peter 1933- DLB-16

Ormond, John 1923- DLB-27

Ornitz, Samuel 1890-1957 ......DLB-28, 44

Ortiz, Simon 1941- DLB-120

Ortnit and *Wolfdietrich*
circa 1225-1250 .... DLB-138

Orton, Joe 1933-1967 .... DLB-13

Orwell, George 1903-1950 ......DLB-15, 98

The Orwell Year Y-84

Ory, Carlos Edmundo de 1923- .. DLB-134

Osbey, Brenda Marie 1957- DLB-120

Osbon, B. S. 1827-1912 .... DLB-43

Osborne, John 1929-1994 .... DLB-13

Osgood, Herbert L. 1855-1918 ...... DLB-47

Osgood, James R., and
Company DLB-49

Osgood, McIlvaine and
Company DLB-112

O'Shaughnessy, Arthur
1844-1881 .... DLB-35

O'Shea, Patrick
[publishing house] DLB-49

Osipov, Nikolai Petrovich
1751-1799 .... DLB-150

Osofisan, Femi 1946- DLB-125

Ostenso, Martha 1900-1963 .... DLB-92

Ostriker, Alicia 1937- DLB-120

Osundare, Niyi 1947- DLB-157

Oswald, Eleazer 1755-1795 .... DLB-43

Otero, Blas de 1916-1979 .... DLB-134

Otero, Miguel Antonio
1859-1944 .... DLB-82

Otero Silva, Miguel 1908-1985 ...... DLB-145

Otfried von Weißenburg
circa 800-circa 875? DLB-148

Otis, James (see Kaler, James Otis)

Otis, James, Jr. 1725-1783 .... DLB-31

Otis, Broaders and Company DLB-49

Ottaway, James 1911- DLB-127

Ottendorfer, Oswald 1826-1900 ..... DLB-23

Otto-Peters, Louise 1819-1895 ...... DLB-129

Otway, Thomas 1652-1685 .... DLB-80

Ouellette, Fernand 1930- DLB-60

Ouida 1839-1908 .... DLB-18, 156

Outing Publishing Company DLB-46

Outlaw Days, by Joyce Johnson DLB-16

Overbury, Sir Thomas
circa 1581-1613 .... DLB-151

The Overlook Press DLB-46

Overview of U.S. Book Publishing,
1910-1945 .... DLB-9

Owen, Guy 1925- DLB-5

Owen, John 1564-1622 .... DLB-121

Owen, John [publishing house] DLB-49

Owen, Robert 1771-1858 ..... DLB-107, 158

Owen, Wilfred 1893-1918 .... DLB-20

Owen, Peter, Limited DLB-112

The *Owl and the Nightingale*
circa 1189-1199 .... DLB-146

Owsley, Frank L. 1890-1956 .... DLB-17

Ozerov, Vladislav Aleksandrovich
1769-1816 .... DLB-150

Ozick, Cynthia 1928- DLB-28, 152; Y-82

P

Pace, Richard 1482?-1536 ....DLB-167

Pacey, Desmond 1917-1975 . . . . DLB-88

Pack, Robert 1929- DLB-5

Packaging Papa: *The Garden of Eden* Y-86

Padell Publishing Company DLB-46

Padgett, Ron 1942- DLB-5

Padilla, Ernesto Chávez 1944- DLB-122

Page, L. C., and Company DLB-49

Page, P. K. 1916- DLB-68

Page, Thomas Nelson
1853-1922 . . . . DLB-12, 78; DS-13

Page, Walter Hines 1855-1918 . . .DLB-71, 91

Paget, Francis Edward
1806-1882 . . . . .DLB-163

Paget, Violet (see Lee, Vernon)

Pagliarani, Elio 1927- DLB-128

Pain, Barry 1864-1928 . . . . .DLB-135

Pain, Philip ?-circa 1666 . . . . .DLB-24

Paine, Robert Treat, Jr. 1773-1811 . . .DLB-37

Paine, Thomas
1737-1809 . . . . DLB-31, 43, 73, 158

Painter, George D. 1914- DLB-155

Painter, William 1540?-1594 . . . . . . .DLB-136

Palazzeschi, Aldo 1885-1974 . . . . . . .DLB-114

Paley, Grace 1922- DLB-28

Palfrey, John Gorham
1796-1881 . . . . .DLB-1, 30

Palgrave, Francis Turner
1824-1897 . . . . .DLB-35

Paltock, Robert 1697-1767 . . . . .DLB-39

Pan Books Limited DLB-112

Panamaa, Norman 1914- and
Frank, Melvin 1913-1988 . . . . .DLB-26

Pancake, Breece D'J 1952-1979 . . . . .DLB-130

Panero, Leopoldo 1909-1962 . . . . . . .DLB-108

Pangborn, Edgar 1909-1976 . . . . .DLB-8

"Panic Among the Philistines": A Postscript,
An Interview with Bryan Griffin Y-81

Panneton, Philippe (see Ringuet)

Panshin, Alexei 1940- DLB-8

Pansy (see Alden, Isabella)

Pantheon Books DLB-46

Paperback Library DLB-46

Paperback Science Fiction DLB-8

Paquet, Alfons 1881-1944 . . . . .DLB-66

Paradis, Suzanne 1936- DLB-53

Pareja Diezcanseco, Alfredo
1908-1993 . . . . .DLB-145

Pardoe, Julia 1804-1862 . . . . DLB-166

Parents' Magazine Press DLB-46

Parisian Theater, Fall 1984: Toward
A New Baroque Y-85

Parizeau, Alice 1930- DLB-60

Parke, John 1754-1789 . . . . DLB-31

Parker, Dorothy
1893-1967 . . . . DLB-11, 45, 86

Parker, Gilbert 1860-1932 . . . . DLB-99

Parker, James 1714-1770 . . . . DLB-43

Parker, Theodore 1810-1860 . . . . DLB-1

Parker, William Riley 1906-1968 . . . DLB-103

Parker, J. H. [publishing house] DLB-106

Parker, John [publishing house] DLB-106

Parkman, Francis, Jr.
1823-1893 . . . . DLB-1, 30

Parks, Gordon 1912- DLB-33

Parks, William 1698-1750 . . . . DLB-43

Parks, William [publishing house] . . . DLB-49

Parley, Peter (see Goodrich, Samuel Griswold)

Parnell, Thomas 1679-1718 . . . . DLB-95

Parr, Catherine 1513?-1548 . . . . DLB-136

Parrington, Vernon L.
1871-1929 . . . . DLB-17, 63

Parronchi, Alessandro 1914- DLB-128

Partridge, S. W., and Company DLB-106

Parton, James 1822-1891 . . . . DLB-30

Parton, Sara Payson Willis
1811-1872 . . . . DLB-43, 74

Pasolini, Pier Paolo 1922- DLB-128

Pastan, Linda 1932- DLB-5

Paston, George 1860-1936 . . . . DLB-149

The *Paston Letters* 1422-1509 . . . . . . DLB-146

Pastorius, Francis Daniel
1651-circa 1720 . . . . DLB-24

Patchen, Kenneth 1911-1972 . . . . DLB-16, 48

Pater, Walter 1839-1894 . . . . DLB-57, 156

Paterson, Katherine 1932- DLB-52

Patmore, Coventry 1823-1896 . . . DLB-35, 98

Paton, Joseph Noel 1821-1901 . . . . . . DLB-35

Paton Walsh, Jill 1937- DLB-161

Patrick, Edwin Hill ("Ted")
1901-1964 . . . . DLB-137

Patrick, John 1906- DLB-7

Pattee, Fred Lewis 1863-1950 . . . . . . DLB-71

Pattern and Paradigm: History as
Design, by Judith Ryan DLB-75

Patterson, Alicia 1906-1963 . . . . . . .DLB-127

Patterson, Eleanor Medill
1881-1948 . . . . .DLB-29

Patterson, Eugene 1923- DLB-127

Patterson, Joseph Medill
1879-1946 . . . . .DLB-29

Pattillo, Henry 1726-1801 . . . . .DLB-37

Paul, Elliot 1891-1958 . . . . .DLB-4

Paul, Jean (see Richter, Johann Paul Friedrich)

Paul, Kegan, Trench, Trubner and Company
Limited .DLB-106

Paul, Peter, Book Company DLB-49

Paul, Stanley, and Company
Limited .DLB-112

Paulding, James Kirke
1778-1860 . . . . .DLB-3, 59, 74

Paulin, Tom 1949- DLB-40

Pauper, Peter, Press DLB-46

Pavese, Cesare 1908-1950 . . . . .DLB-128

Paxton, John 1911-1985 . . . . .DLB-44

Payn, James 1830-1898 . . . . .DLB-18

Payne, John 1842-1916 . . . . .DLB-35

Payne, John Howard 1791-1852 . . . . .DLB-37

Payson and Clarke DLB-46

Peabody, Elizabeth Palmer
1804-1894 .DLB-1

Peabody, Elizabeth Palmer
[publishing house] DLB-49

Peabody, Oliver William Bourn
1799-1848 . . . . .DLB-59

Peace, Roger 1899-1968 . . . . .DLB-127

Peacham, Henry 1578-1644? DLB-151

Peachtree Publishers, Limited DLB-46

Peacock, Molly 1947- DLB-120

Peacock, Thomas Love
1785-1866 . . . . .DLB-96, 116

Pead, Deuel ?-1727 . . . . .DLB-24

Peake, Mervyn 1911-1968 . . . . . .DLB-15, 160

Pear Tree Press DLB-112

Pearce, Philippa 1920- DLB-161

Pearson, H. B. [publishing house] DLB-49

Pearson, Hesketh 1887-1964 . . . . . . .DLB-149

Peck, George W. 1840-1916 . . . . .DLB-23, 42

Peck, H. C., and Theo. Bliss
[publishing house] DLB-49

Peck, Harry Thurston
1856-1914 . . . . .DLB-71, 91

Peele, George 1556-1596 . . . . . . .DLB-62, 167

Pellegrini and Cudahy DLB-46

Pelletier, Aimé (see Vac, Bertrand)

Pemberton, Sir Max 1863-1950 ..... DLB-70

Penguin Books [U.S.] DLB-46

Penguin Books [U.K.] DLB-112

Penn Publishing Company DLB-49

Penn, William 1644-1718 .... DLB-24

Penna, Sandro 1906-1977 .... DLB-114

Penner, Jonathan 1940- Y-83

Pennington, Lee 1939- Y-82

Pepys, Samuel 1633-1703 .... DLB-101

Percy, Thomas 1729-1811 .... DLB-104

Percy, Walker 1916-1990 ... DLB-2; Y-80, 90

Perec, Georges 1936-1982 .... DLB-83

Perelman, S. J. 1904-1979 .... DLB-11, 44

Perez, Raymundo "Tigre"
    1946- DLB-122

Peri Rossi, Cristina 1941- DLB-145

Periodicals of the Beat Generation ... DLB-16

Perkins, Eugene 1932- DLB-41

Perkoff, Stuart Z. 1930-1974 .... DLB-16

Perley, Moses Henry 1804-1862 .... DLB-99

Permabooks DLB-46

Perrin, Alice 1867-1934 .... DLB-156

Perry, Bliss 1860-1954 .... DLB-71

Perry, Eleanor 1915-1981 .... DLB-44

Perry, Sampson 1747-1823 .... DLB-158

"Personal Style" (1890), by John Addington
    Symonds DLB-57

Perutz, Leo 1882-1957 .... DLB-81

Pesetsky, Bette 1932- DLB-130

Pestalozzi, Johann Heinrich
    1746-1827 .... DLB-94

Peter, Laurence J. 1919-1990 .... DLB-53

Peter of Spain circa 1205-1277 ..... DLB-115

Peterkin, Julia 1880-1961 ....DLB-9

Peters, Lenrie 1932- DLB-117

Peters, Robert 1924- DLB-105

Peters, Robert, Foreword to
    Ludwig of Bavaria DLB-105

Petersham, Maud 1889-1971 and
    Petersham, Miska 1888-1960 .... DLB-22

Peterson, Charles Jacobs
    1819-1887 .... DLB-79

Peterson, Len 1917- DLB-88

Peterson, Louis 1922- DLB-76

Peterson, T. B., and Brothers DLB-49

Petitclair, Pierre 1813-1860 .... DLB-99

Petrov, Gavriil 1730-1801 .... DLB-150

Petrov, Vasilii Petrovich
    1736-1799 .... DLB-150

Petrović, Rastko 1898-1949 .... DLB-147

Petruslied circa 854? DLB-148

Petry, Ann 1908- DLB-76

Pettie, George circa 1548-1589 ..... DLB-136

Peyton, K. M. 1929- DLB-161

Pfaffe Konrad
    flourished circa 1172 .... DLB-148

Pfaffe Lamprecht
    flourished circa 1150 .... DLB-148

Pforzheimer, Carl H. 1879-1957 .... DLB-140

Phaer, Thomas 1510?-1560 .... DLB-167

Phaidon Press Limited DLB-112

Pharr, Robert Deane 1916-1992 ..... DLB-33

Phelps, Elizabeth Stuart
    1844-1911 .... DLB-74

Philip, Marlene Nourbese
    1947- DLB-157

Philippe, Charles-Louis
    1874-1909 .... DLB-65

Philips, John 1676-1708 .... DLB-95

Philips, Katherine 1632-1664 .... DLB-131

Phillips, Caryl 1958- DLB-157

Phillips, David Graham
    1867-1911 ....DLB-9, 12

Phillips, Jayne Anne 1952- Y-80

Phillips, Robert 1938- DLB-105

Phillips, Robert, Finding, Losing,
    Reclaiming: A Note on My
    Poems DLB-105

Phillips, Stephen 1864-1915 .... DLB-10

Phillips, Ulrich B. 1877-1934 .... DLB-17

Phillips, Willard 1784-1873 .... DLB-59

Phillips, William 1907- DLB-137

Phillips, Sampson and Company DLB-49

Phillpotts, Eden
    1862-1960 .... DLB-10, 70, 135, 153

Philosophical Library DLB-46

"The Philosophy of Style" (1852), by
    Herbert Spencer DLB-57

Phinney, Elihu [publishing house] ... DLB-49

Phoenix, John (see Derby, George Horatio)

PHYLON (Fourth Quarter, 1950),
    The Negro in Literature:
    The Current Scene DLB-76

Physiologus
    circa 1070-circa 1150 .... DLB-148

Piccolo, Lucio 1903-1969 .... DLB-114

Pickard, Tom 1946- DLB-40

Pickering, William
    [publishing house] DLB-106

Pickthall, Marjorie 1883-1922 ...... DLB-92

Pictorial Printing Company DLB-49

Piel, Gerard 1915- DLB-137

Piercy, Marge 1936- DLB-120

Pierro, Albino 1916- DLB-128

Pignotti, Lamberto 1926- DLB-128

Pike, Albert 1809-1891 ....DLB-74

Pilon, Jean-Guy 1930- DLB-60

Pinckney, Josephine 1895-1957 ....DLB-6

Pindar, Peter (see Wolcot, John)

Pinero, Arthur Wing 1855-1934 .....DLB-10

Pinget, Robert 1919- DLB-83

Pinnacle Books DLB-46

Piñon, Nélida 1935- DLB-145

Pinsky, Robert 1940- Y-82

Pinter, Harold 1930- DLB-13

Piontek, Heinz 1925- DLB-75

Piozzi, Hester Lynch [Thrale]
    1741-1821 .... DLB-104, 142

Piper, H. Beam 1904-1964 ....DLB-8

Piper, Watty DLB-22

Pisar, Samuel 1929- Y-83

Pitkin, Timothy 1766-1847 ....DLB-30

The Pitt Poetry Series: Poetry Publishing
    Today Y-85

Pitter, Ruth 1897- DLB-20

Pix, Mary 1666-1709 ....DLB-80

Plaatje, Sol T. 1876-1932 ....DLB-125

The Place of Realism in Fiction (1895), by
    George Gissing DLB-18

Plante, David 1940- Y-83

Platen, August von 1796-1835 ....DLB-90

Plath, Sylvia 1932-1963 .... DLB-5, 6, 152

Platon 1737-1812 ....DLB-150

Platt and Munk Company DLB-46

Playboy Press DLB-46

Plays, Playwrights, and Playgoers DLB-84

Playwrights and Professors, by
    Tom Stoppard DLB-13

Playwrights on the Theater DLB-80

Der Pleier flourished circa 1250 ....DLB-138

Plenzdorf, Ulrich 1934- DLB-75

Plessen, Elizabeth 1944- DLB-75

Plievier, Theodor 1892-1955 ....DLB-69

Plomer, William 1903-1973 .....DLB-20, 162

Plumly, Stanley 1939- DLB-5

Plumpp, Sterling D. 1940- DLB-41

Plunkett, James 1920- DLB-14

Plymell, Charles 1935- DLB-16

Pocket Books DLB-46

Poe, Edgar Allan
    1809-1849 ....DLB-3, 59, 73, 74

Poe, James 1921-1980 ....DLB-44

The Poet Laureate of the United States
    Statements from Former Consultants
    in Poetry Y-86

Pohl, Frederik 1919- DLB-8

Poirier, Louis (see Gracq, Julien)

Polanyi, Michael 1891-1976 ....DLB-100

Pole, Reginald 1500-1558 ....DLB-132

Poliakoff, Stephen 1952- DLB-13

Polidori, John William
    1795-1821 ....DLB-116

Polite, Carlene Hatcher 1932- DLB-33

Pollard, Edward A. 1832-1872 ......DLB-30

Pollard, Percival 1869-1911 ....DLB-71

Pollard and Moss DLB-49

Pollock, Sharon 1936- DLB-60

Polonsky, Abraham 1910- DLB-26

Polotsky, Simeon 1629-1680 ....DLB-150

Ponce, Mary Helen 1938- DLB-122

Ponce-Montoya, Juanita 1949- DLB-122

Ponet, John 1516?-1556 ....DLB-132

Poniatowski, Elena 1933- DLB-113

Pony Stories DLB-160

Poole, Ernest 1880-1950 ....DLB-9

Poole, Sophia 1804-1891 ....DLB-166

Poore, Benjamin Perley
    1820-1887 ....DLB-23

Pope, Abbie Hanscom
    1858-1894 ....DLB-140

Pope, Alexander 1688-1744 .....DLB-95, 101

Popov, Mikhail Ivanovich
    1742-circa 1790 ....DLB-150

Popular Library DLB-46

Porlock, Martin (see MacDonald, Philip)

Porpoise Press DLB-112

Porta, Antonio 1935-1989 ....DLB-128

Porter, Anna Maria
    1780-1832 ....DLB-116, 159

Porter, Eleanor H. 1868-1920 ....DLB-9

Porter, Henry ?-? DLB-62

Porter, Jane 1776-1850 ....DLB-116, 159

Porter, Katherine Anne
    1890-1980 ... DLB-4, 9, 102; Y-80; DS-12

Porter, Peter 1929- DLB-40

Porter, William Sydney
    1862-1910 ....DLB-12, 78, 79

Porter, William T. 1809-1858 .....DLB-3, 43

Porter and Coates DLB-49

Portis, Charles 1933- DLB-6

Postans, Marianne
    circa 1810-1865 ....DLB-166

Postl, Carl (see Sealsfield, Carl)

Poston, Ted 1906-1974 ....DLB-51

Postscript to [the Third Edition of] *Clarissa*
    (1751), by Samuel Richardson ... DLB-39

Potok, Chaim 1929- DLB-28, 152; Y-84

Potter, Beatrix 1866-1943 ....DLB-141

Potter, David M. 1910-1971 ....DLB-17

Potter, John E., and Company DLB-49

Pottle, Frederick A.
    1897-1987 ....DLB-103; Y-87

Poulin, Jacques 1937- DLB-60

Pound, Ezra 1885-1972 ....DLB-4, 45, 63

Powell, Anthony 1905- DLB-15

Powers, J. F. 1917- DLB-130

Pownall, David 1938- DLB-14

Powys, John Cowper 1872-1963 ....DLB-15

Powys, Llewelyn 1884-1939 ....DLB-98

Powys, T. F. 1875-1953 ....DLB-36, 162

Poynter, Nelson 1903-1978 ....DLB-127

The Practice of Biography: An Interview
    with Stanley Weintraub Y-82

The Practice of Biography II: An Interview
    with B. L. Reid Y-83

The Practice of Biography III: An Interview
    with Humphrey Carpenter Y-84

The Practice of Biography IV: An Interview
    with William Manchester Y-85

The Practice of Biography V: An Interview
    with Justin Kaplan Y-86

The Practice of Biography VI: An Interview
    with David Herbert Donald Y-87

The Practice of Biography VII: An Interview
    with John Caldwell Guilds Y-92

The Practice of Biography VIII: An Interview
    with Joan Mellen Y-94

The Practice of Biography IX: An Interview
    with Michael Reynolds Y-95

Prados, Emilio 1899-1962 ....DLB-134

Praed, Winthrop Mackworth
    1802-1839 ....DLB-96

Praeger Publishers DLB-46

Pratt, E. J. 1882-1964 ....DLB-92

Pratt, Samuel Jackson 1749-1814 ....DLB-39

Preface to *Alwyn* (1780), by
    Thomas Holcroft DLB-39

Preface to *Colonel Jack* (1722), by
    Daniel Defoe DLB-39

Preface to *Evelina* (1778), by
    Fanny Burney DLB-39

Preface to *Ferdinand Count Fathom* (1753), by
    Tobias Smollett DLB-39

Preface to *Incognita* (1692), by
    William Congreve DLB-39

Preface to *Joseph Andrews* (1742), by
    Henry Fielding DLB-39

Preface to *Moll Flanders* (1722), by
    Daniel Defoe DLB-39

Preface to *Poems* (1853), by
    Matthew Arnold DLB-32

Preface to *Robinson Crusoe* (1719), by
    Daniel Defoe DLB-39

Preface to *Roderick Random* (1748), by
    Tobias Smollett DLB-39

Preface to *Roxana* (1724), by
    Daniel Defoe DLB-39

Preface to *St. Leon* (1799), by
    William Godwin DLB-39

Preface to Sarah Fielding's *Familiar Letters*
    (1747), by Henry Fielding
    [excerpt] DLB-39

Preface to Sarah Fielding's *The Adventures of
    David Simple* (1744), by
    Henry Fielding DLB-39

Preface to *The Cry* (1754), by
    Sarah Fielding DLB-39

Preface to *The Delicate Distress* (1769), by
    Elizabeth Griffin DLB-39

Preface to *The Disguis'd Prince* (1733), by
    Eliza Haywood [excerpt] DLB-39

Preface to *The Farther Adventures of Robinson
    Crusoe* (1719), by Daniel Defoe ...DLB-39

Preface to the First Edition of *Pamela* (1740), by
    Samuel Richardson DLB-39

Preface to the First Edition of *The Castle of
    Otranto* (1764), by
    Horace Walpole DLB-39

Preface to *The History of Romances* (1715), by
    Pierre Daniel Huet [excerpts] DLB-39

Preface to *The Life of Charlotta du Pont* (1723), by Penelope Aubin DLB-39

Preface to *The Old English Baron* (1778), by Clara Reeve DLB-39

Preface to the Second Edition of *The Castle of Otranto* (1765), by Horace Walpole DLB-39

Preface to *The Secret History, of Queen Zarah, and the Zarazians* (1705), by Delariviere Manley DLB-39

Preface to the Third Edition of *Clarissa* (1751), by Samuel Richardson [excerpt] DLB-39

Preface to *The Works of Mrs. Davys* (1725), by Mary Davys DLB-39

Preface to Volume 1 of *Clarissa* (1747), by Samuel Richardson DLB-39

Preface to Volume 3 of *Clarissa* (1748), by Samuel Richardson DLB-39

Préfontaine, Yves 1937- DLB-53

Prelutsky, Jack 1940- DLB-61

Premisses, by Michael Hamburger .. DLB-66

Prentice, George D. 1802-1870 ..... DLB-43

Prentice-Hall DLB-46

Prescott, William Hickling 1796-1859 .... DLB-1, 30, 59

The Present State of the English Novel (1892), by George Saintsbury DLB-18

Prešeren, Francè 1800-1849 .... DLB-147

Preston, Thomas 1537-1598 .... DLB-62

Price, Reynolds 1933- DLB-2

Price, Richard 1723-1791 .... DLB-158

Price, Richard 1949- Y-81

Priest, Christopher 1943- DLB-14

Priestley, J. B. 1894-1984 .... DLB-10, 34, 77, 100, 139; Y-84

Primary Bibliography: A Retrospective Y-95

Prime, Benjamin Young 1733-1791 .. DLB-31

Primrose, Diana floruit circa 1630 .... DLB-126

Prince, F. T. 1912- DLB-20

Prince, Thomas 1687-1758 ..... DLB-24, 140

The Principles of Success in Literature (1865), by George Henry Lewes [excerpt] .. DLB-57

Prior, Matthew 1664-1721 .... DLB-95

Pritchard, William H. 1932- DLB-111

Pritchett, V. S. 1900- DLB-15, 139

Procter, Adelaide Anne 1825-1864 .. DLB-32

Procter, Bryan Waller 1787-1874 .... DLB-96, 144

The Profession of Authorship: Scribblers for Bread Y-89

The Progress of Romance (1785), by Clara Reeve [excerpt] DLB-39

Prokopovich, Feofan 1681?-1736 ... DLB-150

Prokosch, Frederic 1906-1989 .... DLB-48

The Proletarian Novel DLB-9

Propper, Dan 1937- DLB-16

The Prospect of Peace (1778), by Joel Barlow DLB-37

Proud, Robert 1728-1813 .... DLB-30

Proust, Marcel 1871-1922 .... DLB-65

Prynne, J. H. 1936- DLB-40

Przybyszewski, Stanislaw 1868-1927 .... DLB-66

Pseudo-Dionysius the Areopagite floruit circa 500 .... DLB-115

The Public Lending Right in America Statement by Sen. Charles McC. Mathias, Jr. PLR and the Meaning of Literary Property Statements on PLR by American Writers Y-83

The Public Lending Right in the United Kingdom Public Lending Right: The First Year in the United Kingdom Y-83

The Publication of English Renaissance Plays DLB-62

Publications and Social Movements [Transcendentalism] DLB-1

Publishers and Agents: The Columbia Connection Y-87

A Publisher's Archives: G. P. Putnam ...Y-92

Publishing Fiction at LSU Press Y-87

Pückler-Muskau, Hermann von 1785-1871 .... DLB-133

Pugh, Edwin William 1874-1930 ... DLB-135

Pugin, A. Welby 1812-1852 .... DLB-55

Puig, Manuel 1932-1990 .... DLB-113

Pulitzer, Joseph 1847-1911 .... DLB-23

Pulitzer, Joseph, Jr. 1885-1955 ..... DLB-29

Pulitzer Prizes for the Novel, 1917-1945 .... DLB-9

Pulliam, Eugene 1889-1975 .... DLB-127

Purchas, Samuel 1577?-1626 ...... DLB-151

Purdy, Al 1918- DLB-88

Purdy, James 1923- DLB-2

Purdy, Ken W. 1913-1972 ...... DLB-137

Pusey, Edward Bouverie 1800-1882 .... DLB-55

Putnam, George Palmer 1814-1872 .... DLB-3, 79

Putnam, Samuel 1892-1950 ....DLB-4

G. P. Putnam's Sons [U.S.] DLB-49

G. P. Putnam's Sons [U.K.] DLB-106

Puzo, Mario 1920- DLB-6

Pyle, Ernie 1900-1945 .... DLB-29

Pyle, Howard 1853-1911 .... DLB-42; DS-13

Pym, Barbara 1913-1980 ...... DLB-14; Y-87

Pynchon, Thomas 1937- DLB-2

Pyramid Books DLB-46

Pyrnelle, Louise-Clarke 1850-1907 ...DLB-42

Q

Quad, M. (see Lewis, Charles B.)

Quarles, Francis 1592-1644 ....DLB-126

The Quarterly Review 1809-1967 ....DLB-110

Quasimodo, Salvatore 1901-1968 ...DLB-114

Queen, Ellery (see Dannay, Frederic, and Manfred B. Lee)

The Queen City Publishing House ...DLB-49

Queneau, Raymond 1903-1976 ......DLB-72

Quennell, Sir Peter 1905-1993 ......DLB-155

Quesnel, Joseph 1746-1809 ....DLB-99

The Question of American Copyright in the Nineteenth Century Headnote Preface, by George Haven Putnam The Evolution of Copyright, by Brander Matthews Summary of Copyright Legislation in the United States, by R. R. Bowker Analysis of the Provisions of the Copyright Law of 1891, by George Haven Putnam The Contest for International Copyright, by George Haven Putnam Cheap Books and Good Books, by Brander Matthews DLB-49

Quiller-Couch, Sir Arthur Thomas 1863-1944 .... DLB-135, 153

Quin, Ann 1936-1973 ....DLB-14

Quincy, Samuel, of Georgia ?-? DLB-31

Quincy, Samuel, of Massachusetts 1734-1789 ....DLB-31

Quinn, Anthony 1915- DLB-122

Quintana, Leroy V. 1944- DLB-82

Quintana, Miguel de 1671-1748 A Forerunner of Chicano Literature DLB-122

Quist, Harlin, Books DLB-46

Quoirez, Françoise (see Sagan, Franççise)

R

Raabe, Wilhelm 1831-1910 ....DLB-129

Rabe, David 1940- DLB-7

Raboni, Giovanni 1932- DLB-128

Rachilde 1860-1953 ....DLB-123

Racin, Kočo 1908-1943 ....DLB-147

Rackham, Arthur 1867-1939 ......DLB-141

Radcliffe, Ann 1764-1823 ....DLB-39

Raddall, Thomas 1903- DLB-68

Radiguet, Raymond 1903-1923 ......DLB-65

Radishchev, Aleksandr Nikolaevich
1749-1802 ....DLB-150

Radványi, Netty Reiling (see Seghers, Anna)

Rahv, Philip 1908-1973 ....DLB-137

Raimund, Ferdinand Jakob
1790-1836 ....DLB-90

Raine, Craig 1944- DLB-40

Raine, Kathleen 1908- DLB-20

Rainolde, Richard
circa 1530-1606 ....DLB-136

Rakić, Milan 1876-1938 ....DLB-147

Ralph, Julian 1853-1903 ....DLB-23

Ralph Waldo Emerson in 1982 ....Y-82

Ramat, Silvio 1939- DLB-128

Rambler, no. 4 (1750), by Samuel Johnson
[excerpt] DLB-39

Ramée, Marie Louise de la (see Ouida)

Ramírez, Sergío 1942- DLB-145

Ramke, Bin 1947- DLB-120

Ramler, Karl Wilhelm 1725-1798 ....DLB-97

Ramon Ribeyro, Julio 1929- DLB-145

Ramous, Mario 1924- DLB-128

Rampersad, Arnold 1941- DLB-111

Ramsay, Allan 1684 or 1685-1758 ...DLB-95

Ramsay, David 1749-1815 ....DLB-30

Ranck, Katherine Quintana
1942- DLB-122

Rand, Avery and Company DLB-49

Rand McNally and Company DLB-49

Randall, David Anton
1905-1975 ....DLB-140

Randall, Dudley 1914- DLB-41

Randall, Henry S. 1811-1876 ....DLB-30

Randall, James G. 1881-1953 ....DLB-17

The Randall Jarrell Symposium: A Small
Collection of Randall Jarrells
Excerpts From Papers Delivered at
the Randall Jarrell
Symposium Y-86

Randolph, A. Philip 1889-1979 .....DLB-91

Randolph, Anson D. F.
[publishing house] DLB-49

Randolph, Thomas 1605-1635 .. DLB-58, 126

Random House DLB-46

Ranlet, Henry [publishing house] DLB-49

Ransom, John Crowe
1888-1974 ....DLB-45, 63

Ransome, Arthur 1884-1967 ....DLB-160

Raphael, Frederic 1931- DLB-14

Raphaelson, Samson 1896-1983 .....DLB-44

Raskin, Ellen 1928-1984 ....DLB-52

Rastell, John 1475?-1536 ....DLB-136

Rattigan, Terence 1911-1977 ....DLB-13

Rawlings, Marjorie Kinnan
1896-1953 ....DLB-9, 22, 102

Raworth, Tom 1938- DLB-40

Ray, David 1932- DLB-5

Ray, Gordon Norton
1915-1986 ....DLB-103, 140

Ray, Henrietta Cordelia
1849-1916 ....DLB-50

Raymond, Henry J. 1820-1869 ... DLB-43, 79

Raymond Chandler Centenary Tributes
from Michael Avallone, James Elroy, Joe
Gores,
and William F. Nolan Y-88

Reach, Angus 1821-1856 ....DLB-70

Read, Herbert 1893-1968 ......DLB-20, 149

Read, Herbert, "The Practice of Biography," in
*The English Sense of Humour and Other
Essays* DLB-149

Read, Opie 1852-1939 ....DLB-23

Read, Piers Paul 1941- DLB-14

Reade, Charles 1814-1884 ....DLB-21

Reader's Digest Condensed
Books DLB-46

Reading, Peter 1946- DLB-40

Reaney, James 1926- DLB-68

Rèbora, Clemente 1885-1957 ......DLB-114

Rechy, John 1934- DLB-122; Y-82

The Recovery of Literature: Criticism in the
1990s: A Symposium Y-91

Redding, J. Saunders
1906-1988 ....DLB-63, 76

Redfield, J. S. [publishing house] DLB-49

Redgrove, Peter 1932- DLB-40

Redmon, Anne 1943- Y-86

Redmond, Eugene B. 1937- DLB-41

Redpath, James [publishing house] ...DLB-49

Reed, Henry 1808-1854 ....DLB-59

Reed, Henry 1914- DLB-27

Reed, Ishmael 1938- ... DLB-2, 5, 33; DS-8

Reed, Sampson 1800-1880 ....DLB-1

Reed, Talbot Baines 1852-1893 .....DLB-141

Reedy, William Marion 1862-1920 ...DLB-91

Reese, Lizette Woodworth
1856-1935 ....DLB-54

Reese, Thomas 1742-1796 ....DLB-37

Reeve, Clara 1729-1807 ....DLB-39

Reeves, James 1909-1978 ....DLB-161

Reeves, John 1926- DLB-88

Regnery, Henry, Company DLB-46

Rehberg, Hans 1901-1963 ....DLB-124

Rehfisch, Hans José 1891-1960 .....DLB-124

Reid, Alastair 1926- DLB-27

Reid, B. L. 1918-1990 ....DLB-111

Reid, Christopher 1949- DLB-40

Reid, Forrest 1875-1947 ....DLB-153

Reid, Helen Rogers 1882-1970 ......DLB-29

Reid, James ?-? DLB-31

Reid, Mayne 1818-1883 ....DLB-21, 163

Reid, Thomas 1710-1796 ....DLB-31

Reid, V. S. (Vic) 1913-1987 ....DLB-125

Reid, Whitelaw 1837-1912 ....DLB-23

Reilly and Lee Publishing
Company DLB-46

Reimann, Brigitte 1933-1973 ....DLB-75

Reinmar der Alte
circa 1165-circa 1205 ....DLB-138

Reinmar von Zweter
circa 1200-circa 1250 ....DLB-138

Reisch, Walter 1903-1983 ....DLB-44

Remarque, Erich Maria 1898-1970 ...DLB-56

"Re-meeting of Old Friends": The Jack
Kerouac Conference Y-82

Remington, Frederic 1861-1909 .....DLB-12

Renaud, Jacques 1943- DLB-60

Renault, Mary 1905-1983 ....Y-83

Rendell, Ruth 1930- DLB-87

Representative Men and Women: A Historical
Perspective on the British Novel,
1930-1960 ....DLB-15

(Re-)Publishing Orwell Y-86

Reuter, Fritz 1810-1874 .... DLB-129

Reuter, Gabriele 1859-1941 .... DLB-66

Revell, Fleming H., Company DLB-49

Reventlow, Franziska Gräfin zu
1871-1918 .... DLB-66

Review of Reviews Office DLB-112

Review of [Samuel Richardson's] *Clarissa*
(1748), by Henry Fielding DLB-39

The Revolt (1937), by Mary Colum
[excerpts] DLB-36

Rexroth, Kenneth
1905-1982 .... DLB-16, 48, 165; Y-82

Rey, H. A. 1898-1977 .... DLB-22

Reynal and Hitchcock DLB-46

Reynolds, G. W. M. 1814-1879 ..... DLB-21

Reynolds, John Hamilton
1794-1852 .... DLB-96

Reynolds, Mack 1917- DLB-8

Reynolds, Sir Joshua 1723-1792 .... DLB-104

Reznikoff, Charles 1894-1976 ... DLB-28, 45

"Rhetoric" (1828; revised, 1859), by
Thomas de Quincey [excerpt] .. DLB-57

Rhett, Robert Barnwell 1800-1876 ... DLB-43

Rhode, John 1884-1964 .... DLB-77

Rhodes, James Ford 1848-1927 ..... DLB-47

Rhys, Jean 1890-1979 ..... DLB-36, 117, 162

Ricardo, David 1772-1823 .... DLB-107, 158

Ricardou, Jean 1932- DLB-83

Rice, Elmer 1892-1967 .... DLB-4, 7

Rice, Grantland 1880-1954 .... DLB-29

Rich, Adrienne 1929- DLB-5, 67

Richards, David Adams 1950- DLB-53

Richards, George circa 1760-1814 ... DLB-37

Richards, I. A. 1893-1979 .... DLB-27

Richards, Laura E. 1850-1943 ...... DLB-42

Richards, William Carey
1818-1892 .... DLB-73

Richards, Grant
[publishing house] DLB-112

Richardson, Charles F. 1851-1913 ... DLB-71

Richardson, Dorothy M.
1873-1957 .... DLB-36

Richardson, Jack 1935- DLB-7

Richardson, John 1796-1852 .... DLB-99

Richardson, Samuel
1689-1761 .... DLB-39, 154

Richardson, Willis 1889-1977 ...... DLB-51

Riche, Barnabe 1542-1617 .... DLB-136

Richler, Mordecai 1931- DLB-53

Richter, Conrad 1890-1968 .... DLB-9

Richter, Hans Werner 1908- DLB-69

Richter, Johann Paul Friedrich
1763-1825 .... DLB-94

Rickerby, Joseph
[publishing house] DLB-106

Rickword, Edgell 1898-1982 .... DLB-20

Riddell, Charlotte 1832-1906 ...... DLB-156

Riddell, John (see Ford, Corey)

Ridge, Lola 1873-1941 .... DLB-54

Ridge, William Pett 1859-1930 ..... DLB-135

Riding, Laura (see Jackson, Laura Riding)

Ridler, Anne 1912- DLB-27

Ridruego, Dionisio 1912-1975 ...... DLB-108

Riel, Louis 1844-1885 .... DLB-99

Riffaterre, Michael 1924- DLB-67

Riis, Jacob 1849-1914 .... DLB-23

Riker, John C. [publishing house] DLB-49

Riley, John 1938-1978 .... DLB-40

Rilke, Rainer Maria 1875-1926 ...... DLB-81

Rinehart and Company DLB-46

Ringuet 1895-1960 .... DLB-68

Ringwood, Gwen Pharis
1910-1984 .... DLB-88

Rinser, Luise 1911- DLB-69

Ríos, Alberto 1952- DLB-122

Ríos, Isabella 1948- DLB-82

Ripley, Arthur 1895-1961 .... DLB-44

Ripley, George 1802-1880 .....DLB-1, 64, 73

The Rising Glory of America:
Three Poems DLB-37

The Rising Glory of America: Written in 1771
(1786), by Hugh Henry Brackenridge and
Philip Freneau DLB-37

Riskin, Robert 1897-1955 .... DLB-26

Risse, Heinz 1898- DLB-69

Rist, Johann 1607-1667 .... DLB-164

Ritchie, Anna Mowatt 1819-1870 ..... DLB-3

Ritchie, Anne Thackeray
1837-1919 .... DLB-18

Ritchie, Thomas 1778-1854 .... DLB-43

Rites of Passage
[on William Saroyan] Y-83

The Ritz Paris Hemingway Award Y-85

Rivard, Adjutor 1868-1945 .... DLB-92

Rive, Richard 1931-1989 ....DLB-125

Rivera, Marina 1942- DLB-122

Rivera, Tomás 1935-1984 ....DLB-82

Rivers, Conrad Kent 1933-1968 ....DLB-41

Riverside Press DLB-49

Rivington, James circa 1724-1802 ....DLB-43

Rivington, Charles
[publishing house] DLB-154

Rivkin, Allen 1903-1990 ....DLB-26

Roa Bastos, Augusto 1917- DLB-113

Robbe-Grillet, Alain 1922- DLB-83

Robbins, Tom 1936- Y-80

Roberts, Charles G. D. 1860-1943 ....DLB-92

Roberts, Dorothy 1906-1993 ....DLB-88

Roberts, Elizabeth Madox
1881-1941 .... DLB-9, 54, 102

Roberts, Kenneth 1885-1957 ....DLB-9

Roberts, William 1767-1849 ....DLB-142

Roberts Brothers DLB-49

Roberts, James [publishing house] ...DLB-154

Robertson, A. M., and Company DLB-49

Robertson, William 1721-1793 .....DLB-104

Robinson, Casey 1903-1979 ....DLB-44

Robinson, Edwin Arlington
1869-1935 ....DLB-54

Robinson, Henry Crabb
1775-1867 ....DLB-107

Robinson, James Harvey
1863-1936 ....DLB-47

Robinson, Lennox 1886-1958 ....DLB-10

Robinson, Mabel Louise
1874-1962 ....DLB-22

Robinson, Mary 1758-1800 ....DLB-158

Robinson, Richard
circa 1545-1607 ....DLB-167

Robinson, Therese
1797-1870 .... DLB-59, 133

Robison, Mary 1949- DLB-130

Roblès, Emmanuel 1914- DLB-83

Roccatagliata Ceccardi, Ceccardo
1871-1919 ....DLB-114

Rochester, John Wilmot, Earl of
1647-1680 ....DLB-131

Rock, Howard 1911-1976 ....DLB-127

Rodgers, Carolyn M. 1945- DLB-41

Rodgers, W. R. 1909-1969 ....DLB-20

Rodríguez, Claudio 1934- DLB-134

Rodriguez, Richard 1944- DLB-82

Rodríguez Julia, Edgardo 1946- DLB-145

Roethke, Theodore 1908-1963 ....DLB-5

Rogers, Pattiann 1940- DLB-105

Rogers, Samuel 1763-1855 ....DLB-93

Rogers, Will 1879-1935 ....DLB-11

Rohmer, Sax 1883-1959 ....DLB-70

Roiphe, Anne 1935- Y-80

Rojas, Arnold R. 1896-1988 ....DLB-82

Rolfe, Frederick William 1860-1913 ....DLB-34, 156

Rolland, Romain 1866-1944 ....DLB-65

Rolle, Richard circa 1290-1300 - 1340 ....DLB-146

Rolvaag, O. E. 1876-1931 ....DLB-9

Romains, Jules 1885-1972 ....DLB-65

Roman, A., and Company DLB-49

Romano, Octavio 1923- DLB-122

Romero, Leo 1950- DLB-122

Romero, Lin 1947- DLB-122

Romero, Orlando 1945- DLB-82

Rook, Clarence 1863-1915 ....DLB-135

Roosevelt, Theodore 1858-1919 .....DLB-47

Root, Waverley 1903-1982 ....DLB-4

Root, William Pitt 1941- DLB-120

Roquebrune, Robert de 1889-1978 ...DLB-68

Rosa, João Guimarães 1908-1967 ....DLB-113

Rosales, Luis 1910-1992 ....DLB-134

Roscoe, William 1753-1831 ....DLB-163

Rose, Reginald 1920- DLB-26

Rosegger, Peter 1843-1918 ....DLB-129

Rosei, Peter 1946- DLB-85

Rosen, Norma 1925- DLB-28

Rosenbach, A. S. W. 1876-1952 ....DLB-140

Rosenberg, Isaac 1890-1918 ....DLB-20

Rosenfeld, Isaac 1918-1956 ....DLB-28

Rosenthal, M. L. 1917- DLB-5

Ross, Alexander 1591-1654 ....DLB-151

Ross, Harold 1892-1951 ....DLB-137

Ross, Leonard Q. (see Rosten, Leo)

Ross, Martin 1862-1915 ....DLB-135

Ross, Sinclair 1908- DLB-88

Ross, W. W. E. 1894-1966 ....DLB-88

Rosselli, Amelia 1930- DLB-128

Rossen, Robert 1908-1966 ....DLB-26

Rossetti, Christina Georgina 1830-1894 ....DLB-35, 163

Rossetti, Dante Gabriel 1828-1882 ... DLB-35

Rossner, Judith 1935- DLB-6

Rosten, Leo 1908- DLB-11

Rostenberg, Leona 1908- DLB-140

Rostovsky, Dimitrii 1651-1709 .....DLB-150

Bertram Rota and His Bookshop Y-91

Roth, Gerhard 1942- DLB-85, 124

Roth, Henry 1906?- DLB-28

Roth, Joseph 1894-1939 ....DLB-85

Roth, Philip 1933- DLB-2, 28; Y-82

Rothenberg, Jerome 1931- DLB-5

Rotimi, Ola 1938- DLB-125

Routhier, Adolphe-Basile 1839-1920 ....DLB-99

Routier, Simone 1901-1987 ....DLB-88

Routledge, George, and Sons DLB-106

Roversi, Roberto 1923- DLB-128

Rowe, Elizabeth Singer 1674-1737 ....DLB-39, 95

Rowe, Nicholas 1674-1718 ....DLB-84

Rowlands, Samuel circa 1570-1630 ....DLB-121

Rowlandson, Mary circa 1635-circa 1678 ....DLB-24

Rowley, William circa 1585-1626 ...DLB-58

Rowse, A. L. 1903- DLB-155

Rowson, Susanna Haswell circa 1762-1824 ....DLB-37

Roy, Camille 1870-1943 ....DLB-92

Roy, Gabrielle 1909-1983 ....DLB-68

Roy, Jules 1907- DLB-83

The Royal Court Theatre and the English Stage Company DLB-13

The Royal Court Theatre and the New Drama DLB-10

The Royal Shakespeare Company at the Swan Y-88

Royall, Anne 1769-1854 ....DLB-43

The Roycroft Printing Shop DLB-49

Royster, Vermont 1914- DLB-127

Ruark, Gibbons 1941- DLB-120

Ruban, Vasilii Grigorevich 1742-1795 ....DLB-150

Rubens, Bernice 1928- DLB-14

Rudd and Carleton DLB-49

Rudkin, David 1936- DLB-13

Rudolf von Ems circa 1200-circa 1254 ....DLB-138

Ruffin, Josephine St. Pierre 1842-1924 ....DLB-79

Ruganda, John 1941- DLB-157

Ruggles, Henry Joseph 1813-1906 ...DLB-64

Rukeyser, Muriel 1913-1980 ....DLB-48

Rule, Jane 1931- DLB-60

Rulfo, Juan 1918-1986 ....DLB-113

Rumaker, Michael 1932- DLB-16

Rumens, Carol 1944- DLB-40

Runyon, Damon 1880-1946 ......DLB-11, 86

Ruodlieb circa 1050-1075 ....DLB-148

Rush, Benjamin 1746-1813 ....DLB-37

Rusk, Ralph L. 1888-1962 ....DLB-103

Ruskin, John 1819-1900 ....DLB-55, 163

Russ, Joanna 1937- DLB-8

Russell, B. B., and Company DLB-49

Russell, Benjamin 1761-1845 ....DLB-43

Russell, Bertrand 1872-1970 ....DLB-100

Russell, Charles Edward 1860-1941 ....DLB-25

Russell, George William (see AE)

Russell, R. H., and Son DLB-49

Rutherford, Mark 1831-1913 ....DLB-18

Ryan, Michael 1946- Y-82

Ryan, Oscar 1904- DLB-68

Ryga, George 1932- DLB-60

Rymer, Thomas 1643?-1713 ....DLB-101

Ryskind, Morrie 1895-1985 ....DLB-26

Rzhevsky, Aleksei Andreevich 1737-1804 ....DLB-150

S

The Saalfield Publishing Company DLB-46

Saba, Umberto 1883-1957 ....DLB-114

Sábato, Ernesto 1911- DLB-145

Saberhagen, Fred 1930- DLB-8

Sackler, Howard 1929-1982 ....DLB-7

Sackville, Thomas 1536-1608 ......DLB-132

Sackville, Thomas 1536-1608 and Norton, Thomas 1532-1584 ....DLB-62

Sackville-West, V. 1892-1962 ....DLB-34

Sadlier, D. and J., and Company DLB-49

Sadlier, Mary Anne 1820-1903 ...... DLB-99

Sadoff, Ira 1945- DLB-120

Saenz, Jaime 1921-1986 .... DLB-145

Saffin, John circa 1626-1710 .... DLB-24

Sagan, Françoise 1935- DLB-83

Sage, Robert 1899-1962 .... DLB-4

Sagel, Jim 1947- DLB-82

Sagendorph, Robb Hansell
1900-1970 .... DLB-137

Sahagún, Carlos 1938- DLB-108

Sahkomaapii, Piitai (see Highwater, Jamake)

Sahl, Hans 1902- DLB-69

Said, Edward W. 1935- DLB-67

Saiko, George 1892-1962 .... DLB-85

St. Dominic's Press DLB-112

Saint-Exupéry, Antoine de
1900-1944 .... DLB-72

St. Johns, Adela Rogers 1894-1988 .. DLB-29

St. Martin's Press DLB-46

St. Omer, Garth 1931- DLB-117

Saint Pierre, Michel de 1916-1987 ... DLB-83

Saintsbury, George
1845-1933 .... DLB-57, 149

Saki (see Munro, H. H.)

Salaam, Kalamu ya 1947- DLB-38

Salas, Floyd 1931- DLB-82

Sálaz-Marquez, Rubén 1935- DLB-122

Salemson, Harold J. 1910-1988 ......DLB-4

Salinas, Luis Omar 1937- DLB-82

Salinas, Pedro 1891-1951 .... DLB-134

Salinger, J. D. 1919- DLB-2, 102

Salkey, Andrew 1928- DLB-125

Salt, Waldo 1914- DLB-44

Salter, James 1925- DLB-130

Salter, Mary Jo 1954- DLB-120

Salustri, Carlo Alberto (see Trilussa)

Salverson, Laura Goodman
1890-1970 .... DLB-92

Sampson, Richard Henry (see Hull, Richard)

Samuels, Ernest 1903- DLB-111

Sanborn, Franklin Benjamin
1831-1917 ....DLB-1

Sánchez, Luis Rafael 1936- DLB-145

Sánchez, Philomeno "Phil"
1917- DLB-122

Sánchez, Ricardo 1941- DLB-82

Sanchez, Sonia 1934- DLB-41; DS-8

Sand, George 1804-1876 .... DLB-119

Sandburg, Carl 1878-1967 ....DLB-17, 54

Sanders, Ed 1939- DLB-16

Sandoz, Mari 1896-1966 .... DLB-9

Sandwell, B. K. 1876-1954 .... DLB-92

Sandy, Stephen 1934- DLB-165

Sandys, George 1578-1644 ......DLB-24, 121

Sangster, Charles 1822-1893 .... DLB-99

Sanguineti, Edoardo 1930- DLB-128

Sansom, William 1912-1976 ...... DLB-139

Santayana, George
1863-1952 .... DLB-54, 71; DS-13

Santiago, Danny 1911-1988 .... DLB-122

Santmyer, Helen Hooven 1895-1986 ....Y-84

Sapir, Edward 1884-1939 .... DLB-92

Sapper (see McNeile, Herman Cyril)

Sarduy, Severo 1937- DLB-113

Sargent, Pamela 1948- DLB-8

Saro-Wiwa, Ken 1941- DLB-157

Saroyan, William
1908-1981 .... DLB-7, 9, 86; Y-81

Sarraute, Nathalie 1900- DLB-83

Sarrazin, Albertine 1937-1967 .... DLB-83

Sarton, May 1912- DLB-48; Y-81

Sartre, Jean-Paul 1905-1980 .... DLB-72

Sassoon, Siegfried 1886-1967 .... DLB-20

Saturday Review Press DLB-46

Saunders, James 1925- DLB-13

Saunders, John Monk 1897-1940 .... DLB-26

Saunders, Margaret Marshall
1861-1947 .... DLB-92

Saunders and Otley DLB-106

Savage, James 1784-1873 .... DLB-30

Savage, Marmion W. 1803?-1872 .... DLB-21

Savage, Richard 1697?-1743 .... DLB-95

Savard, Félix-Antoine 1896-1982 .... DLB-68

Saville, (Leonard) Malcolm
1901-1982 .... DLB-160

Sawyer, Ruth 1880-1970 .... DLB-22

Sayers, Dorothy L.
1893-1957 .... DLB-10, 36, 77, 100

Sayles, John Thomas 1950- DLB-44

Sbarbaro, Camillo 1888-1967 ...... DLB-114

Scannell, Vernon 1922- DLB-27

Scarry, Richard 1919-1994 ....DLB-61

Schaeffer, Albrecht 1885-1950 ....DLB-66

Schaeffer, Susan Fromberg 1941- ...DLB-28

Schaff, Philip 1819-1893 .... DS-13

Schaper, Edzard 1908-1984 ....DLB-69

Scharf, J. Thomas 1843-1898 ....DLB-47

Scheffel, Joseph Viktor von
1826-1886 ....DLB-129

Scheffler, Johann 1624-1677 ....DLB-164

Schelling, Friedrich Wilhelm Joseph von
1775-1854 ....DLB-90

Scherer, Wilhelm 1841-1886 ....DLB-129

Schickele, René 1883-1940 ....DLB-66

Schiff, Dorothy 1903-1989 ....DLB-127

Schiller, Friedrich 1759-1805 ....DLB-94

Schirmer, David 1623-1687 ....DLB-164

Schlaf, Johannes 1862-1941 ....DLB-118

Schlegel, August Wilhelm
1767-1845 ....DLB-94

Schlegel, Dorothea 1763-1839 ....DLB-90

Schlegel, Friedrich 1772-1829 ....DLB-90

Schleiermacher, Friedrich
1768-1834 ....DLB-90

Schlesinger, Arthur M., Jr. 1917- ...DLB-17

Schlumberger, Jean 1877-1968 ......DLB-65

Schmid, Eduard Hermann Wilhelm (see
Edschmid, Kasimir)

Schmidt, Arno 1914-1979 ....DLB-69

Schmidt, Johann Kaspar (see Stirner, Max)

Schmidt, Michael 1947- DLB-40

Schmidtbonn, Wilhelm August
1876-1952 ....DLB-118

Schmitz, James H. 1911- DLB-8

Schnackenberg, Gjertrud 1953- ...DLB-120

Schnitzler, Arthur 1862-1931 ... DLB-81, 118

Schnurre, Wolfdietrich 1920- DLB-69

Schocken Books DLB-46

Schönbeck, Virgilio (see Giotti, Virgilio)

School Stories, 1914-1960 ....DLB-160

Schönherr, Karl 1867-1943 ....DLB-118

Scholartis Press DLB-112

The Schomburg Center for Research
in Black Culture DLB-76

Schopenhauer, Arthur 1788-1860 ....DLB-90

Schopenhauer, Johanna 1766-1838 ...DLB-90

Schorer, Mark 1908-1977 ....DLB-103

Schottelius, Justus Georg
1612-1676 ....DLB-164

Schouler, James 1839-1920 ....DLB-47

Schrader, Paul 1946- DLB-44

Schreiner, Olive 1855-1920 .....DLB-18, 156

Schroeder, Andreas 1946- DLB-53

Schubart, Christian Friedrich Daniel
1739-1791 ....DLB-97

Schubert, Gotthilf Heinrich
1780-1860 ....DLB-90

Schücking, Levin 1814-1883 ....DLB-133

Schulberg, Budd
1914- DLB-6, 26, 28; Y-81

Schulte, F. J., and Company DLB-49

Schupp, Johann Balthasar
1610-1661 ....DLB-164

Schurz, Carl 1829-1906 ....DLB-23

Schuyler, George S. 1895-1977 ...DLB-29, 51

Schuyler, James 1923-1991 ....DLB-5

Schwartz, Delmore 1913-1966 ....DLB-28, 48

Schwartz, Jonathan 1938- Y-82

Schwarz, Sibylle 1621-1638 ....DLB-164

Schwerner, Armand 1927- DLB-165

Schwob, Marcel 1867-1905 ....DLB-123

Science Fantasy DLB-8

Science-Fiction Fandom and
Conventions DLB-8

Science-Fiction Fanzines: The Time
Binders DLB-8

Science-Fiction Films DLB-8

Science Fiction Writers of America and the
Nebula Awards DLB-8

Scot, Reginald circa 1538-1599 .....DLB-136

Scotellaro, Rocco 1923-1953 ....DLB-128

Scott, Dennis 1939-1991 ....DLB-125

Scott, Dixon 1881-1915 ....DLB-98

Scott, Duncan Campbell
1862-1947 ....DLB-92

Scott, Evelyn 1893-1963 ....DLB-9, 48

Scott, F. R. 1899-1985 ....DLB-88

Scott, Frederick George
1861-1944 ....DLB-92

Scott, Geoffrey 1884-1929 ....DLB-149

Scott, Harvey W. 1838-1910 ....DLB-23

Scott, Paul 1920-1978 ....DLB-14

Scott, Sarah 1723-1795 ....DLB-39

Scott, Tom 1918- DLB-27

Scott, Sir Walter
1771-1832 ... DLB-93, 107, 116, 144, 159

Scott, William Bell 1811-1890 ......DLB-32

Scott, Walter, Publishing
Company Limited DLB-112

Scott, William R.
[publishing house] DLB-46

Scott-Heron, Gil 1949- DLB-41

Scribner, Charles, Jr. 1921-1995 ....Y-95

Charles Scribner's Sons DLB-49

Scripps, E. W. 1854-1926 ....DLB-25

Scudder, Horace Elisha
1838-1902 ....DLB-42, 71

Scudder, Vida Dutton 1861-1954 ....DLB-71

Scupham, Peter 1933- DLB-40

Seabrook, William 1886-1945 ....DLB-4

Seabury, Samuel 1729-1796 ....DLB-31

Seacole, Mary Jane Grant
1805-1881 ....DLB-166

The Seafarer circa 970 ....DLB-146

Sealsfield, Charles 1793-1864 ......DLB-133

Sears, Edward I. 1819?-1876 ....DLB-79

Sears Publishing Company DLB-46

Seaton, George 1911-1979 ....DLB-44

Seaton, William Winston
1785-1866 ....DLB-43

Secker, Martin, and Warburg
Limited DLB-112

Secker, Martin [publishing house] .. DLB-112

Second-Generation Minor Poets of the
Seventeenth Century DLB-126

Sedgwick, Arthur George
1844-1915 ....DLB-64

Sedgwick, Catharine Maria
1789-1867 ....DLB-1, 74

Sedgwick, Ellery 1872-1930 ....DLB-91

Sedley, Sir Charles 1639-1701 .....DLB-131

Seeger, Alan 1888-1916 ....DLB-45

Seers, Eugene (see Dantin, Louis)

Segal, Erich 1937- Y-86

Seghers, Anna 1900-1983 ....DLB-69

Seid, Ruth (see Sinclair, Jo)

Seidel, Frederick Lewis 1936- Y-84

Seidel, Ina 1885-1974 ....DLB-56

Seigenthaler, John 1927- DLB-127

Seizin Press DLB-112

Séjour, Victor 1817-1874 ....DLB-50

Séjour Marcou et Ferrand, Juan Victor (see
Séjour, Victor)

Selby, Hubert, Jr. 1928- DLB-2

Selden, George 1929-1989 ....DLB-52

Selected English-Language Little Magazines
and Newspapers [France,
1920-1939] DLB-4

Selected Humorous Magazines
(1820-1950) DLB-11

Selected Science-Fiction Magazines and
Anthologies DLB-8

Self, Edwin F. 1920- DLB-137

Seligman, Edwin R. A. 1861-1939 ...DLB-47

Seltzer, Chester E. (see Muro, Amado)

Seltzer, Thomas
[publishing house] DLB-46

Selvon, Sam 1923-1994 ....DLB-125

Senancour, Etienne de 1770-1846 ...DLB-119

Sendak, Maurice 1928- DLB-61

Senécal, Eva 1905- DLB-92

Sengstacke, John 1912- DLB-127

Senior, Olive 1941- DLB-157

Šenoa, August 1838-1881 ....DLB-147

"Sensation Novels" (1863), by
H. L. Manse DLB-21

Sepamla, Sipho 1932- DLB-157

Seredy, Kate 1899-1975 ....DLB-22

Sereni, Vittorio 1913-1983 ....DLB-128

Serling, Rod 1924-1975 ....DLB-26

Serote, Mongane Wally 1944- DLB-125

Serraillier, Ian 1912-1994 ....DLB-161

Serrano, Nina 1934- DLB-122

Service, Robert 1874-1958 ....DLB-92

Seth, Vikram 1952- DLB-120

Seton, Ernest Thompson
1860-1942 .... DLB-92; DS-13

Settle, Mary Lee 1918- DLB-6

Seume, Johann Gottfried
1763-1810 ....DLB-94

Seuss, Dr. (see Geisel, Theodor Seuss)

The Seventy-fifth Anniversary of the Armistice:
The Wilfred Owen Centenary and the
Great War Exhibit at the University of
Virginia Y-93

Sewall, Joseph 1688-1769 ....DLB-24

Sewall, Richard B. 1908- DLB-111

Sewell, Anna 1820-1878 ....DLB-163

Sewell, Samuel 1652-1730 ....DLB-24

Sex, Class, Politics, and Religion [in the
British Novel, 1930-1959] DLB-15

Sexton, Anne 1928-1974 ....DLB-5

Seymour-Smith, Martin 1928- DLB-155

Shaara, Michael 1929-1988 .... Y-83

Shadwell, Thomas 1641?-1692 ...... DLB-80

Shaffer, Anthony 1926- DLB-13

Shaffer, Peter 1926- DLB-13

Shaftesbury, Anthony Ashley Cooper,
Third Earl of 1671-1713 .... DLB-101

Shairp, Mordaunt 1887-1939 .... DLB-10

Shakespeare, William 1564-1616 .... DLB-62

The Shakespeare Globe Trust Y-93

Shakespeare Head Press DLB-112

Shakhovskoi, Aleksandr Aleksandrovich
1777-1846 .... DLB-150

Shange, Ntozake 1948- DLB-38

Shapiro, Karl 1913- DLB-48

Sharon Publications DLB-46

Sharp, Margery 1905-1991 .... DLB-161

Sharp, William 1855-1905 .... DLB-156

Sharpe, Tom 1928- DLB-14

Shaw, Albert 1857-1947 .... DLB-91

Shaw, Bernard 1856-1950 .... DLB-10, 57

Shaw, Henry Wheeler 1818-1885 ... DLB-11

Shaw, Joseph T. 1874-1952 .... DLB-137

Shaw, Irwin 1913-1984 .... DLB-6, 102; Y-84

Shaw, Robert 1927-1978 .... DLB-13, 14

Shaw, Robert B. 1947- DLB-120

Shawn, William 1907-1992 .... DLB-137

Shay, Frank [publishing house] DLB-46

Shea, John Gilmary 1824-1892 ...... DLB-30

Sheaffer, Louis 1912-1993 .... DLB-103

Shearing, Joseph 1886-1952 .... DLB-70

Shebbeare, John 1709-1788 .... DLB-39

Sheckley, Robert 1928- DLB-8

Shedd, William G. T. 1820-1894 .... DLB-64

Sheed, Wilfred 1930- DLB-6

Sheed and Ward [U.S.] DLB-46

Sheed and Ward Limited [U.K.] ... DLB-112

Sheldon, Alice B. (see Tiptree, James, Jr.)

Sheldon, Edward 1886-1946 ....DLB-7

Sheldon and Company DLB-49

Shelley, Mary Wollstonecraft
1797-1851 ....DLB-110, 116, 159

Shelley, Percy Bysshe
1792-1822 ....DLB-96, 110, 158

Shelnutt, Eve 1941- DLB-130

Shenstone, William 1714-1763 ...... DLB-95

Shepard, Ernest Howard
1879-1976 .... DLB-160

Shepard, Sam 1943- DLB-7

Shepard, Thomas I,
1604 or 1605-1649 .... DLB-24

Shepard, Thomas II, 1635-1677 ..... DLB-24

Shepard, Clark and Brown DLB-49

Shepherd, Luke
flourished 1547-1554 .... DLB-136

Sherburne, Edward 1616-1702 ..... DLB-131

Sheridan, Frances 1724-1766 .....DLB-39, 84

Sheridan, Richard Brinsley
1751-1816 .... DLB-89

Sherman, Francis 1871-1926 .... DLB-92

Sherriff, R. C. 1896-1975 .... DLB-10

Sherry, Norman 1935- DLB-155

Sherwood, Mary Martha
1775-1851 .... DLB-163

Sherwood, Robert 1896-1955 .....DLB-7, 26

Shiel, M. P. 1865-1947 .... DLB-153

Shiels, George 1886-1949 .... DLB-10

Shillaber, B.[enjamin] P.[enhallow]
1814-1890 ....DLB-1, 11

Shine, Ted 1931- DLB-38

Ship, Reuben 1915-1975 .... DLB-88

Shirer, William L. 1904-1993 .... DLB-4

Shirinsky-Shikhmatov, Sergii Aleksandrovich
1783-1837 ....DLB-150

Shirley, James 1596-1666 .... DLB-58

Shishkov, Aleksandr Semenovich
1753-1841 ....DLB-150

Shockley, Ann Allen 1927- DLB-33

Shorthouse, Joseph Henry
1834-1903 .... DLB-18

Showalter, Elaine 1941- DLB-67

Shulevitz, Uri 1935- DLB-61

Shulman, Max 1919-1988 .... DLB-11

Shute, Henry A. 1856-1943 .... DLB-9

Shuttle, Penelope 1947- DLB-14, 40

Sibbes, Richard 1577-1635 .... DLB-151

Sidgwick and Jackson Limited DLB-112

Sidney, Margaret (see Lothrop, Harriet M.)

Sidney, Mary 1561-1621 .... DLB-167

Sidney, Sir Philip 1554-1586 .... DLB-167

Sidney's Press DLB-49

Siegfried Loraine Sassoon: A Centenary Essay
Tributes from Vivien F. Clarke and
Michael Thorpe Y-86

Sierra, Rubén 1946- DLB-122

Sierra Club Books DLB-49

Siger of Brabant
circa 1240-circa 1284 ....DLB-115

Sigourney, Lydia Howard (Huntley)
1791-1865 .... DLB-1, 42, 73

Silkin, Jon 1930- DLB-27

Silko, Leslie Marmon 1948- DLB-143

Silliphant, Stirling 1918- DLB-26

Sillitoe, Alan 1928- DLB-14, 139

Silman, Roberta 1934- DLB-28

Silva, Beverly 1930- DLB-122

Silverberg, Robert 1935- DLB-8

Silverman, Kenneth 1936- DLB-111

Simak, Clifford D. 1904-1988 ....DLB-8

Simcoe, Elizabeth 1762-1850 ....DLB-99

Simcox, George Augustus
1841-1905 ....DLB-35

Sime, Jessie Georgina 1868-1958 .....DLB-92

Simenon, Georges
1903-1989 .... DLB-72; Y-89

Simic, Charles 1938- DLB-105

Simic, Charles,
Images and "Images" DLB-105

Simmel, Johannes Mario 1924- DLB-69

Simmons, Ernest J. 1903-1972 ......DLB-103

Simmons, Herbert Alfred 1930- DLB-33

Simmons, James 1933- DLB-40

Simms, William Gilmore
1806-1870 .... DLB-3, 30, 59, 73

Simms and M'Intyre DLB-106

Simon, Claude 1913- DLB-83

Simon, Neil 1927- DLB-7

Simon and Schuster DLB-46

Simons, Katherine Drayton Mayrant
1890-1969 .... Y-83

Simpkin and Marshall
[publishing house] DLB-154

Simpson, Helen 1897-1940 ....DLB-77

Simpson, Louis 1923- DLB-5

Simpson, N. F. 1919- DLB-13

Sims, George 1923- DLB-87

Sims, George Robert
1847-1922 .... DLB-35, 70, 135

Sinán, Rogelio 1904- DLB-145

Sinclair, Andrew 1935- DLB-14

Sinclair, Bertrand William
1881-1972 ....DLB-92

Sinclair, Catherine
1800-1864 ....DLB-163

Sinclair, Jo 1913- DLB-28

Sinclair Lewis Centennial
Conference Y-85

Sinclair, Lister 1921- DLB-88

Sinclair, May 1863-1946 ....DLB-36, 135

Sinclair, Upton 1878-1968 ....DLB-9

Sinclair, Upton [publishing house] ...DLB-46

Singer, Isaac Bashevis
1904-1991 .... DLB-6, 28, 52; Y-91

Singmaster, Elsie 1879-1958 ....DLB-9

Sinisgalli, Leonardo 1908-1981 .....DLB-114

Siodmak, Curt 1902- DLB-44

Sissman, L. E. 1928-1976 ....DLB-5

Sisson, C. H. 1914- DLB-27

Sitwell, Edith 1887-1964 ....DLB-20

Sitwell, Osbert 1892-1969 ....DLB-100

Skármeta, Antonio 1940- DLB-145

Skeffington, William
[publishing house] DLB-106

Skelton, John 1463-1529 ....DLB-136

Skelton, Robin 1925- DLB-27, 53

Skinner, Constance Lindsay
1877-1939 ....DLB-92

Skinner, John Stuart 1788-1851 ......DLB-73

Skipsey, Joseph 1832-1903 ....DLB-35

Slade, Bernard 1930- DLB-53

Slater, Patrick 1880-1951 ....DLB-68

Slaveykov, Pencho 1866-1912 ......DLB-147

Slavitt, David 1935- DLB-5, 6

Sleigh, Burrows Willcocks Arthur
1821-1869 ....DLB-99

A Slender Thread of Hope: The Kennedy
Center Black Theatre Project DLB-38

Slesinger, Tess 1905-1945 ....DLB-102

Slick, Sam (see Haliburton, Thomas Chandler)

Sloane, William, Associates DLB-46

Small, Maynard and Company DLB-49

Small Presses in Great Britain and Ireland,
1960-1985 ....DLB-40

Small Presses I: Jargon Society Y-84

Small Presses II: The Spirit That Moves Us
Press Y-85

Small Presses III: Pushcart Press Y-87

Smart, Christopher 1722-1771 .....DLB-109

Smart, David A. 1892-1957 ....DLB-137

Smart, Elizabeth 1913-1986 ....DLB-88

Smellie, William
[publishing house] DLB-154

Smiles, Samuel 1812-1904 ....DLB-55

Smith, A. J. M. 1902-1980 ....DLB-88

Smith, Adam 1723-1790 ....DLB-104

Smith, Alexander 1829-1867 .....DLB-32, 55

Smith, Betty 1896-1972 ....Y-82

Smith, Carol Sturm 1938- Y-81

Smith, Charles Henry 1826-1903 ....DLB-11

Smith, Charlotte 1749-1806 ....DLB-39, 109

Smith, Cordwainer 1913-1966 ....DLB-8

Smith, Dave 1942- DLB-5

Smith, Dodie 1896- DLB-10

Smith, Doris Buchanan 1934- DLB-52

Smith, E. E. 1890-1965 ....DLB-8

Smith, Elihu Hubbard 1771-1798 ....DLB-37

Smith, Elizabeth Oakes (Prince)
1806-1893 ....DLB-1

Smith, F. Hopkinson 1838-1915 ....DS-13

Smith, George D. 1870-1920 ......DLB-140

Smith, George O. 1911-1981 ....DLB-8

Smith, Goldwin 1823-1910 ....DLB-99

Smith, H. Allen 1907-1976 ......DLB-11, 29

Smith, Hazel Brannon 1914- DLB-127

Smith, Horatio (Horace)
1779-1849 ....DLB-116

Smith, Horatio (Horace) 1779-1849 and
James Smith 1775-1839 ....DLB-96

Smith, Iain Crichton
1928- DLB-40, 139

Smith, J. Allen 1860-1924 ....DLB-47

Smith, John 1580-1631 ....DLB-24, 30

Smith, Josiah 1704-1781 ....DLB-24

Smith, Ken 1938- DLB-40

Smith, Lee 1944- DLB-143; Y-83

Smith, Logan Pearsall 1865-1946 ....DLB-98

Smith, Mark 1935- Y-82

Smith, Michael 1698-circa 1771 .....DLB-31

Smith, Red 1905-1982 ....DLB-29

Smith, Roswell 1829-1892 ....DLB-79

Smith, Samuel Harrison
1772-1845 ....DLB-43

Smith, Samuel Stanhope
1751-1819 ....DLB-37

Smith, Sarah (see Stretton, Hesba)

Smith, Seba 1792-1868 ....DLB-1, 11

Smith, Sir Thomas 1513-1577 ......DLB-132

Smith, Stevie 1902-1971 ....DLB-20

Smith, Sydney 1771-1845 ....DLB-107

Smith, Sydney Goodsir 1915-1975 ...DLB-27

Smith, William
flourished 1595-1597 ....DLB-136

Smith, William 1727-1803 ....DLB-31

Smith, William 1728-1793 ....DLB-30

Smith, William Gardner
1927-1974 ....DLB-76

Smith, William Henry
1808-1872 ....DLB-159

Smith, William Jay 1918- DLB-5

Smith, Elder and Company DLB-154

Smith, Harrison, and Robert Haas
[publishing house] DLB-46

Smith, J. Stilman, and Company DLB-49

Smith, W. B., and Company DLB-49

Smith, W. H., and Son DLB-106

Smithers, Leonard
[publishing house] DLB-112

Smollett, Tobias 1721-1771 .....DLB-39, 104

Snellings, Rolland (see Touré, Askia
Muhammad)

Snodgrass, W. D. 1926- DLB-5

Snow, C. P. 1905-1980 ....DLB-15, 77

Snyder, Gary 1930- DLB-5, 16, 165

Sobiloff, Hy 1912-1970 ....DLB-48

The Society for Textual Scholarship and
TEXT Y-87

The Society for the History of Authorship,
Reading and Publishing Y-92

Soffici, Ardengo 1879-1964 ....DLB-114

Sofola, 'Zulu 1938- DLB-157

Solano, Solita 1888-1975 ....DLB-4

Sollers, Philippe 1936- DLB-83

Solmi, Sergio 1899-1981 ....DLB-114

Solomon, Carl 1928- DLB-16

Solway, David 1941- DLB-53

Solzhenitsyn and America Y-85

Somerville, Edith Œnone
1858-1949 ....DLB-135

Sontag, Susan 1933- DLB-2, 67

Sorrentino, Gilbert 1929- DLB-5; Y-80

Sorge, Reinhard Johannes 1892-1916 . . . . DLB-118

Sotheby, William 1757-1833 . . . . DLB-93

Soto, Gary 1952- DLB-82

Sources for the Study of Tudor and Stuart Drama DLB-62

Souster, Raymond 1921- DLB-88

The *South English Legendary* circa thirteenth-fifteenth centuries DLB-146

Southerland, Ellease 1943- DLB-33

Southern Illinois University Press Y-95

Southern, Terry 1924- DLB-2

Southern Writers Between the Wars DLB-9

Southerne, Thomas 1659-1746 . . . . . . DLB-80

Southey, Caroline Anne Bowles 1786-1854 . . . . DLB-116

Southey, Robert 1774-1843 . . . . DLB-93, 107, 142

Southwell, Robert 1561?-1595 . . . . . DLB-167

Sowande, Bode 1948- DLB-157

Soyfer, Jura 1912-1939 . . . . DLB-124

Soyinka, Wole 1934- . . . DLB-125; Y-86, 87

Spacks, Barry 1931- DLB-105

Spalding, Frances 1950- DLB-155

Spark, Muriel 1918- DLB-15, 139

Sparks, Jared 1789-1866 . . . . DLB-1, 30

Sparshott, Francis 1926- DLB-60

Späth, Gerold 1939- DLB-75

Spatola, Adriano 1941-1988 . . . . DLB-128

Spaziani, Maria Luisa 1924- DLB-128

The Spectator 1828- DLB-110

Spedding, James 1808-1881 . . . . DLB-144

Spee von Langenfeld, Friedrich 1591-1635 . . . . DLB-164

Speght, Rachel 1597-after 1630 . . . . DLB-126

Speke, John Hanning 1827-1864 . . . DLB-166

Spellman, A. B. 1935- DLB-41

Spence, Thomas 1750-1814 . . . . DLB-158

Spencer, Anne 1882-1975 . . . . DLB-51, 54

Spencer, Elizabeth 1921- DLB-6

Spencer, Herbert 1820-1903 . . . . DLB-57

Spencer, Scott 1945- Y-86

Spender, J. A. 1862-1942 . . . . DLB-98

Spender, Stephen 1909- DLB-20

Spener, Philipp Jakob 1635-1705 . . . DLB-164

Spenser, Edmund circa 1552-1599 . . DLB-167

Sperr, Martin 1944- DLB-124

Spicer, Jack 1925-1965 . . . . .DLB-5, 16

Spielberg, Peter 1929- Y-81

Spielhagen, Friedrich 1829-1911 . . . . DLB-129

"*Spielmannsepen*" (circa 1152-circa 1500) DLB-148

Spier, Peter 1927- DLB-61

Spinrad, Norman 1940- DLB-8

Spires, Elizabeth 1952- DLB-120

Spitteler, Carl 1845-1924 . . . . DLB-129

Spivak, Lawrence E. 1900- DLB-137

Spofford, Harriet Prescott 1835-1921 . . . . DLB-74

Squibob (see Derby, George Horatio)

Stacpoole, H. de Vere 1863-1951 . . . . DLB-153

Staël, Germaine de 1766-1817 . . . . . . DLB-119

Staël-Holstein, Anne-Louise Germaine de (see Staël, Germaine de)

Stafford, Jean 1915-1979 . . . . DLB-2

Stafford, William 1914- DLB-5

Stage Censorship: "The Rejected Statement" (1911), by Bernard Shaw [excerpts] DLB-10

Stallings, Laurence 1894-1968 . . . . .DLB-7, 44

Stallworthy, Jon 1935- DLB-40

Stampp, Kenneth M. 1912- DLB-17

Stanford, Ann 1916- DLB-5

Stanković, Borisav ("Bora") 1876-1927 . . . . DLB-147

Stanley, Henry M. 1841-1904 . . . . .DS-13

Stanley, Thomas 1625-1678 . . . . DLB-131

Stannard, Martin 1947- DLB-155

Stanton, Elizabeth Cady 1815-1902 . . . DLB-79

Stanton, Frank L. 1857-1927 . . . . DLB-25

Stanton, Maura 1946- DLB-120

Stapledon, Olaf 1886-1950 . . . . DLB-15

Star Spangled Banner Office DLB-49

Starkey, Thomas circa 1499-1538 . . . DLB-132

Starkweather, David 1935- DLB-7

Statements on the Art of Poetry DLB-54

Stead, Robert J. C. 1880-1959 . . . . . . DLB-92

Steadman, Mark 1930- DLB-6

The Stealthy School of Criticism (1871), by Dante Gabriel Rossetti DLB-35

Stearns, Harold E. 1891-1943 . . . . DLB-4

Stedman, Edmund Clarence 1833-1908 .DLB-64

Steegmuller, Francis 1906-1994 . . . . .DLB-111

Steel, Flora Annie 1847-1929 . . . . DLB-153, 156

Steele, Max 1922- Y-80

Steele, Richard 1672-1729 . . . . . . DLB-84, 101

Steele, Timothy 1948- DLB-120

Steele, Wilbur Daniel 1886-1970 . . . . .DLB-86

Steere, Richard circa 1643-1721 . . . . . .DLB-24

Stegner, Wallace 1909-1993 . . . . DLB-9; Y-93

Stehr, Hermann 1864-1940 . . . . .DLB-66

Steig, William 1907- DLB-61

Stieler, Caspar 1632-1707 . . . . .DLB-164

Stein, Gertrude 1874-1946 . . . . DLB-4, 54, 86

Stein, Leo 1872-1947 . . . . .DLB-4

Stein and Day Publishers DLB-46

Steinbeck, John 1902-1968 . . . DLB-7, 9; DS-2

Steiner, George 1929- DLB-67

Stendhal 1783-1842 . . . . .DLB-119

Stephen Crane: A Revaluation Virginia Tech Conference, 1989 . . . . Y-89

Stephen, Leslie 1832-1904 . . . . . . DLB-57, 144

Stephens, Alexander H. 1812-1883 . . .DLB-47

Stephens, Ann 1810-1886 . . . . DLB-3, 73

Stephens, Charles Asbury 1844?-1931 . . . . .DLB-42

Stephens, James 1882?-1950 . . . . DLB-19, 153, 162

Sterling, George 1869-1926 . . . . .DLB-54

Sterling, James 1701-1763 . . . . .DLB-24

Sterling, John 1806-1844 . . . . .DLB-116

Stern, Gerald 1925- DLB-105

Stern, Madeleine B. 1912- . . . DLB-111, 140

Stern, Gerald, Living in Ruin DLB-105

Stern, Richard 1928- Y-87

Stern, Stewart 1922- DLB-26

Sterne, Laurence 1713-1768 . . . . .DLB-39

Sternheim, Carl 1878-1942 . . . . . DLB-56, 118

Sternhold, Thomas ?-1549 and John Hopkins ?-1570 . . . . .DLB-132

Stevens, Henry 1819-1886 . . . . .DLB-140

Stevens, Wallace 1879-1955 . . . . .DLB-54

Stevenson, Anne 1933- DLB-40

Stevenson, Lionel 1902-1973 . . . . . . .DLB-155

Stevenson, Robert Louis 1850-1894 . . . DLB-18, 57, 141, 156; DS-13

Stewart, Donald Ogden
    1894-1980 .... DLB-4, 11, 26

Stewart, Dugald 1753-1828 .... DLB-31

Stewart, George, Jr. 1848-1906 ...... DLB-99

Stewart, George R. 1895-1980 .... DLB-8

Stewart and Kidd Company DLB-46

Stewart, Randall 1896-1964 .... DLB-103

Stickney, Trumbull 1874-1904 ...... DLB-54

Stifter, Adalbert 1805-1868 .... DLB-133

Stiles, Ezra 1727-1795 .... DLB-31

Still, James 1906- DLB-9

Stirner, Max 1806-1856 .... DLB-129

Stith, William 1707-1755 .... DLB-31

Stock, Elliot [publishing house] DLB-106

Stockton, Frank R.
    1834-1902 .... DLB-42, 74; DS-13

Stoddard, Ashbel
    [publishing house] DLB-49

Stoddard, Richard Henry
    1825-1903 .... DLB-3, 64; DS-13

Stoddard, Solomon 1643-1729 .... DLB-24

Stoker, Bram 1847-1912 .... DLB-36, 70

Stokes, Frederick A., Company DLB-49

Stokes, Thomas L. 1898-1958 .... DLB-29

Stokesbury, Leon 1945- DLB-120

Stolberg, Christian Graf zu
    1748-1821 .... DLB-94

Stolberg, Friedrich Leopold Graf zu
    1750-1819 .... DLB-94

Stone, Herbert S., and Company DLB-49

Stone, Lucy 1818-1893 .... DLB-79

Stone, Melville 1848-1929 .... DLB-25

Stone, Robert 1937- DLB-152

Stone, Ruth 1915- DLB-105

Stone, Samuel 1602-1663 .... DLB-24

Stone and Kimball DLB-49

Stoppard, Tom 1937- DLB-13; Y-85

Storey, Anthony 1928- DLB-14

Storey, David 1933- DLB-13, 14

Storm, Theodor 1817-1888 .... DLB-129

Story, Thomas circa 1670-1742 ..... DLB-31

Story, William Wetmore 1819-1895 ... DLB-1

Storytelling: A Contemporary
    Renaissance Y-84

Stoughton, William 1631-1701 ..... DLB-24

Stow, John 1525-1605 .... DLB-132

Stowe, Harriet Beecher
    1811-1896 .... DLB-1, 12, 42, 74

Stowe, Leland 1899- DLB-29

Stoyanov, Dimitŭr Ivanov (see Elin Pelin)

Strachey, Lytton
    1880-1932 .... DLB-149; DS-10

Strachey, Lytton, Preface to *Eminent
    Victorians* DLB-149

Strahan and Company DLB-106

Strahan, William
    [publishing house] DLB-154

Strand, Mark 1934- DLB-5

The Strasbourg Oaths 842 .... DLB-148

Stratemeyer, Edward 1862-1930 .... DLB-42

Stratton and Barnard DLB-49

Straub, Peter 1943- Y-84

Strauß, Botho 1944- DLB-124

Strauß, David Friedrich
    1808-1874 .... DLB-133

The Strawberry Hill Press DLB-154

Streatfeild, Noel 1895-1986 .... DLB-160

Street, Cecil John Charles (see Rhode, John)

Street, G. S. 1867-1936 .... DLB-135

Street and Smith DLB-49

Streeter, Edward 1891-1976 .... DLB-11

Streeter, Thomas Winthrop
    1883-1965 .... DLB-140

Stretton, Hesba 1832-1911 .... DLB-163

Stribling, T. S. 1881-1965 .... DLB-9

Der Stricker circa 1190-circa 1250 .. DLB-138

Strickland, Samuel 1804-1867 ...... DLB-99

Stringer and Townsend DLB-49

Stringer, Arthur 1874-1950 .... DLB-92

Strittmatter, Erwin 1912- DLB-69

Strode, William 1630-1645 .... DLB-126

Strother, David Hunter 1816-1888 ... DLB-3

Strouse, Jean 1945- DLB-111

Stuart, Dabney 1937- DLB-105

Stuart, Dabney, Knots into Webs: Some Auto-
    biographical Sources DLB-105

Stuart, Jesse
    1906-1984 .... DLB-9, 48, 102; Y-84

Stuart, Lyle [publishing house] DLB-46

Stubbs, Harry Clement (see Clement, Hal)

Stubenberg, Johann Wilhelm von
    1619-1663 .... DLB-164

Studio DLB-112

The Study of Poetry (1880), by
    Matthew Arnold DLB-35

Sturgeon, Theodore
    1918-1985 .... DLB-8; Y-85

Sturges, Preston 1898-1959 .... DLB-26

"Style" (1840; revised, 1859), by
    Thomas de Quincey [excerpt] DLB-57

"Style" (1888), by Walter Pater DLB-57

Style (1897), by Walter Raleigh
    [excerpt] DLB-57

"Style" (1877), by T. H. Wright
    [excerpt] DLB-57

"Le Style c'est l'homme" (1892), by
    W. H. Mallock DLB-57

Styron, William 1925- DLB-2, 143; Y-80

Suárez, Mario 1925- DLB-82

Such, Peter 1939- DLB-60

Suckling, Sir John 1609-1641? ...DLB-58, 126

Suckow, Ruth 1892-1960 .... DLB-9, 102

Sudermann, Hermann 1857-1928 ...DLB-118

Sue, Eugène 1804-1857 .... DLB-119

Sue, Marie-Joseph (see Sue, Eugène)

Suggs, Simon (see Hooper, Johnson Jones)

Sukenick, Ronald 1932- Y-81

Suknaski, Andrew 1942- DLB-53

Sullivan, Alan 1868-1947 .... DLB-92

Sullivan, C. Gardner 1886-1965 ..... DLB-26

Sullivan, Frank 1892-1976 .... DLB-11

Sulte, Benjamin 1841-1923 .... DLB-99

Sulzberger, Arthur Hays
    1891-1968 .... DLB-127

Sulzberger, Arthur Ochs 1926- ...DLB-127

Sulzer, Johann Georg 1720-1779 ..... DLB-97

Sumarokov, Aleksandr Petrovich
    1717-1777 .... DLB-150

Summers, Hollis 1916- DLB-6

Sumner, Henry A.
    [publishing house] DLB-49

Surtees, Robert Smith 1803-1864 ....DLB-21

A Survey of Poetry Anthologies,
    1879-1960 .... DLB-54

Surveys of the Year's Biographies

A Transit of Poets and Others: American
    Biography in 1982 .... Y-82

The Year in Literary Biography ...Y-83–Y-95

Survey of the Year's Book Publishing

The Year in Book Publishing Y-86

Survey of the Year's Children's Books

The Year in Children's Books Y-92–Y-95

Surveys of the Year's Drama

The Year in Drama
.... Y-82–Y-85, Y-87–Y-95

The Year in London Theatre Y-92

Surveys of the Year's Fiction

The Year's Work in Fiction:
A Survey Y-82

The Year in Fiction: A Biased View Y-83

The Year in
Fiction Y-84–Y-86, Y-89, Y-94, Y-95

The Year in the
Novel Y-87, Y-88, Y-90–Y-93

The Year in Short Stories Y-87

The Year in the
Short Story Y-88, Y-90–Y-93

Survey of the Year's Literary Theory

The Year in Literary Theory Y-92–Y-93

Surveys of the Year's Poetry

The Year's Work in American
Poetry Y-82

The Year in Poetry ... Y-83–Y-92, Y-94, Y-95

Sutherland, Efua Theodora
1924- DLB-117

Sutherland, John 1919-1956 .... DLB-68

Sutro, Alfred 1863-1933 .... DLB-10

Swados, Harvey 1920-1972 ....DLB-2

Swain, Charles 1801-1874 .... DLB-32

Swallow Press DLB-46

Swan Sonnenschein Limited DLB-106

Swanberg, W. A. 1907- DLB-103

Swenson, May 1919-1989 ....DLB-5

Swerling, Jo 1897- DLB-44

Swift, Jonathan
1667-1745 .... DLB-39, 95, 101

Swinburne, A. C. 1837-1909 ..... DLB-35, 57

Swineshead, Richard floruit
circa 1350 .... DLB-115

Swinnerton, Frank 1884-1982 ...... DLB-34

Swisshelm, Jane Grey 1815-1884 .... DLB-43

Swope, Herbert Bayard 1882-1958 .. DLB-25

Swords, T. and J., and Company DLB-49

Swords, Thomas 1763-1843 and
Swords, James ?-1844 .... DLB-73

Sylvester, Josuah
1562 or 1563 - 1618 .... DLB-121

Symonds, Emily Morse (see Paston, George)

Symonds, John Addington
1840-1893 .... DLB-57, 144

Symons, A. J. A. 1900-1941 .... DLB-149

Symons, Arthur
1865-1945 ....DLB-19, 57, 149

Symons, Julian
1912-1994 ....DLB-87, 155; Y-92

Symons, Scott 1933- DLB-53

A Symposium on *The Columbia History of
the Novel* Y-92

Synge, John Millington
1871-1909 .... DLB-10, 19

Synge Summer School: J. M. Synge and the
Irish Theater, Rathdrum, County Wiclow,
Ireland Y-93

Syrett, Netta 1865-1943 .... DLB-135

T

Taban lo Liyong 1939?- DLB-125

Taché, Joseph-Charles 1820-1894 .... DLB-99

Tafolla, Carmen 1951- DLB-82

Taggard, Genevieve 1894-1948 ...... DLB-45

Tagger, Theodor (see Bruckner, Ferdinand)

Tait, J. Selwin, and Sons DLB-49

Tait's Edinburgh Magazine
1832-1861 .... DLB-110

The Takarazaka Revue Company Y-91

Tallent, Elizabeth 1954- DLB-130

Talvj 1797-1870 ....DLB-59, 133

Taradash, Daniel 1913- DLB-44

Tarbell, Ida M. 1857-1944 .... DLB-47

Tardivel, Jules-Paul 1851-1905 ...... DLB-99

Targan, Barry 1932- DLB-130

Tarkington, Booth 1869-1946 ....DLB-9, 102

Tashlin, Frank 1913-1972 .... DLB-44

Tate, Allen 1899-1979 ....DLB-4, 45, 63

Tate, James 1943- DLB-5

Tate, Nahum circa 1652-1715 .... DLB-80

Tatian circa 830 .... DLB-148

Tavčar, Ivan 1851-1923 .... DLB-147

Taylor, Ann 1782-1866 .... DLB-163

Taylor, Bayard 1825-1878 .... DLB-3

Taylor, Bert Leston 1866-1921 ...... DLB-25

Taylor, Charles H. 1846-1921 .... DLB-25

Taylor, Edward circa 1642-1729 ..... DLB-24

Taylor, Elizabeth 1912-1975 .... DLB-139

Taylor, Henry 1942- DLB-5

Taylor, Sir Henry 1800-1886 .... DLB-32

Taylor, Jane 1783-1824 .... DLB-163

Taylor, Jeremy circa 1613-1667 .....DLB-151

Taylor, John
1577 or 1578 - 1653 ....DLB-121

Taylor, Mildred D. ?- DLB-52

Taylor, Peter 1917-1994 .... Y-81, Y-94

Taylor, William, and Company DLB-49

Taylor-Made Shakespeare? Or Is
"Shall I Die?" the Long-Lost Text
of Bottom's Dream? Y-85

Teasdale, Sara 1884-1933 ....DLB-45

The Tea-Table (1725), by Eliza Haywood
[excerpt] DLB-39

Telles, Lygia Fagundes 1924- DLB-113

Temple, Sir William 1628-1699 .....DLB-101

Tenn, William 1919- DLB-8

Tennant, Emma 1937- DLB-14

Tenney, Tabitha Gilman
1762-1837 ....DLB-37

Tennyson, Alfred 1809-1892 ....DLB-32

Tennyson, Frederick 1807-1898 ......DLB-32

Terhune, Albert Payson 1872-1942 ....DLB-9

Terhune, Mary Virginia 1830-1922 .... DS-13

Terry, Megan 1932- DLB-7

Terson, Peter 1932- DLB-13

Tesich, Steve 1943- Y-83

Tessa, Delio 1886-1939 ....DLB-114

Testori, Giovanni 1923-1993 ....DLB-128

Tey, Josephine 1896?-1952 ....DLB-77

Thacher, James 1754-1844 ....DLB-37

Thackeray, William Makepeace
1811-1863 ....DLB-21, 55, 159, 163

Thames and Hudson Limited DLB-112

Thanet, Octave (see French, Alice)

The Theater in Shakespeare's
Time DLB-62

The Theatre Guild DLB-7

Thegan and the Astronomer
flourished circa 850 ....DLB-148

Thelwall, John 1764-1834 ...... DLB-93, 158

Theodulf circa 760-circa 821 ....DLB-148

Theriault, Yves 1915-1983 ....DLB-88

Thério, Adrien 1925- DLB-53

Theroux, Paul 1941- DLB-2

Thibaudeau, Colleen 1925- DLB-88

Thielen, Benedict 1903-1965 ....DLB-102

Thiong'o Ngugi wa (see Ngugi wa Thiong'o)

Third-Generation Minor Poets of the
  Seventeenth Century DLB-131

Thoma, Ludwig 1867-1921 . . . . DLB-66

Thoma, Richard 1902- DLB-4

Thomas, Audrey 1935- DLB-60

Thomas, D. M. 1935- DLB-40

Thomas, Dylan
  1914-1953 . . . . DLB-13, 20, 139

Thomas, Edward
  1878-1917 . . . . DLB-19, 98, 156

Thomas, Gwyn 1913-1981 . . . . DLB-15

Thomas, Isaiah 1750-1831 . . . . DLB-43, 73

Thomas, Isaiah [publishing house] . . . DLB-49

Thomas, John 1900-1932 . . . . DLB-4

Thomas, Joyce Carol 1938- DLB-33

Thomas, Lorenzo 1944- DLB-41

Thomas, R. S. 1915- DLB-27

Thomasîn von Zerclære
  circa 1186-circa 1259 . . . . DLB-138

Thompson, David 1770-1857 . . . . DLB-99

Thompson, Dorothy 1893-1961 . . . . . DLB-29

Thompson, Francis 1859-1907 . . . . . . DLB-19

Thompson, George Selden (see Selden, George)

Thompson, John 1938-1976 . . . . DLB-60

Thompson, John R. 1823-1873 . . . DLB-3, 73

Thompson, Lawrance 1906-1973 . . . DLB-103

Thompson, Maurice
  1844-1901 . . . . DLB-71, 74

Thompson, Ruth Plumly
  1891-1976 . . . . DLB-22

Thompson, Thomas Phillips
  1843-1933 . . . . DLB-99

Thompson, William 1775-1833 . . . . . DLB-158

Thompson, William Tappan
  1812-1882 . . . . DLB-3, 11

Thomson, Edward William
  1849-1924 . . . . DLB-92

Thomson, James 1700-1748 . . . . DLB-95

Thomson, James 1834-1882 . . . . DLB-35

Thomson, Mortimer 1831-1875 . . . . . DLB-11

Thoreau, Henry David 1817-1862 . . . . DLB-1

Thorpe, Thomas Bangs
  1815-1878 . . . . DLB-3, 11

Thoughts on Poetry and Its Varieties (1833),
  by John Stuart Mill DLB-32

Thrale, Hester Lynch (see Piozzi, Hester
  Lynch [Thrale])

Thümmel, Moritz August von
  1738-1817 . . . . DLB-97

Thurber, James
  1894-1961 . . . . DLB-4, 11, 22, 102

Thurman, Wallace 1902-1934 . . . . . . DLB-51

Thwaite, Anthony 1930- DLB-40

Thwaites, Reuben Gold
  1853-1913 . . . . DLB-47

Ticknor, George
  1791-1871 . . . . DLB-1, 59, 140

Ticknor and Fields DLB-49

Ticknor and Fields (revived) DLB-46

Tieck, Ludwig 1773-1853 . . . . DLB-90

Tietjens, Eunice 1884-1944 . . . . DLB-54

Tilney, Edmund circa 1536-1610 . . . DLB-136

Tilt, Charles [publishing house] DLB-106

Tilton, J. E., and Company DLB-49

Time and Western Man (1927), by Wyndham
  Lewis [excerpts] DLB-36

Time-Life Books DLB-46

Times Books DLB-46

Timothy, Peter circa 1725-1782 . . . . . DLB-43

Timrod, Henry 1828-1867 . . . . DLB-3

Tinker, Chauncey Brewster
  1876-1963 . . . . DLB-140

Tinsley Brothers DLB-106

Tiptree, James, Jr. 1915-1987 . . . . DLB-8

Titus, Edward William 1870-1952 . . . . DLB-4

Tlali, Miriam 1933- DLB-157

Todd, Barbara Euphan
  1890-1976 . . . . DLB-160

Toklas, Alice B. 1877-1967 . . . . DLB-4

Tolkien, J. R. R. 1892-1973 . . . . DLB-15, 160

Toller, Ernst 1893-1939 . . . . DLB-124

Tollet, Elizabeth 1694-1754 . . . . DLB-95

Tolson, Melvin B. 1898-1966 . . . . DLB-48, 76

Tom Jones (1749), by Henry Fielding
  [excerpt] DLB-39

Tomalin, Claire 1933- DLB-155

Tomlinson, Charles 1927- DLB-40

Tomlinson, H. M. 1873-1958 . . . DLB-36, 100

Tompkins, Abel [publishing house] . . DLB-49

Tompson, Benjamin 1642-1714 . . . . . DLB-24

Tonks, Rosemary 1932- DLB-14

Tonna, Charlotte Elizabeth
  1790-1846 . . . . DLB-163

Toole, John Kennedy 1937-1969 . . . . . Y-81

Toomer, Jean 1894-1967 . . . . DLB-45, 51

Tor Books DLB-46

Torberg, Friedrich 1908-1979 . . . . . . DLB-85

Torrence, Ridgely 1874-1950 . . . . . . DLB-54

Torres-Metzger, Joseph V.
  1933- DLB-122

Toth, Susan Allen 1940- Y-86

Tough-Guy Literature DLB-9

Touré, Askia Muhammad 1938- . . . DLB-41

Tourgée, Albion W. 1838-1905 . . . . . DLB-79

Tourneur, Cyril circa 1580-1626 . . . . DLB-58

Tournier, Michel 1924- DLB-83

Tousey, Frank [publishing house] DLB-49

Tower Publications DLB-46

Towne, Benjamin circa 1740-1793 . . . DLB-43

Towne, Robert 1936- DLB-44

The Townely Plays
  fifteenth and sixteenth
  centuries DLB-146

Townshend, Aurelian
  by 1583 - circa 1651 . . . . DLB-121

Tracy, Honor 1913- DLB-15

Traherne, Thomas 1637?-1674 . . . . . DLB-131

Traill, Catharine Parr 1802-1899 . . . . DLB-99

Train, Arthur 1875-1945 . . . . DLB-86

The Transatlantic Publishing
  Company DLB-49

Transcendentalists, American DS-5

Translators of the Twelfth Century:
  Literary Issues Raised and Impact
  Created DLB-115

Travel Writing, 1837-1875 . . . . DLB-166

Traven, B.
  1882? or 1890?-1969? DLB-9, 56

Travers, Ben 1886-1980 . . . . DLB-10

Travers, P. L. (Pamela Lyndon)
  1899- DLB-160

Trediakovsky, Vasilii Kirillovich
  1703-1769 . . . . DLB-150

Treece, Henry 1911-1966 . . . . DLB-160

Trejo, Ernesto 1950- DLB-122

Trelawny, Edward John
  1792-1881 . . . . DLB-110, 116, 144

Tremain, Rose 1943- DLB-14

Tremblay, Michel 1942- DLB-60

Trends in Twentieth-Century
  Mass Market Publishing DLB-46

Trent, William P. 1862-1939 . . . . DLB-47

Trescot, William Henry
  1822-1898 . . . . DLB-30

Trevelyan, Sir George Otto
  1838-1928 .... DLB-144

Trevisa, John
  circa 1342-circa 1402 .... DLB-146

Trevor, William 1928- DLB-14, 139

Trierer Floyris circa 1170-1180 ...... DLB-138

Trilling, Lionel 1905-1975 ..... DLB-28, 63

Trilussa 1871-1950 .... DLB-114

Trimmer, Sarah 1741-1810 .... DLB-158

Triolet, Elsa 1896-1970 .... DLB-72

Tripp, John 1927- DLB-40

Trocchi, Alexander 1925- DLB-15

Trollope, Anthony
  1815-1882 .... DLB-21, 57, 159

Trollope, Frances 1779-1863 ... DLB-21, 166

Troop, Elizabeth 1931- DLB-14

Trotter, Catharine 1679-1749 ...... DLB-84

Trotti, Lamar 1898-1952 .... DLB-44

Trottier, Pierre 1925- DLB-60

Troupe, Quincy Thomas, Jr.
  1943- DLB-41

Trow, John F., and Company DLB-49

Truillier-Lacombe, Joseph-Patrice
  1807-1863 .... DLB-99

Trumbo, Dalton 1905-1976 .... DLB-26

Trumbull, Benjamin 1735-1820 ..... DLB-30

Trumbull, John 1750-1831 .... DLB-31

Tscherning, Andreas 1611-1659 .... DLB-164

T. S. Eliot Centennial Y-88

Tucholsky, Kurt 1890-1935 .... DLB-56

Tucker, Charlotte Maria
  1821-1893 .... DLB-163

Tucker, George 1775-1861 .... DLB-3, 30

Tucker, Nathaniel Beverley
  1784-1851 ....DLB-3

Tucker, St. George 1752-1827 ...... DLB-37

Tuckerman, Henry Theodore
  1813-1871 .... DLB-64

Tunis, John R. 1889-1975 .... DLB-22

Tunstall, Cuthbert 1474-1559 ..... DLB-132

Tuohy, Frank 1925- DLB-14, 139

Tupper, Martin F. 1810-1889 .... DLB-32

Turbyfill, Mark 1896- DLB-45

Turco, Lewis 1934- Y-84

Turnbull, Andrew 1921-1970 ..... DLB-103

Turnbull, Gael 1928- DLB-40

Turner, Arlin 1909-1980 ...... DLB-103

Turner, Charles (Tennyson)
  1808-1879 .... DLB-32

Turner, Frederick 1943- DLB-40

Turner, Frederick Jackson
  1861-1932 .... DLB-17

Turner, Joseph Addison
  1826-1868 .... DLB-79

Turpin, Waters Edward
  1910-1968 .... DLB-51

Turrini, Peter 1944- DLB-124

Tutuola, Amos 1920- DLB-125

Twain, Mark (see Clemens,
  Samuel Langhorne)

The 'Twenties and Berlin, by
  Alex Natan DLB-66

Tyler, Anne 1941- DLB-6, 143; Y-82

Tyler, Moses Coit 1835-1900 ....DLB-47, 64

Tyler, Royall 1757-1826 .... DLB-37

Tylor, Edward Burnett 1832-1917 ... DLB-57

Tynan, Katharine 1861-1931 ...... DLB-153

Tyndale, William
  circa 1494-1536 .... DLB-132

                   U

Udall, Nicholas 1504-1556 .... DLB-62

Uhland, Ludwig 1787-1862 .... DLB-90

Uhse, Bodo 1904-1963 .... DLB-69

Ujević, Augustin ("Tin")
  1891-1955 .... DLB-147

Ulenhart, Niclas
  flourished circa 1600 .... DLB-164

Ulibarrí, Sabine R. 1919- DLB-82

Ulica, Jorge 1870-1926 .... DLB-82

Ulizio, B. George 1889-1969 .... DLB-140

Ulrich von Liechtenstein
  circa 1200-circa 1275 .... DLB-138

Ulrich von Zatzikhoven
  before 1194-after 1214 .... DLB-138

Unamuno, Miguel de 1864-1936 ....DLB-108

Under the Microscope (1872), by
  A. C. Swinburne DLB-35

Unger, Friederike Helene
  1741-1813 .... DLB-94

Ungaretti, Giuseppe 1888-1970 ..... DLB-114

United States Book Company DLB-49

Universal Publishing and Distributing
  Corporation DLB-46

The University of Iowa Writers' Workshop
  Golden Jubilee Y-86

The University of South Carolina
  Press Y-94

University of Wales Press DLB-112

"The Unknown Public" (1858), by
  Wilkie Collins [excerpt] DLB-57

Unruh, Fritz von 1885-1970 .... DLB-56, 118

Unspeakable Practices II: The Festival of
  Vanguard Narrative at Brown
  University Y-93

Unwin, T. Fisher
  [publishing house] DLB-106

Upchurch, Boyd B. (see Boyd, John)

Updike, John
  1932- ... DLB-2, 5, 143; Y-80, 82; DS-3

Upton, Bertha 1849-1912 .... DLB-141

Upton, Charles 1948- DLB-16

Upton, Florence K. 1873-1922 ...... DLB-141

Upward, Allen 1863-1926 .... DLB-36

Urista, Alberto Baltazar (see Alurista)

Urzidil, Johannes 1896-1976 .... DLB-85

Urquhart, Fred 1912- DLB-139

The Uses of Facsimile Y-90

Usk, Thomas died 1388 .... DLB-146

Uslar Pietri, Arturo 1906- DLB-113

Ustinov, Peter 1921- DLB-13

Uttley, Alison 1884-1976 .... DLB-160

Uz, Johann Peter 1720-1796 .... DLB-97

                   V

Vac, Bertrand 1914- DLB-88

Vail, Laurence 1891-1968 .... DLB-4

Vailland, Roger 1907-1965 .... DLB-83

Vajda, Ernest 1887-1954 .... DLB-44

Valdés, Gina 1943- DLB-122

Valdez, Luis Miguel 1940- DLB-122

Valduga, Patrizia 1953- DLB-128

Valente, José Angel 1929- DLB-108

Valenzuela, Luisa 1938- DLB-113

Valeri, Diego 1887-1976 .... DLB-128

Valgardson, W. D. 1939- DLB-60

Valle, Víctor Manuel 1950- DLB-122

Valle-Inclán, Ramón del
  1866-1936 .... DLB-134

Vallejo, Armando 1949- DLB-122

Vallès, Jules 1832-1885 .... DLB-123

Vallette, Marguerite Eymery (see Rachilde)

Valverde, José María 1926- DLB-108

Van Allsburg, Chris 1949- DLB-61

Van Anda, Carr 1864-1945 ....DLB-25

Van Doren, Mark 1894-1972 ....DLB-45

van Druten, John 1901-1957 ....DLB-10

Van Duyn, Mona 1921- DLB-5

Van Dyke, Henry
1852-1933 .... DLB-71; DS-13

Van Dyke, Henry 1928- DLB-33

van Itallie, Jean-Claude 1936- DLB-7

Van Rensselaer, Mariana Griswold
1851-1934 ....DLB-47

Van Rensselaer, Mrs. Schuyler (see Van
Rensselaer, Mariana Griswold)

Van Vechten, Carl 1880-1964 ......DLB-4, 9

van Vogt, A. E. 1912- DLB-8

Vanbrugh, Sir John 1664-1726 ......DLB-80

Vance, Jack 1916?- DLB-8

Vane, Sutton 1888-1963 ....DLB-10

Vanguard Press DLB-46

Vann, Robert L. 1879-1940 ....DLB-29

Vargas, Llosa, Mario 1936- DLB-145

Varley, John 1947- Y-81

Varnhagen von Ense, Karl August
1785-1858 ....DLB-90

Varnhagen von Ense, Rahel
1771-1833 ....DLB-90

Vásquez Montalbán, Manuel
1939- DLB-134

Vassa, Gustavus (see Equiano, Olaudah)

Vassalli, Sebastiano 1941- DLB-128

Vaughan, Henry 1621-1695 ....DLB-131

Vaughan, Thomas 1621-1666 ......DLB-131

Vaux, Thomas, Lord 1509-1556 ....DLB-132

Vazov, Ivan 1850-1921 ....DLB-147

Vega, Janine Pommy 1942- DLB-16

Veiller, Anthony 1903-1965 ....DLB-44

Velásquez-Trevino, Gloria
1949- DLB-122

Veloz Maggiolo, Marcio 1936- DLB-145

Venegas, Daniel ?-? DLB-82

Vergil, Polydore circa 1470-1555 ...DLB-132

Veríssimo, Erico 1905-1975 ....DLB-145

Verne, Jules 1828-1905 ....DLB-123

Verplanck, Gulian C. 1786-1870 .....DLB-59

Very, Jones 1813-1880 ....DLB-1

Vian, Boris 1920-1959 ....DLB-72

Vickers, Roy 1888?-1965 ....DLB-77

Victoria 1819-1901 ....DLB-55

Victoria Press DLB-106

Vidal, Gore 1925- DLB-6, 152

Viebig, Clara 1860-1952 ....DLB-66

Viereck, George Sylvester
1884-1962 ....DLB-54

Viereck, Peter 1916- DLB-5

Viets, Roger 1738-1811 ....DLB-99

Viewpoint: Politics and Performance, by
David Edgar DLB-13

Vigil-Piñon, Evangelina 1949- DLB-122

Vigneault, Gilles 1928- DLB-60

Vigny, Alfred de 1797-1863 ....DLB-119

Vigolo, Giorgio 1894-1983 ....DLB-114

The Viking Press DLB-46

Villanueva, Alma Luz 1944- DLB-122

Villanueva, Tino 1941- DLB-82

Villard, Henry 1835-1900 ....DLB-23

Villard, Oswald Garrison
1872-1949 ....DLB-25, 91

Villarreal, José Antonio 1924- DLB-82

Villegas de Magnón, Leonor
1876-1955 ....DLB-122

Villemaire, Yolande 1949- DLB-60

Villena, Luis Antonio de 1951- ...DLB-134

Villiers de l'Isle-Adam, Jean-Marie
Mathias Philippe-Auguste, Comte de
1838-1889 ....DLB-123

Villiers, George, Second Duke
of Buckingham 1628-1687 ......DLB-80

Vine Press DLB-112

Viorst, Judith ?- DLB-52

Vipont, Elfrida (Elfrida Vipont Foulds,
Charles Vipont) 1902-1992 ....DLB-160

Viramontes, Helena María
1954- DLB-122

Vischer, Friedrich Theodor
1807-1887 ....DLB-133

Vivanco, Luis Felipe 1907-1975 ....DLB-108

Viviani, Cesare 1947- DLB-128

Vizetelly and Company DLB-106

Voaden, Herman 1903- DLB-88

Voigt, Ellen Bryant 1943- DLB-120

Vojnović, Ivo 1857-1929 ....DLB-147

Volkoff, Vladimir 1932- DLB-83

Volland, P. F., Company DLB-46

von der Grün, Max 1926- DLB-75

Vonnegut, Kurt
1922- DLB-2, 8, 152; Y-80; DS-3

Voranc, Prežihov 1893-1950 ....DLB-147

Voß, Johann Heinrich 1751-1826 ....DLB-90

Vroman, Mary Elizabeth
circa 1924-1967 ....DLB-33

W

Wace, Robert ("Maistre")
circa 1100-circa 1175 ....DLB-146

Wackenroder, Wilhelm Heinrich
1773-1798 ....DLB-90

Wackernagel, Wilhelm
1806-1869 ....DLB-133

Waddington, Miriam 1917- DLB-68

Wade, Henry 1887-1969 ....DLB-77

Wagenknecht, Edward 1900- DLB-103

Wagner, Heinrich Leopold
1747-1779 ....DLB-94

Wagner, Henry R. 1862-1957 ......DLB-140

Wagner, Richard 1813-1883 ....DLB-129

Wagoner, David 1926- DLB-5

Wah, Fred 1939- DLB-60

Waiblinger, Wilhelm 1804-1830 .....DLB-90

Wain, John
1925-1994 .... DLB-15, 27, 139, 155

Wainwright, Jeffrey 1944- DLB-40

Waite, Peirce and Company DLB-49

Wakoski, Diane 1937- DLB-5

Walahfrid Strabo circa 808-849 .....DLB-148

Walck, Henry Z. DLB-46

Walcott, Derek
1930- DLB-117; Y-81, 92

Waldman, Anne 1945- DLB-16

Walker, Alice 1944- DLB-6, 33, 143

Walker, George F. 1947- DLB-60

Walker, Joseph A. 1935- DLB-38

Walker, Margaret 1915- DLB-76, 152

Walker, Ted 1934- DLB-40

Walker and Company DLB-49

Walker, Evans and Cogswell
Company DLB-49

Walker, John Brisben 1847-1931 ....DLB-79

Wallace, Dewitt 1889-1981 and
Lila Acheson Wallace
1889-1984 ....DLB-137

Wallace, Edgar 1875-1932 ....DLB-70

Wallace, Lila Acheson (see Wallace, Dewitt,
and Lila Acheson Wallace)

Wallant, Edward Lewis
1926-1962 .... DLB-2, 28, 143

Waller, Edmund 1606-1687 .... DLB-126

Walpole, Horace 1717-1797 .... DLB-39, 104

Walpole, Hugh 1884-1941 .... DLB-34

Walrond, Eric 1898-1966 .... DLB-51

Walser, Martin 1927- DLB-75, 124

Walser, Robert 1878-1956 .... DLB-66

Walsh, Ernest 1895-1926 .... DLB-4, 45

Walsh, Robert 1784-1859 .... DLB-59

Waltharius circa 825 .... DLB-148

Walters, Henry 1848-1931 .... DLB-140

Walther von der Vogelweide
circa 1170-circa 1230 .... DLB-138

Walton, Izaak 1593-1683 .... DLB-151

Wambaugh, Joseph 1937- DLB-6; Y-83

Waniek, Marilyn Nelson 1946- ... DLB-120

Warburton, William 1698-1779 .... DLB-104

Ward, Aileen 1919- DLB-111

Ward, Artemus (see Browne, Charles Farrar)

Ward, Arthur Henry Sarsfield
(see Rohmer, Sax)

Ward, Douglas Turner 1930- ... DLB-7, 38

Ward, Lynd 1905-1985 .... DLB-22

Ward, Lock and Company DLB-106

Ward, Mrs. Humphry 1851-1920 ... DLB-18

Ward, Nathaniel circa 1578-1652 ... DLB-24

Ward, Theodore 1902-1983 .... DLB-76

Wardle, Ralph 1909-1988 .... DLB-103

Ware, William 1797-1852 ....DLB-1

Warne, Frederick, and
Company [U.S.] DLB-49

Warne, Frederick, and
Company [U.K.] DLB-106

Warner, Charles Dudley
1829-1900 .... DLB-64

Warner, Rex 1905- DLB-15

Warner, Susan Bogert
1819-1885 .... DLB-3, 42

Warner, Sylvia Townsend
1893-1978 .... DLB-34, 139

Warner Books DLB-46

Warr, Bertram 1917-1943 .... DLB-88

Warren, John Byrne Leicester (see De Tabley,
Lord)

Warren, Lella 1899-1982 .... Y-83

Warren, Mercy Otis 1728-1814 ..... DLB-31

Warren, Robert Penn
1905-1989 ..... DLB-2, 48, 152; Y-80, 89

Die Wartburgkrieg
circa 1230-circa 1280 .... DLB-138

Warton, Joseph 1722-1800 .....DLB-104, 109

Warton, Thomas 1728-1790 ...DLB-104, 109

Washington, George 1732-1799 ..... DLB-31

Wassermann, Jakob 1873-1934 ...... DLB-66

Wasson, David Atwood 1823-1887 ... DLB-1

Waterhouse, Keith 1929- DLB-13, 15

Waterman, Andrew 1940- DLB-40

Waters, Frank 1902- Y-86

Waters, Michael 1949- DLB-120

Watkins, Tobias 1780-1855 .... DLB-73

Watkins, Vernon 1906-1967 .... DLB-20

Watmough, David 1926- DLB-53

Watson, James Wreford (see Wreford, James)

Watson, John 1850-1907 .... DLB-156

Watson, Sheila 1909- DLB-60

Watson, Thomas 1545?-1592 ...... DLB-132

Watson, Wilfred 1911- DLB-60

Watt, W. J., and Company DLB-46

Watterson, Henry 1840-1921 .... DLB-25

Watts, Alan 1915-1973 .... DLB-16

Watts, Franklin [publishing house] ... DLB-46

Watts, Isaac 1674-1748 .... DLB-95

Waugh, Auberon 1939- DLB-14

Waugh, Evelyn 1903-1966 ......DLB-15, 162

Way and Williams DLB-49

Wayman, Tom 1945- DLB-53

Weatherly, Tom 1942- DLB-41

Weaver, Gordon 1937- DLB-130

Weaver, Robert 1921- DLB-88

Webb, Frank J. ?-? DLB-50

Webb, James Watson 1802-1884 .... DLB-43

Webb, Mary 1881-1927 .... DLB-34

Webb, Phyllis 1927- DLB-53

Webb, Walter Prescott 1888-1963 ... DLB-17

Webbe, William ?-1591 .... DLB-132

Webster, Augusta 1837-1894 .... DLB-35

Webster, Charles L.,
and Company DLB-49

Webster, John
1579 or 1580-1634? DLB-58

Webster, Noah
1758-1843 .... DLB-1, 37, 42, 43, 73

Weckherlin, Georg Rodolf
1584-1653 ....DLB-164

Wedekind, Frank 1864-1918 ......DLB-118

Weeks, Edward Augustus, Jr.
1898-1989 ....DLB-137

Weems, Mason Locke
1759-1825 .... DLB-30, 37, 42

Weerth, Georg 1822-1856 ....DLB-129

Weidenfeld and Nicolson DLB-112

Weidman, Jerome 1913- DLB-28

Weigl, Bruce 1949- DLB-120

Weinbaum, Stanley Grauman
1902-1935 ....DLB-8

Weintraub, Stanley 1929- DLB-111

Weisenborn, Gunther
1902-1969 .... DLB-69, 124

Weiß, Ernst 1882-1940 ....DLB-81

Weiss, John 1818-1879 ....DLB-1

Weiss, Peter 1916-1982 .... DLB-69, 124

Weiss, Theodore 1916- DLB-5

Weisse, Christian Felix 1726-1804 ...DLB-97

Weitling, Wilhelm 1808-1871 ......DLB-129

Welch, Lew 1926-1971? DLB-16

Weldon, Fay 1931- DLB-14

Wellek, René 1903- DLB-63

Wells, Carolyn 1862-1942 ....DLB-11

Wells, Charles Jeremiah
circa 1800-1879 ....DLB-32

Wells, Gabriel 1862-1946 ....DLB-140

Wells, H. G. 1866-1946 .... DLB-34, 70, 156

Wells, Robert 1947- DLB-40

Wells-Barnett, Ida B. 1862-1931 .....DLB-23

Welty, Eudora
1909- DLB-2, 102, 143; Y-87; DS-12

Wendell, Barrett 1855-1921 ....DLB-71

Wentworth, Patricia 1878-1961 ......DLB-77

Werder, Diederich von dem
1584-1657 ....DLB-164

Werfel, Franz 1890-1945 .... DLB-81, 124

The Werner Company DLB-49

Werner, Zacharias 1768-1823 ....DLB-94

Wersba, Barbara 1932- DLB-52

Wescott, Glenway 1901- DLB-4, 9, 102

Wesker, Arnold 1932- DLB-13

Wesley, Charles 1707-1788 ....DLB-95

Wesley, John 1703-1791 ....DLB-104

Wesley, Richard 1945- DLB-38

Wessels, A., and Company DLB-46

Wessobrunner Gebet
circa 787-815 ....DLB-148

West, Anthony 1914-1988 ....DLB-15

West, Dorothy 1907- DLB-76

West, Jessamyn 1902-1984 ......DLB-6; Y-84

West, Mae 1892-1980 ....DLB-44

West, Nathanael 1903-1940 .... DLB-4, 9, 28

West, Paul 1930- DLB-14

West, Rebecca 1892-1983 ......DLB-36; Y-83

West and Johnson DLB-49

Western Publishing Company DLB-46

The Westminster Review 1824-1914 ....DLB-110

Wetherald, Agnes Ethelwyn
1857-1940 ....DLB-99

Wetherell, Elizabeth
(see Warner, Susan Bogert)

Wetzel, Friedrich Gottlob
1779-1819 ....DLB-90

Weyman, Stanley J.
1855-1928 ....DLB-141, 156

Wezel, Johann Karl 1747-1819 ......DLB-94

Whalen, Philip 1923- DLB-16

Whalley, George 1915-1983 ....DLB-88

Wharton, Edith
1862-1937 ......DLB-4, 9, 12, 78; DS-13

Wharton, William 1920s?- Y-80

Whately, Mary Louisa
1824-1889 ....DLB-166

What's Really Wrong With Bestseller
Lists Y-84

Wheatley, Dennis Yates
1897-1977 ....DLB-77

Wheatley, Phillis
circa 1754-1784 ....DLB-31, 50

Wheeler, Anna Doyle
1785-1848? DLB-158

Wheeler, Charles Stearns
1816-1843 ....DLB-1

Wheeler, Monroe 1900-1988 ....DLB-4

Wheelock, John Hall 1886-1978 .....DLB-45

Wheelwright, John
circa 1592-1679 ....DLB-24

Wheelwright, J. B. 1897-1940 .....DLB-45

Whetstone, Colonel Pete
(see Noland, C. F. M.)

Whetstone, George 1550-1587 ......DLB-136

Whicher, Stephen E. 1915-1961 ....DLB-111

Whipple, Edwin Percy
1819-1886 ....DLB-1, 64

Whitaker, Alexander 1585-1617 .... DLB-24

Whitaker, Daniel K. 1801-1881 .....DLB-73

Whitcher, Frances Miriam
1814-1852 ....DLB-11

White, Andrew 1579-1656 ....DLB-24

White, Andrew Dickson
1832-1918 ....DLB-47

White, E. B. 1899-1985 ....DLB-11, 22

White, Edgar B. 1947- DLB-38

White, Ethel Lina 1887-1944 ......DLB-77

White, Henry Kirke 1785-1806 .....DLB-96

White, Horace 1834-1916 ....DLB-23

White, Phyllis Dorothy James
(see James, P. D.)

White, Richard Grant 1821-1885 .... DLB-64

White, T. H. 1906-1964 ....DLB-160

White, Walter 1893-1955 ....DLB-51

White, William, and Company DLB-49

White, William Allen
1868-1944 ....DLB-9, 25

White, William Anthony Parker (see Boucher,
Anthony)

White, William Hale (see Rutherford, Mark)

Whitechurch, Victor L.
1868-1933 ....DLB-70

Whitehead, Alfred North
1861-1947 ....DLB-100

Whitehead, James 1936- Y-81

Whitehead, William
1715-1785 ....DLB-84, 109

Whitfield, James Monroe
1822-1871 ....DLB-50

Whitgift, John circa 1533-1604 .....DLB-132

Whiting, John 1917-1963 ....DLB-13

Whiting, Samuel 1597-1679 ....DLB-24

Whitlock, Brand 1869-1934 ....DLB-12

Whitman, Albert, and Company DLB-46

Whitman, Albery Allson
1851-1901 ....DLB-50

Whitman, Alden 1913-1990 ....Y-91

Whitman, Sarah Helen (Power)
1803-1878 ....DLB-1

Whitman, Walt 1819-1892 ....DLB-3, 64

Whitman Publishing Company DLB-46

Whitney, Geoffrey
1548 or 1552?-1601 ....DLB-136

Whitney, Isabella
flourished 1566-1573 ....DLB-136

Whitney, John Hay 1904-1982 .....DLB-127

Whittemore, Reed 1919- DLB-5

Whittier, John Greenleaf 1807-1892 ...DLB-1

Whittlesey House DLB-46

Who Runs American Literature? Y-94

Wideman, John Edgar
1941- DLB-33, 143

Widener, Harry Elkins 1885-1912 ...DLB-140

Wiebe, Rudy 1934- DLB-60

Wiechert, Ernst 1887-1950 ....DLB-56

Wied, Martina 1882-1957 ....DLB-85

Wieland, Christoph Martin
1733-1813 ....DLB-97

Wienbarg, Ludolf 1802-1872 ....DLB-133

Wieners, John 1934- DLB-16

Wier, Ester 1910- DLB-52

Wiesel, Elie 1928- DLB-83; Y-87

Wiggin, Kate Douglas 1856-1923 ....DLB-42

Wigglesworth, Michael 1631-1705 ...DLB-24

Wilberforce, William 1759-1833 ....DLB-158

Wilbrandt, Adolf 1837-1911 ....DLB-129

Wilbur, Richard 1921- DLB-5

Wild, Peter 1940- DLB-5

Wilde, Oscar
1854-1900 ....DLB-10, 19, 34, 57, 141, 156

Wilde, Richard Henry
1789-1847 ....DLB-3, 59

Wilde, W. A., Company DLB-49

Wilder, Billy 1906- DLB-26

Wilder, Laura Ingalls 1867-1957 .....DLB-22

Wilder, Thornton 1897-1975 ....DLB-4, 7, 9

Wildgans, Anton 1881-1932 ....DLB-118

Wiley, Bell Irvin 1906-1980 ....DLB-17

Wiley, John, and Sons DLB-49

Wilhelm, Kate 1928- DLB-8

Wilkes, George 1817-1885 ....DLB-79

Wilkinson, Anne 1910-1961 ....DLB-88

Wilkinson, Sylvia 1940- Y-86

Wilkinson, William Cleaver
1833-1920 ....DLB-71

Willard, Barbara 1909-1994 ....DLB-161

Willard, L. [publishing house] DLB-49

Willard, Nancy 1936- DLB-5, 52

Willard, Samuel 1640-1707 ....DLB-24

William of Auvergne 1190-1249 ....DLB-115

William of Conches
circa 1090-circa 1154 ....DLB-115

William of Ockham
  circa 1285-1347 .... DLB-115

William of Sherwood
  1200/1205 - 1266/1271 .... DLB-115

The William Chavrat American Fiction
  Collection at the Ohio State University
  Libraries Y-92

Williams, A., and Company DLB-49

Williams, Ben Ames 1889-1953 .... DLB-102

Williams, C. K. 1936- DLB-5

Williams, Chancellor 1905- DLB-76

Williams, Charles
  1886-1945 .... DLB-100, 153

Williams, Denis 1923- DLB-117

Williams, Emlyn 1905- DLB-10, 77

Williams, Garth 1912- DLB-22

Williams, George Washington
  1849-1891 .... DLB-47

Williams, Heathcote 1941- DLB-13

Williams, Helen Maria
  1761-1827 .... DLB-158

Williams, Hugo 1942- DLB-40

Williams, Isaac 1802-1865 .... DLB-32

Williams, Joan 1928- DLB-6

Williams, John A. 1925- DLB-2, 33

Williams, John E. 1922-1994 .... DLB-6

Williams, Jonathan 1929- DLB-5

Williams, Miller 1930- DLB-105

Williams, Raymond 1921- DLB-14

Williams, Roger circa 1603-1683 .... DLB-24

Williams, Samm-Art 1946- DLB-38

Williams, Sherley Anne 1944- DLB-41

Williams, T. Harry 1909-1979 ...... DLB-17

Williams, Tennessee
  1911-1983 .... DLB-7; Y-83; DS-4

Williams, Ursula Moray 1911- ... DLB-160

Williams, Valentine 1883-1946 ..... DLB-77

Williams, William Appleman
  1921- DLB-17

Williams, William Carlos
  1883-1963 .... DLB-4, 16, 54, 86

Williams, Wirt 1921- DLB-6

Williams Brothers DLB-49

Williamson, Jack 1908- DLB-8

Willingham, Calder Baynard, Jr.
  1922- DLB-2, 44

Williram of Ebersberg
  circa 1020-1085 .... DLB-148

Willis, Nathaniel Parker
  1806-1867 ..... DLB-3, 59, 73, 74; DS-13

Willkomm, Ernst 1810-1886 .... DLB-133

Wilmer, Clive 1945- DLB-40

Wilson, A. N. 1950- DLB-14, 155

Wilson, Angus
  1913-1991 .... DLB-15, 139, 155

Wilson, Arthur 1595-1652 .... DLB-58

Wilson, Augusta Jane Evans
  1835-1909 .... DLB-42

Wilson, Colin 1931- DLB-14

Wilson, Edmund 1895-1972 .... DLB-63

Wilson, Ethel 1888-1980 .... DLB-68

Wilson, Harriet E. Adams
  1828?-1863? DLB-50

Wilson, Harry Leon 1867-1939 ...... DLB-9

Wilson, John 1588-1667 .... DLB-24

Wilson, John 1785-1854 .... DLB-110

Wilson, Lanford 1937- DLB-7

Wilson, Margaret 1882-1973 .... DLB-9

Wilson, Michael 1914-1978 .... DLB-44

Wilson, Mona 1872-1954 .... DLB-149

Wilson, Thomas
  1523 or 1524-1581 .... DLB-132

Wilson, Woodrow 1856-1924 .... DLB-47

Wilson, Effingham
  [publishing house] DLB-154

Wimsatt, William K., Jr.
  1907-1975 .... DLB-63

Winchell, Walter 1897-1972 .... DLB-29

Winchester, J. [publishing house] DLB-49

Winckelmann, Johann Joachim
  1717-1768 .... DLB-97

Winckler, Paul 1630-1686 .... DLB-164

Windham, Donald 1920- DLB-6

Wingate, Allan [publishing house] .. DLB-112

Winnifrith, Tom 1938- DLB-155

Winsloe, Christa 1888-1944 ...... DLB-124

Winsor, Justin 1831-1897 .... DLB-47

John C. Winston Company DLB-49

Winters, Yvor 1900-1968 .... DLB-48

Winthrop, John 1588-1649 ...... DLB-24, 30

Winthrop, John, Jr. 1606-1676 ..... DLB-24

Wirt, William 1772-1834 .... DLB-37

Wise, John 1652-1725 .... DLB-24

Wiseman, Adele 1928- DLB-88

Wishart and Company DLB-112

Wisner, George 1812-1849 .... DLB-43

Wister, Owen 1860-1938 .... DLB-9, 78

Wither, George 1588-1667 .... DLB-121

Witherspoon, John 1723-1794 ...... DLB-31

Withrow, William Henry 1839-1908 ... DLB-99

Wittig, Monique 1935- DLB-83

Wodehouse, P. G.
  1881-1975 .... DLB-34, 162

Wohmann, Gabriele 1932- DLB-75

Woiwode, Larry 1941- DLB-6

Wolcot, John 1738-1819 .... DLB-109

Wolcott, Roger 1679-1767 .... DLB-24

Wolf, Christa 1929- DLB-75

Wolf, Friedrich 1888-1953 .... DLB-124

Wolfe, Gene 1931- DLB-8

Wolfe, Thomas
  1900-1938 .... DLB-9, 102; Y-85; DS-2

Wolfe, Tom 1931- DLB-152

Wolff, Helen 1906-1994 .... Y-94

Wolff, Tobias 1945- DLB-130

Wolfram von Eschenbach
  circa 1170-after 1220 .... DLB-138

Wolfram von Eschenbach's *Parzival*:
  Prologue and Book 3 .... DLB-138

Wollstonecraft, Mary
  1759-1797 .... DLB-39, 104, 158

Wondratschek, Wolf 1943- DLB-75

Wood, Benjamin 1820-1900 .... DLB-23

Wood, Charles 1932- DLB-13

Wood, Mrs. Henry 1814-1887 ...... DLB-18

Wood, Joanna E. 1867-1927 .... DLB-92

Wood, Samuel [publishing house] DLB-49

Wood, William ?-? DLB-24

Woodberry, George Edward
  1855-1930 .... DLB-71, 103

Woodbridge, Benjamin 1622-1684 ... DLB-24

Woodcock, George 1912- DLB-88

Woodhull, Victoria C. 1838-1927 .... DLB-79

Woodmason, Charles circa 1720-? ... DLB-31

Woodress, Jr., James Leslie
  1916- DLB-111

Woodson, Carter G. 1875-1950 ..... DLB-17

Woodward, C. Vann 1908- DLB-17

Wooler, Thomas
  1785 or 1786-1853 .... DLB-158

Woolf, David (see Maddow, Ben)

Woolf, Leonard
1880-1969 .... DLB-100; DS-10

Woolf, Virginia
1882-1941 ..... DLB-36, 100, 162; DS-10

Woolf, Virginia, "The New Biography," *New York Herald Tribune,* 30 October 1927
.... DLB-149

Woollcott, Alexander 1887-1943 ..... DLB-29

Woolman, John 1720-1772 .... DLB-31

Woolner, Thomas 1825-1892 .... DLB-35

Woolsey, Sarah Chauncy
1835-1905 .... DLB-42

Woolson, Constance Fenimore
1840-1894 .... DLB-12, 74

Worcester, Joseph Emerson
1784-1865 .... DLB-1

Wordsworth, Christopher
1807-1885 .... DLB-166

Wordsworth, Dorothy
1771-1855 .... DLB-107

Wordsworth, Elizabeth
1840-1932 .... DLB-98

Wordsworth, William
1770-1850 .... DLB-93, 107

The Works of the Rev. John Witherspoon
(1800-1801) [excerpts] DLB-31

A World Chronology of Important Science
Fiction Works (1818-1979) DLB-8

World Publishing Company DLB-46

World War II Writers Symposium at the
University of South Carolina,
12–14 April 1995 .... Y-95

Worthington, R., and Company DLB-49

Wotton, Sir Henry 1568-1639 ..... DLB-121

Wouk, Herman 1915- Y-82

Wreford, James 1915- DLB-88

Wren, Percival Christopher
1885-1941 .... DLB-153

Wrenn, John Henry 1841-1911 ..... DLB-140

Wright, C. D. 1949- DLB-120

Wright, Charles 1935- DLB-165; Y-82

Wright, Charles Stevenson 1932- ... DLB-33

Wright, Frances 1795-1852 .... DLB-73

Wright, Harold Bell 1872-1944 .... DLB-9

Wright, James 1927-1980 .... DLB-5

Wright, Jay 1935- DLB-41

Wright, Louis B. 1899-1984 .... DLB-17

Wright, Richard
1908-1960 ....DLB-76, 102; DS-2

Wright, Richard B. 1937- DLB-53

Wright, Sarah Elizabeth 1928- DLB-33

Writers and Politics: 1871-1918,
by Ronald Gray DLB-66

Writers and their Copyright Holders:
the WATCH Project Y-94

Writers' Forum Y-85

Writing for the Theatre, by
Harold Pinter DLB-13

Wroth, Lady Mary 1587-1653 ..... DLB-121

Wyatt, Sir Thomas
circa 1503-1542 .... DLB-132

Wycherley, William 1641-1715 ..... DLB-80.

Wyclif, John
circa 1335-31 December 1384 .. DLB-146

Wylie, Elinor 1885-1928 .... DLB-9, 45

Wylie, Philip 1902-1971 .... DLB-9

Wyllie, John Cook 1908-1968 ..... DLB-140

Y

Yates, Dornford 1885-1960 ..... DLB-77, 153

Yates, J. Michael 1938- DLB-60

Yates, Richard 1926-1992 ... DLB-2; Y-81, 92

Yavorov, Peyo 1878-1914 .... DLB-147

Yearsley, Ann 1753-1806 .... DLB-109

Yeats, William Butler
1865-1939 ....DLB-10, 19, 98, 156

Yep, Laurence 1948- DLB-52

Yerby, Frank 1916-1991 .... DLB-76

Yezierska, Anzia 1885-1970 .... DLB-28

Yolen, Jane 1939- DLB-52

Yonge, Charlotte Mary
1823-1901 .... DLB-18, 163

The York Cycle
circa 1376-circa 1569 .... DLB-146

A Yorkshire Tragedy DLB-58

Yoseloff, Thomas
[publishing house] DLB-46

Young, Al 1939- DLB-33

Young, Arthur 1741-1820 .... DLB-158

Young, Edward 1683-1765 .... DLB-95

Young, Stark 1881-1963 ....DLB-9, 102

Young, Waldeman 1880-1938 .... DLB-26

Young, William [publishing house] ... DLB-49

Yourcenar, Marguerite
1903-1987 .... DLB-72; Y-88

"You've Never Had It So Good," Gusted by
"Winds of Change": British Fiction in the
1950s, 1960s, and After DLB-14

Yovkov, Yordan 1880-1937 .... DLB-147

Z

Zachariä, Friedrich Wilhelm
1726-1777 .... DLB-97

Zamora, Bernice 1938- DLB-82

Zand, Herbert 1923-1970 .... DLB-85

Zangwill, Israel 1864-1926 ......DLB-10, 135

Zanzotto, Andrea 1921- DLB-128

Zapata Olivella, Manuel 1920- DLB-113

Zebra Books DLB-46

Zebrowski, George 1945- DLB-8

Zech, Paul 1881-1946 .... DLB-56

Zeidner, Lisa 1955- DLB-120

Zelazny, Roger 1937-1995 .... DLB-8

Zenger, John Peter 1697-1746 ....DLB-24, 43

Zesen, Philipp von 1619-1689 ...... DLB-164

Zieber, G. B., and Company DLB-49

Zieroth, Dale 1946- DLB-60

Zimmer, Paul 1934- DLB-5

Zingref, Julius Wilhelm
1591-1635 .... DLB-164

Zindel, Paul 1936- DLB-7, 52

Zola, Emile 1840-1902 .... DLB-123

Zolotow, Charlotte 1915- DLB-52

Zschokke, Heinrich 1771-1848 ...... DLB-94

Zubly, John Joachim 1724-1781 ..... DLB-31

Zu-Bolton II, Ahmos 1936- DLB-41

Zuckmayer, Carl 1896-1977 ....DLB-56, 124

Zukofsky, Louis 1904-1978 ......DLB-5, 165

Župančič, Oton 1878-1949 .... DLB-147

zur Mühlen, Hermynia 1883-1951 ... DLB-56

Zweig, Arnold 1887-1968 .... DLB-66

Zweig, Stefan 1881-1942 ....DLB-81, 118